A

COMMENTARY

ON THE

EPISTLE TO THE HEBREWS.

BY

MOSES STUART,

Late Prof. of Sacred Literature in the Theol. Sem. at Andover.

THIRD EDITION, CORRECTED AND ENLARGED.

Wipf and Stock Publishers
EUGENE, OREGON

Entered according to Act of Congress, in the year 1833 by

MOSES STUART,

in the Clerk's Office of the District Court of the District of Massachusetts.

Wipf and Stock Publishers
199 West 8th Avenue, Suite 3
Eugene, Oregon 97401

Commentary on the Epistle to the Hebrews
By Stuart, Moses
ISBN: 1-59244-371-0
Publication date 10/1/2003
Previously published by Warren F. Draper, 1833

ADVERTISEMENT.

WHATEVER fears may have been entertained respecting the application of the principles of criticism to the Sacred Text, and whatever doubts may have led some to decry the cultivation of that species of knowledge which has for its object the grammatical and philological interpretation of that text, it is now almost universally admitted, that such operations are indispensable to the attainment of a solid and satisfactory acquaintance with its contents. The peculiar exigencies of the times call for a more than ordinary attention to such subjects, and a richer stock of materials specially adapted to facilitate their study. For, with all the progress which has been made in matters of general Biblical research, and all the diligence which has been applied to the exposition of the Scriptures, the want of strictly philological and exegetical commentary has been severely felt, both by divines and theological students, and by a very considerable portion of intelligent and well-educated Christians, whose habits of reading bring them into constant contact with difficulties which only such commentary can remove.

To engage in labours of this description, few were better qualified than Professor Stuart. Intimately acquainted with the minutiæ of Hebrew and Greek Grammar; familiar with the diversities which characterize the style of the Sacred Writers; trained by long study of the laws of Biblical exegesis to a matured and refined tact in seizing the point, the bearing, the various shades and ramifications of meaning which are couched under the sacred phraseology; versed in the theological learning of Germany; imbued with a sincere love of Divine truth, and a profound reverence for its dictates;

ADVERTISEMENT.

and, withal, endowed with a manly and richly cultivated intellect—his talents and acquirements peculiarly fitted him for translating and commenting upon the Epistle to the Hebrews :—a task replete with difficulties, but which he has here performed with so much credit to himself, and so much advantage to the church of God.

The ordeal to which this important portion of Scripture has been subjected by the wild and extravagant hypotheses of some of the master-spirits of Germany, rendered it a matter of imperious necessity that it should be submitted to a fresh and full investigation. This, the perusal of the introductory part of the volume will prove that the author has successfully done. Questions respecting style, authorship, and interpretation, which men of such celebrity as Eichhorn, Bertholdt, De Wette, and others, were considered to have completely set at rest, have received the most patient and rigid consideration; and, in most instances triumphantly, in all more or less satisfactorily, the very reverse of their conclusions has been shewn to be in accordance with the real facts of the case.

The very favourable reception which the former edition of the work has met with in this country, and the continued and increasing demand which there has been for copies since it was exhausted, have induced the present publishers to bring out a new and correct impression. May the Divine blessing accompany its more extended circulation, that a more general taste for the close and accurate study of the Sacred Oracles may be created, and a more intimate acquaintance with this important Epistle promoted!

E. HENDERSON.

LONDON, September 24, 1833.

PREFACE.

THE origin of the following work must be ascribed to the duties which my present occupation calls upon me to perform. As the time spent in the study of the Scriptures, at this seminary, has not allowed me to lecture upon all the Epistles of Paul, it has been my custom to select those which appeared to be the most difficult, and, in some respects, the most instructive and important. These are, the epistles to the Romans and the Hebrews. In respect to the latter epistle, many serious exegetical difficulties occur, to remove which much time and extensive study are necessary. But the greatest difficulty of all arises from the fact, that this epistle is anonymous, and that the Pauline origin of it has been more or less doubted or disputed, ever since the latter part of the second century, if not still earlier. This subject I have deemed to be very interesting and important; and I have endeavoured, while discharging my duty of lecturing upon the epistle, to throw what light I could upon the dark places of its literature.

Experience, however, has taught me, that lectures could communicate to students but a very limited and incompetent view of the disputed ground, in regard to the origin of the epistle to the Hebrews. The exceedingly numerous quotations, and appeals to writers ancient and modern, which it was necessary to make, and the almost endless references to the Scriptures, which apposite illustration and argument required, rendered it impossible that a mere lecturer should communicate, or his hearer acquire and retain, any thing like an adequate view of the whole subject.

What was true of the literary introduction to the epistle, was also found to be true in respect to many of the most important exegetical difficulties connected with the interpretation of it. The young student, by the mere repetition or delivery of any lecture upon them, (however particular or plain it might be in the view of an experienced interpreter,) was not able to acquire such a knowledge as would avail thoroughly to free him from his embarrassments, or to render him capable of explaining such matters to others.

The knowledge of these facts, resulting from repeated experience, first led me to the design of publishing, *in extenso*, on the epistle to the Hebrews. The repeated solicitations which have been made, that I would engage in this undertaking, might, perhaps, constitute some apology for embarking in it, if such an apology were necessary. But the time has come, when, in our country, no apology is necessary for an effort to promote the knowledge of the holy Scriptures, or to cast any light upon them. There is an apprehension, at present, somewhat extensive and continually increasing, that no age, nor any body of men pertaining to it, have done *all* which the human faculties, with the blessing of God, are capable of accomplishing. Christians, in this country, are coming more and more to believe, that as the church advances nearer to that state, in which "the knowledge of the Lord shall fill the earth as the waters cover the seas," a better understanding of the Scriptures may be confidently hoped for and expected. It cannot be rationally supposed, that this will be communicated by a miraculous interposition. It must result from candid, patient, long-continued, and radical investigation of the language and idiom of the sacred writers. Interpretations *a priori* have long enough had their sway in the church; and it is very manifest, that a more judicious and truly Protestant mode of thinking and reasoning, in respect to the interpretation of the Scriptures, has commenced, and bids fair to be extensively adopted.

Whether the following sheets will contribute to aid this great object, must be left to the readers of them to decide. I can only say, that I have aimed at the accomplishment of this end, and that, if I have failed in respect to it, one great design of my undertaking and labours is defeated.

Probably some of my readers may think, that the *introductory* dissertations are more extended than was necessary, and that they are too minute and circumstantial. My only reply to this is, that an acquaintance with what has of late years been done, and with what is now doing, to shake the credit of our epistle, and to eject it from the canon of sacred writings to which appeal can be made in proof of Scripture doctrine, would of itself be an ample apology for all the pains I have taken, and all the minuteness of examination into which I have gone. Should it be said, that the German writers, whom I have opposed, are as yet unknown in this country, and that it was inexpedient to make them known; the allegation would only show how little acquainted the person who makes it is, with the actual state of our present knowledge, and with the relations in which we stand to the German authors. Our youth are every day resorting to Germany for education; our colleges are filling up with professors who have been educated there; the language of Germany is becoming an object of classical study in our public seminaries of learning; and in a multitude of ways, through the medium of translations as well as by the knowledge of the German language, is the literature of Germany producing an influence upon our own.

In this state of things, the attacks made upon the Pauline origin, or upon the canonical credit, of the epistle to the Hebrews, cannot be kept back from the knowledge of our intelligent and industrious students. It is better, therefore, to meet the whole matter with an open face, fairly to examine it, and either to yield to the force of arguments suggested by the critics of the old world, or to combat them in such a way as effectually to defend the positions which we take. Christian candour and impartiality demand this. The day of *authority* in the church is passed by; it is to be hoped, that the day of *sound reason* and of *argument* is to follow. It is better to convince men by an appeal to their understandings and their hearts, than it is to terrify them by holding the rod of authority over them, or to deter them from speaking out their convictions by arguments *ad invidiam*. These are the never-failing resource of minds, which are conscious of possessing no better means than such, of convincing others, and which naturally resort to those which are most within their reach.

Our religion seeks no concealment; it fears no assaults. If it will not stand the test of sober reason and of argument, it will not long have place in the world among enlightened men. Those who shrink from such tests, and declaim against the use of our reason, show their want of confidence in the cause which they profess to espouse. If they did but know it, they are already half won over to the ranks of doubters or of unbelievers.

On the subjects of interpretation, one may well say, "Drink deep, or taste not." A half-illuminated interpreter doubts every thing, and sees nothing clearly. Would God, the rising generation of those who are devoted to the study of the Divine word, might feel deeply penetrated with the truth of this! It would be an event highly auspicious to the cause of truth in the world.

In the new translation of the Epistle to the Hebrews which is here furnished, it has been my object to give a more exact view of the features of the original Greek, than is presented by our common English version. Of all the tasks which an interpreter performs, this is the most difficult. To make some kind of translation, is indeed a very easy thing; to follow on in the tracks of some other interpreter, is equally easy. But to translate, so as to make an author, who has composed in another language, altogether intelligible, and yet preserve all the shades, and colouring, and nice transitions, and (so far as may be) even the idioms themselves of the original, is the very highest and most difficult work which an interpreter is ever called to perform. A translation, faithfully presenting the original, is in itself a commentary. It is the sum of all an interpreter's labours, exhibited in the briefest manner possible. Hence the little success that has attended most of the versions which have been made of the Scriptures. Their authors have either abridged or paraphrased the original; more commonly the latter. Neither is admissible, in a translation truly faithful. Whether I have shunned the one and the other, must be left to the judgment of the reader.

I much prefer the Saxon English for a version of the Bible. I have accordingly chosen it whenever I could, and have purposely avoided substituting Latinizing English in its room, unless a regard to the meaning of the original compelled me to do it.

It is proper to advertise the reader, that in the translation I have purposely avoided the usual division into chapters and verses, which is exhibited in our common editions of the Scriptures. I have done this, because the sense is sometimes disturbed by it, and the reader is unwarily led to associate things together in a manner which the writer of the epistle never intended.

The words or phrases which are supplied in the translation, and which are not expressed in the original Greek, I have uniformly included in brackets, so that the reader may at once see the extent of the liberty that has been taken in order to render the version more explicit.

For the sake of accommodation, the designation of the chapters and verses is made upon the margin; and the larger pauses mark the end of a verse, when they occur in a line that is opposite to any number designating a verse.

I have, in most cases, repeated the greater part of the translation, in printing the commentary or notes upon the original. This has been done merely to save the reader the trouble of turning continually back to the version, which is often tedious, and always inconvenient. But I have not been careful always to repeat *verbatim*, in the notes, the words of the translation, as they stand at the commencement of the volume. In fact, the reader may regard the version at the head of the volume, and that contained among the notes, as two different versions. They were, for the most part, made at different times, and in a measure independently of each other. The former is that on which I have bestowed most pains as to diction. The latter is merely designed to facilitate the labours of the student.

The translation is followed by a continuous commentary upon the whole epistle. When difficulties demanded special and extended investigation, I have thrown the result of such investigation into *Excursus* at the end. There, subjects of difficulty can be treated, and studied, with more convenience and more fully, than if intermixed with the usual series of exegetical notes.

I have consulted commentaries both ancient and modern, while composing the exegetical part of the work. Chrysostom, Theodoret, and Theophylact, are the ancient interpreters, who may be read with much interest, and with some profit. I owe to them not a few hints, which I regard as valuable. From more recent critics I have derived very considerable aid, which I would gratefully acknowledge. After all, I have examined other writers, rather for the sake of correcting or enlarging my own impressions, than for the sake of abridging or condensing their works. My uniform method of study has been, to exhaust the resources of my own mind before I applied to others for help. But I have neither despised nor neglected this help; nor have I, in any case, followed the opinion of any critic, unless I was satisfied with the reasons which he gives for it. Critics of very different sentiments and views, I have consulted. Impartial investigation demanded this; and I should be but ill satisfied, in respect to the discharge of my own duty, if I had not done it.

The interpretations which I have adopted and defended, are the result of long-continued and often-repeated labour and study. This, however, does not of itself enhance their value to the reader. They must stand by their own internal value, if they do stand, and not by the length of time during which they have been coming into existence.

I have not made it an object to transcribe other commentators, and continually to refer to them. It is a mode of commentary to which I have a dislike; particularly so, when it is carried to the excess to which many interpreters have carried it. I have therefore retreated as far from it as my views of usefulness and propriety would permit me to do. The reader will have, at least, one advantage from this. He will not be compelled, merely *agere actum*, to read over what he had read before.

To say, that *critical* commentaries on the Scriptures, of the higher kind, are wanting in the English language, would be only to repeat what every biblical student has long felt and confessed. The time has come, when this evil ought, if possible, to be redressed. Whether the attempt to assist in this great work, which I have made in the following sheets, can be justly regarded as a successful one, is not for the writer to judge.

It will be understood, of course, that the work is designed for students in theology, and for those who engage in a truly critical

PREFACE. xi

study of the Scriptures. With commentaries designed for the edification of Christian readers at large, I believe the English world is better supplied than any other part of Christendom. Henry, Patrick, Guise, Orton, Doddridge, Brown, Clark, Scott, and others, have published works of this nature. It is not my design to occupy the ground which they have already occupied. The reader of my work must not expect sermonizing commentary, but an attempt at philological and critical interpretation. *Cuique suum.* I bless God for raising up such commentators as those just mentioned, for Christians at large; but the *professed interpreters* of his word need other aid, and that very different from what their works afford, in order to attain a fundamentally critical knowledge of the original Scriptures.

In regard to the *Excursus*, different opinions will not improbably be entertained respecting them. The expediency of them, their length, and the correctness of some of the positions which they advance, may all be called in question. In matters so difficult and delicate, and which have so long been the theme of controversy, it cannot be expected that there will be, at once, an entire and universal agreement of opinion. The writer of these sheets does not venture to flatter himself with the expectation, that all will adopt his views. Of one thing, however, he is very confident; and this is, that he claims no authority of any kind over the opinions of others. But he thinks it proper to express his sincere desire, that those who may differ from him as to some of the opinions advanced in the Excursus, or in the body of the work, would thoroughly examine the subjects in respect to which they may think him erroneous, before they pass sentence of condemnation. It is not too much, moreover, to request, that they would assign their *reasons* why they differ from him. In this way, differences of opinion may ultimately aid in the discovery of truth, with respect to dark and difficult subjects, and so prove to be of real utility to the church.

Subjects of high and awful interest in religion should not be treated with obtrusive confidence, nor with presumption. I shall most thankfully accept any better light than I now have, let it come from what quarter it may. Being a Protestant, and *nullius addictus jurare in verba magistri*, I deem it not unreasonable to expect, that where I may be in the wrong, I may be convinced by *argument*, not silenced by *authority*. Appeals should ever be made, by Protestants, to the understanding, not *ad invidiam*, nor to current or popular prejudice.

With these explanations of my views and feelings, I submit the work to the friends of exegetical study, not without much solicitude as to the opinion which the wise and the good may entertain respecting it; but still, with some expectation, that it may serve to aid such as are aiming to attain a critical knowledge of the Scriptures, or, at least, excite some to efforts which shall end in the production of better Commentaries on the Scriptures than are yet before the public.

The responsibility of publishing a work like the present, is very great. It is one from which I should shrink, if, on the whole, I could come to the conclusion, that duty permitted me to decline it. As my conviction now is, I must venture to commit it to God, and to the Christian public, hoping that it may contribute, in some measure, to advance the knowledge of a very interesting portion of his Holy Word.

M. STUART.

Theological Seminary, Andover,
March 25th, 1828.

COMMENTARY.

INTRODUCTION.

§ 1. *Preliminary Remarks.*

No part of the New Testament has occasioned so much difference of opinion, and given rise to so much literary discussion among critics, as the Epistle to the Hebrews. The principal reason of this seems to be, that this epistle does not exhibit, either in the beginning of it or elsewhere, any express evidence of having been addressed to any particular church, nor any designation of the author's name. If it had been expressly inscribed to a particular church, and if the author had originally affixed his name to it, there would of course have been as little occasion for dispute, respecting the persons to whom it was addressed, or in regard to the author of it, as there has been in the case of the epistles to the Romans, Corinthians, or Galatians.

At an early period of the Christian era, the eastern and the western churches were divided in opinion respecting the author and canonical authority of this epistle. In modern times, and especially of late, every topic which its literary history could suggest, has been the subject of animated discussion. It has been disputed whether it is an epistle, an essay, or a homily; whether it was written by Paul, Apollos, Barnabas, Clement of Rome, or by some other person; and whether it was originally written in Hebrew or in Greek. There has also been a difference of opinion as to the place where, and the time when, it was written. On every one of these topics, critics have been and still are divided. Nor has this division been occasioned merely by a difference in theological opinions. The subjects of dispute have, in this case, been generally regarded rather as topics of *literature*, than of religious sentiment or doctrine. Men of very different views and feelings, in other respects, have often been found united in the same ranks, when questions respecting the epistle to the Hebrews have been disputed. Such too is the case, even at the present time. All the learning and ability, which have as yet been summoned to the contest, have failed to achieve a victory so complete, as to bring about a general acknowledgment that all ground for further dispute is fairly removed.

The student who is unacquainted with these facts, and who has merely read the epistle to the Hebrews with the same views and feelings which he has entertained while reading the *acknowledged* epistles of Paul, finds himself thrown into a situation not a little perplexing, when he begins to make such critical inquiries respecting the epistle in question, as are usually made respecting any ancient writing. He finds philologists and critics, of great reputation in the church, strangely divided and opposed to each other, in respect to every topic to be examined. What he reads in one author, which perhaps for a time satisfies his mind, he finds controverted, shaken, or overthrown by another; who again, in his turn, receives castigation from a third; while a fourth, a fifth, and a sixth, differ each from all his predecessors. The curiosity of the inquirer thus becomes roused, and he begins to pursue some train of thought or investigation, with the hope, or perhaps with confidence, that it will lead him to an important and satisfactory result. He presses forward with eagerness, peruses and re-peruses modern critics, dives into the recesses of the ancient ones, and finds, perhaps, after all his toil, that he has been pursuing a phantom, which recedes as fast as he advances. Perplexed with doubt, and wearied at last with the pursuit, he becomes exposed to the danger of entirely abandoning his object, or of settling down in the cold and comfortless conclusion, that nothing satisfactory can be known in regard to it.

Such, or not much unlike to this, will be the experience, I believe, of nearly every one who sets out with his mind unfettered by any notions of early education, and determined seriously and thoroughly to investigate and weigh for himself all the evidence which can be found, in respect to the topics suggested by the literary history of the epistle to the Hebrews. He who begins such an investigation, with his mind already made up that Paul wrote this epistle, and directed it to the Hebrews of Palestine, may indeed spare himself most of the perplexity, in which an inquirer of the class just named, will be involved. But then, if his mind is already made up, what need is there of further investigation? And why not spare himself the time and trouble which it must cost?

Minds of a different order, however, will doubtless wish to examine for themselves; to "prove all things," and then "to hold fast that which is good," if indeed they may be able to distinguish what is of this character. It is for such that the following investigations are intended; and it is only to persons of this class, that they can be particularly useful, even supposing that they are conducted in such a manner as the subject demands. The writer commenced them in the discharge of his duty, as a lecturer upon the epistle in question. He found many unforeseen and unexpected obstacles in his path. He had been accustomed, with those around him, to regard Paul as the author of the epistle to the Hebrews; and he did not well know, until he came to examine, how long, and how extensively, this had been doubted. Men of high reputation in the church, and who admitted the canonical authority of the epistle, he found to have been doubtful in regard to the question, Who was the author of it? Neither Luther nor Calvin admitted it to be from the hand of Paul; and so early, at least, as the latter part of the second century, more or less of the Western churches seem to have disputed or rejected its authority.

With such facts before him, he became deeply interested in the subject, and resolved, if possible, to satisfy his own mind. For this purpose, he directed his attention principally toward the original sources of evidence, although he has not neglected any writer of importance among modern critics. The results of his investigation he now gives to the public, in hope that if they do not serve to satisfy the minds of others, they will, at least, excite some to engage in the discussion of the topics presented, until, sooner or later, light enough is poured in, to scatter the remaining darkness which rests upon them.

§ 2. *Is the epistle to the Hebrews appropriately called an* epistle, *or is it a homily or essay?*

Berger, a late critic of some eminence and considerable acuteness, has advanced and endeavoured to support the opinion, that this epistle (so called) was originally a homily or address to some assembly of Christians, which was afterwards reduced to writing by some of the preacher's friends or hearers. Others also have doubted, whether it is properly named an epistle. But none have argued on this topic so much at length, or with so much effort, as Berger. On this account, it may be proper briefly to consider the principal arguments which he has advanced; *briefly*, because the topic seems not to be of sufficient importance to justify one for occupying much time in the discussion of it.

(1.) 'The writer himself of the epistle to the Hebrews,' says Berger, 'calls it λόγος παρακλήσεως, a *hortatory address*, xiii. 22, which accords well with the contents of the piece.'

But Paul, one may reply, often uses the word παρακαλέω in his *epistles*. May not, then, an epistle of his in which παρακαλέω is used, be appropriately enough styled a λόγος παρακλήσεως? May not any epistle, containing precept and exhortation, be so denominated? An instance exactly in point, is the circular letter respecting the question about circumcision, sent by the apostolic council at Jerusalem to the churches in Antioch, Syria, and Cilicia; which is called a παράκλησις, Acts xv. 31. The words of Luke are, "When they had read, [the epistle,] they rejoiced ἐπὶ τῇ παρακλήσει."

(2.) 'The writer of the epistle to the Hebrews uses λαλεῖν instead of γράφειν; which is rather characteristic of a *hortatory* address than an *epistle*.'

But an appeal to the Greek Concordance shews that λαλεῖν is used every where in the epistles contained in the New Testament; and a corresponding word of the same import, is in fact used in the epistolary style of all nations and languages. No evidence, therefore, in favour of Berger's opinion, can be deduced from such an usage in the epistle to the Hebrews.

(3.) Berger supposes the basis of our present epistle to the Hebrews to have been the address of Paul to the church at Antioch in Pisidia, as recorded in Acts xiii. 14—41. Some disciple and friend of his, he conjectures, reduced this discourse to writing, commenting or enlarging upon various parts of it; and finally adding of himself, to the original discourse, the four last verses of our present epistle. It is to these four verses he supposes the copyist to refer, when he says, "I have written to you διὰ βραχέων, *briefly*," viz. by adding only the four last verses of the epistle, as properly his own.

To these considerations we may reply, first, that the address of Paul to the church of Antioch, in Pisidia, exhibits two very important topics, as prominent parts of the discourse, which are not at all commented on (one of them is not even adverted to) in the epistle to the Hebrews; I mean the subject of John the Baptist's testimony concerning Christ, and the resurrection of Jesus, Acts xiii. 24, 25, 30—37. Would it not be strange, that a commentator should entirely pass by the prominent topics of the discourse which he designed to explain or enforce?

Secondly, διὰ βραχέων ἐπίστειλα ὑμῖν does not admit of the reference which Berger supposes; for it is necessarily connected with the *preceding* part of the epistle to the Hebrews, and not (as he asserts) with the *succeeding* part; to which it can be attached only by doing violence to the ordinary laws of language.

(4.) 'The word ἀμὴν, in Hebrews xiii. 21, shews that the *original* discourse ended there, and that what follows is only an addition made by the transcriber.'

The answer is, that ἀμὴν here stands after a *doxology*, where Paul always inserts it; and he frequently introduces it in this way in the very middle of his letters. E. g. Rom. i. 25. ix. 5. xi. 36. xv. 33. xvi. 20. Gal. i. 5. Eph. iii. 21. etc. It follows, that in this case, the insertion of ἀμὴν cannot afford any valid proof that our epistle ended with it.

(5.) 'The whole epistle is a regular series of reasoning, a connected chain of discourse; like to an essay or a homily, and not after the manner of a familiar letter.'

But, it may well be asked in reply to this, May not and do not men reason, and regularly discuss subjects, in familiar letters or epistles? Has not Paul discussed and reasoned in his epistles to the Romans, the Galatians, the Ephesians, and in others? Is there any more regularity of structure in the epistle to the Hebrews, than there is in that to the Romans? Surely the regularity and orderly discussion, exhibited by any composition, can never prove that this composition was not an epistle. At most, it can only serve to show that it was not an *ordinary* epistle on topics of little moment. Nor because a great part, or even the whole, of an epistle is of such a tenor, that it might have been *spoken* as an *address* or a *homily*, will it prove that it was not originally, or was not designed to be, an epistle. For every species of composition in use among men, is employed in epistolary writing.

The reasons of Berger, then, for the opinion which he has advanced, will not bear the test of examination. I may add, that the whole question is but little if anything better than logomachy. Of what consequence can it be, whether the so-called epistle to the Hebrews, was, in its first conception, designed to be an epistle or a homily? But whatever the original design was, I cannot believe, with Berger, that our epistle is a kind of commentary on an original discourse of Paul. That the author (the original author) of the epistle wrote down his own conceptions, or at least *dictated* them to an amanuensis, appears to me so deeply stamped on every part of the composition, that it seems hardly possible for a discerning and unprejudiced reader not to perceive it. But whether or not the author first spoke the words which the letter contains, to some assembly, and afterwards reduced them to writing, can make no difference as to the tenor and general character of the epistle; so that dispute about this would be only dispute about the *name* to be given to the writing; and how would this differ from logomachy?

However, if this must be disputed, we can easily satisfy ourselves respecting it. The address every where is like that of an epistle, viz. in the second person plural; with the single exception, that the writer occasionally uses a κοίνωσις, that is, he includes himself with those whom he addresses, and so employs the *first person plural*. But this is a practice so common in epistolary correspondence, that it occasions no difficulty in the case under consideration.

It is true, the mode of address would be the same in regard to the particular just noticed, if the epistle had originally been a homily. But other particulars render such a supposition utterly inadmissible. The epistle every where supposes the persons addressed to be *absent* from the writer, not present before him, as in the case of a homily. How could he, in a *homily*, ask them to " pray that he might be *restored to them?*" Heb. xiii. 19. How could he promise to " *make them a visit*, in company with Timothy, if he should come speedily?" xiii. 23. The first of these cases, at least, belongs to that part of the epistle, which Berger acknowledges to be the *original* discourse of Paul.

I add, that I am unable to see how any one can well imagine, (as Berger does, and as Origen long ago conjectured,) that the hand of a *commentator* is discernible in this epistle. The whole tenor of it, from beginning to end, contradicts this. Did ever any writing come more warmly and fully from the heart? Here is no patchwork; no congeries of heterogeneous materials; no designed, exegetical *commentary*; no trace of a copyist or reporter. It is one uniform, unbroken, continuous work; produced by the mighty impulse of one and the same mind, fraught with knowledge of the subject which it discusses, glowing with benevolent feelings toward those who are addressed, and agitated with alarm at the danger to which they are exposed. Sooner should I think of dividing into parcels the Iliad, the Eneid, or the Paradise Lost, and assigning respective parts to different poets, than of introducing the hand of a copyist, or a mere commentator, into the epistle to the Hebrews. Be it written where, when, or by whom it may have been, *one* mind performed the great work, and stamped it with characteristics too plain to be obscured, too deep to be erased

§ 3. *General considerations respecting the present inscription to the epistle.*

In what latitude is the word *Hebrews*, used in the inscription to this epistle, to be understood?

Certainly not as designating *all* Hebrews of every country. To the *unbelieving* Jews most evidently it was not addressed. From beginning to end, the persons addressed are regarded as having made a profession of the Christian faith; for the great object of the epistle, as all agree, is to guard them against apostacy from this faith.

To the believing Jews of *every* country, it could not have been primarily and immediately addressed. It is altogether improbable that *all* such, in every country, were in special danger of apostacy, when this letter was written. We know from the epistles of Paul, that many churches planted by him, and made up in part of Jews, were, at the period when our epistle must have been written, in a very flourishing condition, and eminent for Christian faith and holiness of life. Other circumstances mentioned in the epistle, and pertaining to those whom he addressed, cannot be applied to *all* the believing Hebrews of that period. The writer speaks of the great fight of afflictions and the loss of property, to which those had been subjected for the sake of religion whom he addresses, x. 32—34; occurrences which surely had not taken place, in *every* church where Jews were found.

A still more convincing argument, in favour of the sentiment just advanced, is drawn from what the writer himself has stated, at the close of his letter. He asks the prayers of those whom he addresses, that he may be speedily restored to them, xiii. 19; and promises, if Timothy return in a short time, that he will in his company pay them a visit, xiii. 23. He could not mean that he would, in company with Timothy, visit *all* the churches where Jews were to be found throughout the world. And could Timothy be known to them all? Or could the circumstances of Timothy, and of the writer himself, be so well known by them all, as the manner of address here necessarily supposes?

These considerations render it quite clear, that whosoever the Hebrews were that are named by the present inscription, they must have been those of some particular church and country. And even if we pay no regard to the *inscription*, (but suppose it, after some time had elapsed, to have been affixed to the epistle by another hand, as it probably was,) the fact that *Jewish converts* are addressed, and such too as belonged to some *particular* church or region, is, from the internal evidence of the epistle just stated, too plain to admit of any considerable doubt.

§ 4. *To what church was the epistle to the Hebrews written?*

A question replete with difficulties, and which has been much agitated by late critics. We can easily satisfy ourselves, that the epistle was designed for Jewish converts; and exclusively (in a certain sense of this word) designed for them, i. e. originally adapted to them throughout, in its texture and mode of reasoning. But *where* did these converts live? No salutation, such as stands at the head of nearly all the apostolic epistles, gives us information on this point. The conclusion of the letter, moreover, contains nothing definite enough to settle this question. We are left, then, to gather from ecclesiastical tradition and from internal evidence, such information as is necessary to determine it. But the first of these has been regarded by many critics, particularly by recent ones, as too indefinite or too imperfect to satisfy the mind of an inquirer; and the second is so indeterminate, at least it has been often considered so indeterminate, as to afford no *convincing* evidence, but rather to give occasion for constant diversity of opinion. The same passages, for example, have often been quoted, in some instances, to support conclusions directly opposed to each other; and in other cases, *definite* conclusions have been drawn in support of particular opinions, from texts which appear to be capable of conveying only a *general* idea.

The task of examining the principal opinions which have been advanced in respect to the original destination of the epistle to the Hebrews, is tedious and appalling; but it has become absolutely necessary to every one, who makes any just pretensions to acquaintance with the literary history of this epistle. I shall be as brief as the nature of the discussion, and justice to the arguments of others, will permit; and I shall examine only those opinions which the authors of them have endeavoured to support by arguments, omitting a particular discussion of those which have been thrown out as mere conjecture. For a *mere conjecture* that the epistle was directed to Jewish converts at Rome, in Spain, or at Babylon, (such conjectures have been made by critics of no small note,) is sufficiently answered by a *conjecture* that it was directed to Jewish converts at some other place. If no weight be laid in the scales, it requires none to adjust the balance.

In our investigation respecting the question under consideration, we meet with critics who have maintained, that the epistle was written to Jewish Christians in Galatia; at Thessalonica; at Corinth; or to dispersed Hebrews in Asia Minor at large, who had fled from Palestine in order to avoid the persecutions to which they were there exposed. The majority of critics, however, have held, as nearly all the ancient churches did, that the epistle was directed to the Hebrews of Palestine. I proceed to examine each of these opinions, in the order here suggested.

§ 5. *Was the Epistle written to the Church in Galatia?*

The opinion, that the epistle was directed to Jewish converts in Galatia, has been advanced and maintained with no small degree of acuteness and learning by Storr, late Professor of Theology at the University of Tübingen. I shall present a summary of the arguments which he uses to establish it; and in order to avoid repetition, and also to render the discussion as perspicuous as may be, I shall examine the validity of each argument, as it is adduced.

He begins by observing, that the epistle to the Hebrews could not be directed to the church in Palestine, because it appears from Heb. ii. 3, that the persons to whom it was addressed were not such as heard Christ speak in person; from xii. 4, and xiii. 7, that they had as yet suffered no bloody persecution; and from vi. 10, xiii. 3, 10, and x. 34, that so far from having received charity from other churches, they had themselves contributed to the support of others. Now, as neither of these things can, in his view, be truly said respecting the church in Palestine, he concludes, that our epistle must have been directed to some church abroad.

I shall not stop here to examine, whether a proper interpretation of the passages on which he relies to support his opinion, will in fact support it, as this subject must be examined in another place. I must content myself, at present, with simply remarking, that if he has rightly construed the texts to which he refers, they only serve to show, at most, that the church in Palestine was *not* the one to which the epistle was directed; leaving the question still untouched, whether it was sent, as he maintains, to the church in Galatia. As my present intention is to examine only *positive* arguments in favour of his opinion, I pass this consideration without further remark.

Most, if not all of the arguments on which Storr relies, are grounded on what he supposes to be *probabilities*. The general nature of them may be thus stated. " Certain facts relative to the Galatians and the Hebrews, are known from history, and from the epistles which bear their names. But these facts cannot well be accounted for on any other ground, than by the supposition, that the epistles to the Hebrews and Galatians were *cotemporaneously* written, and directed *severally* to the Jewish and Gentile parts of the same church. This being admitted, several things, otherwise strange or inexplicable, may be easily accounted for; and consequently, we may or must admit such a composition and direction of these epistles."

Let us examine the particulars, which go to make up the general argument that I have just stated.

(1.) "As the epistle to the Hebrews was not written to the churches in Palestine, and as all the churches abroad consisted of a mixture of Jews and Gentiles, it is a singularity very striking, and at first appearance inexplicable, how it should come to pass that the epistle to the Galatians is written exclusively to Gentile converts, and the epistle to the Hebrews exclusively to Jewish ones. But all appearance of difficulty vanishes, if we suppose that the two epistles were sent, at the same time, to the church in Galatia; each to the respective party for whom it was intended. A supposition which removes such difficulties, must be regarded as a probable one."

This supposition is not wanting in ingenuity; and at first view, it may be regarded as not being destitute of probability. But then, the critic must ask, How far can we be allowed to draw conclusions, in respect to subjects of this nature, from mere *conjectural* probabilities? I may conjecture thousands of circumstances, in themselves probable, which would liberate me from difficulties presented by particular passages, or by whole books of the Old Testament and the New; on which conjectures, however, it would be very uncritical and unsafe for me to build conclusions, in respect to any matter of *fact*. Even if we allow the *probability*, then, of Storr's conjecture, it cannot add much real weight to the cause which he endeavours to support.

Such a probability, however, cannot well be allowed. There are circumstances, in the epistles to the Galatians and the Hebrews, relative

TO THE CHURCH IN GALATIA? 9

conjecture that the epistle was directed to Jewish converts at Rome, in Spain, or at Babylon, (such conjectures have been made by critics of no small note,) is sufficiently answered by a *conjecture* that it was directed to Jewish converts at some other place. If no weight be laid in the scales, it requires none to adjust the balance.

In our investigation respecting the question under consideration, we meet with critics who have maintained, that the epistle was written to Jewish Christians in Galatia; at Thessalonica; at Corinth; or to dispersed Hebrews in Asia Minor at large, who had fled from Palestine in order to avoid the persecutions to which they were there exposed. The majority of critics, however, have held, as nearly all the ancient churches did, that the epistle was directed to the Hebrews of Palestine. I proceed to examine each of these opinions, in the order here suggested.

§ 5. *Was the Epistle written to the Church in Galatia?*

The opinion, that the epistle was directed to Jewish converts in Galatia, has been advanced and maintained with no small degree of acuteness and learning by Storr, late Professor of Theology at the University of Tübingen. I shall present a summary of the arguments which he uses to establish it; and in order to avoid repetition, and also to render the discussion as perspicuous as may be, I shall examine the validity of each argument, as it is adduced.

He begins by observing, that the epistle to the Hebrews could not be directed to the church in Palestine, because it appears from Heb. ii. 3, that the persons to whom it was addressed were not such as heard Christ speak in person; from xii. 4, and xiii. 7, that they had as yet suffered no bloody persecution; and from vi. 10, xiii. 3, 10, and x. 34, that so far from having received charity from other churches, they had themselves contributed to the support of others. Now, as neither of these things can, in his view, be truly said respecting the church in Palestine, he concludes, that our epistle must have been directed to some church abroad.

I shall not stop here to examine, whether a proper interpretation of the passages on which he relies to support his opinion, will in fact support it, as this subject must be examined in another place. I must content myself, at present, with simply remarking, that if he has rightly construed the texts to which he refers, they only serve to show, at most, that the church in Palestine was *not* the one to which the epistle was directed; leaving the question still untouched, whether it was sent, as he maintains, to the church in Galatia. As my present intention is to examine only *positive* arguments in favour of his opinion, I pass this consideration without further remark.

Most, if not all of the arguments on which Storr relies, are grounded on what he supposes to be *probabilities*. The general nature of them may be thus stated. " Certain facts relative to the Galatians and the Hebrews, are known from history, and from the epistles which bear their names. But these facts cannot well be accounted for on any other ground, than by the supposition, that the epistles to the Hebrews and Galatians were *cotemporaneously* written, and directed *severally* to the Jewish and Gentile parts of the same church. This being admitted, several things, otherwise strange or inexplicable, may be easily accounted for; and consequently, we may or must admit such a composition and direction of these epistles."

Let us examine the particulars, which go to make up the general argument that I have just stated.

(1.) " As the epistle to the Hebrews was not written to the churches in Palestine, and as all the churches abroad consisted of a mixture of Jews and Gentiles, it is a singularity very striking, and at first appearance inexplicable, how it should come to pass that the epistle to the Galatians is written exclusively to Gentile converts, and the epistle to the Hebrews exclusively to Jewish ones. But all appearance of difficulty vanishes, if we suppose that the two epistles were sent, at the same time, to the church in Galatia; each to the respective party for whom it was intended. A supposition which removes such difficulties, must be regarded as a probable one."

This supposition is not wanting in ingenuity; and at first view, it may be regarded as not being destitute of probability. But then, the critic must ask, How far can we be allowed to draw conclusions, in respect to subjects of this nature, from mere *conjectural* probabilities? I may conjecture thousands of circumstances, in themselves probable, which would liberate me from difficulties presented by particular passages, or by whole books of the Old Testament and the New; on which conjectures, however, it would be very uncritical and unsafe for me to build conclusions, in respect to any matter of *fact*. Even if we allow the *probability*, then, of Storr's conjecture, it cannot add much real weight to the cause which he endeavours to support.

Such a probability, however, cannot well be allowed. There are circumstances, in the epistles to the Galatians and the Hebrews, relative to the condition of the persons respectively addressed, which serve to evince, that the Galatian church could not, at the *same* time, have been addressed by both of these letters. This I shall have farther occasion to show, in the sequel. In the mean time, it may suffice to remark here, that it is far from being certain, as Storr assumes it to be, that the epistle to the Galatians is addressed *exclusively* to Gentile converts. When the apostle speaks of their being "shut up under the law, before the gospel was preached;" and of "the law having been their instructer to bring them to Christ," Gal. iii. 23, 24 ; can those whom he thus addresses have been only *Gentiles?* And when he speaks of their "having been in a state of minority before Christ came;" of their "having been νήπιοι, and in bondage to the elements of the world," i. e. the ritual ceremonies of the Mosaic law, Gal. iv. 1—3 ; it seems to be very far from being obvious that only Gentile converts are addressed. Indeed, so plainly do these passages appear to respect Jews, that a critic of no less note than Noesselt, considers it as certain, that Jewish converts *only* are addressed in the epistle to the Galatians ; an opinion incapable, no doubt, of being defended, but still serving to show that Storr has, in the case before us, taken much more for granted than can be readily allowed.

Moreover, it is not so *singular* as Storr represents it to be, that Jewish converts should be exclusively addressed in one case, and Gentile ones in another. The church at Ephesus, for example, consisted, beyond all doubt, of a mixture of Jews and Gentiles. Yet, in the epistle which Paul wrote to them, he has addressed only the Gentiles, (τὰ ἔθνη— ἀκροβυστία, Eph. ii. 11, also iii. 1.) But who ever thought it necessary, in order to account for this, to suppose that Paul also wrote another letter, at the same time, to the Jewish part of the church at Ephesus?

Besides, what object could be answered by writing two *separate* letters at the same time ? Was it not a matter of course, that the whole church should be made acquainted with an apostolic letter to one part of it ? Is there not abundant evidence, that the letters of the apostles were regarded and treated by the early churches as encyclical, or (as we call them) *circulars ?* When Peter wrote his second epistle to various churches in Asia Minor, he adverts to Paul's epistles as being already known to them, 2 Pet. iii. 16. And when Clement of Rome, within the first century, wrote his epistle to the Corinthians, he made extracts from nearly all the epistles of Paul, without even naming them; which certainly implies, that he regarded the Corinthian church as being already well acquainted with them. Such being the state of knowledge respecting the apostolic epistles, in the early churches, it is a very improbable supposition, that either the epistle to the Galatians, or that to the Hebrews, was designed to be kept secret from the Jewish or Gentile Christians in Galatia, if written to them. Indeed, an arrangement of this nature would have worn the appearance of a worldly policy, and of a kind of double-dealing; which is far from being characteristic of Paul, and which would have served rather to alienate than to reconcile those who were ready to renounce his authority.

The *possibility*, that the two letters should have been written at the same time, may, for the sake of argument, be conceded. But the *necessity* of such a supposition, on grounds alleged by Storr, is contradicted by the state of the epistle to the Ephesians, which is addressed to *Gentiles only.* If the probability of it has not already been shown to be little or nothing; in the sequel, I trust, this will be made satisfactorily apparent.

(2.) "The epistle to the Hebrews," says Storr, "has no salutation, (which all the other epistles of Paul have;) it wants the usual greeting at the close; and it nowhere exhibits the name of the author. These facts, now, are easily accounted for, if we suppose that this epistle was sent at the same time with that to the Galatians, which Paul says he wrote *with his own hand,* Gal. vi. 11. It is probable, that the epistle to the Hebrews was written by the aid of an amanuensis; and as it was sent along with an epistle written and subscribed by Paul in his own hand-writing, a salutation and subscription were unnecessary or superfluous."

But why so? Why did not the longer epistle to the Hebrews need as many marks of authenticity as the shorter one to the Galatians? Is the subject less important? Are the persons addressed less regarded by the writer? And why should the fact, (if it be one, for this too is mere conjecture,) that an amanuensis wrote one letter, supersede all effort to authenticate it, when Paul has been so careful to render the other letter authentic, which was written with his own hand? During such a contest between parties as existed in Galatia, is there any probability that either letter would be left deficient as to evidences of genuineness, when the whole weight of the apostle's authority was needed to check the growing evil there? Would not the apostle at least intimate plainly in one letter, that he had written another? So far from salutation or subscription being superfluous, in such a case, the one or the other, or rather both of them, would seem to be peculiarly needed, in order that neither letter should fail of its proper destination, or have its genuineness disputed.

(3.) "In Gal. vi. 16. it is said, 'As many as walk by this rule, peace be on them, and mercy be upon *the Israel of God.*' Now the phrase, *Israel of God*, means the *Jewish* converts in Galatia, in distinction from the *Gentile* ones; and this conveys an intimation, that the apostle had written to these Jewish converts, as well as to them, the Gentile ones."

This argument, however, is built upon an exegesis of the passage quoted, which is inadmissible. The *Israel of God* is plainly a figurative name for true Christians. Paul had shown in the previous part of his epistle, that those " who are of the faith," whether Jews or Gentiles, are the children of Abraham, iii. 7, 29. At the close, he pronounces a blessing on such as adopt the principles, and obey the injunctions, which he had communicated; and concludes it, very appositely to his purpose, by calling such the Israel of God, καὶ ἐπὶ τὸν Ἰσραὴλ τοῦ Θεοῦ. The καὶ which stands before this clause, seems clearly to be *explicative*, and not *conjunctive;* amounting merely to our English *namely, even, to wit,* or to some word of the same import, and placing τὸν Ἰσραὴλ in apposition with the preceding ἐπ' αὐτοὺς.

But even supposing the apostle does advert here only to the *Jewish* converts, as such; where is the intimation to be found that he had written to them? Or, if he had, that the letter was the same with our present epistle to the Hebrews?

(4.) "The epistles to the Hebrews and to the Galatians must have been written about the same time; and probably both were written at Corinth, during Paul's first abode there. Here Paul found Priscilla and Aquila, who had fled from Italy, on account of Claudius' decree which banished the Jews from Rome, Acts xviii. 1, 2; and at the close of the epistle to the Hebrews, the writer says, *They of Italy* (οἱ ἀπὸ τῆς Ἰταλίας) *salute you*, which means, " Priscilla and Aquila from Italy salute you." The coincidence of such circumstances renders it probable that the epistle to the Hebrews was written at Corinth.—And as to the epistle to the Galatians, it was written between the time of Paul's second and third visit to Galatia; and consequently must have been written during some of his journeys recorded in Acts xvi. xvii. and xviii., which are occupied with the history of the apostle in the interval of time between those visits. But if written during this interval, when can it with so much probability be considered to have been written, as within the eighteen months' abode of Paul at Corinth, during the same time? Consequently, it is probable that both letters were written at the same place, and about the same time; and it may therefore be concluded, that the supposition of their having been sent to Galatia at the same time, is correct."

Ingenious and specious as this may appear at first view, it is far from being satisfactory, when we come to examine its parts in detail. In respect to those circumstances, which Storr represents as showing that the epistle to the Hebrews was written at Corinth, they are far from being decisive. Supposing (with him) that οἱ ἀπὸ τῆς 'Ιταλίας, in the greeting at the close, means Priscilla and Aquila; is it necessary that the salutation from them should have been sent from Corinth? Did they not afterwards travel with Paul to Ephesus? Acts xviii. 18, 19. And were they not probably at Rome during his captivity there? In Rom. xxvi. 3, a salutation is sent to them as being at Rome; and of course they were there before Paul went thither as a prisoner, because his epistle to the Romans was written before that event, Rom. i. 9—12. How then can we assume that Corinth is the only place from which Paul sent, or could send, the salutation of these Italians to Galatia?

But another consideration must be brought into our account. Storr's exegesis of the expression οἱ ἀπὸ τῆς 'Ιταλίας is altogether improbable. How should two strangers, *lately* (προσφάτως) come from Rome to Corinth, Acts xviii. 2, be so well acquainted with the church in Galatia, (situated in the interior and very remotest part of Asia Minor, and having but little intercourse with the world,) that it was not necessary even to name them to this church, but simply to advert to them by the periphrasis, οἱ ἀπὸ τῆς 'Ιταλίας? How did the Galatians know that Priscilla and Aquila were at Corinth? Or how could they distinguish them from any other Jews that fled from Rome, after the edict of Claudius proscribing the Jews was published? Besides, in all other cases where Paul sends greetings from these Italians, or to them, he calls them by name; e. g. 1 Cor. xvi. 19. 2 Tim. iv. 19. Rom. xvi. 3. This view of the subject, therefore, renders highly improbable the very circumstance which Storr has *assumed* as a *fact*, in order to make out that the epistle to the Hebrews was written at Corinth.

Next, as to the epistle to the Galatians. It was written, he says, between Paul's second and third journey to Galatia; therefore, most probably, *during his stay at Corinth*, which happened in that interval of time.

But, if we follow the account of Luke in the Acts, it is difficult, nay, impossible, to defend the supposition of Storr, that the epistle to the Galatians was written after the second visit of Paul to Galatia. Acts xvi. 6, gives us the first intimation of a visit to Galatia by Paul; and his second visit is described in Acts xviii. 22, 23, which was *after he had left Corinth*, and travelled through Palestine and Asia Minor. I know, indeed, some critics have *conjectured* that Paul made a journey to Galatia previously to the one first mentioned by Luke in Acts xvi. 6. But of what avail are *conjectures* in such cases, when they are supported neither by the epistle to the Galatians, nor by the history of Paul?

Nothing, then, but *supposition* is offered by Storr, to show that either the epistle to the Hebrews, or that to the Galatians, was written at Corinth, or that both were written about the same time; and of course, these circumstances cannot be assumed as *proved*, or even as rendered probable, in order to build the conclusion on them, that the epistle to the Hebrews, and the epistle to the Galatians, were written simultaneously to the same church.

(5.) "Timothy originated from the neighbourhood of Galatia, and was no doubt in company with Paul during his journey there, as mentioned in Acts xvi. 6. It is a singular circumstance, that although the apostle so often joins his name with his own, in the salutations contained in his other letters, he has not joined him in his epistle to the Galatians church; *specially singular*, in as much as Timothy must have been so well known to the Galatians, and as he was with Paul at Corinth. But this apparent singularity is accounted for, when we suppose that Timothy was sent with both the letters in question to the Galatians; who, of course, would receive his salutation from his own mouth."

But is it not more singular still, I ask, that Paul should say, at the close of the epistle to the Hebrews, *Know ye that our brother Timothy is* ἀπολελυμένον, i.e. either *sent away* on some errand, or *set at liberty*? Was it necessary to tell the Galatian church this, when Timothy was before their eyes *in propria persona*? I know indeed that Storr, in order to avoid this striking incongruity, has translated γινώσκετε τὸν ἀδελφὸν Τιμόθεον ἀπολελυμένον thus, *Receive honourably our brother Timothy who is sent to you;* but it is a violence done to the natural import of the language, which no other respectable critic that I know of has sanctioned, and to do which, I must think, nothing but the eagerness of supporting a favourite theory could have led this excellent writer.

(6.) "The epistle of Paul to the Galatians, both in matter and manner, has many striking coincidences with the epistle to the Hebrews."

No doubt this is true. But it is equally true also of other epistles of Paul: with the exception, that the subject in the epistle to the Galatians particularly resembles, in some important respects, that of the epistle to the Hebrews, and is prosecuted more extensively in the latter epistle, than in any of the other acknowledged epistles of Paul. Noesselt has used the same argument, in order to prove that the epistle to the Hebrews must have been written to the church in Thessalonica; and Weber, to show that it was written to the Corinthians. Might it not be used, with similar effect, to show also that it was written to the Romans? Such an argument may be of some weight, in the question whether Paul, or some other person, wrote the epistle to the Hebrews; but it cannot be of much avail to show that this epistle was written to the church at Galatia, rather than to some other church.

(7.) But the argument on which Storr seems to place most reliance of all, and which, if well founded, is of a *historical*, and not of a conjectural nature, is that deduced from 2 Pet. iii. 14—16.

As this passage is not only adduced by Storr, for the purpose of showing that the epistle to the Hebrews was written to the Galatians, but by him and many other critics of great reputation, for the purpose of proving that Paul must have been the author of the epistle to the Hebrews; in order to save repetition, I shall here examine it in reference to both of these topics, since I must of necessity institute an examination of it, with respect to the topic now under discussion.

The passage runs thus: "Wherefore, beloved, since ye are in expectation of these things [viz. the changes described in the preceding context], make strenuous efforts that ye may be found of him [Christ] in peace, without spot and blameless; and consider the delay of our Lord to come, as a matter of favour: as also our beloved brother Paul, according to the wisdom given to him, *hath written to you;* as [he has done] likewise in all his epistles, speaking in them of these things: in which are some things hard to be understood; which the ignorant and the unstable pervert, as they do the other Scriptures, to their own destruction."

To understand the nature of the argument drawn from this, we must advert to some circumstances mentioned in the epistles of Peter. His first epistle is directed to the churches in Pontus, Galatia, Cappadocia, Asia, and Bithynia, 1 Pet. i. 1. His second is directed to the same churches; for he says, "This second epistle, beloved, I write to you in which I am to stir up your pure minds by way of remembrance," 2 Pet. iii. 1. To the above-named churches in Asia Minor, then, the second epistle of Peter was directed.

The nature of Storr's argument may now be understood. It is this: "All the epistles of Paul, excepting that to the Hebrews, have designated the churches to which they were sent; the epistle to the Hebrews does not. Peter says, that Paul had written a letter to the churches in Asia Minor, whom he addresses, *as our beloved Paul hath writen* TO YOU. Now this cannot advert to any of his letters which have *inscriptions*, as they are not directed to the afore-named churches in Asia Minor. Consequently, Peter must refer to the epistle to the Hebrews, which is the only one that has no inscription. It follows, therefore, not only that Paul wrote this letter, but that he wrote it to some of the churches addressed by Peter. Most probably, then, it was written to Galatia. Especially is this credible, since the epistle to the Hebrews contains those very warnings and sentiments to which Peter adverts, as being comprised in the letter of Paul to the churches in Asia Minor, whom he addresses."

One is tempted, at first view, to acquiesce in a statement seemingly so probable, and to conclude, that the inference drawn by Storr is substantially supported. A closer examination, however, suggests formidable difficulties, which must not be passed over in silence.

I omit, at present, any consideration respecting the genuineness of the second epistle of Peter, so much called in question, and disputed by many churches of ancient times. It is unnecessary here to take other ground in regard to it, than Storr himself has taken; which is, to admit its genuineness.

What then does the passage of Peter, now in question, teach us?

(1.) That Paul had written a letter to the churches whom Peter addressed, ἔγραψεν ὑμῖν. (2.) That he had urged on them the same considerations which Peter himself had urged; *even as our beloved brother Paul hath written to you.* (3.) That in all his epistles (viz. all that had been read by them,) he had urged the same, or the like, considerations; *as likewise in all his epistles, speaking in them concerning these things.*

The question, on which the point under discussion mainly turns, is What are the *things* to which Peter refers, as treated of in common by him and by Paul?

To find an answer to this, we may make three suppositions. First, they are *all* the subjects treated of in the preceding part of Peter's epistle; or, secondly, they are those comprised in the preceding part of the third chapter; or thirdly, they are those things suggested by the immediate context, in connexion with the passage already cited.

Now, the *first* of these suppositions cannot be admitted; for Paul is so far from treating, in all his epistles, of every subject comprised in the whole of Peter's second epistle, that he has nowhere treated of some of them. If Peter, then, referred to the epistles of Paul which are now extant, it is clear he did not mean to say, that Paul had in *every* epistle of his discussed the *same* subjects, as he himself had done, throughout his second letter.

But Storr urges in a special manner the *second* supposition, viz. that the *subjects* presented to view in the *third* chapter of Peter's second epistle, are particularly treated of in the epistle to the Hebrews; and consequently, that Peter must have referred to *these* subjects, and to *that* epistle. The sum of the *third* chapter of Peter is, 'That the heavens and the earth are perishable; that they will be destroyed by fire; that the delay to destroy the ungodly must not be imputed to slackness on the part of the Lord, who puts off this catastrophe on account of his long-suffering towards men; and that the time when they shall be dissolved by fire, will come speedily, and unexpectedly, and then the heavens and the earth will be destroyed, and a new heaven and a new earth created.' Such is the context. Then follows the exhortation; "Beloved, keep yourselves unspotted and blameless; and regard the delay of your Lord's coming as a favour; *even as our beloved brother, Paul, has written to you,*" &c. Now *where* has Paul written any thing respecting the dissolution of the material elements of the universe by fire, and the creating of new heavens and a new earth instead of them? I do not find this subject treated of in the epistle to the Hebrews; nor is it touched upon in *all* the epistles of Paul; it is only adverted to in *some* of them.

It is then, *thirdly*, the exhortation in the immediate context, *to keep themselves unspotted and blameless, in view of their Lord's coming,* which Peter means to say had been urged by Paul on the persons whom he addressed, as well as by himself. This is the plain *grammatical construction*; and it is the only one which will bear examination, by comparing it with the contents of Paul's epistles.

But exhortation of such a nature is far from being contained only in the epistle to the Hebrews. The epistles to the Corinthians, Philippians, the first to the Thessalonians, the first to Timothy, and that to Titus, contain direct exhortations of this sort, and the other epistles of Paul, repeated intimations of the same nature. If the argument is good, then, to prove that the epistle to the Hebrews was written to the Galatians, because it contains such sentiments and exhortations; the same argument might prove that any of the other epistles of Paul were written to the same church, because they contain the like sentiments.

But there is one of the churches in Asia Minor to which Peter wrote, namely, that of Galatia, to which a letter of Paul now extant is addressed. May not this be the very epistle to which Peter adverts, and not the epistle to the Hebrews? In chapter vi. 7—9, is a passage of warning and exhortation, grounded on the doctrine of future retribution. This may be the very passage to which Peter adverts; or if any should think it too *general* to satisfy the reference which he makes, then the exhortation may have been in a letter now lost. That some of Paul's letters are lost, is pretty certain, from 1 Cor. v. 9—11. See also Phil. iii. 1. Evidently one of John's epistles is lost. "I wrote to the church," says he, in his second epistle, verse 9, "but Diotrephes, who loves pre-eminence, did not receive us." We have no remains of the epistle to which he here adverts. The letter of Paul, which Peter mentions, may have shared the same fate. At most, the epistle to the Hebrews, even supposing it to be proved that Paul wrote it, has no special claim to be considered as the one adverted to by Peter.

If then it cannot be shown (as I am fully persuaded it cannot) that Peter, in the passage under consideration, adverts to the epistle to the Hebrews, it cannot, of course, be shown from Peter's testimony, that Paul wrote this epistle. This argument has, indeed, been often and strongly urged, in order to establish this point, by modern and late critics; but it will not abide the test of examination. The ancient church, it is well known, never brought it forward to support the opinion that Paul was the author of the epistle to the Hebrews. Storr himself, who urges it very strongly, concedes that it was never employed by the Christian fathers. It does not follow, indeed, that it has no validity, because it was not employed by them. But it would seem, at least, that the proof to be derived from it is not so *obvious*, nor so *conclusive*, as some modern critics have deemed it.

(8.) Storr adduces "the special circumstances of the churches addressed in the epistles to the Galatians and to the Hebrews, as a ground for the opinion, that both epistles were directed to the church in Galatia. The Galatians," says he, " had for a *long* time been Christians; so had the Hebrews. The Galatians were persecuted and misled by false teachers, and were in danger of defection from Christianity; so were the Hebrews."

Now, so far from finding evidence of sameness, in the representations of the two epistles, respecting these circumstances, I find proof of dissimilarity so great as to exclude all hope of supporting the opinion of Storr, and to show that the admission of it would do great violence to the laws of probability. To the Galatians Paul says, " I marvel that ye are *so soon* removed from him who called you to the grace of Christ, unto another gospel," Gal. i. 6. To the Hebrews he says, " When for the time [i. e. plainly the long time since they professed Christianity] ye ought to be teachers, ye have need again to be taught the first elements of religion," Heb. v. 12. And again, " Call to mind the *former days* in which, when ye were enlightened, ye endured a great fight of afflictions," x. 32. And again, the writer calls on them to " remember the example of their *former teachers*, who were deceased," xiii. 7.

Then as to persecution, the Hebrews had suffered the loss of their property by it, x. 34; but there is no intimation of this in respect to the Galatians. Indeed, there is no proof, that out of Palestine persecution was such, in the apostolic age, (one or two instances only excepted,) as to deprive men of either property or life. The Roman magistracy did not permit this, either out of Palestine or in it; so long as they were in authority. This is evident from several passages of history in the Acts; e. g. Acts xviii. 12. 17, xix. 35—40. Acts xvi. xxvi. Then there is a great difference between the kind of persecution animadverted upon in the epistle to the Galatians, and in that to the Hebrews. In the *former*, Christians are addressed as in danger, from their pressure, of incorporating Judaism with Christianity, and making the continued profession of it essential to salvation; in the *latter*, they are every where addressed, as in danger of a final and total renunciation of the Christian religion. In the one, they are dehorted from superadding the Jewish ceremonies to Christianity; in the other, from utterly abandoning the Christian religion.

But further; Paul says, in Gal. vi. 11, " Ye see how LARGE a letter I have written to you with my own hand." Yet this epistle consists of only *six* chapters of a moderate length. How then could Paul say to a part of the *same* church, in a letter accompanying this, " I beseech you, brethren, to bear with a word of exhortation from me, for I have written unto you διὰ βραχέων IN A FEW WORDS," or *briefly*, Heb. xiii. 22. Yet this *brief* epistle is more than twice as long as the *large* letter which accompanied it. Could Paul so forget himself, on such an occasion as this?

Again, Paul often adverts, in his epistle to the Galatians, to the fact that he was the first who taught them the doctrines of Christianity. Yet in the Epistle to the Hebrews, there is not a word of this; but, plainly, the whole manner of the letter, and specially the manner in which he speaks of the teachers of those whom he addresses, implies that he had not himself planted the church to which his letter was directed.

But what determines the question beyond all hope of supporting the views of Storr, is, that in the epistle to the Galatians, their *teachers* are animadverted upon with great severity, on account of their improper conduct and erroneous doctrines. They are represented as perverting the gospel of Christ; as having an erroneous zeal for selfish purposes, iv. 17, v. 13; and the apostle even proceeds so far as to express a wish that they might be cut off from the church, v. 12. But how totally different is the character given of teachers, in the epistle to the Hebrews! " Obey your teachers, and be subject to them; for they watch over your souls, as they who must give an account;" i. e. they are altogether worthy of your confidence and obedience, xiii. 17. And at the close of the letter, he sends his affectionate salutations to them, xiii. 24.

These considerations seem to remove all probability, and even possibility, that the epistle to the Hebrews was, as Storr maintains, written at the same time and place as the epistle to the Galatians, and that it was also directed to the same church.

The excellent character and distinguished acuteness of Storr, entitle almost any opinion which he has seriously defended, to examination; but I cannot resist the impression, that he has utterly failed in defending the sentiment which has now been examined.

I have, throughout this investigation, proceeded on the supposition that Paul wrote the epistle to the Hebrews; which Storr fully believed, and the belief of which is necessary, in order that one may adopt the sentiment which he has maintained in respect to its destination. Whether there is sufficient reason to believe that Paul was the author of the epistle, will be a subject of discussion in a subsequent part of this

Introduction. In the mean time, I shall concede this point, (while examining the question relative to its destination,) to all the writers who have assumed it, in supporting their respective opinions. Such is the case with all those, whose various opinions relative to the destination of our epistle, still remain to be examined.

§ 6. *Was the epistle directed to the church at Thessalonica?*

The character which has just been given of Storr, will also apply, in respect to some of its prominent traits, to Noesselt, late professor of Thelogy at Halle, who has maintained, in an essay devoted to this purpose,* that the epistle to the Hebrews was written to the churches in Macedonia, or rather to the church at Thessalonica. Semler had done this before him; but on somewhat different grounds, and with less plausible reasons. On this account, I shall now, without particularly adverting to the efforts of Semler, proceed to examine the more ably supported opinion of Noesselt.

The general principle, to which Noesselt makes an appeal in his argument, is, in itself, considered correct. He endeavours to show, that " there are circumstances mentioned in the epistle to the Hebrews, in Paul's epistles to the Thessalonian church, and in the life of this apostle, which afford a very striking agreement; so striking as to render it altogether probable, that Paul must have directed to this church, the epistle which is now inscribed, *To the Hebrews;* and that he must have written it during his abode of eighteen months at Corinth, as recorded in Acts xviii." Let us examine these circumstances.

(1.) " When Paul visited Corinth for the first time, he found Priscilla and Aquila there, who had recently fled from Italy, on account of the decree of Claudius, which banished the Jews from Rome, Acts xviii. 1, 2. At the close of the epistle to the Hebrews, he says, ' They of Italy salute you;' meaning Priscilla and Aquila. Here then is a circumstance in the epistle to the Hebrews, which accords with the circumstances of Paul, during his first visit to Corinth."

But, as I have before remarked, (p. 11,) Paul was in company with these Italians at other places besides Corinth. From some of these other places, then, he *might* have written this salutation. Besides, is there any probability, (as I have before asked,) that two strangers, who had *recently* (προσφάτως) come from a city so distant as Rome, should

* Contained in his Opuscula.

be so well known to the Thessalonians in the extreme north-eastern part of Greece, that they need not even be named, but simply called οἱ ἀπὸ τῆς Ιταλίας, in a greeting or salutation ? And particularly so, as neither of them were officers in the church, or public teachers. In all other cases, as has been already shown, Paul expressly *names* these persons, when he adverts to them. Why should he depart here from his usual custom ?

(2.) " Paul says, at the close of the epistle to the Hebrews, that Timothy was ἀπολελυμένον, *sent away ;* and Paul had sent Timothy from Berea to Thessalonica, while Paul himself was at Athens, a little before he came to Corinth : comp. Acts xvii. 13—16. Here then is a concurrence of circumstances, which favours the opinion that the epistle to the Hebrews was written by Paul at *Corinth,* and directed to the Thessalonians."

To understand the nature of this argument, and the reply which I have to make, it is necessary to advert, for a moment, to the history of Paul's journeys at the time now under consideration. Paul, in company with Silas and Timothy, first preached the gospel at Thessalonica, where a church was formed ; but, being vehemently opposed by some of the Jews, they went to Berea, a neighbouring city, Acts xvii. 10. Thither the persecuting Jews of Thessalonica followed them ; in consequence of which, Paul, leaving Silas and Timothy there, withdrew to Athens. Here he resided a short time, and then went on his first visit to Corinth, Acts xvii. 1—15, xviii. 1. At this last place, he staid eighteen months, Acts xviii. 11. Now Noesselt supposes, that before Paul left Athens, he sent Timothy (who was still at Berea, Acts xvii. 10. 14) back to Thessalonica, in order to make inquiries respecting the state of the church there ; and that this is the meaning of that passage at the close of the epistle to the Hebrews, *Ye know,* (as he would translate it,) *that our brother Timothy is sent away.*

But as there is nothing of all this in the history which Luke has given of Paul and Timothy, Acts xvii, and as the whole must therefore be founded on *conjecture,* it might be sufficient, on the other hand, to *conjecture* that Paul did *not* send Timothy from Berea to Thessalonica, as Noesselt supposes.

However, respect for so excellent a critic as Noesselt, would rather demand some argument, to show that this conjecture cannot be well founded. I would observe, then, that in order to render his position probable, he assumes as a fact, that the epistle to the Hebrews was written *before* the epistles to the Thessalonians ; a supposition not capable of being rendered *probable*, much less of being proved.

It will be admitted, that there is not a word in our present first epistle to the Thessalonians, respecting any *previous* letter addressed to them ; a circumstance not to be imagined, provided the apostle had written such a laboured epistle to them as that to the Hebrews is, and on such an important question. Besides, it appears altogether probable from Acts xviii. 1—6, that Silas and Timothy arrived at Corinth soon after Paul had gone there ; so that the absence of Timothy, supposed by Noesselt to have taken place at the time when the epistle to the Hebrews was written, cannot be rendered at all probable, from this part of Paul's history; for it cannot be thought *probable*, that such an epistle as that to the Hebrews would be written by Paul *immediately* after his arrival at Corinth, amidst all the agitation and dispute and hazard occasioned by his first preaching there. But even conceding that this *might* have been done, is it probable that Paul, who (according to Noesselt) had just before, while at Athens, sent Timothy to Thessalonica, and who knew that he was *now there*, should gravely write to the Thessalonians, *Ye know that our brother Timothy is sent away;* when this same Timothy, *in propria persona*, was present with the very church to whom this was written?

(3.) "In Heb. x. 34. Paul says, *Ye had compassion on my bonds;* or, according to another reading, of equal authority, *Ye had compassion on those who were bound*, i.e. the prisoners. This refers to Paul's imprisonment, as related in Acts xvi. 23—40 ; and to the sympathy which the Thessalonians evinced for him in these circumstances."

But this imprisonment was at Philippi, *before* Paul had visited Thessalonica, and before the Thessalonians could know that he was in their region, except by report. This imprisonment lasted but a *few hours;* it ended in a most triumphant deliverance, by the interposition of Divine power, and in the shame and mortification of the magistracy who had ordered it. The whole occurrence, instead of demanding compassionate sympathy, was a matter of *triumph* and *congratulation*. Or, if otherwise, it was not an affliction in respect to which the Thessalonians could compassionate Paul, as they could not know of its having happened, until it was past.

(4.) " The Hebrews are praised for their liberality ; and so are the Thessalonians."

To which I reply, So are other churches. Does it follow, because they exhibited this trait of character which was *common* among Christians in the apostolic age, that the Thessalonian church must have been the same which is thus recommended in the epistle to the Hebrews?

(5.) "The persons to whom the epistle to the Hebrews was addressed, had suffered persecution, Heb. x. 32, xii. 4; which was also the case with the Thessalonians, 1 Thess. ii. 14—16, 2 Thess. i. 11."

So had many other churches. But neither at Thessalonica, nor scarcely any where else, except in Palestine, do we know of a persecution, at this period, which involved the loss of property and the hazard of liberty and life. The epistle to the Hebrews speaks of their being despoiled of their property, x. 34; a circumstance not to be found in the account of the persecution at Thessalonica, and one which makes directly against the supposition of Noesselt.

(6.) "The Thessalonians were in danger of defection from the faith, so that Paul was obliged to send Timothy to confirm them, 1 Thess. iii. 2, 3; and the same danger is every where adverted to, in the epistle to the Hebrews."

This argument is built on an erroneous exegesis. That Timothy made a visit to *confirm* the Thessalonians, does not surely imply that they were in special danger of apostasy. When Paul is said to have gone through Asia Minor *confirming* the churches, Acts xv. 36—41, xvi. 4—6, xviii. 23, are we to draw the inference that all the churches there were in the same danger of apostasy as the persons to whom the epistle to the Hebrews is addressed? If not, this argument of Noesselt has no force to establish the opinion which he advocates.

(7.) "There is a great similarity between the epistle to the Hebrews and the epistle to the Thessalonians."

So there is, also, between the epistle to the Hebrews and all the epistles of Paul. This argument, then, proves too much. It may serve to show that Paul probably wrote the epistle to the Hebrews; but it can have no important influence on the question, *To whom* did he write this epistle?

Most of the similarities, moreover, which are produced by Noesselt, are similarities of a *general* nature in respect to sentiments of piety and morality. Must there not be a similarity, of course, in these respects, in all the epistles of Paul, provided he always taught the same doctrines of Christianity?

But the *dissimilarities* between the epistles to the Thessalonians and the Hebrews, Noesselt has not proceeded to develop. Yet there are some; and some so striking, as to render the supposition which he defends, altogether improbable. The Hebrews addressed in our epistle, had been for a *long* time Christians; but if Noesselt's supposition be true, they had been so only a *few months*, at most, when Paul wrote his first epistle to them; for Paul had only made a rapid journey from Thessalonica to Athens, and thence to Corinth; and soon after his arrival there, and (as Noesselt thinks) before Timothy had come to him, he wrote the epistle in question.

I may add, the author of the epistle to the Hebrews nowhere adverts to his having *first* planted Christianity among them. But Paul, in his epistle to the Thessalonians, very frequently adverts to this circumstance.

Further, the epistle to the Hebrews is directed to a church almost wholly (if not altogether) *Jewish;* while it is plain, from Acts xvii. 4, 5, that only a *few* Jews had early joined the Thessalonian church; and plainer still, that this church was principally made up of Gentiles, from Paul's first epistle to them, i. 9, where he says, " Ye have *turned from idols*, to serve the living God." Now, circumstances so widely diverse and opposite, cannot be predicated of the same church, while they have respect only to an interval of time, which, at the most, cannot exceed the eighteen months that Paul abode at Corinth.

Finally, Paul's two epistles to the Thessalonians, throughout, are filled with commendations of the Thessalonian church, for their firmness and stedfastness in the faith of the gospel. Not a word of their Jewish prejudices. Not a reference to the imminent danger of apostacy, which is every where developed in the epistle to the Hebrews. Noesselt accounts for this, by the supposition, that Paul's first epistle to them, viz. that to the Hebrews, (as he supposes,) had produced a thorough reformation among them. But when Paul's *first* epistle to the Corinthians had effected a reformation, in respect to various particulars of far less importance than those treated of in the epistle to the Hebrews, how does the apostle fill his *second* letter with commendations, which have a direct reference to his former admonitions? Could it be otherwise here, if the epistle to the Hebrews had been written before our present epistles to the Thessalonians, and produced such an effect as Noesselt supposes?

On the whole, then, the supposition of Noesselt must be abandoned; not only because it is not well supported, but because it involves difficulties and improbabilities so great as to render it altogether incredible.

§ 7. *Was it directed to Hebrews, who were sojourners in Asia Minor?*

Bolten (who has distinguished himself, in a peculiar manner, by a translation of the New Testament, with constant reference to the Syriac or Syro-Chaldaic language, in which he supposes many of the original documents must have been composed,) has advanced the opinion, that the Hebrews, addressed in our epistle, were those who had fled from Palestine, about A.D. 60, on account of the persecutions there, and were scattered abroad Asia Minor. To this he thinks the οἱ καταφυγόντες in vi. 18, refers; as also the passage in xiii. 14, which speaks of their having *no abiding city*. He finds parallels of such a meaning, in 3 John verses 5 and 7, where *strangers* are mentioned, and those *who have gone abroad* (ἐξῆλθον) *for his* (Christ's) *name's sake;* in 1 Pet. i. 1, where *sojourners of the dispersion* are mentioned; and in James i. 1, where the οἱ ἐν τῇ διασπορᾷ are addressed.

I am unable, however, to find any history of a persecution in Palestine, at the period which he mentions, or any account of a dispersion of Jewish Christians abroad, at that period. As to the texts which he cites, in favour of his supposition, they will not bear the construction which he has put upon them. *We who have fled*, Hebrews vi. 18, is inseparably connected with the clause which follows, viz. *to lay hold on the hope set before us*, i. e. in the gospel. Besides, the writer does not say *you* who have fled, but *we*, i.e. Christians. So also in xiii. 14, it is *we* (viz. Christians) *who have no abiding city*, i. e. no permanent place of happiness in the present world. The passage in 3 John verses 5, 7, probably refers to Gentile Christians, who became exiles; and those in James and Peter have respect merely to Jews who *lived* in foreign countries, in distinction from those who lived in Palestine.

Besides, how could the apostle address *wandering* fugitives, scattered over Asia Minor, and destitute of a home, as in a condition to bestow charity? xiii. 1, 2. 16. How could he speak of them as having stated teachers? xiii. 17, 24. How could he expect his letter to reach them; or promise them a visit with Timothy, xiii. 23, in case he should speedily return?

Respectable as the critic is who has advanced this opinion, it seems to be quite destitute of probability, and entitled to but little consideration.

§ 8. *Was the epistle addressed to the church at Corinth?*

Michael Weber, who has distinguished himself in some respects as a critical writer on the canon of the New Testament, has advanced, and endeavoured to support the opinion, that the epistle to the Hebrews was written to the church at Corinth. He labours, in the first place, to show that Paul wrote no less than five letters to the Corinthians. The first was one which has been lost, and which Paul mentions in our present 1 Cor. v. 9—13. The second and third were our first to the Corinthians, and so much of the second as includes chapters i.—ix., with the two last verses of the epistle; the fourth, our present epistle to the Hebrews; and the fifth, the remainder of the second epistle to the Corinthians; all which, he thinks, were written in the order now suggested.

Proceeding on the ground of such an arrangement of Paul's letters, he endeavours to support his opinion, that the epistle to the Hebrews was written to the Corinthians, by arguments which I shall now examine.

(8.) " The Hebrews became Christians at an early period, and so did the Corinthians; the Hebrews were Judaizing Christians, and so were the Corinthians. An agreement in these respects renders it probable, that the epistle to the Hebrews was sent to the church at Corinth."

But Paul did not visit Corinth until A.D. 51 or 52, after he had repeatedly traversed the various countries of Asia Minor, and founded several churches in Macedonia. It cannot, therefore, be called an *early* period, at which the Corinthians were converted. Paul established few, if any, new churches, *after* the establishment of this at Corinth; at least, history does not give us any account of them.

In respect to the Corinthians being *Judaizing* Christians, the proof is altogether wanting. The apostle has taken no notice of any contest or question of this nature among them. He has indeed, in 2 Cor. iii. 6—18, drawn a parallel between the Mosaic and Christian dispensations; but it is of a general nature, and touches none of the points usually contested by Judaizing Christians. In 2 Cor. xii. 13—23, to which Weber appeals for proof of his assertion, it is plain, that some Judaizing teacher (or teachers) is adverted to by Paul; whose conduct he describes in terms which convey very strong disapprobation. But this, instead of aiding to establish the position of Weber, seems absolutely to overthrow it; for in the epistle to the Hebrews, the *teachers* (as we have already had occasion to remark, p. 21,) are *commended*, as being altogether worthy of confidence and obedience, Heb. xiii. 17. 24. We have already seen, moreover, that the church at Corinth consisted, at first, of but few Jews; as is plain from the history of Paul's planting it, Acts xviii.

(2.) " There is a most striking resemblance between the epistle to the Hebrews and the epistle to the Corinthians."

This, Weber labours to establish, by a comparison of the methods in which each quotes the Old Testament; of the ἅπαξ λεγόμενα; and of the similitudes employed.

That there is a similarity, I should readily concede. But resemblance, and even striking resemblance, is not confined merely to the epistles addressed to the Corinthians and to the Hebrews. Storr finds it between the epistles to the Galatians and to the Hebrews; Noesselt, between the epistles to the Thessalonians and to the Hebrews; and it may be easily shown, (as it will be hereafter,) that the epistle to the Hebrews has a striking resemblance to *all* the epistles of Paul, in a variety of respects. Why should we, or how can we, limit this to the epistles addressed to the Corinthians?

But in various respects, in which Weber has undertaken to make out a likeness between the epistle to the Hebrews and the epistle to the Corinthians, it seems to me that he has entirely failed. In the epistle to the Hebrews, repeated reference is made to personal sufferings and loss of property, through persecution, Heb. x. 33, 34, xii. 4; but in the epistle to the Corinthians, we discover no traces of such persecution; nor does the history of the church at Corinth give us any knowledge of persecution having early prevailed there. At all events, when our present first epistle to the Corinthians was written, it is clear that no such event had taken place at Corinth; for Paul says, 1 Cor. x. 13, *no trial hath befallen you but such as is common to men.* Now, as the epistle to the Hebrews speaks of *the great fight of afflictions*, x. 33, 34, which they endured, when they were first enlightened, here is an absolute contradiction of Weber's supposition, instead of a confirmation of it.

(3.) "The warnings, exhortations, and commendations for charity bestowed, are alike in the epistles to the Corinthians and to the Hebrews."

But the same resemblances which Weber finds between these epistles, Noesselt finds between the epistles to the Thessalonians and to the Hebrews. Such resemblances may be found, also, in other epistles. But they are of a nature too *general* to afford any evidence of weight in such a question as the one before us. Does not every Christian church need *warning, reproof, consolation?* And is not every one that is charitable, entitled to *commendation?* It is not, therefore, from a comparison of general expressions of this nature, that the sameness of churches addressed can be proved. There must be something particular, local, and *sui generis*, to make such proof valid.

(4.) The greeting at the close of the epistle to the Hebrews, Ἀσπάζονται ὑμᾶς οἱ ἀπὸ τῆς Ἰταλίας, Weber understands (like the critics whom I have already examined) as referring to Priscilla and Aquila; and compares it with the greeting from the same persons, in 1 Cor. xvi. 19.

But in the latter place they are *expressly* named, so that there is a striking *dissimilitude*, instead of resemblance, in the manner of the salutation.

(5.) He further compares several ideas in the epistle to the Corinthians and the epistle to the Hebrews ; such as warnings taken from the example of ancient Israel, 1 Cor. x. 1—12, and Heb. iii. 16—18 ; the doctrine that God chastises his children for their good, 1 Cor. xi. 32, and Heb. xii. 5—11 ; and some other things, about which similar views in both epistles are expressed.

The words, however, which are employed in these two cases, are, for the most part, quite diverse. And even if they were not, could Paul write on such subjects to no more than *one* church ? And must that church be *only* at Corinth ?

(6.) " But, the epistle to the Hebrews is called λόγον παρακλήσεως ; and also in 2 Cor. vi. 1, Paul says, παρακαλοῦμεν."

True ; but the same Paul repeatedly says παρακαλέω in his epistles to the Romans, Ephesians, Philippians, Thessalonians, and elsewhere. Was the epistle to the Hebrews written to these churches, because παρακαλέω is a word common to it and to the epistles directed to them ?

(7.) " In 1 Cor. iv. 18, 19, xvi. 2—7, the apostle has expressed his desire or determination to pay the Corinthians a visit ; and at the close of the epistle to the Hebrews, the same determination is expressed, Heb. xiii. 23."

But were there no other churches which the apostle desired or determined to visit, besides that at Corinth ? And could he express the desire or determination to visit no other ? Even if all this should be admitted, the determination to pay a visit, as expressed in our first epistle to the Corinthians, was abandoned when he wrote the second, i. 15 seq. ; which, according to Weber's own arrangement, was written before our epistle to the Hebrews.

(8.) " From 1 Cor. xvi. 10, it appears, that Timothy, when this letter was written, was absent from Paul ; and in the epistle to the Hebrews, xiii. 23, he is said to be sent away (ἀπολελυμένον.) Here again is a similarity of circumstances."

Granted; but was not Timothy constantly employed in this manner, on errands of Paul to the churches? Was he absent *only once*? And could Paul tell no other church of his absence, but that of Corinth? Besides, our second epistle to the Corinthians, (written, according to Weber himself, *before* our epistle to the Hebrews,) makes it clear that Timothy had returned; for he is joined with Paul in the salutation at the beginning of the epistle, 2 Cor. i. 1.

(9.) "Since the writer of the epistle to the Hebrews says, xiii. 22, I have written to you διὰ βραχέων, *briefly*, this refers to our *second* epistle to the Corinthians, [which, according to Weber, consisted of the first nine chapters;] and the meaning of this phrase is, 'My last epistle to you (viz. the second epistle to the Corinthians) was short;' implying, at the same time, that the present one is longer or more copious."

But such an explanation the text will not bear. "I beseech you, brethren," says the writer, "bear with my address to you, because (or, since) I have written briefly;" he evidently means, *briefly* in comparison with the importance of the subject and the occasion; briefly in comparison with the copiousness which his interested feelings for them and the cause of truth would have prompted. "I have written briefly," is an apology for the letter to the Hebrews which the writer was then concluding; and, not for a *former* one to the church at Corinth. The incongruity of a supposition, such as Weber makes, is manifest from the meaning of the very language which he quotes to support it. For how could the apostle say that he had written *briefly*, in the second epistle to the Corinthians, and imply that he had written copiously in the epistle to the Hebrews; when, even abridged as Weber makes the former, it would be almost as long as the latter?

We have seen the inconclusive nature of Weber's arguments, and their insufficiency to establish his opinion. It may now be observed, in addition, that the subjects treated of in the epistle to the Corinthians, and in that to the Hebrews, are widely different, in general, and quite dissimilar. Not a word in the epistle to the Hebrews of internal disorder, tumult, and parties in the church; no precepts about separation of husband and wife; none concerning meats offered to idols; none about the abuse of spiritual gifts; no discussion about the resurrection of the body; nothing about the denial of Paul's authority; which, with various matters relating to decorum, constitute the principal subjects discussed in our present epistles to the Corinthians. On the other hand, in the epistles to the Corinthians there is nothing about apostacy;

nothing relative to persecution ; nothing in commendation of their teachers ; no apparent apprehension expressed respecting a Judaizing spirit in the church. If the epistles to the Corinthians have resemblances in expression and doctrine to the epistle to the Hebrews, (as all Paul's epistles certainly have a resemblance to it,) are they not still so diverse as to the matters treated of, and as to the circumstances of the parties addressed, as to render hopeless all attempts to show that our present epistles to the Hebrews and to the Corinthians were addressed to one and the same church ?

§ 9. *Was the Epistle sent to Spain or to Rome ?*

Ludwig has conjectured, that the epistle to the Hebrews was written to a church in Spain ; and Wetstein, that it was written to the church at Rome. But these conjectures are altogether unsupported by the authors of them, and therefore need not delay our present investigation. We have the same liberty to conjecture, that it was written to some other place ; and the argument (if it be one) would be equally good.

§ 10. *Was it written to the church in Palestine ?*

I have examined the most specious opinions which modern criticism has offered, in order to show that the epistle to the Hebrews was not directed to the church in Palestine, but to some church abroad. In ancient times, so far as I have been able to discover, there was but one opinion on this subject ; and this has been adopted and defended by a majority of distinguished critics, in modern and recent times. This opinion is, that THE EPISTLE WAS ADDRESSED TO THE HEBREW CHURCH OF PALESTINE. We come now to examine whether there is satisfactory evidence, that this opinion is well founded.

Many arguments have been employed to establish this supposition, which appear to be incapable of bearing the test of examination. Lardner and Michaelis, who in many respects were able critics, have brought together a number of such arguments. Regard for the opinions of such men, seems to render it necessary to subject these arguments to a brief review.

(a) Lardner adduces Heb. i. 2. *God—hath in these last days spoken unto* us *by his Son;* which, he thinks, must designate those whom Christ *personally* addressed, i. e. the Jews.

But although it *may* have such a meaning, it is equally plain that it may have a different one, viz. *spoken unto Christians,* or *to men in general.* Thus the word *us* is in other places employed; e. g. Luke i. 1. *The things fully credited by* us, i. e. by Christians.

(b) " Heb. iv. 2. *Unto* us *is the gospel preached, as well as unto them.*"
To this passage the remarks just made will apply, with the same force as to Heb. i. 2.

(c) " Heb. ii. 1—4. *How shall we escape if we neglect so great salvation, which at the first began to be spoken by the Lord, and was confirmed unto us by them that heard him; God also bearing them witness by signs and wonders,* &c. Now Palestine was the place where miracles were performed."

But miracles were also performed out of Palestine, by those who had heard Christ, as well as in it. And how then can it be a proof, that those addressed in the passage under examination belonged exclusively to Palestine? The meaning is, (or at least *may be,*) that Christianity was confirmed to *the men of that age,* by the miracles which were wrought by the immediate disciples of Christ. This sentiment, of course has nothing necessarily *local* attached to it.

(d) " Those addressed by the epistle to the Hebrews were wel. acquainted with the sufferings of Christ; as the Christians of Judea must have been, i. 3. ii. 9. 18. v. 7, 8. ix. 14. 28. x. 12. xii. 2, 3 xiii. 12."

And so were all to whom the apostles preached. Christ *crucified* was the grand theme, the prominent subject, of apostolic preaching, 1 Cor. ii. 2. Gal. vi. 14.

(e) " Heb. v. 12. *But when for the time ye ought to be teachers of others, ye have need to learn the first principles;* which most suitably applies to Christians in Judea, to whom the gospel was first preached."

But if the epistle to the Hebrews was written after A. D. 60, (as is altogether probable, and as Lardner himself supposes,) then the same thing might be said to many other churches out of Palestine, who were among the *early* converts.

(f) " What is said of apostates, in ch. vi. 4—6, and x. 26—29, is peculiarly applicable to apostates in Judea."

But this may be very properly applied, also, to apostates elsewhere, in any other churches where the gospel had been fully preached.

(g) Heb. xiii. 13, 14. *Let us therefore go forth to him* [viz. Jesus] *without the camp, bearing his reproach; for here we have no permanent city, but we seek one which is to come.* This, Lardner and

Michaelis both suppose, was addressed to Christians in Jerusalem, warning them to flee from that city, because the destruction of it would speedily take place.

But it seems quite plain to me, that this passage is merely an exhortation to self-denial, and to patient endurance of suffering on account of Christ, and after his example, couched in figurative language, and applicable to Christians in general of that or any other time or place.

(h) To these arguments, Michaelis has added, Heb. x. 25—37. *Exhorting one another; and this so much the more, as ye see the day drawing near.—Yet a very little time, and he who is coming will come, and will not delay.* This, Michaelis thinks, is a warning to Christians in Jerusalem, that the destruction of the city was near at hand.

The obvious reply is, that the same consideration is addressed by Paul to churches and persons abroad; e. g. to the Philippians, iv. 5; to the Thessalonians, 1 Thess. v. 2—6, also v. 23; to Timothy, 1 Tim. vi. 14, 15; and by the apostle James, v. 8, when writing to the twelve tribes dispersed abroad. How can such a warning, then, (admitting that the interpretation of it by Michaelis is correct,) be considered as determining the *locality* of the epistle? The fall of *Jerusalem* surely would not endanger the *personal* safety of those who lived in Macedonia, and other places abroad.

(i) " Heb. xiii. 9. *It is good that the heart should be confirmed by grace, not by meats; for those who are conversant with them are not profited.* This must apply specially to the Jews of Palestine."

But were there not Christian Jews, in other places, superstitiously attached to doctrines concerning distinctions of meats and drinks? Were not such to be found at Rome, in Galatia, at Colosse? If so, how can this text apply *exclusively* to Jews in Palestine?

On such arguments, then, dependence cannot well be placed, in order to establish the opinion which Michaelis and Lardner defend. It cannot be denied, indeed, that a peculiar significancy would be attached to several of the passages that have now been examined, provided it could first be shown that the epistle to the Hebrews was originally directed to Jews in Palestine. But it must be conceded, that these passages (in themselves considered) are not sufficiently discriminating, to determine the question whether it was so directed. If no other than such arguments can be adduced, then must we abandon the idea of being able to offer such proof as will satisfy a critical inquirer, that the epistle to the Hebrews was directed to the Hebrews of Palestine.

That such, however, was the first *original* direction, I am inclined to believe; and to this belief the following considerations have led me.

(1.) The *inscription* to this epistle most naturally leads to this supposition, and helps to strengthen it.

I am willing to concede the point here, (for I think it may be shown to the satisfaction of every one who is well acquainted with the principles of critical inquiry,) that this inscription is not *a manu auctoris*. Such is not the manner of the epistles. They contain *within themselves* the direction which the writer gave them. Thus, Rom. i 1—7, " Paul an apostle—to the church at Rome : 1 Cor. i. 1, 2. Paul an apostle—to the church of God at Corinth : Eph. i. 1, Paul an apostle—to the saints at Ephesus : James i. 1, James a servant of God, to the twelve tribes in dispersion : 1 Pet. i. 1, Peter an apostle, to the sojourners in dispersion; 2 John v. 1, The elder, to the elect lady : Jude ver. 1, Jude a servant of Jesus Christ—to those who are sanctified :" and so of other epistles. Moreover, there are reasons why the titles of the sacred books in general, throughout the Old and New Testaments, should not be regarded as coming from the hand of those who originally composed the books. Some of these inscriptions or titles are incongruous with the contents of the book, or chapter, to which they are prefixed. But one fact, on which I do not remember to have seen any comments made, is very striking. None of the New Testament writers, when they quote the Scriptures, ever appeal to the *names* of the Old Testament books. Nothing could have been more to their purpose, than to employ these names for the sake of guiding their readers, had they been at that time affixed to the books. But they have no where employed them. Even when they quote the prophets, it is the name of the *person* who wrote, and not the name of a *book* as such, to which they appeal.

Such is the universal practice of the New Testament writers ; and such is that of Clemens Romanus, who wrote during the first century. In writing to the Corinthians, he names, indeed, the epistle of Paul to them; but how could he do otherwise ? But in all the numerous quotations which he makes of the other New Testament books, he does not once call any of them by name.

Such facts show satisfactorily, that the present names of Scripture books did not then exist ; for had they existed, appeal had been made to them, for the same purposes, and from the same necessity, as we now make it every day.

Admitting now, that the inscription, $\dot{\eta}$ πρὸς Ἑβραίους ἐπιστολὴ, is not original, and that it was superadded by some later editor or transcriber of this epistle; it is a very natural and pertinent question, *Why was such a title given to the epistle in question?* The obvious answer must be, Because the editor or transcriber, who gave it, supposed that the epistle was intended for the Hebrews. And whoever the author of the title or inscription was, it is quite certain that he lived at an early period. Nor can there be any reasonable doubt, that he gave such a title to our epistle, as agreed with the general tradition and common opinion of the Christian church at that period. For we find this title, not only in all our present Greek manuscripts, (which would not indeed settle the question of its very remote antiquity,) but in all the early versions, the Syriac, and others; also in the manuscripts of the old Itala, and the ante-Hieronymean Latin versions, the Codex Regius and San Germanensis only excepted. There is, indeed, a catalogue of canonical books from the fragments of an anonymous author, who lived near the close of the second century, (published by Muratori in his Antiqq. Ital. tom. iii. p. 854,) in which the epistle to the Hebrews is supposed to be called [epistola] *apud Alexandrinos.* But the whole passage of this writer is so obscure, and his ignorance respecting the contents of the epistle to the Hebrews so profound, (as will hereafter be shown,) that nothing is to be abated, on his account, from the statement which has just been exhibited. The fathers of the second century give the same title to our epistle which it now has; for it is by this name that Pantenus, Clemens Alexandrinus, Tertullian, and Origen, (with the whole series of fathers after them,) make their appeal to it. This shows, beyond reasonable doubt, that from whatever source the title arose, it arose *early*, and early became general, or rather universal, in the church, wherever the epistle was received.

But although the fact is certain, in respect to the *early* origin and currency of this title, one question remains, about which there has been no small dispute among critics. What is the meaning of the word *Hebrews?* Does this name apply only to the Jews of Palestine who spoke the Hebrew language? Or is it equally applicable to all the descendants of the Hebrews, who lived in foreign countries, and adhered to the Jewish religion? On this question turns the whole evidence to be derived from the title, in respect to the main subject under consideration. If the first be true, then does it show, that soon after the epistle was written, the church in general believed it to have been directed to the Jews in Palestine, if the second, then it does not at all help to show, whether the early church held it to be written to the Christian community of Hebrews in Palestine, or out of it. Viewed in this light, the question as to the meaning of the word *Hebrews* becomes a matter of no inconsiderable importance, and should therefore be radically investigated. The writers of the New Testament may be fairly presumed to have used the word *Hebrew*, according to the prevailing *usus loquendi* of the times when they wrote; and in all probability, too, of the time when the title was given to our epistle, which could not be long afterwards. But they have uniformly employed it to designate the Palestine Jews, or those who had imbibed their opinions and spoke their language. In Acts vi. 1, the Palestine Christians are expressly called 'Εβραῖοι, in contradistinction from the foreign Jews, who are called 'Ελληνισταὶ : *there arose a murmuring of the* HELLENISTS *against the* HEBREWS, *because their widows were neglected in the daily administration*. In conformity with this passage, (which is fundamental in the question now under consideration,) the dialect of Palestine is repeatedly called 'Εβραὶς or Εβραϊκὸς, in the New Testament; e. g. Acts xxi. 40, xxii. 2, Luke xxiii. 38. John v. 2, xix. 13, 17. Agreeably to this, 'Εβραΐζειν means, *to speak or write Hebrew;* as Josephus says, τὰ τοῦ Καίσαρος διήγγειλε 'Εβραΐζων, Bell. Jud. vi. 2, i. e. *he narrated Cesar's history in the Hebrew tongue*. To have a knowledge of the Hebrew language, and to speak it, was deemed among the Jews a matter of great importance, or a very valuable acquisition, Acts xxi. 40, xxii. 2. Hence Paul, when speaking of the ground of precedence which he might claim above the false teachers at Philippi, says, that *he is a Hebrew of the Hebrews*, i. e. one of full Hebrew descent, and acquainted with the Hebrew language. Although he was born at Tarsus, he was brought up at the feet of Gamaliel in Jerusalem, Phil. iii. 5. To this same fact he seems to appeal again, in a similar case, 2 Cor. xi. 22. *Are they Hebrews? So am I.*

With this *usus loquendi* of the New Testament agree other facts, which seem to place the question beyond reasonable doubt, as to what the usage of the apostolic age was, in respect to the meaning of the word in question.

The Hebrew Christians of Palestine early possessed a spurious Gospel, which long continued to have currency among them. Universal consent gave to this Gospel, written in the Syro-Chaldaic or Palestine dialect of the time, the name Εὐαγγέλιον καθ' 'Εβραίους; evidently because it was used or approved by people of Palestine who spoke the so-called Hebrew language. The early fathers, it is well known, drew the conclusion from the title to our epistle, that it was originally written in the Hebrew language. Thus Clemens Alexandrinus asserts that it was written, 'Εβραίοις 'Εβραϊκῇ φωνῇ, and interpreted by others, Euseb. H. Ecc. vi. 14. In the same way, Eusebius declares that it was addressed, 'Εβραίοις διὰ τῆς πατρίου γλώττης, to the Hebrews in their native tongue, Hist. Ecc. iii. 28; and Jerome says that Paul wrote, *ut Hebræus, Hebræis, Hebraicè*, i. e. *as a Hebrew, to the Hebrews, in the Hebrew language;* Catal. Scriptt. verb. Paulus.

Now, how could these fathers reason thus, unless they had understood the word *Hebrews* as necessarily meaning, according to the *usus loquendi* of that age, *those who spoke the Hebrew language*?

Bertholdt declares boldly, that not a single example can be found, in early times, of Jewish Christians out of Palestine being called Hebrews, Einleit. p. 2875. I would express my own conviction in a more guarded manner, and say, I have not been able to find any instance where this is the case.

Yet Eichhorn has ventured to assert, that the name *Hebrew* never has any reference to *language*, but always to *religion* or *origin*. His proof is, first, a passage from Eusebius' Hist. Ecc. iii. 4, in which the historian asserts, that Peter addressed his epistle, πρὸς τοὺς ἐξ 'Εβραίων ὄντας ἐν διασπορᾷ Πόντου. But this implies simply, that those whom Peter addressed were descended from the Hebrews, or belonged to those of the circumcision. Another passage to which he appeals, is in Philo, (de Abrahamo, p. 338 D. edit. Par.) where he says, that *Sarah advised Abraham to take as a concubine* [Hagar], *who by descent was an Egyptian*, τὴν τε προαίρησιν 'Εβραῖαν, *but by choice a Hebrew;* which he construes as meaning, *who had embraced the religion of the Hebrews*. But the antithesis here does not admit of this sense. By *descent* she was of the *Egyptian nation*, but by *voluntary choice* she attached herself to the *Hebrew nation*, is plainly the meaning of the passage; so that it fails altogether in affording ground for the conclusion which Eichhorn adduces from it.

Carpzoff, to whom Eichhorn is indebted for this quotation, has adduced several others, to show that the word *Hebrew* is used to characterize the *religion* of the Jews, rather than their *language* or *nation*. Exercitt. in Heb. Prolog. c. 1. But so far are they from affording satisfaction to my mind, that I do not think them worthy the labour of an examination in this place.

The result of this inquiry is, then, that 'Εβραῖοι, in the inscription to our epistle, means, and, according to the *usus loquendi* of the age, must mean, *the Hebrews of Palestine*, i. e. Hebrews in a country where the Hebrew language was *vernacular*.

If I have offered sufficient evidence to establish this, then does the title to our epistle go far towards showing what the original destination of the epistle was. If an ancient epistle has no direction within itself, and contains no unequivocal passages indicative of locality, in what way can we ascertain the original direction of it better than by tradition? Do we not appeal in all similar cases to tradition, in order to show when and where authors were born, lived, and wrote? where and when books were written? And seldom, indeed, can we trace back tradition, in a manner so satisfactory and definite as in the case just considered.

Thus much for the *external* testimony, in regard to the opinion that Palestine was the place to which our epistle was directed; the voice of antiquity, and the title of the letter, constituting strong presumptive evidence that such was the case. But does the *internal* condition of the epistle itself agree with this? And does it furnish no objections, which will overbalance the weight of tradition? Something must be said relative to these questions, before we can make our ultimate conclusion. I proceed then,

(2.) To examine whether the internal condition of the epistle agrees with and confirms the supposition which I am now endeavouring to defend.

The most superficial reader cannot help being impressed, on a slight reading of this epistle, with the idea that it is addressed to Jewish converts. In respect to this, indeed, all critics, ancient and modern, are of one opinion. But a close examination discloses a peculiarity of appeal, in this epistle, to the Mosaic ritual, which can be found no where else in the New Testament.

In the Acts of the Apostles, and in the acknowledged epistles of Paul, we find, indeed, numerous traces of dispute and difficulty with Jews who lived in countries remote from Palestine. But the disputed questions turn upon points of circumcision, of meats clean and unclean, points which respected the sabbaths, and the holidays that the Jews had been accustomed to observe. Concerning the priesthood, the temple, and the ritual of sacrifices, we find no questions of difficulty agitated.

The obvious reason of this seems to be, that but very few of the foreign Jews, regularly, or even at all, attended the services of the temple. The great body of those who lived in the countries more distant from

Palestine, plainly could not attend the feast at Jerusalem three times in each year, according to the prescription of Moses. The time and expenses necessary to do this, could not be spared.

This is not matter of mere conjecture. We know that the most numerous colony of Jews, any where to be found at that period, as well as the most learned and rich, was that at Alexandria in Egypt. Hither they had been transplanted, about 284 years A. C. by Ptolemy Philadelphus, who had overrun Palestine with his army. They were allowed great privileges under the reign of this prince; so that many were allured to Egypt, in his time, and the number of Jews in that country became quite large. Under Ptolemy Philometor, not far from 175 A. C., Onias, son of the high-priest Onias at Jerusalem, who had fled to Egypt for safety, asked leave of Ptolemy and his queen Cleopatra, to build a temple at Leontopolis in that country, which was a town in the prefecturate of Heliopolis. This leave he obtained; and there he built a temple, and constituted priests and Levites as ministers for its services. In his petition for obtaining this liberty, he states, that while on his military expeditions in the service of the king, he had seen temples used by the Jews for their religious services, in Celosyria, Phenicia, and Leontopolis. Joseph. Antiq. Jud. xiii. 6, edit. Colon. Allowing this statement to be true, it would appear, that at least many of these foreign Jews had then already lost their zeal for attendance on the temple worship at Jerusalem. That the Jews in Egypt did not, in general, attend the feasts at Jerusalem, is well known. They only sent an occasional deputy there, by way of testifying their respect and fraternal sympathy.

If the Jews in Egypt did thus, we may well suppose that the Jews at a greater distance from Palestine imitated them in their remissness, with respect to attendance on the temple worship at Jerusalem. The nature of the case shows, that as a body they could not have been habitually present at the holy feasts; and that most of them, indeed, never frequented Jerusalem at all. In fact, this city could not have accommodated the one-fourth part of the worshippers from abroad, had all the foreign Jews gone up to the feasts held there.

The natural consequence of not being familiar with the temple rites and priesthood, was a diminution of zeal in the foreign Jews with respect to things of this nature; until, in the end, they became to them matters of minor importance, or even of comparative indifference. Hence, Paul had no disputes with the foreign Jews about these things. At least, no marks of such disputes appear in the history of this apostle by Luke, nor in the letters of Paul himself.

But here is a point, respecting which the epistle to the Hebrews differs widely from all the other epistles of the New Testament. It is not with the question whether circumcision is to be retained or rejected; not with the dispute about meats offered to idols; not with prescriptions about new-moons and sabbaths, that the writer is concerned. The whole epistle turns on different subjects. It is the favourite idea of pre-eminence, so tenaciously attached by zealous Jews to all parts of the Mosaic *ritual*, which the writer discusses. The dignity or rank of those, through whose mediation the law was given; the temple-apartments, furniture, rites, and sacrifices; the order and honour of the priesthood; in a word, the whole apparatus of the Levitical service, both daily and annual, are the subjects of which he treats, and the things which he compares with the corresponding parts of the Christian dispensation, in order to show the superiority of the latter. Were angels employed in order to introduce the law? Christ, who has obtained a name and place far more exalted than they, himself introduced the new dispensation. Was Moses the beloved and honoured leader of God's chosen people, placed at the head of the Jewish dispensation? He was placed there as a *servant;* but Christ, at the head of the new dispensation, as a *Son.* Was the high-priest of the Jews a mediator between God and the people, who offered up their annual propitiatory sacrifice, and went into the holy of holies, into the immediate presence of the Divinity, on their account? The office of this high priest, from its very nature, and from the brevity of human life, was short and limited: but Christ is high priest *for ever;* he has entered the holy of holies in the highest heavens, and has once for all offered a propitiatory sacrifice of everlasting efficacy. Was the temple a magnificent structure, the sacred character of which inspired awe? Magnificent and sacred as it was, it was merely a copy of the temple in which Jesus officiates, reared by God himself, and eternal in the heavens. Was the blood of goats and bullocks annually presented before the shrine of Jehovah by the Jewish high-priest, on the great day of atonement? Jesus, by his own blood, entered the sanctuary of the eternal temple, and made an atonement which needs not to be repeated. In a word, were all the implements of temple-service, all which pertained to the order and persons of the priesthood, venerable and holy? All these things were merely similitudes of the more perfect temple and priesthood of him, who is the great high priest of the Christian dispensation.

Who, now, were possessed of these *specific* views in respect to the Mosaic ritual, which the writer thus brings into comparison? To whom could the writer of the epistle to the Hebrews (as he constantly does) appeal, as being familiarly acquainted with every thing that pertained even to the minutest parts of the Jewish ritual, and priesthood, and sacred places, and utensils, and the very location of these utensils? To whom, I ask, but to the Palestine Jews? To those who from childhood were familiar with all these objects, and who had been inspired by education with the most profound reverence for them, and with zeal to maintain their importance.

Why are not these subjects brought into view, in Paul's letters to other churches? Disputes he had with the Jews, as the epistles to the Romans, Corinthians, Galatians, Colossians and Thessalonians, in a word, as all his epistles, testify. But not about the temple ritual, and priesthood, and holy places, and utensils. The disputes concerned other rites of Judaism, which could be generally practised by Hebrews living in foreign countries; and not those, in which only a few devotees would feel a particular interest.

I cannot resist the impression, when I read the 7th, 8th, 9th, and 10th chapters of the epistle to the Hebrews, that the appeal is made to those who have an intimate knowledge, and strong jealousy for the honour of the whole Mosaic ritual there brought to view. I am fully aware, that pilgrims (so to speak) annually resorted from all parts of the world, where the Jews were settled, to Jerusalem. So they do still. But how few must these have been, from countries more remote! The supposition that the great body of the church, or the whole church, addressed in the epistle to the Hebrews, (if these Hebrews belonged to foreign countries,) possessed the intimate personal knowledge of the Jewish ritual, holy places, and utensils, which the writer evidently supposes those to possess whom he addresses, does, in itself considered, seem to be very improbable.

It is rendered still more so, by some additional facts, which ought to be here stated. In the latter part of Paul's ministry, his disputes abroad about Judaism appear to have generally subsided, and he was every where received by the foreign churches with great cordiality and affection. It was only at the first planting of the churches abroad, at the period when the transition was to be made from Judaism to Christianity, (which was indeed a great transition in respect to *externals*,) that disputes arose, and passions were awakened, which occasioned much trouble and anxiety to the apostle. More light, and a better understanding of the nature of Christianity, appeased these disputes, wherever Judaism had not the strong grasp which the *constant* practice of the *ritual* gave it.

Not so in Palestine. The very last visit which the apostle made there, before he was sent a prisoner to Rome, occasioned a tumult among the zealots for the law; who even joined in persecuting him. "Thou seest, brother," said the other apostles to him, "how many thousand Jews are become believers, and they are all ζηλωταὶ τοῦ νόμου," *zealots for the observance of the law*, Acts xxi. 20; the correctness of which sentiment was abundantly confirmed by the sequel. That the *zealots for the law* here means particularly the Jews of Palestine, is evident from ver. 21, which follows.

That the Palestine Christians adhered with far greater tenacity to the Jewish ritual than the Jews abroad, is clearly shown moreover by the fact that, while the foreign Jews soon abandoned altogether the rites of Judaism, the zealots for the Mosaic ritual in Palestine even separated, at last, from the community of other Christians, rejected all the epistles of Paul from the canon of the New Testament, and retained in all their strictness the ceremonies of the law. I refer to the sects of the Nazarenes and Ebionites, the first heresies that rent asunder the church of Christ; and which would not bear at all with the catholic spirit of Paul's preaching and epistles.

All these circumstances united, have strongly impressed me with the idea, that the whole texture and manner of the epistle to the Hebrews almost of necessity implies, that those to whom it was originally addressed were habitually attendants on the services of the temple, and intimately and *personally* acquainted with all its rites and ceremonies. Of course, I must regard them as belonging to Palestine, or its near neighbourhood.

In addition to these considerations, which apply generally to the epistle in question, there appear to be some particular references made to circumstances, which would seem to presuppose a personal and familiar knowledge, on the part of those addressed, with objects in and about Jerusalem and the temple. E. g. when the writer says, xiii. 12, "Wherefore Jesus, that he might purify the people by his own blood, suffered without the gate," viz. the gate through which criminals were led to execution. This implies, that the readers were supposed to be acquainted with the *locality* of Jerusalem. And in ix. 5, after recounting the apartments and various sacred utensils of the temple, the writer says, *Concerning which things*, οὐκ ἔστι, *it is not my purpose* [or it is unnecesary] *to speak particularly;* by which there is an appeal made to the knowledge of his hearers, that seems to imply a *local* and *personal* acquaintance with the circle of objects which are designated.

I freely acknowledge these circumstances are not so peculiar and exclusive, that it is not possible to apply them to Jews who resided abroad, and habitually visited Jerusalem. But where was the *community* abroad, who *as a body* did this? And then, *probability*, and not *demonstration*, is what we seek for, in an argument of this nature. If demonstration, or what is equivalent to it, had been found in the epistle itself, there had not been such endless dispute about it.

It is a striking fact also, that *only Jews* are addressed throughout the epistle. Where were the churches abroad that consisted only of Jews? I am aware, this argument may be met by asking the question,' Could not the writer address the Jewish part of a church abroad, and not the Gentile? The *possibility* of this cannot be denied. The *probability* that it was so, does not, in this case, seem to be very great. For is it not natural to suppose, that the Gentile part of the church would have been more or less infected with the feelings of the Jewish part; and that some of them, at least, would have also been in danger of apostacy? Could the writer, who shows such deep solicitude to prevent this awful catastrophe, fail to have warned his Gentile brethren against their danger; and to have exhorted and encouraged them to persevere? If this be *possible*, we must still grant, when we consider the characteristics of the writer, that it is at least highly *improbable*.

Nor can it be alleged, as an adequate reply to this, that the epistles to the Ephesians and Galatians are exclusively addressed to Gentile converts. For, in regard to the first, no such urgent and fundamental question, as that treated of in the epistle to the Hebrews, comes under discussion. It is probable, moreover, that by far the greater part of this church were gentiles. And with respect to the epistle to the Galatians, although Storr has assumed it as a point which admits of no question, that it is directed to Gentile converts only, yet Noesselt (as we have seen) is of opinion, that it is addressed altogether to Jewish converts, and says, that no one except Beausobre denies this. Opusc. Fascic. i. p. 293. Neither he nor Storr can establish their respective opinions, from the contents of the epistle. Most apparent is it, that, in general, converts from the heathen are addressed. But when the apostle says, Gal. iv. 9, " Why should ye turn *again* to the weak and beggarly elements of the world, to which ye desire *again* to be in bondage," viz. to the Jewish ritual, can he address only converts from the *heathen*? And when he says, too, ver. 1, " Be not again entangled in the yoke of bondage," can he address only those who were formerly heathens? An appeal, then, to the epistles addressed to the Ephesians and Galatians, as being *exclusively* addressed to only one part of churches made up of both Jews and Gentiles, is not satisfactory in the case before us; for the Galatian church is plainly addressed as a mixed body; and the church at Ephesus appears to have been principally made up of Gentiles. It is not comparing *par cum pari*. The peculiar circumstances of which the epistle to the Hebrews treats, show that a warning to the Gentile part of that church to whom it was sent, if such church were among the Gentiles, and consisted in part of them, was a thing, to all appearance, of indispensable necessity.

Here then is another circumstance, which contributes to render it probable that some church in Palestine was addressed by the epistle to the Hebrews. It is *possible*, that there may have been some churches abroad wholly made up of Jews; but history has given no account of any such; and not only the *possibility* but the *probability* of it must be shown, before the argument now adduced is deprived of its force.

Again, the persons addressed are requested to " call to mind their sufferings in former days, when they were first enlightened, and when they took joyfully the spoiling of their goods, and suffered other evils from persecution," x. 32. 34. This, indeed, may *possibly* have been true of other churches abroad; but we have no historical information of persecutions abroad, in the earliest age of Christianity, which were permitted by the civil government to proceed so far as to destroy or confiscate property, and to imprison persons for any length of time. Palestine was the place for such occurrences, from the very first. I am aware that Paul went with a commission to Damascus, that he might cast Christians into prison. But the very terms of that commission directed him to bring those whom he should apprehend " bound to Jerusalem," Acts ix. 2. Indeed, it is plainly the case, that at this period the Roman magistracy every where abroad opposed persecution; for it was contrary to the established maxims of the Roman government, to intermeddle with the religion of their provinces. Often did this magistracy interfere, to protect Christians whom the violence of the Jews had assailed; Acts xviii. 12—17. xix. 35—40. Acts xxi. etc. Still, I have admitted that it is *possible* such early persecution, as the epistle to the Hebrews speaks of, may have taken place abroad; but this has not been rendered *probable*, by producing any historical records which testify to it. The solitary instance of Antipas at Pergamos, Rev. ii. 13, is the only one I have been able to find. In all probability, he, like Stephen, was destroyed by the rage of a lawless mob. Of course, until more evidence on this subject can be produced, the argument from the passage in our epistle, which has been just cited, adds no inconsiderable weight to the evidence in favour of the supposition which I am endeavouring to defend.

(3.) If it can be rendered probable that Paul wrote the epistle to the Hebrews, I should think it almost certain that it must have been written to Jews in Palestine; for throughout the whole epistle, there is not one word which shows the writer to have been the instrument of their conversion, or even to have been their religious teacher. What church abroad could be thus addressed by Paul? For what one had not been either planted or nurtured by him? I do not deny the possibility of there having been some one; but the evidence that there actually was, at the time when our epistle was written I have not been able to find.

And besides this, it is peculiar to the epistle to the Hebrews, that not one word is said, which implies that their teachers were lacking in any thing pertaining either to their knowledge, or the duties demanded by their office. All is commendation. How natural is this, and easy to be accounted for, if these teachers were apostles or immediate disciples of Christ himself; and such were the teachers of the churches in Palestine. On the whole, this is a circumstance which increases the probability of the opinion that I am assaying to defend.

Internal evidence, then, is not wanting, which accords with the testimony given by the inscription of the epistle to the Hebrews. Indeed, the concurrence of both kinds of evidence is such, as to afford grounds of probability as strong as could be expected in regard to a question of this nature, which respects a matter so ancient and so difficult. Direct and positive proof, incapable of being in any way questioned or contradicted, can neither be required nor justly expected. But there is evidence enough, as it appears to me, to render the opinion of the ancient church, that the epistle to the Hebrews was directed to Christians in Palestine altogether probable.

Objections, however, drawn from the epistle itself, against this opinion, have been often and strongly urged by critics of late; and these cannot, with due respect to the authors of them, be passed over in silence.

OBJECTION 1. "Heb. ii. 3. 'How shall we escape, if we neglect so great salvation, which at the first began to be spoken by the Lord, and was confirmed unto us by them that heard him?' From this passage it appears that Christ had not personally taught those to whom this epistle is addressed; they had only been instructed by *those who heard him*, viz. the apostles and immediate disciples of Christ.

It is remarkable that this same verse is adduced and relied on, by Lardner, to support the opinion that the Hebrews of Palestine only could have been addressed by it; and by Storr, to prove that those could *not* have been the persons addressed. The argument is equally valid in both cases, i. e. it amounts to nothing in either. For the simple sentiment of the text is, " How can we escape punishment, if we neglect the gospel first published by the Lord of glory in person, and then abundantly confirmed by miracles which were wrought by the apostles and immediate disciples of Christ ?"

Now, this might be said to any church of that period, in any country; and to any church on earth, from that period down to the present hour. Of course, it determines nothing relative to the question, whether our epistle was directed to a church in, or out of Palestine.

OBJECTION 2. " Heb. xii. 4. ' Ye have not resisted unto blood, striving against sin;' i. e. against injurious and unjust opposition. How could this be said to the church at Jerusalem, which had been called to witness the martyrdom of Stephen and others, and the bloody death of James; and who had lived in the fire of persecution ever since its first establishment ?"

This argument has appeared so conclusive to many critics, that they have abandoned the idea of supporting the ancient opinion, that our epistle was directed to the church in Palestine. Its first appearance inclined me to the same conclusion. A more particular examination of it, however, has led me to doubt altogether of its validity.

" Call to mind," says the writer, " your severe afflictions in former days, when ye were first enlightened," x. 32—34. That is, your former persecutions, which were severe, ye bore with patience and cheerfulness, although ye suffered imprisonment and loss of property. Now, indeed, ye are tried, continues the writer, but not in the highest degree. " Ye have not yet resisted unto blood." How then does the history of the church in Palestine comport with this sentiment? A question which must necessarily be investigated here.

The first persecution was that which arose at the time of Stephen's martyrdom, Acts vi. vii. This happened probably in A. D. 37 or 38. During this persecution many were imprisoned, severely beaten, and subjected to various insults and outrages; but there is no satisfactory evidence, that any blood was shed except that of Stephen. Paul, in giving an account of his former conduct, says, that he persecuted Christianity unto death, Acts xxii. 4, which was in fact the case with respect to

Stephen; and no doubt he designed to do so, in respect to many others. But in telling us what he actually effected, he says that he arrested Christians, beat them in the synagogues, Acts xxii. 4, 19, compelled them to blaspheme, and shut them up in prison, Acts xxvi. 10, 11. But the voice of Jesus arrested him, on his way to Damascus; and in confessing his crime, he avows that he imprisoned believers and beat them in the synagogues. But he does not state that he was guilty of blood, except in the case of Stephen, Acts xxii. 19, 20. As this passage contains, we have reason to believe, a *full* confession of his guilt, it may serve to explain the doubtful passage in Acts xxvi. 10, where he says, *when they were slain*, (ἀναιρουμένων αὐτῶν) *I gave my vote against them.* The plural number here (ἀναιρουμένων) has led many to suppose that Paul was concerned in *frequent* murders. But any one versed in the narrations of the New Testament, cannot but know how frequently the plural number is used to designate the occurrence of facts, in which *only one* person is concerned, i. e. where the sense of the passage requires it to be understood only as in the singular. It is thus that the thieves on the cross are said to have reviled the Saviour, although *only one* of them did so, Matt. xxvii. 44, Mark xv. 32, comp. Luke xxiii. 39; thus, that the demoniacs at Gadara are said to have been exceedingly fierce, when *only one* of them was so, Matt. viii. 28—34, comp. Mark v. 1—18, Luke viii. 26—38; and thus, in other cases, presented by the Scriptures,* and (I may add) by other writings also, too numerous to be here recounted. Nothing is said, in the history of the first persecution, of any Christians suffering martyrdom besides Stephen. Nothing in Paul's confession to the Saviour, which specifies the blood that he had shed. The conclusion seems to be, then, that only the blood of Stephen was shed on this occasion, although doubtless Paul then *meant* to add to the number of martyrs; he gave his vote for this purpose, Acts xxvi. 10, and abused Christians in various ways, such as the spite and malice of Jews suggested. But they were not *destroyed*. It must be remembered, in regard to this persecution, that it was limited to *Jerusalem;* with the exception only that Paul *designed* to extend it to Damascus, Acts viii. 12, xxvi. 10.

Saul's conversion, however, appears to have put an end to this persecution; for we read, after his first visit to Jerusalem, that the churches in

---

* See Matt. xx. 30—34, and comp. Mark x. 46—52, xviii. 35—43. See also Matt. xxviii. 1, Mark xvi. 1, 2, with which comp. Luke xxiv. 1, 9, 10, and John xx. 1, 11, 18.

Judea, Galilee, and Samaria, were in a state of peace and prosperity, and were multiplied, Acts ix. 31.

Persecution again broke out under Herod Agrippa, (about A. D. 44,) who, to gain favour with the Jews, pretended great zeal for the law; and, to do them a pleasure, undertook to harass Christians. How widely he extended his efforts to vex them, the sacred historian has not told us; it is simply said that he undertook κακῶσαί τινας τῶν ἀπὸ τῆς ἐκκλησίας, and that he put to death James the brother of John, and cast Peter into prison, Acts xii. 1, 3. It is very probable, since Herod lived a part of his time at Cesarea, that he may have extended his vexations to the churches there, in order to increase his popularity in that city, which was the capital of his kingdom. Be this as it may, we read of only one death on this occasion; *James he destroyed,* ἀνεῖλε; but others, ἐκάκωσε. This persecution happened so early as A. D. 44.

Herod died a short time after this, at Cesarea, smitten by a divine hand on account of his having impiously received praise as a God. With his death the persecution ceased; for the Roman procurators who followed, allowed of no open persecution. It was not until the departure of Festus, and before the arrival of his successor Albinus, (nineteen or twenty years after the persecution of Herod,) that the Jews were again engaged in any open or violent outrages against Christians. James the younger, and some others with him, were then destroyed by Ananus the high-priest. But this act of violence was disapproved by the considerate and sober part of the Jews, and Ananus himself was thrust out of office, by the interference of the succeeding Roman governor, on account of this act of cruelty, Josephus Antiq. xx. These are all the persecutions unto blood, in Palestine and before the destruction of Jerusalem, of which we have any historical information. The last of these probably occurred, after the epistle to the Hebrews was written. Vexation, proceeding from personal insult, contumely, excommunications, malice, and blind fiery zeal, on the part of the unbelieving Jews, no doubt, the Christians in Palestine suffered very frequently, during the period before the destruction of Jerusalem. But restraint of personal liberty, and destruction of property or of life, were not permitted by the Roman government, while the civil administration of Judea was actually in their hands.

Compare now these facts, (which I have not seen fully developed by any of the critics who have written on our epistle,) with the passage which is at present under consideration. Our epistle is directed to Christians **as a body, and not to the** *teachers* or *officers* of the churches; for these are separately spoken of, Heb. xiii. 7, 17. and a salutation is sent to them, Heb. xiii. 24, as not being a party to the epistle, but a separate class of persons. The investigation which we have instituted shows that *only teachers*, and not *private Christians*, had suffered martyrdom in Judea. An epistle to private Christians in Palestine, then, and not addressed to their teachers, might say, and might truly say, " Ye have not yet resisted unto blood, striving against sin ;" although some of their *teachers* had suffered martyrdom.

Eichhorn, denying that our epistle was written to a church in Palestine, asks, as though it were incapable of contradiction, " Did not blood often flow at Jerusalem, and (since this was the metropolis of the country) in Palestine at large ?" And then he concludes it to be impossible, that our epistle should say to Hebrew Christians in Palestine, " Ye have not resisted unto blood." But had he minutely investigated the history of these persecutions, he might have spared his conclusion, and refrained from the assurance with which it is stated. If, however, we should admit all that is contended for, viz. that in the persecution of the time of Stephen, and under Herod Agrippa, many *private* Christians were destroyed ; even then, the passage of the epistle, which we are considering, offers no formidable difficulty. Plainly the principles of interpretation demand no more, than that what is said, in the verse under consideration, should have respect to the generation of Christians *then living*, and the persecution *then pending*, when the epistle was written. One generation of Christians, who were adults, or in advanced life, when they were converted, (which might have been on or near the day of Pentecost,) must have necessarily passed off the stage, in a period of almost thirty years. But many of the generation now addressed may have been Christians, and probably were so, at the time when Herod persecuted the church ; which accords well with what our epistle says, " Remember the former days, when, soon after your conversion, ye endured a great fight of afflictions," x. 32—34. But after that, when Herod was dead, there was a remission of severities. Now again, the violence of the Jews had begun to show itself; but the Roman government overawed it, so as to restrain it from shedding blood. Such a state of things agrees well with the language of our epistle. *Ye have not*, i. e. in your present struggle, *resisted unto blood*. This expression has not *necessarily* any respect to preceding times of persecution, but only to that which was then pending. In this way the laws of exegesis are satisfied. But if not, if the expression must be referred to past times, it is, as we have already seen, capable of historical vindication, when applied to the Hebrews. Private persons had not resisted unto blood.

My apology for dwelling so long on this subject is, the interesting facts in the history of the church with which it is connected; and the hasty conclusions, or imperfect investigations respecting it, which I have found in all the writers whom I have had opportunity to consult. Even Schroeckh, in his great work on Ecclesiastical History, has omitted any detailed account of the primitive persecutions, and has given us nothing which is adapted to satisfy a particular inquirer.

OJECTION 3. " Heb. xiii. 24. *They of Italy salute you.* What did the church in Italy know of the church in Palestine, that they should send salutations to them? Or if, as most critics have averred, *they of Italy* means Priscilla and Aquila, how should the church of Palestine know any thing of these private Jews, who had only travelled from Rome to Corinth, from Corinth to Ephesus, and thence back again to Rome?"

In regard to the first part of this objection, it is sufficient to ask, How could Peter send a salutation from the church at Babylon, 1 Peter v. 13, to the churches in Pontus, Galatia, Cappadocia, Asia, and Bithynia? 1 Peter i. 1. How could Paul, writing to the Corinthians from Ephesus, say, " *The churches of Asia salute you?*" 1 Cor. xvi. 19. Was then the church at Babylon *personally* acquainted with all those churches in Asia, to whom their salutation is sent by Peter? Or were the churches of Asia *personally* acquainted with the Corinthians? Neither the one, nor the other. Neither was necessary; for what is more common than salutations, sent by a mutual friend, from some persons, to others whom they have never seen?

But farther: had *they of Italy* never heard of the church in Palestine? And might they not sympathize with them in their trials and dangers, and send them an affectionate expression of their regard in a salutation? Such objections cannot surely help to support the cause, in aid of which they are adduced.

As to Aquila and Priscilla (if the οἱ ἀπὸ τῆς 'Ιταλίας means them, which is very improbable,) a sympathy in them, as Jews, for their Christian brethren in Palestine, is surely not a matter of wonder. And an expression of this in a salutation, is as little so.

OBJECTION 4. " The writer of the epistle to the Hebrews, has in various places eulogized them for the charity which they had so cheerfully manifested, and continued to manifest, on various occasions, Heb. vi. 10; in particular, for their compassion towards those who were in bonds, i. e. imprisoned, x. 32 seq. He exhorts them also to continue their benefactions of this nature, by a liberal hospitality, Heb. xiii. 1, 2, and 16. How could such things be addressed to the church in Palestine? and how could that church be praised for contributions to others when its members were so poor, from the first, that they had even been assisted by the contributions of churches from abroad?"

But this argument fails of producing conviction, because it is built on an interpretation of the epistle which is not admissible, and on an assumption of facts altogether improbable and unsupported. The writer tells them, that God will not forget their labour of love, in that they have ministered to the saints, and do still minister, vi. 10 ; that they have had compassion on those who were in bonds, x. 34 ; that they must not forget to entertain strangers, xiii. 2 ; and that God is well pleased with their sacrifices of hospitality (κοινωνίας,) xiii. 16. Here is nothing said, or even intimated, of making contributions for churches abroad. They are commended for being liberal to the saints, who were in need or in prison; and exhorted to continue their hospitality to strangers, i. e. to receive with liberality and kindness brethren that were strangers from abroad (probably, preachers,) who visited them. Who can doubt that a characteristic, so peculiarly exhibited by Christians in general of the primitive age, was manifested by the churches in Palestine? a country which so many strangers visited.

But when it is said, that the church in Palestine was supported by contributions from abroad, why should this be predicated, as it is by many critics, of *all* the Christian churches in Palestine? There is no support for this opinion to be derived from history. When the famine occurred in the time of Claudius, Acts xi. 27—30, a collection was made at Antioch, and sent to Judea ; which appears, however, to have been distributed at Jerusalem, Acts xii. 25. In respect to all the other collections mentioned in Paul's epistles, Jerusalem is evidently the place for which they were destined. See Rom. xv. 25—31. 1 Cor. xvi. 1—3. 2 Cor. viii. ix. εἰς ἁγίους; comp. 1 Cor. xvi. 1—3. Gal. ii. 1—10. If now we consider the circumstances of the church at Jerusalem, this will not excite any surprise. For, first, in this metropolis Jewish zeal was more displayed than elsewhere; and Christians here were, of course, peculiarly exposed to persecution and want. Secondly, the multitude of Christian Jews, who still resorted to the temple in order to pay their services there, and who would naturally consort with the Christians at Jerusalem, rendered necessary the charity of the churches abroad, in order that the Christians of the Jewish metropolis might support their hospitality. But as to other churches in Palestine, we know nothing of their poverty. We know that many Christians in that country had possessions, and sold them in order to put the avails into the public treasury of the church, soon after the day of Pentecost, Acts ii. 44, 45. Indeed, it is beyond all the bounds of probability, to suppose that of the many thousand Jews in Palestine, who had become Christians, *all* were poor, and in need of foreign charity. Poverty of this nature was not very common among the Jews, who were always an active and industrious nation. Above all, the supposition that the Hebrew Christians were unable to perform the common rites of hospitality, and to aid in any way such as were thrown into prison, or to furnish them with aliment, is destitute of every degree of probability; and therefore it can form no solid objection to the idea, that the epistle to the Hebrews was addressed to some church or churches in Palestine. Why is it necessary to suppose that the church at Jerusalem, and that *exclusively*, was addressed?

Moreover, the very objection itself affords an argument for the position which it is designed to oppose. In what country were the *prisoners* to whom compassion had been shown? Prisoners they were, evidently, on account of their Christian faith. We have seen that neither liberty nor life were, at this period, in jeopardy abroad, on account of religion, because of the restraint over the Jews exercised by the Roman government. We have no history that proves such jeopardy to have been matter of fact. The mere temporary imprisonment of Paul and Silas, on a charge of sedition, and as preparatory to trial, (Acts xvi.) proves nothing to the purpose. Accounts of other imprisonments besides this, out of Palestine, cannot be shown in the history of the primitive church, at least within the Roman provinces abroad. Palestine was the only place where Christians were imprisoned. Even when Paul went to Damascus, he expected to bring his prisoners to Jerusalem, Acts ix. 2. *Palestine* then was the place where compassion to Christian prisoners was needed, and where it was to be shown; and there, as it seems to me, it was exhibited by those whom the epistle to the Hebrews addresses.

OBJECTION 5. " Heb. xiii. 23. ' Know ye that our brother Timothy is *set at liberty*, ἀπολελυμένον, with whom, if he come soon, I will pay you a visit.' How could the church in Palestine know any thing of Timothy, who was never there? and what particular concern can they be supposed to have had with a visit of Timothy to them?"

But, first, it is altogether probable that Timothy was with Paul at

Jerusalem, during his last visit there, before his imprisonment. It is certain from Acts xx. 4, that Timothy set out with him and several others, from Troas, to go to Jerusalem; and equally certain, that although the history of Paul's voyage to Palestine, at that time, is traced with a minuteness that is unusual, not a word is mentioned of Timothy's being left behind, or being separated for any time from him; although it is the custom of Luke to mention such a fact, whenever it occurs; e. g. Acts xix. 22, xvii. 14, xx. 5. 13, 14. Indeed, it is altogether against probability, that Timothy would have separated from Paul, on this occasion; as it was announced to Paul, on his way, that bonds and imprisonment awaited him at Jerusalem, Acts xxi. 4, xx. 23; not to mention the desire which Timothy, who had been educated as a Jewish proselyte, must have had, to see Jerusalem, and the interesting objects which it presented.

The sequel of this journey was, that Paul was kept two years as a prisoner at Cesarea; with full liberty of access, however, to all his friends and acquaintance. Is there any probability that Timothy, who was so ardently attached to Paul, as to have followed him every where, from the very first of his acquaintance with him, would have now immediately deserted him; or, even if he was then abroad, that he would not have come to aid his necessities? So far then as the objection is built on Timothy's ignorance of the Jews in Palestine, or theirs of him, it appears altogether improbable.

Besides, even supposing Timothy had not been personally there, did not the churches there know that he was the favourite companion and helper of Paul? And was he not commended to the Jews, by the *fact* that, after he became a Christian, he had submitted to the rite of circumcision on their account? If Paul wrote the epistle in question, or any other person intimately connected with Timothy, he might very naturally give the churches in Palestine, and specially the church at Cesarea, information that he was *sent away* (ἀπολελυμένον,) *or set at liberty*, and that when he should return, he would pay them a visit in his company.

OBJECTION 6. "But how could Paul pray to be *restored* to the churches in Palestine? Hebrews xiii. 19. He had just been sent to Rome as a prisoner, by the persecuting spirit of the Jews of Palestine; how could he expect or wish to return thither again?"

This objection is built on the assumption, that Paul was the author of our epistle. Conceding this point then, for the sake of argument, it may be asked, in reply, If Paul had been at Rome, and was dismissed there by the emperor himself, on an appeal to him personally as a judge in respect to the Jews, might not the apostle well expect that the Jews would in future be overawed, and not venture to attack him again on account of his religion? Besides, it was only at *Jerusalem* that he was exposed to dangerous persecution. At Cesarea, he remained a kind of prisoner at large, without any tumult or excitement, for two whole years. Might he not desire to be restored to the brethren *there*, who had treated him in a friendly manner, and administered to his necessities while he was among them as a prisoner? Besides, Paul was not a man to be deterred from a desire to go, or from actually going, to any place where he thought it his duty to go, by any prospect of persecution or of sufferings; as his history abundantly testifies.

OBJECTION 7. "The Ebionites, a sect made up of Palestine Jews, appear to have known nothing of the epistle to the Hebrews. How could this be, if it had been directed to any of the churches in Palestine?"

If Paul was the author of this epistle, then it is very easy to answer this objection; for the Ebionites rejected all the epistles of Paul from their canon, (as Eusebius expressly testifies,) because Paul every where appears in them, wherever occasion demands it, in opposition to a Judaizing spirit. They, on the other hand, separated from other Christians out of zeal for the rites of the Jewish law. Nay, the manner in which Eusebius mentions this fact, seems to imply that the Ebionites were acquainted with the epistle to the Hebrews, and rejected it, together with Paul's acknowledged epistles; for Eusebius reckoned this epistle to be certainly one of Paul's; and he mentions the rejection of Paul's epistles by these sectarians, in a manner which seems to imply, that the *whole* of these epistles, as reckoned by himself, were rejected by them.*

To the same purpose Irenæus testifies, Advers. Hæres. i. 26. "Apostolum Paulum [Ebionitæ] recusant, apostatam eum legis dicentis."

Moreover, if some other person, and not Paul, had been the author of

---

* Eusebius (Hist. Ecc. iii. 27,) says, that *the Ebionites rejected* ALL *Paul's epistles, because they believed him to be an apostate from the law,* οὗτοι δὲ τοῦ μὲν ἀποστόλου πάσας τὰς ἐπιστολὰς ἀρνητέας ἡγοῦντο εἶναι δεῖν, ἀποστάτην ἀποκαλοῦντες αὐτὸν τοῦ νόμου. Now, as in L. iii. 25, of the same author, the epistle to the Hebrews is implicitly reckoned as one of Paul's epistles, and clearly as one of the books of Scripture which are ὁμολογούμενοι, (comp. Lib. iii. 25, and iii. 3,) it appears that Eusebius means to say, that the Ebionites rejected the epistle to the Hebrews; for he undoubtedly held this to be one of Paul's. Of course, he supposes the Ebionites to have been acquainted with it, or to have had opportunity of being acquainted with it.

the epistle to the Hebrews, the sentiments which it contains respecting the Jewish ritual, would have occasioned its rejection from the canon of the Ebionites. That they did not retain it, then, as part of their New Testament Scriptures, is no argument against its having been directed to the church in Palestine.

OBJECTION 8. "But if the epistle to the Hebrews was directed to the church in Palestine, why was it not written in the dialect of tha country, instead of the Greek language? Is it not improbable, that any writer would address, in Greek, Jews who spoke the Hebrew language?"

There are critics, both of ancient and modern times, who maintain that the original epistle was in Hebrew; believing, as Jerome says, that the author, *ut Hebræus, Hebræis Hebraicè scripsit*. But as I am not persuaded of the correctness of this opinion, I will not advance it here, as a reply to the objection which we are now considering.

It is well known, and abundantly evident from the writings of the New Testament, that the Greek language was generally understood over all Hither Asia. The conquests of Alexander, and the governments established by him, had made Greek the language of courts, of literature, and of all well-informed people. In the larger and more commercial towns, this knowledge extended in some measure to the common people, as well as to those of a more elevated rank.*

The Greek votaries, who went up to Jerusalem every year to perform their religious services there, must have rendered the Greek language somewhat current in this metropolis. It was the language by which all the inhabitants of western Asia, when they met as strangers, held intercourse with one another. If the epistle to the Hebrews, then, was written in Greek, and directed to the church at Jerusalem, it *might* have been understood by them.

But if the epistle to the Hebrews was directed to Cesarea, there is still more reason to suppose it would have been easily understood there. In that city there were a great multitude of Greeks, even a majority of its inhabitants, Joseph. Bell. Jud. iii. 14, p. 854, edit. Colon., πλέον ὑφ' Ἑλλήνων ἐποικουμένην. The Jews who lived there, were, in general, men devoted to commerce, or to concerns of a public nature, and must have well understood the Greek language. No serious difficulty, then, lies in the way of supposing this epistle to have been sent to some part

---

* See this subject illustrated, in a very able and satisfactory manner, by Hug, in his Einleit. in Das. N. Test. Theil ii. § 10

of *Palestine,* and that it was intelligible there, although written in the Greek language.

On the other hand, is it not apparent, that the author of our epistle designed it should be *encyclical,* so that Jews far and near might ultimately peruse it, in order that they might become weaned from their attachment to the Levitical rites, and substitute Christianity in the place of the Mosaic religion? Such a design would have been in some measure defeated, by writing it in Hebrew; for Greek was by far the most general language.

Taking all these facts into view, that it was written in Greek, does not appear to constitute any solid objection to its having been directed to some part of Palestine.

OBJECTION 9. " How could this epistle have been directed to Palestine, when the ground of argument in it, in several places, is furnished by the *Septuagint* version, and not by the Hebrew Scriptures? How could Jews in *Palestine* be convinced, by an appeal of this nature?"

But who does not know, that the Palestine Jews of that day regarded the Septuagint version as being of divine authority? Josephus gives full credit to the account of Aristeas, respecting the miraculous manner in which this version was made; as may be seen in his Antiq. xii. 2, edit. Colon. There could be no danger, that the Jews of Palestine would object to such an appeal, or to such a mode of argument.

RESULT.

I have now examined all the objections against the opinion, that the epistle to the Hebrews was directed to Palestine, with which I have met, and which seem to be of sufficient magnitude to deserve attention. I am unable to perceive that they are very weighty; and surely they come quite short of being *conclusive.* On the other hand, the positive proof, I acknowledge, is only of a circumstantial nature, and falls short of the weight which direct and unequivocal testimony in the epistle itself would possess. But uniting the whole of it together; considering the intimate knowledge of Jewish rites, the strong attachment to their ritual, and the special danger of defection from Christianity in consequence of it, which the whole texture of the epistle necessarily supposes, and combining these things with the other circumstances above discussed, I cannot resist the impression, that the universal opinion of the ancient church respecting the persons to whom our epistle was addressed, was well founded, being built upon early tradition and the contents of the epistle; and that the doubts and difficulties thrown in the way by modern and recent critics, are not of sufficient importance to justify us in relinquishing the belief that Palestine Christians were addressed by the epistle to the Hebrews. Thousands of facts, pertaining to criticism and to history, are believed and treated as realities, which have less support than the opinion that has now been examined.

There remains but one question more, relative to the original destination of this epistle, concerning which inquiry is now to be made.

§ 11. *Was it directed to* ALL *the churches in Palestine, or only to* ONE? *And if only to one, was this the church at Jerusalem, or at some other place?*

This question cannot be answered, as is sufficiently evident from what has been already said, by adducing any *direct* testimony concerning it. *Probability*, made out from circumstantial evidence, is all, at the most, which criticism can achieve. Perhaps it may fail, even in respect to this.

While engaged in the investigations necessary to complete the views above presented, it often occurred to me as not improbable, that the epistle to the Hebrews was originally directed to the church at Cesarea. The reasons of this I will now briefly state.

Cesarea, Καισάρεια παράλιος, *Cesarea by the sea*, was built by Herod the Great, in a most splendid manner, and named by him in honour of the Roman emperor Augustus. Previously to this, it was an insignificant village, called Στράτωνος πύργος, *the tower of Strato*. Although it lay out of the district of Judea, (as *anciently* defined by the Jews,) and within the borders of Phenicia, yet it was within the Roman procuratorship of Judea, and was the capital of the Roman prefects or procurators. Josephus calls it " the greatest city of *Judea*," and says, (as has been already mentioned,) that *the majority of the inhabitants were Greeks*, Bell. Jud. iii. 14, p. 854, edit. Colon.

Here Cornelius, the first convert to the Christian faith from the Gentiles, was stationed. On occasion of his conversion, a church was gathered here, and the miraculous gifts of the Spirit imparted to it, Acts x. 44—48. This was the earliest church that was gathered, out of the ancient limits of Judea.

Paul had repeated opportunities for acquaintance with Christians here. After his first journey to Jerusalem, he returned to Tarsus, through Cesarea, Acts ix. 30. After preaching at Corinth, and on going to revisit the churches in Asia, Paul landed here, Acts xviii. 22. On his

CHURCHES OF PALESTINE IN GENERAL? 59

fourth visit to Palestine, he lodged here at the house of Philip the Evangelist, one of the seven deacons named in Acts vi. Here he abode *many days*, ἡμέρας πλείους, Acts xxi. 8—10. Here, at the time just mentioned, when Agabus had predicted, that in case Paul went to Jerusalem, he would be bound as a culprit there, and delivered up to the heathen tribunals, the men of the place (οἱ ἐντόπιοι,) as well as his own travelling companions, besought him with tears and strong entreaties to refrain from going thither, Acts xxi. 12, 13.

When, after this, he had been up to Jerusalem, and was sent away under a guard of Roman soldiers, he was brought again to Cesarea; where he remained *two whole years* a kind of prisoner at large, none of his friends being forbidden to approach or assist him, Acts xxiv. 23, 27.

At Cesarea dwelt a rich and powerful body of Jews. In the time of Felix, these Cesarean Jews, boasting of their riches and of Herod as the founder of the city, treated with contempt the Syrian part of the population. This raised a tumult, and at last occasioned mutual assaults, in which the Syrians were worsted. Felix was obliged to check the overbearing power of the Jewish party, by commissioning the Roman soldiery to kill and plunder them, Antiq. Jud. xx. 6, p. 695, edit. Colon.

The Jews here, it appears also, were strong zealots for the temple worship. Herod Agrippa, while king of Judea, very probably in order to ingratiate himself with the rich men of this his capital, as well as with those of Jerusalem, pretended a very strong zeal for Judaism. This he exhibited, by causing James the brother of John to be slain with the sword, by imprisoning Peter, and vexing others of the church, Acts xii. 1, seq. Now, considering that Cesarea was his capital, and that to ingratiate himself with the Jews there, who were rich and powerful, would be a great object for a prince so wholly devoted as he was to the interests of ambition; is it probable that his vexations of the church were limited to Jerusalem?

Let us now put all these facts together, and compare them with the contents of our epistle, on the supposition that Paul wrote it. From the epistle to the Hebrews it no where appears, that the *writer* was the *first* teacher of the church whom he addresses, but the contrary is plainly implied. Now, history tells us that Peter planted the church at Cesarea, and not Paul, Acts x. The teachers of the church addressed in the epistle to the Hebrews, are applauded without any exception as to their doctrine or behaviour; and so this might well be, for the first teachers at Cesarea were apostles and primitive evangelists. Philip the evangelist was stationed there, when Paul made his last visit to Jerusalem, Acts xxi. 8, seq.; and this Philip had four daughters, who were prophetesses, i. e. teachers of the Christian religion. Does not this show a flourishing state of the church there? The persons to whom the epistle to the Hebrews is addressed, had often bestowed charity to relieve the necessities of Christians, and particularly of those who were imprisoned, Heb. x. 34, vi. 10. How aptly this fits the circumstances of Paul among the Cesareans, it is easy to perceive. He was a prisoner among them for the space of two years. Well might he say, " Ye had compassion τοῖς δεσμοῖς μου, *on my bonds*," as the common text reads; or (which comes after all to the same thing) τοῖς δεσμίοις, *on the imprisoned*. Paul's gratitude for this, probably led him to speak of it repeatedly; and so it stands in the epistle to the Hebrews. The eulogy, which the writer of that epistle bestows on those whom he addresses, certainly becomes very significant, on supposition that it was written by Paul under such circumstances.

The Hebrews addressed in our epistle had been early made converts to Christianity, v. 12, x. 32. The church at Cesarea was the first gathered out of the ancient limits of Judea. Its first converts, indeed, were Gentile proselytes, Acts x.; but it cannot with any probability be supposed, that, flourishing as it was when Paul paid his last visit to it, before his imprisonment, Acts xxi. 8, seq., there were no Jews who belonged to it; for Cesarea contained (as we have seen) a large number of Hebrew residents. Herod Agrippa persecuted the church in A. D. 44, which was some twenty years before the epistle to the Hebrews was written; and Cesarea was Herod's capital. May not the Christians in it have suffered at that time? The Hebrews, in our epistle, had lost their property in some early persecution, and had been imprisoned, x. 32, seq.; and the persecuting Herod, who had the power of life and death, had also the power of confiscation and imprisonment; for he was made a *sovereign* by the Roman emperor. Under him the church at Cesarea may have experienced, and very probably did experience, such vexations. Certainly the church at Jerusalem experienced them at this time, Acts xii. 1, seq.

The epistle to the Hebrews presents images drawn from the Grecian games and public shows, x. 32, xii. 1, seq. At Cesarea, Herod the Great had instituted all the Grecian games, and built a splendid theatre; so that such allusions would be very forcible and pertinent, if addressed to those who lived there. The writer of our epistle mentions Timothy, to the church whom he addresses, as his special friend, and one in whom they would feel a deep interest; and as Timothy, it cannot well be doubted, was at Cesarea with Paul more or less of the time that he was a prisoner there for two years, the church at that place must have been well acquainted with him. Paul requests their prayers, that he himself may be restored to them, xiii. 19; and the frequent visits which he had made the Cesareans, the strong attachment they had manifested to him, and the long residence he had made among them, correspond well with a request so plainly founded in their affectionate regard for him, and in his for them.

Again, Cesarea was only two days' journey from Jerusalem, and the Jews there were zealots for the traditions of their fathers. Resistance to the Roman power, which finally brought on the destruction of the Jewish commonwealth, first began here, from the wounded spirit of Jewish pride and national feeling. These facts render it probable, that the Jews there had a full and intimate acquaintance with all the Mosaic ritual; and that the Christian Jews must, from the power, wealth, and overbearing spirit of the others, have been hard pressed, (by persecution on the one hand, and the imposing pomp of the temple service on the other,) to make defection from the Christian religion. Finally, as the majority of the inhabitants here were Greeks, and of course the current language in this splendid capital was Greek, this may account for it, that our epistle was written in Greek instead of the Palestine dialect. From this place, it could not fail to be circulated abroad, as there must have been comers and goers to and from this place, from all parts of Palestine. For Paul to subscribe his name to this epistle was not *necessary*, in case he sent it by a friend, as doubtless he must have done; and besides this, the circumstances mentioned in it, of being restored to them, and of coming to them with Timothy, would be sufficient of themselves to disclose the author to the Cesarean Christians. And designed, as the letter in all probability was, to be a circular among the Jews, they who were abroad, reading it without the name of the author, would not so readily have those prejudices awakened, which had lately shown themselves to be very violent among the Jews who were zealous for the honour of the Mosaic law, whenever Paul had made his appearance among them.

I grant, at once, that all this is *supposition*. But in the absence of all positive testimony, if a supposition can be presented, which contains nothing improbable in itself, and explains a variety of characteristic passages in our epistle, and accords well with the facts which history has recorded, may it not be received, at least, as a *probability*, until the fallacy of it be exposed, or a more probable one is advanced?

The points of coincidence just recited, forced themselves upon me, unsought and unexpected, in the course of my investigation. They are not offered from the love of novelty, nor with any overweening confidence as to the approbation which others may give them.

One objection to the view here given seems to be, that the church at Cesarea, in the time of Origen and Eusebius, (both of whom lived there,) do not appear to have retained a tradition that our epistle was directed to them. At least, neither of these fathers, so far as I know, make mention of such a tradition; which they probably might have done, had it existed in their times. Still, if our epistle was designed to be a *circular*, and, for that reason, a direction to any particular church was omitted in it, the Cesarean church, if they were the *first* who received it, might not have considered it appropriately theirs, in the same manner as the Corinthians, Galatians, and others, did the letters addressed to them.

Another objection to the idea, that our epistle was directed to the church at Cesarea, may be drawn from the probability, that the church there must have consisted, in fact, of Gentiles; especially as Greeks constituted a majority of the population of that city. What was really fact, however, in regard to this, at the time when the epistle was written, we have no historical means of ascertaining. It is certainly a very possible case, that, at the time when the epistle to the Hebrews was written, the church at Cesarea might have been principally made up of Jews; or at least have contained a majority of members, who were Hebrews. Or, there may have been more than one church at Cesarea, (a thing altogether probable;) and the Jews there, who were such uncommon zealots for the law, might have established a religious community of their own, separate from that of the Gentile Christians, whom the former would regard with an eye of jealousy, if not of distrust. If the author of our epistle designed it for the good of the Hebrews in *general*, he would have written just in the manner which he has adopted, whether the church whom he addressed contained some Gentiles or not.

Upon the whole, it is a plain case, that confident and positive assertions in regard to any one particular church, cannot be made with propriety. The most which I would say here is, that more reasons seem to offer themselves in favour of the supposition, that our epistle was originally sent to the church at Cesarea, than in favour of any other place I cannot, therefore, but regard it as a *probable* event.

§ 12. *Antiquity and canonical authority of the epistle.*

Its *antiquity* may be established by evidence internal and external. The allusions made to the temple service, in the epistle itself, necessarily imply that this service was then performed, when the letter was written, Heb. ix. 9. " Which [former tabernacle with its services] was a significant emblem in respect to the present time; *in which* gifts and sacrifices *are* offered, that cannot render tranquil the conscience of him who performs this service." Again, in chap. viii. 4, 5. the writer says, " For if he [Jesus] had performed his service on earth, then he could not be a priest; seeing *there are priests* who, according to the prescription of the law, *perform* their service in a tabernacle which is merely a copy of the heavenly one." Both of these passages clearly imply, that the temple rites were then performed, at the time when the writer composed our epistle.

Now, as the whole temple service ceased, of course, with the destruction of Jerusalem, in A. D. 70, it is clear that our epistle must have been written before that period; and consequently it belongs to the apostolic age.

Another argument also in proof of this is, that the particular views which the epistle throughout gives of temptation to apostacy, are evidently grounded on the then existing rites of the Jewish temple-worship. The state of feeling among the Jews at large, (which resulted from strong attachment to these rites, and the zeal with which their views of these things were maintained,) and their extreme jealousy of every thing which had a tendency to diminish the supposed importance of their ritual, together with the imposing splendour and magnificence of the Levitical ceremonies, as then practised, all concurred to tempt those Hebrews who had embraced Christianity, and renounced the common views of their countrymen, to relapse into their former views and habits. The shape in which this whole subject presents itself, in the epistle to the Hebrews, manifestly implies that the Levitical institutions were then in full vigour. Of course, the age in which this was the case, must have been the apostolic.

It is equally plain, that our epistle was written in the *latter* part of the apostolic age. Those whom it addresses are represented as having been Christians long enough to be qualified, had they been properly attentive to their duty in learning the principles of Christianity, to become teachers of it, v. 12. The *former* days, when they were first enlightened, are spoken of by the writer, x. 32, in distinction from the time then current. They are addressed also as having witnessed the death of their first teachers, xiii. 7; and their then present teachers are commended to their affectionate regard, xiii. 17. All these circumstances imply that some time must have passed away since the gospel was first preached among them, and they had been converted to Christianity. In other words, the epistle must have been written in the latter part of the apostolic age. The specific year I shall not here endeavour to ascertain, as it will hereafter be a subject of inquiry.

With the internal marks of antiquity, exhibited by the epistle itself, corresponds the external testimony that can be gathered respecting it. Clement of Rome is the most important witness that can be adduced, in regard to the point before us. His epistle to the Corinthians, (commonly named his *first* epistle,*) is the most considerable, certainly the most important and best authenticated, relic of ecclesiastical antiquity, which belongs to the first century of the Christian era. According to the general voice of the ancients, the author of this espistle is the Clement whom Paul mentions as one of his fellow-labourers, and as having his name written in the book of life, Philip. iv. 3. He was the *third* bishop of Rome, according to Irenæus (contra Hæres. III. 3,) Eusebius (Hist. Ecc. III. 13. 15. 21. 34. 38,) and Jerome (Viri Illus. v. Clemens.) In the name of the church at Rome, and as their bishop, he addressed an epistle to the church at Corinth. This epistle, as all agree, must have been written within the first century; probably about A. D. 96.

* It is called *first*, because there is a *second*, which bears his name, and which has usually been printed in connexion with the first. The first was so greatly esteemed by the churches in the early ages, that it was read publicly to Christian assemblies, in like manner as the books of the New Testament. It is very often cited, with great encomiums, by nearly all the Christian fathers! It has been assailed, indeed, by a few critics, in modern times; and what relic of antiquity has not? It, doubtless, like most ancient books, has suffered somewhat in regard to the purity of its text, by frequent transcription, and by negligence. But, on the whole, it is a venerable and a precious relic of the primitive age of Christianity; and it is very generally admitted to be such.—The *second* epistle is quoted by none of the early fathers; and it differs in style and method so much from the *first*, that there can scarcely be a doubt of its spuriousness. Vide Clem. Rom. edit. Wotton p. ccvi.

Several critics of high reputation are disposed to assign to it a much earlier date. For example, Pearson, Pagi, Dodwell, Wake, and Le Clerc date it at a period antecedent to the destruction of Jerusalem, i. e before A. D. 70. If their opinion be correct, the testimony of Clement's epistle will be still stronger in proof of the antiquity and authority of our epistle to the Hebrews; for this testimony, in such a case, must have been given within some eight or ten years after our epistle was written, and during the apostolic age. But be this as it may, I am willing to assume the latest date, which can with any show of probability be assigned to Clement's epistle, viz. A. D. 96; for this will be only about thirty years after the epistle to the Hebrews was most probably written.

It will be seen, in the sequel, that the testimony of Clement will serve to cast light upon the two points of inquiry which constitute the object of the present section, viz. the antiquity and the authority of our epistle.

I shall first exhibit the evidence that Clement has quoted this epistle, and then subjoin some remarks on his testimony. I enter into the examination of this matter the more formally and fully, because of the important bearing which the testimony of a writer so early and respectable as Clement must evidently have upon the authority of our epistle, and indirectly upon its origin; and also because the subject has been, (at least, so it seems to me,) imperfectly treated, and passed over with a slight examination, by nearly all the critics whom I have had an opportunity to consult.

It is a singular circumstance, that no book of the New Testament should have been so frequently quoted by Clement, as the epistle to the Hebrews. That such is the fact, any one may satisfy himself, who will take the pains to examine his quotations as referred to in Wotton's edition of this author, or the detail of them as exhibited by Lardner, Credibil. of Gosp. Hist. I. p. 49. seq.

The quotations made by Clement from the epistle to the Hebrews may be arranged under four different classes; viz.

§ 12. ANTIQUITY AND CANONICAL

I.

Passages in which the exact words, or nearly so, of the epistle are quoted.

HEBREWS.

CLEMENT.

No. 1.

No. 1.

i. 3. Ὃς ὢν ἀπαύγασμα τῆς δόξης .... 4. Τοσούτῳ κρείττων γενόμενος τῶν ἀγγέλων ὅσῳ διαφορώτερον παρ' αὐτοὺς κεκληρονόμηκεν ὄνομα.

7. Λέγει· Ὁ ποιῶν τοὺς ἀγγέλους αὐτοῦ πνεύματα, καὶ τοὺς λειτουργοὺς αὐτοῦ πυρὸς φλόγα.

5. Τίνι γὰρ εἶπέ ποτε τῶν ἀγγέλων· Υἱός μου εἶ σύ, ἐγὼ σήμερον γεγέννηκά σε; ———

13. Πρὸς τίνα δὲ τῶν ἀγγέλων εἴρηκέ ποτε· Κάθου ἐκ δεξιῶν μου, ἕως ἂν θῶ τοὺς ἐχθροὺς σου ὑποπόδιον τῶν ποδῶν σου;

Cap. 36. Ὃς ὢν ἀπαύγασμα τῆς μεγαλοσύνης αὐτοῦ, τοσούτῳ μείζων ἐστὶν ἀγγέλων ὅσῳ διαφορώτερον ὄνομα κεκληρονόμηκε.

Γέγραπται γὰρ οὕτως· Ὁ ποιῶν τοὺς ἀγγέλους αὐτοῦ πνεύματα, καὶ τοὺς λειτουργοὺς αὐτοῦ πυρὸς φλόγα.

Ἐπὶ δὲ τῷ υἱῷ αὐτοῦ, οὕτως εἶπεν ὁ δεσπότης· υἱὸς μού εἶ σύ, ἐγὼ σήμερον γεγέννηκά σε.

...καὶ πάλιν λέγει πρὸς αὐτόν· Κάθου ἐκ δεξιῶν μου, ἕως ἂν θῶ τοὺς ἐχθρούς σου ὑποπόδιον τῶν ποδῶν σου.

No 2.

No. 2.

Heb. vi. 18..... ἐν οἷς ἀδύνατον ψεύσασθαι Θεόν......

Cap. xxvii..... οὐδὲν γὰρ ἀδύνατον παρὰ τῷ Θεῷ, εἰ μὴ τὸ ψεύσασθαι.

No. 3.

No. 3.

Heb. xi. 37..... περιῆλθον ἐν μηλωταῖς, ἐν αἰγείοις δέρμασι.

Cap. xvii. οἵτινες ἐν δέρμασιν αἰγείοις καὶ μηλωταῖς περιεπάτησαν.

No. 4.

No. 4.

Heb. x. 37. Ἔτι γὰρ μικρὸν ὅσον ὅσον, ὁ ἐρχόμενος ἥξει καὶ οὐ χρονιεῖ.

Cap. xxiii..... συνεπιμαρτυρούσης καὶ τῆς γραφῆς· ὅτι ταχὺ ἥξει καὶ οὐ χρονεῖ.

AUTHORITY OF THE EPISTLE. 67

HEBREWS. CLEMENT.
II.

Passages containing the sentiment, with more or less contraction of the expression, or an exchange of the original word for a synonymous one.

No. 5.
Heb. iv. 12.......καὶ κριτικὸς ἐνθυμήσεων καὶ ἐννοιῶν καρδίας.

No. 5.
Cap. xxi.....οὐδὲν λέληθεν αὐτὸν τῶν ἐννοιῶν ἡμῶν, οὐδὲ τῶν διαλογισμῶν ὧν ποιούμεθα.
(Again, near the end)......ἐρευνητὴς γὰρ ἐστιν ἐννοιῶν καὶ ἐνθυμήσεων.

No. 6.
Heb. xi. 5. Πίστει 'Ενὼχ μετετέθη, τοῦ μὴ ἰδεῖν θάνατον.

7. Πίστει χρηματισθεὶς Νῶε.

8. Πίστει καλούμενος Ἀβραὰμ ὑπήκουσεν ἐξελθεῖν εἰς τὸν τόπον, κ. τ. λ.

31. Πίστει 'Ραὰβ ἡ πόρνη οὐ συναπώλετο τοῖς ἀπειθήσασι, δεξαμένη τοὺς κατασκόπους μετ' εἰρήνης.

No. 6.
Cap. ix.....'Ενὼχ, ὃς ἐν ὑπακοῇ δίκαιος εὑρεθεὶς μετετέθη, καὶ οὐχ εὑρέθη αὐτοῦ θάνατος.
....Νῶε πιστὸς εὑρεθεὶς ......
Cap. x. Ἀβραὰμ ...... πιστὸς εὑρέθη ἐν τῷ αὐτὸν ὑπήκοον γενέσθαι τοῖς ῥήμασι τοῦ Θεοῦ, οὗτος δι' ὑπακοῆς ἐξῆλθεν ἐκ τῆς γῆς, κ. τ. λ.
Cap. xii. Διὰ πίστιν καὶ φιλοξενίαν ἐσώθη 'Ραὰβ ἡ πόρνη.

III.

Passages which are a paraphrastic imitation of the epistle to the Hebrews; or in which the style or phraseology of this epistle is more or less exhibited.

No. 7.
Heb. xi. 36—39. Ἕτεροι δὲ ἐμπαιγμῶν καὶ μαστίγων πεῖραν ἔλαβον, ἔτι δὲ δεσμῶν καὶ φυλακῆς. Ἐλιθάσθησαν, ἐπρίσθησαν, ἐπειράσθησαν, ἐν φόνῳ μαχαίρας ἀπέθανον ....καὶ οὗτοι πάντες μαρτυρηθέντες διὰ τῆς πίστεως.

No. 7.
Cap. xlv. (Ἐγκύπτετε εἰς τὰς γραφὰς τὰς ἀληθεῖς ῥήσεις πνεύματος τοῦ ἁγίου......οὐ γὰρ εὑρήσεται δικαίους ἀποβεβλημένους, ἀπὸ ὁσίων ἀνδρῶν.) Ἐδιώχθησαν δίκαιοι, ἀλλ' ὑπὸ ἀνόμων· ἐνεφυλακίσθησαν, ἀλλ' ὑπὸ ἀνοσίων· ἐλιθάσθησαν ὑπὸ παρανόμων· ἀπεκτάνθησαν ὑπὸ τῶν μιαρῶν καὶ ἄδικον ζῆλον ἀνειληφότων Ταῦτα πάσχοντες εὐκλαιῶς ἤνεγκαν.

§ 12. ANTIQUITY AND CANONICAL

HEBREWS.
No. 8.

Heb. xii. 1, 2...... τοσοῦτον ἔχοντες περικείμενον ἡμῖν νέφος μαρτύρων....δι᾽ ὑπομονῆς τρέχωμεν τὸν προκείμενον ἡμῖν ἀγῶνα. ἀφορῶντες εἰς τὸν τῆς πίστεως ἀρχηγὸν, κ. τ. λ.

No. 9.
Heb. xii. 5—11. (comp. Prov. iii. 11, 12.)....υἱέ μου, μὴ ὀλιγώρει παιδείας Κυρίου, μηδὲ ἐκλύου ὑπ᾽ αὐτοῦ ἐλεγχόμενος. ῞Ον γὰρ ἀγαπᾷ Κύριος, παιδεύει, μαστιγοῖ δὲ πάντα υἱὸν ὃν παραδέχεται....Οἱ μὲν.... κατὰ τὸ δοκοῦν αὐτοῖς ἐπαίδευον [ἡμᾶς,] ὁ δὲ [Θεὸς] ἐπὶ τὸ συμφέρον, εἰς τὸ μεταλαβεῖν τῆς ἁγιότητος αὐτοῦ.

No. 10.
Heb. iv. 14, seq. ῎Εχοντες οὖν ἀρχιερέα μέγαν.... ᾽Ιησοῦν.... οὐ ἔχομεν ἀρχιερέα μὴ δυνάμενον συμπαθῆσαι ταῖς ἀσθενείαις ἡμῶν.... προσερχώμεθα...... ἵνα....χάριν εὕρωμεν εἰς εὔκαιρον βοήθειαν.

CLEMENT.
No. 8.
Cap. xix. Πολλῶν οὖν καὶ μεγάλων καὶ ἐνδόξων μετειληφότες παραδειγμάτων (Wotton, πράξαιων) ἐπαναδράμωμεν ἐπὶ τὸν ἐξ ἀρχῆς παραδεδομένον ἡμῖν τῆς εἰρήνης σκόπον καὶ ἀτενίσωμεν εἰς τὸν πατέρα, κ. τ. λ.

No. 9.
Cap. lvi. ᾽Αναλάβωμεν παιδείαν ἐφ᾽ ᾗ οὐδεὶς ὀφείλει ἀγανακτεῖν.... ὃν γὰρ ἀγαπᾷ Κύριος παιδεύει, μαστιγοῖ δὲ πάντα υἱὸν ὃν παραδέχεται ......γὰρ ἀγαθὸς ὢν παιδεύει ὁ Θεὸς εἰς τὸ νουθετηθῆναι ἡμᾶς διὰ τῆς ὁσίας παιδείας αὐτοῦ.

No. 10.
Cap. xxxvi.....᾽Ιησοῦν Χριστὸν τὸν ἀρχιερέα τῶν προσφορῶν ἡμῶν, τὸν προστάτην καὶ βοηθὸν τῆς ἀσθενείας ἡμῶν· Cap. lviii....διὰ τοῦ ἀρχιερέως καὶ προστάτου ἡμῶν I. Χριστου......

IV.

Passages similar to texts in the Old Testament, but which Clement probably quoted from the epistle to the Hebrews.

No. 11.
Heb. iii. 2. Πιστὸν ὄντα τῷ ποιήσαντι αὐτὸν, ὡς καὶ Μωϋσῆς ἐν ὅλῳ τῷ οἴκῳ αὐτοῦ.
5. Καὶ Μωϋσῆς μὲν πιστὸς ἐν ὅλῳ τῷ οἴκῳ αὐτοῦ, ὡς θεράπων.

No 12.
Heb. xii. vi. ῞Ον γὰρ ἀγαπᾷ Κύριος, κ.τ.λ. Vide supra, under No. 9.

No. 11.
Cap. xvii. Μωϋσῆς πιστὸς ἐν ὅλῳ τῷ οἴκῳ αὐτοῦ ἐκλήθη.

Cap. xliii. ῾Ο μακάριος πιστὸς θεράπων ἐν ὅλῳ τῷ οἴκῳ, Μωϋσῆς.

No. 12.
Cap. lvi....ὃν γὰρ ἀγαπᾷ Κύριος, κ. τ. λ.

AUTHORITY OF THE EPISTLE. 69

I shall now subjoin a few remarks on the preceding view

No. 1. Some parts of the passage, here extracted from Clement, may be found in the Old Testament as well as in the epistle to the Hebrews; but other parts of it are appropriate only to the latter. This, as well as the application itself of the passages taken from the Old Testament, shows, beyond any reasonable doubt, that Clement must have had the first chapter of the epistle to the Hebrews distinctly in his mind, when he wrote the passage which is presented in the comparison.

That Clement, in his letter, has added more of the second psalm than is found in the epistle to the Hebrews, forms no argument that he quoted directly from the second psalm, rather than from Heb. i. In his view, clearly, the whole of the second psalm applied to the Messiah. To the quotation made from it by the writer of our epistle, Clement adds two other verses, in order to amplify and confirm the view of the subject which he has introduced.

To this statement we may the more readily accede, since it is often the manner of Clement, in making his quotations of Scripture, to intermingle passages taken from different parts of the Bible, without any notice, or any sign of transition from the one to the other.*

No. 2. That Clement does not introduce this passage with the *formula* of a quotation, is no proof that it is not one; for he *often* extracts passages both from the Old and the New Testament, *without using any formula of quotation*, or without any intimation that he is about to quote. The singularity of the expression itself, exhibited in No. 2, and the fact that it is peculiar to the epistle to the Hebrews, are the grounds on which I should rest the probability, that Clement had in his mind distinctly the manner of expression in our epistle, when he wrote the sentence presented in the comparison.

No. 3. This is so plainly and exactly a quotation, of an expression *sui generis* in the epistle to the Hebrews, that to doubt whether it be in reality copied from this epistle, would be to doubt whether Clement has quoted in any case, except where he has given express notice of it. But

---

* E. g. Clement, (Epist. c. 50,) after quoting from Isaiah xxvi. 20, adds another quotation (from what book it is uncertain) without any note of transition. So in cap. liii. after quoting Deut. ix. 12, seq., he goes on to quote other passages, from different places, without any notice of transition. And so, frequently, in his epistle, where he arranges together various quotations.

a doubt of this nature can never be cherished by any one who has read Clement's epistle, and examined the method of his quotations.

No. 4 appears to me a case of quotation from Heb. x. 37, which has the formula of appeal to the Scriptures prefixed, συνεπιμαρτυρούσης τῆς γραφῆς. The passage quoted is found, in the sense in which it is used by Clement, in the epistle to the Hebrews. Another passage from which we might suppose the quotation to be taken, viz. Mal. iii. 1, is quoted at length, in immediate connexion with the one exhibited in the table, plainly because Clement deemed it to be a parallel one; so that we cannot choose the passage in Malachi, as the source of his quotation. There remains, then, besides Heb. x. 37, only Hab. ii. 3, which affords any special resemblance to the quotation of Clement. But the passage in Habakkuk relates wholly to a *vision*, or *prophecy*, and not to a *person*, as in Heb. x. 37; and to a *person*, Clement evidently applies it. The probability is then altogether in favour of the supposition, that the passage is quoted from the epistle to the Hebrews.

No. 5 is so alike in Clement and in our epistle, I can hardly persuade myself that the expression in the latter was not in Clement's mind, when he wrote the passages here extracted from him. Still, it does not appear to be a case, I readily concede, on which a conclusion respecting actual quotation or imitation can be built with entire certainty.

No. 6, although it does not exhibit an exact use of the *language* in our epistle, contains, in my view, one of the most convincing proofs of quotation. The arrangement of these examples together, as in the epistle to the Hebrews; the manner of characterising their actions or their rewards, viz. that they flowed from *faith;* and the almost exact similarity of ideas, in cases where these are peculiar to the writer of our epistle, all combine to prove (I had almost said) the certainty that Clement had Heb. XI. before his eyes, or at least before the eye of his mind. In what other part of Scripture are these examples so arranged together? And where else is found such a method of presenting them to our view? In fact, imitation thus exact, of a passage so peculiar in its style and manner, is better proof that the passage was before the eye of Clement, or at least in his mind, than exact coincidence of language in some cases would be. In a short passage, such coincidence might be accidental, arising merely from similarity of views or of idiom. But *accidental* coincidence as to the mode of reasoning and representation here, seems to be fairly out of the question.

No. 7 seems to be a kind of parody upon the corresponding passage in the epistle to the Hebrews, or paraphrastic imitation of it. The extraneous matter which Clement inserts, has evident reference to the preceding context in his own epistle.

No. 8. In Clement's epistle, the passage is in the sequel of the sentence, extracted in No. 3. Now, as the writer of the epistle to the Hebrews has exhibited the same order of thought, Heb. xi. 37, and xii. 1, 2, is it not probable that Clement had the corresponding passages of that epistle in his mind, when he wrote the one presented by the comparison? The similarity of costume in the two passages can hardly fail to strike the attentive reader.

No. 9 may be somewhat doubtful, because it may have arisen from the passage in Prov. iii. 11. The whole strain of reasoning upon it, however, inclines me to believe, that Clement had in his mind the corresponding passage in the epistle to the Hebrews.

No. 10 exhibits an appellation of the Saviour, (ἀρχιερέα) which is peculiar to our epistle. There is, moreover, an evident similarity between Christ as δυνάμενον συμπαθῆσαι ταῖς ἀσθενείαις ἡμῶν, Hebrews iv. 15, and Clement's προστάτην καὶ βοηθὸν τῆς ἀσθενείας ἡμῶν.

Nos. 11 and 12 cannot, of course, be much relied on in the present case; as no decisive reason can be offered, to prove that Clement *must* have quoted from our epistle. From the tenor of the passages, and the context, I am inclined to believe that he did; but I cannot attach much weight to this supposition.

In order now to make a fair estimate of the comparison which has been made, and the weight of evidence to be adduced from it, it is necessary that we should have correct views of the manner of Clement's quotations in general, and the principles on which they are grounded.

I have examined the whole of this writer's quotations, both from the Old and New Testament, with a view to ascertain, whether any thing can be determined as to the *authority* which he attaches to them, from the *manner* in which they are made; and also to ascertain, by a view of the whole, what his particular manner of quotation is. The result of this examination I will now briefly state.

(1.) Clement names no book of either Testament. He appeals, indeed, to the words of the prophets; but their names he evidently uses to indicate their *persons*, and not (as we do) the titles of their books. The importance of this fact, considered in connexion with the same usage by the writers of the New Testament, in respect to a critical examination of the genuineness of the titles prefixed to the books of Scripture, has been already adverted to in the preceding part of this introduction, § 10. p. 35.

(2.) Clement habitually appeals to the books of either Testament, with or without a formula which gives notice of a citation. He often prefixes γέγραπται, λέγει, εἶπεν ὁ Θεὸς, φησιν ὁ Λόγος ἅγιος, and the like formulas, to his quotations. But nearly as often, particularly in the New Testament, he cites without any notice or formula at all; evidently taking it for granted that his readers will at once recognise the quotation, without any pains on his part to designate it.

(2.) I find no satisfactory evidence of quotation from the Apocrypha, or any apocryphal writer now known. The instances of quotation from the Wisdom of Solomon (chap. XII. XXVII.,) alleged by Wotton, are plainly too far fetched to appear probable; and the reference to the book of Judith, (C. LV. of Clement,) is only a reference to the story concerning her, which Clement evidently believed. There are, it is true, a few cases of apparent quotation, either from books not found in our present Scriptures, or from traditionary accounts; just as there are some quotations of this nature in the New Testament, which are not found in the Hebrew Scriptures. But there is no satisfactory evidence, that Clement received any of the known apocryphal writings, either of the Old Testament or the New, as canonical.

With these facts in view, I cannot well account for it, that Eichhorn, in his introduction to our epistle, should say, when speaking of the weight of Clement's testimony in respect to its canonical authority; " Clement indeed acknowledged the existence of the epistle, because he has borrowed whole passages from it. But still, he no where cites it *formally;* as is the case, when he makes use of the other canonical writings of the New Testament. How much then can be educed from him, in respect to the credit to be attached to this epistle? Would he not have *formally* cited it, and named Paul as the author of it, if he had regarded it as canonical, and as coming from Paul?" (Einl. § 271.)

From this he concludes, that we can merely prove the existence of it in Clement's day; but nothing in respect to the credit which he attached to it.

But, as we have already seen, Clement is just as far from *formally* citing the other books of Scripture, as he is from *formally* citing our epistle. Often as he has quoted Paul's epistles, he never once appeals to his name, except in connexion with the mention of the first epistle to the Corinthians, where he could not well avoid it. With this exception, he has not even once named a single book of the New Testament, copiously as he has every where drawn from it.

Allowing, then, that Clement has not *formally* cited the epistle to the Hebrews, it amounts to no proof that he has not used it as Scripture. But we are not obliged to allow so much. In No. 1. above cited, from Heb. i. 7, it appears that Clement has prefaced his quotation with γέγραπται γὰρ οὕτως; which is one of the highest appeals that he makes to the volume of inspiration. This very passage, too, is produced by Eichhorn as an example of Clement's quoting from our epistle; but the γέγραπται γὰρ is wholly overlooked.

There is another instance also in Clement (c. XXIII.,) where the quotation from Heb. x. 37 is quite probable, and which is prefaced by συνεπιμαρτυρούσης τῆς γραφῆς; supra No. 4. If No. 7 be regarded, also, as a paraphrastic imitation by Clement of the corresponding passage in the epistle to the Hebrews, then is this a third direct appeal to the divine authority of our epistle; for he introduces the passage by saying, "Search in the Scriptures the true sayings of the Holy Spirit."

Thus much for the allegation of Eichhorn, that Clement has no where cited our epistle *formally*, as he does the canonical Scriptures. But further. The conclusion which this writer draws from the *assumed* facts stated by him, is as erroneous as the facts themselves. One might indeed have expected, in a matter so weighty as that of Clement's testimony, and one in which the evidence is so accessible, that so manifest an error in regard to Clement's mode of quotation should not be committed. Nothing can be more evident to a critical reader of Clement, than that no conclusion can be drawn from the *mode* of his quotation, against the supposition that he believed the book quoted to be canonical. The fact that he appeals to our epistle more frequently than to any other part of the New Testament; that he no where appeals, so far as we can discover, to any apocryphal writings of either Testament; above all, that he appeals to our epistle by quoting passages from it in order to confirm and impress the truths which he is inculcating, and appeals to it in the same way and for the purposes as he appeals to the most acknowledged parts of Scripture; the fact, too, that Clement was the companion and fellow-labourer of Paul, and was also bishop of the church at Rome, the metropolis of the world; that he wrote in the name of the church there

74 § 12. ANTIQUITY AND CANONICAL

to the church at Corinth,* and that he addressed to them passages from the epistle to the Hebrews, in such a way as to imply that this epistle was already well known and familiar to them; these facts, taken all together, make on my own mind a strong impression, that the evidence is as clear and convincing, that in the age of Clement our epistle was considered a part of the sacred writings of the Scripture, as it is that any other book of the New Testament was considered as a part of them.

Such was the impression which in ancient times Eusebius had, from reading Clement's epistle. Speaking of monuments preserving apostolic doctrines, he says, ['Επιστολῇ] καὶ τοῦ Κλήμεντος ἐν τῇ ἀνωμολογουμένῃ παρὰ πᾶσιν, ἣν ἐκ προσώπου τῆς 'Ρωμαίων ἐκκλησίας τῇ Κορινθίων διετυπώσατο· ἐν ᾗ τῆς πρὸς Ἑβραίους πολλὰ νοήματα παραθεὶς, ἤδη δὲ καὶ αὐτολεξεὶ ῥητοῖς τισὶν ἐξ αὐτῆς χρησάμενος, σαφέστατα παρίστησιν ὅτι μὴ νεὸν ὑπάρχει τὸ σύγγραμμα· ὅθεν εἰκότως ἔδοξεν, αὐτὸ τοῖς λοιποῖς ἐγκαταλεχθῆναι γράμμασι τοῦ ἀποστόλου, that is, " [We count also the epistle] of Clement, acknowledged by all, which he wrote in behalf of the church at Rome to the church at Corinth; in which, exhibiting many of the sentiments of the epistle to the Hebrews, he makes use of some expressions taken from it in the very words of the epistle, by which he most clearly shows that this epistle is no recent composition; whence it seems likely, that it is to be reckoned among the other writings of the apostle [Paul.]" Hist. Ecc. III. 38. I am not able to see how one who reads critically the epistle of Clement, can avoid the conviction that he has quoted it as Eusebius avers, and that he has appealed to it as Scripture.

Of other writers, belonging to the first half century after the apostolic age, we have but few remains; and most of these are imperfect. Some near resemblances to passages in our epistle to the Hebrews may be found in them; but after a careful examination of them, I have not thought them sufficiently definite and important to become the subject of discussion here; I shall merely subjoin them, and leave them to the consideration of the reader.

The following are the passages usually compared.

Heb. III. 5. Μωϋσῆς μὲν πιστὸς ἐν ὅλῳ τῷ οἴκῳ αὐτοῦ ὡς θερά-   Barnabas, Epist. c. XIV. Μωϋσῆς, θεράπων ὤν, ἔλαβεν [viz.

* C. i. Ἡ ἐκκλησία τοῦ Θεοῦ ἡ παροικοῦσα 'Ρώμην, τῇ ἐκκλησίᾳ κ. τ. λ. is the commencement of Clement's epistle.

πων..... 6. Χριστὸς δὲ ὡς υἱὸς ἐπὶ τὸν οἶκον αὐτοῦ, οὗ οἶκός ἐσμεν ἡμεῖς.

Heb. x. 25. Μὴ ἐγκαταλείποντες τὴν ἐπισυναγωγὴν ἑαυτῶν καθὼς ἔθος τισίν.

Heb. xii. 17...... μετανοίας γὰρ τόπον οὐχ εὗρε.

Heb. iv. 12..... κριτικὸς ἐνθυμήσεων καὶ ἐννοιῶν καρδίας .... οὐκ ἔστι κτίσις ἀφανὴς ἐνώπιον αὐτοῦ.

Heb. vi. 20. Ἰησοῦς .... ἀρχιερεὺς γενόμενος, comp. vii. 3. 24. iv. 14.

Heb. xiii. 9. Διδαχαῖς ποικίλαις καὶ ξέναις μὴ περιφέρεσθε ...... ἐν οἷς οὐκ ὠφελήθησαν οἱ περιπατήσαντες.

Heb. x. 28, 29. Ἀθετήσας τις νόμον Μωϋσέως χωρὶς οἰκτιρμῶν ἐπὶ δυσὶν ἢ τρισὶ μάρτυσιν ἀποθνήσκει· Πόσῳ δοκεῖτε χείρονος ἀξιωθήσεται τιμωρίας, ὁ τὸν υἱὸν τοῦ Θεοῦ καταπατήσας, κ. τ. λ.

τὰς πλάκας.] Αὐτὸς δὲ ὁ Κύριος ἡμῖν ἔδωκεν, εἰς λάον κληρονομίας, κ. τ. λ.

Barnabas, Epist. c. iv. Non separatim debetis seducere vos, tanquam justificati. [Old Latin version; the original Greek here being lost.]

Hermas, Simil. viii. 8. His igitur non est locus penitentiæ.

Polycarp, Epist. c. iv..... λέληθεν αὐτὸν οὐδὲν, οὔτε λογισμῶν οὔτε ἐννοιῶν, οὔτε τι τῶν κρυπτῶν τῆς καρδίας.

Polycarp, Martyr. ...... διὰ τοῦ αἰωνίου ἀρχιερέως Ἰησοῦ Χριστοῦ; (quoted in Euseb. Hist. Ecc. p. 133. D.; so, also, in the Latin version of Polycarp, published by Usher.) Add, from the same version, c. xii. .... et ipse sempiternus pontifex, Dei filius, Christus Jesus. Lardner, ii. 830.

Ignatius, Epist. ad Magnesios, c. viii. Μὴ πλάνασθε ταῖς ἑτεροδοξίαις, μηδὲ μυθεύμασιν τοῖς παλαιοῖς ἀνωφελέσιν οὖσιν.

Ignatius, Epist. ad Ephes. c. xvi. Εἰ δὲ οἱ τοὺς ἀνθρωπίνους οἴκους διαφθείροντες, θανάτῳ καταδικάζονται· πόσῳ μᾶλλον οἱ τὴν Χριστοῦ ἐκκλησίαν νοθεύειν ἐπιχειροῦντες αἰωνίαν τίσουσι δίκην, ὑπὲρ ἧς σταυρὸν καὶ θάνατον ὑπέμεινεν ὁ Κύριος Ἰησοῦς, κ. τ. λ.

The passages may be found in Cotelerius; or in Lardner, Cred. i. pp. 43, 44, 131, 217; ii. 830; i. 177; edit. 1734. See also Eich. Einleit. § 271, note 2. Several of them, (specially one from Polycarp, naming Christ the *eternal high priest*,) look very much like a *quotation*

§ 12. ANTIQUITY AND CANONICAL AUTHORITY.

But in a matter so weighty, it is not best to place very much dependence on them, as the similarity may be accidental.

Justin Martyr is the first considerable writer of the second century, whose works are come down to us. He was born about A. D. 103, and flourished about A. D. 140. In his dialogue with Trypho the Jew, the following passage occurs. " This is he, who, after the order of Melchizedek, is king of Salem, and eternal priest of the Most High," p. 341. He elsewhere calls Christ, αἰώνιον τοῦ Θεοῦ ἱερέα καὶ βασιλέα, καὶ Χριστὸν μέλλοντα γίνεσθαι, p. 323. c. In another place, he says of Christ, Καὶ ἄγγελος δὲ καλεῖται καὶ ἀπόστολος, Apolog. i. p. 96. D; which name (ἀπόστολος) is given him only in the epistle to the Hebrews.

In addition to the facts already stated, respecting the early existence and credit of the epistle to the Hebrews, it should be noted, that the *Peshito*, or old Syriac version of the New Testament, made, in all probability, during the second century; and the old Latin versions, made during the same period, and probably within the first half of it; both contain the epistle to the Hebrews, Bertholdt Einleit, p. 637, seq., 717, seq. This is a fact of very great importance; for these versions were in common use and authority among the churches of the East and West. It is not pretended that either of these versions, at this period, comprised any book which is now known to be apocryphal. Undoubtedly they did not comprise any which were then deemed apocryphal. Here then is palpable evidence, that the epistle to the Hebrews was widely circulated among Christians a short time after the apostolic age. In the west, the *Itala* and old Latin versions comprised it; in Greece, or the middle region, the church at Corinth are addressed by Clement as being familiar with it; and in the east, the Syrian church, wide spread as it was, comprised it in their canon.

From near the close of the second century onward, the history of the canonical credit of our epistle intermingles itself with the controverted question, *whether Paul was the author of it*. On this account, I shall not separately pursue the history any farther at present, as it must necessarily be investigated in the course of discussing that important question which still remains for consideration.

The sum of what has been shown, under our present head of discussion, is, that the epistle to the Hebrews was written before the destruction of Jerusalem, probably but a short time before this event; that in about thirty years, at most, it had acquired such currency and credit, that the church at Rome, the metropolis of the world, in a letter addressed by their bishop to the church at Corinth, made repeated appeals to it as a book of divine authority, and in such a way as to imply a knowledge and acknowledgment of it, by the Corinthian church, similar to their own; that Justin Martyr, about A. D. 140, has evidently appealed to its contents as sacred; that about this time, or not long after, it was inserted among the canonical books of the New Testament, by the churches of the East and the West; and that, consequently, it must have had, at a period very little after the apostolic age, a currency and a credit not at all, or at most very little, inferior to that of other acknowledged books of the New Testament. *Better* evidence than this of early and general reception by the churches, it would be difficult to find, in respect to a considerable number of books in the New Testament; with *less* than this we are obliged to content ourselves, respecting several of them.

But admitting the early existence and general credit of this epistle, there still remains the most difficult of all the questions which have been raised respecting it, " Who was its author ? Was it Paul, or some other person ?" This very important question deserves, and must receive, a particular and thorough discussion.

§ 13. *Was Paul the writer of the epistle to the Hebrews?*

From whatever source the epistle to the Hebrews is derived, every reader of it must perceive that it comes from a man of deep feeling, of a benevolent heart, of extensive knowledge, and of views, in respect to the *spiritual* nature of Christianity, as exalted as can be found any where in the New Testament. Every attentive reader of the Mosaic law, moreover, must feel, that the epistle to the Hebrews is the best key to unlock the treasures which are secreted there; and that it affords us a disclosure, in respect to the general nature and object of the Jewish dispensation, which Christians much need, and which can no where else be found in a manner so full and satisfactory.

But this, however correct or important it may be, cannot establish the fact that Paul wrote the epistle. We must not virtually assume this position from reasons *a priori*, or because we may wish it to be so. It is as uncritical to believe without any evidence, as it is to reject evidence when it is offered. It is uncritical also to establish (or rather attempt establishing) a position that concerns a simple matter of *fact*, by any reasoning *a priori*. To investigate the present question in a becoming and candid manner, we must lay aside prejudice either in respect to the affirmative or negative of it; and also our previous opinions, which have been derived merely from education, and have not been established on the basis of proper evidence.

The epistle to the Hebrews has no *subscription*. Consequently, we are left either to conjecture who the author was, or to gather it from evidence external or internal. *Conjecture,* in respect to an epistle, the claims of which are supposed to be *authoritative,* can give no real satisfaction to the thorough inquirer. *Circumstantial evidence* is that, then, to which we must necessarily resort, since the signature of the author is wanting.

I make these observations here, because it has seemed to me, that very much more has been demanded by some critics, in order to prove that Paul wrote this epistle, than the nature of the case admits, or even requires. Their demands would amount to nothing less than the signature of the writer himself, or direct testimony that he wrote it, given by witnesses then present.

In the investigation of the question, " Who was the author of an anonymous letter that is almost 1800 years old, written in an age and country where literary records (if they at all exist) are accidental and not designed?" how can it be justly required, that proof of a direct, unequivocal, and positive nature should be produced? Where is the anonymous letter of antiquity, that could ever be assigned to any particular author, if demands such as these were made in respect to it?

The question is not, whether the point in dispute can be rendered *certain* by plain and indubitable testimony, (for then how should it ever have been disputed?) but, all things considered, whether there is not a *probability* in favour of supposing Paul to be the author of it—a probability deduced from evidence external and internal, which is sufficient to quiet our reasonable doubts, and to command our prevailing belief.

It is not modern critics only, who have been divided on this question. The ancient Christians early differed in opinion about it, for several centuries; the Latin, or Occidental Christians, after the second century, generally rejecting it from their canon, as they did not reckon it to be Paul's; while the Greek, or rather the Oriental, Christians generally received it as coming from the hand of the apostle Paul.

I shall divide the evidence, in respect to this question, into external and internal. By the former, I mean whatever can be gathered from the Christian fathers, or ancient writers, or the tradition of the churches, respecting the epistle; and by the latter, the characteristics of the epistle in respect to sentiment, style, and diction, compared with the acknowledged letters of Paul, and also certain facts which are adverted to in the epistle itself. The great deficiency of genuine early Christian records, for many years after the completion of the New Testament, is a fact acknowledged and lamented by all who study either the early history of the church, or that of its sacred books. A few fragments only we have, of Barnabas, Clement of Rome, Papias, Hermas, Ignatius, Polycarp, and some others; in most instances too short, and too imperfectly preserved, to afford any strong ground of satisfaction to the critical inquirer.

§ 14. *Testimony of the Alexandrine Church.*

The evidence, that the epistle to the Hebrews was early recognized as one of the sacred books, has been already exhibited. The first testimony that we have respecting Paul's being the author of the epistle, is that of Pantænus, the head of the celebrated Christian school at Alexandria in Egypt, who flourished about A. D. 180. This testimony was inserted by Clement of Alexandria, the disciple of Pantænus, and his successor in the famous school just mentioned, in a work of his entitled Ὑποτυπώσεις, *Institutions,* or *Sketches.* This work is now lost; but Eusebius has preserved an extract from it, in his Ecclesiastical History, lib. vi. c. 14. Pantænus himself was the most learned Christian of the age in which he lived, and one whose weight and authority in the churches was very great.

Clement, in the extract preserved by Eusebius, is endeavouring to assign a reason, why Paul had not subscribed his name to the epistle to the Hebrews. After giving his opinion in regard to this point, he adds, " As our worthy presbyter [so he usually calls Pantænus] has already said, Since the Lord himself was sent by the Almighty as an apostle to the Hebrews, Paul being an apostle to the Gentiles, on account of modesty, does not subscribe himself as the apostle to the Hebrews, both out of reverence for his Lord, and, because being a preacher, and an apostle to the Gentiles, by a kind of supererogation he wrote to the Hebrews."*

---

* "Ἤδη δὲ ὡς ὁ μακάριος ἔλεγε πρεσβύτερος, ἐπεὶ ὁ Κύριος ἀπόστολος ὢν τοῦ παντοκράτορος ἀπεστάλη πρὸς Ἑβραίους, διὰ μετριότητα ὁ Παῦλος ὡς ἂν εἰς τὰ ἔθνη ἀπεσταλμένος οὐκ ἐγγράφει ἑαυτὸν Ἑβραίων ἀπόστολον· διά τε τὴν πρὸς τὸν κύριον τιμὴν, διά τε τὸ ἐκ περιουσίας καὶ τοῖς Ἑβραίοις ἐπιστέλλειν, ἐθνῶν κήρυκα ὄντα καὶ ἀπόστολον. Lib. vi. 14.

Two points are equally clear from this testimony; the first, that Pantænus entertained no doubt of Paul's being the author of the epistle to the Hebrews, the whole passage implying as well as asserting this; the second, that still, either from the suggestions of his own mind, or from those made by others, objections had been raised against this opinion, because the epistle lacked the usual subscription or inscription of Paul. The attempt to solve these doubts, necessarily implies that they had been suggested from one of these sources; but from which, we cannot tell with any certainty.

I am very ready to allow, with some recent critics, that the attempt at solution is but a poor specimen of critical reasoning, and is insufficient to accomplish what Pantænus designed to accomplish. For how was it necessary, as he seems to suppose, that Paul should have subscribed himself *an apostle to the Hebrews*, if he had put his name to the epistle? If he declined doing this, "because his Lord and Master was the apostle of God to them," as Pantænus says, still he might (as on other occasions he actually does) have called himself *an apostle of Jesus Christ;* or he might, as he twice does, have called himself *a servant of Jesus Christ*, Phil. i. 1, Tit. i. 1; or he might, as he twice does, have simply written his name *Paul*, 1 Thess. i. 1, 2 Thess. i. 1. Why should he have been any more *diffident* with respect to doing this, in the present case, than in any other?

As to his *diffidence* arising from being an apostle to the Gentiles, which made him, as Pantænus supposes, decline subscribing his name in an epistle to the Hebrews, so much weight cannot well be attributed to it. The writer of our epistle has told the persons addressed, of his circumstances, and of his companions; he has also asked their prayers, that "he might be speedily restored to them;" all which necessarily implies, that his name was not designed to be wholly concealed, and could not be so concealed, from those whom he *directly* and *originally* addressed: so that neither of Pantænus' reasons for Paul's declining to subscribe his name, appears to have any considerable weight in it.

Eichhorn and Bertholdt, it must be acknowledged, have refuted the good father's *critical reasoning*, on which I have just animadverted; but they should not (as they appear to have done) substitute this for a confutation of his *testimony* also. Bertholdt moreover maintains, that Pantænus has simply expressed an *opinion*, that Paul wrote the epistle to the Hebrews; an opinion *merely his own*, and not founded on any tradition. This he endeavours to prove, by the following argument:—

" It is clear, that Pantænus' expressions imply the existence of persons, in his time, who maintained the opinion, that Paul was not the author of the epistle to the Hebrews. Now, if general tradition maintained that he was, how could there be any such persons? For at this time it was easy to trace a tradition of this nature up to its primary source." Einleit. p. 2918.

But has there ever been a period, since the Gospels or Epistles were written, in which more or less of them were not discarded by some, and doubted by others? Have there not been some such men as Ebionites, Alogi, Marcionites, and others of a similar character, in every age, and almost in every country? And can it be a valid objection to a book, or to testimony respecting it, that such men have rejected it, or doubted it? If so, then the whole New Testament must be given up at once; and the effort to maintain its genuineness, abandoned as a task utterly hopeless; for what part of it has not been discarded by some of these, or such like, sectarians?

Does Pantænus, I ask, tell us whence the doubts in question arose; whether from his own mind, from heretics, or from the members of the catholic church? Not a word of this. Be it, then, that they came from whatever quarter you please, or from all quarters; the weight of his testimony is increased, rather than diminished, by the objections. For how does the case now stand? Pantænus had objections to the apostolic origin of the epistle suggested, by members of the catholic church, by heretics, and by his own mind; yet such was the strength of his conviction, arising from the evidence opposed to these doubts, that he hesitates not in the least to consider it as an established point, that Paul was the author of this epistle. He speaks of it as being certainly his.

Now, whence did Pantænus derive such a conviction? Pantænus, who was at the head of the first Christian school in the world; who resided near Palestine, and where constant communication was all the time kept up with that country; Pantænus, who lived within a century after the apostolic age. It cannot be shown, nor in any way rendered probable, that he had any favourite or peculiar sentiment to be supported by the epistle to the Hebrews, which was the reason why he defended its apostolic origin. I am aware of the allegation made by some, that the epistle to the Hebrews was already received in the churches as one of the sacred books; and that, as some doubted respecting it, because it wanted an apostle's name to sanction it, Pantænus, in order to save its credit, and defend the custom of the churches in receiving it as canonical, assigned the reasons produced above, why Paul did not subscribe his name to it. But is not this, after all, conceding the very point which it is meant to deny? "The epistle to the Hebrews was already received by the churches; therefore Pantænus defends it!" Indeed? And how came it to be received? Whence this general credit already obtained; a credit so strong, a custom of reception so general, as to inspire Pantænus with entire confidence in its canonical authority, and raise him above all the objections which had been suggested? And how comes it, that no epistles should have made their way into the canon, amid all the conflicting opinions, and various apocryphal and supposititious writings, of the early ages of the church, but those which either bear an apostle's name, or were by *general consent* assigned to an apostle? This is a fundamental question, in respect to the great subject of the authority of our New Testament canon. It is an *articulus stantis vel cadentis auctoritatis*, in respect to it. And the answer to this question plainly is, that the catholic church in the primitive age, taken as a body, were governed by the maxim, that no book or epistle could be properly regarded as canonical, except such as was written by an apostle.

I am far from denying, that particular churches, and even particular regions of country, did, near the close of the second century, and afterwards, regard as sacred, some of the apocryphal books of the Old Testament and of the New. The quotations from them by the Christian fathers, is conclusive evidence of this. But, then, such books, for the time being, were of course estimated as holding a rank entitled to the credit of inspired books. And in respect to the *apocryphal* writings of the New Testament, it is clear that they were regarded, (where they were admitted as canonical,) as either coming from the hands of apostles, or as having been written with their approbation, or under their inspection. Nothing can be more evident, than that there was a constant verging of the church, as a body, toward the point of limitation, in respect to *canonical credit*, that has just been stated. That some churches and persons should have committed mistakes, respecting the extent to which the principle adverted to would carry them, is not at all to be wondered at, considering the state of literary knowledge at that period. But that such mistakes were not committed by the predominant part of the churches, is demonstrated from the state of the New Testament, ever since the earliest period; the received books of which are only those, which were regarded as being of apostolic origin, or revision, and *generally* believed to be so.

Such being the fact, we may ask, and we ought to ask, How came the epistle to the Hebrews into the canon; so that Clement of Rome in the very first century, and Pantænus in the next, refer to it as Scripture? Why, plainly, because an apostolic origin was attributed to it. Pantænus regards this as certainty; and Pantænus says that the apostle who wrote it was *Paul, διὰ τε τὸ* . . . . *τοῖς 'Εβραίοις 'επιςέλλειν* [Παῦλον.]

I readily concede, that he is not a witness contemporary with Paul. But he is a witness, (and one of the very best the age afforded, in which he lived, and was so distinguished as a man of knowledge) of what the opinion of the churches *then* was. Is it not evident, that in the passage under consideration, he is defending the *usual* opinion of the churches, in regard to our epistle; and that he is *not* merely delivering his own *private* sentiments? The manner in which he speaks, plainly declares this.

Moreover, that he did speak the opinion which was *prevalent* and *general* at this period, is rendered still more probable by the fact, that at least as early as the time in which he lived, probably earlier, the Syriac translation in the East, and the old Latin version in the West, as we have already seen, were completed; both of which went into general use in those countries, and both of which comprise the epistle to the Hebrews. In regard to the Syriac, it may be further noted, that while it was made too early, as it would seem, to comprise the 2d epistle of Peter, and the 2d and 3d epistles of John, (which for various reasons came later into circulation than the other epistles,) it still comprises the epistle to the Hebrews. Are not these facts, then, when taken together, good evidence, that the credit of this epistle was early and widely diffused, and that it was regarded at a very early period, by the great body of the churches, as of apostolic origin? To which of the apostles it was assigned by current belief, and of course by current tradition, Pantænus informs us.

Let it be distinctly noted, that all this took place within about a century after the apostolic age, (and probably less;) " when tradition," as Bertholdt says, " might be easily traced back to its origin." Does not, then, the testimony of Pantænus, whom Photius (Cod. 118) represents to be not only a hearer of those who had seen the apostles, but of some of the apostles themselves, supported as it is by concurrent testimony of the canon of the churches in the East and in the West, amount to satisfactory evidence, in regard to general ecclesiastical tradition at the time in which this father lived? And if so, does not this plead strongly for the probability, that Paul was the author of the epistle?

I am unable to distinguish the testimony in question of Pantænus, from that of other writers, whom Bertholdt quotes as good support for the genuineness of other books of the New Testament. How many hundred testimonies has he quoted, where the witness does not say whether he delivers his own opinion, or recites tradition ! Yet Bertholdt takes these, and such like testimonies, as legitimate evidence, when he sets out to establish the genuineness of any books of the New Testament, or of any ancient writing. Why, then, should he resort to the extraordinary, the unsupported, (I may say improbable,) supposition, that Pantænus has, in the case before us, only delivered his own *private opinion* ? Even if it were so, the question, ' On what was the opinion grounded ? what induced him to believe so ?' would present serious difficulties, in respect to the suggestions which Bertholdt has made ; as I have already shown.

At any rate, the principle which Bertholdt assumes here, would render it utterly impossible ever to establish the genuineness of any of the New Testament books ; and, I may add, of any other ancient book. A principle fraught with such consequences, cannot, either with propriety or safety, be admitted into our critical investigations.

The importance of this discussion, which treats of testimony so early and respectable, in regard to the subject in question, will, I hope, be a sufficient apology for the length to which it has been protracted.

Pantænus was succeeded, in his school, by the celebrated Clement of Alexandria, near the close of the second century. Clement, as he tells us in the first book of his *Stromata*, (p. 274. Lardner, Cred. ii. 462,) had travelled in Greece, Italy, the East, and Egypt, in quest of knowledge, and employed masters in all these countries. With Pantænus he settled down in Egypt ; and he represents this teacher, though last in time, as first in merit. He compares him to the Sicilian bee, that had gathered flowers from the prophetic and apostolic meadows ; and represents him as filling the minds of his hearers with pure knowledge.

Clement, then, was well qualified to judge what was the general usage and tradition of the churches, in respect to the canon of Scripture ; as he had traversed a great part of the regions where churches were planted. His testimony (extracted from a work of his, entitled 'Υποτυπώσεις,) is preserved by Eusebius, in his Ecc. Hist. l. vi. c. 14. " In his book," says Eusebius, " Clement affirms that Paul is the author of the epistle to the Hebrews ; and that, as it was addressed to Hebrews, it was originally written in their language, and afterwards translated by Luke, for the use of the Greeks; which is the reason, why the colouring of the style is the same in this epistle and in the Acts of the Apostles. The reason why Paul did not affix his name at the head of it, probably is, because the Hebrews had conceived a prejudice against him, and were suspicious of him. Very prudently, therefore, he did not place his name at the head of the epistle, so as to divert them from the perusal of it.*

Eichhorn and Bertholdt have endeavoured to show here, also, that Clement's testimony is only his own *private* opinion, or at most, that of his master, Pantænus. Eichhorn attacks the apology which Clement makes for Paul's omitting to prefix his name to the epistle; and seeming to triumph over this, he dismisses the whole of the testimony along with it. Bertholdt has pursued a course somewhat different. Pantænus he represents as giving one reason why the name of Paul is omitted; Clement, another. This contradiction, he avers, proves that neither Pantænus nor Clement rested on tradition as their support, but only followed their own conjecture.

This conclusion is somewhat singular. What is the point in question? Simply, whether Paul wrote the epistle to the Hebrews. Pantænus says that he did; Clement asserts the same; both, as it appears, without any doubt or hesitation in their own minds. How came they by this confidence? Clement derived it, says Bertholdt, from his master Pantænus. But from whom did Pantænus derive it? Whence did he get so much confidence respecting this point, as to overcome all the obstacles thrown in the way of such a belief? He appears to have been a man of great sobriety, knowledge, diligence, and excellence of character. He was no innovator; nor does it appear that he had any pride of speculative opinions and conceits to foster. But because he *answers the doubts*, that had been suggested against Paul's being the author of the epistle to the Hebrews, in *one* way, and Clement in *another*, "this," says Bertholdt, "is *contradiction;* and it shows that neither of these fathers grounded his opinion on tradition, but on his own conjectures." *Contradiction* in what? Are these two fathers agreed on the great point in

---

* Ἐν δὲ ταῖς Ὑποτυπώσεσι .... τὴν πρὸς Ἑβραίους ἐπιστολὴν Παῦλον μὲν εἶναι φησί· γεγράφθαι δὲ Ἑβραίοις Ἑβραϊκῇ φωνῇ· Λουκᾶν δὲ φιλοτίμως μεθερμηνεύσαντα ἐκδοῦναι τοῖς Ἕλλησιν. Ὅθεν τὸν αὐτὸν χρῶτα εὑρίσκεσθαι κατὰ τὴν ἑρμηνείαν ταύτης τῆς ἐπιστολῆς καὶ τῶν πράξεων. Μὴ προγεγράφθαι δὲ τὸ, Παῦλος ἀπόστολος, εἰκότως· Ἑβραίοις γὰρ φησιν ἐπιστέλλων πρόληψιν εἰληφόσι κατ' αὐτοῦ, καὶ ὑποπτεύουσιν αὐτὸν, συνετῶς πάνυ οὐκ ἐν ἀρχῇ ἀπέτριψεν αὐτοὺς τὸ ὄνομα θείς.— Lib. vi. 14.

question, viz. whether Paul was the author of the epistle? This is conceded. Where, then, is the contradiction? "They are not agreed how the doubts raised against it should be solved." What follows? "Why, as Bertholdt avers, " that they grounded not their opinions on tradition." That is, (if this have any appropriate meaning,) that tradition had not brought down to them *the mode of solving these doubts;* since they were not agreed in the *mode* of solving them. But what if tradition had, as is most probable, handed down to them neither doubts nor solutions; and that the solutions they proposed were of *newly-raised* doubts, which about this time began to appear in some of the Occidental churches—solutions drawn, as I would most freely concede, from their own personal views, rather than from tradition; what, I ask, has the *manner* of solving these doubts to do with the main point at issue? Nothing at all; and be it, that Eichhorn has triumphed over both the good fathers, Pantænus and Clement, in showing the incompetency of their reasoning to solve the doubts then raised, it leaves their testimony, as to the great point at issue, quite untouched.

I am not disposed, however, to concede so much to Eichhorn's reasoning, in respect to the assertions of Clement. If Paul did write the epistle to the Hebrews, and direct it to a church in Palestine, every one acquainted with his history knows, that the Hebrews in that country, at least very many of them, were affected towards him as Clement has represented them to be; and this might be a proper and adequate reason, for not setting down his name at the head of his epistle.

" But Paul," says Eichhorn, " has not shrunk from openly professing his name on all other occasions." This may be true. But to what other part of the church did he write, circumstanced as the Jews of Palestine were? Does not a prudent man change the *mode* of his address, as circumstances may require?

" But, after all, the author has not concealed himself. At the close of the epistle he has developed circumstances which must certainly make him known." I grant it, in respect to the church whom he immediately and primitively addressed; but the case would not be the same in respect to other churches, for whom, also, there can be but little doubt, the epistle was ultimately designed. At least, those who read it, would first have been subjected to the influence of its reasoning, and its eloquent and powerful remonstrances, before they would come to make the inquiries about the author, suggested by the circumstances at the close. May not the author, who could write such an epistle, well have trusted to its power in disarming prejudices, which the appearance merely of a name at the outset might have heightened? And might not Clement, who travelled through the East, and over so many countries, have thus become acquainted with the manner in which the difficulty was commonly solved, which he proposes? This solution, although Eichhorn thinks it to be so incompetent, is still a much more probable one than that of Pantænus; nay, I must think that it is in itself by no means destitute of probability. How can it be shown in any way to be incongruous, that such a reason should have influenced Paul to withhold his name?

But further, Bertholdt says, "Another proof that Clement did not ground his testimony on tradition, is, that he declares the epistle to have been originally written in Hebrew; and that Luke translated it into the Greek language; and thus he merely undertakes, in his own way, to account for the diversity of the style from that of Paul, and its similarity to that of the Acts of the Apostles?"

Be it so then, for the sake of argument. But still, what is the amount of this? Nothing more than that Clement undertakes to meet an objection, raised from the *style* of the epistle; and to show how this style could be somewhat diverse from Paul's, and yet the epistle derive its origin from that apostle. How can this determine, that Clement did not ground his belief of Paul's being the author of the epistle, on the tradition of the church, rather than on his own conjecture?

In fact, that Clement should have remained entirely unmoved in his opinion, by all objections made to Paul's being the author of our epistle, proves just the reverse of what Bertholdt has endeavoured to establish. It proves, beyond all reasonable controversy, the *strength* and *constancy* of his opinion, which triumphed over all such obstacles; and which to do this, must, as it seems to me, have been supported, in his own mind, by the general voice of the churches among whom he had travelled.

But further to invalidate the testimony of Pantænus and Clement, Bertholdt suggests, that " they were inclined to favour the epistle to the Hebrews, on account of the Alexandrine spirit which reigns in it," [he means the spirit of allegorizing and finding secondary senses to language;] and "to establish the credit of a favourite letter, they attributed it to Paul, being supported in this by the apparent similarity which it has to his writings."

Now, since this is altogether *gratuitous conjecture*, it might not improperly be answered by *conjecture* that such was not the case. I will suggest, however, that it is by no means certain, either that Pantænus or Clement were natives of Alexandria. The probability is, that they came there partly as learners, but principally as teachers; and that their opinions were not formed merely by the fashion of interpreting the Scriptures at Alexandria. Besides, what ground is there to suppose that these fathers, conscientious and deeply imbued with reverence for the Scriptures as they were, would have been persuaded, by attachment to the Alexandrine spirit of allegory, to foist a book into the canon of the New Testament as Paul's, when they had no evidence on which to ground such an opinion? And how comes it, that at this very period, this same epistle was inserted in the canon, in the *Itala* of the western churches, and the *Peshito* or old Syriac version of the eastern ones? Did Pantænus and Clement effect this? They had no concern with the management of either of these churches. Christians then in the East and West, far distant from Alexandria, did ascribe canonical authority to this epistle; and if they did so, there is, of course, good reason to believe, that they ascribed the epistle to an apostle as the author. What probability can there be, then, that Clement and Pantænus ascribed this epistle to Paul, merely on the ground of their own *private* opinion or local prejudices?

The sum of testimony for the second century has now been presented. Its importance is greatly magnified by its proximity to the time when the epistle was written, and when tradition respecting it might be traced back, as Bertholdt avers, without much difficulty, by a sober and interested inquirer. That at the close of the first century, the epistle to the Hebrews was not only extant, but in full credit as a canonical writing at Rome, we have seen in the examination of the testimony of Clement of Rome. That at the close of the second century, it occupied a place in the canon of the eastern, the western, and the intermediate churches, follows from the testimony that has now been examined. That Paul was the author of this epistle, appears to have been the firm belief of the most celebrated theological school then existing; and that this belief harmonized with that of the churches in general, who required evidence of apostolic origin or approbation, in order to entitle an epistle to a place in the canon, seems quite probable, and is contradicted by no circumstances with which we are acquainted.

We may now advance to the former part of the third century, and examine a few of the principal witnesses.

The celebrated Origen, second to none of the fathers (except Jerome) as a critic, and in general learning superior to them all, the disciple and the successor of Clement at Alexandria, is, in all respects, a most important witness to be examined. He spent his life in the study and explanation of the Scriptures; and his testimony in regard to the canon of Scripture, at the time when he flourished, (A. D. 220,) is of greater weight than that of any other individual of the same period. The most explicit testimony of Origen is, that which Eusebius has preserved, Ecc. Hist. vi. 25; being an extract from one of Origen's homilies on the epistle to the Hebrews. The passage runs thus in Eusebius: " In respect to the epistle to the Hebrews, Origen decides thus in his homilies upon it. ' The character of the style of the epistle to the Hebrews has not the unpolished cast of the apostle's language, who professes himself to be a man unlearned in speech, i. e. in phraseology. Besides, this epistle, in the texture of its style, is more conformed to Greek idiom; as every one must confess, who is able to distinguish differences in style. Moreover, the ideas in this epistle are admirable, and not inferior to those which are confessedly apostolic; and this every one must concede is true, who has attentively read the writings of the apostles.' A little further on he adds, ' If I were to give my opinion, I should say, the phraseology and the texture belong to some one relating the apostle's sentiments, and, as it were, commenting on the words of his master. *If any church therefore hold this to be an epistle of Paul, let it receive commendation on account of this;* FOR IT IS NOT WITHOUT REASON (οὐ εἰκῇ,) THAT THE ANCIENTS HAVE HANDED IT DOWN (παραδεδώκασι, *have had a tradition*) AS BEING OF PAUL. Who wrote the epistle, [γράψας, penned it, or committed it to writing,] God [only] knows with certainty; but the report which has reached us is, that some affirm it to be written by Clement, bishop of Rome; and some, by Luke, who wrote the Gospel and the Acts.'"* Euseb. Hist. Ecc. vi. 25. Lard. iv. p. 235.

* ...... περὶ τῆς πρὸς Ἑβραίους ἐπιστολῆς ἐν ταῖς εἰς αὐτὴν ὁμιλίαις ταῦτα διαλαμβάνει· ὅτι ὁ χαρακτὴρ τῆς λέξεως τῆς πρὸς Ἑβραίους ἐπιγεγραμμένης ἐπιστολῆς οὐκ ἔχει τὸ ἐν λόγῳ ἰδιωτικὸν τοῦ ἀποστόλου, ὁμολογήσαντος ἑαυτὸν ἰδιώτην εἶναι τῷ λόγῳ, τουτέστι τῇ φράσει. Ἀλλὰ ἐστὶν ἡ ἐπιστολὴ συνθέσει τῆς λέξεως Ἑλληνικωτέρα, πᾶς ὁ ἐπιστάμενος κρίνειν φράσεων διαφορὰς ὁμολογήσαι ἄν. Πάλιν τε αὖ ὅτι τὰ νοήματα τῆς ἐπιστολῆς θαυμάσιά ἐστι, καὶ οὐ δευτέρα τῶν ἀποστολικῶν ὁμολογουμένων γραμμάτων· καὶ τοῦτο ἂν συμφήσαι εἶναι ἀληθὲς πᾶς ὁ προσέχων τῇ ἀναγνώσει τῇ ἀποστολικῇ. Τούτοις μεθ' ἕτερα ἐπιφέρει λέγων· Ἐγὼ δὲ ἀποφαινόμενος εἴποιμ' ἄν, ὅτι τὰ μὲν νοήματα τοῦ ἀποστόλου ἐστίν· ἡ δὲ φράσις καὶ

This passage has been appealed to for different purposes, by writers of different sentiments; by some, in order to show that Origen doubted, by others to show that he did not doubt, about Paul's being the author of the epistle in question. Omitting an account of what others have said, let us endeavour to elicit the sentiments of Origen, by considering this passage in connexion with other passages to be found in his writings.

(1.) It is plain that Origen felt the force of the objection against the authorship of Paul, drawn from the style and manner of the epistle, in the same way as his preceptor Clement had before done; and to meet this objection, he suggests a reason *similar* to that which Clement had suggested. Clement says, that the epistle was first written in Hebrew, and then translated by Luke into Greek; and thus he endeavours to account for the supposed diversity of style between this epistle and those of Paul. But Origen does not appear to have at all supposed that it was written, at first, in Hebrew. He supposes it to have been for substance delivered, dictated, or spoken by the apostle, and penned down by some one who used his own diction, commenting, as it were, on the words of his master. In this way, the *sentiments* are regarded as apostolic and authoritative, while the *diction* is considered as arising from one not an apostle; and thus the full *credit* of the epistle is maintained, while the objection to this credit, drawn from the diversity of style, is apparently removed.

(2.) It should be noted, that Origen does not say, whether the objections against the epistle to the Hebrews being the production of Paul, arose from his own mind, or from the allegations of others. Most probably from both sources. He appears to have had a full conviction, that there was a diversity of style in it; and to remove the difficulty about the credit of the epistle, which arose in his mind from this circumstance, he resorted to the supposition just mentioned. We can have no reasonable doubt, that at this time there were some, who alleged that this epistle did not come from the hand of Paul; as Pantænus

ἡ σύνθεσις, ἀπομνημονεύσαντός τινος τὰ ἀποστολικὰ, καὶ ὡσπερεὶ σχολιογραφήσαντος τὰ εἰρημένα ὑπὸ τοῦ διδασκάλου. Εἴ τις οὖν ἐκκλησία ἔχει ταύτην τὴν ἐπιστολὴν ὡς Παύλου, αὕτη εὐδοκιμείτω καὶ ἐπὶ τοῦτο. Οὐ γὰρ εἰκῇ οἱ ἀρχαῖοι ἄνδρες ὡς Παύλου αὐτὴν παραδεδώκασι. Τίς δὲ ὁ γράψας τὴν ἐπιστολὴν, τὸ μὲν ἀληθὲς Θεὸς οἶδεν· ἡ δὲ εἰς ἡμᾶς φθάσασα ἱστορία, ὑπὸ τινων μὲν λεγόντων, ὅτι Κλήμης ὁ γενόμενος ἐπίσκοπος Ῥωμαίων ἔγραψε τὴν ἐπιστολὴν· ὑπὸ τινων δὲ, ὅτι Λουκᾶς ὁ γράψας τὸ Εὐαγγέλιον καὶ τὰς Πράξεις. Ecc. Hist. vi. 25.

and Clement had, before this, made an effort to remove objections against it.

(3.) The very manner in which Origen attempts to remove objections, shows that he gave full credit to the *apostolic origin* of the epistle. "The *thoughts*," he avers, "are apostolic, and worthy of an apostle; but the *diction* is derived from another." And when he says, "*It is not without reason that the ancients have handed it down as belonging to Paul;*" and then adds, "but who wrote it, God only knows with certainty, some attributing it to Luke, and some to Clement:" nothing can be plainer, than that he means here to suggest, that he considers it to be uncertain who *penned* it, i. e. *reduced it to writing;* for he had just asserted that the *thoughts* were *suggested* by the *apostle,* while the *diction* arose from him who reduced them to writing. To suppose (as has been supposed) that Origen means to assert, that God only knows from whom the *sentiments* of the epistle sprung, or who the author was, in this sense, is to suppose that Origen has directly contradicted himself, in the very same paragraph. Therefore,

(4.) When Origen says, that some attribute it to Luke, and some to Clement; the probability clearly is, (from the connexion in which this stands,) that he means to say, "Some attribute the penning or writing of it down, to the one or the other of these persons." If this be so, (and it appears to be very plain that it is,) it only serves to show, that Origen did not consider the tradition about Luke and Clement as well established; and especially so, as the traditionary reports were not agreed respecting the amanuensis or recorder of the epistle. It is *possible,* I acknowledge, that Origen means to say, that some attributed the real authorship to Luke or Clement; although I cannot think that this opinion has any *probable* support, in the passage of Origen now under consideration, if it be explained by any just rules of interpretation.

(5.) It is clear that Origen ascribes his own belief, and the belief of the churches of his time, that the epistle was Paul's, to ancient tradition. "If any church receive this epistle as Paul's, let it be commended for this; for it is not without reason, that the ancients (οἱ ἀρχαῖοι) have handed it down (παρδεδώκασι) as Paul's." Here two things are asserted; first, that the tradition of its being Paul's is well grounded, in Origen's view, οὐκ εἰκῇ παραδεδώκασι; and secondly, that it is an ancient tradition, for οἱ ἀρχαῖοι ἄνδρες have so thought.

I cannot well account for it, that Eichhorn and Bertholdt have kept out of sight this direct testimony of Origen to the tradition of the churches.

Eichhorn has indeed quoted it (§ 271,) but made no comment upon it; while Bertholdt has broken the paragraph into two parts, and quoted what precedes the clause in question, in one place (p. 2944,) and that which follows it in another (p. 2956;) while he has *wholly omitted* the clause under consideration. The opinion of Pantænus and Clement, that Paul wrote this epistle, had previously been ascribed by these critics either to their own conjectures, or to the influence which the views of the church of Alexandria had over them, in respect to this subject. Origen also is represented by them, as struggling between his own convictions and the prejudices of the times, in respect to the point in question, and as falling at last upon the conjecture, that " the *sentiments* are the apostle's, while the *diction* is another's," in order to reconcile his own views, and the current prejudices of the Alexandrine church. These critics have been very careful to render *prominent* the expression of Origen—*who wrote it, God* [only] *knows, report attributing it to Clement and to Luke;* and they have quoted this too, without adverting at all to the evident meaning of it, which is, " who penned or wrote it down is uncertain, report attributing it to different men; using the expression just as if Origen had simply said, " *who was the author of the epistle, God only knows.*" See Berth. Einl. § 648. Eichh. § 271. Besides this, Bertholdt represents Origen as asserting, that an *ancient* tradition, brought down even to his time, attributed the *authorship* of the epistle to Luke (p. 2955,) or to Clement (p. 2958;) but that Origen, believing neither of these ancient traditions, declared that " God only knows who *composed* it." One cannot help remarking, how leaning towards a favourite hypothesis will help to obscure one part of testimony, and make another to stand out in relief. That οἱ ἀρχαῖοι ἄνδρες have not, as Origen asserts, *without reason declared the epistle to be Paul's*, this critic has passed over with profound silence. On the other hand, " it is an ancient tradition," he says, " propagated down to the time of Origen, that either Clement or Luke *composed* it." But Origen himself does not say this. His words are simply, " Who wrote it [i. e. penned it down,] God knows, ἡ δὲ εἰς ἡμᾶς φθάσασα ἱστορία, *but a report has come to us*, that it was either Clement or Luke." Now, where is the *ancient* tradition, brought even down to Origen's time, ascribing the *composition* of the epistle to two different men, neither of whom Origen believed to be the author? So far from this, Origen says not a word here of *ancient* tradition; nor even of tradition at all. He does not say that either ἱστορία παλαιὰ, or παράδοσις παλαιὰ, brings down this report; but simply ἡ εἰς ἡμᾶς φθάσασα ἱστορία,

i. e. *report has come to us* ; or, *it is reported; there is a report ; report says*—that either Luke or Clement wrote it. Now, he might have used the same expression, I freely concede, if such report had been ancient; but he might use the same, too, in reference merely to the reports of his day; at which time, no doubt, various difficulties were raised, in some of the churches, respecting the Pauline origin of the epistle. Certainly, then, Bertholdt has no right to represent Origen in the manner he does, as averring that *ancient* tradition assigned the *authorship* of the epistle to Luke or to Clement.

Indeed, the language which Origen employs, in this case, would seem to be *designedly* different from that which he employs in the sentence wholly omitted by Bertholdt, which runs thus ; " If any church holds this epistle to be Paul's, it deserves commendation for this ; because οὐκ εἰκῆ *the ancients have handed it down* to us, that it is Paul's. Observe the expressions οἱ ἀρχαῖοι and παραδεδώκασι, words altogether appropriate to the designation of truly ancient tradition, and not to be mistaken ; while the report concerning Luke and Clement is announced simply by ἡ εἰς ἡμᾶς φθάσασα ἱστορία, leaving it wholly indeterminate whether this report is recent or ancient ; for φθάσασα surely does not of course designate the *antiquity* of the report. Why Bertholdt should thus magnify this part of Origen's assertion, and wholly omit all notice of the other, which cannot be misunderstood, and is not liable to misconstruction, is best known to himself. But thus much may he properly said, If the testimony of the ancients (or moderns) is to be managed in this way, then we may assert, with equal truth, our inability to prove any thing, or our ability to prove *aliquid ex aliquo*.

That Origen was not in the doubtful state about the epistle, which the critics just named represent him to be, may be clearly evinced from other passages in his writings, even if the one already examined were to be regarded as dubious. For example ; Comm. on John, (ii. p. 18, ed. Huet.,) " According to this, the *apostle* says,"* and then quotes Heb. v. 12. That by this apostle he meant Paul, other passages in the same commentary clearly show. E. g. " In the epistle to the Hebrews, the same Paul says,"† p. 56 ; again, " Paul in the epistle to the Hebrews,"‡ p. 162. In his book against Celsus, he says ; " For it is written by

---

* Κατὰ τοῦτὸ φησιν ὁ ἀπόστολος, ὅτι, κ. τ. λ. loc. cit.
† Καὶ ἐν τῇ πρὸς Ἑβραίους, ὁ αὐτὸς Παῦλὸς φησι, κ. τ. λ. loc. cit.
‡ Ὁ δὲ Παῦλος, ἐν τῇ πρὸς Ἑβραίους, κ. τ. λ. loc. cit.

Paul, in his letter to the Corinthians.... and the *same apostle* says ;"*
and then he quotes Heb. v. 12, Contra Cels. p. 482, ed. Bened. In
his treatise on prayer, he quotes the epistle to the Hebrews, as an epistle
of the same apostle who wrote the epistle to the Ephesians, De Oratione
i. p. 250, ed. Bened. In a homily, preserved in a Latin translation, he
says, " Paul himself, the greatest of the apostles, writing to the Hebrews, says ;"† then he quotes Heb. xii. 18, 22, 23. He also appeals
to this epistle as *authoritative*, in establishing any position ; c. g. Comm.
in John ii. 57, 58, ed. Huet.

These testimonies can leave no doubt what the opinion of Origen was,
as to the real *authorship* of the epistle, however he might account for
what he deemed the peculiar colouring of the style. It is surely quite
a subordinate question, Who was the amanuensis or translator of Paul?
The important questions are, Did the *sentiments* originate from him?
And is he the real author of them? If Origen has not developed his
opinion respecting these questions beyond all doubt, I know not that
it is in the power of language to do this. If he has not most explicitly
averred, that the *then ancient* tradition taught this, and for good reasons,
I am unable to conceive how he could have averred it.

(6.) Let us ask, how far back must this testimony have gone, in order
to be *ancient* in Origen's time? Nothing can be weaker, than the
assertion that Origen refers, in his ἀρχαῖοι ἄνδρες, to Clement and Pantænus; both of whom were his contemporaries, and lived until he was
about thirty years of age. Pantænus died about 211, as Jerome affirms;
Clement, about A. D. 217 or 220 ; and Origen was born A. D. 184 or
185. Now, as Origen lived but little more than a century from the apostolic
age, nothing can be plainer, than that the οἱ ἀρχαῖοι ἄνδρες must mean,
either those who were conversant with the apostles, or at least the generation succeeding them. This not only confirms what I have already
endeavoured to prove, from Clement of Rome, from the testimony of
the Italic and Syriac versions, and from Pantænus and Clement, viz.
that the epistle to the Hebrews was *canonical* in the *primitive* age of the
church ; but it shows, beyond reasonable doubt, that Pantænus and
Clement believed Paul to be the author of the epistle to the Hebrews,

---

* Γέγραπται γὰρ παρὰ τῷ Παύλῳ ἡμῶν Κορινθίοις ἐπιστέλλοντι . . . . ὁ δὲ αὐτὸς
. . . . φησί, καὶ γεγόνατε χρείαν ἔχοντες, κ. τ. λ. loc. cit.

† Ipse ergo apostolorum maximus . . . . Paulus . . . . dicit, ad Hebræos scribens,
etc. Homil. III. in Num. p. 281, edit. Benedict.

in common with the churches of their times, on the ground of ecclesiastical tradition, and not from their own conceit, or their own prejudices in favour of Alexandrine notions.

(7.) It appears that Origen was strongly impressed with the conviction, that the style of the epistle to the Hebrews was different from the usual one of Paul. Yet so firm was his conviction, that the epistle for substance did originate from Paul, that he has not only often ascribed it directly to him, *obiter*, but given us at large his view, viz. that he considered Paul as the author of the *thoughts* or *ideas*. At the same time, he endeavours to account for it, without prejudice to this opinion, or to church tradition, that the costume of the epistle is not Pauline, by supposing a disciple of Paul to have recorded the conceptions of his master in his own language. That Origen should have adhered to what he declares to be the tradition of the *ancients*, respecting the author of this epistle, under such circumstances, and beset with such doubts, exhibits, in a most striking manner, the strength of his convictions, and the weight of tradition in its favour.

The allegation made by Eichhorn and Bertholdt, that Origen conceded the epistle to the Hebrews to be Paul's, from forbearance to the prejudices of the church at Alexandria, and out of love to the allegory which is in it, the credit of which he would wish to defend, has no real support. In regard to his prejudices in favour of the church at Alexandria, we cannot suppose them to have been very strong; for he was banished from this place, in the midst of his public labours, when he was about 48 years of age; and he spent the last 22 years of his life principally at Cesarea and in its neighbourhood, never returning again to Alexandria. Yet in works, published long after he resided at Cesarea, he ascribes to Paul the epistle to the Hebrews. And in regard to the *allegory* of this epistle, if this were the principal reason for receiving it into the canon, then why did he not also receive the epistle of Barnabas, the Shepherd of Hermas, and many other pieces of a similar nature, in which the ancient church abounded? We may well be permitted to ask, indeed, why should we ascribe any other motive to Origen for receiving this epistle, than what he declares to have been a sufficient and commendable one in the churches, viz. that *the ancients*, NOT WITHOUT REASON, *had handed it down as Paul's*?

The opinion of the church at Alexandria appears to have been uniformly the same, after the age of this great man. I shall very briefly notice it here; as testimony later than Origen's, from this quarter, can amount but to little more than proof, that the opinions of himself and his predecessors continued to be held without variation.

Dionysius, bishop of Alexandria, received the epistle to the Hebrews as canonical, and as the work of Paul, about A.D. 247; as did Theognostus, probably a teacher in the famous Christian school at Alexandria, about 282. It was received as Paul's by Alexander, bishop in the same city, about 313; by the celebrated Athanasius, bishop of the same place, about 326; by Didymus, master of the catechetical school there, about 370; and by Cyril, bishop of Alexandria, about 412.

It is unnecessary to proceed any farther on, than down to the time of Jerome and Augustine; whose opinion in favour of this epistle being Paul's, is universally acknowledged; and whose influence over the western churches occasioned the gradual, and finally the universal, reception of it, by all those churches in that quarter where it had been rejected.

§ 15. *Testimony of the Eastern Churches.*

From Egypt let us now repair to the Eastern region, and see what the tradition of the churches was in that quarter.

We have already seen that Justin Martyr, a native of Samaria, quotes from our epistle about 140. After Justin, there were no considerable writers, in this part of the church, whose works are still extant, until the time of Eusebius. Methodius, however, bishop first of Olympus in Lycia, and afterwards of Tyre, seems pretty plainly to ascribe this epistle to Paul, about 292, Lard. vii. 261. It was probably received as such by Pamphylius, presbyter at Cesarea, about 294; as it stands in the midst of Paul's epistles, in a manuscript copied from one of Pamphilus, id. vii. 325.

But the most important testimony from this quarter, (next after that of Origen, who lived at a period so much earlier, and spent here the most important part of his life, viz. the last twenty-two years of it,) remains to be recited. I refer to the testimony of Eusebius of Cesarea, the well-known historian of the church, who has taken so much pains to collect evidence from all quarters, respecting the canon of Scripture. I shall produce his testimony in a collected view, in order to facilitate the comparison of it; and then subjoin a few remarks.

Lib. III. c. iii. " Fourteen epistles are *clearly* and *certainly* Paul's; although it is proper to be known, that some have rejected that which is written to the Hebrews, alleging, with the church at Rome, that it is spoken against, as not belonging to Paul."* A little after this, in the same book, c. xxv., he reckons among the books of Scripture, which he calls ὁμολογούμενοι, (i. e. *not contradicted*, or *gainsayed*, viz. by such authority as to create any doubts, or to any considerable extent, in the church,) the *epistles* of Paul ; in which, beyond all question, he includes the epistle to the Hebrews ; for he afterwards particularizes the epistle of James, of Jude, the 2d Peter, and 2d and 3d John, as those books which are ἀντιλεγόμενοι, i. e. *called in question, contradicted*.† In the same book, c. xxxviii., after saying that Clement of Rome had made many extracts from the epistle to the Hebrews, he adds, " Wherefore, not without reason, this epistle is reckoned among the writings of Paul. For when Paul had written to the Hebrews, in their vernacular language, some say that Luke made a translation of it, and some, that this Clement did, of whom we have been speaking.‡ In Lib. VI. c. xx., he mentions, that " Caius, in a dispute against Proclus, held at Rome in the time of Zephyrinus, blames the temerity and audacity of his opponents in composing new writings, and mentions only thirteen epistles of Paul, not numbering that which is inscribed to the Hebrews. Moreover, even to the present time, this epistle is reckoned, by some of the Romans, as not belonging to Paul."§

In Eusebius, we meet with the first ecclesiastical writer, who has

* Τοῦ δὲ Παύλου πρόδηλοι καὶ σαφεῖς αἱ δεκατέσσαρες· ὅτι γε μὴν τινες ἠθετήκασι τὴν πρὸς Ἑβραίους, πρὸς τῆς Ῥωμαίων ἐκκλησίας, ὡς μὴ Παύλου οὖσαν αὐτὴν ἀντιλέγεσθαι φήσαντες, οὐ δίκαιον ἀγνοεῖν. Hist. Ecc. iii. 3.

† Μετὰ δὲ ταύτην [sc. τὴν τῶν Πράξεων γραφὴν] τὰς Παύλου καταλεκτέον ἐπιστολάς· αἷς ἑξῆς, κ. τ. λ. .... ταῦτα μὲν ἐν ὁμολογουμένοις. Τῶν δὲ ἀντιλεγομένων ...... ἡ λεγομένη Ἰακώβου ...... καὶ Ἰούδα, ἥτε Πέτρου δευτέρα ἐπιστολὴ, καὶ ἡ ὀνομαζομένη δευτέρα καὶ τρίτη Ἰωάννου. Hist. Ecc. iii. 25.

‡ Ἐν ᾗ [sc. ἐπιστολῇ Κλήμεντος] τῆς πρὸς Ἑβραίους πολλὰ νοήματα παραθεὶς, ἤδε δὲ καὶ αὐτολεξεὶ ῥητοῖς τισιν ἐξ αὐτῆς χρησάμενος, σαφέστατα περίεσιν ὅτι μὴ νεὸν ὑπάρχει τὸ σύγγραμμα. Ὅθεν εἰκότως ἔδοξεν αὐτὸ τοῖς λοιποῖς ἐγκαταλεχθῆναι γράμμασι τοῦ ἀποστόλου. Ἑβραίοις γὰρ διὰ τῆς πατρίου γλώττης ἐγγράφως ὡμιληκότος τοῦ Παύλου, οἱ μὲν τὸν εὐαγγελιστὴν Λουκᾶν, οἱ δὲ τὸν Κλήμεντα τοῦτον αὐτὸν ἑρμηνεῦσαι τὴν γραφήν. Lib. iii. 38.

§ Ἦλθε δὲ εἰς ἡμᾶς καὶ Γαΐου λογιωτάτου ἀνδρὸς διάλογος, ἐπὶ Ῥώμης κατα Ζεφυρῖνον, πρὸς Πρόκλον τῆς κατὰ Φρύγας αἱρήσεως ὑπερμακοῦντα κεκινημένος· ἐν ᾧ τῶν δὶ ἐναντίας τὴν περὶ τὸ συντάττειν καινὰς γραφὰς προπέτειάν τε καὶ τόλμαν ἐπιστομίζων, τῶν τοῦ ἱεροῦ ἀποστόλου δεκατριῶν μόνων ἐπιστολῶν μνημονεύει, τὴν πρὸς Ἑβραίους μὴ συναριθμήσας ταῖς λοιπαῖς. Ἐπεὶ καὶ εἰς δεῦρο παρὰ Ῥωμαίων τισὶν, οὐ νομίζεται τοῦ ἀποστόλου τυγχάνειν. Lib. vi. 20.

H

designedly made out a full and regular catalogue of the canon of the New Testament; and who made extensive investigation, in regard to the opinions of the church respecting this subject. From a view of his testimony, collected and compared together, it is clear—

(1.) That there were, in the East, some who doubted whether Paul wrote the epistle to the Hebrews; and that they appealed, in support of this opinion, to the church at Rome. It is clear, too, that in the time of Zephyrinus, (about 212,) there were persons in the Western church, and probably at Rome, who denied that this epistle was written by Paul; for Caius reckons only thirteen epistles of Paul, probably omitting that to the Hebrews. And that this denial continued down to the time of Eusebius, in the church at Rome, (his words are, παρὰ 'Ρωμαίων τισιν, *by some of the Romans,)* is clearly signified by this historian.

(2.) His assertion of the Pauline origin of the epistle to the Hebrews, is as unequivocal and strong as language can well make it. " Fourteen epistles of Paul," (of course, the epistle to the Hebrews included, there being but thirteen without it,) "*are* CLEARLY *and* CERTAINLY Paul's, πρόδηλοι καὶ σαφεῖς. And again, he reckons this epistle among the books which are ὁμολογούμενοι, i. e. *generally recognized, admitted.* These declarations Eusebius makes, with a full view of the objections urged against this epistle by some. It is clear, then, that he did not consider those objections as respectable enough, or sufficiently extensive, or well grounded, to raise any serious doubts in his own mind about this matter, or to weigh at all against the current and general opinion of the church on this subject. Consequently, nothing can be more directly to the purpose, for demonstrating the strength and generality of the opinion in the church, at the time of Eusebius, that Paul wrote the epistle to the Hebrews, than this testimony. For as Eusebius has been careful, even when asserting that the epistle is clearly and certainly Paul's, to note that there are some who dissent from this opinion, and also to collect, in various instances, accounts of disagreement in respect to it, it may be regarded as quite certain, that he viewed opposition to it as neither well founded, nor extensive enough to raise any serious doubts about the correctness of the common opinion of the churches.

(3.) It is pretty evident, that Eusebius had heard of the objections drawn from the style of the epistle, which Clement of Alexandria and Origen had before endeavoured to answer. Eusebius thinks that Paul wrote it in Hebrew, and says that some attributed the translation of it to

Luke, and some to Clement. His own opinion is, that the translation is to be ascribed to the latter.

It will be recollected, now, that Origen, residing at the same place, (Cesarea,) had, nearly a century before, mentioned the very same report or tradition. The passage in Eusebius shows, therefore, the uniformity of the tradition; it serves also to show, that when Origen adverts to it, he means to say, (as I have above supposed him to say,) that God only knows who *penned* or *wrote down* the epistle; not, *who was the author of the sentiments*, for these he directly attributes to Paul; just as Eusebius attributes the *authorship* to Paul, and the *diction* to Clement.

(4.) One thing more is evident, from the testimony of Eusebius. While he records, with fidelity, the fact that there were some in that quarter of the church who doubted the Pauline origin of this epistle, he tells us, at the same time, that *those who did deny it, alleged the example of the church at Rome, in order to justify themselves in so doing.* The necessary implication of course is, that they could not support themselves by any creditable example in the Oriental churches. Would they have made an appeal for support, to a church abroad at so great a distance, if they could have found it at home, and in their own quarter? Most surely not; for at that period, the church of Rome was inferior in credit to a number of other churches in the East. The very nature of this appeal shows, that respectable support for the denial of the Pauline origin of our epistle, could not be found in the East.

Eichhorn has, indeed, cited the above testimony of Eusebius; but he has passed it without comment, excepting the single remark, that " the reason of Eusebius, for supposing Paul to have written the epistle to the Hebrews, was, that it was very old, and was cited so far back as the time of Clement of Rome;" a reason which, if it were well founded, would of course make Paul the author of all very old ecclesiastical writings, which had been often cited, and were anonymous.

Bertholdt has exhibited more sensibility to the testimony of Eusebius. He confesses that Eusebius founds his judgment, respecting the books of the New Testament, on the tradition of the Oriental church. The repeated asseverations of Eusebius as to this point, did not permit him to conclude otherwise; although Eichhorn has left out of sight every circumstance of this nature. But then, says Bertholdt, " did this tradition go back to the apostolic age? Undoubtedly not," he answers; " it went back only to Pantænus and Clement of Alexandria, who grounded it only upon supposition, or on their own personal views and feelings."

And then he goes on to assert, that " the epistle to the Hebrews was first favourably received at Alexandria, because it was so congenial to the allegorizing spirit of that place; thence the credit of it diffused itself to Antioch in Syria; and what Antioch and Alexandria believed concerning it, would, in process of time, be believed by all the other churches in Egypt, and in the East. Thus it came about, that in Eusebius' time there was such a general consent among the churches of his neighbourhood, in the belief that Paul was the author of the epistle to the Hebrews."

It is not *necessary* to answer this, except by saying, that from beginning to end, it is a series of *suppositions*, wholly unsupported by a single historical *fact*, and wholly incapable of being supported by any *known facts*. The examination through which we have already passed, has, I trust, afforded sufficient evidence, that the suppositions in question are *contrary to facts*, and destitute therefore of any actual support, as well of any tolerable degree of probability. What connexion had Antioch with Alexandria? And how should a single Egyptian church and school, planted and instituted late in the apostolic age, if not after it, influence all the churches of the East, planted by Paul and the other apostles, and nurtured by their personal hearers and disciples, so as to make them receive a supposititious book into their canon? And why should not a multitude of other allegorical books, (like the Shepherd of Hermas,) written in or near the apostolic age, have been advanced to a place in the canon by the Alexandrine church, and thence have diffused their credit among all the Eastern churches? But it is unnecessary to proceed with such questions. If principles of argument, and methods of weighing testimony respecting ancient writings, may be adopted, like those which Eichhorn and Bertholdt have adopted here, in order to maintain the theory which they had espoused, any ancient writing whatever may be proved to be either spurious or genuine, as shall best suit the notion of any individual. He has only to make out a series of bold and confident *suppositions*, and his work is done.

I deem it unnecessary to detail the testimony of writers in the Oriental churches, subsequent to the time of Eusebius. I shall merely advert to them, because it is not denied by any respectable critics, that, subsequent to this period, the epistle to the Hebrews was generally regarded in the East as Paul's.

Archelaus, bishop of Mesopotamia, received the epistle to the Hebrews as Paul's, about A. D. 300; as did the author of the Synopsis of Scripture ascribed to Athanasius, and written about 320; Adamantius, about 330; Cyril of Jerusalem, about 348; the council of Laodicea, about 363; Epiphanius, about 368; Basil, about 370; Gregory Nazianzen, about 370; Gregory Nyssen, about 371; Ephrem Syrus, about 370; Diodore of Tarsus, about 378; and Chrysostom, about 398. Others might be named, which are mentioned in Lardner's collection of testimonies, but it is superfluous. The object on account of which these have been adduced, is merely to show the unity and universality of the opinion, in the Oriental churches, that Paul wrote the epistle to the Hebrews subsequently to the time of Eusebius, on whose testimony I have already dwelt.

In fact, not a single writer of any respectability in the catholic church, in all the East, has been produced, who rejected this epistle; an extraordinary circumstance, indeed, if the belief of its apostolic origin was not altogether a predominant one in Egypt, and throughout all the eastern world. That there were individuals in this part of church, who doubted or denied the authenticity of it, will certainly be admitted by every unprejudiced inquirer. But that there was any thing like a respectable or widely diffused party, who denied it, can be supported by no competent evidence whatever.

§ 16. *Testimony of the Western Churches.*

In the Western churches, the case was certainly different. We come now to take a view of their opinion.

We have already seen, that Clement of Rome, at the close of the apostolic age, has frequently quoted this epistle, and in the same way, and for the same purposes, that he does other parts of the Scripture; and, consequently, we cannot entertain reasonable doubts, that he regarded it as a part of the sacred records. Eusebius long ago drew the same conclusion. " Clement," says he, " in his epistle acknowledged by all, which he wrote to the Corinthians in behalf of the church at Rome, exhibits many sentiments that are contained in the epistle to the Hebrews, making use of the very words of the epistle in several sentences, by which he shows most clearly, that this writing is not recent; whence it seems probable, that it is to be reckoned among the other writings of the apostle," Ecc. Hist. iii. 38. (See the original Greek, on p. 74, above.) That ·it had such credit, in this quarter of the church, for some time after this, is sufficiently manifest from the fact, that the old

Latin version comprises it; which was probably made before A. D. 150, or (as almost all acknowledge) before A. D. 200.

The first *negative* evidence to be found among the Western churches, respecting the question before us, is that of Irenæus, bishop of Lyons in France, during the latter part of the second century. Neither the country from which he sprung, nor the time of his birth or death, are known with any certainty. Eichhorn has placed him at A. D. 150, evidently in order to throw his testimony as far back toward the apostolic age as possible. Lardner places him at A. D. 178, a much more probable era. He was a disciple of Polycarp, when very young; for he states himself, that when a child, he was a hearer of Polycarp, in Hither Asia, v. 20.

Photius (fl. A. D. 858) tells us in his Bibliotheca, that Stephen Gobar, a writer of the middle ages, says, that Irenæus and Hippolytus declare " the epistle to the Hebrews not to be Paul's," Cod. 152. Eich. p. 519. Whence Gobar drew his conclusion, Photius does not inform us; nor does it any where appear. In all the writings of Irenæus, now extant, no such assertion is contained; but then several of his writings are lost. That Irenæus was acquainted with the epistle to the Hebrews, and that he has cited it, is directly testified by Eusebius, who says, that " he wrote a book of various disputations, in which he mentions the epistle to the Hebrews, and the book called the Wisdom of Solomon, quoting some expressions from them," * v. 26. But Eusebius does not say whether he quotes them as Scripture, or not; and as the book of Irenæus, to which he adverts, has perished, we have now no certain means of judging. Storr, Cramer, and some other critics, have called in question this assertion of Gobar, and have supposed that it is only a conclusion which he drew from the fact, that Irenæus had not quoted the epistle to the Hebrews in his works. But this reasoning must, of course, be merely hypothetical. We have the bare assertion of Gobar, without the grounds; and as Irenæus has made no use of the epistle to the Hebrews, in his works still extant, the probability seems to be, that Gobar has given a correct statement. The passages produced by Lardner, as possible quotations, have indeed a close affinity with some passages in the epistle to the Hebrews; but still they may have been taken from the Old Testament, instead of this epistle. (Lard. i. 368—370.) Neither can the

* Καὶ βιβλίον τι [sc. ἔγραψε Εἰρηναῖος] διαλέξεων διαφόρων, ἐν ᾧ τῆς πρὸς Ἑβραίους ἐπιστολῆς, καὶ τῆς λεγομένης Σοφίας Σολομῶντος, μνημονεύει ῥητά τινα ἐξ αὐτῶν παραθίμενος, κ. τ. λ. Hist. Ecc. v. 26.

fact, that Irenæus has quoted the epistle to the Hebrews, (which is sufficiently vouched for by Eusebius,) determine the question in respect to the nature of his testimony; for surely he may have quoted books, which he did not regard as Scriptural. On the whole, in the present state of evidence, it would seem, that we ought to admit it as probable, that Irenæus did not include the epistle to the Hebrews in his canon; but on what ground, is uncertain. It may, indeed, have been the case, that this epistle, originally addressed to Hebrews in Palestine, had not yet obtained circulation and credit among that part of the church in Asia Minor, where Irenæus lived when he was a youth. It is not improbable, too, that he went in early life, with Polycarp his teacher, to Rome; and that he remained there until he was sent to Lyons in France, where he became the successor of Photinus, in the bishopric of that city. In this way it may be accounted for, that Irenæus came to cherish doubts respecting the epistle to the Hebrews; which, we shall see, began to be somewhat extensively cherished in the Roman churches during the latter half of the second century.

At the same time, one cannot but remark, that it appears quite singular, when Eusebius expressly mentions Irenæus as having quoted the epistle to the Hebrews, that he should not, on this occasion or some other, have at all adverted to the fact of his having denied the Pauline origin of this epistle, if such were the fact. This is the more singular, because Eusebius has devoted a chapter of considerable length, in his work, entirely to giving an account of the manner which Irenæus had mentioned the sacred books; and in this chapter there is not a word of Irenæus quoted, respecting the epistle to the Hebrews. Ecc. Hist. v. 8.

Moreover, Eusebius has evidently been careful and particular, on all occasions where the epistle to the Hebrews was treated of, to mention objections to it; or where persons of consideration in the church were named who rejected it, to state this fact. Eusebius also must have had the writings of Irenæus, in a more perfect state and much more complete, than Gobar who lived so long afterwards. And as Irenæus was a writer for whom Eusebius evidently cherished a high respect, it is really very difficult to account for it, that he should not have once adverted to the opinion which Gobar affirms was held by Irenæus.

Difficult, however, as this would seem to be, the supposition that Irenæus did *not* acknowledge our epistle, is somewhat strengthened by the united asseveration of Gobar and Photius himself, (Eichhorn, p. 519,) that Hippolytus, (whom Photius calls a disciple of Irenæus, and who probably flourished about A. D. 220,) asserts of the epistle to the Hebrews, that it is not Paul's, Eichhorn, p. 520. This Hippolytus is called, by Eusebius, a bishop of some place; but neither he, nor Jerome, knew its name. The probable opinion is, that it was Portus Romanus. Lard. iii. 89, seq. The assertion in question was made, as Photius states, in a book of Hippolytus against heresies, which he compiled from a work of Irenæus. But as the work is lost, all that remains is the statement of Gobar and Photius; which seems, however, to be entitled to credit.

In accordance with this denial of the Pauline origin of our epistle, is the testimony of Eusebius in respect to Caius. Caius is called, by Photius, a presbyter of the church of Rome; which is quite probable, although Eusebius and Jerome simply state that he was a presbyter, without naming the place of his residence. He flourished, it is most probable, about A. D. 210. The statement of Eusebius is as follows.

"There hath come to us a dialogue of Caius, a most eloquent man, held at Rome under Zephyrinus, with Proclus, a patron of the Montanist heresy; in which, reproving the rashness and audacity of his opponents in forging new writings, he makes mention of only thirteen epistles of the holy apostle, not numbering that to the Hebrews with the others; and even to the present time, some of the Romans do not reckon it to be Paul's." Lard. iii. 24. Eus. vi. 20. See the original, on p. 97, above.

The new writings or scriptures here mentioned, were the prophecies which the enthusiastic Montanists feigned to have delivered by inspiration; Montanus having declared himself to be the Paraclete. See Eus. v. 14. 18. Jerome states, that Caius denied the epistle to the Hebrews to be Paul's; De Vir. Illus. voc. Caius. But Eusebius and Photius simply say, that he omitted it in his account of the canonical books; which, however, virtually implies, under such circumstances, what Jerome declares.

In what circumstances this dialogue was composed; whether it was first actually held, for substance, with Proclus, and afterwards written down; or whether it was only written (like the dialogues of Plato, Cicero, and others,) in order to represent the sentiments of Proclus, and confute them; whether it was held publicly, with the approbation of Zephyrinus and his presbyters, or not, we are not informed, and have no certain means of discovering. But I think it must be regarded as probable, that Caius would not venture upon the publication of such a dialogue at Rome, without the concurrence or approbation of the church there.

Other evidence also is adduced, that doubts whether the epistle to the Hebrews was Paul's had already begun at Rome, and in the West, toward the close of the second century. Muratorius (Antiq. Ital. Medii. Ævi. tom. iii. p. 854,) has published a fragment of an anonymous author, who probably lived near the close of the second century, that contains a catalogue of books which he deemed canonical, and which lacks the epistle to the Hebrews, those of James, Peter, and 3d John; while it contains some apocryphal books. Speaking of Paul's epistles, this anonymous writer says, " Fertur [epistola] etiam ad Laodicenses. Alia *apud Alexandrinos* Paulli nomine ficta ad hæresia Marcionis, et alia plura; quæ in catholicam ecclesiam recipi non potest, fel enim cum melle misceri non congruit." That is, " An epistle is in circulation, addressed to the Laodiceans. Another is current with the Alexandrians, forged in the name of Paul, for the sake of promoting the heresy of Marcion, and many other things, which the catholic church cannot receive, for it is not proper to mingle gall with honey."

Critics have supposed, that by the *alia apud Alexandrinos*, this writer means the *epistle to the Hebrews*, which was received by the Greeks or Alexandrians. But surely it must be very doubtful, whether our epistle to the Hebrews is meant, as this anonymous writer admits several books not canonical into his catalogue, and excludes several others which are so. Besides, he mentions another fictitious epistle, viz. that to the Laodiceans. Why may not this *epistle among the Alexandrians, forged in the name of Paul, in favour of the Marcion heresy*, be wholly different from our epistle to the Hebrews; which has not, and never had, the name of Paul affixed to it? And then how could this writer say, *forged in favour of the Marcionite heresy?* a heresy which denied the divine origin of the Jewish religion, and rejected the God of the Old Testament; two fundamental articles on which our epistle to the Hebrews is built. Nothing could be more directly opposed to Marcion, than this epistle. The probability, therefore, is, that our epistle to the Hebrews is *not* designated by the anonymous writer in question. But if it really be the fact, that he did mean to designate it, his consummate ignorance of the nature of its contents forbids us to attach any weight of importance to his testimony.

But more definite and satisfactory evidence, that, about the close of the second century, there were doubts among the western churches whether our epistle was of apostolic origin, may be adduced from the works of Tertullian. This father, who flourished about A. D. 200, says in his book *De Pudicitia* (c. 20,) "There is *an epistle of Barnabas inscribed to the Hebrews;* therefore by a man of such authority, that Paul placed him next to himself in respect to abstinence; "Am I and Barnabas only without power to do this?" And, certainly, this epistle of Barnabas is more received among the churches, than the apocryphal *Pastor* of adulterers," [he means the Shepherd of Hermas.] " Warning therefore the disciples, that leaving the first principles," &c. [quoting Heb. vi. 1, &c.*

That Tertullian also alludes to the epistle to the Hebrews in other passages, seems to me quite probable, from the instances of this nature produced by Lardner, ii. 608—612. But it no where appears, what credit he attached to this epistle. It is plain from the passage quoted, that he ascribed it to Barnabas; and not improbable, that the churches in his neighbourhood, and perhaps at Rome, did the same, at this period. It is also plain, that he does not ascribe *full* canonical credit to it, because he does not consider it as the work of an apostle; otherwise he would have vehemently urged its authority upon his opponents, as the passage which he quotes seems extremely apposite to his purpose, which was, to prove that lapsed Christians could not again be received into the bosom of the church. That there was a division of opinion among the churches of his day, in the region where he lived, at least, seems to be plainly indicated, by his saying that this epistle was more correct, and of more authority in the churches, than the *Shepherd of Hermas;* which latter, however, we know to have been early admitted as part of the sacred records, by a number of churches in the West.

On the whole, it is plain that Tertullian did not admit our epistle to be Paul's; and that there were churches in that region, who doubted or denied that it was his.

Cyprian, bishop of Carthage, comes next as a witness for the negative of our question. He flourished about A. D. 248, i. e. the next generation after Tertullian, who died about A. D. 220. From Cyprian, however, no direct testimony can be adduced. It is agreed, that he no

* Volo, tamen, ex redundantia alicujus etiam comitis apostolorum testimonium superinducere, idoneum confirmandi de proximo jure disciplinam magistrorum. Exstat enim et Barnabæ titulus ad Hebræos, adeo satis auctoritatis viro, ut quem Paulus juxta se constituerit in abstinentiæ tenore; "Aut ego solus et Barnabas non habemus hoc operandi potestatem?" Et utique receptior apud ecclesias epistola Barnabæ, illo apocrypho pastore mœchorum. Monens itaque discipulos, " Omissis omnibus initiis," &c. *De Pudicitia*, c. 20.

where quotes the epistle to the Hebrews in his works; which we cannot well account for, if he admitted its authority. There is but one passage hitherto produced from him, which seems to have a bearing on our question. It is as follows; " The apostle Paul, who was mindful of this authorized and well-known number, [he is speaking of the number *seven*,] writes to seven churches."* This would of course exclude the epistle to the Hebrews, as there are seven churches addressed besides this. But still, I cannot consider this testimony so decisive as Lardner and Eichhorn do, in respect to Cyprian's canon. For, as the epistle to the Hebrews has no address, Cyprian may have had reference only to such of Paul's epistles as have an address to churches prefixed, which are seven in number. I do not, therefore, regard this passage as amounting to much. The fact that Cyprian has nowhere quoted the epistle to the Hebrews, considering how many writings he has left behind him, and how many occasions he had to quote the sentiments contained in it, renders it probable, either that he was unacquainted with the epistle, or that he did not admit its canonical authority.

Novatus, a presbyter of Rome, (A. D. 251,) the founder of the Novatian sect, is supposed by some critics not to have received the epistle to the Hebrews. This inference is drawn from the fact, that he does not appeal to it, in behalf of the sentiments which he maintained, respecting the exclusion of the lapsed heretics from re-admission to the church. There are passages in his writings, however, in which he seems to refer to the epistle to the Hebrews, e. g. " It is asserted of Christ, by prophets and apostles, that he sitteth at the right-hand of the Father ;"† comp. Heb. i. 3. Again, " Christ is found to be greater and better, not than one angel only, but than all the angels."‡ The last of these passages, in particular, looks very much like a quotation from Heb. i. 4. Be the case as it may, respecting Novatus himself, his followers, about thirty years afterwards, admitted the epistle in question; as is clear from the testimony of Philaster (about A. D. 380) on this subject, who states, that they received the usual canon of the Old and New Testament. Philast. Hæres. 82.

* Et apostolus Paulus, qui hujus numeri legitimi et certi meminit, ad septem ecclesias scribit. De Exhort. Mart. cap. xi.

† Aut eum sedere ad dextram Patris, et a prophetis et ab apostolis approbatur. De Reg. Fid. c. xxvi.

‡ Qui non uno, sed omnibus angelis et major et melior invenitur. De Reg Fid. c. xx.

This is all the negative testimony that I have been able to find, in the churches of the west, previously to A. D. 400; excepting what is implied in the statements of some of the Latin writers, to whom I shall now advert.

We have already seen, in the passage cited from Tertullian, an intimation of a difference of opinion among the Western churches, in respect to the epistle to the Hebrews, as if some received and some rejected it. Lactantius, about 306, who does not often quote Scripture, at least with any good degree of accuracy, seems to me to have some indubitable references to the epistle to the Hebrews, which Lardner has drawn out at length (vii. 185—188;) but as they only seem to recognize the authority of the epistle, but do not ascribe it to Paul, I shall not adduce them here.

The epistle to the Hebrews was clearly received as Paul's by Hilary, bishop of Poictiers, about A. D. 354; by Lucifer, bishop of Cagliari, about 354; by Victorinus, a famous rhetorician at Rome, about 360; by Ambrose, bishop of Milan, about 374; by Philaster, bishop of Brescia, in Italy, about 380; who states, however, that there were some who did not admit it to be Paul's ; by Gaudentius, his successor, about 387 ; by the celebrated Jerome, about 392 ; by Ruffinus about 397 ; and by Augustine, about 400.

But the testimony of Augustine and Jerome whose influence appears to have been effectual in re-establishing the credit of the epistle to the Hebrews among the Western churches, deserves to be adduced here, as it serves to show, that the Latin churches had not been united in respect to the point in question.

Jerome, in his epistle to Dardanus, has the following passage. " This is to be maintained, that this epistle, which is inscribed to the Hebrews, is not only received by the churches of the East, as the apostle Paul's, but has been, in past times, by all ecclesiastical writers in the Greek language ; although most [Latins] think that Barnabas or Clement was the author. And it matters not whose it is, since it belongs to some ecclesiastical man, and is daily commended by the reading of it in the churches. But if the custom of the Latins does not receive it among the canonical writings,"* &c. Again ; " Among the Romans, it is not

---

* Illud nostris dicendum est, hanc epistolam, quæ inscribitur ad Hebræos, non solum ab ecclesiis Orientis, sed ab omnibus retro ecclesiasticis Græce sermonis scriptoribus quasi apostoli Pauli suscipi ; licet plerique eam vel Barnabæ, vel Clementis

received down to the present time as an epistle of Paul."* This general assertion means only that " such is, or has been, the predominant custom among the Romans ;" as is plain from a passage in his epistle to Evagrius, where he says, " which epistle to the Hebrews all the Greeks receive, and *some* of the Latins."† In his epistle to Paulinus, he says, " Paul the apostle writes to seven churches ; for his eighth epistle to the Hebrews is placed by *most* out of the number of his."‡ And again, in his Comm. on Matt. xxvi. he says, " Paul in his epistle to the Hebrews, although *many* of the Latins doubt concerning it, says,"|| &c.

On a comparison of all these different passages together, the following appears to be the result of Jerome's testimony.

(1.) The majority of the Roman churches in his time did not receive the epistle as Paul's ; " it is placed by most out of the number of Paul's epistles."

(2.) But some of the Latin churches did receive it still, in accordance with the custom of the Greek, i. e. Oriental churches ; *omnes Græci recipiunt, et nonnulli Latinorum.*

(3.) The *reception* or *rejection* of this epistle, as described by Jerome, refers (one passage only excepted) to receiving it as *Paul's*, or refusing to admit *Paul* as the author. Jerome does not say, that the Roman churches condemned it as spurious. Nay, that he does not mean to say this, is very plain from his own express words ; for after averring that " most persons [Romans] regard it as written either by Barnabas or by Clement," he goes on to say, *nihil interesse cujus sit, cum ecclesiastici viri sit, et quotidie ecclesiarum lectione celebretur.* That is, it matters not about the person of the author, since he was an ecclesiastical man, and the churches every day read his epistle. But how much this means exactly, it is difficult to say ; for the writer adds, *Quod si Latinorum*

---

arbitrenter. Et nihil interesse cujus sit, cum ecclesiastici viri sit, et quotidie ecclesiarum ectione celebretur. Quodsi autem Latinorum consuetudo non recipit inter scripturas canonicas, etc.—Epist. ad Dardanum.

* Apud Romanos, usque hodie, quasi Pauli epistola non habetur. Opp. tom. iii. p. 46.

† Quam epistolam ad Hebræos, omnes Græci recipiunt, et *nonnulli Latinorum.*—Epist. ad Evagrium.

‡ Paulus Apostolus ad septem ecclesias scribit ; octava enim ad Hebræos a *plerisque* extra numerum ponitur.—Epist. ad Paulinum.

|| Paulus, in epistola sua quæ scribitur ad Hebræos, licet de ea *multi Latinorum* dubitent, etc. loc. cit.

consuetudo non recipit inter canonicas scripturas, &c. By *canonical,* Jerome seems to understand *apostolical,* or having that authority which the writings of an apostle has. So much is plain, then, viz. that in the day of this writer, the churches made a distinction between writings *apostolic* and *not apostolic;* and if so, it must have been by giving to the former a rank higher, and more authoritative, than the latter. On the whole, we must understand Jerome as meaning to aver, that while *some* of the Latin churches admitted Paul to be the author of the epistle to the Hebrews, and regarded this epistle as canonical in the highest sense, most of these churches doubted whether Paul was the author, and consequently gave the epistle but a secondary place in their canon; or rather, they read it, with the other books of Scripture, for edification, but (probably) did not appeal to it as *authoritative.*

The testimony of Augustine corresponds well with this. " *Many* say, that [the epistle to the Hebrews] is Paul's; but some deny it.* And again; " In the epistle to the Hebrews, which the illustrious defenders of the catholic faith use as a witness, faith is called, &c."†

The council at Carthage, held A. D. 397, reckon this epistle among the divine and canonical writings, and attribute it to Paul.‡

I have now traced the history of this epistle down to the fourth century, in the Egyptian, the Eastern, and the Western churches. Lower down, it is altogether unnecessary to trace it; as all admit that it has had a general currency in the Christian churches every where, since that period.

§ 17. Result.

We now come to the result of this investigation. In the Egyptian and Eastern churches, there were, it is probable, at a pretty early period, some who had doubts whether Paul wrote the epistle to the Hebrews; but no *considerable* person or party is definitely known to us, who entertained these doubts; and it is manifest, from Origen and Eusebius, that there was not, in that quarter, any important opposition to the general and constant tradition of the church, that Paul did write

---

* *Plures* apostoli Pauli dicunt, [sc. epistolam ad Hebræos;] *quidam* vero negant. De Civitate Dei, xvi. 22.

† In epistola quippe ad Hebræos, qua teste usi sunt illustres catholicæ regulæ defensores, fides esse dicta est, etc. De Fide, Spe, et Caritate, c. viii.

‡ Sunt autem canonicæ Scripturæ . . . . . Pauli epistolæ tredecim, ejusdem ad Hebræos una. Can. 47.

§ 17. RESULT. 111

it. Not a single witness of any considerable respectability is named, who has given his voice, in this part of the church, for the negative of the question which we are considering. What Jerome avers, appears to be strictly true, viz. *ab ecclesiis Orientis et ab omnibus retro ecclesiasticis Græci sermonis scriptoribus, quasi apostoli Pauli suscipi.*

In the Western churches, a diversity of opinion prevailed; although the actual quantity of negative testimony, that can be adduced, is not great. Yet the concessions of Jerome and Augustine leave no room to doubt the fact, that the *predominant* opinion of the Western churches, in their times, was in the negative. In early times, we have seen that the case was different, when Clement of Rome wrote his epistle, and when the old Latin version was brought into circulation. What produced a change of opinion in the West, we are left to conjecture. The scanty critical and literary records of those times, afford us no means for tracing the history of it. But this is far from being a singular case. Many othes changes in the opinions of the churches have taken place, which we are, for a similar reason, as little able to trace with any certainty or satisfaction.

Storr has endeavoured to show, that Marcion occasioned this revolution, when he came from the East to Rome, and brought with him a collection of the sacred books, in which the epistle to the Hebrews was omitted. But it is very improbable, that an extravagant man, excommunicated by the Roman church itself, should have produced such a revolution there in sentiment. Others have, with more probability, attributed it to the zealous disputes at Rome against the Montanist party, whom the epistle to the Hebrews was supposed particularly to favour. The Montanists strenuously opposed the reception again into the bosom of the church, those persons who had so lapsed as to make defection from the Christian faith. The passages, in Heb. vi. 4—8, and x. 26—31, at least seem strongly to favour the views which they maintained. The church at Rome carried the dispute against the Montanists very high; and Ernesti, and many other critics, have been led to believe, that the epistle to the Hebrews was ultimately rejected by them, because the Montanists relied on it as their main support.

As a matter of fact, this cannot be established by direct historical evidence. But, in the absence of all testimony in respect to this subject, it must be allowed as not improbable, that the epistle to the Hebrews may have, in this way, become obnoxious to the Romish church. Many such instances might be produced, from the history of the church. The

Ebionites, the Manicheans, the Alogi, and many ancient and modern sects, have rejected some part of the canon of Scripture, because it stood opposed to their party views. The Apocalypse was rejected by many of the Oriental churches, on account of their opposition to the Chiliasts, who made so much use of it. And who does not know, that Luther himself rejected the epistle of James, because he viewed it as thwarting his favourite notions of *justification;* yea, that he went so far as to give it the appellation of *epistola straminea?* It cannot be at all strange, then, that the Romish church, exceedingly embittered by the dispute with the Montanists, should have gradually come to call in question the apostolic origin of our epistle; because it was, to their adversaries, a favourite source of appeal, and because (unlike Paul's other epistles) it was anonymous.

That *all,* even of the Montanists, however, admitted the apostolic origin of our epistle, does not seem to be true. Tertullian, who took a very active part in favour of this sect, had, as we have already seen, doubts of such an origin; or rather, he ascribed it to Barnabas.

But whatever might have been the cause that the epistle in question was pretty generally rejected by the churches of the West, the *fact,* that it was so, cannot be reasonably disputed. A majority of these churches, from the latter half of the second century to the latter half of the fourth, seem to have been generally opposed to receiving this epistle as Paul's; although there were some among them who did receive it.

It remains, then, to balance the testimony thus collected together and compared. The *early* testimony is, of course, immeasurably the most important. And there seems to me sufficient evidence, that this was as general and as uniform, for the first century after the apostolic age, as in respect to many other books of the New Testament; and more so, than in respect to several. I cannot hesitate to believe, that THE WEIGHT OF EVIDENCE FROM TRADITION, IS ALTOGETHER PREPONDERANT IN FAVOUR OF THE OPINION, THAT PAUL WAS THE AUTHOR OF OUR EPISTLE.

§ 18. *Internal evidence that the epistle is Paul's.*

We come, then, next to inquire, whether the *internal condition* of the epistle corresponds with and confirms this tradition. The evidence drawn from this, may be divided into two kinds: first, *that which arises from circumstances mentioned or adverted to in the epistle;* and, secondly, *that which arises from the style and manner of it.*

§ 19. Evidence that it was Paul's, from circumstances mentioned or adverted to in the epistle.

As our epistle no where exhibits the author's name, we can appeal, for internal testimony respecting the author of it, only to accidental circumstances which are developed in it.

(1.) The most striking one is that contained in xiii. 23, " Know ye, that our brother Timothy is ἀπολελυμένον, with whom, if he come speedily, I will pay you a visit." From the first acquaintance of Timothy with Paul, he had been his intimate friend and constant companion. That he was with Paul at Rome, during his imprisonment, we know for certainty; because Paul has united him in the salutation prefixed to the epistles written to the Philippians, Colossians, and to Philemon, during his captivity in that city. Timothy was greatly beloved and confided in by Paul, as the manner in which he speaks of him, in several of his epistles, abundantly shows; and Paul often calls him (as here) his *brother*. But the meaning of the word ἀπολελυμένον, as applied to Timothy, has been much contested; some rendering it, *set at liberty*, i. e. from prison; others, *sent away*, i. e. on some errand of Paul's. Giving to ἀπολελυμένον the first meaning assigned it, viz. *liberated*, objectors have said that " we have no account of Timothy's having been imprisoned during the life of Paul, and therefore, the occurrence of his imprisonment must have taken place after Paul's death; consequently the epistle must have been written by some *other* friend of Timothy, who calls him *brother*, in accordance with the usual style of the primitive Christians."

Nothing, however, can be more unsafe or uncritical, than the supposition that the Acts of the Apostles, or Paul's epistles, give us a *full* and *complete* account of all which happened to the various persons who are named in them. E. g. Aristarchus is called by Paul, in Col. iv. 10, his fellow-prisoner; as is Epaphras, in Philem. v. 23; but where is the history of their imprisonment? The supposition by Bertholdt, that another Timothy, different from him who is so often mentioned in the sacred records, may be meant here, is doubtless a *possible* one; but is it a *probable* one? Have we any kind of ecclesiastical voucher, that there was another Timothy, who distinguished himself in the apostolic age? It is *possible* that one Virgil wrote the Eneid, and another the Georgics; yet who thinks it to be *probable*? But if this be insufficient, Bertholdt alleges that a different person from Paul may have been the intimate

I

§ 19. INTERNAL EVIDENCE.

friend and travelling companion of Timothy, while Paul was imprisoned at Rome; and that the passage we are considering, may have come from him. Eichhorn thinks it must have been written by such a friend of Timothy, after the death of Paul; as, during his life, Timothy closely adhered to this apostle. All this, no doubt, is *possible ;* and a great many other hypotheses, which could be easily made, present no *impossibility.* But are they *probable?* And is not the language, which we are considering, more appropriate to the known relation of Paul and Timothy, than to the relation of any other person of that period with Timothy, concerning whom we have any knowledge? The spontaneous feeling of Christian readers, in all ages, has fully answered this question.

But what was the imprisonment which is adverted to by the word (ἀπολελυμένον? To suppose with Schmidt, (Hist. Antiq. Canon,) and many others, that it was an imprisonment at Rome with Paul, is evidently preposterous; for how, if Timothy were already at Rome, could Paul, or any one else there, say, *if he come,* or *return, speedily?* Must not Timothy have been *absent,* when this was said? If Timothy had been imprisoned abroad, and was then *liberated* (ἀπολελυμένον,) would he not have been the immediate bearer of the news himself to the apostle? I do not allege this as a certain fact, for possibly there may have been circumstances to prevent it. But then, it is not in itself very probable, that Paul in confinement at Rome would obtain information about Timothy, (who, if absent, was doubtless among some of the churches where Paul had been,) any sooner than those to whom he wrote our epistle; and who, as it appears from the manner in which Paul speaks of him to them, had a special regard for him.

Why, moreover, raise up all these difficulties in order to maintain an interpretation of ἀπολελυμένον which accords no better with the *usus loquendi* of the sacred or classical writers, than the rendering, *dismissed* or *sent away?* a sense so exactly consentaneous with the relation between Paul and Timothy. See Schleus. in voc. ἀπολύω, No. 3. In Philip. ii. 19, (this epistle was written while Paul was a prisoner at Rome,) the apostle speaks of sending Timothy to them shortly, so soon as he should see how it would go with him, in respect to being liberated from prison, ii. 23; at the same time expressing a hope, that he should himself come to them shortly, v. 24. What then is more natural than the supposition, that he did send Timothy to them; and that, during his absence, Paul wrote the epistle to the Hebrews, in which he tells them, that Timothy was sent away, that he is now assured that he himself would be speedily

§ 19. INTERNAL EVIDENCE. 115

set at liberty, and that he intends to pay them a visit in company with Timothy, if he should shortly return, viz. from Philippi? Many facts are believed by Bertholdt, and all other critics, which have less of verisimilitude to support them than this. Indeed, one cannot well see, how mere circumstantial evidence could be better adapted to make the impression of *probability* than this.

I do not feel the weight of the objection, made by alleging that Timothy was unknown to the church in Palestine, and that they could have no special interest with respect to the information in question. For, first, Timothy was the well-known and beloved companion of Paul, in all his journeyings during his later years; and must have been known as such, wherever Paul was known. Next, there can be no reasonable question, that he was with Paul during his last visit to Jerusalem, previously to the apostle's captivity for two years at Cesarea. Is there any probability, even if he were not with Paul during his journey to Jerusalem, that he did not frequently visit him in his afflictions? And would not the church at Cesarea, therefore, be well acquainted with him? Specially so, as Timothy would be the more acceptable to the Palestine Jewish Christians, on account of his having received the rite of circumcision, after he became a convert to Christianity.

Now, as all these circumstances do plainly accord with Paul's situation while a prisoner at Rome; with his relation to Timothy; and with the manner in which he employed him; and as we have not a syllable of testimony that they are applicable to any other person; I do not see how we can be justified, in denying that the evidence deducible from them is sufficient to render it quite probable, that Paul was the author of our epistle.

(2.) In Heb. xiii. 18, 19, the writer asks the prayers of those whom he addressed, that he might speedily be restored to them; and in Heb. xiii. 23, he expresses a confident expectation of " speedily paying them a visit." From these passages it is clear, that the writer was then in a state of imprisonment; and, also, that he was assured of a speedy liberation, which would enable him to pay the visit that he had encouraged then to hope for.

Compare this, now, with the situation of Paul at Rome, during the latter part of his imprisonment there. In his epistle to the Philippians, (written during that period,) he expresses his entire confidence that his life will be prolonged, so that he shall yet promote their religious profit and joy; τοῦτο πεποιθὼς οἶδα, ὅτι μενῶ καὶ συμπαραμενῶ πᾶσιν ὑμῖν, εἰς τὴν ὑμῶν

§ 19. INTERNAL EVIDENCE.

προκοπὴν καὶ χαρὰν τῆς πίστεως, Phil. i. 25. Again, in Phil. ii. 24, he says, πέποιθα δὲ ἐν Κυρίῳ, ὅτι καὶ αὐτὸς ταχέως ἐλεύσομαι, *I trust in the Lord, that I myself shall speedily come* [*to you*.] In the epistle to Philemon, (also written during the same imprisonment, (he says, ἐλπίζω γὰρ, ὅτι διὰ τῶν προσευχῶν ὑμῶν χαρισθήσομαι ὑμῖν, *for I hope, that by your prayers I shall be restored to you*, ver. 22. So confident was Paul of this, that he bids Philemon *prepare lodgings for him*, ἑτοίμαζέ μοι ξενίαν, ver. 22.

It appears very plainly, then, from these passages, that the writer had a satisfactory assurance in his mind of being speedily set at liberty; although, it is probable, a *formal* declaration of his acquittal had not yet been made by the Roman emperor. This last conclusion I gather from Phil. ii. 23, where Paul declares to the church whom he is addressing, " that he shall send Timothy to them immediately, ὡς ἂν ἀπίδω τὰ περὶ ἐμὲ, *whenever I shall know how my affairs issue.*" By this it appears, that he was in daily expectation of receiving *official* notice of the determination of the emperor in respect to his case, but that he had not yet received it. That he had private information, however, of the way in which his case was likely to terminate, and information which pretty fully satisfied his mind, is evident from the manner in which he speaks in the passages quoted above, of his intended visit to the Philippians, and to Philemon.

Supposing, now, as soon as an intimation was made by the Roman emperor, that Paul would be set at liberty, that intelligence respecting it was immediately communicated to the apostle, by *those of Cesar's household* (Phil. iv. 22,) who were his Christian friends; and supposing that, agreeably to his promise made to the Philippians ii. 23, he then immediately sent away Timothy to them; and supposing still further, (which surely cannot be regarded as improbable,) that there was some little delay in *formally* making out his sentence of acquittal, and carrying it into execution by actually liberating him from prison; then how obviously easy and natural is the expression in Heb. xiii. 23, " Know that our brother Timothy is sent away; with whom, if he speedily return, I shall pay you a visit?" On the supposition that the *close* of the epistle to the Hebrews was written at this juncture of time, nothing can be more probable than that the promised mission of Timothy, adverted to in Phil. ii. 23, is referred to in Heb. xiii. 23; and consequently that ἀπολελυμένον here means *sent away, dismissed*, (as all must acknowledge it *may* mean,) and not, *liberated*, or, *set at liberty*.

§ 19. INTERNAL EVIDENCE. 117

The circumstances adverted to, or implied, in Heb. xiii. 23, Phil. ii. 23, and Philem. ver. 22, have other correspondencies which deserve particular notice. In the two latter passages, it is plain that the writer *expects* his liberty, and means to send away Timothy to Philippi. In the former, he is *assured* of his liberty, and only waits for the return of Timothy, in order that he may set out to visit the Hebrews whom he had been addressing. In case Timothy did not return *speedily* (τάχιον,) it is plainly implied in Heb. xiii. 23, that the writer meant to set out on his journey without him. There was, then, some uncertainty in his mind, respecting the time when Timothy would return. How well all this accords with the journey of Timothy to a place so remote from Rome as Philippi, cannot fail to strike the mind of every considerate reader.

Now, laying aside all favouritism for any previous opinions respecting our epistle, can it be reasonably doubted, that here is a concurrence of circumstances so striking, as to render it highly probable that Paul wrote it? More especially so, when we consider that the epistle must have been written, about the same period of time when these circumstances happened; for it proffers internal evidence of being written before the destruction of Jerusalem; and yet written so late, that the period when the Hebrews were first converted to Christianity is adverted to as being already a considerable time before, Heb. v. 12, and is called τὰς πρότερον ἡμέρας, x. 32. Now, the imprisonment of Paul, at Rome, happened probably A. D. 62 or 63, which was some thirty years after the gospel had begun to be preached abroad, and about seven years before the destruction of Jerusalem.

Taking all these circumstances together, it must be acknowledged that there is an extraordinary concurrence of them, which cannot but serve much to increase the probability that our epistle was written by Paul, near the close of his liberation at Rome.

The objections which Bertholdt makes against the arguments just presented, do not seem to be weighty. "Would *Paul*," he asks, " promise to revisit Palestine, when the people of that very country had sent him into captivity at Rome? A very improbable circumstance, indeed!"

But a nearer consideration of the circumstances attending Paul's case, will remove the appearance of so great improbability. For, first, Paul had been kept a prisoner, at Cesarea, two years before his removal to Rome, Acts xxiv. 25—27; and at Rome he lived two years more, in a similar condition, Acts xxviii. 30. These, with the time occupied by his going to Rome, and returning from it, would make nearly a five years' interval between his leaving Palestine and revisiting it. Might not some of his fiercest persecutors have died during this period? Or, might they not have laid aside their furious, persecuting zeal?

But, in the next place, supposing our epistle to have been sent to the church at Cesarea, where Paul had been treated with so much kindness during his imprisonment; could there have been any fear in his mind, with respect to paying them a visit? And even if we suppose that Cesarea was not the place to which the letter was directed, but that it was sent to the Christians at Jerusalem; yet the objection brought forward by Bertholdt will not be of much validity. Paul was not to be deterred from going to Jerusalem, by the prospect of persecution. From the time when he first made his appearance there, after his conversion, the Jews had always showed a bitter enmity against him, and persecuted him. Yet this did not deter him from going, again and again, to that city. And why should it now deter him, any more than formerly?

Besides, he was now liberated from the accusations of the Jews, by the sentence of the emperor himself. Would they venture to do again, the very thing which the court of Rome had decided to be unlawful? Might not Paul well expect, with the decision of the emperor in his hand, to find his personal liberty for the future respected?

"But," says Bertholdt, "we have no account that Paul paid a visit to Palestine, after his liberation."

True. But what argument this can furnish, against the probability that he did pay such a visit, I do not perceive. Bertholdt himself, in the very paragraph which contains this objection, says, "Who does not know, that the accounts of what befell the apostles, and primitive teachers of Christianity, are very incomplete?" Every one knows, that Luke breaks off the history of Paul, with the account of his imprisonment at Rome. Has any writer given us a well-authenticated *supplement* to this? And can the want of any history of Paul, after the period of his imprisonment at Rome, be a proof that he never travelled to any particular place, or that he did not live and preach there? Surely this cannot be urged with any show of propriety.

I add only, that analogy would lead us to suppose that Paul, when liberated, would go to Palestine, and then to the other churches in Asia Minor. Such was the general course of his travels; see Acts xviii. 2, seq. It is altogether consonant, then, with the usage of Paul, to suppose that he would visit the church at Palestine, after his imprison

§ 19. INTERNAL EVIDENCE. 119

ment at Rome; and therefore natural to suppose that Heb. xiii. 23, refers to such an event.

(3.) If the reading in Heb. x. 34, "for ye had compassion *on my bonds*," (τοῖς δεσμοῖς μου,) be correct, it is another argument that Paul is the author of our epistle; for his bonds in Palestine, whither the letter was sent, are well known. That he obtained compassion there, particularly during his two years' imprisonment at Cesarea, will not be questioned. But as the reading δεσμοῖς μου is controverted, and δεσμίοις (*the prisoners*) is preferred by some good critics, I do not think proper to urge this argument; although the evidence is about equally in favour of δεσμοῖς μου, δεσμοῖς, and δεσμίοις.

(4. The salutation in Heb. xiii. 24, agrees with the supposition that Paul wrote this epistle; ἀσπάζονται ὑμᾶς οἱ ἀπὸ τῆς Ἰταλίας. Paul, writing from Rome, which had communication, of course, with all parts of Italy, and with the Italian churches, may very naturally be supposed to have sent such a salutation. Indeed, the circumstances render this quite probable.

The objections made against this, do not strike me as forcible. Eichhorn alleges, that οἱ ἀπὸ τῆς Ἰταλίας must mean *people who had come from Italy*, i. e. who had left Italy, and were *locally* out of it, when the writer sent a salutation from them. Consequently, he concludes, the writer of the epistle could not have been Paul, during his imprisonment at Rome.

This interpretation, however, is not founded in the *usus loquendi* of the Greek language. From the many proofs of this, which might be offered, I select only a few cases. Matt. xxi. 11, Ἰησοῦς . . . . . ὁ ἀπὸ Ναζαρέτ, *Jesus the Nazarene*; οἱ ἀπὸ Θεσσαλονίκης Ἰουδαῖοι, *the Thessalonian Jews*. In this last case, the Jews *at* Thessalonica, not *out of* it, are meant; as is plain from the last part of the verse, which speaks of them as going to Berea, *after* they had heard the report of Paul's preaching there. So οἱ ἀπὸ Ἱεροσολύμων γραμματεῖς, *the Jerusalem scribes*, Matt. xv. 1.

In the same manner, other prepositions, of the like signification with ἀπὸ, are used with the article : e. g. οἱ ἐκ ἐριθείας, *the contentious*; οἱ ἐκ νόμου, *sticklers for the law*; τὸ ἐξ οὐράνου, *heavenly*; οἱ ἐκ τῆς Καίσαρος οἰκίας, *Cæsar's domestics*.

So far is Eichhorn's remark from being well founded, in regard to the meaning of such a phrase as οἱ ἀπὸ τῆς Ἰταλίας, that one may venture to say, it is incapable of such a meaning as he gives it. It is only when ἀπὸ, in such a connexion, is preceded by ἀφίστημι, ἀναβαίνω, ἐξέρχομαι, ἔρχομαι, καταβαίνω, &c. that it denotes, *being out of a country*. Οἱ ἀπὸ denotes, *belonging to*. Consequently the salutation in Heb. xiii. 24, means simply, *The Italians* [i. e. Italian Christians] *salute you*.

But here again, it is asked, " How came Italians to salute a church in Palestine? If Paul wrote our epistle, at *Rome*, why did he not say, ἀσπάζονται ὑμᾶς οἱ ἀπὸ τῆς Ῥώμης? What acquaintance had the *Romans* with the church at Palestine?

This objection, however, will not bear examination. The Romans surely were *Italians;* and it is a matter of indifference, whether the writer at Rome said οἱ ἀπὸ τῆς Ῥώμης, or οἱ ἀπὸ τῆς Ἰταλίας, if he meant to send only the salutation of Christians who resided at Rome. But is it at all probable, that there were not Christians often at Rome, from various parts of Italy, who were acquainted with Paul, and who cherished a friendly interest for the church whom he was addressing? If these also, as well as the *Romans*, wished to send the expression of their friendly regards to the Hebrews; what other phraseology could Paul have adopted, that would be more appropriate than οἱ ἀπὸ τῆς Ἰταλίας, which would embrace Christians in general, who lived in the country where the writer was?

Then, why should this be thought so strange, when an example of the very same nature may be produced from the acknowledged writings of Paul? This apostle, writing from Ephesus (1 Cor. xvi. 8,) to the church at Corinth, says, *The churches of Asia salute you*, xvi. 19. May not the same questions be urged here, as objectors urge in the case above? May we not ask, How could the Asiatics be *personally* known to the Corinthians? And why should Paul speak of *the churches of Asia*, and not of that at Ephesus? Plainly, the reason of this was, that Christians from different parts of Asia Minor, (which is here meant,) were collected together in Ephesus, its capital, where they had intercourse with Paul, and knew that he was addressing the Corinthians, and desired an expression of their brotherly affection toward them. What is more common, every day, than for single individuals, or societies of men, who have never had any personal intercourse together, to exchange friendly salutations? Could not Paul as well send the salutation of οἱ ἀπὸ τῆς Ἰταλίας, as of οἱ ἀπὸ τῆς Ἀσίας?

Such are the various circumstances adverted to in our epistle, whicn serve to render it probable that Paul was the author of it. From its nature, this evidence is *indirect;* but evidence of such a kind is, not unfre-

§ 20. INTERNAL EVIDENCE.

quently, as convincing as that which appears to be more direct. The prefixing or suffixing of a writer's name to an epistle, is a more easy and obvious method of interpolation, than the insertion of minute circumstances, which imply a very intimate acquaintance with a writer's condition and circumstances.

Will any one undertake to show, that the circumstances, which are brought into view above, may be more probably attached to some other person than to Paul? If not, then the probability from them is in favour of Paul as the author of our epistle.

§ 20. *Evidence that the epistle is Paul's from a similarity of sentiment, and also from the form, method, style, and diction of the composition.*

The preceding section treated of the facts or external circumstances, to which various passages of our epistle adverts; and what is gathered from these may be called, in a certain respect, a kind of *external* evidence. But a comparison of our epistle with the other acknowledged writings of Paul, remains yet to be made. This is a species of evidence, on which some have relied with great confidence; and it is remarkable, that it has been appealed to with equal confidence, both by those who defend, and by those who assail, the Pauline origin of the epistle to the Hebrews. Even in very ancient times, so early as the third century, the same occurrence took place. One might, perhaps, naturally enough conclude from this, that no very satisfactory evidence on either side would be obtained; but that the epistle contains things to which both parties may appeal, with some tolerable show of reason. Before coming, however, to such a conclusion, we ought at least to make a thorough investigation, and to weigh well all the arguments which are adduced to support the respective opinions to which I allude.

A comparison between our epistle and the acknowledged letters of Paul, may have respect to the *doctrines* taught in both; or to the *form* and *method*, as well as the *style* and *diction*, of the epistle. When these shall have passed in review before us, the allegations, with regard to a *dissimilarity* between the epistle to the Hebrews and other epistles of Paul, may be further discussed.

§ 21. Similarity of DOCTRINES between the epistle to the Hebrews, and the acknowledged epistles of Paul.

Are the sentiments, in our epistle, such as Paul was wont to teach? Do they accord with his, not only in such a general way as we may easily suppose the sentiments of all Christians in the apostolic age harmonized with each other, but have they the colouring, the proportion, the characteristic features of Paul's sentiments? Are they so stated and insisted on, as Paul is wont to state and insist on his?

The resemblance in respect to doctrine may be arranged, for the sake of perspicuity and distinction, under the following heads:

I. General preference of Christianity above Judaism.

There can, indeed, be no reasonable doubt, that all the apostles and primitive teachers of Christianity, who were well instructed in the principles of this religion, must have acknowledged and taught its superiority over the ancient religion of the Jews. The very fact, that they were Christians, necessarily implies this. But still, it is quite certain, that the preference of the new above the ancient religion, is taught by Paul in a manner different from that of other writers of the New Testament; and with more emphasis, in his writings, than in any other parts of the sacred volume.

The grounds of preferring Christianity to Judaism, may be classed under the following particulars.

(1.) *The superior degree of light, or religious knowledge, imparted by the gospel.*

In his acknowledged epistles, Paul calls Judaism, τὰ στοιχεῖα τοῦ κόσμου, Gal. iv. 3; and again, τὰ ἀσθενῆ καὶ πτωχὰ στοιχεῖα, Gal. iv. 9. He represents it as adapted to children, νήπιοι, Gal. iv. 3, who are in a state of nonage and pupilage, Gal. iv. 2, or in the condition of servants rather than that of heirs, Gal. iv. 1.

On the other hand, Christians attain to a higher knowledge of God, Gal. iv. 9; they are no more as servants, but become sons, and obtain the privileges of adoption, Gal. iv. 5, 6. They are represented as τέλειοι, 1 Cor. xiv. 20; as being furnished with instruction adequate to make them ἄνδρας τελείους, Eph. iv. 11—13. Christianity leads them to see the glorious displays of himself which God has made, with an unveiled face, i. e. clearly, 2 Cor. iii. 18 ; while Judaism threw a veil over these things, 2 Cor. ii. 13. Christianity is engraven on the hearts of its votaries, ἡ διακονία τοῦ πνεύματος, 2 Cor. iii. 8; while Judaism was engraven on tablets of stone, ἐντετυπομένη ἐν λίθοις, 2 Cor. iii. 7. Such is a brief sketch of Paul's views in respect to this point, as presented in his acknowledged epistles. Let us now compare these views with those which the epistle to the Hebrews discloses.

This epistle commences with the declaration, that God, who in times past spake to the fathers by the prophets, hath, in these last days, spoken to us by his Son, Heb. i. 1, ii. 1, seq. Judaism was revealed only by the mediation of angels, ii. 2 ; while Christianity was revealed by the Son of God, and abundantly confirmed by miraculous gifts of the Holy Ghost, ii. 3, 4. The ancient covenant was imperfect, in respect to the means which it furnished for the diffusion of knowledge ; but the new covenant provides that all shall know the Lord, from the least to the greatest, viii. 9—11. The law was only a sketch or imperfect representation of religious blessings ; while the gospel proffers the blessings themselves, x. 1. The worthies of ancient times had only imperfect views of spiritual blessings ; while Christians enjoy them in full measure, xi. 39, 40.

(2.) *The gospel holds out superior motives and encouragements to virtue and piety.*

Paul represents the condition of the Jews, while under the law, as like to that of children, immured and kept under the eye of masters and teachers, Gal. iii. 23, iv. 2; as being in bondage, Gal. iv. 3 ; as servants, iv. 1 ; as children, iv. 3 ; and as having the spirit of bondage, Rom. viii. 15. This servile spirit, which inspired them with fear, Rom. viii. 15, gives place, under the Christian religion, to the spirit of adoption, by which they approach God with filial confidence, Rom. viii. 15—17. Christianity has liberated us from pedagogues, and made us partakers of the privileges of sons and heirs, Gal. iii. 25, seq. iv. 4, seq. The liberty of the gospel affords urgent motives for the practice of virtue, Gal. v. 1, seq. v. 13, seq. The spirit imparted under the gospel furnishes aid, and creates special obligation, to mortify our evil passions and affections, Rom. viii. 12—17. Circumcision is now nothing, and uncircumcision nothing ; but obedience to the commands of God is the all-important consideration, 1 Cor. vii. 19. Not circumcision or uncircumcision is matter of concern, under the Christian religion, but a new creation, i. e. a spiritual renovation, Gal. vi. 15, and faith which worketh by love, Gal. v. 6.

Turn we now to the epistle to the Hebrews. There we find, that the sacrifices prescribed by the Jewish law, could not quiet and purify the conscience of the worshipper, ix. 9; nor deliver him from the pollution of sin, in order that he might, in a becoming manner, worship the living God; which is effected only under the gospel, ix. 14. The law served to inspire its votaries with awe and terror, Heb. xii. 18—21; but the gospel with cheering confidence, xii. 22—24. Now, we may obtain grace to serve God in an acceptable manner, xii. 28. We have a covenant established on better promises than the ancient one, viii. 6—13; and are urged by more powerful motives to a holy life under the gospel, xii. 25—29.

It must be admitted, in respect to the particulars of the comparison just drawn, that the *diction* of the passages generally, in the epistle to the Hebrews, presents no very striking resemblances to that in Paul's acknowledged epistles. But this, as will be easily seen by inspecting all the passages drawn into the comparison, may very naturally result from the different topics with which the passages from our epistle stand connected. The *mode* of introducing these topics is different, because it arises from different occasions of introducing them. But the fundamental ideas in both are the same. Other writers also of the New Testament urge the obligations of Christians to peculiar holiness of life; but what other writers, except Paul, urge it from *comparative* views of the Jewish and Christian dispensations?

(3.) *The superior efficacy of the gospel, in promoting and ensuring the real and permanent happiness of mankind.*

Paul represents the law as possessing only a condemning power, and subjecting all men to its curse, in consequence of disobedience, Gal. iii. 10. It is the ministry of death, 2 Cor. iii. 7; the ministry of condemnation, 2 Cor. iii. 9; by it none can obtain justification or pardoning mercy, Gal. iii. 11, Rom. iii. 20.

On the contrary, Christianity is the ministry of pardon, τῆς δικαιοσύνης, 2 Cor. iii. 9; it holds out forgiveness of sins for the sake of Christ, gratuitous pardon on account of him, Rom. iii. 24, 25, Eph. i. 7. Through him, we are allowed to cherish the hope of future glory, Rom. v. 1, 2; and this without perfect obedience to the law, Rom. iii. 21, Gal. ii. 16; Acts xiii. 38, 39. And to such blessings, under the gospel, is attached

§ 21. INTERNAL EVIDENCE.

a most important circumstance, in order to heighten their value, viz. that they are *perennial*, and not (like the Mosaic institutions) liable to abolition, 2 Cor. iii. 11.

In correspondence with all this, the epistle to the Hebrews represents the Mosaic dispensation, as one which was calculated to inspire awe and terror, Heb. xii. 18—21; the offerings and sacrifices which it enjoined, could never tranquillize and purify the conscience of the worshipper, ix. 9; for it was impossible that the blood of bulls and goats should take away sin, x. 4, 11. The blood of Christ has made a real expiation, procured forgiveness, and liberated the conscience from an oppressive sense of guilt, ix. 11—14; v. 9; vi. 18—20. Christ by his death has delivered us from the condemning power of sin, and freed us from the oppressive fear which it occasions, ii. 14, 15. He has procured access to God, and is ever ready to aid those who approach him, vii. 29; ix. 24. The offering which he has made for sin has a perennial influence, and without repetition remains for ever efficacious, ix. 12, 25—28; x. 12; vii. 23—28.

Other writers also of the New Testament have set before us the blessings of the gospel, and these as connected with what Christ has done and suffered. But what other writer, except Paul, has charged his picture with such a contrast between the Mosaic and Christian dispensations, and thrown so much shade over the one, and light over the other? If the hand of Paul be not in the epistle to the Hebrews, it is the hand of one who had drunk deeply of his doctrines, and in a high degree participated of his feelings and views.

(4.) *The Jewish dispensation was only a type and shadow of the Christian.*

Thus Paul often represents it. Meats and drinks, feasts and new moons, and sabbaths, are σκιὰ τῶν μελλόντων, but the σῶμα is Christ, Col. ii. 16, 17. The passage through the Red Sea was typical of Christian baptism; and the manna, of our spiritual food, 1 Cor. x. 1—6. The occurrences under the ancient dispensation were typical of things under the new, 1 Cor. x. 11. In like manner, Paul calls Adam τύπος τοῦ μέλλοντος, i. e. a type of Christ, Rom. v. 14, comp. 1 Cor. xv. 45—47. The Mosaic institution did but darkly shadow that, which is clearly revealed under the gospel, 2 Cor. iii. 13—18. Hagar and Sarah may be considered as allegorically representing the law and the gospel, or the two covenants, Gal. iv. 22—31. The law was only our pedagogue until the coming of Christ, under whom full privileges are enjoyed, Gal. iii. 23—25, iv. 1—5.

The epistle to the Hebrews, in like manner, represents the Jewish rites and ordinances only as a παραβολὴ, i. e. a *significant emblem* of blessings under the gospel; and these rites were imposed only until the time of reformation, ix. 9—14. The law was only σκιὰ of good things to come; while the gospel proffered the very things themselves, x. 1. All the Levitical ritual, the temple itself and all its appurtenances, were only a ὑπόδειγμα of the temple in which Christ ministers, and of the functions which he performs, viii. 1—9, ix. 22—24; they were a designed emblem of the objects of the new dispensation, ix. 9.

The question may be emphatically put here,—What other parts of the New Testament, the writings of Paul excepted, furnish us with views of such a nature as these exhibit? Manifestly Pauline is both the sentiment, and the costume which the writer has put upon it.

(5.) *While the Christian dispensation is designed for perpetuity, the Jewish institutes are abolished on account of their imperfection.*

Paul represents the Law as having no glory, in comparison with Christianity, 2 Cor. iii. 10; it was designed to be abolished, when the perennial dispensation of Christ should be introduced, 2 Cor. iii. 11. 13. The veil over the ancient dispensation rendered it obscure, and hindered the Jews from fully comprehending it; but the time was come, under the gospel, when that veil was removed, and the glory of God was seen with open face, 2 Cor. iii. 13—18. The law being altogether incapable of justifying sinners, gives place to another and gratuitous method of justification, Rom. iv. 14—16. Christians are dead to the law, and affianced to another covenant, Rom. vii. 4—6. The law was incompetent to effect the designs of divine benevolence, and therefore gives place to a more perfect dispensation, Gal. iii. 21—25; iv. 1—7; v. 1. It was void of power to justify the sinner, and therefore the interposition of Christ became necessary, Rom. viii. 3, 4; Gal. ii. 16.

On the other hand, the writer of the epistle to the Hebrews represents the new covenant as inspiring better hopes than the ancient one did, and the latter as taxable with defects, viii. 6—8. The old covenant is antiquated, and ready to expire, ἐγγὺς ἀφανισμοῦ, viii. 13 Christ is appointed high-priest according to a new order of priesthood, different from the Levitical one; because the dispensation, by which the latter received its appointment, was weak, and incompetent to effect the introduction

§ 21. INTERNAL EVIDENCE. 127

of such hopes as the gospel inspires, vii. 17—19. Burnt-offerings and sacrifices can never take away sin, Christ only can effect this; so that, when his offering is made, it needs not to be repeated, but is of sufficient and everlasting efficacy, x. 1—14.

Other writers of the New Testament have also appealed to the efficacy of Jesus' atoning blood; but who, besides Paul, has thrown this whole subject into an attitude of contrast with the inefficiency of the Jewish dispensation?

Thus much for our first general head, by way of comparing the *sentiments* of Paul with those of our epistle, in respect to the grounds of preference over Judaism, which Christianity affords.

II. The person and work of the Mediator, Jesus Christ.

Under this head, the following particulars are entitled to our consideration:—

(1.) *The* PERSON *of the Mediator is presented in the same light, by the writer of the epistle to the Hebrews, and by Paul.*

Paul, in various passages, represents Christ as the image of God, as the resemblance or likeness of the Father; as humbling himself, or condescending to assume our nature, and suffer death in it; and as being exalted in consequence of this, i. e. as a reward of his benevolence and obedience, to the throne of the universe, and made head over all things. Thus, in Philip. ii. 6—11, Christ being ἐν μορφῇ Θεοῦ, took on himself our nature, and obeyed or subjected himself, in the same, unto death, even the death of the cross; in consequence of which, God hath given him a name above every other, so that all in heaven or on earth must bow the knee to him. In Col. i. 15—20, Christ is represented as the image of the invisible God; as having created all things in heaven and in earth; all things are said to consist by him; over all he has a distinguished pre-eminence; and by his sufferings and death he has produced a reconciliation among the creatures of God, and made expiation for sin, so that God treats the pardoned sinner as if he were innocent. In 2 Cor. viii. 9, Paul says, that the Lord Jesus Christ, who was rich, became poor on our account, that we through his poverty might become rich. In Eph. iii. 9, God is said to have created all things by Jesus Christ; and in 1 Cor. viii. 6, all things are said to be by him. In 1 Cor. xv. 25—27, it is declared, that he must reign until all things are put under his feet.

The peculiarity of this Pauline representation consists, in presenting Christ as the *image* of God; in specificating the act of humility by which he became incarnate, *he humbled himself*, ἐκένωσε σεαυτὸν—*though rich, he became poor;* in presenting his obedience and sufferings, as the ground of his elevation to the throne of the universe, in the mediatorial nature; in representing him as head over all, both friends and enemies, and as reigning until his enemies be made his footstool; and finally, in representing God as having created all things *by him.*

If we turn now to the epistle to the Hebrews, we find the same representations there. The Son of God is the reflection of the Father's glory, his exact image or resemblance, χαρακτὴρ, i. 3. God made all things by him, i. 2. He directs all things by his powerful word, i. 3. He was in a state of humiliation, (ἠλαττωμένον,) lower than the angels, ii. 9. He took part in flesh and blood, that he might, by his own death, render null and void the destructive power of the devil, ii. 14. On account of the suffering of death, he is exalted to a state of glory and honour, ii. 9. He endured the sufferings of the cross, making no account of its disgrace, but having a regard to the reward set before him, which was a seat at the right hand of God, xii. 2. All things are put under his feet, ii. 8. x. 13; where the very same passage from the Old Testament is quoted, which Paul quotes in 1 Cor. xv. 25—28, and it is applied in the same manner.

Is all this, now, mere *accident?* What other writer of the New Testament presents such speciality of views respecting Christ's resemblance to God, his mediatorial character, his obedience, sufferings, and exaltation in our nature to the throne of the universe? No other writer presents them in the same connexion, employs the same images for comparison, or brings the topics to view in the same light. There is a peculiarity of representation so distinctly marked here, so exclusively Pauline in its manner, that if Paul himself did not write the epistle to the Hebrews, it must have been some one, who had drunk in so deeply of his instructions, as to become the very image of the fountain whence he drew.

(2.) *The death of Christ as a propitiatory sacrifice for sin, and the reconciliation of sinners to God by means of this sacrifice.*

Other writers, indeed, of the New Testament, besides Paul, teach this doctrine. But there is in his letters a peculiar and urgent manner of enforcing it. Oftener than any other writer, does he recur to this interesting theme; and in all his representations, it stands in high relief.

§ 21. INTERNAL EVIDENCE.

The general annunciation of it is often repeated. Christ came into the world to save sinners, 1 Tim. i. 15. He died for our sins, I Cor. xv. 3. He was given up or devoted to death, on our account, Rom. viii. 32. Our redemption was wrought by him, Rom. iii. 24. He was given up, i. e. to death, on account of our offences, Rom. iv. 25. He gave up himself for our sins, Gal. i. 4. ii. 20. He gave up himself an acceptable sacrifice for us, Eph. v. 2. He was our paschal lamb, 1 Cor. v. 7. By his blood we have redemption, or forgiveness of sin, Eph. i. 7. Col. i. 14. He gave himself a ransom for all, 1 Tim. ii. 6. 1 Cor. vi. 20. vii. 23. These may serve as a specimen of the general statement which Paul so frequently makes of this subject.

But he also recurs very often to this topic, in his reasonings at length, and insists upon it with particularity. In his epistle to the Romans, he labours at length to prove the universal guilt of men, in order to show that salvation by Christ is necessary for all, Rom. iii. 22—27. v. 12—21. He urges the impossibility of obtaining this salvation by the law, Rom. iii. 20. 28. viii. 3. Gal. ii. 16. 21 ; averring that Jesus, by his death, has effected what the law could not do. Assuming our nature, he became a sin-offering for us, Rom. viii. 3. He became a propitiatory sacrifice on our account, so that through him we may obtain pardoning mercy, Rom. iii. 24—26. As all men have come into a state of condemnation through Adam, so all men may come into a state of pardon through Christ, Rom. v. 12—21. comp. 2 Cor. v. 14. 19—21. Now, since Christ died for us, Christians may regard God as no more inclined to punish them as guilty, for they are in a state of peace and pardon, Rom. v. 1. 8—11. viii. 32. Now we may hope for abounding grace and happiness, Rom. v. 17. vi. 23. viii. 17. 32. Jesus at the right hand of God is ever ready to aid us, Rom. viii. 34. Jesus is the Mediator between God and man, to make reconciliation, 1 Tim. ii. 5, 6.

It were easy to add many other passages of the same tenor, from the acknowledged writings of Paul; but these are sufficient to exhibit his views, and the mode in which he inculcates them.

In the epistle to the Hebrews, we find the same sentiments, urged with the same ardour. Christ, by the sacrifice of himself, made expiation for our sins, i. 3. By the grace of God, assuming our nature, he tasted death for all, ii. 9. He became, through his sufferings, the author of eternal salvation to believers, ver. 8, 9.

But no where is there more speciality of argument to establish this great point, than in Heb. vii. viii. ix. and x.; nearly all of which is occupied with it. The Jewish offerings are altogether insufficient to make expiation, ix. 9—14. vii. 11. 19. x. 1. 11. Those offerings needed constant repetition; and even then, they could never remove sin, v. 1—3. vii. 27, 28. ix. 6, 7. 25. x. 4. 11. Christ by offering up himself has effected this, i. 3. vii. 27. ix. 25, 26. By his own blood, not with that of beasts, he entered into the eternal sanctuary, once for all making expiation for sin, ix. 12—15. x. 10—12. 14. 19. By his death, he has delivered us from the oppressive fear of condemnation, ii. 14, 15. He has tranquillized and purified the conscience of penitent sinners, which the law could not do, ix. 9. 14. He is the Mediator of a new covenant, ix. 15. xii. 24; which is better than the ancient one, vii. 22. viii. 6. He is exalted to the throne of the universe, ii. 6—10; and he is ever ready and able to assist us, iv. 14—16. vii. 25. He has introduced us to a dispensation, which speaks not terror only, like the law, but offers abounding grace and happiness, xii. 18—29.

Such are some of the more striking *traits of doctrine*, and *peculiarities in the mode of representing them*, common to the acknowledged epistles of Paul and to the epistle to the Hebrews.

§ 22. *Form and method of the epistle to the Hebrews, compared with those of Paul's acknowledged epistles.*

These topics may be considered, either in a general point of view, as it respects the arrangement of the epistle at large; or specially, as having reference to various particulars which it exhibits.

(1.) *The general method or arrangement of this epistle, is like to that of Paul.*

Most of all does it resemble his two epistles to the Romans, and to the Galatians; which exhibit first a theoretical or doctrinal, then a practical, part. The epistle to the Romans is principally occupied, to the end of the tenth chapter, with the doctrinal part; and the remainder with practical matter and salutations. In like manner, the epistle to the Galatians, as far as the end of the fourth chapter, is principally doctrinal discussion; while the remainder is hortatory and practical. In some degree, the same thing may be said of the epistles to the Ephesians Colossians, Philippians, and Thessalonians. But that to the Romans is most distinctly marked of all.

Turning now to the epistle to the Hebrews, we find that it is composed on a similar plan. As far as chapter x. 19, it is principally doctrinal It has, however, like Paul's other epistles, occasional exhortation inter-

§ 22. INTERNAL EVIDENCE. 131

mixed, which the strength of the writer's feelings plainly appears to have forced from him. Hence to the end, it is hortatory and practical.

In the epistle to the Romans, just before the salutatory part begins, the writer earnestly asks for a special interest in the prayers of those whom he addressed, in order that he may be delivered from the power of persecution; and he follows this request with a petition, that the God of peace might be with them, and concludes with an *Amen*, Rom. xv 30—33. The very same order, petition, style, and conclusion, appear at the close of the epistle to the Hebrews, xiii. 18—21. The writer begs an interest in their prayers, that he may be restored to them the sooner; commends them to the *God of peace*, (an expression used no where else but in Paul's writings, and in the epistle to the Hebrews;) and concludes with an *Amen*, before the salutation.

Is all this arrangement, to which we have now adverted, merely *accidental;* or does it look as if it must have come from the hand of the same writer? I know, indeed, it has been said, that the order of nature and propriety would lead every man, writing an epistle which contained doctrinal discussion and practical exhortation, to arrange them in such a manner that the former should precede; and that this arrangement, therefore, cannot with probability be represented as exclusively *Pauline*. With the views of rhetorical propriety, which are entertained by classical scholars of the present day, I readily acknowledge that such an order is almost spontaneous. But then, another question arises here. Why has not Paul adopted this in all his epistles? And why has neither John, nor James, nor Peter, nor Jude, adopted it? All these apostles have commingled doctrine and practice throughout their epistles. *Regularly* arranged discussion of doctrine, they do not exhibit. In this respect, the only similars to the epistle to the Hebrews are to be found in the epistles of Paul. But if the general arrangement here adverted to, be not considered as of much weight in the matter before us, it must be admitted, that there is a striking resemblance between the close of the practical part, just before the salutations or greetings, in the epistles to the Romans and to the Hebrews. Here, also, we find the exclusively Pauline phrase, *the God of peace*, employed in the same way, in both epistles.

(2.) *The manner of appealing to and employing the Jewish Scriptures, in Paul's acknowledged epistles and in the epistle to the Hebrews, is the same.*

I do not refer here to the *formulas* of quotation, by which a passage from the Old Testament is introduced. I have compared those formulas presented by the epistle to the Hebrews, with those in Paul's epistles; but I do not find any thing peculiar enough in either, to mark Paul's writings with any certainty; as I shall endeavour to show, in its proper place. Every where, in the New Testament, a great variety of such formulas is found, as also in the epistles of Paul. I refer now, in a particular manner, to the *method* in which, and the *frequency* with which, the Jewish Scriptures are employed; and that in a similar way, both in the epistle to the Hebrews, and in the acknowledged epistles of Paul. Paul often quotes and combines passages of Scripture, without any notice of quotations; e. g. Rom. ix. 7. 21. x. 6—8. 18. xi. 33, 34. xiii. 9. In Rom. iii. 10—18, several passages from different parts of the Scriptures are combined together, without any notice that this is done. In the same manner does the writer of the epistle to the Hebrews proceed; e. g. iii. 2. vi. 14. x. and xi. throughout; also, in xii. 5, 6. 12, 13. and xiii. 6, quotations, with a general appeal, are made from different parts of Scripture connected together. Paul makes a very frequent and copious use of the Jewish Scriptures, in all the argumentative part of his epistles; so does the writer of the epistle to the Hebrews. Paul often appeals to the Jewish Scriptures, as *prophetically* declaring the abrogation of the Mosaic economy, and to Abraham, as having received a covenant which the law could not annul; the same does the writer of the epistle to the Hebrews. Paul employs the Old Testament, in every way in which the Jews of that time were usually accustomed to reason from it. Sometimes he appeals to direct and prophetic assurances; sometimes to similarity of sentiment; sometimes he accommodates passages, which in the original have a local or temporary meaning, to designate something then extant, or happening at the time in which he wrote; sometimes he appeals to the history of the Old Testament, for analogical cases to confirm or impress the doctrine or truth which he inculcates; and sometimes he uses the Old Testament language as a vehicle of thought, in order to express his own ideas. The very same traits characterize, in a most visible manner, the method in which the Old Testament is employed throughout the epistle to the Hebrews; as every attentive reader must plainly see, without my delaying here to specify individual cases.

In a particular manner does Paul employ passages of the Jewish Scripture, and Scripture history, κατ' ἄνθρωπον; in other words, he uses them by way of *argumentum ad hominem*, or *argumentum ex concessis*.

§ 22. INTERNAL EVIDENCE.   133

It is thus that he allegorizes, on the two sons of Sarah and Hagar, in Gal. iv. 24, seq.; on the command of Moses, not to muzzle the ox which treadeth out the corn, Deut. xxxv. 4, the spirit of which he applies to the maintenance of religious teachers, in 1 Cor. ix. 9; on the rock from which the Israelites obtained water, Exod. xvii. 6, which he considers as an emblem of Christ, in 1 Cor. x. 2, seq.; on the veil over Moses' face, Exod. xxxiv. 33, which he applies to the comparative obscurity that rested on the Jewish revelation, in 2 Cor. iii. 13, 14; on the declaration that a man should leave his father and mother, and cleave to his wife, and that they twain should become one flesh, Gen. ii. 24, which he applies to the union of Christ and his church, in Eph. v. 31, 32.

How conspicuous this method of reasoning is, in the epistle to the Hebrews, need not be insisted on to any attentive reader. The whole comparison between Christ and Melchisedek, Heb. vii., is of a similar nature with those already mentioned. The temple and all its apparatus, and the holy place, which the high-priest entered with his expiatory offerings of blood, are types and shadows of the temple, of the offering, and of the great High-priest presenting it in the heavens, Heb. viii. 1—5. ix. 1—9. Indeed, the strain of argumentation, throughout, is often *ad hominem*, or *ex concessis*. The argument that Christ is a more exalted personage than the angels, than Moses, than the high-priest; that Christ's priesthood, the temple in which he officiates with all its apparatus, the offering of blood which he makes, and his official duties as a priest, are all spiritual, heavenly, elevated above all the corresponding things in the Jewish dispensation, to which the Jew adhered with so strong an attachment, and by which he was tempted to make defection from his Christian profession, is peculiarly *ad hominem*. We who are not Jews, and who have never felt the power of their prejudices, need not, in order to produce in us a conviction of the importance of Christianity, to be addressed with comparisons drawn from ritual types, and from the analogy of such objects. But these were all familiar to the Jew, and were not only attractive to him, but, in his view, of the highest importance. No one, indeed, can reasonably find fault, that the writer addresses the Jews *as such*; reasons with them *as such*; and makes use of those arguments, whether *ad hominem* or *ex concessis*, which he knew would produce the most powerful effect in persuading them to hold fast the truths of Christianity. There is nothing in this, which is inconsistent with the maxim of that apostle, who became " all things to all men ;"

with the Jews, demeaning himself, and reasoning as a Jew, and in like manner with the Gentiles, in order that he might win both to Christianity.

But it is not my object, here, to defend the *manner* of argumentation employed in Paul's acknowledged epistles, and in the epistles to the Hebrews. I design merely to show, (what cannot be denied,) that the same method of reasoning from sentiments and objects presented by the Old Testament, is exhibited by both, and in a manner which cannot well escape the attention of the inquisitive reader.

I will only ask now, What other writers of the New Testament have exhibited the traits of composition, which I have noted under this head, in the same degree, or with the same frequency? Nay, I venture to affirm, that there is scarcely an approximation, in any of their writings, to those of Paul, either in regard to the frequency or the latitude of the usage in question.

But it may be said, " This only shows, that these other writers named were not the authors of the epistle to the Hebrews ; not that Paul wrote this epistle."

It seems to me, however, to go somewhat further. It proves that the characteristics peculiar to Paul's epistles and to the epistle to the Hebrews, were not the general or universal characteristics of writers of that age ; and, of course, that either Paul, or one who had drunk in deeply of his doctrine and manner, must have written the epistle in question.

(3.) *The manner of Paul's reasoning, in respect to separating his premises from his conclusion, or his protasis from his epitasis, bears a striking resemblance to that which is found in the epistle to the Hebrews.*

The peculiarity I have in view, is the enthymeme or imperfect form of syllogism, and unfinished sentences and comparisons ; which, it has been often observed, are characteristic of Paul's mode of writing. He states the major, or major and minor terms, of a syllogism ; or the first parts of a sentence or comparison ; and then, leaving it in this unfinished state, he turns aside to illustrate or confirm some hint, which was suggested to his mind by what he had stated ; or some train of thought is introduced, to which the natural association of ideas would lead ; and after descanting on this, he returns, and with, or without, repeating his proposition or sentence at first commenced, presents in full the conclusion, or epitasis, which is required to complete it.

§ 22. INTERNAL EVIDENCE. 135

A striking example of this occurs in Rom. v. 12—18. " Wherefore," says he, " as by one man sin entered the world, and death by sin; and so death passed upon all men, in that all have sinned," ver. 12. The premises being thus stated, he turns aside to descant on the universality of sin, its pernicious consequences, and the salutary effects of the blessing which is proffered by Christ; and it is not until he reaches the 18th verse of the chapter, that the proposition which he had commenced is repeated, and the conclusion fully brought out, where it is thus stated: " Therefore, as by one offence, condemnation came upon all men; so, by the obedience of one, the blessing of justification unto life comes upon all men."

So in Rom. ii. 6, Paul says, " Who [God] will render to every man according to his works;" and after nine verses of explanatory matter, which was suggested by the mention of *rendering to every man according to his works*, he adds, at last, the remainder of the sentence which he had begun, viz. " in the day when the secret doings of men shall be judged by Jesus Christ, according to the gospel which I preach," Rom. ii. 16.

So in Eph. iii. 1, the apostle says, " For this cause, I Paul, the prisoner of Jesus Christ for you Gentiles;" then, leaving the sentence thus commenced, he proceeds on, twelve verses, with thoughts suggested by the mention of his being a messenger to the Gentiles; and, finally, in the 13th verse, he adds the conclusion of the sentence commenced in the first, viz. " I desire that ye faint not at my tribulations for you, which is your glory."

In the same way has the writer of the epistle to the Hebrews constructed some of his reasonings and sentences. In Heb. iv. 6, he says, " Seeing, then, it remains that some should enter into [the rest,] and they to whom the good tidings were formerly proclaimed, did not enter in through unbelief—;" the sentence is then suspended, until the writer introduces another quotation from the Psalms, and reasons upon it, in order to prove that the rest in question could not have been such a rest as the land of Canaan proffered. After this, and in the 9th verse, we have the concluding part of the sentence or syllogism, viz. " there remaineth then a rest for the people of God." How entirely this coincides with the Pauline manner above exhibited, must strike the mind of every one who considers it.

So in Heb. v. 6, the writer introduces the divine appointment of Christ as a priest after the order of Melchisedek, with a design to show

§ 22. INTERNAL EVIDENCE.

that this was an appointment of the most *solemn* nature, and of a higher order than that of the Jewish priests. He then suspends the consideration of this topic, and introduces another, in verses 7—9; after which he resumes the former topic. But no sooner does he do this, than he turns aside once more, in order to descant upon the difficulties which present themselves in the way of an ample discussion of it. These result from the very imperfect state of religious knowledge among those whom he addresses, verses 11—14; the criminality and danger of which state he dwells upon at large, in chap. vi. intermixing threats and encouragements. It is not until we come to chap. vii. 1, that the subject of Melchisedek's priesthood is resumed ; where it is treated of, at full length.

So in Heb. ix. 7, the writer says, that " the Jewish high-priest entered into the holy place, once in each year, with the blood of victims, in order to make atonement." This is designed as one member of a comparison ; but the other member follows only in ix. 12, after descanting on several matters suggested by what the writer had stated. There the antithesis is stated, viz. " Jesus, the high-priest of future blessings, entered the sanctuary of the temple not made with hands, with his own blood accomplishing eternal redemption," ix. 12.

Such is the suspended connexion here, even if we adopt that method of interpretation which will make it as close as possible. But an attentive consideration of the whole preceding context, will perhaps render it probable to the attentive reader, that Heb. ix. 11, may be the antithesis of the latter part of viii. 4, and first part of viii. 5 ; where the ὑπόδειγμα and σκιὰ τῶν ἐπουρανίων, are in contrast with the μελλόντων ἀγαθῶν and the μείζονος καὶ τελειοτέρας σκηνῆς, οὐ χειροποιήτου, of ix. 11.

How much such suspensions resemble the manner of Paul, need not be again insisted on. Instances of this nature might easily be increased; but no attentive critical reader can help observing them, as they abound in the epistle to the Hebrews.

The instances above produced may serve to show, that, as to *form* and *method*, in regard either to general arrangement, or the deducing of arguments from the Old Testament, or the exhibition of a peculiar manner in the statement of these arguments, there is a striking similarity between the acknowledged writings of Paul and the epistle to the Hebrews.

To the method of argument which I have thus far employed, in order to show the probability that Paul wrote the epistle to the Hebrews, some objections have been, and may be, raised.

§ 23. INTERNAL EVIDENCE.

It may be asked, " Did not Paul's hearers, disciples, and intimate friends, who travelled with him, daily conversed with him, and for years heard his instructions, cherish the same views of doctrine that he did? And in writing the epistle to the Hebrews, might not an attentive hearer of Paul, and a reader of his epistles, exhibit the same sentiments? And further; if the same general manner, in which the contents of his epistle are arranged, or the contents of some of them, be found in the epistles to the Hebrews; or if the particular manner in which he quotes or employs passages of tha Jewish Scriptures, or interprets them; or if even his method of stating arguments, and employing imperfect syllogisms or sentences, be found in this epistle; still, may not some favourite disciple of his, some devoted follower and successful imitator of his manner, be naturally supposed to have derived all this from hearing him, and reading his letters? And how, then, can arguments of this nature *prove* that Paul wrote the epistle in question?

Prove it, in the way of demonstration, they certainly cannot; nor is this the purpose for which they are adduced. But of this, more hereafter. At present, I merely observe, that the force of these objections is very much diminished, if in comparing the epistle to the Hebrews with the writings of Paul, it shall appear, that not the strain of sentiment only; nqt merely the general arrangement of the contents of the epistle, or the particular manner of it in respect to various ways of reasoning, or constructing syllogisms and sentences; but even the *idiomatical* and *distinctive style* and *diction* itself of Paul abound in it. These, none but a writer that was a mere copyist or plagiarist could exhibit. But such a writer is one of the last men who can be justly suspected of having composed an epistle like that to the Hebrews.

These suggestions naturally lead us, in the next place, to a comparison, in respect to *phraseology* and *words*, between the acknowledged writings of Paul, and the epistle to the Hebrews.

§ 23. *Comparison of the phraseology and diction of the epistle to the Hebrews, and the acknowledged epistles of Paul.*

1. The similarity of phraseology and diction, where the same words or synonymous ones, are employed; or where the shade of thought or representation is peculiar and homogeneous, although the language may be somewhat diverse.

Heb. i. 2. Δι' οὗ ['Ιησοῦ Χριστοῦ] καὶ τοὺς αἰῶνας [Θεὸς] ἐποίησε.

Eph. iii. 9. Τῷ [Θεῷ] τὰ πάντα κτίσαντι διὰ 'Ιησοῦ Χριστοῦ.

§ 23. INTERNAL EVIDENCE.

Heb. i. iii. Ὃς ὢν ἀπαύγασμα τῆς δόξης καὶ χαρακτὴρ τῆς ὑποστάσεως αὐτοῦ.
Col. i. 15. Ὅς ἐστιν εἰκὼν τοῦ Θεοῦ τοῦ ἀοράτου.
Phil. ii. 6. Ὃς ἐν μορφῇ Θεοῦ ὑπάρχων.
2 Cor. iv. 4. Ὅς ἐστιν εἰκὼν τοῦ Θεοῦ.
Heb. i. 3. Φέρων τε τὰ πάντα τῷ ῥήματι τῆς δυνάμεως αὐτοῦ.
Col i. 17. Τὰ πάντα ἐν αὐτῷ συνέστηκε.

Heb. i. 5. Υἱὸς μου εἶ σύ, ἐγὼ σήμερον γεγέννηκά σε.
Acts xiii. 33. Υἱὸς μου εἶ σύ, ἐγὼ σήμερον γεγέννηκά σε; used here by Paul, and applied in both passages (but nowhere else in the New Testament) to Christ.

Heb. i. 4. Τοσούτῳ κρείττων γενόμενος τῶν ἀγγέλων, ὅσῳ διαφορώτερον παρ' αὐτοὺς κεκληρονόμηκεν ὄνομα.
Eph. i. 21. Ὑπεράνω ...... παντὸς ὀνόματος ὀνομαζομένου οὐ μόνον ἐν τῷ αἰῶνι τούτῳ, ἀλλὰ καὶ ἐν τῷ μέλλοντι.
Phil. ii. 9. Ὁ Θεὸς ...... ἐχαρίσατο αὐτῷ ὄνομα τὸ ὑπὲρ πᾶν ὄνονα ἵνα ἐν τῷ ὀνόματι Ἰησοῦ πᾶν γόνυ κάμψῃ ἐπουρανίων, κ. τ. λ

Heb. i. 6. Τὸν πρωτότοκον ......
Rom. vii. 29. Εἰς τὸ εἶναι αὐτὸν τὸν πρωτότοκον.
Col. i. 15. Πρωτότοκος πάσης κτίσεως. V. 18. Πρωτότοκος. This appellation is applied to Christ nowhere else, excepting in Rev. i. 5.

Heb. ii. 2. Ὁ δι' ἀγγέλων λαληθεὶς λόγος.
Gal. iii. 19. Ὁ νόμος....διαταγεὶς δι' ἀγγέλων. Comp. Acts vii. 53.
Here is the same sentiment, λόγος and νόμος being synonymes; as, for substance, λαληθεὶς and διαταγείς are. However, Stephen once uses a similar expression, Acts vii. 53.

Heb. ii. 4. Σημείοις τε καὶ τέρασι, καὶ ποικίλαις δυνάμεσι, καὶ πνεύματος ἁγίου μερισμοῖς.
1 Cor. xii. 4. Διαιρέσεις δὲ χαρισμάτων εἰσί, τὸ δὲ αὐτὸ πνεῦμα.
1 Cor. xii. 11. Πάντα δὲ ταῦτα ἐνέργει τὸ ἓν καὶ τὸ αὐτὸ πνεῦμα, διαιροῦν ἰδίᾳ ἑκάστῳ καθὼς βούλεται.
Rom. xii. 6. Ἔχοντες δὲ χαρίσματα κατὰ τὴν χάριν τὴν δοθεῖσαν ἡμῖν διάφορα ...... all spoken of the miraculous gifts of the Holy Spirit,

§ 23. INTERNAL EVIDENCE. 139

and characterized by the same shade of thought, viz. the *various* or *different gifts* of this nature distributed by him.

Heb. ii. 8. Πάντα ὑπέταξας ὑποκάτω τῶν ποδῶν αὐτοῦ.
1 Cor. xv. 27. Πάντα γὰρ ὑπέταξεν ὑπὸ τοὺς πόδας αὐτοῦ.
Eph, i. 22. Καὶ πάντα ὑπέταξεν ὑπὸ τοὺς πόδας αὐτοῦ.
Phil. iii. 21. Ὑποτάξαι ἑαυτῷ τὰ πάντα ...... phraseology applied to designate the sovereignty conferred upon Christ, and found only in Paul and in our epistle.

Heb. ii. 10. Δι᾿ ὃν τὰ πάντα, καὶ δι᾿ οὗ τὰ πάντα.
Rom. xi. 36. Ἐξ αὐτοῦ, καὶ δι᾿ αὐτοῦ, καὶ εἰς αὐτὸν τὰ πάντα.
Col. i. 16. Τὰ πάντα δι᾿ αὐτοῦ καὶ εἰς αὐτόν.
1 Cor. viii. 6. Εἷς Θεὸς....ἐξ οὗ τὰ πάντα· καὶ εἷς Κύριος....δι᾿ οὗ τὰ πάντα .... a method of expression, employed to designate God as the author of all things, and also the lord and possessor of them, which is appropriate to Paul, and to our epistle.

Heb. ii. 14. Ἵνα .... καταργήσῃ τὸν τὸ κράτος ἔχοντα τοῦ θανάτου, τοῦτ᾿ ἔστι τὸν διάβολον.
2 Tim. i. 10. Καταργήσαντος μὲν τὸν θάνατον. Καταργέω, employed in the sense of *abolishing*, *rendering null*, is exclusively Pauline. No other writer of the New Testament employs it at all, except Luke; and he but once, and then in a quite different sense from that attached to it by Paul, Luke xiii. 7.

Heb. ii. 16. Σπέρματος Ἀβραὰμ, to designate Christians.
Gal. iii. 29. Εἰ δὲ ὑμεῖς Χριστοῦ, ἄρα τοῦ Ἀβραὰμ σπέρμα ἐστέ.
Gal. iii. 7. Οἱ ἐκ πίστεως, οὗτοι εἰσιν υἱοὶ Ἀβραάμ.
Rom. iv. 16. Ἀβραὰμ, ὅς ἐστι πατὴρ πάντων ἡμῶν.
The appellation, *seed* or *sons of Abraham*, applied to designate Christians, is found only in Paul and in our epistle.

Heb. iii. 1. Κλήσεως ἐπουρανίου.
Phil. iii. 14. Τῆς ἄνω κλήσεως τοῦ Θεοῦ.
Rom. xi. 29. Ἡ κλῆσις τοῦ Θεοῦ. The phrase *heavenly* or *divine calling*, applied to designate the proffered mercies of the gospel, is limited to Paul and to our epistle.

Heb. iv. 12. Ζῶν γὰρ ὁ λόγος τοῦ Θεοῦ .... καὶ τομώτερος, ὑπὲρ πᾶσαν μάχαιραν δίστομον.

§ 23. INTERNAL EVIDENCE.

Eph. vi. 17. Τὴν μάχαιραν τοῦ πνεύματος, ὅ ἐστι ῥῆμα Θεοῦ. The comparison of the word of God to a sword, is found only in Paul and in our epistle.

Heb. v. 8. Καίπερ ὢν υἱὸς, ἔμαθεν ἀφ' ὧν ἔπαθε τὴν ὑπακοήν.
Phil. ii. 8. Ἐταπείνωσεν ἑαυτὸν, γενόμενος ὑπήκοος, μέχρι θανάτου. The idea of *obedience* in the *humiliation and sufferings* of Christ, constitutes the speciality and the similitude of these two passages.

Heb. v. 13. Νήπιος γὰρ ἐστι, i. e. *a child in religion, comparatively ignorant, uninformed..*
1 Cor. iii. 1. Ὡς νηπίοις ἐν Χριστῷ, in the same sense.
Eph. iv. 14. Ἵνα μηκέτι ὦμεν νήπιοι, in the same.
Rom. ii. 20. Διδάσκαλον νηπίων, in the same.
Gal. iv. 3. Ὅτε ἦμεν νήπιοι, in the same. This phraseology is limited to Paul and to our epistle.

Heb. v. 14. Τελείων δὲ ἐστιν ἡ στερεὰ τροφή.
1 Cor. xiv. 20. Ταῖς δὲ φρεσὶ τέλειοι γίνεσθε. The word τέλειοι is here the antithesis of νήπιοι, and means *well instructed, mature.* In this sense, it is employed only in Paul and in our epistle.

Heb. vi. 1. Τελειότητα, *an advanced, mature state,* i. e. of Christian knowledge.
Col. iii. 14. Σύνδεσμος τῆς τελειότητος, *the bond* or *cement of a matured Christian state.* The word τελειότης, in such a sense, is limited to Paul and to our epistle.

Heb. vi. 3. Ἐάνπερ ἐπιτρέπῃ ὁ Θεὸς.
1 Cor. xvi. 7. Ἐὰν ὁ Κύριος ἐπιτρέπῃ ...... a phrase no where else employed.

Heb. vi. 10. Τῆς ἀγάπης ἧς ἐνεδείξασθε εἰς τὸ ὄνομα αὐτοῦ, διακονήσαντες τοῖς ἁγίοις καὶ διακονοῦντες.
2 Cor. viii. 24. Τὴν οὖν ἔνδειξιν τῆς ἀγάπης ὑμῶν .... εἰς αὐτοὺς ἐνδείξασθε. The similarity consists in employing ἐνδείξασθαι τὴν ἀγάπην in both cases, constructed with εἰς before the object that follows.
Heb. viii. 5. Οἵτινες ὑποδείγματι καὶ σκιᾷ λατρεύουσι τῶν ἐπουρανίων.
Heb. x. 1. Σκιὰν γὰρ ἔχων ὁ νόμος τῶν μελλόντων.
Col. ii. 17. Ἅ ἐστι σκιὰ τῶν μελλόντων .... language respecting the

§ 23. INTERNAL EVIDENCE. 141

figurative nature of the Jewish dispensation, which is appropriate to Paul and to our epistle.

Heb. viii. 6. Κρείττονός έστι διαθήκης μεσίτης.
1 Tim. ii. 5. Εἶς μεσίτης .... Χριστὸς Ἰησοῦς.
Gal. iii. 19, 20. Ἐν χειρὶ μεσίτου. Ὁ δὲ μεσίτης ἑνὸς οὐκ ἔστι·
The word *mediator*, applied to designate Christ or Moses, is appropriate to Paul and to our epistle.

Heb. viii. 10. Καὶ ἔσομαι αὐτοῖς εἰς θεὸν, καὶ αὐτοὶ ἔσονταί μοι εἰς λαὸν.
2 Cor. vi. 16. Καὶ ἔσομαι αὐτῶν θεὸς, καὶ αὐτοὶ ἔσονταί μοι λαὸς.
Both passages are quoted from the Old Testament. The resemblance consists in the quotation and application of the same passage in both places, and in the same manner.

Heb. viii. 10. Καὶ ἐπὶ καρδίας αὐτῶν ἐπιγράψω αὐτοὺς.
Rom. ii. 15. Τὸ ἔργον τοῦ νόμου γραπτὸν ἐν ταῖς καρδίαις αὐτῶν.
2 Cor. iii. 3. Ἐγγεγραμμένη .... ἐν πλαξὶ καρδίας σαρκίναις.
The passage in Hebrews is a quotation. But the other passages serve to show that such a phraseology was familiar to Paul, and that he probably derived it from the Old Testament passage, quoted in Heb. viii. 10.

Heb. ix. 15. Θανάτου γενομένου εἰς ἀπολύτρωσιν τῶν ἐπὶ τῇ πρώτῃ διαθήκῃ παραβάσεων.
Rom. iii. 25. Διὰ τῆς ἀπολυτρώσεως .... εἰς ἔνδειξιν τῆς δικαιοσύνης αὐτοῦ, διὰ τὴν πάρεσιν τῶν προγεγονότων ἁμαρτημάτων.
In these two passages the peculiar idea is expressed, that the efficacy of Christ's atoning blood extends back to past ages; an idea nowhere else brought to view in the same manner.

Heb. x. 19. Ἔχοντες .... παῤῥησίαν εἰς τὴν εἴσοδον τῶν ἁγίων ἐν τῷ αἵματι Ἰησοῦ.
Rom. v. 2. Δἰ οὗ τὴν προσαγωγὴν ἐσχήκαμεν τῇ πίστει εἰς τὴν χάριν ταύτην.
Eph. ii. 18. Δἰ αὐτοῦ ἔχομεν τὴν προσαγωγὴν .... πρὸς τὸν πατέρα.
Eph. iii. 12. Ἐν ᾧ ἔχομεν τὴν παῤῥησίαν καὶ τὴν προσαγωγὴν ἐν πεποιθήσει.
The idea of *access* to God, or παῤῥησία, bold, *free access*, or *liberty of address*, is designated in this manner only by Paul and in our epistle.

Heb. x. 28. Ἐπὶ δυσὶν ἢ τρισὶ μάρτυσιν ἀποθνήσκει.
2 Cor. xiii. 1. Ἐπὶ στόματος δύο μαρτύρων καὶ τριῶν σταθήσεται πᾶν ῥῆμα.
1. Tim. v. 19. Ἐπὶ δύο ἢ τριῶν μαρτύρων. Such an expression is found elsewhere, only in the words of Christ, Matt. xviii. 16.

Heb. x. 30. Ἐμοὶ ἐκδίκησις, ἐγὼ ἀνταποδώσω.
Rom. xii. 19. Ἐμοὶ ἐκδίκησις, ἐγὼ ἀνταποδώσω.

The similarity consists in quoting the same passage, and applying it to show that punishment is the awful prerogative of the Deity, and that he will inflict it.

Heb. x. 32. Ἄθλησιν.... τῶν παθημάτων.
Phil. i. 30. Τὸν αὐτὸν ἀγῶνα ἔχοντες, οἷον εἴδετε ἐν ἐμοί.
Col. ii. 1. Ἡλίκον ἀγῶνα ἔχω περὶ ὑμῶν.
1 Thess. ii. 2. Ααλῆσαι.... τὸ εὐαγγέλιον.... ἐν πολλῷ ἀγῶνι.

The phrase *contest*, in respect to afflictions, is peculiar to Paul and to our epistle.

Heb. x. 33. Ὀνειδισμοῖς τε καὶ θλίψεσι θεατριζόμενοι.
1. Cor. iv. 9. Θέατρον ἐγενήθημεν τῷ κόσμῳ, κ. τ. λ......language peculiar to Paul and to our epistle.

Heb. x. 33. Κοινωνοὶ τῶν οὕτως ἀναστρεφομένων γενηθέντες, *participating*, i. e. *sympathising* with the afflicted.
Phil. iv. 14. Συγκοινωνήσαντές μου τῇ θλίψει, *sympathising in my affliction*. The same figurative expression stands in both passages.

Heb. x. 38. Ὁ δὲ δίκαιος ἐκ πίστεως ζήσεται.
Rom. i. 17. Ὁ δὲ δίκαιος ἐκ πίστεως ζήσεται.
Gal. ii. 11. Ὅτι ὁ δίκαιος ἐκ πίστεως ζήσεται.

The passage is a quotation. But the application, and use of it, appear to be exclusively Pauline.

Heb. xii. 1. Τρέχωμεν τὸν προκείμενον ἡμῖν ἀγῶνα.
1 Cor. ix. 24. Οὕτω τρέχετε ἵνα καταλάβητε.
Phil. iii. 14. Τὰ μὲν ὀπίσω ἐπιλανθανόμενος, τοῖς δὲ ἔμπροσθεν ἐπεκτεινόμενος, κατὰ σκοπὸν διώκω.

The resemblance here is, that Christian efforts are, in each passage,

§ 23. INTERNAL EVIDENCE. 143

compared to *a race*; a comparison found only in Paul and in our epistle.

Heb. xiii. 18. Πεποίθαμεν γὰρ, ὅτι καλὴν συνείδησιν ἔχομεν.
Acts xxiii. 1. Paul says, Ἐγὼ πάσῃ συνειδήσει ἀγαθῇ πεπολίτευμαι....
a manner of speaking found nowhere else.

Heb. xiii. 20. Ὁ δὲ Θεὸς τῆς εἰρήνης.
Rom. xv. 33. Ὁ δὲ Θεὸς τῆς εἰρήνης. Also in Rom. xvi. 20. 1 Cor. xiv. 33. 2 Cor. xiii. 11. Phil. iv. 9. 1 Thess. v. 23. An expression used by no other writer of the New Testament.

Heb. xiii. 18. Προσεύχεσθε περὶ ἡμῶν.
1 Thess. v. 25. Προσεύχεσθε περὶ ἡμῶν.
Natural as this may appear at the close of a letter, it is peculiar to Paul and to our epistle.

To the instances of phraseology thus collected, may be added the greeting and benediction at the close of the epistle to the Hebrews, which is altogether Pauline.

II. Words which are found, among the New Testament writers, only in Paul and in our epistle ; or, if found elsewhere, are used in a sense different from that in which they are here employed.

Ἀγὼν, in the sense of *Christian effort*, either in performing duties, or bearing trials, Heb. xii. 1. 1 Tim. vi. 12. 2 Tim. iv. 7.

Ἀδελφοὶ, *brethren of Christ*, considered in respect to his human nature, Heb. ii. 12, 17. Rom. viii. 29.

Ἀδόκιμος, *inept, unfit*, Heb. vi. 8. Tit. i. 16.

Αἰδὼς, *reverence, modesty*, Heb. xii. 28. 1 Tim. ii. 9.

Αἱρέομαι, *to choose*, Heb. xi. 25. 2 Thess. ii. 13. Phil. i. 22.

Ἄκακος, *innocent*, Heb. vii. 26. Rom. xvi. 18.

Ἀσθένεια, *sin, sinful infirmity*, Heb. v. 2. Rom. v. 6.

Διαθήκη, *will, testament*, Heb. ix. 16. Gal. iii. 15. It is doubtful, however, whether διαθήκη has the sense of *testament*, in the latter passage.

Ἐλπὶς προκεκειμένη, *proffered Christian happiness*, Heb. vi. 18. Col. i. 5.

Ἐκλύω, *to be despondent*, Heb. xii. 3. Gal. vi. 9.

Ἐνδυναμόω, *to give strength*; (passively) *to receive strength*, Heb. xi. 34. 2 Tim. iv. 17. 1 Tim. i. 12.

Καταργεῖν, to annul, abolish, abrogate, Heb. ii. 14. Rom. iii. 3, 31 vi. 6. 1 Cor. i. 28. Gal. v. 11, and elsewhere often in Paul's epistles.

Καύχημα, glorifying, rejoicing, Heb. iii. 6. Rom. iv. 2. 1 Cor. ix. 15.

Κληρονόμος, lord, possessor, applied to Christ, Heb. i. 2. Rom. viii. 17.

Λατρεύειν, (δουλεύειν, a synonyme,) Θεῷ ζῶντι, Heb. ix. 14. 1 Thess. i. 9.

Μὴ (οὐ) βλεπόμενα, the invisible objects of the future world, Heb. xi. 1. 2 Cor. iv. 18.

'Ομολογία, religion, religious, or Christian profession, Heb. iii. 1. iv. 14. x. 23. 2 Cor. ix. 13.

"Ονομα, majesty, or dignity, Heb. i. 4. Phil. ii. 9, 10. Eph. i. 21. But although this sense of ὄνομα in Heb. i. 4, is adopted by some eminent critics, still it is more probable that it has the sense of *appellation*; see Heb. i. 5, seq.

Οὐ κτίσις, nothing, Heb. iv. 13. Rom. viii. 39.

Τελειόω, to consummate in happiness, to bestow the reward consequent on finishing a victorious course, Heb. ii. 10. vii. 28. x. 14. Phil. iii. 12.

'Υπόστασις, confidence, Heb. iii. 14. ii. 1. 2 Cor. ix. 4. xi. 17.

'Ιερουσαλὴμ ἐπουράνιος, the abode of the blessed, Heb. xii. 22 ; comp. 'Ιερουσαλὴμ ἄνω, Gal. iv. 26, in the like sense.

III. Peculiarity of *grammatical construction*, in regard to the use of the passive verb, instead of the active.

Thus in Heb. vii. 11, we find the phrase, ὁ λαὸς γὰρ ἐπ' αὐτῇ νενομοθέτητο, *for the people under it* [the Levitical priesthood] *received the law*; where the nominative case of the person who is the *object* (not the *subject*) in the sentence, is joined with the passive of the verb; and this mode of construction is employed, instead of the *active* voice of the same verb, followed by the *dative* of the person who is the *object*; e. g. νενομοθέτητο λαῷ.

The like construction is found in Paul's acknowledged writings. E. g. Rom. iii. 2, ὅτι [αὐτοῖ] ἐπιστεύθησαν τὰ λόγια τοῦ Θεοῦ, *they were intrusted with the oracles of God*, instead of saying, *the oracles of God were ntrusted to them*. Rom. vi. 17—εἰς ὃν παρεδόθητε τύπον διδαχῆς, *into which model of doctrine ye have been delivered*, instead of *which form or model of doctrine was delivered to you*. 1 Tim. i. 11, ὃ ἐπιστεύθην

§ 24. INTERNAL EVIDENCE. 145

ἐγὼ, *with which I was entrusted*, instead of *which was intrusted to me*, ὃ ἐπιστεύθη μοι.

This is a minuteness of grammatical construction, which a copyist of Paul would not be likely either to notice or to imitate. It affords, therefore, the more striking evidence, that all proceeded from the same hand.

Finally, Paul frequently employs an adjective of the neuter gender, in order to designate *generic quality,* instead of using a synonymous noun : e. g. τὸ γνωστὸν, Rom. i. 19 ; τὸ χρηστὸν, Rom. ii. 4 ; τὸ δυνατὸν, Rom. ix. 22 ; τὸ ἀδύνατον, Rom. vii. 3 ; τὸ ἀσθενὲς, 1 Cor. i. 25. Compare τὸ ἀμετάθετον, Heb. vi. 17 ; τὸ φανταζόμενον, Heb. xii. 21 ; τὸ χωλὸν, xii. 13.

§ 24. *Remarks on the Comparisons made in the preceding sections.*

In the first place, without any hesitation, I concede thus much to those critics, who make light of the evidence drawn from such a comparison as has now been made, viz. that no evidence of this nature can ever afford what is equivalent to a *demonstration* of the fact, for the support of which it is adduced. But, then, *demonstration* is what such a case neither admits nor demands. If the writer's name were affixed to the epistle, it would not amount to proof of this kind; for, might it not have been put there by another person, in order to answer some designs of his own? Nay, unless witnesses have given us testimony, who themselves saw Paul write the epistle, the proof is not of the highest kind that is *possible ;* nor even then would their testimony establish the fact, unless we could be well assured of their credibility. By such a criterion, however, the genuineness of no writing, ancient or modern, can be examined. It is *generally* enough for us, that an author's name is affixed to a writing. *Prima facie*, it is evidence that it belongs to him ; and it must be regarded as *sufficient* evidence, until it is contradicted either expressly, or by implication.

Let us suppose now, that, after an author has published many pieces, and his style and sentiments have become well known, he publishes a composition of any kind, without affixing his name to it; can there be no adequate, no *satisfactory* evidence, that it belongs to him ?

This is the very question before us. I grant that *similarity*, or even *sameness* of *sentiment*, in different pieces, does not certainly prove identity of authorship; for the friends, or imitators, or disciples of any distinguished man, may imbibe the same sentiments which he inculcates,

§ 24. INTERNAL EVIDENCE.

and exhibit them in similar words and phrases. I grant that the primitive teachers of Christianity were agreed, and must have been agreed, (supposing that they were under divine guidance,) as to the fundamental doctrines of the gospel. But in respect to the *mode of representing* them; in regard to the style, and diction, and urgency with which particular views of doctrine are insisted on; what can be more various and diverse than the epistles of Paul, and James, and Peter, and John?

The reply to this, by critics who entertain sentiments different from those which I have espoused, is, that " the writer of the epistle to the Hebrews was an intimate friend, or a studious imitator, of Paul; a man of talents, who, with unqualified admiration of the apostle's sentiments, mode of reasoning, and even choice of words, closely imitated him in all these particulars. Hence the similarity between the writings of Paul and the epistle to the Hebrews."

The *possibility* of this cannot be denied. Designed imitation has, in a few instances, been so successful as to deceive, at least for a while, the most sharp-sighted critics. Witness the imitation of Shakspeare which a few years ago was palmed upon the English public, as the work of that distinguished poet himself. Witness also the well-known and long controverted fact, in respect to the pieces ascribed to Ossian, which are now known to be a forgery. But, after all, such attempts have very *seldom* been successful, even where the most strenuous efforts have been made at close imitation; and these, with all the advantages which a modern education could afford. How few, for example, of the multitudes, who have aimed at copying the style of Addison or Johnson with the greatest degree of exactness, have succeeded even in any tolerable measure; and none in such a way, that they are not easily distinguished from the models which they designed to imitate.

Just so it was, in the primitive age of the church. The Christian world was filled with gospels and epistles, ascribed to Paul, and Peter, and other apostles and disciples. Yet no one of these succeeded in gaining any considerable credit among the churches; and what little was ever gained by any of them, proved to be temporary, and of very small influence. This was not owing to want of exertion; for strenuous efforts were made by writers to imitate the apostolic manner of writing, so as to gain credit for their supposititious pieces. But all of them failed. Indeed, nothing can be more egregious, or striking, than the failure. A comparison of any of the *apocryphal* writings of the New Testament, with the *genuine* writings of the same, shows a difference

§ 24. INTERNAL EVIDENCE. 147

heaven-wide between them, which the most undistinguishing intellect can hardly fail to discern.

If, then, the writer of the epistle to the Hebrews was an imitator, a designed and close imitator, of the apostle Paul, he has succeeded, in such a way as no other writer of those times, or any succeeding ones, ever did. He has produced a composition, the sentiments of which, in their shade, and colouring, and proportion, (so far as his *subjects* are common with those in the acknowledged epistles of Paul,) are altogether Pauline. Nay, he has preserved not only the order of writing which Paul adopts; but his mode of reasoning, his phraseology, and even his choice of peculiar words, or words used in a sense peculiar to the apostle. The imitation goes so far, it extends to so many particulars, important and unimportant, that, if our epistle was not written by Paul, it must have been an imitation of him which was the effect of settled design, and was accomplished only by the most strenuous effort.

But here, while I acknowledge the *possibility* of such an imitation, I must, from thorough conviction, say, that the *probability* of it does seem to be very small. With Origen, I must, after often-repeated study of this epistle, say, *The sentiments are wonderful, and in no way behind those of the acknowledged writings of the apostles:* τὰ νοήματα τῆς ἐπιστολῆς θαυμάσιά ἐστι, καὶ οὐ δευτέρα τῶν ἀποστολικῶν ὁμολογουμένων γραμμάτων, Euseb. Hist. Ecc. vi. 25. I cannot find any higher intensity of mind; any more exalted conceptions of the true nature of Christianity, as a *spiritual* religion; any higher views of God and Christ, or of the Christian's privileges and his obligations to believe in, love, and obey the Saviour; any more noble excitements to pursue the Christian course, unawed by the threats and unallured by the temptations of the world; or any so awful representations of the fearful consequences of unbelief, and of defection from Christianity. The man who wrote this epistle, has no marks of a plagiarist, or of an imitator, about him. Nothing can be more free and original than his thoughts, reasonings, and mode of expressing them. It is most evident, that they flow directly and warm from the heart. They are " thoughts that breathe, and words that burn." Where, in all the ancient world, did ever a plagiarist, or an imitator, write in this manner? A man who could form such conceptions in his mind, who could reason, and exhort, in such an impressive and awful manner; has he any need of imitating—even Paul himself? No; it may be said of him, (what Paul, on another occasion, said of himself in comparison with his brethren,) that "he was not a whit behind the very chiefest of the apostles."

Then, how could such a man be concealed, in the first ages of the church, when the memory of those who were very distinguished has been preserved so distinct, and with so much care and reverence, by ecclesiastical tradition? Men, who can write in this manner, cannot remain concealed any where. And the writer of such an epistle, it would seem, must have acted a part not less conspicuous than that of the great apostle of the Gentiles himself.

But antiquity, we are told, has attributed this epistle to distinguished men in the early church; to Clement of Rome, to Luke, or to Barnabas; each of whom is known to have been the warm friend and admirer of Paul.

I know this has been often alleged. But, fortunately, there are extant writings of each of these persons, with which our epistle may be compared; and which serve to show how little foundation there is for such an opinion. But of this, more hereafter. I merely say, at present, that the great body of critics, for some time past, have agreed in rejecting the opinion, which ascribes our epistle to either of the authors just mentioned.

Who, then, did write it, if Paul did not? And what is to be gained, by endeavouring to show the *possibility* that some other person wrote it, when so many circumstances unite in favour of the general voice of the primitive ages, that this apostle was the author? That the church, during the first century after the apostolic age, ascribed it to some one of the apostles, is clear from the fact, that it was inserted among the canonical books of the churches in the East and the West; that it was comprised in the *Peshito;* in the old Latin version; and was certainly admitted by the Alexandrine and Palestine churches. Now, what apostle did write it, if Paul did not? Surely neither John, nor Peter, nor James, nor Jude. The difference of style is too striking, between their letters and this, to admit of such a supposition. But what other apostle, except Paul, was ever distinguished in the ancient church as a writer? None; and the conclusion, therefore, seems to be altogether a probable one, that he was the writer. Why should all the circumstances which speak for him, be construed as relating to some unknown writer? Are the sentiments unworthy of him? Are they opposed to what he has inculcated? Do they differ from what he has taught? Neither. Why not, then, admit the *probability* that he was the author? Nay, why not admit that the probability is as great as the nature of the case (the epistle being anonymous) could be expected to afford? Why should there be any more objection to Paul as the author of this epistle, than to any other man?

My own conviction, if I may be permitted to express it, is as clear in respect to this point, as from its nature I could expect it to be. I began the examination of the subject unbiassed, if I was ever unbiassed in the examination of any question; and the evidence before me has led me to such a *result*.

But the arguments, which are urged against the opinion that I have now endeavoured to defend remain to be examined. They must not be passed over in silence, nor any of them be kept out of sight, to which importance can reasonably be attached.

§ 25. *Objections.*

The objections made to the opinion, that Paul was the author of our epistle, are numerous. All the hints which ancient writers have given, by way of objection, have been brought forward, of late, and urged with great zeal and ability. Arguments internal and external, of every kind, have been insisted on. Indeed, the attack upon the Pauline origin of our epistle has been so warmly and powerfully made, by the last and present generation of critics on the continent of Europe, that most who are engaged in the study of sacred literature, seem inclined to think that the contest is over, and that victory has been won. So much, at least, must be conceded, viz. that those who admit the Pauline origin of this epistle, must make more strenuous efforts than they have yet made, in order to defend their opinion, and to satisfy objectors. To do this, is indeed a most laborious, and in many cases exceedingly repulsive task; for of such a nature are many of the objections, thrown out at random, and asserted with confidence, that an attack which cost but a few moments' effort on the part of the assailant, costs days and weeks of labour, on the part of him who makes the defence.

The question, however, is too important to be slightly treated. ˙ Nor will it suffice for those who defend the Pauline origin of our epistle, merely to select a few specimens of argument on the part of their opponents, and, showing the insufficiency or inaccuracy of these, make their appeal to the reader's sympathies, assuring him, that the rest of the arguments employed by their opponents are of a similar nature. There are readers, (and such are the men whose opinion on subjects of this nature is most to be valued,) who will not be satisfied with cursory, hasty, half-performed examination; and who, when you show them that one or more of an opponent's arguments is unsound, will not believe it to follow, of course, that all of them must be so. Above all, one must expect, that many doubters of the genuineness of our epistle, will not be satisfied with having only one side of the question presented. It is reasonable that they should not; and if the objections, which have weight in their minds, cannot be as satisfactorily answered, as from the nature of the case might be justly expected, then let them have so much weight as is properly due to them.

It is but fair to warn the reader, that in entering on this part of our subject, his patience will be tried, by the length and minuteness of the examination. Perhaps those only, who fully know the present state of critical effort and opinion with respect to the literature of our epistle, will be able to find an adequate apology for such particularity as the sequel exhibits. But such probably will feel, that the time has come, when objections must either be *fully* and *fairly* met, or those who defend the Pauline origin of our epistle must consent to give up their opinion, if they would preserve the character of candour. The present leaning of criticism is strongly against this origin; and it is high time that the subject should receive an ample discussion.

Whether the question at issue has been deeply, fundamentally, and patiently examined, by the principal writers who have given a tone to the present voice of critics, I will not venture either to affirm or to deny. I shall leave it to the reader, when he shall have gone through with an examination of these writers, to speak his own feelings.

§ 26. *Objections by Bertholdt considered.*

Bertholdt has collected and embodied all the objections made by previous writers, which are worthy of particular consideration, in his Introduction to the books of the Old and New Testament. To these he has added some, which apparently were originated by himself. I shall briefly state his objections; subjoining to each, as I proceed, such remarks as the nature of the case may seem to demand.

(1.) " It is a suspicious circumstance, and against the opinion that Paul wrote the epistle to the Hebrews, that he has not subscribed his name; since he says, in 2 Thess. iii. 17, that it was his practice to do this in order to show that letters, purporting to be his, might thus be certainly known as being genuine."

§ 26. OBJECTIONS BY BERTHOLDT. 151

The reply to this is obvious. After Paul had written his first epistle to the Thessalonian church, in which he had mentioned the *second coming* of Christ, it appears that some one had written another letter, counterfeiting his name, in which *the day of the Lord* had been represented as *very near*. On this account, Paul says, in his second letter to the same church, " Be not agitated by any message, or by any epistle as from me, in respect to the day of the Lord, as being already at hand," ii. 2. And then, to avoid the effects of any misrepresentation of this nature, for the future, he says, at the close of the letter, iii. 17, " This salutation from me, Paul, by my own hand. This is the proof [viz. of the genuineness of my letter] in every epistle [i. e. to your church;] so I write."

Let it now be noted, that the epistles to the Thessalonians were the first, in regard to time, which Paul wrote to any church; at least, the first that are now extant. Under circumstances like these, when letters to the Thessalonians had been forged in his name, can the assurance that he subscribes all his letters to them with his own hand, be taken as a proof, that, in all his future life, he should never address an *anonymous* letter to any church, in any circumstances?

(2.) " No good reason can be given why Paul should conceal his name. Does he not intimate, at the close of the letter, that he is yet in prison, but expects soon to be set at liberty? Does he not ask their prayers that he may be speedily restored? And does he not promise them a visit, in company with Timothy, if his return be speedy? Why should Paul attempt to conceal himself, when he has developed circumstances which evidently imply that he was not concealed, and that he did not desire to be so?"

But if this objection be of any validity, it is just as valid in respect to any other person, as to the writer of this letter. Why should any other writer attempt to conceal himself, when most clearly the tenor of the letter implies, that he must be known to those whom he immediately addresses? If there be any incongruity here, it applies just as much to any other writer, as to Paul.

But is there no good reason imaginable, why Paul should have withheld his name? If he designed the epistle to be a *circular* among the Jews generally, (which from the nature of the discussion, comprising topics so interesting to them all, I am altogether inclined to believe was the case,) then might he not, as a measure of prudence, omit prefixing or subscribing his name directly, lest the prejudices of those Christians who were zealots for the law might be excited, on the *first* inspection of his epistle? *Ultimately*, he might be, and must be known, if the letter was traced back to the church to whom it was first sent, and the inquiries made respecting it, which the circumstances mentioned at the close of it would naturally suggest. To this the writer would probably feel no objection; trusting that the arguments suggested in it might disarm prejudiced readers, before they came to the certain knowledge of the author. Is it an unknown, unheard-of case, that men should write letters, anonymously at first, but afterwards avow them? Or that they should write letters, anonymous, but so circumstanced, and designedly so circumstanced, that inquiry might ultimately lead to a knowledge of the author?

Granting, however, that neither the reason of Clement of Alexandria, nor of Eusebius, nor of Jerome, nor the reason now given, for the apostle's withholding his name, is satisfactory; still is there no possibility that adequate reason may have existed for the letter being sent without the subscription of the writer's name, of which reason we are ignorant? Let it be whoever it may, that wrote the letter, does not the same difficulty, in every case, attend the explanation of its being *anonymous*? I can see no difference; unless we assume the position, that the writer meant it should be attributed to an apostle, and therefore concealed his own name. Such a writer, we cannot with any probability suppose the author of our epistle to have been. All—all is sincerity, fervent benevolence, ingenuous and open-hearted dealing, throughout the whole.

Besides, is the case in hand one that has no parallel? Certainly not. The first epistle of John is altogether destitute of the author's name, or of any internal marks that will lead us to know him, except what are contained in the style itself. Why should it be more wonderful, that *Paul* should write an anonymous letter, than that *John* should do it?

(3.) "The Jews of Palestine had a great antipathy to Paul, and always persecuted him, when he came among them. How can it be supposed, that he should have addressed to them a letter, with the expectation that it would be read and regarded by them?"

That some of the zealots for the law, in Judea, were strongly opposed to Paul, is sufficiently evident from the history of his visits to Jerusalem. But, that the apostles and teachers there were his warm and decided friends, is equally evident from the same source. Moreover, that there were private Christians there, who cherished a very friendly feeling toward him, is evident from Acts xxi. 17, where, on his last visit there, *the brethren* (οἱ ἀδελφοὶ) are said *to have received him gladly*. The persetution, which ensued at this time, was first excited, as the historian expressly states, by Jews from Asia Minor, xxi. 27. But it is unnecessary to dwell on this. At Ptolemais, xxi. 7, and at Cesarea, xxi. 8 seq., he had warm friends; and at the latter place, he abode two whole years as a prisoner, before his removal to Rome. Were there no friends of his, then, in *Palestine*, among whom he could hope to find a listening ear? no Christians, on whom he could hope that his arguments would make an impression? And after all, did he ever cease to speak to the Jews, to admonish them, to dispute with them, in order to vindicate the religion which he had embraced, because they were prejudiced against him? How unlike himself, then, does the objection which we are considering represent Paul to be! He did not *confer with flesh and blood;* he believed that the armour in which he was clad, was " mighty, through God, to the pulling down of strong holds."

(4.) " But there is internal evidence, from the style of the epistle to the Hebrews, and from circumstances mentioned in it, which render it impossible to believe that Paul was the author of it."

This objection is a very ancient one. It was felt, as we have seen, by Clement of Alexandria; deeper still, by Origen; and adverted to by Eusebius, and other fathers of the church. It would seem, that there must be some real foundation for an objection, so long, so often, and confidently urged. Late critics have attributed an irresistible power to it. Eichhorn and Bertholdt maintain, that it lies so upon the very face of the whole epistle, that every reader must be impressed with it. So strong, indeed, are their impressions with respect to it, that they seem to require no other argument, in order to satisfy them that Paul could not have written the epistle to the Hebrews.

That there are cases, where the general character of the style of one piece, is so plainly different from another, as to leave no doubt on the mind of a discerning reader that both did not, nay even could not, come from the same pen, certainly cannot be called in question. Who could ever attribute the epistles of John, to Paul, or to Peter, or to James? But, that there are other cases, where the characteristic marks are not so discernible, and about which there may be a great difference of feeling in respect to the style, is well known. For example; the book of Deuteronomy is ascribed by one set of critics, of high acquisitions and refined taste, of great acuteness and discriminating judgment, to Moses as the author, because it betrays every where, as they think, the most indubitable marks of his style and spirit. Another class of critics,

§ 26. OBJECTIONS BY BERTHOLDT.

equally eminent for literary acquisition and discrimination, confidently draw the conclusion, that Moses could not have been the author, from the feeling which they have, on reading it, that it is composed in a manner totally diverse from the style and spirit of Moses.

Just such is the case, in regard to the speech of Elihu, in the book of Job. One party reject it as spurious, because their *critical taste* leads them to do so; and another holds it to be genuine, for the like reason.

Isaiah, too, has met with the same fate. The last 26 chapters are now familiarly called Pseudo-Isaiah, by one party of critics; while another strive to vindicate the whole book as genuine.

Each party is equally confident, and equally satisfied of the validity of their arguments. But what is the humble inquirer to do, in the midst of all these contests of taste and of opinion? How can he trust his *feelings* to decide, with confidence, in a case where the most acute and distinguishing critics differ in respect to the judgment that a critical tact should give? He cannot do it with safety. In what way, then, shall one who examines for himself, be able to arrive at any satisfactory conclusion? My answer, in all such cases, would be, MAKE THE ACTUAL COMPARISON; collate sentiment with sentiment, phrase with phrase, words with words. This is the kind of proof that is *palpable*, and is not left to the uncertain tenor of feeling, excited by mere insulated perusal; a feeling which, in cases where the composition read is in a *foreign* language, must be a very uncertain guide; and which, even in our own vernacular language, not unfrequently misleads us.

Origen, as he avers, found, in the epistle to the Hebrews, the *thoughts* of Paul; but the *words*, he thinks, are better Greek (ἑλληνικώτερα) than the apostle wrote. He, therefore, resorts to the supposition, that a translator had given to it its present Greek costume, who had received the *sentiments* from the mouth of Paul. But Eichhorn does not limit the difference, between the style of this epistle and those of Paul, to the quality of the Greek. " The manner of it," says he, " is more tranquil and logical than that in which Paul with his strong feelings could write. Every thing is arranged in the most exact order. The expression is well rounded, choice, and very clear in the representation which it makes. Paul is altogether different; he is unperiodical, involved, obscure, writes poor Greek, is given to rhapsody and aphorism," Einl. § 260. Bertholdt has repeated the same sentiment, in almost the same words, in his Introduction to this epistle, § 646.

§ 26. OBJECTIONS BY BERTHOLDT.

If I might be allowed to express my own feelings, after having, for many years, annually devoted myself to the explanation of this epistle, translated it with all the care which I could bestow upon it, and minutely weighed every expression and word in it, I should say, that nothing could be more unfortunately chosen, than the epithet, " ruhig," *equable, tranquil, void of excitement,* which these distinguished critics have applied to its style. I appeal to every man's feelings who reads it, and ask, Are there, in the whole book of God, any warnings so awful as here, and expressed with such mighty energy ? Are there any threats of punishment for unbelief, so tremendous and impassioned as those in this epistle ?

Then, as to " every thing being arranged in such exact order," as they aver, " conclusion following conclusion, all in the manner of a good rhetorician ;" the instances above produced, and which might easily be increased, of enthymemes, and suspended construction, exactly in the manner of Paul, may help to judge of this. Moreover, let any one make the attempt to translate this epistle into his own vernacular language, and he will then see whether all is so *well rounded* and *perspicuous,* as these critics represent it to be. I find ellipsis as frequent here, as in Paul's acknowledged writings. Any good translation, that exhibits the supply of these ellipses, and marks them by the common mode in which they are printed, demonstrates this to the eye. Hebraism I find here, as well and as often as in Paul. In short, I cannot but feel, in reading the epistle to the Hebrews, that the writer has reached the very summit of eloquence, and energy, and vivid representation, in many passages of his composition ; and I am constrained to make a similar acknowledgment, in respect to many passages of the known epistles of Paul. I cannot perceive any striking diversity in regard to these characteristics.

To what cause, now, can it be attributed, that feelings so very different, in respect to the character of the style, should arise in the minds of men, when they read the epistle in question ? Two reasons for this, I apprehend, may be given. The first and principal one is, that the main topics of this epistle are so diverse from those generally treated of in the acknowledged epistles of Paul, that they required, of course and from necessity, a variety of words, phrases, and ideas, that either are not common, or are not at all to be found in his other epistles. This I regard as chiefly the ground of the judgment which has so often been passed in respect to *dissimilarity* of style. The other is, that one comes to the reading of this epistle, with his feelings impressed by the circumstance,

§ 26. OBJECTIONS BY BERTHOLDT.

that there is a want of direct evidence about the author; and consequently so tuned, as to be strongly agitated by any thing, which may seem to increase or diminish the probability that Paul was the author of it. That the doctrinal views, contained in this epistle, have made many willing to get rid of its canonical authority, if it could be done, is not by any means improbable. After all, however, in a question where there is such a difference of sentiment in regard to style, among those who are capable of judging, the appeal must be made, and can be made, only to *actual comparison.* Such an appeal I have endeavoured to make. To array mere *feeling* or *apprehension*, arising from the perusal of the epistle, against *actual comparison*, can never be to judge by making use of the best means of judging. Origen's authority, in this case, cannot go far with any one who chooses to examine and decide for himself. Origen, with all his talents and learning, was far enough from being a Cicero or a Quintilian, in respect to taste and nice discernment of differences of style. He makes assertions equally confident, in other cases, that will not bear the test of examination; and assertions, too, that have respect to the Greek language, his mother tongue. For example, he says that the want of the article before θεὸς, in John i. 1, proves that the writer cannot have meant to designate the *supreme God* by this word. Now, whether the supreme God be meant, or not, can never be determined by such a rule; for it is usual, in the Greek language, that the *predicate* of a proposition should be without the article, while the *subject* commonly has it. Moreover, in the very same chapter, θεὸς stands without the article, in more than one instance, incontrovertibly, for the supreme God; e. g. in verses 6. 12, 13. 18. Whether Origen's opinion, then, about the style of the epistle to the Hebrews, is well founded or not, is a proper subject of *examination.* The result of comparison has shown, that in respect to sentiment, phraseology, and diction, the epistle is filled with the peculiarities of Paul. I doubt whether any one of Paul's acknowledged epistles, compared with the others, will supply more, or more exact resemblances.

I know, indeed, that no critic can be argued out of feelings of this sort in respect to style. But he may reasonably be called upon to state the ground of those feelings; specially so, when he asserts, with a confidence which is intended to influence others, that the style of the epistle to the Hebrews cannot be Paul's.

(5.) But Bertholdt has made the appeal to *fact.* He has produced words and expressions which, he says, " are not Pauline, and which

§ 26. OBJECTIONS BY BERTHOLDT.

serve satisfactorily to show, that Paul could not have written the epistle to the Hebrews." I proceed to examine them.

(a) In Hebrews xiii. 7. 17. 24, the word ἡγούμενοι is used for *teachers ;* Paul *every where* employs the word διδάσκαλοι for this purpose," p. 2937.

The allegation, that Paul *every where* uses the word διδάσκαλοι to designate *teachers*, is far from being correct. He uses, besides this, the words πρεσβύτερος, 1 Tim. v. 1. 17. 19 ; Tit. i. 5 ; ἐπίσκοπος, Acts xx. 28 ; Phil. i. 1 ; 1 Tim. iii. 2 ; Tit. i. 7 ; ποιμὴν, Eph. iv. 11. Very natural for Paul it must have been, to apply a variety of appellations to Christian ministers, which would correspond with those applied to religious teachers in the Jewish synagogues. These were פַּרְנָס, *pastor, leader, guide, prefect ;* מַנְהִיג, *leader, guide ;* נָגִיד, *ruler, prefect ;* and אַלּוּף, *guide, director.* What could be more natural, then, than for Paul, when writing to Hebrews, to call the teachers in their churches ἡγούμενοι, which corresponds quite well with all of the above appellations, that they had been accustomed to give to their religious teachers ? Besides, the argument of Bertholdt, if admitted, would prove too much. The same mode of reasoning must lead us to conclude, that those epistles, in which Christian teachers are called ἐπίσκοποι, cannot be reckoned as Paul's, because διδάσκαλοι is not used instead of ἐπίσκοποι. The same may be said, in respect to the use of the words ποιμένες and πρεσβύτεροι. The consequence would be, that several of Paul's now acknowledged epistles could not be ascribed to him. But who, that knows the variety of appellations employed to designate teachers in the Jewish synagogues, can attribute any critical weight to the fact, that such a variety of Greek terms is used, corresponding with the Hebrew appellations that were familiar to those whom our author addressed ? And of all these Greek names of pastors, certainly, none better corresponds with the Hebrew ones, than the word ἡγούμενοι, employed in our epistle.

It may be added, too, that Paul employed a term here, not at all *unique ;* for the same appellation is given to teachers, in Luke xxii. 26 ; Acts xiv. 12 ; xv. 22.

(b) " In the epistle to the Hebrews, κατέχειν βεβαίαν is used for *holding fast,* Heb. iii. 6. 14 ; and κατέχειν ἀκλινῆ, in Heb. x. 23 ; while Paul uses only κατέχειν simply, 1 Cor. xi. 2 ; xv. 2 ; 1 Thess. v. 21."

On examination, I find the verb κατέχω, in the sense of *holding fast, carefully retaining,* to be exclusively *Pauline.* This word, then, affords an argument, to establish a conclusion, the reverse of that for which it is adduced by Bertholdt. The addition of βεβαίαν or ἀκλινῆ is evidently for the purpose merely of *intensity* ; just as we may join an adverb to a verb for this purpose, or we may refrain from the use of it, and still employ the same verb simply in the same sense. What could be more natural, now, than for the writer of the epistle to the Hebrews to employ words of intensity, while in the state of strongly excited feeling in which he wrote ?

(c) " In the epistle to the Hebrews, we find εἰς τὸ διηνεκὲς, vii. 3, and εἰς τὸ παντελὲς, vii. 25, used to designate the idea of *for ever ;* while Paul always uses εἰς τοὺς αἰῶνας."

Our author also employs αἰών, in the epistle to the Hebrews, no less than nine times in the like way; viz. i. 8 ; v. 6 ; vi. 20 ; vii. 17. 21. 24. 28 ; xiii. 8. 21. Is it a matter of wonder, then, that he should sometimes employ other words for the same purpose, which were synonymous ; specially, if those words belonged both to common and to Hebrew Greek ? Such is the fact, in respect to both the words in question. Διηνεκὲς is used by Ælian, Var. Hist. i. 19 ; by Appian, Bell. Civ. i. p. 682 ; Heliod. Ethiop. i. p. 25. Lucian, V. H. i. 19 ; by Symmachus, translator of the Hebrew Scriptures into Greek, Ps. xlviii. 15. Παντελὲς is used by Ælian, vii. 2 ; xii. 20 ; by Josephus, Antiq. vi. 2, 3 ; and by Luke, xiii. 11.

But whether the sense of the word παντελὲς, in Heb. vii. 25, is *for ever*, may be doubted. Its etymology would lead to the sense of *prorsus, omnino*, i. e. *entirely, altogether, thoroughly ;* and so, many critics have construed it. Such is clearly the meaning of παντελῶς, e. g. Jos. Antiq. iv. 6, 5 ; 2 Macc. iii. 12. 31 ; vii. 40 ; and so Bretschneider construes εἰς τὸ παντελὲς, in Heb. vii. 25, in his recent Lexicon.

But supposing it does mean *for ever*, in the case before us, can the argument, derived from the employment of such synonymes with εἰς τοὺς αἰῶνας, as belong to common and to Hebrew Greek, be of any validity to show that Paul could not have written our epistle ?

(d) " Αἰῶνες, in the sense of *universe*, is used only in the epistle to the Hebrews, i. 2 ; xi. 3. Paul employs other terms to designate the same idea, such as τὰ πάντα, &c."

Paul, in the phrase τῷ βασιλεῖ τῶν αἰώνων, 1 Tim. i. 17, has employed the word in the same sense as it is used in the epistle to the Hebrews ; and, as the use of the word αἰὼν, in such a sense is limited to Paul and to our epistle, so far as the New Testament is concerned, it would seem to prove the reverse of what Bertholdt has adduced it to establish.

§ 26. OBJECTIONS BY BERTHOLDT.

(e) "The word πίστις is *always* used by Paul, in the *restricted* sense of πίστις εἰς Ἰησοῦν Χριστὸν ; in the epistle to the Hebrews, it is employed in a much wider latitude." So Bertholdt, p. 2939; and to the same purpose Eichhorn Einlet. p. 462. This objection has been repeated, greatly magnified, and dwelt upon, by Schulz, *Brief an die Hebrüer*, p. 112, seq.; and by Seyffarth, *de Epist. ad Heb. indole*, § 33. These latter writers represent πίστις, when used by Paul, as always having reference to Christ or the Christian religion, as such; whereas πίστις, in our epistle, relates, they aver, only to God or to things future, and means a firm confidence in the declarations of God respecting them; a sense in which, as they think, Paul never employs the word.

I have united the objections and views of these writers under one head, in order to save the repetition of this subject. It deserves an attentive consideration.

There can be no doubt that Paul, in a multitude of cases, employs πίστις to designate belief in Christ as our Saviour and Redeemer. He often employs it to designate that state of mind, which trusts in his propitiatory sacrifice or blood as the means of salvation, in opposition to any trust or confidence in our own merit as the ground of acceptance. But to aver, that the author of our epistle does not disclose similar views in regard to the nature and importance of *faith* or *belief* in Christ, seems to be quite contrary to the whole tenor of the epistle. What is the object of the whole? Plainly, to prevent apostacy, i. e. renunciation of belief in Christ. But why is such a renunciation criminal and dangerous? Because Christ is of infinite dignity, and because, when belief in his blood is renounced, " there remaineth no further sacrifice for sin." To what purpose is the awful example of the effects of unbelief, proposed in chapter iii., except to warn the Hebrews against renouncing belief in Christ? To what purpose are the parallels drawn, in chapter iii.—x., between Christ and Moses; Christ and Melchisedek; and also between the great High Priest of the Christian religion, and the Jewish priests; between the sacrifice offered by the former, and the sacrifices made by the latter—but for the sake of warning the Hebrews against renouncing their *faith in Christ?* Plainly for no other purpose. All the warnings, reproofs, and tremendous denunciations in the epistle, converge to the same point; they all have a bearing upon the same specific object.

In respect to the allegation, that *faith*, in our epistle, is employed to denote belief or confidence in the declarations of God, specially with regard to the objects of a *future* world; this is true. But it is true, also, that Paul, in his acknowledged epistles, employs it in a similar manner. E. g. in Rom. iv. 17—23, Paul represents Abraham, under the most unpromising circumstances, as believing that God would raise up from him, already νενεκρωμένον, a numerous progeny. This belief he represents as an act of faith, ἐπίστευσε—μὴ ἀσθενήσας τῇ πίστει—οὐ διεκρίθη τῇ ἀπιστίᾳ—πληροφορηθεὶς—ἐλογίσθη τῷ Ἀβραὰμ [ἡ πίστις] εἰς δικαιοσύνην. On the other hand, our epistle, xi. 8, seq., represents Abraham as going out from his country, and sojourning in a strange land, πίστει. By *faith*, also he obtained a son, even when he was νενεκρωμένος, xi. 12, from whom a numerous progeny was to spring. Both these accounts characterise this whole transaction in the same way. Both describe the same acts as being *faith*, on the part of Abraham. Both describe his physical state, by calling him νενεκρωμένον. Both treat the whole transaction as a rare instance of the power of faith, and appeal to it as an example most worthy of imitation. Surely here is something different from *discrepancy* of views in these writers. Is there not a *coincidence*, which is altogether striking, both in the manner and language of the epistles?

But there are other circumstances in the account of Abraham, which deserve distinct notice. Paul, in Rom, iv. 17, seq., represents Abraham as believing the divine assurance, that he should become the father of many nations; the assurance of that God, " who restoreth the dead to life, and calleth things that are not, into being." In this expression, the apostle evidently refers to the belief which Abraham entertained, that, in case he offered up Isaac as a sacrifice, God could and would raise him from the dead, or call another son into being, from whom a numerous progeny should descend.

So in Heb. xi. 17, seq., the writer represents Abraham as offering up Isaac, in *faith* that God was able to raise him from the dead, from whence, as it were, he did obtain him, i. e. Isaac sprung from one apparently νενεκρωμένος, ver. 12. In both cases the writers have characterised the state of Abraham's mind, on this occasion, by representing it as *faith*, ἐπίστευσε, πίστει. In both, they disclose the same specific views of the point on which the faith of Abraham rested, and they characterise it in the same way.

§ 26. OBJECTIONS BY BERTHOLDT.

Is not here a minute coincidence of thought, expression, and manner of representing faith, which creates strong presumption in favour of the opinion, that the writer in both cases was the same person.

Again, in Heb. xi., Noah is represented as being divinely admonished respecting future occurrences, and as preparing an ark for his safety, in consequence of his *faith* in the admonition which he had received. The writer, then, proceeds to say, that by this act, he became an heir, τῆς κατὰ πίστιν δικαιοσύνης, *of that justification which is by faith;* the very expression, and the very idea, which Paul so often repeats in his acknowledged epistles, viz. those to the Romans and Galatians. What other writer of the New Testament, except Paul, has employed such an expression ?

It is true, indeed, that the author of our epistle does represent faith, in Heb. xi., as confidence in the declarations of God respecting future things. But it is equally true, that this was the view of it which he was naturally led to present, from the circumstances of the case before him. His appeal was to the worthies of former days, as examples of *belief*. Belief in what ? Not in Christianity surely, which had not then been revealed. Could the writer, when characterizing the actual nature of their *faith*, represent it as a belief in that which was *not yet disclosed* to them ? Surely not; but he must represent, and does represent it, as a belief in what God *had disclosed* to them. The nature of the case rendered it impossible that their faith should be represented in any other light than this.

Just so Paul, in Rom. iv., represents the faith of Abraham as *justifying faith*, and appeals to it in proof of the fact, that faith is a means of justification. Yet not a word is said there of Abraham's belief in Christ. In what respect does this case differ from that of all the examples cited in Heb. xi. ? Rather, is there not a *sameness of principle* in the two instances of faith ? Both respect *future* things depending on the promise of God ; neither have any special reference to Christ.

The truth is, that *faith*, in its *generic* nature, is *belief*, or *confidence in the promises* or *revelations of God*. Now, whether these respect things future, things of another world, or things past, or the nature, character, offices, and work of the Messiah, faith receives them all. Faith, therefore, in the ancients, who gave entire credit to what was revealed to them, was the same *principle* as faith in him who believes in Christ, because Christ is proposed to him. Circumstances only make any apparent difference in the case. The *disposition* is always the same.

M

§ 26. OBJECTIONS BY BERTHOLDT.

That Paul thought thus of this subject, is clear enough from the example of Abraham, which he cites as a signal instance of justifying faith, in Rom. iv. But, besides this, we have other proof that Paul has not always represented faith as having reference only to Christ, but also represented it, as it commonly appears in our epistle. So 2 Cor. v. 7, *We walk by faith, and not by sight*, i. e. we live as those who confide or believe in the realities of a future world, not like those who regard only visible objects. So too, in 1 Cor. xiii. 13. In 1 Thess. i. 8, we have ἡ πίστις ὑμῶν ἡ πρὸς τὸν Θεὸν; 1 Cor. xii. 9, πίστις ἐν τῷ αὐτῷ πνεύματι. So in 1 Cor. xiii. 2; 2 Cor. iv. 13; Eph. vi. 16; 1 Thess. v. 8, and in many other passages, faith has a variety of meanings, and is not limited to belief in Christ only.

I am unable to see, therefore, why this argument should be so strenuously urged, as it is by Schulz and others, and relied upon as so decisive. I can see no other difference between the *faith* of our epistle, and that which the writings of Paul present, than what the nature of the examples to which our author appealed necessarily requires. When Paul makes a like appeal, he treats the subject in the same way, Rom. iv. And nothing can be farther from correctness, than to aver that Paul always employs πίστις in the sense of *Christianity, believing on Christ*. Merely opening a Greek lexicon or concordance, on the word πίστις, is ample refutation of this assertion. Paul employs the word, in all the latitude which is elsewhere given it in the New Testament; and that embraces a great variety of specific significations, nearly all of which range themselves under the general idea of *confidence in the divine declarations*.

That it is the great object of our epistle to inculcate belief in Christ, and to warn the Hebrews against unbelief, I suppose will not be denied. What foundation, then, can Schulz have for saying, that "the Pauline idea of belief is altogether foreign to this writer?" Above all, how could he add, "A sentence, like the Pauline one, ὃ οὐκ ἐκ πίστεως, ἁμαρτία ἐστὶ, would sound strange enough in the epistle to the Hebrews." Yet, strange as it may seem, in Heb. ix. 6, we have, χωρὶς δὲ πίστεως ἀδύνατον εὐαρεστῆσαι [Θεῷ.]

On the whole, the representation of faith, in our epistle, as it respects the case of Abraham and Noah, is not only exactly the same as that of Paul's, but, in the mode of representation, are found such strong resemblances, as to afford no inconsiderable ground for supposing that the writer of both must have been the same person.

§ 26. OBJECTIONS BY BERTHOLDT. 163

(f) " Σαρκικὸς, in the sense of *transient, temporary*, is used only in the epistle to the Hebrews."

But, first, this is a disputed reading. Not to rely on this, however, σαρκικὸς in the sense of *weak, imperfect*, is common in Paul; a sense substantially the same with the one demanded here. Bretschneider renders it, in Heb. vii. 16, *ad naturam animalem spectans*; which is a *usual* sense, but not admissible here, on account of the antithesis, ζωῆς ἀκαταλύτου. Let it be, then, an ἅπαξ λεγόμενον as to sense here; are there not such in nearly all of Paul's epistles? E. g. ἐξουσία, 1 Cor. xi. 10, in the sense of *veil;* in 1 Cor. ix. 12, in the sense of *property;* and so of many other words.

(g) " The phrase οἰκουμένη μέλλουσα, Heb. ii. 5, for the *Christian dispensation*, is no where found in Paul's acknowledged epistles, in which he always employs αἰὼν μέλλων."

But are not οἰκουμένη and αἰὼν employed as *synonymes* in the New Testament? Both correspond to the Heb. עוֹלָם. Besides, in Heb. vi. 5, this very phrase, αἰὼν μέλλων, is employed by the writer in the sense of *Christian dispensation*. Must the same writer always employ the very same phraseology, when he has a choise of synomymous words?

Besides, it is not true that Paul uses the phrase αἰὼν μέλλων for the *Christian dispensation*. Once only does he employ it, Eph. i. 21, and then simply in the sense of *future world*.

(h) " But where is Christ called a *High Priest* and *an Apostle*, except in Heb. iii. 1.? It cannot be imagined, that the reverence which the apostles bore to their Master, would permit them to call him an *apostle*."

As to the appellation ἀρχιερεὺς, nothing could be more natural, than for the writer of the epistle to the Hebrews to apply this to Christ. He labours to prove, that Christianity has a preference over Judaism in *all* respects; that, consequently, it has a *High-priest* exalted above the Jewish one. How could the writer avoid calling Christ a High Priest? If Paul has no where done this in his acknowledged epistles, it may be for the obvious reason, that he has no where drawn such a comparison in them.

In respect to ἀπόστολος, Wetstein has shown, on John ix. 7, that one of the names which the Jews applied to their expected Messiah, was שָׁלִיחַ , i. e. *sent, apostle*. Besides, a common name of a prefect of the Jewish *synagogue*, was שְׁלִיחַ הַצִּבּוּר, ἀπόστολος τῆς ἐκκλησίας; in the Apocalypse, ἄγγελος τῆς ἐκκλησίας. Now, the object of the writer,

M 2

§ 26. OBJECTIONS BY BERTHOLDT.

in Heb. iii. 1, seq. is, to compare Christ as appointed over the household of God, with Moses in a similar office. Since then שָׁלִיחַ meant *curator ædis sacræ, ædituus,* and such an office was the very object of comparison, nothing can be more natural, than that our author should have named Christ שָׁלִיחַ i. e. ἀπόστολος. See Comm. on Heb. iii. 1.

And why should it be considered as incompatible with that *reverence* which Paul had for Christ, that he should call him ἀπόστολος? The same Paul, in Rom. xv. 8, calls Jesus Christ διάκονον τῆς περιτομῆς. Is διάκονος, a *more honorable* appellation than ἀπόστολος? Or because Paul calls Christ διάκονος in this case, are we to draw the inference, that he did not write the epistle to the Romans, since this word is nowhere else applied by him in this manner? Such a conclusion would be of the same nature, and of the same validity, as that which Bertholdt has drawn from the use of ἀπόστολος and ἀρχιερεὺς in the epistle to the Hebrews.

Thus much for *words* and *phrases.* Bertholdt next brings forward *sentiments* in the epistle to the Hebrews, which are diverse, he says, from Paul's, if not in opposition to them.

(1.) " In Heb. x. 25, seq., the speedy coming of Christ is mentioned; and so it is often by Paul. But in the epistle to the Hebrews, it is evidently a *moral* coming, a *moral* change; whereas Paul every where speaks of it as an *actual visible* coming of Christ."

This difficulty depends entirely upon the writer's exegesis. Whatever the nature of the coming of Christ may be, I venture to say, it is palpably represented in the same manner, in the epistle to the Hebrews and in the epistles of Paul. Indeed, so far has the representation, in the epistle to the Hebrews, appeared to be from being *plainly a moral* one, that some of the most distinguished commentators have understood it, as having respect to the *natural* changes that are to take place, when Christ shall come at the end of the world. So Storr; and others, also, before and after him. Paul surely has little or nothing, which more certainly designates the *actual, visible* coming of Christ, than this epistle. Comp. 1 Cor. iv. 5, 6. Phil. i. 10. iv. 5. 1 Thess. iii. 13. v. 1—6; ver. 23. 1 Tim. vi. 13—16. Tit. ii. 11—13. Compare, also, with these representations, 2 Thess. ii. 1—10, where Paul explains his views in respect to the coming of Christ. Indeed, so much alike is the representation of this subject, in the epistle to the Hebrews and in Paul's epistles, that many critics have used this very circumstance as a proof, that the author of both must have been the same person; an argument not valid however, because the same representation is common to other writers of the New Testament. Still, the mention of this serves to show, that the exegesis of Bertholdt, in this case, is not to be relied on with such confidence as he places in it.

(2.) " According to the epistle to the Hebrews, the propitiatory office of Christ continues *for ever* in the heavenly world, vii. 24, seq.; whereas Paul, on the contrary, considers the atonement for men as already *completed* by the death and resurrection of Jesus, Rom. iv. 25."

This argument is surely not well chosen. The author of the epistle to the Hebrews says, in so many words, that the High Priest of Christianity had no daily necessity, like the Jewish priests, to make offerings first for his own transgressions and then for those of the people; " for this he did once for all, when he made an offering of himself, vii. 27." And again : " Nor had he need often to repeat the sacrifice of himself, (as the high priest yearly enters into the holy place with blood not his own;) for then he must have suffered often since the foundation of the world ; but now, in this last age, he has appeared, once for all, to put away sin by the sacrifice of himself. And as all men die, once for all, and then go to the judgment; so Christ was offered up, once for all, to take away the sins of many; and when he shall make his second appearance, it will not be to atone for sin, but to bestow salvation on those who look for him," ix. 25—28. How can words make it more certain, that the author of the epistle to the Hebrews considered the propitiation or atonement as entirely *completed,* by the death of Christ ?

It is true, indeed, that the same author also represents Christ as for ever living, and exercising the duties of his office as an intercessor (or helper) for the saints, before God : " He, because he continueth for ever, hath an unchangeable priesthood; whence he is able to save to the uttermost those who come unto God through him, since he ever lives to intercede for ($\dot{\epsilon}\nu\tau\nu\gamma\chi\acute{a}\nu\epsilon\iota\nu$, *to help*) them," vii. 24, 25. With which agrees another representation, in ix. 24 ; " Christ has entered into heaven itself, henceforth to appear before God for us."

But are these sentiments foreign to Paul, as Bertholdt alleges ; " Who shall accuse the elect of God?—God acquits them. Who shall pass sentence of condemnation upon them ? Christ, who died for them? Rather, who is risen again, who is at the right hand of God, and who intercedes for ($\dot{\epsilon}\nu\tau\nu\gamma\chi\acute{a}\nu\epsilon\iota$, *helps*) them," Rom. viii. 33.

Here is not only the very same idea as in the epistle to the Hebrews, but even the very same term ($\dot{\epsilon}\nu\tau\nu\gamma\chi\acute{a}\nu\epsilon\iota\nu$) is used in both. Instead then of affording any evidence *against* the opinion, that Paul wrote the epistle to the Hebrews, the point in question affords evidence in favour of it. Paul, and Paul only, of all the apostolic authors, has presented the idea of the *intercession* of Christ in the heavenly world. To say the least, the whole mode of representing this subject is Pauline. The only difference between the epistle to the Romans and the epistle to the Hebrews, is, that in the latter case, the nature of the argument which the writer had employed, required him to represent Christ as performing the functions of a priest in the heavenly world. But it is palpably the intercessory function, which he is represented as continuing there to perform, in the passages which I have cited.

(3.) " The doctrine respecting the *Logos*, in the epistle to the Hebrews, is of Alexandrine hue, and evidently resembles that of John, and not of Paul. E. g. the divine Logos (Λόγος Θεοῦ) is quick and powerful, &c., iv. 12, 13 ; also, Christ is a priest, κατὰ δύναμιν ζωῆς ἀκαταλύτου, vii. 16. So, too, when Christ is represented as making an offering διὰ πνεύματος αἰωνίου, ix. 14, this, as well as the other cases, coincides with the views and representations of John, and not of Paul."

If now a critic will do such violence to the laws of exegesis, as to construe these passages so as to make them have respect to the doctrine of the *Logos*, the best way to answer him would be, to show that his principles of interpretation are without any good foundation. I cannot turn aside to do this here, as it more properly belongs to the exegetical part of the work. I shall content myself with merely observing, that one of the last ideas, which can well be deduced from the passage respecting the λόγος Θεοῦ just referred to, is that which Bertholdt has deduced from it; a deduction, which does equal violence to the context, and to the whole strain of reasoning, in our epistle. And where does *John* speak of Christ's *eternal priesthood,* or of his offering made in heaven διὰ πνεύματος αἰωνίου ?

At the conclusion of the arguments which I have now reviewed, Bertholdt adds, " With such real discrepancies between the epistle to the Hebrews and those of Paul, it is impossible that identity of authorship should exist," p. 2943.

If, indeed, the discrepancies were made out as clearly as Bertholdt supposes them to be, there might be some difficulty in supposing identity of authorship ; at least we could not suppose this, without at the same time conceding, that the writer was at variance in some measure with himself. But the conclusion which Bertholdt here draws, of course

§ 27. OBJECTIONS BY SCHULZ. 167

depends entirely on the fact, that all his allegations in respect to discrepancies of style and sentiment are well supported. Whether this be so, must now be left to the reader to judge.

But there are other recent writers, who remain to be examined, that have gone into the subject under discussion much more thoroughly and copiously than Bertholdt. I refer in particular to Dr. Schulz of Breslau, in the introduction to his *Translation of the Epistle to the Hebrews, with brief notes*, published A. D. 1818; and to Seyffarth, in his tract, *De Epistolæ ad Heb. indole maxime peculiari*. This last work especially has been spoken of with strong commendations by many critics; and Heinrichs, who in the first edition of his *Commentary on the Hebrews* defended the Pauline origin of our epistle, has, in the second edition of the same, declared himself a convert to the side of those who disclaim Paul as the author; attributing his conviction principally to the essay of Seyffarth just mentioned. As these works are the latest critical attempts to discuss at length the question under examination, and as they have manifestly had no small degree of influence upon the views of most of the continental critics of the present time, a particular examination of them becomes necessary.

§ 27. *Objections of Schulz considered.*

That Dr. Schulz is a man entitled to high respect for acuteness and strength of intellectual power, is sufficiently manifest from his work on the Sacrament, entitled *Die Christl. Lehre vom heil. Abendmahle, nach dem Grundtexte des N. Testaments*, A. D. 1824; a work which, from the talent it developes, and the discussion that it has excited, bids fair perhaps to bring this long-controverted subject to some close in the Lutheran church. His acquisitions of a *philological* nature are such, also, that great expectations were excited among not a few in Germany (if the Reviews are to be credited,) when it was announced that Dr. Schulz's commentary on our epistle was about to appear. I make these remarks principally to show, that a particular attention to his work is not only allowable on the present occasion, but really necessary, if one would even seem to preserve the attitude of impartiality.

This work was published a year before Bertholdt's volume, which contains the views that I have just examined. But this writer informs us, that he had not seen the work of Schulz when his own went to the press; consequently, this author, as far as we are now concerned, may be considered as posterior to Bertholdt.

§ 27. OBJECTIONS BY SCHULZ.

Nearly the whole *Introduction* of Schulz is devoted to the consideration of the question, Who was the author of the epistle to the Hebrews? or rather, to showing that Paul was not the author, pp. 1—158. Previously to writing this, the author had been engaged in controversy on the subject with his colleague Scheibel. The whole work bears the appearance of a heated, if not an exasperated state of mind; and while it discloses some vivid thoughts and pungent considerations, it also discloses some adventurous remarks and extravagant criticisms; to which the sequel of this examination will bear testimony.

The first fifty pages are devoted to the examination of Meyer's *Essay on the internal grounds for supposing that the epistle to the Hebrews was written by Paul.** In this are some remarks worthy of consideration, and which may serve to show that Meyer, in some cases, has pushed his comparisons too far. It is not to my purpose, however, to review this; as the subject has already been presented above, in § 21. My only object is, to select from Schulz such arguments against the Pauline origin of our epistle, as have not already been examined, in order that the reader may obtain a full view of our subject. These arguments I shall now subjoin, with such remarks upon each, as the nature of the case may seem to require.

(1.) "It is incomprehensible, and indeed quite impossible, that, if Paul wrote this epistle, early Christian antiquity should have been so doubtful about it, and the epistle itself have been received by the church so late, and with so much difficulty; and, after all, received only by some, and not at all by the generality of Christians. Such a fate did no other book of the New Testament meet with; not even the epistles which are addressed to individual persons," p. 58.

This objection borrows all its importance from assuming the fact, that our epistle was early and generally doubted in the churches, and at last but partially and doubtingly received. Whether Schulz had any good right to assume such a fact, must be left to the judgment of those who have read and weighed with impartiality the historical evidence already laid before them. It is unnecessary to retrace the ground here, which has once been passed over. The state of facts is far enough from showing, that all early Christians were doubtful about this epistle; nor can it be rendered probable, in any way, that doubts about it, at any period,

---

* Printed in Ammon and Bertholdt's Kritisches Journal der neuesten Theol. Literatur. II. 225, seq.

§ 27. OBJECTIONS BY SCHULZ.

had their origin in any *ancient* tradition that the epistle was not written by Paul. The doubts suggested are merely of a *critical* nature, or else they originated in *doctrinal* opinions, which seemed to be thwarted by our epistle.

Nor is it correct, that other parts of the New Testament were not early doubted by some churches; nay, some of it was doubted by many. Witness the fact, that Eusebius, Ecc. Hist. III. 25, classes among the ἀντιλεγόμενοι, James, Jude, 2 Peter, 2 John, and 3 John. Witness the fact, that the old Syriac version (Peshito) does not comprise either of these epistles, that of James excepted. Who, that is acquainted with the early state of criticism, and the history of our Canon, does not know that the ancient churches were not, for a long time, agreed in respect to all these epistles? Yet neither Schulz, nor any considerate critic, would decide that these books were spurious, because doubts had been raised respecting them. Are not the Gospels of Matthew, Luke, and John doubted, and called in question, by some learned critics, even at the present time? Shall they be given up, because they are called in question?

(2.) "The epistle to the Hebrews is altogether *unique;* so much so, that no other writer of the New Testament could have produced it. Every one who can comprehend peculiarities, and is able to distinguish them, must acknowledge this to be so. Nothing more than this fact needs to be considered, in order to decide the matter," p. 59.

If the writer here means that the *style* is *unique*, then I must refer to the evidences of the contrary in the preceding pages. If he means that the selection of particular *words* is *unique*, this is to be hereafter considered, when the selection, which Dr. Schulz has made, comes to be examined. If he means, that the *matter* is *sui generis*, I readily accede; but I demur to the allegation. Must Paul always write on one and the same subject to all the churches? Were their circumstances and wants all just the *same?* E. g. Is the first epistle to the Corinthians just like that to the Romans, Philippians, Colossians, Thessalonians, &c.; or is it a kind of ἅπαξ λεγόμενον, or ἅπαξ λογιζόμενον, compared with all the other epistles of Paul? Surely none of the others has much resemblance to it, in respect to the *matters* treated of. Does it then follow, that this epistle is *spurious*, because the subjects of it are *sui generis?* And is it any better evidence, that the epistle to the Hebrews does not belong to Paul, because the subjects of which it treats are *peculiar?* When we can prove that the wants of all churches are one and the same; and that an apostle who addresses them can write, or ought to write, only upon one subject, and in one way; then, and not till then, can this argument of Schulz have any weight in deciding the question before us.

(3.) "The Hebrews addressed in this epistle are of a peculiar class. They seem to have regarded themselves as a species of *illuminati*, elect, and favourites of heaven ; as animated by the Holy Spirit dwelling in them ; they are represented as despising the world, as inclined to mystical and allegorical views, as aiming at the acquisition of unearthly objects, &c. The epistle wins much for its exegesis, by such a supposition," p. 67, seq.

But supposing, now, all this to be correct, (which it would be difficult enough satisfactorily to prove,) how would it show that Paul did not write our epistle to them? And, surely, if the Hebrews had such views of themselves, what the apostle says, in chapter v. vi., and in some other places, was well adapted to humble them, and bring them to sober consideration.

The proof, on which Dr. Schulz relies for the establishment of his assertion, is drawn from the use, by the writer of our epistle, of such terms as ἅγιοι, φωτισθέντες, τέλειοι, ἁγιαζόμενοι, λάος τοῦ Θεοῦ, &c. But these are terms applied to Christians, everywhere in the New Testament, and to the use of which nothing peculiar in our epistle can be justly attributed.

(4.) "The author of this epistle was a Judaizing Christian, who grants that Judaism is still to continue, yea, to have a perpetual duration. Not a trace of any thing is to ·be found, which intimates an equal participation in the privileges of the gospel by Jews and Gentiles," pp. 74. 80.

The *first* of these allegations is, so far as I know, *altogether new*. Nothing more need be said in respect to it, than to refer the reader to chapters viii.—x. for most ample and satisfactory confutation. I had ever thought, before reading Dr. Schulz, that the writer of our epistle was the last of men who could be justly accused of *Judaizing*. If his views do not agree with those of Paul in respect to this matter, I am unable to see how language could express them.

In regard to the *second* allegation ; it is sufficient to say, that the object of the writer did not lead him to treat of the subject to which it relates. Are there not other epistles of Paul which do not bring this subject to view? And must a writer always repeat the same topics ? In what part of the first epistle to the Corinthians does Paul treat of the equal participation of Jews and Gentiles in the privileges of the gospel, and maintain the equal right of the latter ; as he does in the epistles to the Romans and Galatians? And is it not enough to say, that he did not do this, because the occasion did not demand it?

(5.) "But Christ, in our epistle, appears every where as the *Son of God*, as *Apostle*, and *High Priest*. Where is he so represented by Paul?" p. 81, seq.

In regard to the appellation, *Son of God*, it is often enough given to Christ by Paul. In respect to ἀπόστολος and ἀρχιερεὺς, he is not so called, indeed, by the apostle in his acknowledged epistles. The only reason why the writer of our epistle calls him so, is obviously one drawn from the nature of the comparison instituted between him and Moses, and between him and the Jewish high-priest. The nature of the composition, and the object of the writer, rendered this unavoidable. In the acknowledged epistles of Paul, no such occasion is presented of using the appellations in question. See above, p. 163.

(6.) "The design of the writer is *hortatory*. The motives which he urges to continue stedfast in the Christian belief, and in the practice of Christian virtue, are drawn, (1.) From the great dignity of the Messiah; (2.) From the danger to which apostacy would expose them. This danger is augmented by the consideration, that the *end of the world is near at hand*, p. 86, seq. Storr, and others, who differ in their exegesis of passages which declare this, scarcely deserve contradiction," p. 91.

The whole force of this rests, of course, upon the correctness of Dr. Schulz's exegesis. From his views, in regard to such passages as x. 36, seq. and xii. 26, seq., I feel myself compelled entirely to dissent. But even if they are allowed, I see not how they can establish the fact, that Paul did not write our epistle, provided we stand upon the same ground with Dr. Schulz. He will not deny that Paul had exalted views of the dignity of the Saviour, and of the obligation of Christians to continue stedfast in their acknowledgment of him. He believes that Paul, too, expected the end of the world to be actually near at hand. What is there, then, in the sentiments of our epistle, inconsistent with these views of Paul, as understood by him?

(7.) "Our author says nothing of Christ as judge of the world, but uniformly attributes judgment to God. Nor does he say a word of Hades, Gehenna, Satan, (excepting in ii. 14, 15,) the resurrection of the dead, and generally of the closing scene of all things; of which matters Paul treats so copiously," p. 95, seq.

But surely the final close or destruction of all material things is sufficiently intimated, in i. 10, seq.; future punishment, in iv. 11, seq., vi. 4, seq., x. 26, seq., xii. 29. That the names *Hades* and *Gehenna* do not occur in our epistle, would be a singular argument to prove that Paul did not write it. Where, in all the acknowledged epistles of Paul, is either of these words to be found, excepting in one solitary quotation, in 1 Cor. xv. 55, which exhibits ᾅδης? As to *Satan*, this appellation does not indeed occur; but its equivalent διάβολος occurs, in ii. 14. The word *Satan* does not occur in Galatians, Ephesians, Philippians, Colossians, 2 Timothy, Titus, Philemon: are these epistles, therefore, *spurious?*

In regard to *the resurrection of the dead*, it is sufficient to refer to vi. 2, xi. 35, and what is implied in xii. 22, seq.

That the writer of our epistle did not make frequent mention of these topics is easily accounted for, on the ground that he was more immediately occupied with other subjects. Are there not several of Paul's acknowledged epistles which omit the same topics? But who undertakes to prove from this, that they are spurious?

(8.) "But not a word of Christ's resurrection; a theme on which Paul everywhere descants," p. 97.

What, then, does Heb. xiii. 20, mean? And what is implied in viii. 1; i. 3; x. 12; xii. 2; ii. 9; v. 7—9? And will Dr. Schulz point out the places, where Paul discusses this subject in his epistles to the Galatians, Colossians, in the second to the Thessalonians, in the first to Timothy, and some others?

(9.) "If Paul did not become wholly unlike himself, and change his very nature, he could not have written the epistle to the Hebrews; which not only contains ideas foreign to his, but opposed to his," p. 101.

This is *assertion*, not *argument*. The only way to convince those who differ in opinion from us, is to offer *arguments* for what we avouch; not merely to assume or assert it to be true.

(10.) "The grand point of Paul's doctrines is, that Christ is the *Saviour of all;* that he died, or made atonement, *for all.* There is nothing of this in our epistle. Paul everywhere makes *belief in Christ* essential to salvation, and looks with contempt upon Jewish rites and ceremonies. But our author evidently handles Judaism with a sparing hand, and treats with honour the shell, from which he endeavours to extract the nut," p. 102, seq.

In regard to the first of these allegations, the reader is referred to Heb. ii. 9—11; v. 9; ix. 15. 28; xiii. 10; which afford hints sufficiently plain, that the writer did not regard the Messiah as the Saviour of the Jews only. But to treat, in our epistle, of the extent of his salvation among the Gentiles, plainly was not apposite to the particular design he had in view; and he might abstain from this topic, out of regard to the prejudices which those whom he addressed probably entertained (in common with most Jews) respecting it. Are there none of the acknowledged Pauline epistles, which do not treat of this subject? And must Paul always bring it into view, whether to do so would be timely or untimely, apposite or inapposite to the object of his epistle?

In respect to the *Judaizing* spirit of the writer, I must refer once more to chap. viii.—x.; and what has already been said above, in examining the fourth objection. And with regard to belief in Christ as essential to salvation, the great object of all the epistle to the Hebrews is to urge it. Dispute with one who denies this, would surely be in vain.

(11.) " Paul no where represents Christ as a priest, nor his intercession as procuring favours for them," p. 109, seq.

In respect to this objection, I refer the reader to what has already been said, pp. 163 (h) and 165 (2.)

(12.) " Paul has no where drawn a parallel between Christ and Moses," p. 111.

But he did something very much like it, when he represented Moses and Christ as *mediators*, Gal. iii. 19, seq. And if he has not formally done it in any of his acknowledged epistles, it is enough to say, it was because the occasion did not call for it.

(13.) " Our author says nothing of the *kingdom of God*, or the *kingdom of Satan*, or of the *gospel of Jesus Christ;* ideas predominant in Paul's epistles," p. 115.

But is not a kingdom ascribed to Christ, in Heb. i. 8, 9; i. 10, seq., ii. 7, seq.; x. 13; xii. 2? And are not Christians represented as belonging to it, in xii. 28? And are the second epistle to the Corinthians and the epistle to the Philippians not genuine, because the first of these phrases is not in them? Is not the power or reign of Satan recognized, in Heb. ii. 14, 15? And as to εὐαγγέλιον, see iv. 2; iv. 6. Apply, too, the same method of reasoning to Paul's acknowledged epistles. Εὐαγγελίζω is a favourite word with this apostle; yet Philippians, Colossians, 2 Thessalonians, 1 Timothy, 2 Timothy, Titus, Philemon, do not exhibit it. The word εὐαγγέλιον, too, is not found in the epistle to Titus. But is not the *thing*, which it indicates, found there? It is; and so it is in Hebrews, as frequently as the nature of the case required: e. g. i. 1; ii. 1. 3; iv. 1, 2; v. 12; vi. 1, seq., x. 25; xiii. 8, 9. 17.

(14.) "How such expressions respecting the resurrection, as occur in 1 Cor. xv. 5, seq. Rom. vi. 4; xi. 15. Phil. iii. 20, seq. Col. ii. 13. 1 Thess. iv. 15, seq. 2 Thess. ii. 2 Tim. ii. 18, with Acts xxiv. 15; xxvi. 6, seq., are to be reconciled with the views of the resurrection presented in our epistle, those who defend the genuineness of the epistle may be called on to account for," p. 116.

In some of these citations, I can find no reference at all to the resurrection. In others, (e. g. Col. ii. 13,) there is simply a *figurative* or *moral* use of the term. As to the remainder, I can perceive no discrepancy between them and Heb. vi. 2; xi. 35, and what is implied in xii. 22, seq. As Schulz has not pointed out in what the discrepancy consists, I am unable to apprehend it.

(15.) "But 1 Cor. xv. 24, seq. is at variance with Heb. i. 2. 8, seq. 12, 13. vii. 24 seq. comp. v. 16; ix. 14, p. 116."

Just as much as it is with Luke i. 33. Dan. ii. 44; vii. 14; Mic. iv. 7. John xii. 34. Isa. ix. 6. Ps. lxxxix. 36. 2 Sam. vii. 16; and no more. What interpreter, who has carefully studied the idiom of the Scriptures, does not know that לְעוֹלָם, לָנֶצַח, and εἰς τοὺς αἰῶνας τῶν αἰώνων, are applied to things to which a time of continuance is assigned, that is not liable to interruption by any *adventitious* circumstances, and which are to endure to the full period for which they were designed? So it is with *the world, the mountains, the hills;* they are לְעוֹלָם, εἰς τοὺς αἰῶνας. So also, the *mediatorial reign* is not to be interrupted, but to continue until all the designs of God in the redemption of men are completed. Then, of course, it must cease; as no more mediatorial offices are to be performed.

And why, too, should Dr. Schulz suggest such a consideration, as a proof that Paul did not write the epistle to the Hebrews, when he makes no difficulty at all in suggesting, that the sacred writers are not unfrequently at variance with themselves? To allege the fact of *variance*, then, either with each other or with themselves, is no valid argument, on the ground upon which he stands. He is not, here, consistent with himself. And, besides, has not Paul himself recognised the *perpetuity* of Christ's dominion, in his acknowledged epistles? See Rom. ix. 5.

(16.) "The writer of our epistle, entangled with types and allegories, knows not how to say any thing respecting Christianity, except what he finds an analogy for in Judaism; so that his work is made up of parallels between the old and new dispensation, spun out to an excessive length...... The limited circle in which this writer moves, his evident deficiency in activity of mind, and in unfolding his own views, are altogether unlike the active, creative mind of Paul, that master-spirit, who moves with such perfect freedom, and controls at pleasure all his own views, without any subjection to the influence of others, or even being at all affected by any thing of Jewish origin; all of which was entirely at his command...... Whoever should attribute this singular production to Paul, would show that he was little acquainted with him," p. 119.

Yet, in p. 124, Dr. Schulz says, " One finds in the unknown author [of our epistle,] more orderly deduction, more learned accuracy, and, for the most part, a well-arranged, gradual ascent, from the point where he starts, which he usually establishes by quotations from the Old Testament, to the sublime region, to which, as true, eternal, and heavenly, he directs every thing, and where he ends every thing; finally, more luxurious, oratorical qualities, than in Paul."

How this consists with the preceding representation, the writer of both may well be required to show. The reader, I am sure, must find difficulty enough to make them harmonize. But, at any rate, the accusation that the writer of the epistle to the Hebrews is not master of his own subject and own thoughts, is, so far as I know, *new;* and one which (as I shall confidently believe, until I see more evidence to the contrary,) it is unnecessary to answer.

(17.) " Heb. ii. 1, 2, proves that Paul could not have been the writer of our epistle; for he did not receive his gospel from others, but was immediately taught it by Christ himself, Gal. i. 11, 12; v. 15—19;" p. 125, seq.

On the subject of this objection, the reader is referred to p. 33 (c). I add here only, that if the use of the *first person plural* by the writer, necessarily makes him one, in all respects, with those whom he is addressing, then the author of our epistle did himself need the admonitions which he has so powerfully and feelingly addressed to others: see ii. 1. 3; iii. 6; iv. 1, 2. 11. 13. 16; vi. 1—3. 18. 19; x. 22—25, 26. 39; xi. 40; xii. 1. 9, 10. 28; xiii. 10. 13. 15. Nay, he must have included himself among those who were shaken in their Christian belief, and who were in imminent hazard of final apostacy.

On the other hand; nothing can be plainer, than that he uses *we* or *ye* indifferently, for the persons whom he addresses; e. g. *we*, in xii. 1, 2;

§ 27. OBJECTIONS BY SCHULZ.

ye, in xii. 3—8; *we*, in xii. 9, 10; *ye*, in xii. 14—25; *we*, in xiii. 25—28; and often in the same manner elsewhere, the address being still most manifestly made to the very same persons. He often employs, also, the first person plural (ἡμεῖς,) to designate *merely himself;* e. g. in Heb. ii. 5; vi. 9. 11; xiii. 18. This, in like manner, he interchanges with the first person singular: e. g. xiii. 18; comp, xiii. 19. 22, 23.

How can it be, now, that Dr. Schulz should so strenuously urge the argument drawn from the use of the *first person plural*, to show that the writer of our epistle received his knowledge of the gospel from apostles and disciples, and of course that he could not be Paul? Yet he not only urges it at length, pp. 125—130, but declares, that " it affords a decisive proof, that the apostle Paul could not have written the epistle in question," p. 126. Especially, how could he urge such an argument, when the same use of the first person plural runs through all the Pauline epistles: e. g. ἡμεῖς and ἐγὼ for the writer himself, Gal. i. 8; comp. i. 9—24; Gal. ii. 5; comp. ii. 1—4, and ii. 6, 7. So ἡμεῖς and ὑμεῖς for the persons addressed, Gal. iii. 1—12; iii. 13—25; iii. 26—29; iv. 6—20; iv. 26—31, et alibi. Is it possible, then, to attribute any weight to such an argument as that in question?

(18.) " The manner of citing or appealing to the Old Testament, by Paul and by the writer of the epistle to the Hebrews, is very different. Paul appeals to it as a *written record;* but the writer of our epistle every where cites it as the immediate word of God, or of the Holy Ghost. Paul's formulas of citation are, γέγραπται, καθὼς γέγραπται, ἡ γραφὴ λέγει, ἐγράφη, κατὰ τὸ γεγραμμένον, ὁ λόγος γεγραμμένος, Μωϋσῆς γράφει—λέγει, ὁ νόμος λέγει, ἐν Μωϋσέως νόμῳ γέγραπται, Δαβὶδ λέγει, Ἡσαΐας λέγει—κράζει, ἐν τῷ Ὡσηὲ λέγει, and κατὰ τὸ εἰρήμενον; which are not used in a single instance, in the epistle to the Hebrews. Instead of these formulas, the author uses λέγει—μαρτύρει—τὸ πνεῦμα τὸ ἅγιον, λέγει ὁ θεὸς; or the abridgments of these formulas, viz. λέγει, εἴρηκε, μαρτύρει, φησὶ. Does not such a diversity necessarily imply diversity of authorship?" p. 120, seq.

To this representation of Dr. Schulz, Seyffarth has not only assented, but, in his *Essay on the Peculiarities of the Epistle to the Hebrews,** he has placed the modes of appeal to the Jewish Scriptures at the head of these *peculiarities,* so far as the style of the author is concerned; " referenda huc est, præ ceteris omnibus, *loca Vet. Test. laudandi singularis ratio.*" Dr. Schulz, moreover, says, " that plainly Paul

* De epistolæ ad Heb. indole, §§ 58—60.

makes less frequent use, in general, of the Old Testament Scriptures, than is made of them in the epistle to the Hebrews;" an objection which has been frequently alleged by others.

The result of an attentive and repeated examination of our epistle, and of all the acknowledged Pauline epistles, in respect to the *mode* and *frequency* of quotation, has led me to conclusions somewhat different from those which Schulz and Seyffarth have adopted. I shall present them, with my reasons for adopting them.

(a) The writer of the epistle to the Hebrews is by no means uniform in his mode of appeal to the Jewish Scriptures. In *twenty-one* cases, viz. i. 5; i. 6; i. 7; ii. 12; iii. 7; iv. 3; v. 5, 6; vi. 4; vii. 17; vii. 21; viii. 5; viii. 8; ix. 20; x. 5; x. 8; x. 9; x. 15; x. 30; xii. 26; xiii. 5, he has used εἶπεν, εἴρηκε, λέγει, λέγων, ματύρει, φησὶ, with a nominative *never expressed*, except in three instances, viz. Heb. iii. 7; vi. 14, by implication, and x. 15. In *fourteen* of these cases, we may gather from the context, that Θεὸς, or Κύριος, is the probable nominative, i. e. the one which the writer meant his readers should supply. *Four* of the cases have Χριτὸς, or Ἰησοῦς, for a nominative, viz. ii. 13; x. 5; x. 8; x. 9, which is implied ; *two* of them have τὸ πνεῦμα τὸ ἅγιον expressed, viz. iii. 7; x. 15; and *one* only has Θεὸς expressed, and that because it was unavoidable, vi. 14.

In *five* cases more, which are introduced merely with πάλιν, καὶ, or δὲ, viz. i. 5; i. 8; i. 10; ii. 13; x. 30, but stand connected with a preceding quotation, the grammatical connexion requires us to supply εἶπε, λέγων, λέγει, &c., i. e. Κύριος or Θεὸς λέγει, εἶπε, &c. In two cases of the like nature, viz. ii. 13; ii. 14, Ἰησοῦς or Χριτὸς is the implied nominative. In the whole, there are *twenty-five* instances of quotation in which the nominative is *not* expressed, in *nineteen* cases of which it probably is Θεὸς, and Χριτὸς in the other *six*. There are *two* cases only, in which the nominative τὸ πνεῦμα τὸ ἅγιον is expressed ; and *one* only where Θεὸς is actually inserted.

If one might trust to the representations of Dr. Schulz and Seyffarth, he must, of course, be led to believe, that these are all the kinds of quotation which our epistle presents. This, however, is not the case. In ii. 6, we have διεμαρτύρατο δέ που τὶς, viz. Δαβὶδ; in iii. 15, ἐν τῷ λέγεσθαι, *when it is said*, (like שֶׁנֶּאֱמַר in the Mishna;) in iv. 4, εἴρηκε γάρ που, sc. ἡ γραφὴ plainly, which formula is repeated by πάλιν in iv. 5 ; in iv. 7, we find ἐν Δαβὶδ λέγων, *saying by David;* in ix. 20, Μωϋσῆς—

λέγων; in xi. 18, ἐλαλήθη, (like וַיֹּאמֶר;) in xii. 5, παρακλήσεως; in xii. 20, τὸ διαςελλόμενον; in xii. 21, Μωϋσῆς εἶπε; in xii. 27, τὸ δὲ; in xiii. 6, ὥςε ἡμᾶς λέγειν, so that we may say. Besides this, we have, in iii. 5; x. 37; and xi. 21, quotations without any direct sign or notice of appeal; not to mention several references or partial quotations which might easily be subjoined. In the whole, there are *fifteen* instances of quotation, (i. e. about *three-eighths* of all the quotations,) where the appeal is *different* from that which Schulz and Seyffarth attribute to our author, and on which they have built their argument against the Pauline origin of our epistle.

(b) There is a similar variety of appeal in the acknowledged Pauline epistles. E. g. καθὼς γέγραπται, γέγραπται γὰρ, or ἐν νόμῳ γέγραπται, are used in Romans sixteen times: viz. i. 17; ii. 24; iii. 4; iii. 10; iv. 17; viii. 36; ix. 13; ix. 33; x. 15; xi. 8; xi. 26; xii. 19; xiv. 11; xv. 3; xv. 9; xv. 21. In 1 Corinthians, nine times: viz. i. 19; i. 31; ii. 9; iii. 19; ix. 9; x. 7; xiv. 21; xv. 45; xv. 54. In 2 Corinthians, three times: viz. iv. 13; viii. 15; ix. 9. In Galatians, four times: viz. iii. 10; iii. 13; iv. 22; iv. 27. In all, thirty-two. Ἡ γραφὴ λέγει is used eight times: viz. Rom. iv. 3; ix. 17; x. 11; xix. 2; probably Rom. xv. 10; xv. 11. 1 Cor. vi. 16. Gal. iv. 30. Ἡσαΐας λέγει, four times: viz. Rom. x. 16; x. 20; x. 21; xv. 12. Ἡσαΐας κράζει, Rom. ix. 27; Ἡσαΐας προείρηκε, ix. 29; Μωϋσῆς λέγει, x. 19; Μωϋσῆς γράφει, x. 5; Δαβὶδ λέγει, iv. 16; xi. 9; ὁ νόμος ἔλεγε, vii. 7; ἡ ἐκ πίςεως δικαιοσύνη λέγει, x. 6; τί λέγει, [sc. ἡ ἐκ πίςεως δικαιοσύνη,] x. 9; χρηματισμὸς λέγει, xi. 4.

There are *ten* cases of quotation without any formula of appeal; viz. Rom. ix. 7; x. 13; x. 18; xi. 34; xii. 20; 1 Cor. ii. 16; x. 26; xv. 27; Gal. iii. 11; iii. 12; not to mention many cases where partial reference is made, in both the phraseology and thought of the apostle, to passages in the Old Testament.

Where an appeal is expressly made to the Old Testament by Paul, in his acknowledged epistles, there is, then, a small majority of cases in which καθὼς γέγραπται, or its equivalents, are used, if we take the whole together. But, in the epistle to the Romans, the other methods of quotation *predominate*. The ground of such appeals as Δαβὶδ, Ἡσαΐας, Μωϋσῆς—λέγει, will be the subject of remark by and by.

(c) The assertion of Schulz, that Paul no where uses the formula of appeal Θεὸς, Κύριος—λέγει, comes next to be examined; for on this have he and Seyffarth grounded the conclusion, that the same writer could

§ 27. OBJECTIONS BY SCHULZ.

not have been the author of the Pauline epistles and of the epistle to the Hebrews. Assertions made at random, on this subject, cannot decide it Let the appeal be made to *facts*. Rom. ix. 12, ἐρρήθη αὐτῇ, viz. to Rebecca. But by whom was it said By Jehovah, Gen. xxv. 23. It is the λόγος Κυρίου or Θεοῦ, then, to which appeal is necessarily made here. Rom. ix. 15, τῷ Μωϋσῇ λέγει, [sc. ὁ Κύριος vel ὁ Θεός.] Rom. ix. 25, ἐν τῷ Ὡσηὲ λέγει, [sc. ὁ Θεός,] just the same as in Heb. iv. 7, ἐν Δαβὶδ λέγων; i. e. *saying by Hosea, saying by David*.

In 2 Cor. vi. 2, λέγει γὰρ [sc. ὁ Κύριος;] vi. 16, εἶπεν ὁ Θεός; vi. 17, λέγει Κύριος; vi. 18, λέγει Κύριος παντοκράτωρ; Gal. iii. 16, οὐ λέγει, [sc. ὁ Θεός.]

So much for the assertion, that Paul has *never* used the formula of appeal, ὁ Θεὸς λέγει, or λέγει Κύριος. Dr. Schulz will surely not object, that the nominative Κύριος or Θεὸς is not *expressed* in all these cases; for it *never* is so, in the epistle to the Hebrews, with the exception of only one instance, viz. Heb. vi. 14. But other resemblances remain to be pointed out.

In Rom. xiii. 9, τὸ γὰρ is prefixed to a quotation; and again, ἐν τῷ, Rom. xiii. 9. In the same way is τὸ δὲ used, Heb. xii. 27. In Rom. iv. 18, we find the perfect participle used, κατὰ τὸ εἰρημένον; in Heb. xii. 20, τὸ διαστελλόμενον. In Rom. ix. 12, ἐρρήθη; Heb. xi. 18, ἐλαλήθη, and (equivalent to this) ἐν τῷ λέγεσθαι, iii. 15.

In regard to the assertion of Schulz and Seyffarth, " that Θεὸς, Χριστὸς, or πνεῦμα ἅγιον, is *always* the nominative to λέγει, εἶπε, &c., in the epistle to the Hebrews," the following formulas may be consulted; viz. Heb. ii. 6, διεμαρτύρατο δέ που τὶς, [sc. Δαβὶδ]; iv. 4, εἴρηκε γὰρ [sc. ἡ γραφή]; which is repeated by necessary implication, in iv. 5; ix. 20, Μωϋσῆς......λέγων xii. 21, Μωϋσῆς εἶπε, (either a quotation of a sacred traditional saying, or a reference to the Scriptures *ad sensum:*) all cases of the same nature as those which occur in Paul's acknowledged epistles.

Besides these, we have, in xii. 5, a quotation referred to by calling it παράκλησις, (comp. Rom. xi. 4, χρηματισμὸς λέγει;) and in xiii. 6, we are pointed to a text of Scripture by the expression, ὥστε ἡμᾶς λέγειν. There are several instances, also, of quotation without any formula o appeal; just as in Paul's acknowledged epistles.

(d) There is as great a difference between Paul's *acknowledged* epistles, in regard to the formulas and the frequency of quotation from the Old Testament, as there is between the epistle to the Hebrews and some of Paul's acknowledged epistles; nay, even a greater difference. E. g. in the first epistle to the Corinthians, the only formula of quotation is the verb γέγραπται, viz. 1 Cor. i. 19; i. 31; ii. 9; iii. 19; iii. 20; ix. 9; x. 7; xiv. 21; xv. 24; one case only excepted, vi. 16. Four times, quotation is made without any formula, viz. 1 Cor. ii. 16; x. 26; xv. 27; xv. 32. Now, in the epistle to the Romans, out of forty-eight quotations, only sixteen are introduced with the same formula; the others exhibiting all the variety above described. On the other hand, the second epistle to the Corinthians is equally divided between the formulas, ὡς γέγραπται, and λέγει, εἶπε [sc. ὁ Θεὸς or Κύριος]; there being three of each kind, viz. ὡς γέγραπται, 2 Cor. iv 13; viii. 15; ix. 9; λέγει, εἶπε [ὁ Θεὸς], vi. 2; vi. 16; vi. 17. It has also two quotations without any formula, ix. 7; xiii. 1. The epistle to the Galatians has four formulas with γέγραπται, Gal. iii. 10; iii. 13; iv. 22; iv. 27; one with Θεὸς implied, iii. 16; and two without any formula, iii. 11; iii. 12.

In all the other Pauline epistles, to the Ephesians, Philippians, Colossians, Thessalonians, to Timothy and Titus, there are not more than four or five quotations of Scripture to be found.

Suppose now, that we take the epistle to the Romans, (one of the most undoubted of all Paul's epistles,) as the model of this writer's quotations. Then the argument is conclusive, (on the ground which Schulz and Seyffarth have taken against the genuineness of all his other acknowledged epistles, unless it be the second to the Corinthians, and that to the Galatians. Above all, what shall we say of the great majority of his epistles, which never quote the Old Testament at all? Can it be, that the same man wrote these, who has directly appealed no less than *forty-eight* times to the Old Testament, in the epistle to the Romans, not to mention many other implicit references? And can it be, when his formulas of reference are so diverse, as they are between this epistle and the first to the Corinthians, that the same person was the author of both? It is easy now to perceive, that if arguments can be built on such circumstances as these, then the genuineness of the greater portion of the Pauline epistles must of course be denied. Is Dr. Schulz prepared for such a conclusion?

(e) A word as to the *greater frequency* of quotations, in the epistle to the Hebrews. Let us compare it with that to the Romans, which it most of all resembles, in respect to discussion and method of argument. In the epistle to the Romans, there are, at least, *forty-eight* quotations;

in that to the Hebrews, *thirty-four*. More may be made in each, if we reckon all the cases of like phraseology or resemblances to the Old Testament, in the turn of thought, which may be found in both. Now, the proportion of the epistle to the Romans to that of the Hebrews, in regard to *length*, is as fourteen to ten ; the number of quotations as forty-eight to thirty-four; which would average nearly three and a half to a page, in each epistle ; the proportion being nearly the same in both, but the excess on the side of the epistle to the Romans. So much for the assertion, that the *frequency* of quotation in our epistle proves that Paul was not the author of it. If there be any weight in such an argument, it lies equally against the genuineness of the epistle to the Romans, compared with Paul's other epistles, which have no quotations at all.

(f) On the whole, then, the objection, drawn either from the *method* or the *frequency* of quotation, *(singularis ratio præ ceteris omnibus* of our epistle, as Seyffarth calls it,) vanishes away upon close examination; or if adhered to, must disprove the genuineness of a major part of the acknowledged epistles of Paul. That Paul, in our epistle, should have more frequently than elsewhere used λέγει, εἶπεν, εἴρηκε, is altogether consonant with what we may suppose him to have done, when addressing the Hebrews. The usual and almost the only mode of quoting, prevalent among the Jews, in ancient times, appears to have been such : at least if we may judge of it as it appears in the Mishna, where שֶׁנֶּאֱמַר נֶאֱמַר, *it is said, as it is said, which is said,* is almost the only formula in use. There is an obvious reason for this. Every Jew, being conversant with the Old Testament Scriptures, would of course know what was the kind and weight of the appeal, made by λέγει, εἶπε, (נֶאֱמַר) ; i. e. he would at once refer it to divine testimony. Hence, this abridged and natural mode of quotation prevails in our epistle. But in writing to churches made up of both Jews and Gentiles, the latter of whom were of course less familiar with the Old Testament, and knew less where to look for passages quoted, it was more natural for the apostle, (as he has done in the epistle to the Romans,) to say Μωϋσῆς λέγει, Ἐσαΐας λέγει, &c., so that the reference might be more definite. This is a sufficient reason to account for any differences in the *formula* of quotation, between our epistle and the other epistles of Paul. The difference itself has, however, as we have seen, been greatly over-rated. Nothing important, most plainly, can be made of it by higher criticism, in performing its office upon our epistle. What can be more improbable, too, than that such a master-spirit as Paul should cast all his letters in the same mould;

182 § 27. OBJECTIONS BY SCHULZ.

always use the same round of expression; mechanically apply the same formulas of quotation; and for ever repeat the same sentiments in the same language? And because he has not done so, in the epistle to the Hebrews, must it be wrested from him, by criticism which exacts such uniformity in a writer? Where is the writer of epistles, ancient or modern, who possessed any talents and free command of language, whose letters can be judged of by such a critical test as this?

(19.) " The appellations given to the Saviour, in Paul's acknowledged epistles and in the epistle to the Hebrews, are so diverse, as to afford strong evidence that both did not originate from the same person. E. g. in the Pauline epistles, these appellations are either, ὁ κύριος ἡμῶν Ἰησοῦς Χριστὸς, Ἰησοῦς Χριστὸς ὁ κύριος ἡμῶν, Χριστὸς Ἰησοῦς ὁ κύριος ἡμῶν, or ὁ κύριος Ἰησοῦς Χριστὸς. In innumerable passages is Christ referred to by these appellations; which are so characteristic of Paul's writings, that they are to be regarded as nearly the *constant established formulas*, by which he adverts to the Saviour. On the contrary, in the epistle to the Hebrews, the writer uses most commonly υἱὸς τοῦ Θεοῦ or ὁ υἱὸς; he also employs, at times, ὁ κύριος or ὁ Ἰησοῦς simply. *Twice* only has he connected Ἰησοῦς Χριστὸς. This must appear *striking* to every unprejudiced person, and of importance," p. 139, seq.

Striking, indeed, the argument may appear, in the form stated by Schulz; but an investigation, through the medium of a Concordance, will present a very different result from that which he has presented.

(a) In regard to υἱὸς τοῦ Θεοῦ or ὁ υἱὸς being the most *frequent* appellation given to Christ by the writer of our epistle, the facts stand thus. Omitting dubious references, and all the names of Christ that are appellatives suggested merely by the occasion, (such as ἀπόστολος, ἀρχιερεὺς, ἀρχηγὸς σωτηρίας—τῆς πίστεως, μεσίτης, σωτὴρ, and κληρόνομος,) the writer refers to the Messiah, by some one of his usual titles, in thirty-two places; in four of which only he calls him υἱὸς τοῦ Θεοῦ, viz. Heb. iv. 14; vi. 6; vii. 3; x. 29. In eight other places he calls him υἱὸς; viz. i. 1, 5 bis, 8; iii. 6; v. 5. 8; vii. 28. In the Pauline epistles, these designations are used seventeen times: viz. Rom. i. 3, 4. 9; v. 10; viii. 3. 29. 32. 1 Cor. i. 9; xv. 28. 2 Cor. i. 19. Gal. i. 16; ii. 20; iv. 4. 6. Eph. iv. 13. Col. i. 13. 1 Thess. i. 10.

(b) Κύριος is so far from being limited to the epistle to the Hebrews, in its application to Christ, that, if I have counted rightly, it is found in the acknowledged Pauline epistles, applied in the same way, one hundred and forty-seven times, and is the most frequent appellation of any except

§ 27. OBJECTIONS BY SCHULZ. 183

Χριστός. The cases where κύριος stands united with 'Ιησοῦς, 'Ιησοῦς Χριστός, &c. are exempted from this enumeration.

On the other hand, the writer of our epistle is so far from making a frequent use of this designation, that he has employed it singly in two places only, or at most three, viz. ii. 3; vii. 14; probably xii. 14. That Schulz should make a representation so singularly incorrect, respecting the appellation κύριος, can be accounted for in no other way, than by supposing that he never examined his Concordance, for the sake of investigating the question respecting the use of it.

But further; in the epistle to the Romans, κύριος is applied to Christ not more than seventeen times; some may think still less, in as much as the exegesis, in a few of the cases, may be doubtful. In the first epistle to the Corinthians, however, (which is about the same length,) the same appellation is given to Christ forty-five times; while, in the epistle to Titus it does not occur at all. Further, 'Ιησοῦς Χριστός, or Χριστός 'Ιησοῦς, is used, in the epistle to the Romans, as connected with κύριος only fourteen times; in 1 Corinthians, only eleven. 'Ιησοῦς κύριος is used in Romans twice; in 1 Corinthians, thrice. Κύριος Χριστός only in Rom. xvi. 18. Such a variety of usage in these different epistles, must, if Schulz's method of arguing is correct, prove that Paul could not have written them all.

(c) 'Ιησοῦς, without being connected with the other usual appellations of Christ, is employed in our epistle seven times: viz. ii. 9; vi. 20; vii. 22; x. 19; xii. 2. 24; xiii. 12. In the Pauline epistles, sixteen times; viz. Rom. iii. 26; viii. 11. 1 Cor. xii. 3. 2 Cor. iv. 5; iv. 10 bis; iv. 11 bis. iv. 14. xi. 4. Eph. iv. 21. Phil. ii. 10. 1 Thess. i. 10; ii. 15; iv. 14 bis. In the epistles to the Galatians, Colossians, 2 Thessalonians, 1 Timothy, 2 Timothy, Titus, and Philemon, it is not found at all.

(d) Χριστός is used, in like manner, by our author, six times, viz. ii. 6. 14; v. 5; vi. 1; ix. 11. 14. 24. 28; xi. 26; in the Pauline epistles one hundred and ninety-eight, if I have rightly counted.

(e) 'Ιησοῦς Χριστός, instead of being used only twice, as Schulz avers, is used three times; Heb. x. 10; xiii. 8. 21, omitting iii. 1, where it stands also in the *textus receptus*.

(f) In xiii. 20, Κύριον 'Ι. Χριστόν is used by the writer, just as Paul employs it.

(g) Those designations of Christ in the Pauline epistles, which Schulz has mentioned as the usual and only appellations of him by Paul, do not collectively amount to more than *sixty-eight*, if we take the number as stated by himself (who, however, as is usual with him, has in haste over looked some instances;) while, in the same epistles, other appellations which he does *not* acknowledge, are used with far greater frequency; e. g. κύριος is used *one hundred and forty-seven times*, and Χριστός, *one hundred and ninety-eight;* the former being an appellation which this writer holds out as characteristic of our epistle to the Hebrews, and *neglected* by Paul. Truly this matter is *striking* (if I may use Dr. Schulz's own language;) and if the epistle to the Hebrews can be wrested from Paul only by arguments such as this, those who ascribe it to this apostle have not much reason for apprehension, in regard to the safety of their cause.

Even if the facts stated by Schulz were correct, it would not follow that Paul could not be the author of our epistle. The predominant appellation of the Saviour in the Pauline epistles is simply Χριστός; as we have just seen. Yet, in the second epistle to the Thessalonians, this appellation, simply used, occurs but once, (iii. 5.) and in both the epistles to Timothy, and in that to Titus, it does not once occur. Does it follow from this, then, that Paul did not write these epistles? If not, then, supposing the facts alleged by Schulz to be correct, no critical argument could be safely built upon them. But they are so far from being correct, that one finds it difficult to account for it, how any man, who expected others to examine for themselves, and not to receive what he says as *authoritative*, should have thrown out before the public such affirmations as every tyro, with a Greek Concordance in his hand, would be able to disprove. Truly Professor Schulz must not blame his readers, if they are slow and cautious about admitting his allegations, on subjects where accuracy, and diligence, and patience are necessary, in order to produce correct results.

Seyffarth has brought forward the same argument, but with a somewhat different statement of facts; yet full of inaccuracies and errors. He concludes, as the sum of the whole, " that the writer of the epistle to the Hebrews has given to the Saviour appellations, which are indicative of less reverence than those which Paul bestows upon him," and that " there is a great difference between the usage of Paul, in this respect, and that of our epistle," p. 90.

On the whole, nothing can be plainer, than that the usage in our epistle, with respect to the appellations in question, differs no more from the usual Pauline one, than the usage of several of his acknowledged epistles differs from that of others belonging to him. Consequently, no weight can be attached to this objection.

§ 27 OBJECTIONS BY SCHULZ.

(20.) " The writer of our epistle has made use of a great many words and phrases, in order to express ideas which Paul expresses, (either always or usually,) by different words or phrases," p. 138, seq.

This objection is drawn out at great length, and requires a minuteness of consideration and philological exhibition which is truly appalling. But having commenced the work, it must not be left unfinished. The importance of the subject under discussion, is the apology on which I must rely for justification, as to the length and minuteness of the examination. General assertions may satisfy those who think *in generals*, and reason *in generals;* but the true critic demands *facts*, and of course *detail*, in an investigation dependent on facts.

It will shorten our work, however, and be of no small importance with respect to the satisfaction which the reader's mind is to experience, if some acknowledged, or at least just, principles of reasoning in regard to such a topic, can be premised, before we enter upon particulars.

The following principles seem to be such, as, it may reasonably be expected, will be assented to by all sober and judicious critics; in particular, by all who have not a special end to accomplish by the denial of them.

(a) The same writer, if a man of knowledge and talents, (both of which will be conceded to Paul,) does *not*, in an extensive correspondence either on matters of business or sentiment, *always express the same ideas by the same words or phrases;* much less, always repeat the same ideas, whatever may be the nature of the subject which the occasion demands. I appeal to all the volumes of letters extant, in proof of this.

(b) The same writer, at different periods of life, in different circumstances and states of mind and feeling, exhibits a variety of style in his epistles; especially where the subjects themselves are very diverse. The appeal in proof of this, I make to well-known facts, and to every one's own experience, who has been long accustomed to write letters on a variety of grave and important topics. In particular will the case be as now represented, if a writer's lot, at one period of his life, be cast among men and authors, who differ in style and modes of thinking and expression, from those with whom he has, at another time, been associated.

(c) It follows, then, that differences in the choice of expression, in two epistles, in order to convey the same idea, (above all, when this stands in connexion with diverse subjects,) is no good proof that the same person did not, or could not, write both. Indeed, no man who is not a writer of the most sterile genius, and of a mind the most mechanical, nay, absolutely insusceptible of excitement or of improvement, will always limit himself to the same round of expression. While there will be occasional words and expressions, which will mark some characteristics appropriate to a writer of knowledge and talents, yet in the great body of them, there will not be a mechanical sameness either of thought or of expression; but every letter will take its colouring, more or less, from the occasion and the state of mind which prompted it.

(d) If any person refuses to accede to principles so plain and reasonable as these, it would be easy to show him, (as will be seen hereafter,) that any one of Paul's acknowledged epistles may be proved to be spurious, on a different ground, just as easily as the epistle to the Hebrews. Schulz and Seyffarth have undertaken to prove, that Paul did not write the epistle to the Hebrews, because it contains many words, either not employed by Paul, or not employed by him in the same sense; and also some favourite expressions, not found in his acknowledged epistles. At first view, the number of such words or expressions, as exhibited by them, seems very great; nay, quite appalling, before examination. Most critics of the present day seem to have been influenced principally by this consideration, in giving up the Pauline origin of our epistle. But a widely-extended examination of this subject has ended in producing different impressions upon my own mind. In am fully persuaded, now, that there is scarcely any one of Paul's *acknowledged* epistles, which cannot be proved to be spurious, if the grounds of argument assumed by the above-named writers is tenable. I will pledge myself (I do not say it at a venture) to produce as many peculiarities, as many ἅπαξ λεγόμενα or ἅπαξ λογιζόμενα, for example, in the epistle to the Romans, in the first to the Corinthians, or in the second to the Corinthians, (in proportion to the length of these epistles, and compared with the other acknowledged epistles of Paul,) as there are in the epistle to the Hebrews. If this can be done, then is the argument equally good against either of these epistles, which are among the most undoubted of all the writings of Paul. The proof of this I shall by and by produce, by laying before the reader the result of the principles which I have ventured to call in question, by applying them to the first epistle of Paul to the Corinthians.

(e) Dr. Schulz himself, who has laboured with so much zeal and confidence to fix upon our epistle the charge of peculiarities in style, expression, and favourite phrases, has, in another part of his work, and before

§ 27. OBJECTIONS BY SCHULZ. 187

his mind became heated with this subject, made the following remarks, which are well worthy of attention.

" We give up words, and phrases, and thoughts, [in the epistle to the Hebrews,] which occur but seldom in the books of the New Testament, or in Paul's epistles. We shall not insist upon the ἅπαξ λεγόμενα or the ἅπαξ λογιζόμενα; for why must a writer of numerous works necessarily repeat, oftentimes, his ideas in general, or his favourite phrases? Why must he often do this in *all* his works, and not use some of them merely in particular passages? Every writer will do the latter, and must do it, when, either by accident or by design, he falls only once upon some particular idea. But in regard to a writer, whose whole works we do not possess, (perhaps only a small part of them,) how can we pronounce sentence upon many phrases and thoughts, or deduce any argument at all from them? And such is the case before us. What now appears, in the letters of Paul still extant, to be ἅπαξ εἰρημένον, he may have said and written numberless times, in works now lost." p. 52.

He then proceeds very justly to ask, " whether it is the design of any New Testament writer, in any one particular book, to represent the whole scheme of Christian doctrine complete in all its parts? And if not, whether that, which in one book differs from the contents of another, is to be considered as *departure* or *contradiction*, in respect to that other?" And then he adds, " It is quite surprising, and deserving of reprobation, that any one should call in question expressions against which no objections can be made, when they are consonant with the *usus loquendi*, and are genuine Greek; and also, that any one should produce them as grounds of suspicion against a book, because they do not occur in other compositions of a similar nature. In the epistle to the Hebrews, there are many of this kind." p. 53.

These remarks are no less just than striking. I freely give to them my entire and hearty approbation; and I am willing, with such principles in view, to join issue with the author, as to his list of words and phrases which he brings forward, in his attack upon our epistle. Nine parts in ten of all that he has advanced, of this nature, would be excluded from the argument by his own sentence.

To reduce the view, which I must now give of the words and phrases adduced by Schulz, to as short a compass as will be consistent with my design, I shall first remark on those words which require to be separately discussed; and then I shall class together those to which some general principle will apply in common. I follow mostly the order of Schulz,

§ 27. OBJECTIONS BY SCHULZ.

step by step, merely because this is more convenient for those who may wish to compare what is here written with the remarks of this author.

I. Words and phrases, instead of which Paul employs other and different ones.

(1.) " Εὐλάβεια, Heb. v. 7, xii. 28, is used in the sense of *piety, devotedness to God;* it is equivalent to εὐσέβεια as employed by Paul, 1 Tim. ii. 2. iii. 16, &c. Neither of these writers employs the word used by the other." p. 141.

The sense of εὐλάβεια, in Heb. v. 7, it is altogether probable, is *fear*, which is the *classical* sense of the word ; and this is probably the sense, too, in Heb. xii. 28, as its adjunct αἰδοῦς seems to indicate. Schulz's objection is founded on an exegesis far from being certain, and indeed quite improbable. But if we allow his interpretation to be true, the objection amounts only to this, that Paul, at one time, has employed εὐσέβεια (the proper Greek word) in order to express the idea of *piety ;* and at another time, in writing to the Hebrews, he has used εὐλάβεια, (corresponding to the Heb. יִרְאָה *reverence, piety,*) to express the same idea. What could be more natural for a Hebrew, than to do this ?

(2.) " Our author uses διαπαντὸς ; Paul, πάντοτε, and very frequently repeats it." p. 141.

Διαπαντὸς is common among the Evangelists, and in the Septuagint. Paul uses it, in the citation from the Old Testament, in Rom. xi. 10. Paul, then, was familiar with the word. In our epistle, it is found only *twice ;* viz. ix. 6; xiii. 15. In this same epistle we find the *Pauline* πάντοτε also; viz. in vii. 25. Now, as to the epistle to the Romans, Galatians, Ephesians, and 2 Timothy, each has the word πάντοτε but *once ;* the first epistle to Timothy, and that to Titus, not at all. . If the fact that πάντοτε is used no more than once, is proof that our epistle is not Pauline, then surely these other epistles must be ranked in the same class. The same fact must surely afford the same argument in both cases. But as this proves more than Schulz is willing to allow, we may suppose he will not insist on such an argument.

(3.) " Our epistle uses ἀνακαινίζειν and ἐγκαινίζειν: for which Paul employs ἀνακαινοῦν and ἀνανεοῦσθαι." p. 143.

'Ανακαινίζειν occurs only once, Heb. vi. 6. 'Εγκαινίζειν but twice, Heb. ix. 18; x. 20. On the other hand, ἀνακαινοῦν is found in Paul only twice, 2 Cor. iv. 16. Col. iii. 10 ; and ἀνανεοῦσθαι but once, Eph. iv. 23. Now as ἀνακαινίζω, ἀνακαινόω, and ἀνανεόω, are all either of classic or Septuagint usage, and are of the same signification, the use of one or the

§ 27. OBJECTIONS BY SCHULZ. 189

other, so few times as they are employed in the Pauline epistles and in ours, can afford no argument in favour of a different writer. As to ἐγκαινίζειν, *to consecrate, to initiate*, it is a verb of a different meaning from the others, and is not used in the sense in which Paul employs either ἀνακαινόω or ἀνανεόω.

(4.) " There is, in our epistle, an abundance of verbs ending in -ίζω, such as can be no where else found in the New Testament; above all, in Paul's epistles." p. 142.

(a) The greater part of the verbs in -ίζω, produced by Schulz as appropriate to our epistle, are found often in the New Testament, and in Paul; viz. λογίζεσθαι, in other writers of the New Testament 6 times, in Paul 34, in the epistle to the Hebrews but once; ἐμφανίζειν in New Testament 8, in Hebrews only twice; καταρτίζειν, New Testament 5, Paul 5, Hebrews 3; καθαρίζειν, New Testament 24, Paul 3, Hebrews 3; κομίζειν, New Testament 5, Paul 3, Hebrews 3; μερίζειν, New Testament 7, Paul 5, Hebrews 1; ὁρίζειν, New Testament 6, Paul 1, Hebrews 1; ἐγγίζειν, New Testament 38, Paul 2, Hebrews 2; χωρίζειν, New Testament 5. Paul 6, Hebrews 1; φωτίζειν, New Testament 5, Paul 4, Hebrews 2; καθίζειν, New Testament 40, Paul 4, Hebrews, 4; χρηματίζεσθαι, New Testament 5, Paul 1, Hebrews 3. All these verbs, moreover, are common to the Septuagint and to classic Greek.

(b) Other verbs of this class, adduced by Schulz, are used in our epistle only once; viz. ἀναλογίζεσθαι, xii. 3; ἀνταγωνίζεσθαι, xii. 4; καταγωνίζεσθαι, xi. 33; θεατρίζειν, x. 33; πρίζειν, xi. 37; and τυμπανίζεσθαι, xi. 35. The three last are *denominatives*, for which the Greek language offered no other forms; so that no choice, in this case, was left to the writer. All of them are of classic or Septuagint usage.

(c) Προσοχθίζειν, Heb. iii. 10, is a quotation from the Septuagint; of which the use of the same word, in iii. 17, is a simple repetition.

It turns out, then, that of the *great multitude* of words in -ίζω, peculiar to our epistle, only six are employed, exclusively by it; and of these six, three are *denominatives*, and *necessarily* employed, as there was no choice of other forms; while the other three occur but *once* each, and are all compound verbs, common to the Septuagint and to the classics. But Schulz has not ventured to present us with a view of the numerous verbs in -ίζω, employed by the New Testament writers and by Paul, which are *not* used at all in our epistle. Selecting only under a single letter, (as a specimen of what might be gathered from the whole,) we find the fol-

§ 27. OBJECTIONS BY SCHULZ.

owing, καθοπλίζομαι, καταβιβάζομαι, καταδικάζω, κατακλύζομαι, κατακρημνίζω, καταλιθάζω, καταναθεματίζω, καταποντίζομαι, κατεξουσιάζω, κατεργάζομαι, κατοπτρίζομαι, καυματίζω, καυτηριάζομαι, κλάζω, κιθαρίζω, κλυδωνίζομαι, κολάζομαι, κολαφίζω, κοπάζω, κουφίζω, κράζω, κραυγάζω, κρυσταλλίζω, κτίζω; *twenty-four* under only one letter; which our author, with all his alleged partialities for -ίζω, never uses. Surely this is an argument unfortunately chosen, and very incorrectly stated.

(5.) " 'Εντέλλεσθαι is used in our epistle; Paul uses παραγγέλλω, διατάσσω, or ἐπιτάσσω." p. 145.

'Εντέλλεσθαι is employed only twice, ix. 20; xi. 22. In the New Testament it is used fifteen times, although not employed by Paul. Paul employs παραγγέλλω only in 1 Corinthians, 1 Thessalonians, 2 Thessalonians, and 1 Timothy; διατάσσω only in 1 Corinthians, Galatians, and Titus; ἐπιτάσσω only once in Philemon. Do not these words differ as much from each other, as each of them does from ἐντέλλεσθαι; and will not the reasoning be the same, to prove that Galatians and Titus or Philemon are spurious, as that our epistle is? And what shall be said of all those epistles, where none of these words are at all employed?

(6.) " Our author employs καθίζω in a *neuter* sense, i. 3; viii. 1; x. 12; xii. 2; Paul employs this verb in a *transitive* sense." p. 143.

In the quotation by Paul, 1 Cor. x. 7, it is used in a *neuter* sense; as it is in 2 Thess. ii. 4. It has a transitive sense only in 1 Cor. vi. 4; Eph. i. 20. It occurs in no other case, in Paul, so that his usage is equally divided. In our epistle, it occurs in the same formula in all the four instances where it is employed; and all of these instances refer to Ps. cx. 1, (Sept. cix. 1,) where is the like usage of κάθου.

(7.) " Abstract appellations of God, such as θρόνος τῆς χάριτος, πνεῦμα τῆς χάριτος, θρόνος τῆς μεγαλοσύνης, are unheard of in Paul's writings." p. 144.

What, then, is πνεῦμα ἁγιωσύνης, Rom. i. 4; θειότης, i. 20; ἀλήθειαν τοῦ Θεοῦ, *true God*, i. 25; also ψεῦδος, *false god*, ibid.; and πνεῦμα ζωῆς, viii. 2? Is the usage of employing *abstract* words for *concrete* ones, foreign to the style of Paul? Every one who reads this apostle with attention, will be able to answer this question.

(8.) " Our epistle calls Christ ἀπαύγασμα τῆς δόξης, i. 3; Paul says, εἰκὼν τοῦ Θεοῦ ἀοράτου, 2 Cor. iv. 4; Col. i. 15; and μορφὴ Θεοῦ, in Phil. ii. 6." p. 144.

Is not μορφὴ Θεοῦ as different from εἰκὼν Θεοῦ ἀοράτου, as ἀπαύγασμα

§ 27. OBJECTIONS BY SCHULZ. 191

τῆς δόξης is from the same? And if this argument prove any thing, does it not prove that the epistle to the Philippians, which employs μορφὴ Θεοῦ, (and not εἰκὼν Θεοῦ,) must also be spurious?

(9.) " In our epistle κακουχέω is used, xi. 37; xiii. 3; Paul uses θλίβω instead of this." p. 145.

Paul uses ςενοχωρέομαι three times, in his second epistle to the Corinthians, (and not once any where else,) to express the same idea that he elsewhere expresses by θλίβω. Is this epistle therefore spurious?

(10.) " Our epistle employs ἐνθύμησις and ἔννοια, for which Paul uses διαλογισμὸς and λογισμὸς." p. 145.

Λογισμὸς is found in 2 Cor. x. 4; but διαλογισμὸς in Romans, first Corinthians, Philippians, and first Timothy. Is the second Corinthians spurious, because it does not use διαλογισμὸς?

(11.) " Our epistle uses ἀκλινὴς; for which Paul employs ἑδραῖος, ἀμετακίνητος, or μὴ μετακινούμενος." p. 145.

Ἀκλινὴς is used once only, Heb. x. 32. So ἀμετακίνητος is used only in 1 Cor. xv. 58, and μὴ μετακινούμενος only in Col. i. 23. Now, as in first Corinthians and in Colossians both, Paul uses ἑδραῖος as well as these words, in order to express the same idea, shall the like choice of a synonyme, in another letter, be denied him? And is it reasonable that it should expose his letter to the charge of spuriousness, because that, out of various synonymes, he has sometimes taken one, and sometimes another?

(12.) " Συμπαθεῖν, μετριοπαθεῖν, and παθεῖν, are current in our epistle; Paul uses συμπάσχειν and πάσχειν." p. 145.

Paul uses πάσχειν five times only, in four of which the *present* tense is required, and of course this form must be used, as there is no present παθέω. He also employs ἐπάθετε twice; viz. in Gal. iii. 4, and 1 Thess. ii. 14. Our epistle has this same form, but only *three* times, v. 8; ix. 26; xiii. 12. Here, then, are the same forms, in both Paul and our epistle. Besides, are not πάσχω, συμπάσχω, and συμπαθέω, commingled forms, and every where exchanged for each other? As to μετριοπαθεῖν, it is used but once, Heb. v. 2, and is there employed in its *classical* sense.

(13.) " In our epistle, we find μετέσχε, κατάσχωμεν; but in Paul, μετέχειν, κατέχειν." p. 145.

Once only is μετέσχε used, Heb. ii. 14. On the other hand, the *Pauline* μετέχων is also employed once, in Heb. v. 13. Besides, in all Paul's acknowledged epistles, μετέχω occurs only five times, and all of

§ 27. OBJECTIONS BY SCHULZ.

these are in the first epistle to the Corinthians. Is this the only epistle which is genuine? As to κατάσχωμεν, it is found in our epistle only twice, iii. 6; iii. 14; while the alleged Pauline κατέχειν is also used in x. 43. Besides, are not both of these one and the same verb, in different tenses? And may not the writer of different epistles employ even a different tense of the same verb, when the case demands it, without hazarding the reputation of his letters in respect to genuineness?

(14.) "Verbal nouns feminine, particularly such as end in -σις, are unusually frequent in our epistle; and, when put in the accusative by εἰς, they are employed instead of the infinitive mode with εἰς τὸ before it; which latter is the construction that Paul employs, even to excess, and in a manner not consentaneous with Greek idiom." p. 146.

Paul is no stranger to the employment of nouns in -σις with εἰς before them in the accusative, in the sense of the infinitive mode with εἰς τὸ; e. g. Rom. i. 17; iii. 25; v. 18; xiv. 1; 1 Cor. xi. 24, 25. In regard to other feminine nouns, put in the accusative with εἰς, and used as the infinitive with εἰς τὸ, see Rom. i. 5. 16; iii. 7; v. 16; vi. 19. 22; ix. 21 bis, 22, 23; x. 1. 10; xi. 9; xv. 18; xvi. 26. 1 Cor. i. 9; ii. 7; v. 5; x. 31; xvi. 15. All these cases have respect to nouns feminine only; very many cases might be added of nouns of the masculine form, employed in the same way. The above instances of the feminine forms are selected from only *two* epistles of Paul. I have found more than forty cases, of the same kind, in his remaining acknowledged epistles.

On the other hand; as to the excessive and unclassical use of the infinitive with εἰς τὸ, by Paul, I do not find it to be as Schulz has stated it. In Romans, I find fifteen cases of infinitives with εἰς τὸ; in 1 Cor. there are five cases; in 2 Cor. there are four; in Gal. one; in Eph. three; in Phil. four; in Col. not one; in 1 Tim., 2 Tim., Titus, and Philemon, not one. But in our epistle, we have the infinitive with εἰς τὸ, in ii. 17; vii. 25; viii. 3; ix. 14. 28; x. 2, (διὰ τὸ;) x. 15, (μετὰ τὸ;) xii. 10; xiii. 21; i. e. seven cases, just the same as the Pauline ones, and two more (x. 2. 15) of the same nature. If the want of *frequency* with respect to this construction proves the spuriousness of our epistle; what does the same thing prove, in respect to the longer epistle, called the first to the Corinthians, which exhibits it only *five* times? And what is to be said of the five epistles named above, which do not at all exhibit this *favourite* construction of Paul?

In regard to the frequency of nouns ending in -σις, the proportion is

§ 27. OBJECTIONS BY SCHULZ. 193

not greater than in several of the Pauline epistles; as any one may determine by consulting a Greek concordance.

(15.) " Our epistle uses παροξυσμὸς; Paul ζῆλος." p. 148.

Παροξυσμὸς is used only once, Heb. x. 24, and there not in the sense of ζῆλος.

(16.) " Our epistle uses πρεσβύτεροι for *ancients?* Paul uses πατέρες." p. 149.

Paul uses πατέρες, in this way, only in Rom. ix. 5; xi 28; xv 8. As to πρεσβύτεροι, it is a common word for זְקֵנִים, *ancients*, Matt. xv. 2. Mark vii. 3. 5. also Sept. What should hinder Paul from selecting either of these synonymes at his pleasure?

(17.) " Our author uses προβλέπομαι; Paul uses προετοιμάζω, προορίζω, προτίθημι. Our author uses ἀντικαθίστημι; Paul ἀνθίστημι," p. 149.

Προβλέπομαι occurs only in xi. 40, and is synonymous, in some of its meanings, with the other verbs named. Besides, is there not as much departure from *uniformity*, in employing the several words, προετοιμάζω, προορίζω, προτίθημι, as there is in using προβλέπομαι? And is not ἀντικαθίστημι a classic and Septuagint word, and synonymous with ἀνθίστημι? Must a writer never employ but one and the same word?

II. Words employed in the epistle to the Hebrews in a sense different from that in which Paul uses them.

Some of the objections, drawn from words of this class, have already been noticed above.

(18.) " Μακροθυμία, μακροθυμεῖν means *patient waiting* or *expectation*, in our epistle; in Paul, it means *lenity towards others*." p. 150.

Paul employs it in other senses than that of *lenity*. E. g. Col. i. 11, *patient endurance of evil;* so 2 Tim. iii. 10 prob. iv. 2, see Wahl's Lex. In the same sense it is probably used in Heb. vi. 12. 15. But if this be not allowed; it is enough to say that μακροθυμία, in the sense of *patient expectation*, is agreeable to Hellenistic usage. See Job vii. 16. Sept., and James v. 7, 8.

(19.) " Καταλείπεσθαι and ἀπολείπεσθαι are used, by our author, in the sense of *restare, reliquum esse;* they are not so used by Paul." p. 150.

Καταλείπεσθαι is used, *actively* in the like sense, in Rom. xi. 4; and this sense is classic and Hellenistic. Ἀπολείπεσθαι is used in the active voice by Paul, in 2 Tim. iv. 13. 20, in a sense as kindred to the use of it in our epistle (where it is *passive*,) as one of these voices can be to the other, in regard to a verb of this nature.

o

(20.) "Ὑπόστασις, in our epistle, has a different sense from that in Paul's epistles." p. 150.

I am not able to perceive the difference between ὑπόστασις in 2 Cor. ix. 4; xi. 17; and in Heb. iii. 14; xi. 1. These are all the instances in which this word is employed by Paul or in our epistle, excepting Heb. i. 3, where the word is used in the classical sense of the later Greek writers. See Wahl's Lex. on ὑπόστασις.

(21.) "Λόγος, in Hebrews, means *word given, assurance, declaration*; in Paul, *doctrine, command, word* in opposition to *deed.*" p. 150.
So in Heb. xiii. 7, λόγος means *doctrine*, as also in v. 13; vi. 1. On the other hand, in 1 Cor. xv. 54, it means *assurance* or *declaration*; as also in Rom. ix. 6. 9. 1 Cor. iv. 19. 2 Cor. i. 18. 1 Tim. i. 15; iii. 1; iv. 9. Surely there is no ground for distinction here. In the sense of *account*, too, Paul and our epistle agree; e. g. Rom. xiv. 12. Heb. iv. 13; xiii. 17.

(22.) "Τάξις, in Hebrews, means *series, succession;* Paul uses it for *good order, arrangement.*" p. 150.

Τάξις, in the Septuagint, answers to תִּורָה *prescribed order* or *arrangement,* Prov. xxix. 24 [xxxi. 26]; to עֶרֶךְ, Job xxviii. 13, Aquila's translation. In the Sept. Job xxiv. 5; xxxvi. 28, it has the sense of *prescribed arrangement.* This sense fits, equally well, 1 Cor. xiv. 40. Col. ii. 5, and all the cases where it is used in our epistle; viz. v. 6. 10; vi. 20; vii. 11. 17. 21. all of which are merely the same instance of τάξις repeated. But, even if this exegesis be not admitted, still, it is enough to say, that τάξις is employed in both the senses named by Schulz, in the Septuagint Greek, and also in classic authors. May not Paul, like any other writer, employ the word, in different parts of his writings, (as he does a multitude of other words,) with different shades of meaning?

(23.) "Πλείων is used by our author in the sense of *præstantior;* by Paul, only for *more.*" p. 151.
In Heb. iii. 3; vii. 23, πλείων is used in the sense of *more;* certainly in the last instance. On the other hand, in the sense of *præstantior,* it occurs only once, xi. 4. And this sense is supported both by classic and Septuagint usage.

III. Favourite expressions, and peculiar phraseology.

Of these, Schulz has collected together a great number; so great, that if they are truly what he names them, they must render the genuineness of our epistle *suspected*, to every critical reader. But whether he has

§ 27. OBJECTIONS BY SCHULZ 195

rightly attributed to these words and expressions the characteristics which he gives them, remains to be examined.

(24.) "The use of γὰρ, in our epistle, is excessive; so much so, that a translator, if he means to avoid misleading his readers, must often pass it over unnoticed. Paul is less frequent in the use of this particle; and employs it only in cases where it has a meaning." p. 152.

In the New Testament before me, the epistle of Paul to the Romans occupies fourteen pages; that to the Hebrews, ten. In Romans, I find γὰρ one hundred and forty-five times, i. e. on an average, more than ten to a page; in our epistle, I find it ninety-one times, i. e. on an average, a little more than nine to a page. So much for this *favourite* particle of the author of our epistle.

(25.) "The words προσφέρειν and προσφορὰ, are used times almost without number, in our epistle, in respect to Christ's offering up himself before God, by means of his death; Paul does not use the verb at all, nor the noun but once, Eph. v. 2, in this sense." p. 153.

These words are employed in respect to the offering by Christ, in Heb. ix. 14. 25. 28; x. 10. 12. 14. *six* instances; which, considering the nature of the comparison between Christ's death and the Jewish offerings, is rather to be wondered at for *unfrequent*, than for frequent occurrence. But is it not truly surprising, that Schulz should produce, as examples which have respect to the *offering* made by the *death of Christ*, προσφέρειν and προσφορὰ in Heb. v. 1. 3. 7; viii. 3, 4; ix. 7. 9; x. 1, 2. 5. 8. 11. 18; xi. 4. 17; xii. 7? all of which refer to *Jewish* offerings, excepting xii. 7, which has wholly another sense. Nor is the language of our epistle limited to προσφέρειν and προσφορὰ. The writer uses ἀναφέρω, in vii. 27 bis; ix. 28; xiii. 15; which is also used by other New Testament writers, e. g. James ii. 21. 1 Pet. ii. 5. 24. As to the *frequency* with which προσφορὰ is used, it is found only in five instances; two of these (x. 5. 8,) are quotations from the Old Testament; and the other three, (x. 10. 14. 18,) are all plainly occasioned by the quotations just named, as they are employed in reasoning upon it. No where else, in our epistle, does the writer use this word; but he employs θυσία no less than fifteen times, which word Paul has also employed five times. Considering the nature of the discussion in our epistle, is there any ground for the objection made by Schulz?

(26.) "Ἐγγίζειν τῷ Θεῷ, and προσέρχεσθαι τῷ Θεῷ are frequent forms in our epistle; but not so in Paul." p. 153.

The first of these phrases occurs only once, vii. 19. The *frequency*

o 2

of it, therefore, should not have been alleged. But the same verb as applied to *time*, is used in Heb. x. 25, and in Rom. xiii. 12. That ἐγγίζειν τῷ Θεῷ was a usual form of Hebrew Greek, is evident from James iv. 8.

In respect to προσέρχεσθαι, it is nearly a synonyme with ἐγγίζειν, and is used a great number of times in the New Testament, and by Paul in 1 Tim. vi. 3, but in the figurative sense of *attending to, giving heed to*. The use of it in our epistle, (it is employed seven times,) is occasioned by its correspondence with the Hebrew הִקְרִיב, which describes *the action of approaching God with an offering* ; an idea which, from the nature of the comparisons instituted, must of necessity frequently occur.

(27.) " Such forms as λαμβάνειν πεῖραν—μισθαποδοσίαν—ἀρχὴν—τιμὴν—νεκροὺς—ἐπαγγελίαν—ἐπαγγελίας, are frequent, and *peculiar* to our epistle." p. 153.

In Paul, too, we have λαμβάνειν χάριν—ἀποστολὴν—σημεῖον—καταλλαγὴν—περισσείαν—ἀφορμὴν—πνεῦμα δουλείας—πνεῦμα υἱοθεσίας—κρίμα—πνεῦμα τοῦ κόσμου—μισθὸν—βραβεῖον—στέφανον—ἄρτον—οἰκοδομὴν—ὀψώνιον—ὑμᾶς—πρόσωπον—ἐπαγγελίαν—μορφὴν—ἐντολὴν—ὑπόμνησιν. Is not this equally *peculiar* ?

(28.) " Διαθήκη, and the compounds and derivatives of τιθέναι are *unusually* frequent in our epistle." p. 154.

Διαθήκη is employed by Paul nine times; but in our epistle, where the nature of the comparison lies between the old covenant and the new, the more frequent use of this word was altogether to be expected. Out of the seventeen instances, however, in which our author uses it, six are quoted from the Old Testament, viz. viii. 8, 9 bis, 10 ; ix. 20 ; x. 16 ; and three more are in phrases transferred from the Old Testament, viz. ix. 4 bis, x. 29 ; so that eight instances only belong properly to our author's style. Could a less number than this be rationally expected, considering the nature of the discussion ?

As to the uncommonly frequent use of the compounds and derivatives of τίθημι, in our epistle, the following is the result of comparison. Διατίθημι, four times in Hebrews, two of which are in quotations, viz. viii. 10 ; x. 16. In the other two cases, the word is employed in a sense different from the one usual in the New Testament, viz. ix. 16, 17. Μετάθεσις is one of the ἅπαξ λεγόμενα of our epistle ; (see on these § 29.) Μετατίθημι is used three times; also in Gal. i. 6 ; ἀθετεῖν, Hebrews once, Paul six times ; ἀθέτησις, Hebrews twice; νομοθετεῖν, Hebrews twice, (νομοθεσία in Rom. ix. 4 ;) ἐπίθεσις, Hebrews once, Paul twice ; πρόθεσις,

§ 27. OBJECTIONS BY SCHULZ. 197

Hebrews once, Paul six times; ἀποτίθημι, Hebrews once, Paul four times. Can the position of Schulz be supported, when the result of investigation turns out thus?

(29.) " Τελειοῦν, to bring to perfection, to advance to the highest mark, is a *favourite* expression of our epistle." p. 154.

It is employed in ii. 10; v. 9; vii. 28; xii. 23; but in a different acceptation in vii. 19; ix. 9; x. 1. 14; xi. 40; perhaps the last instance belongs to the other category. To the former alleged *peculiar* sense of τελειόω, Paul is no stranger, Phil. iii. 12; comp. 2 Cor. xii. 9. Other Hellenists, also, employ it in the same manner; Luke xiii. 32. The derivate forms, τελείωσις and τελειότης, vii. 11, xii. 2, occur once only in this epistle. Τελείωσις, also, in Luke i. 45.

(30.) " Κρείττων is employed frequently, by our author, in a sense altogether peculiar, viz. in the sense of *more excellent*." p. 154.

In the same sense Paul uses it, 1 Cor. xii. 31; a sense, moreover, which is common to classic and Hellenistic usage.

(31.) " Αἰώνιος is unusually frequent; e. g. αἰώνιος joined with σωτηρία—κρίμα—πνεῦμα—λύτρωσις—κληρονομία—διαθήκῃ, &c." p. 154.

But Paul uses αἰώνιος ζωή—χρόνος—Θεὸς—βάρος—αἰώνια βλεπόμενα—αἰώνιος ὄλεθρος—παράκλησις—κράτος—δόξη. Paul uses the word twenty-four times; our epistle only *six*.

(32.) " Ζωὴ and ζῆν are used very frequently by our author, to denote *perpetuity*, *lasting continuance*." p. 155.

So they are by Paul; e. g. Rom. ix. 26. 2 Cor. iii. 3; vi. 16. 1 Thess. i. 9. 1 Tim. iii. 15; iv. 10; and this sense is frequent in the New Testament.

(33.) " The frequent use of πᾶς in the *singular*, in our epistle, is striking." p. 155.

Our epistle makes ten pages in the edition of the New Testament lying before me; and I find πᾶς, in the singular, sixteen times in it, i. e. on an average, about once and a half to each page. The epistle to the Ephesians makes four and a half pages, and I find the same πᾶς in it twenty-three times, i. e. on an average more than five times to each page. So much for the *strikingly frequent* use of πᾶς in our epistle!

(34.) " The words ὅθεν, χωρὶς, ἐάνπερ, and ἀδύνατον, are unusually frequent in our epistle." p. 155.

Ὅθεν is not used in the acknowledged epistles of Paul, (see, in respect to ἅπαξ λεγόμενα, § 29;) but in the New Testament it is common. Χωρὶς Paul uses fifteen times. Ἐάνπερ is peculiar to Hebrews, and occurs

§ 27. OBJECTIONS BY SCHULZ.

thrice. Ἀδύνατον is employed four times in our epistle, twice by Paul, and four times by the other writers of the New Testament.

(35.) "Compounds of words with εὖ, are *favourite* forms with our author." p. 155.

The following results will show how far this is well founded. Εὔθετος occurs in Hebrews *once*; εὐθύτης, once; εὐάρεστον, Hebrews 1, Paul 8; εὐαρεστέω, Hebrews 3; εὐαρεστῶς, Hebrews 1; εὐλάβεια, Hebrews 2; εὐλαβέομαι, Hebrews 1; εὐποιΐα, Hebrews 1; εὐπερίστατος, Hebrews 1; εὐλογία, Hebrews 2, Paul 9; εὐλογεῖν, Hebrews 6, Paul 8; εὔκαιρος, Hebrews 1; εὐδοκεῖν, Hebrews 3, Paul 11.

On the other hand, compare the compounds of this sort in Paul, which do not occur in our epistle; viz. εὐγενὴς, εὐαγγέλιον, εὐαγγελιστὴς, εὐδοκία, εὐεργεσία, εὐθέως, εὐκαιρέω, εὐκαίρως, εὐλογητὸς, εὔνοια, εὐμετάδοτος, εὐοδοῦμαι, εὐπρόσδεκτος, εὐπρόσεδρος, εὐπροσωπέω, εὐσέβεια, εὐσεβεῖν, εὐσεβῶς, εὔσημος, εὔσπλαγχνος, εὐσχημόνως, εὐσχημόνη, εὐσχήμων, εὐτραπελία, εὐφημία, εὔφημος, εὐφραίνω, εὐχαριστέω, εὐχάριστία, εὐχάριστος, εὔχρηστος, εὐψυχέω, εὐωδία. Can there be any foundation, now, for the assertion of Schulz?

(36.) "Compounds with ἀνὰ are unusually frequent, in our author." p. 156.

The fact stands thus. *Once* only are ἀναδέχομαι, ἀναθεωρέω, ἀνακαινίζω, ἀνάγω, ἀνακάμπτω, ἀναλογίζομαι, ἀνασταυρόω, ἀνατέλλω, used in our epistle. Ἀναφέρω is employed four times. In Paul, on the other hand, we find, ἀναβαίνω 7, ἀναγγέλλω 2, ἀναγινώσκω 8, ἀνάγνωσις 2, ἀνάχω 1, ἀναζάω 2, ἀναζωπυρέω 1, ἀναθάλλω 1, ἀνάθεμα 5, ἀνακαίνωσις 2, ἀνακαινόω 1, ἀνακαλύπτω 2, ἀνακεφαλαίομαι 2, ἀνακόπτω 2, ἀνακρίνω 10, ἀναλαμβάνω 4, ἀνάλυσις 1, ἀναλύω 1, ἀναλίσκω 1, ἀναλογία 1, ἀραμένω 1, ἀνανεόω 1, ἀνανήφω 1; ἀναξίος 1, ἀναξίως 2, ἀναπαύω 4, ἀναπέμπω 1, ἀναπολόγητος 2, ἀναπληρόω 5, ἀνασατόω 1, ἀνατίθημι 1, ἀνατρέπω 2, ἀναψύχω 1; all of which are wanting in the epistle to the Hebrews. Is there any *want of frequency*, in compounds of this sort, in the writings of Paul? Rather, is there not even a *want of frequency*, with respect to words of this class, in our epistle?

(37.) "Good periods, with comparisons by ὅσον—τοσοῦτο, with εἰ γὰρ—πῶς δέ, with καθὼς, &c. are not so frequent in Paul's writings as here." p. 156.

In what other epistle has Paul had so frequent occasion for *comparisons*?

(38.) "Σωτηρία, in the sense of *Christian happiness*, is peculiar to our epistle. Ἀντιλογία is also peculiar." p. 156.

§ 27. OBJECTIONS BY SCHULZ. 199

(a) Our epistle does not limit the word σωτηρία to such a sense. It is employed in its usual acceptation, in ii. 10; xi. 7; and probably in v. 9 · vi. 9; ix. 28. On the other hand, Paul uses σωτηρία for *Christian happiness*, Rom. x. 1. 10; xi. 11. Eph. i. 13; 1 Thess. v. 8, 9. 2 Thess. ii. 13. 2 Tim. iii. 15.

(b) As to ἀντιλογία, it is not found, it is true, in Paul's acknowledged epistles; but it is in Jude, ver. 11; and the verb, ἀντιλέγω, is in Rom. x. 21. Tit. i. 9; ii. 9.

(39.) " Μαρτυρεῖν and μαρτυρεῖσθαι, in the sense of *bearing honorary testimony*, are *peculiar* to our epistle." p. 156.

They are not. See Rom. x. 2; 1 Tim. v. 10; and often in the Gospels, as may be seen in any of the New Testament lexicons.

(40.) "The following habitual expressions, so often employed by Paul, are wanting in our epistle : viz. οὐ θέλω ὑμᾶς ἀγνοεῖν—θέλω ὑμᾶς εἰδένα.—τοῦτο δὲ φημι—γνωρίζω (γνωρίζομεν) δὲ ὑμῖν—οἶδα γὰρ—οἴδαμεν δὲ, &c.—γινώσκειν δὲ ὑμᾶς βούλομαι—τὶ οὖν ἐροῦμεν—ἀλλ' ἐρεῖ τις—ἐρεῖς οὖν μοι—ἢ ἀγνοεῖτε—μὴ γένοιτο—τὶ οὖν—τὶ γὰρ—ἄρα οὖν—μενοῦνγε." p. 157, seq.

If the want of these forms of expression in our epistle proves it to be spurious, then the same argument must prove a great part of Paul's epistles to be so. E. g. οὐ θέλω ὑμᾶς ἀγνοεῖν is not in Galatians, Philippians, Colossians, 2 Thessalonians, 1 Timothy, 2 Timothy, Titus, Philemon. *Favourite* as Schulz represents this phrase to be, it is found only in Romans twice, 1 Corinthians twice; and in 2 Corinthians, οὐ γὰρ θέλομεν ὑμᾶς ἀγνοεῖν once.

Θέλω δὲ ὑμᾶς εἰδέναι is once in 1 Cor. xi. 3, and wanting in all the other Pauline epistles; an expression, therefore, *singularly* favourite.

Τοῦτο δὲ φημι is in 1 Corinthians twice, and wanting in all the rest of Paul's works.

Γνωρίζω (γνωρίζομεν) δὲ ὑμῖν, Paul uses four times. The verb is employed some twenty times, in all his epistles, but not in the formula mentioned by Schulz.

Οἶδα, οἴδαμεν, &c. is used often by Paul, indeed unusually so; in our epistle less frequently. In x. 30 we have οἴδαμεν, and five other cases of derivatives from εἴδω or εἰδέω occur.

Γινώσκειν δὲ ὑμᾶς βούλομαι, occurs only in Phil. i. 12.

Τὶ οὖν ἐροῦμεν, in Romans six times, and no where else. Which then is spurious, the epistle to the Romans, or all the others?

Ἐρεῖς οὖν μοι, only twice, Rom. ix. 19; xi. 19.

Ἐρεῖ τις, only *once*, 1 Cor. xv. 37.

Ἡ ἀγνοεῖτε, only twice, Rom. vi. 3. vii. 1.

Μὴ γένοιτο, only in Galatians and Romans.

Τί γάρ, not in Galatians, Ephesians, Colossians, first Thessalonians second Thessalonians, first Timothy, second Timothy, Titus.

Τί οὖν, not in any of Paul's epistles, except Romans, first Corinthians and Galatians.

Ἆρα οὖν, only in the epistle to the Romans, Galatians once, Ephesians once, first Thessalonians once, second Tessalonians once. Ἆρα is used by our author too, iv. 9; xii. 8.

Μενοῦνγε, in Romans, Philippians ; but no where else in Paul's epistles.

Certain is it, then, that the same argument which would prove the spuriousness of our epistle, would also prove the spuriousness of more or less of Paul's acknowledged epistles ; for there is not a single phrase mentioned by Schulz, in all his list of " favourite expressions often repeated by Paul," which is not wanting in more or less of his acknowledged epistles. The words οἶδα, οἴδαμεν, &c. only, are to be expected. Many of these *favouritisms* we see, too, upon examination, turn out to belong only to some *single* epistle ; e. g. θέλω δὲ ὑμᾶς εἰδέναι, τοῦτο δὲ φημι, γινώσκειν δὲ ὑμᾶς βούλομαι, τί οὖν ἐροῦμεν, ἐρεῖς οὖν μοι, ἐρεῖ τις, and ἢ ἀγνοεῖτε. It is difficult to conceive how a man of Schulz's intelligence could willingly risk the hazard of such arguments as these.

I have omitted no argument of a philological nature, which Dr. Schulz has brought forward, excepting a few ἅπαξ λεγόμενα, of which I shall hereafter take notice. If the reader hesitates in regard to the sufficiency of some parts of the answers to Schulz, which I have laid before him, I request him to suspend his decision, until he shall have read through the sequel ; in which the general method of argument used by Schulz and Seyffarth, will be the subject of further observation. Before I proceed to this, however, the allegations of Seyffarth, (in cases wherein they differ from those of Schulz, and from those made by Bertholdt and others, which have already been examined,) must be considered. I do not aim at writing a *regular review* of Seyffarth's whole book ; but merely to pass in review such arguments of his, as have not already been examined, omitting only those, on which it cannot well be supposed that he placed any important reliance.

§ 28. *Objections of Seyffarth examined.*

I shall first examine the objections drawn from the alleged " peculiarity of the matters treated of" in our epistle.

(1.) " Paul concerns himself only with those churches he himself established. He was not the founder of any church purely Hebrew. The person who, in our epistle, addresses the Hebrews, must have sustained a relation to them very different from that which Paul sustained." § 47.

Is any thing plainer, however, through the whole epistle, than the fact, that the writer of it was not a founder or bishop of the church whom he addresses? Not a hint of either of these relations is discoverable. The circumstances, then, agree altogether with the condition of Paul, who did not found, or preside over, the Hebrew churches.

But the assumption, that Paul never concerned himself with any churches of which he was not himself the founder, is manifestly erroneous. Did not this apostle write his epistle to the Romans, before he ever saw Rome? See Rom. i. 13. xv. 24. Are not the expressions, in this epistle, as affectionate and as authoritative, to say the least, as in the epistle to the Hebrews? Paul, surely, had a very deep sympathy and tender concern for his Jewish brethren. See Rom. ix. 1, seq. x. 1, seq. xi. 1, seq. Compare, for expressions of kindness, Heb. vi. 10, seq. x. 32 seq., in particular v. 34, if the reading δεσμοῖς μου be adopted; and Titmann, in his recent edition of the New Testament, has adopted it.

(2,) " Paul no where treats formally of the dignity of Jesus; nor does he any where employ such arguments as our epistle exhibits, against defection from Christianity." p. 104.

Paul no where else treats of the resurrection, in such a manner as the 1 Cor. xv. does; nor of many other subjects, discussed in that epistle; does it follow, that Paul did not write the first epistle to the Corinthians, because it has these *peculiarities?* Besides, the fact is not correctly stated by Seyffarth. Surely Rom. ix. 5. Eph. i. 20—23. Phil. ii. 6—11. Col. i. 13—19, contain something about the dignity of Christ; not to mention many other passages. That the apostle has no where, except in our epistle, entered into a formal comparison of Christ with others, is true; but it is enough to say, that no where else did the occasion demand it.

(3.) ' Paul every where inveighs against Jewish opinions; urges justification χωρὶς ἔργων νόμου, and ἐκ πίστεως; dwells on the glorious

§ 28. OBJECTIONS BY SEYFFARTH.

advent of the Messiah; and urges the equal right of the Gentiles to the blessings of the Christian religion. Not a word of all this, in the epistle to the Hebrews." p. 105.

And where is there any thing of all this, in the first epistle to the Corinthians? Must a writer always speak of the very same subjects, and in the same way? And if he does not, but speaks *pro re nata*, is it any just ground of suspicion, that such of his letters as are not exactly like certain other ones, cannot be genuine?

(4.) " It is wonderful, that our epistle should represent the devil as the cause of death, ii. 14; Paul knows nothing of such a cause, see 2 Tim. i. 10. 1 Cor. xv. 55." p. 106.

This objection is built on an exegesis of Heb. ii. 14, which cannot be supported; see the Commentary on this passage. But if the exegesis were correct, it would not follow, that the apostle might not, in one passage, express a sentiment which he has no where else expressed. See, for example, 1 Cor. xv. 22—28. After all, it is not true, that Paul does not recognise Satan as the author of the condemning sentence which Adam incurred; see 1 Tim. ii. 13, 14. 2 Cor. xi. 3, comp. with Rom. v. 12, seq.

(5.) " Paul, when he writes to any church, enters into a particular consideration of all their wants, and woes, and dangers; e. g. in his epistles to the Romans, Corinthians, and Galatians." p. 107, seq.

And does Paul any where show a deeper sympathy for those whom he addresses, than the writer of our epistle exhibits? Must every epistle which a man writes, be *de omni scibili*, or *de omni re possibili?* As Paul was not bishop of the church whom he addresses in our epistle, it was not to be expected that he would use the same degree of freedom, in all respects, which he uses in some others of his epistles. Particularly, may we well suppose, that he would be sparing in localities and personalities, if his epistle was designed to be *encyclical;* as we have good reason to believe it was.

(6.) " Our epistle every where urges to $\tau\epsilon\lambda\epsilon\iota\acute{o}\tau\eta\tau a$; not so Paul. With our author, too, the sonship of Christ is the great $\tau\epsilon\lambda\epsilon\iota\acute{o}\tau\eta\varsigma$ of religion; not so in Paul. See 1 Cor. iii. 11, where it is reckoned as the *foundation.* Where too has Paul compared Christ to the angels?" p. 110.

That Paul does not urge forward those whom he addresses, to a higher degree of Christian knowledge and virtue, is an allegation which I believe to be *novel*, and which needs to be met only when something is

§ 28. OBJECTIONS BY SEYFFARTH.

brought forward to substantiate it. As to the doctrine of Christ's *Sonship* being reckoned as the *foundation* of Christianity, I find nothing of it in 1 Cor. iii. 11, where Christ, in his mediatorial person or character simply, is represented. That Paul's acknowledged epistles have not run a parallel between Christ and the angels, is true enough; but how are we to show that Paul never could do this in one epistle, because he has not done it in another?

(7.) " There is more pure and continuous argument in our epistle, than in those of Paul."

There is more pure and continuous argument in the epistle to the Romans, than there is in the epistles to the Ephesians, Philippians, Colossians, and Thessalonians; but is this any proof, that Paul did not write the latter epistles? And must the tenor of all the epistles which any man writes, however diverse the occasion and the subject may be, always be one and the same?

(8.) " Paul cites the Old Testament with great freedom, at one time following the Septuagint, and at another the Hebrew. Our author keeps close to the Septuagint."

The case is too strongly stated. It is not exactly correct, in either respect. But if it were, it does not follow, that in writing to those who had the Greek Scriptures in their own hands, and were habitually conversant with them, Paul would not keep closer than usual to the words of the ancient oracles. It is altogether natural that he should do so.

I. Objections drawn from peculiar phrases.

(9.) " The following phrases are *sui generis*, and *maxime peculiares*, in our epistle; viz. διαφορώτερον ὄνομα κληρονομεῖν, εἶναι εἰς πατέρα, δόξῃ στεφανοῦν, πεποιθότα εἶναι, ἀρχὴν λαμβάνειν λαλῆσαι, ἀρχιερεὺς τῆς ὁμολογίας, μαρτύριον τῶν λελαλημένων, παῤῥησία τῆς ἐλπίδος, στοιχεῖα τῆς ἀρχῆς τῶν λόγων τοῦ Θεοῦ, διϊκνεῖσθαι ἄχρι μερισμοῦ ψυχῆς τε καὶ πνεύματος, προσέρχεσθαι θρόνῳ χάριτος, ἐξ ἀνθρώπων λαμβάνεσθαι, περικεῖσθαι ἁμαρτίαν, ἀφιέναι τὸν τῆς ἀρχῆς λόγον, καὶ ἐπὶ τὴν τελειότητα φέρεσθαι, γεύσασθαι δωρεᾶς ἐπουρανίου, μιμηταὶ τῶν διὰ πίστεως κληρονομούντων, ἄγκυρα ἐλπίδος, προκειμένη ἐλπὶς, ἱερεὺς εἰς τὸ διηνεκὲς, ἐντολὴ ἀποδεκατοῦν, μετατιθεμένη ἱερωσύνη, ζωὴ ἀκατάλυτος, κεχωρισμένος ἀπὸ τῶν ἁμαρτωλῶν, δικαιώματα λατρείας, περικεκαλυμμένος χρυσίῳ, στάσιν ἔχειν, παύεσθαι προσφερομένην, διδαχαὶ ξέναι, and θυσία αἰνέσεως," p. 83.

Admitting, now, that the same phraseology cannot be found in Paul's epistles; is not the Greek of these phrases classic or Hellenistic? Is it not such as a writer might choose, without any uncommon peculiarities? But without insisting on this, I have only to remark, at present, that the same kind of argument which Seyffarth adduces, if it be valid, will prove any one of Paul's epistles to be spurious, with equal force. I must refer the reader, for the illustration and proof of this, to § 29 in the sequel.

II. Objections from the peculiar forms and juncture of words, in our epistle.

(10.) " Our author makes a peculiarly frequent use of composite words. His epistle contains five hundred and thirty-four words of this sort; while Paul, in his epistle to the Romans, uses only four hundred and seventy-eight." p. 91.

Without following on, in the steps of Seyffarth, to examine whether his enumeration is correct, I take it as he has presented it. I open my New Testament at the epistle to the Colossians accidentally, and proceed to count the *composite* words; which amount, if I have made no mistakes, to one hundred and seventy-eight; the number of pages is three. The epistle, then, averages fifty-nine composite words to a page. The epistle to the Hebrews occupies ten pages, and has, according to Seyffarth, five hundred and thirty-four composite words, i. e. on an average, fifty-three to a page. If it is spurious for this reason, *a fortiori* the epistle to the Colossians must be counted spurious also.

(11.) " Our author is partial to the use of participles, and of the genitive absolute. He employs eighty-four active participles, and one hundred and seven passive and middle ones, and seven cases of the genitive absolute; while in the epistle to the Romans, there are only ninety active participles, and forty-two passive, and no cases of the genitive absolute." p. 81.

Allowing the enumeration of Seyffarth to be correct, the average number of participles, on each page, will be for Hebrews, nineteen; for Romans, ten. Put now this principle to the test, in some other epistles. If I have rightly counted, the epistle to the Colossians has active participles thirty-four, passive forty, pages three, average number of participles to a page, twenty-four. Ephesians has active participles sixty, passive twenty-four, pages four and a half, average to a page, twenty-three. Of course, if our epistle is spurious, because it employs so many as nineteen participles to each page, then these epistles must be spurious, which employ twenty-three or twenty-four to a page.

And as to the genitive *absolute*, the second Corinthians (which has active participles ninety-seven, passive seventy-seven, pages nine, average to a page, nineteen, the same as in our epistle,) has the genitive absolute three times. Can any thing be more inconclusive, now, than such a species of reasoning?

(12.) "Our author has peculiar junctures of words; e. g. ἔσχατον ἡμέρων, τὸ ἀμετάθετον τῆς βουλῆς, κοινωνέω with the genitive, διαφορώτερος παρὰ, ῥῆσαι πρὸς τινα, ἀνάστασις τῶν νεκρῶν, παθήματα θανάτου, ἀγαγεῖν εἰς δόξαν, κρατῆσαι with the accusative, εὐαγγελίζω with the accusative, ἀδύνατον with the infinitive after it, αἱ πρότερον ἡμέραι, καταβάλλειν θεμέλιον." p. 81.

Some of these phrases are Pauline: e. g. ἀνάστασις νεκρῶν, Rom i. 4; xv. 12. 21. 24. Phil. iii. 11. So εὐαγγελίζω with the accusative, Rom. x. 5 bis. 2 Cor. xi. 7. Gal. 9. In regard to the others, if they prove any thing, they will prove too much; for the same kind of argument would show, (as we shall hereafter see,) that the first epistle to the Corinthians is spurious. The phrases in question are all either classic or Alexandrine Greek; and how can it be shown, then, that it was either impossible or improbable that Paul should employ them?

III. *Objections drawn from the use of words employed, in our epistle, in a sense different from that which Paul attaches to them.*

(13.) "Υἱὸς Θεοῦ, in our epistle, designates the higher nature of Christ, and not the Messiah simply. In Paul, it has the latter sense." p. 60, seq.

Paul also uses it in the former sense, in Rom. i. 3, 4; viii. 3. 32, and probably in 2 Cor. i. 19. In our epistle, it is used in the sense, alleged by Seyffarth to be the exclusive one, only in i. 2, and perhaps vii. 3. In other cases, it is employed in the usual sense of *Messiah;* viz. in i. 5 bis. 8; iv. 14; v. 5. 8; vi. 6; vii. 28; x. 29.

(14.) "Κληρονόμος *lord, possessor,* is peculiar to our epistle." p. 63.

Not so. In Rom. iv. 13, 14; viii. 17. Gal. iii. 29; iv. 7. Tit. iii. 7 it is used in the same way. Indeed, the usage of κληρονόμος, in this sense, is *Pauline,* instead of *anti-pauline.*

(15.) "Our author uses ὑπόστασις in the sense of *fundamentum,* Heb. i. 3; Paul no where employs it in such a sense." p. 66.

In Heb. i. 3, ὑπόστασις is *unique.* In iii. 14. 1. ὑπόστασις means *confidence;* so in Paul, 2 Cor. ix. 4. xi. 17.

(16.) "Ἔργον, in the sense of *beneficence,* Heb. vi. 10, is peculiar to our epistle." p. 76.

The meaning attributed to ἔργον here, is deduced merely from the context, viz. from ἀγάπης which follows it. The sense of ἔργον itself

§ 28. OBJECTIONS BY SEYFFARTH.

here does not differ from that which it has in Eph. ii. 10. Col. i. 10. Tit. ii. 14; specially 2 Cor. ix. 8. 1 Tim. vi. 18. So also in Matt. xxvi. 10. Acts ix. 36.

(17.) "Πηλίκος in our epistle, vii. 4, means *quam insignis, how distinguished;* Paul applies it only to *magnitude*, Gal. vi. 11." p. 77.

These two instances are the only ones, in which πηλίκος occurs in the New Testament. Πηλίκος properly signifies, *of what magnitude*. It may be applied either in a *physical* or *moral* sense. In Gal. vi. 11, it is applied in the former sense, (so also in the Septuagint, Zach. ii. 2.) in Heb. vii. 4. it is used in the latter sense; at least, it designates *greatness of rank* or *condition*. Can any thing be more natural than the derivation of this *secondary* sense of the word, in such a case from the primary one?

(18.) "Οἶκος, Heb. viii. 8. 10, is used in the sense of *tota gens*, Paul does not employ it in this sense." p. 77.

It is sufficient to reply, that both of these instances are not our author's own words; they are quotations from the Septuagint. As to the writer's own use of οἶκος, he employs it in the usual sense, viz. *household*. See Heb. iii. 2—6; x. 21; xi. 7, and comp. 1 Cor. i. 16; 1 Tim. iii. 4, 5. 12. 15; v. 4. 2 Tim. i. 16. iv. 19, &c. also Acts vii. 10; x. 2, &c.

(19.) "'Επισυναγωγὴ is peculiar to our epistle," p. 77.

It is employed but once, Heb. x. 25. Only once more is it found in all the New Testament, and that is in 2 Thess. ii. 1, in a sense like that in Heb. x. 25. If any thing can be fairly deduced from this, it is in favour of the Pauline origin of our epistle.

(20.) "Κοσμικὸν, in the sense of *exornatum*, Heb. ix. 1, is peculiar. Paul uses κόσμιος and κεκοσμημένος." p. 78.

The exegesis of this word is manifestly erroneous. See Heb. ix. 11. 24; xii. 22. Rev. xxi. 2.

(21.) "Περικαλύπτω is used, Heb. ix. 4, to express the *covering* of vessels; in Tim. ii. 9, for the *veiling* of women." p. 79.

Περικαλύπτω is not used in 1 Tim. ii. 9, nor any where in Paul's acknowledged epistles. It is used only in Mark xiv. 65. Luke xxii. 64; and there, in the same sense as in Heb. ix. 4.

(22.) "Συνείδησις is used, in our epistle, in the sense of *animus, mens;* by Paul, in the sense of *conscience.*" p. 79.

So is it used in the sense of conscience, too, by our author, in xiii. 18, and probably x. 22. In x. 2, it means *consciousness*. Only in

§ 28. OBJECTIONS BY SEYFFARTH. 207

Heb. ix. 9. 14, has it the sense of *mens, animus;* which also it seems to have in 2 Cor. v. 11.

(23.) " Άναιρέω is used in the sense of *abolishing*, Heb. x. 9 ; Paul uses καταργέω.' p. 80.

'Αναιρέω is used but once; and then in a sense which is common in the Septuagint and in classic authors. Καταργέω is also employed by our author, Heb. ii. 14, and in the same sense in which Paul employs it; which sense is exclusively Pauline. Comp. Luke xiii. 7.

In regard to the words αἰών, τάξις, and ἡγούμενοι, on which Seyffarth also charges peculiarity of signification, in our epistle, they have been already examined above. See pp. 157. 158. 194.

IV. Ἅπαξ λεγόμενα of our Epistle.

Nearly one half of Seyffarth's Essay is occupied with reckoning up words of this class, §§. 16—28. It is singular, that he should bring into this computation words that occur in the quotations made from the Septuagint ; e. g. ἑλίσσειν, παραπικρασμὸς, προσόχθιζω, τροχιά, ὄρθος, &c. ; as if these were chargeable, as peculiarities, upon the idiom of our epistle. Yet such is the ardour with which arguments of this nature have been urged by him, Schulz, and others, that the bounds of sober reflection are not unfrequently overleaped, and objections undistinguishingly pressed into service, by these writers.

I subjoin a catalogue of these ἅπαξ λεγόμενα, because I wish to put the reader in possession of all that is adduced to overthrow the Pauline origin of our epistle. The force of the argument, I shall examine in a subsequent section.

I remark here only, that I find, by actual examination, this whole class of so-called ἅπαξ λεγόμενα, almost without exception, are words both of classical and of Septuagint or Alexandrine usage. The employment, therefore, of words belonging to both these kinds of Greek, can mark nothing very peculiar in the style or choice of words adopted by our author. The instances alleged by Seyffarth are the following; viz.

Chap. I. Πολυμερῶς καὶ πολυτρόπως, ἀπαύγασμα, χαρακτήρ, μεγαλωσύνη, ἑλίσσειν.* II. Παραῤῥυεῖν, μισθαποδοσία, συνεπιμαρτυρέω, βραχύ, παραπλησίως, ἱλάσκεσθαι. III. Μέτοχος, θεράπων, παραπικρασμὸς,* προσοχθίζω.* IV. Ὑπόδειγμα, ἀφανής, τραχηλίζω, βοήθεια, εὔκαιρος. V. Μετριοπαθεῖν, ἱκετηρίαι, αἴτιος, προσαγορευθεὶς, νωθρὸς, αἰσθητήρια, ἕξις. VI. Παραδειγματίζω, βοτάνη, ἐπιτυγχάνω governing the genitive, ἀντιλογία, ἀμετάθετος. VII. Κοπή, ἀπάτωρ, ἀμήτωρ, ἀγενεαλόγητος, ἀφωμοιωμένος, διηνεκὲς, ἀκροθίνια, πατριάρχης, ἱερατεία, συναντάω,

§ 28. OBJECTIONS BY SEYFFARTH.

ἀθέτησις, ἀπαράβατος, παντελὲς, ἀμίαντος. VIII. Ἔπηξε, δῶρα, ἀναφέρω, χρηματίζω, νομοθετεῖν, διατίθέναι, ἵλεως εἶναι,* παλαιοῦν, ἀφανισμὸς. IX. Ἐγκαινίζομαι, ῥαντίζω, αἱματεκχυσία, ἀντίτυπος, συντέλεια τῶν αἰώνων. X. Ἀνώτερον, πρόσφατος, ἀκλινὴς, παροξυσμὸς, ἑκουσίως, φόβερος, ἐνυβρίζειν, ἄθλησις, θεατρίζειν, ὀνειδισμὸς, χρονίζειν. XI Εὐαρεστεῖν, ἄστρα, ἀναρίθμητος, παρεπίδημος, τρίμηνον, ἀστεῖος, διάταγμα, συγκακουχεῖν, κατάσκοπος, παρεμβόλη, τυμπανίζειν, καταγωνίζεσθαι, μελώπη, δέρμα, προβλέπομαι. XII. Τοιγαροῦν, νέφος, ἀφορῶντες, ἀναλογίζομαι, κάμνειν, ἀντικαθιστάναι, ἐκλανθάνειν, ὀλιγωρεῖν, νόθος, παριέναι, τροχιὰ,* ὀρθὸς,* ἐνοχλεῖν, πρωτοτοκία, μετέπειτα, ψηλαφᾶν, γνόφος. διαστέλλομαι, φαντασία, ἔντρομος, ἔκφοβος, πανήγυρις, σείω, ἀσάλευτος, καταναλίσκω. XIII. Βοηθὸς, ἡγούμενος, ἀναθεωρέω, εὐποιΐα, ἀλυσιτελὴς.

The whole number is one hundred and eighteen; from which are to be substracted those six marked with an asterisk, as they are *quoted from the Septuagint*, and belong not to our author. The amount then of ἅπαξ λεγόμενα is one hundred and twelve. And they are collected, too, with an unsparing hand; e. g. ἀπάτωρ, ἀμήτωρ, ἀγενεαλόγητος, τρίμηνον, ἔντρομος, ἔκφοβος, and many other words like these, where it is difficult to see how the author of our epistle could avoid choosing the very terms which he has employed, if we consult the connexion in which they stand.

This list appears, indeed, quite large and formidable to any one, who has not put to the test the principle of reasoning to which it must appeal, if any weight be allowed it in the scale of evidence against our epistle. That principle I shall bring to the test, by subjecting one of Paul's *acknowledged* epistles to an examination, in the same way, and on the same grounds, which Seyffarth, Schulz, and others, have thought proper to adopt in the examination of our epistle.

§ 29. *Objections made against the genuineness of our Epistle, compared with those which may be made against the First Epistle to the Corinthians.*

It often struck me, while engaged in the toilsome and protracted labour of examining the preceding objections made against the Pauline origin of our epistle, by Schulz and Seyffarth, that the only just method of weighing the whole force of the arguments, which they deduce from peculiarities of phraseology and the choice of words by our author, would be, to carry the same principles of reasoning along with us, to the examination of one of Paul's *acknowledged* epistles, and see whether as great a list of expressions and words, foreign to the other acknowledged epistles of Paul, might not be found, as in the epistle to the Hebrews

§ 29. NATURE OF OBJECTIONS EXAMINED. 209

This task, so far as I know, has never yet been performed by any critic. And yet, such an experiment seems to be obvious and necessary, in order that we may judge, with any confidence, in regard to the alleged *singularities* of our epistle. I have gone through with the appalling labour of performing such a work; and I shall now present the reader with the results of this undertaking.

In making choice of an epistle among the acknowledged writings of Paul, I found some difficulty. I chose, at last, the first epistle to the Corinthians; because, like that to the Hebrews, it presents several topics that are peculiar to itself. In this respect it has more resemblance to our epistle, than any other of Paul's acknowledged letters. Consequently, a comparison of its peculiarities of phrase and diction, with the other epistles of Paul, would be more like a comparison of our epistle with these, and would be more just, than a similar comparison of any other of Paul's epistles.

I divide the *peculiarities* of the first epistle to the Corinthians, into two great classes.

I. Phraseology peculiar to this Epistle, and found no where in the other acknowledged writings of Paul.

1 Cor. i. 1 Ἡγιασμένοι, as a title of Christians, used no where else by Paul. 2 Ἐπικαλούμενοι τὸ ὄνομα τοῦ Κυρίου I. X. as a periphrasis for the idea of *Christians*. 5 Ἐν παντὶ ἐπλουτίσθητε ἐν αὐτῷ. 9 Εἰς κοινωνίαν τοῦ υἱοῦ αὐτοῦ. 10 Παρακαλῶ ὑμᾶς διὰ τοῦ ὀνόματος τοῦ Κυρίου I. X....... Paul says, διὰ I. Χριστοῦ, Rom. xv. 30.—τὸ αὐτὸ λέγητε, be in unison—κατηρτισμένοι ἐν τῷ αὐτῷ νοΐ. 13 Μεμέρισται ὁ Χριστὸς: is Christ divided? ...... Paul uses μερίζω, in the sense of *impart*, e. g. Rom. xii. 3. 2 Cor. x. 13. 16 Λοιπὸν οὐκ οἶδα, Paul commonly uses τὸ λοιπὸν, Eph. vi. 10. Phil. iii. 1; iv. 8. 2 Thess. iii. 1. 17 Σοφίᾳ λόγου, ... Paul uses λόγον σοφίας, Col. ii. 23.—κενωθῇ ὁ σταυρὸς. 18 Ὁ λόγος ὁ τοῦ σταυροῦ. 21 Μωρίας τοῦ κηρύγματος. 25 Μωρὸν τοῦ Θεοῦ. 27 Μωρὸν τοῦ κόσμου. 25 Ἀσθενὲς τοῦ Θεοῦ. 27 Ἀσθενῆ τοῦ κόσμου. 26 Βλέπετε τὴν κλῆσιν—σοφοὶ κατὰ σάρκα—δυνατοί, for *those in an elevated station*. 30 Ὃς ἐγενήθη ἡμῖν σοφία .... δικαιοσύνη τε καὶ ἁγιασμὸς καὶ ἀπολύτρωσις.

II. 1 Ὑπεροχὴν λόγου.—τὸ μαρτύριον τοῦ Θεοῦ. 2 Οὐ γὰρ ἔκρινά τι εἰδέναι, *I determined not to make known*. 4 Πειθοῖ σοφίας λόγοι—ἀπόδειξις πνεύματος καὶ δυνάμεως. 5 Σοφίᾳ ἀνθρώπων, *human subtlety*. 6 Σοφία τοῦ αἰῶνος τούτου, ... in 1 Cor. σοφία is used *seventeen* times, in the epistle to the Romans only *once*, and that in a quotation, Rom. xi. 33. 7 Προώρίζεν .... πρὸ τῶν αἰώνων. 8 Ἄρχοντες τοῦ αἰῶνος τούτου—κύριος τῆς δόξης. 10 Ἀποκαλύπτειν διὰ τοῦ πνεύματος— πνεῦμα ἐρευνᾷ—τὰ βάθη τοῦ Θεοῦ. 13 Διδακτοῖς ἀνθρωπίνης σοφίας λόγοις—διδακτοῖς πνεύματος—πνευματικοῖς πνευματικὰ συγκρίνοντες. 14 Ψυχικὸς ἄνθρωπος— πνευματικῶς ἀνακρίνεται.

P

III. 1 Σαρκικοῖς, as applied to *persons*. 3 Κατὰ ἄνθρωπον περιπατεῖτε. 6 Ἐγὼ ἐφύτευσα, applied to the labour of a religious teacher—Ἀπολλὼς ἐπότισε, *Apollos supplied with water*, applied to the same—Θεὸς ηὔξανε, *made to increase*, (Hiphil of the Hebrews,) no where employed in this sense by Paul in his other epistles, nor appropriated to designate such a shade of thought. 8 Λήψεται κατὰ τὸν ἴδιον κόπον .... Paul says, κατὰ τὰ ἔργα, e. g. Rom. ii. 6. 2 Cor. xi. 15. 2 Tim. iv. 14. 9 Συνεργοὶ Θεοῦ—Θεοῦ γεώργιον—Θεοῦ οἰκοδομή. 10 Σοφὸς ἀρχιτέκτων. 11 Θεμέλιον τίθεικα. 12 Ἐποικοδομεῖν χρυσὸν, ἄργυρον, κ. τ. λ. 13 Ἡ ἡμέρα δηλώσει— ἐν πυρὶ ἀποκαλύπτεται—τὸ πῦρ δοκιμάσει. 14 Μισθὸν λαμβάνειν. 15 Ἔργον κατακαίειν—σωθῆναι ὡς διὰ πυρός. 18 Μωρὸς γίνεσθσι. 21 Ἐν ἀνθρώποις καυχᾶσθαι. 23 Ὑμεῖς Χριστοῦ, Χριστὸς Θεοῦ, *ye are Christ's, Christ is God's*.

IV. 1 Ὑπηρέτης Χριστοῦ—οἰκόνομοι μυστηρίων. 3 Εἰς ἐλαχιστὸν εἶναι—ἡμέρα, *day of trial, trial*. 4 Ἐμαυτῷ συνειδεῖν. 5 Πρὸ καιροῦ κρίνειν—βουλαὶ τῶν καρδιῶν—ἔπαινος γίνεται τινί. 6 Μετασχηματίζειν εἰς, *to transfer figuratively*—τὸ μὴ ὑπὲρ ὃ γέγραπται φρονεῖν, *not to think of one's self more highly than the Scriptures allow;* Paul uses παρ' ὃ .... φρονεῖν in such a case, Rom. xii. 3, and employs φρονεῖν ὑπὲρ in the sense of *having a regard for*, Phil. i. 7; iv. 10.—θυσιοῦν ὑπὲρ .... κατὰ. 7 Διακρίνειν τινὰ, *to make one to differ*. 8 Κεκορεσμένοι εἶναι—βασιλεύειν, *to be in a happy* or *prosperous state*. 9 Ἐσχάτους ἀποδεῖξαι—θέατρον γενέσθαι. 10 Μωροὶ διὰ Χριστὸν—φρόνιμοι ἐν Χριστῷ—ἰσχυροὶ applied to *persons*— ἔνδοξοι in the same manner. 13 Περικαθάρματα τοῦ κόσμου—πάντων περίψημα— ἕως ἄρτι. 14 Ἐντρέπων, act. voice, *putting to shame;* no where else, except with a passive meaning. 15 Παιδαγωγοὶ ἐν Χριστῷ—πατέρες [ἐν Χριστῷ]—ἐν Χριστῷ .... γεννᾶν. 17 Ὁδοὺς ...... τὰς ἐν Χριστῷ, *Christian doctrines*. 19 Ἐὰν ὁ Κύριος θελήσῃ. 20 Βασιλεία τοῦ Θεοῦ .... οὐ ἐν λόγῳ .... ἐν δυνάμει. 21 Ἐν ῥάβδῳ ἐλθεῖν.

V. 1 Ὅλως ἀκούεται—γυναῖκα ..... ἔχειν, *to cohabit with a woman*. 2 Πενθεῖν, *to be sorrowful;* Paul, *to make sorrowful*, 2 Cor. xii. 21. 3 Ἀπὼν ἐν σώματι, (Paul, ἀπεῖναι ἐν σαρκὶ, Col. ii. 5.)—παρὼν τῷ πνεύματι. 4 Συναχθέντων ὑμῶν, καὶ τοῦ ἐμοῦ πνεύματος, is altogether *unique*, in the shade of idea. 5 Εἰς ὄλεθρον τῆς σαρκὸς, ἵνα τὸ πνεῦμα σωθῇ, is altogether peculiar. 7 Ἐκκαθαίρειν .... ζύμην— τὸ πάσχα ἡμῶν (Χριστὸς) ἐτύθη. 8 Ἑορτάζειν ἐν ζύμῃ παλαιᾷ—ζύμη κακίας καὶ πονηρίας—ἀζύμοις εἰλικρινείας καὶ ἀληθείας. 10 Πόρνοι τοῦ κόσμου τούτου—ἐκ τοῦ κόσμου ἐξελθεῖν, *to withdraw entirely from converse with men*. 12 Τοὺς ἔσω, *those within the church*.

VI. 1 Πρᾶγμα ἔχειν, *to have ground for a suit at law*. Οἱ ἅγιοι τὸν κόσμον κρινοῦσι—ἀνάξιοι κριτηρίων. 3 Ἀγγέλους κρινοῦμεν, altogether *sui generis*. 4 Καθίζειν, *to make to sit as judges*. 5 Πρὸς ἐντροπὴν λέγω, also in xv. 34.—διακρῖναι ἀνὰ μέσον. 6 Κρίνεται μετὰ, goes to law with—ἄπιστος, used eleven times in this epistle, and *not once* in Romans, Colossians, Galatians, Ephesians, Thessalonians, Philippians, 2 Timothy, 7 Κρίματα, *law-suits*—ἀποστερέομαι, *to suffer one's self to be defrauded*—ἀποστερέω, *to defraud*. 9 Ἄδικοι, for Heb. רְשָׁעִים. Paul uses the word but once, and then in the singular number, Rom. iii. 5, and in quite a different

§ 29. NATURE OF OBJECTIONS EXAMINED. 211

way. 11 Δικαιωθῆναι ἐν ὀνόματι Ἰησοῦ. 12 Πάντα μοι ἔξεστι—συμφέρει, five times in this epistle, and no where else in all of Paul's acknowledged epistles, except *twice* in 2 Cor.—ἐξουσιάζεσθαι ὑπό τινος. 15 Μέλη Χριστοῦ—πόρνης μέλη. 16 Κολλώμενος Κυρίῳ—κολλώμενος τῇ πόρνῃ. 20 Ἀγοράζεσθαι τιμῆς—δοξάζειν ἐν τῷ σώματι. VII. 1 Γυναικὸς ἅπτεσθαι, to cohabit with. 2 Ἔχειν γυναῖκα to marry or possess a wife. 5 Ἐπὶ τὸ αὐτὸ ἦτε, ye may come together. 14 Ἁγιάζω, in a sense *sui generis*—ἀκάθαρτος, in a sense peculiar; so also ἅγιος, which follows. 19 Ἡ περιτομὴ οὐδὲν .... Paul says, οὔτε περιτομή τι ἰσχύει, Gal. v. 6; vi. 15.— ἡ ἀκροβυστία οὐδὲν ἐςι—τήρησις ἐντολῶν .... Paul says, ὑπακοὴ πίςεως, Rom. i. 5; xvi. 26; or ὑπακοὴ simply, Rom. v. 19; vi. 16; xv. 18; xvi. 19; or he uses ὑπακούω, Rom. vi. 12; vi. 17; x. 16, et sæpe. 20 Κλῆσις, condition in life, rank; no where so employed by Paul. 21 Μή σοι μελέτω, be not solicitous—μᾶλλον χρῆσαι, prefer. 25 Ἐπιταγὴν ἔχειν—ἠλεημένος ὑπὸ Κυρίου .... Paul uses ἠλεήθην simply, Rom. xi. 30. 2 Cor. iv. 1. 1 Tim. i. 13. 16. 26 Καλὸν ἀνθρώπῳ .... Paul uses καλὸν simply, in the same sense, e. g. Rom. xiv. 21. Gal. iv. 18. 29 Τὸ λοιπὸν, hereafter, *for the future*. 31 Χρᾶσθαι τῷ κόσμῳ—τὸ σχῆμα τοῦ κόσμου. 32 Μεριμνᾷν τὰ τοῦ Κυρίου. 33 Μεριμνᾷν τὰ τοῦ κόσμου .... Paul uses μεριμνᾷν τὰ περὶ. 34 Ἁγία εἶναι σώματι καὶ πνεύματι. 35 Πρὸς τὸ συμφέρον, *for the profit*. 37 Ἀνάγκην ἔχειν. 40 Δοκεῖν πνεῦμα Θεοῦ ἔχειν, truly *unique*, in the epistles.

VIII. 1 Γνῶσιν ἔχειν. 4 Οὐδὲν εἶναι ἐν κόσμῳ—οὐδεὶς ἕτερος. 6 Ἡμῖν εἷς Θεὸς, ὁ πατὴρ, κ. τ. λ. The whole verse is unique. 7 Συνείδησις, *conscientious scruples*. 12 Ἁμαρτάνειν εἰς, to sin against—τύπτειν συνείδησιν. 13 Βρῶμα σκανδαλίζει ...... Paul, διὰ βρῶμα λυπεῖσθαι, Rom. xiv. 15.

IX. 1 Τὸ ἔργον μου .... ἐν Κυρίῳ. 2 Ἄλλοις .... ὑμῖν .... ἀπόστολος .... Paul uses the gen., ἐθνῶν ἀπόστολος, Rom. xi. 13; ἀπόστολοι ἐκκλησιῶν, 2 Cor. viii. 23; ὑμῶν ἀπόστολος, Phil. ii. 25—σφραγὶς τῆς ἀποστολῆς. 5 Γυναῖκα περιάγειν—7, 13 Ἐσθίειν ἐκ, to eat of .... Paul uses simply the accusative, e. g. Rom. xiv. 2. 2 Thess. iii. 12. 11 Σπείρειν πνευματικὰ—θερίζειν σαρκικὰ, *to have one's temporal wants supplied*. 12 Ἐξουσία, property. 16 Ἀνάγκη .... ἐπίκειταί μοι .... Paul, ἐξ ἀνάγκης 2 Cor. ix. 7; κατ' ἀνάγκην, Philem. v. 14. 17 Οἰκονομίαν πιστευθῆναι. 19 Ἐλεύθερος ἐκ .... Paul uses ἐλεύθερος ἀπὸ Rom. vii. 3. 20 Κερδαίνειν, *to win over* .... in a different sense, Phil. iii. 8. 22 Γίνεσθαι τοῖς πᾶσι τὰ πάντα. 24 Βραβεῖον λαμβάνειν. 25 Φθαρτὸς .... ἄφθαρτος στέφανος. 26 Αἴρα δέρειν.

X. 1, 2 The whole of the description presented in these two verses is *sui generis*, and found no where in Paul. 3 Βρῶμα πνευματικὸν—πόμα πνευματικόν. 4 Πνευματικῆς πέτρας—and specially the idea of the whole phrase, πνευματικῆς ἀκολουθούσης πέτρας. So also ἔπινον ἐκ .... Paul uses πιεῖν (2 aor.) with the accusative, Rom. xiv. 21. 11 Τύποι συμβαίνειν .... Paul, τύπος simply, Rom. v. 14; or γίνεσθαι τύπος, 1 Thess. i. 7; 1 Tim. iv. 12—τὰ τέλη τῶν αἰώνων .... Paul, ἔσχαται ἡμέραι, 2 Tim. iii. 1. 13 Πειρασμὸς ἀνθρώπινος εἴληφε, singular both as to

p 2

§ 29. NATURE OF OBJECTIONS EXAMINED.

the verb and adjective, joined with πειρασμός. 15 Ὡς φρονίμοις λέγω. 16 ποτήριον τῆς εὐλογίας—κοινωνία αἵματος—κοινωνία σώματος. 17 Εἷς ἄρτος ..... εἶναι, said of Christians communing at the Lord's table. 18 Ἰσραὴλ κατὰ σάρκα—κοινωνοὶ θυσιαστηρίου. 19 Τί οὖν φημι. 20 Δαιμονίοις θύειν—κοινωνοὺς δαιμονίων γίνεσθαι. 21 Ποτήριον δαιμονίων—τράπεζα δαιμονίων. 27 Καλέω, in the sense of *inviting to a meal*. 32 Ἀπρόσκοποι, with the dative after it—πάντα πᾶσιν ἀρέσκειν.

XI. 2 Παραδόσεις κατέχειν. 3 Θέλω δὲ ὑμᾶς εἰδέναι—παντὸς ἀνδρὸς κεφαλὴ Χριστὸς—κεφαλὴ Χριστοῦ Θεός. 4 Κατὰ κεφαλῆς ἔχειν, *to cover the head*. 5 Καταισχύνειν, *to dishonour*, ... Paul, *to disappoint*, Rom. v. 5; ix. 33; x. 11—τὸ αὐτὸ τῇ *the same thing as*, i. e. αὐτὸ with the dative after it. 7 Ἀνὴρ .... εἰκὼν καὶ δόξα Θεοῦ—γυνὴ δόξα ἀνδρός. 9 Οὐ ἀνὴρ ἐκ γυναικός, κ.τ.λ. 10 Ἐξουσία, *veil* or *token of power*—ἄγγελοι, *spies*. 12 Ὁ ἀνὴρ διὰ τῆς γυναικός. 14 Φύσις ἐιδάσκει. 17 Συνέρχεσθαι εἰς τὸ κρεῖττον .... εἰς τὸ ἧττον. 20 Κυριακὸν δεῖπνον. 23 Παραλαβεῖν ἀπὸ .... Paul uses παραλαβεῖν παρά, Gal. i. 12; 2 Thess. iii. 6. 24 Τὸ σῶμα ὑπὲρ ὑμῶν κλώμενον. 25 Μετὰ τὸ δειπνῆσαι .... Paul no where uses μετὰ before the inf. mode preceded by τό.—ἡ καινὴ διαθήκη ἐν τῷ ἐμῷ αἵματι. 27 Ἔνοχος ἔσται τοῦ σῴματος καὶ τοῦ αἵματος τοῦ Κυρίου. 29 Κρίμα ἐσθίειν καὶ πίνειν τινὶ —διακρίνειν τὸ σῶμα τοῦ Κυρίου. 30 Ἀσθενεῖς, *sickly*—ἱκανοί, *many* .... Paul uses it in the sense of *able*, *sufficient*, 2 Cor. ii. 6. 16; iii. 5. 2 Tim. ii. 2. 31 Διακρίνειν, *to examine*. 34 Διατάσσομαι, *to set in order, arrange* .... Paul uses it for co*m*mand, Tit. i. 5.

XII. 3 Ἐν πνεύματι Θεοῦ λαλεῖν—λέγειν ἀνάθεμα Ἰησοῦν—εἰπεῖν Κύριον Ἰησοῦν. 6 Ἐνεργεῖν τὰ πάντα ἐν πᾶσι .... Paul, ἐνεργεῖν τὰ πάντα, Eph. i. 11. 7 Φανέρωσις τοῦ πνεύματος. 10 Διακρίσεις, *powers of distinguishing* .... Paul, in a different sense, Rom. xiv. 1—γένη, *kinds* .... Paul uses γένος for *descent, lineage*, Phil. iii. 5. 15 Εἰς ἓν σῶμα βαπτισθῆναι—εἰς ἓν πνεῦμα ποτισθῆναι .... Paul uses ποτίζω no where except in a quotation from the Old Testament, Rom. xii. 20. Vs. 15—17. Where is any representation like this, in all the Pauline epistles? Paul introduces the same general image, in Rom. xii. 4, 5, as is founded in 1 Cor. xii. 12—14; but he does not pursue it into detail. 23 Τιμὴν περιτιθέναι. 24 Διδόνα τιμήν .... Paul, ἀποδιδόναι τιμήν, Rom. ii. 7—τὸ αὐτὸ μεριμνᾶν. 26 Μέλος δοξάζεται—συγχαίρω used absolutely, without any dative following it .... Paul employs the dative after it, Phil. ii. 17, 18. 27 Ἐκ μέρους, Paul uses ἀπὸ μέρους, Rom. xi. 25; xv. 15. 24. 2 Cor. i. 13; ii. 5. 28 Τιθέναι ἐν τῇ ἐκκλησίᾳ, *to constitute officers in the church*. 28 Where else are such officers in the church mentioned, as ἀντιλήψεις, κυβερνήσεις, δυνάμεις?

XIII. 1 Γλῶσσαι ἀγγέλων. 2 Εἰδεῖν μυστήριον—ὄρη μεθιστάνειν. 3 Ψωμίζειν τὰ ὑπάρχοντα. 6 Στέγειν, *to cover over*. 8 Γλῶσσαι παύσονται, the idea of *speaking in a variety of languages*, is not found attached to γλῶσσα, in any of the Pauline epistles. 12 Βλέπειν δὲ ἐσόπτρου .... ἐν αἰνίγματι .... πρόσωπον πρὸς πρόσωπον —γινώσκειν ἐκ μέρους.

§ 29. NATURE OF OBJECTIONS EXAMINED. 213

XIV. 2 Πνεύματι λαλεῖν μυστήρια. 3 Λαλεῖν οἰκοδομὴν.... παράκλησιν.... παραμυθίαν. 5 Οἰκοδομὴν λαβεῖν. 6 Λαλεῖν ἐν ἀποκαλύψει, κ. τ. λ. 7 Φωνὴν διδόναι—διαστολὴν διδόναι. 9 Εἰς ἀέρα λαλεῖν. 10 Τυγχάνω, to happen, to be;.... Paul, in the sense of obtaining, 2 Tim. ii. 10. 11 Δύναμις, force of, in the sense of meaning—εἶναι βάρβαρὸς τινι. 14, 15 Προσεύχεσθαι γλώσσῃ... πνεύματι... νοΐ—ψάλλειν πνεύματι... νοΐ. 16 Εὐλογεῖν τῷ πνεύματι. 19 Λαλεῖν διὰ νοὸς. 20 Παιδία γίνεσθαι ταῖς φρεσὶ—ταῖς φρεσὶ τέλειοι γίνεσθαι. 22 Εἰς σημεῖον εἶναι.... Paul, σημεῖὸν ἐστι, 2 Thess. iii. 17. 27 Κατὰ δύο, ἢ τρεῖς. 32 Πνεύματα προφητῶν προφήταις ὑποτάσσεται. 33 Ἀκαταστασίας Θεὸς. XV. 1 Δί οὗ [εὐαγγελίου] σώζεσθε. 3 Ἐν πρώτοις, first.... Paul, πρῶτος, Rom. x. 19. 8 Ἔσχατον πάντων. 10 Εἰμὶ ὅ εἰμι. 14 Κενὸν κήρυγμα, κενὴ πίστις. 15 Ψευδομάρτυρες τοῦ Θεοῦ. 17 Εἶναι ἐν ἁμαρτίαις. 20 Ἀπαρχὴ τῶν κεκοιμημένων. 21 Δί ἀνθρώπου ὁ θάνατος...... Paul, διὰ τῆς ἁμαρτίας ὁ θάνατος, Rom. v. 12.——δί ἀνθρώπου ἀνάστασις νεκρῶν. Vs. 24—28, a passage altogether sui generis. 29 Βαπτιζόμενοι ὑπὲρ τῶν νεκρῶν. 38 Σῶμα διδόναι. 40 Σῶμα ἐπίγειον. 42 Σπείρεσθαι ἐν φθορᾷ—ἐγείρεσθαι ἐν ἀφθαρσίᾳ—σπείρεσθαι ἐν ἀτιμίᾳ—ἐγείρεσθαι ἐν δόξῃ, κ. τ. λ. 44 Σῶμα ψυχικὸν—σῶμα πνευματικὸν. 47 Ὁ δεύτερος ἄνθρωπος, ὁ Κύριος ἐξ οὐρανοῦ. 49 Φορεῖν εἰκόνα. 50 Σὰρξ καὶ αἷμα, κ. τ. λ. 51 Μυστήριον λέγειν...... Paul, μυστήριον λαλεῖν, Col. iv. 3. 52 Ἐσχάτῃ σάλπιγξ. 53 Δεῖ γὰρ τὸ φθαρτὸν, κ. τ. λ. 56 Κέντρον θανάτου, ἡ ἁμαρτία--δύναμις ἁμαρτίας, ὁ νόμος. 57 Διδόναι νῖκος.

XVI. 2 Μία σαββάτων—τιθέναι παρ ἑαυτῷ. 7 Ἐν παρόδῳ ἰδεῖν. 9 Θύρα ἀνέῳγε μεγάλη καὶ ἐνεργὴς. 22 Ἤτω ἀνάθεμα, μαρὰν ἀθά. 24 Ἡ ἀγάπη μου μετὰ, κ. τ. λ. The whole closing salutation is sui generis.

Such is the almost incredible mass of *peculiar* phraseology, in the first epistle to the Corinthians. It is possible that there may be instances, among so many, where I may, through the tedium of such an examination, have overlooked some phrase of the same kind in Paul's other epistles. If this be so, the student, who has in his hands a Greek Concordance, will be able easily to detect it. In the mean time, I venture to affirm with entire confidence, (having repeated my investigations a second time,) that the number of such mistakes, at most, is not sufficient to affect in any degree the nature of the argument, or the force of the appeal. I remark only, that where I have appealed to Paul, as not having employed a particular word or phrase, or as not using it in a like sense, I mean, of course, that Paul has not done this in his other *acknowledged* epistles.

If any one is disposed to object to this array of phrases *sui generis*, in the first epistle to the Corinthians, and to aver, that many of them are nearly like those used by Paul, and that others are occasioned by the peculiarity of the subjects of which the writer treats, and that, in

214 § 29. NATURE OF OBJECTIONS EXAMINED.

general, they are collected with an unsparing hand ; I have only to reply, that, in all respects, they are as fairly and as sparingly collected as those brought forward by Schulz and Seyffarth. For the correctness of this, I make the appeal to every unprejudiced man, who has read attentively and critically the essays of these authors, in which they have brought forward their objections against the genuineness of our epistle.

As a counterpart for the appalling list of one hundred and eighteen ἅπαξ λεγόμενα, in the epistle to the Hebrews, which Seyffarth has presented, I offer,

II. The ἅπαξ λεγόμενα, in the first epistle to the Corinthians.

Ἄγαμος, ἀγενὴς, ἀγνωσία, ἀγοράζω, ἀδάπανος, ἄδηλος, ἀδήλως, ᾅδης, ἄζυμος, αἴνιγμα, ἀκατακάλυπτος, ἀκολουθέω, ἀκρασία, ἄκων, ἀλλάζω, ἀμέριμνος, ἀμετακίνητος, ἀμπέλων, ἀνά, ἀνακρίνω, ἀνάμνησις, ἀνάξιος, ἀναξίως, ἀνδρίζομαι, ἀντίληψις, ἀπάγω, ἀπελεύθερος, ἀπερισπάστως, ἀπόδειξις, ἀπολούω, ἀποφέρω, ἄργυρος, ἀροτριῶν, ἅρπαξ, ἄρρωστος, ἀρχιτέκτων, ἀσθενέστερος, ἀστὴρ, ἀστατέω, ἀσχημονέω, ἀσχήμων, ἄτιμος, ἄτομος, αὐλέω, αὐλὸς, αὔριον, ἄφωνος, ἄψυχος.

Βρόχος, βιωτικὸς, γάλα, γεώργιον, γογγύζω, γραμματεὺς, γυμνητεύομαι, δειπνέω, δεῖπνον, διαίρεσις, δίδακτος, διερμηνευτὰς, διερμηνεύω, διόπερ, δουλαγωγέω, δράσσομαι, ἐγκοπὴ, ἐγκρατεύομαι, εἰδωλεῖον, εἰδωλόθυτον, εἰσακούω, ἔκβασις, ἐκγαμίζω, ἐκδέχομαι, ἐκνήφω, ἐκπειράζω, ἔκτρωμα, ἐλεεινὸς, ἐνέργημα, ἔννομος, ἔνοχος, ἐντροπὴ, ἐξαίρω, ἐξεγείρω, ἔξεστι, ἐξουσιάζω, ἑορτάζω, ἐπαινέω, ἐπιβάλλω, ἐπιθανάτιος, ἐπιθυμητὴς, ἐπισπάομαι, ἐπιτοαυτό, ἑρμηνεία, ἔσοπτρον, ἑτερόγλωσσοι, εὐγενὴς, εὐκαιρέω, εὐπρόσεδρος, εὔσημος, εὐσχημοσύνη, εὐσχήμων, ἠχέω, the form ἤτω from εἰμὶ, θάπτω, θέατρον, θηριομαχέω, θύω, ἴαμα, ἰσχυρότερος, κάθαρμα, καίω, καλάμη, κατακαίω, κατακαλύπτομαι, κατάκειμαι, καταστρώννυμι, καταχράομαι, κείρω, κέντρον, κιθάρα, κιθαρίζω, κινδυνεύω, κλάω, κλάζω, κόκκος, κομῇ, κομάω, κορέννυμι, κρεῖσσον, in the sense of the adverb *better*, vii. 38, κριτήριον, κτῆνος, κυβέρνησις, κύμβαλον, κυρίακος.

Λιθάζω, λογία, λοιδορέω, λοίδορος, λύσις, μαίνομαι, μάκελλον, μακαριώτερος, μαλακὸς, μαρὰν ἀθὰ, μέθυσος, μέλει, μετέχω, μηνύω, μοιχὸς, μολύνω, μύριοι, μωρία, νὴ, νῖκος, νηπιάζω, ξυράω, ὀλοθρευτὴς, ὅλως, ὁμιλία, ὁσάκις, ὄσφρησις, οὐαὶ, οὐδέποτε, οὐδέπω, οὐθὲν, οὕπω, ὄφελος, παιδίον, παίζω, πανταχοῦ, παραγίνομαι, παραμένω, παραμυθία, πάροδος, παροξύνομαι, πάσχα, πειθὸς, περιάγω, περιβόλαιον, περικάθαρμα, περισσότερον, περιτίθημι, περίψημα, περπερεύομαι, πνευματικῶς, ποιμαίνω, ποίμνη, πόμα, πορνεύω, πορνὴ, ποτήριον, προσεδρεύω, προσκυνέω, προφητεύω, πτηνὸν, πυκτεύω, πωλέω, ῥάβδος, ῥιπῇ, σαλπίζω, σελήνη, σῖτος, στάδιος, συγγνώμη, συγκεράννυμι, συζητητὴς, συμμερίζομαι, σύμφωνος, συνέρχομαι, συνάγω, συνειδέω, συνήθεια, συστέλλω, σχολάζω, τάγμα, τήρησις, τοίνυν, τύπτω, ὑπέρακμος, ὑπηρέτης, ὑπωπιάζω, φιλόνεικος, φρὴν, φυτεύω, χαλκὸς, χοϊκὸς, χόρτος, χρηστεύομαι, ψευδομάρτυρ, ψυχικος, ὡσπερεί. In the whole, 230 words.

§ 29. NATURE OF OBJECTIONS EXAMINED. 215

In order now to estimate the comparative force of the argument, from these ἅπαξ λεγόμενα, we must take into the account the comparative length of the first epistle to the Corinthians, and of our epistle. In the Bible lying before me, the former occupies thirteen pages, the latter ten; i. e. the former, in respect to length, is to the latter, as thirteen to ten. Now, in the epistle to the Hebrews are found one hundred and eighteen ἅπαξ λεγόμενα, according to the reckoning of Seyffarth; in the epistle to the Corinthians, if I have reckoned rightly, (I have repeated, a second time, the whole examination,) there are two hundred and thirty. Consequently, in the epistle to the Hebrews, the average number of ἅπαξ λεγόμενα is a little short of *twelve* to a page ; while the average number in the first epistle to the Corinthians is (within a small fraction) *eighteen* to a page.

Certain it is, then, that if the number of ἅπαξ λεγόμενα in our epistle proves that it was not from the hand of Paul, it must be more abundantly evident that Paul cannot have been the author of the first epistle to the Corinthians, which has a proportion of one-half more ἅπαξ λεγόμενα than our epistle.

Such is the basis of the arguments, so confidently adduced by Schulz and Seyffarth, and so much applauded and trusted in by many other critics. It has been often said by logicians, that " what proves too much, proves nothing." This is *well said;* and applied to the case before us, it will show, at once, that the very same means used to overturn the opinion that Paul was the author of our epistle, would overturn the opinion that he wrote any other particular epistle, which is universally acknowledged as coming from his hand.

But what shall we say, when, in addition to all the ἅπαξ λεγόμενα of words, we reckon up the *phrases* of the same sort, which have been adduced above ? Is not here a mass of evidence apparently overwhelming ? Surely, if the first epistle to the Corinthians had been anonymous, the whole body of modern writers, who have attacked the Pauline origin of the epistle to the Hebrews, must have, with one unanimous voice, disclaimed the first epistle to the Corinthians as belonging to Paul. In all respects which have any reference to the number of *peculiar* phrases and words that are ἅπαξ λεγόμενα, the first epistle to the Corinthians presents far stronger evidence of *not* being Pauline than our epistle does.

So unsafe is this argument, although often produced and much relied upon, in respect to the important subject which we are examining !

How much easier, too, is it to make assertions at hazard, on a subject of this nature, than it is to go through with the excessive labour of verifying such assertions, by means of that great rectifier of wandering critics—a Greek Concordance? Had this been done, long ago, the world had been spared a great deal of useless labour, and literature the record of many a hasty conclusion, from premises unexamined and unestablished.

But further, the argument against the genuineness of the first epistle to the Corinthians could be easily amplified, by appealing still farther to the same kind of arguments as are adduced against our epistle. For example, how easy to ask, " If the first epistle to the Corinthians be Paul's, how is it possible, that in so long a letter there is no discussion of Paul's favourite topics in which he was so deeply interested? How comes it about, that we have nothing about justification by faith, without the deeds of the law; nothing of the vanity and folly of Jewish rites and ceremonies; nothing which asserts the equal rights of Jews and Gentiles, and blames the Judaizing teachers and zealots who refused to acknowledge this? Where has Paul ever descanted, as here, on the subject of spiritual gifts; on the marriage relation, conditions, habits, and dress of women; on the Lord's supper; on the support of preachers; on the comparative value of spiritual gifts, and of faith, hope, and love; and, above all, on the controverted and speculative questions of his time, respecting the manner in which the bodies of the saints would rise from their graves, when the last trumpet should sound? Where else has Paul, or any other sacred writer, intimated, that the regal power of the Messiah would cease after the day of judgment, and that he would be subjected to the Father? Is there any parallel to this epistle, either for matter or manner, in all the acknowledged writings of Paul ?"

I might proceed still further, and collect a large number of favourite expressions, often repeated, in this epistle, but which seldom or never occur in the other Pauline epistles. Many such I have noticed, in the course of my investigations; many more than Dr. Schulz has been able to collect from the epistle to the Hebrews. And if the *two* epistles to the Corinthians were to be the subject of investigation, instead of the first only, the list of ἅπαξ λεγόμενα and ἅπαξ λογιζόμενα, and of favourite idioms and peculiar ideas, might be swelled to an enormous catalogue. I have observed, as I feel quite well satisfied, more ἅπαξ λεγόμενα in the second epistle to the Corinthians in proportion to its

§ 29. NATURE OF OBJECTIONS EXAMINED.

length, than in the first; and quite as many peculiar phrases. In a word, after such an investigation as I have been through, I am bold to say, that there is not a single epistle of Paul's which may not be wrested from him, by arguments of the very same kind, as those by which the genuineness of our epistle is assailed, and in all respects of equal validity.

Unfortunately for the cause of criticism, so just and obvious an investigation has not hitherto been entered upon. Most of those who have doubted the genuineness of the epistle to the Hebrews, have seemed to consider it as quite proper to make out from it all the *specialities* possible, and then to reason from them, without any fear of mistake. I have examined their arguments in detail, because I wished to show how many hasty and incorrect assertions have been brought forward as arguments. I have now exhibited the application of the *principles*, on which their whole argument stands, to one of Paul's epistles, the genuineness of which no critic calls in question. The result is so plain, that it cannot be mistaken.

"But," it will be asked, "can we never reason, in any case, from *dissimilarity of language* in different compositions, to *different* persons as authors?" No doubt we may, in some cases. But not unless the difference be greater than in the case before us. It has been shown above, how many striking traits of resemblance to the other letters of Paul there are in our epistle. While these remain, the discrepancy can never be made out to be great enough to build a sound argument upon it. If the question were to be asked, Whether the author of the epistle to the Romans could have written the first epistle of John? the answer would be easy, nay, almost absolutely certain, from *internal* evidence. But, after all the striking resemblances which can be shown between our epistle and Paul's letters; after proving from actual examination, that the list of peculiarities, in one of his most conspicuous and acknowledged epistles, is much greater than in our epistle; after making all the reasonable abatements which must be made, from the peculiarity of the subjects which are discussed in our epistle, and of the condition of those to whom it was addressed; after reflection upon the acknowledged fact, that every writer's style is more or less altered by advancing age; by the circumstances of haste or leisure in which he writes; by the topics themselves which he discusses; by the degree of excitement which he feels at the time; above all, taking into consideration the fact, that every writer who travels to many different countries, resides in many different places, and is conversant with a great variety of men and of dialects, is much more liable to change his style somewhat, than he who always resides in the same place, and is conversant with the same men and books; after taking, I say, all these things into consideration, can any man have reasonable grounds to be satisfied, that the peculiarity of style and diction in our epistle is such, that its Pauline origin is to be rejected on account of them? I will not undertake to answer for others; but for myself, I can say with a clear and an abiding conviction, I do not feel that such an argument can stand before the impartial tribunal of criticism.

§ 30. *Objections by De Wette.*

While the preceding sheet was under the press, the Historical and Critical Introduction to the New Testament, by W. M. L. De Wette, came to hand. It was published at Berlin, during the last year; and exhibits the views of its celebrated author, in regard to the origin of our epistle.

De Wette is the well-known author of a commentary on the Psalms, of a translation of about one-half of the Old and New Testaments, of a Hebrew Archæology, of an historical and critical Introduction to the Old Testament, and of some other works in the departments of sacred criticism and moral science; all of which have attracted great attention on the continent of Europe, on account of the distinguished genius and extensive erudition of the author. He is now a Professor, in the University of Bâsle, in Switzerland.

De Wette takes side, as from his habits of thinking and reasoning he might be expected to do, with those who deny the Pauline origin of our epistle. His arguments are very brief, (as the nature of his book required them to be;) and I am not a little surprised to find, that, among them all, there is not a single one which is not drawn from the works that have been already examined above.

In regard to the external evidence, he has given many of the principal citations, which are adduced in the preceding part of this discussion, pp. 79—112. But some important ones he has omitted, which speak most unequivocally against the views he gives of the opinion of the fathers. For example, he merely refers to Euseb. Ecc. Hist. vi. 25, in respect to the very important testimony of Origen, which the reader will find on p. 89 seq. above; simply remarking that " Origen gives up the writing down of the epistle by Paul, and only attributes the *matter* of it to him," (p. 285.) In a note, he subjoins, " When he [Origen] speaks

§ 30. OBJECTIONS BY DE WETTE. 219

of the tradition of the churches, it is probable that he means only the Alexandrine church." In regard to such a probability, I must refer the reader to what is said above, p. 95. (7.) The probability is very strong, that all of Origen's homilies must have been published in Palestine; for he was licensed to preach but a few months before he was driven from Alexandria; see Lardner's Credib. iii. 194. Whether Origen would, under such circumstances, be likely to retain any superstitious veneration for the church at Alexandria, every reader will be able to judge, so as to satisfy his own mind. It will be remembered, that the testimony in question of Origen, is from one of his *Homilies* on the epistle to the Hebrews.

In the same manner, he has merely made a simple reference to the important testimony of Jerome, in his epistle to Dardanus, cited above, p. 108; while he has inserted at full length all the passages which might serve to show that Jerome had doubts in his own mind, in regard to the Pauline origin of our epistle. This he avers to have been the fact. But whether there is any just foundation for such an assertion, has already been examined above, p. 108 seq. Jerome, no doubt, felt himself obliged to use great caution, in regard to the manner in which he spoke of the epistle to the Hebrews, because the prevailing sentiment of the western churches, in his time, was against the Pauline origin of it. More than this can never be fairly deduced, from any of the language which he employs. The passages in his epistle to Dardanus, in his commentary on Matt. xxvi., and in his book *De Viris Illustribus* c. v. (supra, pp. 108, 109,) can never be made to speak less than a decided, definite opinion, on the part of Jerome himself, in respect to the Pauline origin of our epistle. How should he have been the occasion of revolutionizing the whole of the western churches, in regard to the sentiment under consideration, if this were not the case?

Other testimonies, too, De Wette has omitted, which are in favour of the Pauline origin of our epistle. In stating the opposition of the Latin churches to this sentiment, he has brought forward the doubts of Jerome, and of his contemporaries. He has followed these on, down to the seventh century, by quoting from Primasius and Isidore Hispaliensis. But he has not once hinted, that in this same western church, all those distinguished bishops who are mentioned above (p. 108,) admitted our epistle to be Paul's; excepting that he has adduced some of the testimony of Jerome and Augustine.

Besides, he has advanced the broad position, that " the western churches originally (anfänglich) denied this epistle to be Paul's." The passages adduced in proof of this, are Euseb. Ecc. Hist. vi. 20, cited above, p. 97;) v. 26, (supra p. 102;) the passages from Photius, Gobar, and Hippolytus, (supra p. 102;) Tertullian, de Pudicitia, c. 20, (supra p. 106 seq.;) Cyprian, de Martyr. c. xi., (supra p. 106;) Jerome, Epist. ad Paulinum, (supra p. 109;) and Philastrius, de Hæres, c. 89, who speaks only of the opinion of others, himself believing the epistle to be Paul's. But De Wette has not said a word, in this connexion, of all the evidence adduced in § 12 above, which has relation to this subject; nor of the division of opinion that existed in the Latin churches of later times, and before the days of Jerome, in respect to the subject in question.

Again, in stating the testimony of the eastern churches, De Wette has merely brought forward Eusebius, as testifying to the opinions of his own times; see Eusebius' testimony above, p. 96 seq. At the same time, he intimates that there were doubts, in that part of the church, in regard to the Pauline origin of our epistle. He has not, however, produced a single author from the East who has expressed any such doubts, (and this for a very imperious reason;) while, at the same time, he has sedulously omitted all those, cited on p. 101 above, who undoubtedly ascribed our epistle to Paul.

Is this, now, an *impartial* examination and statement of evidence, on this great question? And has an author, who writes in this hasty manner, without extended examination, and without deliberation, any right to find fault with others, when they refuse to receive his allegations with implicit credit, and betake themselves to such an examination as may detect imperfect representation and statements evidently dictated by partiality?

Next, *as to the internal grounds of proof* that our epistle does not belong to Paul.

These are, without exception, the same as had been before advanced by Eichhorn, Ziegler, Bertholdt, Schulz, and Seyffarth; all of which have been examined in the preceding pages. De Wette states, very categorically, that the language of our epistle is very different from that of Paul; and he appeals to Schulz as having most fully shown this, in the work which has been already examined. How far the case is as Schulz has represented it, must now be left to the reader to judge for himself.

What most of all surprises me, is, that De Wette should produce, as special proof of the alleged discrepancy of style, the formulas of quotation, examined p. 176 seq. (18.) above; and also the appellations given to the Saviour by the writer of our epistle, examined in p. 182 seq. (19.) above; two of the most unlucky of all the arguments which Schulz and Seyffarth have adduced. It requires, indeed, a great deal of patience and labour to examine this matter to the bottom; more, I am quite inclined from bitter experience to believe, than De Wette consumed in writing the whole of the article in his Introduction, which has respect to our epistle.

Besides these two cases of *diversity* of style, De Wette has proceeded to cite a large list of words; all of which are taken from Schulz and Seyffarth, and have already been the subject of particular examination. With an adventurous step, and without even opening his Greek Concordance for investigation, he has followed his leaders in this hazardous path, and even selected the words examined above, on p. 197 (34.,) p. 198 (37.,) not omitting the most unfortunate of all Dr. Schulz's *guesses*, viz. the phrases on p. 199 (40.,) above. The word πίστις, too, has come in for its usual share of *discrepancy*, (see above, p. 159, e,) and also βασιλεία τοῦ Θεοῦ and τελείωσις.

He avers, moreover, after Schulz, that the comparison and symbolical use of the Old Testament passages and ordinances, is foreign to the manner of Paul, and like to that of Philo. (See on this subject p. 131 seq. (3.) above.) He asserts, too, that Paul could not have represented Christianity so correspondent with Judaism, nor Christ as high priest; nor would he have been silent about his office of apostle to the heathen, nor concealed the fact, that the Christian religion was designed as well for Gentiles as Jews.

Yet, how many of Paul's epistles there are, in which these topics are not insisted on, and which De Wette himself does not suppose to be spurious, he does not seem once to have thought of. How is it possible that such a writer as Paul should be limited to one circle of objects, and reasoning, and expression? De Wette would not like to have the genuineness of his own works tried by such a rule of scrutiny.

On the question, To whom was our epistle directed? De Wette has exhibited a singular method of treating the subject. He endeavours to present difficulties that lie in the way of supposing that it was directed to any church; and then comes to the conclusion, that probably it was not originally an *epistle*, but the composition of some companion of Paul, who added the personal allusions toward the close of the letter, for the sake of giving credit to it as a composition of the apostle; so that all investigation about either the author of the epistle, or the persons to whom it is directed, is in vain and useless, pp. 292—294. It seems after all, then, that the author of our epistle is a dissembler and dishonest man; aiming to stand upon the credit of Paul, because he fears that his own credit is insufficient. But can any candid reader of our epistle refuse to see the unequivocal marks of sincerity, candour, high-raised benevolent feeling, and spiritual comprehensive views, every where exhibited? I repeat it, had the writer of such a piece any need of propping up himself, by the aid of even Paul's name and authority? Then how futile, nay foolish, the attempt to do so, if his style, diction, manner, reasoning, quotations, circle of thought—in a word, every thing—is so *toto cœlo* diverse from that of Paul, as Schulz, Seyffarth, and De Wette represent it! Where were the eyes and understandings of the readers? Could they not detect the imposture? And then what would become of the epistle, and of the reputation of the man who wrote it? One ought to have better reasons than these, to abandon the convictions which a thorough investigation will force upon him.

§ 31. *Objections by Boehme.*

The work of De Wette, noticed in the preceding section, was accompanied by a recent work of C. F. Boehme, comprised in a volume of about 800 pages; which contains an introduction to our epistle, and a translation of the same, followed by a copious commentary. Of the author little is known in this country, and, if I may judge by such reviews of books in Germany as I have perused, little is said in his own country respecting him. The work was printed at Leipsic in 1825.

Like the critics whose works have been examined in the preceding sections, Boehme sets out with the most unqualified assertions respecting the discrepancies of style and manner, between the author of our epistle, and all the other writers of the New Testament. He asserts, that " as to the form and method of his work, the rhetorical construction of it, and the constant and accurate observance of order, our author far excels the other contemporary sacred writers." He extols the art which the writer of our epistle uses, in order to persuade those whom he addressed to follow his advice; in particular, he gives as examples of this, Heb. iii. 7—iv. 13, where the writer very dexterously, as he says, turns the promise of rest in the land of Canaan, into a promise of rest in the heavenly world; to which he adds Heb. xi. 8—16, where, he avers, that " the author by the aid of his rhetorical art, and *contra fidem historiæ*,

§ 31. OBJECTIONS BY BOEHME.

has rendered it *aliquatenus probabile,* that Abraham and the other patriarchs had a spiritual rest in view."

With many other eulogies he loads the author of our epistle, on account of his art, his eloquence, and his excellent Greek ; and from all this, (as was to be anticipated,) he comes to the conclusion, that the author could not be Paul, nor any of the other writers of the New Testament, being far superior to them all.

Into the historical and critical examination of this question, however, he does not even pretend to go. He avers, that to do so would be merely *agere actum.* He considers the works of Schulz, Seyffarth, and Ziegler, as having finally settled the question, beyond any hope of retrieve by those who advocate the Pauline origin of our epistle; and after appealing to the authors just named, and to the considerations which he has himself suggested, in respect to the discrepancies of style and manner between the author and Paul, he concludes by saying, " that Paul was not the author, *satis superque demonstratum est, a nobis aliisque.*"

This is indeed a summary method of despatching a question of this nature; certainly it is a method, which spares writers and readers a great deal of severe labour and study. Unfortunately, however, for all these rhetorical appeals to the mere feelings and imagination of men, there are some, at least, who believe in the Pauline origin of our epistle, that are too φιλόπονοι to shrink from bringing the whole matter to the test of actual investigation, and who will insist upon it, that those who make assertions are bound in duty to prove them.

The work of Boehme, under examination, is not one which bids fair to bring any accession of strength to the cause of those who deny the Pauline origin of our epistle; and all which I could wish to say respecting his suggestions, has been already said in the preceding pages.

I cannot deny, however, that he has exhibited something *new* in his book. He has endeavoured to show, that Silas, or Silvanus, was the author of our epistle, and that it was directed to the church at Antioch; conjectures, which not only have not a single voice of ancient testimony in their favour, but which are destitute of any circumstances that render them even in a slight degree probable. I cannot help thinking of Boehme's introduction to his work, much as one of his countrymen thinks of a certain author, who has made some noise of late in the medical world : " He has some new things, and some true things; but his new things are not true things, and his true things are not new things."

§ 32. Hebraisms of the Epistle.

All the writers, who have declared against the Pauline origin of our epistle, have appealed to Origen's declaration, 'Αλλὰ ἐςὶν ἡ ἐπιςολὴ συνθέσει τῆς λέξεως Ἑλληνικωτέρα, *the epistle* [to the Hebrews] *in the texture of its style is more conformed to the Greek idiom*, [than the epistles of Paul]. Eichhorn, Bertholdt, Ziegler, Schulz, Seyffarth, De Wette, Boehme, and others, have one and all urged this consideration, and insisted upon it, that Origen's judgment, on this point, must be considered as decisive.

In respect to the general principles of criticism, which are to regulate our investigation of such a matter, I have already said all which I wish to say, p. 215 seq. (4.) The actual comparison of our epistle with the acknowledged epistles of Paul has also been made, pp. 173—209 above. It may, however, be of some importance to add, in this place, a list of some of the Hebraisms which occur in our epistle, in order to meet the very categorical assertion of De Wette and Boehme, that " the style of our epistle is not only very different from that of Paul, but he composes in purer Greek, and with a far more oratorical diction."

Words and phrases used in a Hebraistic sense, or in a way different from what is usual in the Greek classics.

CHAP. I. 1 Πατράσι, *ancestors of old time*, אָבוֹת. Seldom or never does classical Greek so employ this word. Ἐπ' ἐσχάτου τῶν ἡμερῶν, *the time of the Messiah, the last age of the world*, אַחֲרִית הַיָּמִים; purely Hebrew. 2 Κληρονόμος, *lord, ruler,* יוֹרֵשׁ; in classic Greek, one who takes by lot or by testament. 3 Δόξα, *splendor, brightness, radiance,* כָּבוֹד; in Greek, opinion, sentiment, maxim, fame, honour. Ὑποστάσεως αὐτοῦ, *of his substance,* i. e. *of himself,* נַפְשׁוֹ עַצְמוֹ. Καθαρισμὸν .... τῶν ἁμαρτιῶν, *expiation for sin,* הַכִּפּוּרִים, (Sept. καθαρισμὸς, Exod. xxix. 36; xxx. 10;) see Comm. in loc. Μεγαλωσύνη, *majesty, excellence,* גֹּדֶל אַדֶּרֶת; not found in the classics. Ἐν ὑψηλοῖς, *in heaven, in the world above,* בַּמְּרוֹם, Sept. ἐν ὑψηλοῖς. 4 Κεκληρονόμηκεν, *obtained,* יָרַשׁ; Greek, to acquire by lot, to inherit. Same word in i. 14.

I omit purposely all the *quotations* which follow here, and all throughout the epistle, which are made from the ancient Scriptures; because, as they were doubtless made, in general, from the Septuagint version, they cannot be justly considered as properly belonging to the style of our author. If the Hebraisms in all these quotations were to be added to the list of those in the rest of the epistle, it would make it to appear something very different from 'Ελληνικωτέρα. Whether Origen did, or did not, mean to exclude them, no one, so far as I know, has yet attempted to show.

II. 2 Λόγος, *commination, command*, or *revelation*, דָּבָר ; not so in the classics. 3 Σωτηρίας, *the Christian religion with its threats and promises*; certainly not a classical sense of the word. 4 Δυνάμεσι, *miraculous powers, miracles*, נִפְלָאוֹת, עֹז, גְּבוּרָה, all of which the Septuagint translate by δύναμις; in the classics, not so. Θέλησιν, a word unknown to the Attics. 5 Οἰκουμένην μέλλουσαν, *the gospel dispensation*, הָעוֹלָם הַבָּא; purely Jewish. 10 Δόξαν, *future happiness, a glorious condition in another world;* peculiar to Helenistic Greek. 11 'Αγιάζων and ἁγιαζόμενοι, *making atonement for*, and, *those for whom atonement is made*, or, *who are expiated*, קָדַשׁ and כִּפֶּר are both rendered by ἁγιάζω in the Septuagint; in the classics, ἁγιάζω means to consecrate, to make or declare sacred. 'Αδελφοὺς, *socios, amicos, ejusdem naturæ participes*, אָחִים ; classics, either children of the same parents, or near relatives, kindred by descent. 12 'Εκκλησία, *public religious assembly*, קָהָל, עֲצָרָה, מִקְרָא ; classics, public civil assembly. 14 Σαρκὸς καὶ αἵματος, *human nature, corporeal state* or *condition*, בָּשָׂר, נֶפֶשׁ=דָּם, see Gen. ix. 4, and in the New Testament, 1 Cor. xv. 50. Matt. xvi. 17. Gal. i. 16. al.; not so used in the classics. Καταργήσῃ, *to destroy, to render null* or *inefficacious ;* classics, to be idle, to remain sluggish or inactive. Διάβολον, *Satan*, שָׂטָן, *the devil;* classics, a slanderer, an accuser. 16 'Αγγέλων, *angels, heavenly messengers*, מַלְאָכִים ; in the classics, ἄγγελος means messenger, or message. Σπέρματος, *progeny*, offspring, זֶרַע, frequent in the New Testament, and three times in our epistle ; rarely, if ever, has it this sense among the classics. The *frequency* of it is Hellenistic.

III. 1 'Αδελφοὶ ἅγιοι, קְדוֹשִׁים, Ps. xvi. 3 et sæpe, *professed people of God, worshippers of God;* in a sense different from the ἅγιος of the classics. Κλήσεως ἐπουρανίου, *invitations* or *privileges of the gospel ;* no parallel in common Greek. 'Απόστολον καὶ ἀρχιερέα τῆς ὁμολογίας ; such a combination is utterly foreign to the classics. 2 Οἴκῳ in the sense of *worshippers of God, the assembly of the faithful*, בֵּית אֱלֹהִים, בַּיִת; peculiar to Hellenistic Greek. So 13 Καθ' ἑκάστην ἡμέραν, כָּל הַיּוֹם, *continually, constantly.* Σκληρύνω, קָשָׁה, חָזַק, applied to the heart or mind; literally used only in the classics. 16 Παρεπίκραναν, מָרָה,

סָרַר, not of classic usage. 17 Προσώχθιζε, קוּט; not a classic word. Ἁμαρτήσασι, חַטָּאִים, sinners, violators of divine precepts ; classic usage, to miss the mark, to fail, &c.; the sense of sinners or offenders, as in our epistle, is seldom and doubtful in the classics. Κῶλα, carcases corpses, פְּגָרִים; in common Greek, members, limbs. 18 Κατάπαυσιν מְנוּחָה, rest, future rest or happiness; Greek, a causing of rest, stilling, quieting.

IV. 2 Εὐαγγελισμένοι, בָּשַׂר, used here in a more appropriate and peculiar sense than in the classics. Ὁ λόγος τῆς ἀκοῆς, שְׁמוּעָה שָׁמַע, found in Paul, 1 Thess. ii. 13; the words are classic, but the combination is altogether diverse from any in the classics. 12 Ζῶν, perpetual, enduring, or active, חַי, as in אֵל חַי; not in the classics. 13 Οὐκ .... κτίσις, לֹא כֹל, Greek οὐδὲν, no creature, nothing; κτίσις, in the classics, means, the act of creating. 14 Οὐρανοὺς, שָׁמַיִם, the Hebrew idea of the firmament above. Ὁμολογίας, religion, professed subjection to Christ, Sept. for נֶדֶר, votum. 15 Ἀσθενείας, moral weaknesses, Sept. for מִכְשׁוֹל stumbling, and צֶלַע claudicatio; classics, physical weakness, with various shades. 16 Θρόνος τῆς χάριτος, without a parallel in the classics.

V. 3 Προσφέρειν, to offer gifts and sacrifices to God, הִקְרִיב, הֵרִים, הֵבִיא; in Greek, not appropriate to this sacred rite. 7 Εἰσακουσθεὶς, delivered, saved, Sept. for הוֹשִׁיעַ, עָנָה. 12 Τὰ στοιχεῖα τῆς ἀρχῆς τῶν λογίων; such an expression is wanting in the classics. Γάλακτος .... τροφῆς, not a classical metaphor. 13 Λόγου δικαιοσύνης, Christian or religious doctrine; without an example in the classics.

VI. 1 Νεκρῶν ἔργων deadly, destructive works, הוֹרְגִים, הָרַג occidere, Septuagint, νεκρός. 2 Βαπτισμῶν διδαχῆς, ἐπιθέσεώς τε χειρῶν, foreign to the classics; as is κρίματος αἰωνίου. 4 Πνεύματος ἁγίου, רוּחַ הַקָּדוֹשׁ; an expression and an idea foreign to all the classics. 5 Καλὸν .... ῥῆμα, promise of good, so דָּבָר טוֹב often in Hebrew; classics, declaration, any thing uttered. Δυνάμεις μέλλοντος αἰῶνος, miraculous powers under the gospel dispensation; an utter stranger to the classic authors.

Βοτάνην, any kind of fruit which the earth produces, עֵשֶׂב; in Greek, simply herbage, vegetation. 10 Εἰς τὸ ὄνομα αὐτοῦ, toward him, toward his cause, for his sake, (לִשְׁמוֹ,) ὄνομα being pleonastic, as in Hebrew. 12 Μακροθυμίας, patient waiting, אָרְכָּה, prolongatio, Sept.; which I cannot find in the classics. Τῆς ἐπαγγελίας, the promised blessing; classic sense, promise.

VII. 1 Θεοῦ ὑψίστου, עֶלְיוֹן; the words are classic Greek, but the

§ 32. HEBRAISMS OF THE EPISTLE. 227

combination is Hebrew. Κοπῆς, *slaughter,* מַכָּה; Greek, hewing, cutting out. 3 'Απάτωρ, ἀμήτωρ, *without any genealogy of parents;* the classic writers apply these words to their gods, and to orphan children, in quite a different sense. 4 'Ακροθινίων, *spoils* in general, (see Gen. xiv. 20 ;) classics, first fruits, part of the spoils of war presented to the gods. Πατριάρχης, רֹאשׁ הָאָבוֹת; I cannot find any trace of this word in the classics. 5 'Αποδεκατόω, *to tithe, to take a tenth part,* עָשַׂר; peculiar to Hebrew Greek. Εξεληλυθότας ἐκ τῆς ὀσφύος, 'Αβραὰμ, יֹצְאִים מֵחֲלָצִים; the Greeks said, γεννᾶσθαι ὑπό τινος, in such a case, so that the above expression is purely Hebrew. 6 Δεκατόω, as ἀποδεκατόω in v. 5. 10 'Εν τῇ ὀσφύι τοῦ πατρὸς, see above on v. 5. 11 Τελείωσις, in a sense *sui generis.* 16 Σαρκικῆς, *perishable, short-lived,* בָּשָׂר; not found in the classics in such a sense. 20 'Ορκωμοσίας, peculiar to our epistle ; the classic ὀρκωμόσια (with antepenult accent) is an adjective, ἱερὰ being understood after it. 22 Διαθήκης, in the sense of the Hebrew בְּרִית.

VIII. 2 'Αγίων, plur., קֹדֶשׁ קָדָשִׁים; classics, ἅγιον. Σκηνῆς, *the divine* אֹהֶל, סֻכָּה ; classics, a common tent or dwelling. 6 Μεσίτης, in a different sense from what is usual in the classics. The long quotation from the Septuagint that follows, is not more Hebraistic than the surrounding context.

IX. 1 Δικαιώματα, *ordinances, arrangements,* מִשְׁפָּטִים ; classics, sentence of justice, decision, just action or requisition. 5 'Ιλαστήριον, כַּפֹּרֶת, Septuagint word ; classics, ἱλαστήριος -ία, -ον, adjective. 9 Παραβολὴ, *symbol;* classics, comparison, similitude in speech or writing. 11 'Αρχιερεὺς μελλόντων ἀγαθῶν, unlike any thing in the classics. 12 Ταύτης τῆς κτίσεως, *of the present world ;* κτίσις in the classics, means, the act of creating. Εὐράμενος, form *sui generis.* 13 Κεκοινωμένους, *the unclean,* חֹלִים, חֲלָלִים ; Greek κοινόω to communicate, to share, to render common. 'Αγιάζει, *purifies,* קָדַשׁ ; Greek, to consecrate, to devote. 16 Φέρεσθαι *accidere, to happen;* it is *sui generis.* 18 'Εγκεκαίνισται, *was ratified ;* classics, to renew. 22 Αἱματεκχυσίας, *sui generis.* 26 Καταβολῆς κόσμου, a combination unknown to the classics. Συντελείᾳ τῶν αἰώνων, *the end of the former dispensation ;* no where in common Greek. 28 'Αμαρτίας, *sin-offering, sacrifice for sin,* אָשָׁם חַטָּאת ; not in the classics.

X. 1 Εἰκόνα, *complete image, perfect delineation,* (in distinction from σκιὰ, an *imperfect* sketch,) תַּבְנִית ; the Greek εἰκὼν is simply, image. Τελειῶσαι, in a more pregnant sense than any classic usage gives to it,

13 Τεθῶσιν οἱ ἐχθροὶ αὐτοῦ ὑποπόδιον τῶν ποδῶν αὐτοῦ, a phrase purely Hebraistic in its hue; see Ps. cx. 1. [2.] 20 Ζῶσαν, qualifying such a word as ὁδὸν, is a combination unknown to the classics. 22 Ἐῤῥαντισμένοι τὰς καρδίας, altogether Hebrew in its hue. 25 Ἡμέρα, *the day of the Lord, the day of terror*, יוֹם יְהוָה, יוֹם, altogether in a Hebrew sense. 27 Πυρὸς ζῆλος, אַף חָרוֹן, exactly Hebrew. 29 Κοινὸν, *an unclean thing;* see under ix. 13. 32 "Ἄθλησιν . . . παθημάτων, a method of expression foreign to the classics. 35 Παῤῥησίαν, *confidence, Christian trust;* classics, boldness or freedom of speech. Μισθαποδοσίαν, *reward; sui generis.*

XI. 3 Αἰῶνας, *worlds*, עוֹלָמִים, entirely Jewish. Ῥήματι, *command*, אָמַר דָּבָר; Greek, saying, thing said. 5 Ἰδεῖν θάνατον, רָאָה מָוֶת, רָאָה שַׁחַת. Οὐχ εὑρίσκετο, אֵינֶנּוּ; foreign to the classics. 6 Μισθαποδότης I cannot find in classic Greek. 7 Κόσμον, *the ungodly, the world who were sinful;* not of classic usage. Δικαιοσύνης, *justifying, of justification;* classics, equity, uprightness. 9 Συγκληρονόμων, *joint-possessors;* foreign, in this sense, to common Greek. 19 Ἐν παραβολῇ, peculiar method of expression. 34 Στόματα μαχαίρας, *the edge of the sword*, פִּי־חָרֶב, unknown to the classic authors. 37 Ἐν φόνῳ μαχαίρας, *with the murderous sword*, a Hebrew combination.

XII. 6 Παιδεύει, *chastises*, יָסַר, and ver. 7 παιδείαν, *chastisement*, מוּסָר: the meanings here given to these two words are seldom, if ever, given in the classics. 9 Τῆς σαρκὸς ἡμῶν πατέρας, a Hebrew, not a classic combination of ideas; σαρκὸς meaning the *physical* man, in distinction from the *mental* one. Τῷ πατρὶ τῶν πνευμάτων: Hebrew, אֱלֹהֵי הָרוּחוֹת לְכָל בָּשָׂר, Num. xvi. 22, xxvii. 16; foreign to all the classics. 10 Ἁγιότητος, can hardly be found, I believe, in the classics. It is a Hellenistic term, corresponding to קֹדֶשׁ. 11 Καρπὸν εἰρηνικὸν, *peaceful fruit*, i. e. happy fruit, פְּרִי שָׁלוֹם; εἰρηνικὸν here manifestly bearing the Hebrew-Greek, and not the classic sense. 14 Οὐδεὶς ὄψεται τὸν Κύριον, so יְהוָה לֹא יִרְאֶה פְּנֵי יְהוָה לֹא יִרְאֶה; the whole form of expression is manifestly Hebraistic. 16 Βρώσεως μιᾶς, *one meal;* classics, the act of eating, or food. The certainty that *meal* is the idea here, arises from the adjunct μιᾶς. Πρωτοτόκια, Heb. בְּכוֹרָה; not used in the classics. 19 Μὴ προστεθῆναι αὐτοῖς λόγον, לְדַבֵּר בִּלְתִּי יֹסֵף עוֹד, a Hebrew and not a Greek mode of expression. 22 Μυριάσι, רִבּוֹת, רִבּוֹ, the usual Hebrew expression for a large indefinite number; the Latins said, *sexcenti.* 23 Ἀπογεγραμμένων ἐν οὐρανοῖς, כָּל הַכָּתוּב לַחַיִּים, Is. iv. 3. Comp. Ex. xxxii. 32. Ps. lxix. 28. Dan. xii. 1., Luke x. 20, &c. An expression altogether Hebraistic.

XIII. 3 Ὄντες ἐν σώματι, in a frail dying state; not so expressed in the classics. The mode of expression comes from the Hebrew, בָּשָׂר. 7 Ἡγουμένων, teachers, spiritual guides, מַנְהִיג אַלּוּף; classic sense never that of teachers. 8 Χθὲς καὶ σήμερον, אֶתְמוֹל וְהַיּוֹם; where, in all the classics, is the like of this, in order to designate all past and present time? 15 Θυσίαν αἰνέσεως .... καρπὸν χειλέων; the idea of sacrifice of praise, is Hebrew, Lev. vii. 12, זֶבַח הַתּוֹדָה, comp. Ps. l. 14. 23. As to καρπὸν χειλέων, there is nothing in the classics like it. Plainly it has its original in the Hebrew, נְשַׁלְּמָה פָרִים שְׂפָתֵינוּ, Hos. xiv. 3, we will render to thee the calves [i. e. the offering, the fruit] of our lips, or rather, we will render to thee calves with our lips. 16 Θυσίαις, as applied to εὐποιΐας καὶ κοινωνίας, is purely a Hebrew application. 17 Ὑπὲρ τῶν ψυχῶν ὑμῶν, for you, לְנַפְשֹׁתֵיכֶם; the Greeks, ὑπὲρ ὑμῶν.

In this selection, I have aimed at taking only the more obvious words and phrases. It might be much enlarged, by more strenuously urging the principle, in all respects, of dissimilarity to the Greek classic writers. That an idea is *peculiar* to the Christian dispensation, and unknown to the classic authors, has not been the basis of my selection in any case, unless at the same time there is a phraseology, which is as foreign to the Greeks as the idea itself. If all the *ideas* which are not *classical*, were to be the guiding principle in our selection, there would be no end of examples. But this would not be a fair and proper method of proceeding. It is the *diction*, and *phraseology*, and the sense which is given to the words employed, that are asserted to be Ἑλληνικώτερα. In this shape have I endeavoured to meet the thing; and the reader has the result before him.

With such a result in view, what matters it, whether De Wette, Schulz, Seyffarth, or even Origen himself, tells us that our epistle is almost *classical* Greek, and that all runs smoothly and oratorically on? As to this last assertion, I have only to ask, that those who make it would translate and explain Heb. ii. 9, 10.; iii. 3, 4. 15; iv. 3—9; v. 5. 7—9; vi. 1, 2; vii. 1—3. 8, 9. 15, 16; ix. 9, 10. 15—17. 27, 28; x. 5—9. 20; xi. 3. 39, 40; xii. 18—24. 27, 28; xiii. 7—9. 11—13; to which I might easily add many other passages. If they will find Greek more elliptical, more involved, more intricate and dark, in all the epistles of Paul, I will thank them for the discovery.—I must add, also, that the list of Hebraisms and unclassical usage, in our epistle, would have been much more swelled, if I had not omitted to repeat the same words, so often as I found them repeated and used in a Hebraistic or in a Hebraistic or unclassical manner. Such words are ἀδελφὸς, ἅγιος ἁγιάζω, ἁμαρτία, ἀσθένεια, δικαίωμα, ἐγκαινίζω, ἐπαγγελία, καθ' ἡμέραν, κληρονόμος, κληρονομέω, κατάπαυσις, λόγος ἀρχῆς, μισθαποδοσία, μεγαλωσύνη, μεσίτης, νεκρὸς, οἶκος, σὰρξ, τελειόω, and others.

I make the appeal now with boldness, and call upon those who assert the *almost classic* style and manner of our epistle, to produce more true Hebraisms, and more idioms foreign to the Greek classics, in any of Paul's acknowledged epistles. I will even venture to make another offer; which is, that I will show that some at least of his acknowledged epistles exhibit less Hebrew colouring, when they shall have shown that some of them exhibit more.

It does not signify to beat the air, in this contest. *Assertions* are one thing; *facts* are another. If Origen and all the Greek fathers were to assert, that our epistle is Ελληνικώτερα than Paul's, it could not make it so. "To the work of *examination*," would be my reply. Let every critic go to this work, for himself, if he knows enough of Hebrew idiom to do it: and the result will be an abiding conviction, that Origen had as little reason for the assertion in question, as he had for the adventurous remark which he has made, on the use of the Greek article by the sacred writers. Origen's assertion, and every other man's, on this subject, can be brought to the test; and he who subjects them to this process, I am persuaded, will find himself brought, at last, if he will examine *impartially* and *fully*, to a firm conviction that they are *mere* assertions, and nothing more.

§ 33. *Alexandrine hue of the Epistle.*

Eichhorn, who has so strenuously insisted that Paul is not the author of our epistle, has endeavoured to show, that it is probably of Alexandrine origin. But the arguments which he adduces for this purpose, seem to me incapable of standing the test of a critical examination.

(1.) "The author of the epistle to the Hebrews treats the ancient Jewish Scriptures as containing a mysterious and secret sense, concealed under the words. He also regards the various ritual observances of the ancient law, only as types and shadows of things under the Christian dispensation, Heb. x. 1; ix. 8. Philo of Alexandria expresses the same views, De confus. Ling. p. 348." Eichh. Einleit. p. 442.

That the general views of the author of our epistle in regard to the meaning and object of Jewish rites coincided with those of Philo, I should not be at all disposed to deny. But who is going to show us, that these were not founded in truth? If, as I believe, the Jewish dispensation had its origin in divine communications and directions, there can be no rational doubt that it had some important end in view. Surely, now, the sacrifices and various rites of external purification could never, in and of themselves, be deemed an object worthy of special divine interposition and command. Their connexion with some higher and more spiritual object and end, was what stamped their highest real value upon them. In any other point of view, they could scarcely be thought worthy of the character of Him who requires men to worship him in spirit and in truth.

That a man of such enlarged views as Philo, should have seen and felt this, and that Paul should have done the same, is not a matter of wonder to any one, who considers the tendency of an enlightened mind to look on the *spiritual* design of religion as infinitely the most important and interesting part of it.

What can be more diverse, however, than the particular form which Philo gives to his speculations on this subject, and that in which the ideas of our author are developed? Philo allegorizes on every thing, and every where, almost without distinction. The historical facts in the book of Genesis, the connexion of Abraham with Sarah and Hagar, and all other occurrences related in the Pentateuch, are, if occasion presents an opportunity, converted into allegory, and made the theme of exuberant speculative mysticism. Neither is there one word in all, which has any relation to the Messiah, or to his atoning sacrifice.

How very different the types and shadows presented by our epistle are, the intelligent and critical reader need not be informed. All is brought to bear on one single point—the death of Christ, the propitiatory sacrifice for sin made by it, and the effectual reconciliation to God accomplished in this manner.

To reason, then, as Eichhorn has done, is just the same, as to bring forward the allegation, that Philo believed in the existence of one supreme God: that the writer of the epistle to the Hebrews did the same, and then draw the inference, that the writer of this epistle must therefore have lived, or at least been nurtured, at Alexandria. I venture to say, that there never has been so rational an account of the *object* of the Jewish ritual, as the author of our epistle gives: nor one so worthy of the great Author of the old and the new dispensations, nor so consonant with the fundamental maxim, that " God is a spirit, and requires men to worship him in a spiritual manner."

(2.) " Philo intimates, that the higher mysteries of the Jewish religion are only for the initiated, μύσαις. In like manner our epistle, v. 11; vi. 3." Einleit. p. 444.

I can find no trace of reserve in our epistle, in regard to the ἀμύστοις, or *uninitiated*. The expression of deep regret, that those whom the writer addresses had not made higher acquisitions of religious knowledge, I can easily find. Severe reproof for such negligence, I see; but not a word about any distinctions between μύσται and ἄμυστοι, *initiated* and *uninitiated*, am I able to discover. Philo, in respect to this, is more than half a Grecian Platonist; but the writer of our epistle practises no concealment at all.

(3.) " The Alexandrine author of the book of Wisdom has praised wisdom on account of its nature and qualities, and then adduced historical examples to illustrate all this, Wisd. i—ix; x. 1; xvi. 1. So, the author of the epistle to the Hebrews, after urging and eulogizing faith, adduces historical examples of it, in chap. xi., in order more strongly to impress its importance." p. 445.

To which one may reply, that from the days of the author of our epistle, down to the present time, almost every practical writer on religion, and every preacher on the subject of faith, has done the same. But does this prove, that every such writer and preacher was born or nurtured at Alexandria? Can a thing, so obvious to the common sense of all men, as the appropriate method of treating a subject, be adduced, to establish a special relation between any two men, as to country or education.

(4.) " Many thoughts and expressions, in the epistle to the Hebrews, resemble those of Philo," p. 446, seq.

So Eichhorn, who has occupied several pages with detailing expressions which afford such resemblances. So Schulz, also, who has ocupied fourteen pages with alleged parallels of this nature, printed in opposite columns. I have examined all these with attention, and must confess, that the impression made upon me by them, is very different from that which Eichhorn and Schulz appear to have received.

To any considerate man, who makes this examination, it will very naturally occur, that the author of our epistle and Philo were contemporaries. At least, the former must have come upon the stage before the latter left it. Then, both were educated as Jews; both were deeply read in the Jewish Scriptures, above all, in the law of Moses. Both

§ 33. ALEXANDRINE HUE OF THE EPISTLE. 233

thought, reasoned, and expressed themselves as Hebrews, writing in Greek. Both had the same views, fundamentally, of the great points of the religion of Moses. Both had high moral feelings, and a deep interest in them. Could it be possible, now, that there should not be points of resemblance between Philo and our author, when writing on similar subjects! Surely not, any more than that there should not be points of similarity between the sentiments of a Christian divine in any particular age and country, and those of another, near the same age, in a different country.

Both Philo and our author often appeal to the Jewish Scriptures. And because they deduce from them like sentiments, does this prove that our author must have been of the Alexandrine school? Why is not the argument just as good the other way, viz. to prove that Philo must have belonged to some other country, i. e. to that in which our author lived? All that such resemblance can prove is, that both belonged to the *Mosaic school;* and who will deny this?

I may venture, however, to go farther, and to aver, that the *dissimilarity* of *style,* between our epistle and the works of Philo, as they appear in the copious extracts made by Schulz, is so great, that one might almost as well think of proving an alliance between some heathen writer of Greek and our epistle, as between the latter and Philo. The moment Philo departs from his Septuagint text, he goes off to an idiom as different from that in our epistle, as can well be conceived of in a Hebrew, writing on moral subjects, and making the Old Testament the basis of his speculations. Every critical reader who inspects the parallels of Dr. Schulz can judge for himself of this; and to every such one the appeal is fearlessly made, in regard to the point in question.

The writers whom I am now controverting, are indebted to J. B. Carpzoff, (Exercitt. Sac. in Paulli epist. ad Hebræos, ex Philone Alexandrino, Helmst. 1750,) for the materials, which they have wrought up into the form of an argument for the Alexandrine origin of our epistle. But they do not once seem to have reflected, that if the same iron diligence, which Carpzoff has exhibited in his work, had been applied to the acknowledged epistles of Paul, in the same way, as large a harvest of resemblances might have been gathered. In regard to allegory, for example, (which is a main point of alleged resemblance,) what could be more obvious, than to appeal to 1 Cor. x. 1—6; x. 11. Rom. v. 14. 1 Cor. xv. 45—47. 2 Cor. iii. 13—18. Gal. iv. 22—31; also to Col. ii. 16, 17. Gal. iii. 23—25; iv. 1—5? May it not be said of these passages, (as Jerome says of our epistle, and which has been so often quoted with confidence,) "*spirant quiddam Philonianum?*" Let the experiment be made by another Carpzoff, and I venture to predict, that, assuming the principle of argument which is assumed by Eichhorn and Schulz, we may easily show, that Paul himself must have been an Alexandrian, and been educated in the Philonian school.

One hint more, and I dismiss the subject. Is not the Septuagint Alexandrine Greek? Are not the Apocryphal books connected with the Old Testament, Alexandrine Greek? Does not the *whole* New Testament Greek bear a close resemblance to the style of these two classes of books? Are not Paul's epistles Hebrew-Greek, like all the rest? How can it be shown, then, that the author of our epistle was an Alexandrian, because he writes Alexandrine Greek? If the argument be valid for this purpose, which Eichhorn and Schulz employ, then may we prove, that all the New Testament writers were Alexandrians. *Quod nimium facit, nihil facit.*

§ 34. *Result.*

The conclusion, then, to be deduced, from the preceding examination, seems to be, that the arguments drawn from the style and diction of the epistle to the Hebrews, are not to be relied on as deciding the question against the Pauline origin of it. No case of this nature can be determined by *assertion.* Allegations made for such a purpose, if found to be contradicted by *facts,* are not to determine the manner in which the question before us is to be decided.

One other thing may be said with truth, which has an important bearing on this question. If the *internal* evidence is altogether insufficient to decide the point at issue in the negative, the *external* is equally so. Indeed, the *historical* evidence against the Pauline origin of our epistle is, as we have seen, so little, so vague, and for the most part so indirect, that we may well say, " the objections have never been of an *historical* nature, but of a *conjectural* one." They have arisen more from taste and feeling, than from tradition or testimony.

On the whole, I must acquiesce in the opinion of Origen, which I repeat as the general voice of antiquity; IT IS NOT WITHOUT REASON THE ANCIENTS HAVE HANDED IT DOWN TO US, THAT THIS EPISTLE IS PAUL'S. Nor should I differ materially from those who, with Eusebius, can say, τοῦ δὲ Παύλου πρόδηλοι καὶ σαφεῖς αἱ δεκατέσσαρες, *fourteen epistles are* CLEARLY *and* CERTAINLY *Paul's.* I consider, however, the form of the proposition, as stated by Origen, to be the most becoming, in regard to a point so controverted, and to contain, for substance, all which it is necessary or expedient for us to assert and to believe.

§ 35. *Was Barnabas the Author?*

Whoever is satisfied with the arguments in favour of the Pauline origin of our epistle, may dispense with the examination, whether any other person than this apostle has a title to be considered as the author. But as past experience must lead one to believe, that unanimity in regard to this subject is not yet to be expected, but that some may still incline to adopt opinions about the authorship of our epistle, which were avowed or defended in ancient times; it seems to be necessary, briefly at least, to examine the claims of some others, as well as those of Paul.

The doubts raised in ancient times, whether Paul wrote the epistle to the Hebrews, occasioned conjectures with regard to several other persons. Among the remains of ancient Christian writings, we find some hints that Barnabas was the author of our epistle. We first meet with these, in the essay of Tertullian, de Pudicitia, c. 201. " Extat," says he, " enim et Barnabæ titulus ad Hebræos," i. e. *there is extant an epistle of Barnabas, inscribed to the Hebrews.* This is simple assertion, without any reference to the *reasons* why Tertullian supposes Barnabas to be the author. He does not intimate whether he gathers it from tradition, or assumes it as a matter of mere opinion. He speaks of it as a thing which he believes; which seems to imply that others in that quarter of the church were probably of the same opinion. But we find no mention of this opinion again, until so late as the end of 4th century, when Jerome adverting to it says, "Most [of the Latins] believe, that the epistle to the Hebrews belongs to Barnabas, or Clement;" see Berth. p. 2953, and Jerome in his Epist. ad Dardanum. Again, in his catalogue of ecclesiastical writers, under the word *Paulus*, he says, " The epistle to the Hebrews is thought not to be his, on account of the discrepancy of the style; but to belong to Barnabas, according to Tertullian; or to the evangelist Luke, according to some; or to Clement of Rome." The same thing Philastrius (A.D. 380) repeats, Hæres. c. 89. And in modern times Cameron and Schmidt have undertaken to defend the hypothesis, that Barnabas was the author of this epistle; Bertholdt, ubi supra.

This is all the evidence which history gives us, in respect to this subject; and this surely is too slender to build any opinion upon, which can lay claim to critical confidence.

But all hope of defending this opinion, with any degree of plausibility. is removed by a comparison of the epistle to the Hebrews with an epistle of Barnabas still extant, and undoubtedly the same that was extant in the days of Tertullian, as the quotations from it by the ancient Christian fathers evince. I produce here a few short extracts from this epistle, to enable every one to judge for himself, whether the author of the one epistle can be rationally supposed to have written the other.

Chap. IX. Μάθετε οὖν, τέκνα, περὶ πάντων πλουσίως, ὅτι Ἀβραάμ, ὁ πρῶτος περιτομὴν δοὺς, ἐν πνεύματι προβλέψας εἰς τὸν υἱὸν περιέτεμε, λαβὼν τριῶν γραμμάτων δόγματα· λέγει γὰρ· Καὶ περιέτεμεν Ἀβραὰμ ἐκ τοῦ οἴκου αὐτοῦ ἄνδρας δέκα καὶ ὀκτὼ καὶ τριακοσίους. Τίς οὖν ἡ δοθεῖσα τούτῳ γνῶσις; Μάθετε τοὺς δεκαοκτὼ πρώτους, εἶτα τοὺς τριακοσίους. Τὸ δὲ δέκα ὀκτὼ, ἰῶτα δέκα, ἦτα ὀκτώ· ἔχεις Ἰησοῦν. Ὅτι δὲ σαυρὸς ἐν τῷ Τ ἔμελλεν ἔχειν τὴν χάριν, λέγει καί, Τριακοσίους. Δηλοῖ οὖν τὸν μὲν Ἰησοῦν ἐν τοῖς δυσὶ γράμμασι· καὶ ἐν ἑνὶ, τὸν σαυρόν. Οἶδεν ὁ τὴν ἔμφυτον δωρεὰν τῆς διδαχῆς αὐτοῦ θέμενος ἐν ἡμῖν. Οὐδεὶς γνησιώτερον ἔμαθεν ἀπ' ἐμοῦ λόγον· ἀλλὰ οἶδα ὅτι ἄξιοί ἐσὲ ὑμεῖς. i. e. Children, learn abundantly in regard to all things; for Abraham, who first instituted circumcision, practised this rite, looking forward in the Spirit to the Son, receiving the doctrine of the three letters. For [the Scripture] says, And Abraham circumcised, of his household, three hundred and eighteen men. What instruction is imparted by this? Learn as to the first eighteen, then as to the three hundred. As to eighteen, ἰῶτα signifies ten, and ἦτα eight; this means *Jesus*. And because the cross, signified by T, would possess grace, it says, *three hundred*. It points out Jesus, therefore, by the two letters, and the cross by one. He knows this, who has conferred upon us the engrafted gift of his doctrine. No one has learned more genuine doctrine of me; but I know that ye are worthy of it." Cotelerius, Pat. Apostol. tom. i. p. 28.

So, then, because Abraham circumcised three hundred and eighteen persons, (which, by the way, is not said in the Scriptures, see Gen. xvii. 23–27; comp. Gen. xiv. 14, which gave occasion to the mistake,) the system of Gospel truth is disclosed in this mysterious number; and this because ἰῶτα stands for *ten*, ἦτα for *eight*, and ταῦ for *three hundred*, i. e. here is Jesus, and he crucified. Where, in all the New Testament, is any thing like such egregious trifling as this?

See, now, how the same Barnabas can explain the ceremony of the red heifer, the ashes of which were sprinkled upon offenders. After stating the ceremony, and that the ashes were sprinkled by three children,

§ 36. WAS LUKE THE AUTHOR? 237

he thus proceeds :—Ὁ μόσχος οὗτός ἐςιν ὁ Ἰησοῦς· οἱ προσφέροντες, ἄνδρες ἁμαρτωλοὶ, οἱ προσενέγκαντες αὐτὸν ἐπὶ σφαγὴν· εἶτα οὐκέτι ἄνδρες, οὐκέτι ἁμαρτωλῶν ἡ δόξα. Οἱ δὲ ῥαντίζοντες παῖδες, εὐαγγελιζόμενοι ἡμῖν τὴν ἄφεσιν τῶν ἁμαρτιῶν, καὶ τὸν ἁγνισμὸν τῆς καρδίας, οἷς ἔδωκε τοῦ εὐαγγελίου τὴν ἐξουσίαν, (οὖσι δεκαδύο εἰς μαρτύριον τῶν φυλῶν, ὅτι δεκαδύο αἱ φυλαὶ τοῦ Ἰσραὴλ,) εἰς τὸ κηρύσσειν. Διὰ τὶ δὲ τρεῖς παῖδες οἱ ῥαντίζοντες; Εἰς μαρτύριον Ἀβραὰμ καὶ Ἰσαὰκ καὶ Ἰακὼβ, ὅτι οὗτοι μεγάλοι τῷ Θεῷ. Ὅτι δὲ τὸ ἔριον ἐπὶ τὸ ξύλον; Ὅτι ἡ βασιλεία τοῦ Ἰησοῦ ἐπὶ τῷ ξύλῳ· διότι οἱ ἐλπίζοντες εἰς αὐτὸν ζήσονται εἰς τὸν αἰῶνα. Διὰ τὶ δὲ τὸ ἔριον καὶ τὸν ὕσσωπον; Ὅτι ἐν τῇ βασιλείᾳ αὐτοῦ ἡμέραι ἔσονται πονηραὶ καὶ ῥυπαραὶ, ἐν αἷς ἡμεῖς σωθησόμεθα· ὅτι καὶ ἀλγῶν τὴν σάρκα διὰ τοῦ ῥύπου τοῦ ὑσσώπου ἰᾶται. Καὶ διὰ τοῦτο οὕτω γενόμενα, ἡμῖν μὲν ἐςι φανερὰ, ἐκείνοις δὲ σκοτεινά· ὅτι οὐκ ἤκουσαν φωνῆς τοῦ Κυρίου.

But enough. If all were cited, which betrays a feeble and puerile mind, the whole epistle must be transcribed. Let him who needs further argument on this subject, peruse the whole epistle to the Hebrews, and then read through the epistle of Barnabas. It is impossible that he should not feel the almost indescribable difference between the two writers.

Here, then, is a case, where the possibility of mistake in judging is very small. The difference between this writer, and him who wrote the epistle to the Hebrews, in respect to style, precision, clearness, energy, brevity—in a word, every thing which characterizes any writing—is heaven-wide. The most obtuse perception cannot fail to discern it. It is a hopeless case, to plead the cause of an hypothesis like this.

§ 36. *Was Luke the Author?*

The first suggestion among the ancient fathers, that Luke had any part in the composition of the epistle to the Hebrews, is found in a fragment of Clement of Alexandria, preserved by Eusebius, Ecc. Hist. vi. 14, in which Clement asserts, that " Paul wrote the epistle to the Hebrews in the Hebrew tongue, and that Luke carefully translated it into the Greek." See note, p. 85. The same opinion, or tradition, Origen mentions thus : " If I may give my opinion, I should say, the thoughts are the apostle's ; but the phraseology and composition belong to some one who relates what the apostle said, and as it were comments on the words of his master. But who wrote [i. e. wrote down] the epistle, God only knows. Report, which has come down to us, says, either that Clement of Rome wrote it, or that Luke the Evangelist did." p. 89, supra.

Both Bertholdt and Eichhorn have adduced Origen as asserting, that report attributed the epistle to the Hebrews to Luke as the *real author;* which the context in Origen by no means allows. I cannot but understand him as saying merely, that " the ancients had a report, that either Luke or Clement *wrote down* the epistle;" which corresponds with the opinion of Clement of Alexandria, Origen's teacher in early life. We have seen that afterwards, among the Latin churches, either Luke, or Clement, was regarded as the real author of this epistle; for so the testimony of Jerome and Philastrius, cited in the preceding section, would seem to indicate.

We have no *historical* ground, then, on which we can build the opinion, that Luke was the author of this epistle. An uncertain tradition of the fourth century is surely insufficient. And even if Origen be understood as asserting, that tradition, in his day, assigned the composition of our epistle to Luke; he also asserts, at the same time, that traditionary testimony was at variance with itself, as one party assigned it to Clement of Rome. He evidently credits neither the one nor the other; at least, not in such a way as to be fully persuaded in his own mind; for he says " Who wrote down the epistle, τὸ μὲν ἀληθὲς Θεὸς οἶδε."

The same uncertainty both Jerome and Philastrius exhibit, in the testimony to which allusion has just been made.

It is no doubt true, that the style of Luke approximates much nearer to that of the epistle to the Hebrews, than the style of Barnabas; so that a comparison, in this respect, does not lead to so clear and satisfactory a result in this case, as in that. But the situation of Luke, (born and educated abroad, as he was, and never having resided long in Palestine,) hardly leads one to believe that he was so deeply versed in rabbinical lore, and in Jewish feelings and modes of thinking, as the author of the epistle to the Hebrews must have been.

The main difficulty, however, is the *want* of any *external* evidence that Luke was the author. And as there are, at least, no internal circumstances, or evidence from style, which speak much in favour of such an opinion, it must be abandoned as improbable, and altogether unsupported.

§ 37. *Was Clement of Rome the author?*

Origen is the first, who mentions Clement as the possible writer of the epistle to the Hebrews. In what sense he does this, has been already considered. Jerome and Philastrius, long afterwards, mention that some in the Latin churches attributed the epistle to the Hebrews to Clement of Rome. The evidence of this from testimony, then, is not entitled to any degree of credit, sufficient to create serious doubts whether Clement may not have been the author.

The internal evidence, drawn from a comparison of the epistle to the Hebrews with Clement's first epistle to the Corinthians, by no means favours the supposition in question. Clement has often cited the epistle to the Hebrews. But this seems to me abundant proof, that he did not write that epistle himself; for, as we have already seen, he appeals to it as Scripture, in order to establish and confirm sentiments which he is inculcating, and in the same manner as he does elsewhere to the other Scriptures. Is this to be supposed, in case he himself wrote that epistle? Did Clement attribute scriptural authority to his own epistle? Or did the church, whom he addressed, attribute scriptural authority to any epistles, but to those of an apostle? Does he any where in his letter appeal to other epistles than such? The obvious answer to these inquiries determines the question, whether Clement wrote the epistle to the Hebrews, in the negative.

But further. The difficulty of style is so great, between the epistle of Clement and that to the Hebrews, as to make it sufficiently evident that both did not proceed from the same pen. I refer not merely to the choice of words, (although this might be easily shown to be considerable,) but to the general spirit and manner of the execution. There is an energy, originality, vividness of conception, and intensity of feeling, displayed every where in the epistle to the Hebrews, which is wholly wanting in Clement's epistle. It is plain, kind, faithful; but it is moderate, comparatively tame, made up of many extracts from the Old Testament and from Paul, and of imitations, as close as might be, of the latter. But what a wide difference there is, after all, between the original writer and the imitator, every one must feel who reads both. The one is a feeble rivulet, gliding gently along, which, but for the occasional contributions it receives from other streams, would become absorbed by the earth over which it passes, and cease to flow; the other a mighty stream, overflowing all its banks, supplying with water, and fertilizing all the country through which it passes. It really seems to me, that a man might as well mistake a canal on the banks of the Nile for the noble river itself, as mistake Clement for the author of the epistle to the Hebrews.

§ 38. *Was Apollos the Author?*

A supposition never made by any of the ancient churches, and first ventured upon, I believe, by Luther, Com. in Gen. xlviii. 20. Postil. Ecc. Test. S. Johann. Evang. p. 44. But this opinion has since been applauded or defended by Le Clerc, Heumann, Müller, Ziegler, and Bertholdt, p. 2974.

The difficulties attending the supposition are, (1.) We have no *external evidence* in favour of it; no voice of antiquity being raised to testify, that Apollos has left one single line of any written composition behind him, much less such an epistle as that to the Hebrews. (2.) We have no *internal* evidence of such a fact; for there is no testimony of this nature in the epistle itself; and there can be no evidence drawn from the style of it compared with the style and diction of Apollos, inasmuch as we have no writing of Apollos, with which the comparison can be made. It follows, therefore, that those who believe Apollos to be the author, must believe so without any evidence external or internal. It is not worth our time to refute such a belief.

§ 39. *In what language was the Epistle originally written?*

On this question, there has been a difference of opinion among critics, both in ancient and modern times. Clement of Alexandria says that "Paul wrote the Hebrews in the Hebrew language, and that Luke carefully translated it into Greek," Euseb. Hist. Ecc. vi. 14. Eusebius in the same manner says, that "Paul wrote to the Hebrews in his vernacular language, and that, according to report, either Luke or Clement translated it," Euseb. iii. 28. So Jerome also; "Scripserat ut Hebræus Hebræis Hebraice," (Catal. Vir. Illust. voc. Paulus;) and then he adds, "that this epistle was translated into Greek, so that the colouring of the style was made diverse, in this way, from that of Paul's." Of the same opinion, in respect to this, was Clement of Alexandria: and Origen, as we have seen above, supposes that the *thoughts* contained in the epistle were Paul's, while the *diction* or *costume* of it must be attributed to the person who wrote down the sentiments of the apostle.

By the *Hebrew language*, no one can reasonably doubt, these fathers meant the *Jerusalem dialect*, which was spoken in the days of the apostles, and not the ancient Hebrew, which had long ceased to be a vernacular language.

It is quite plain also, that these fathers were led to the conclusion, that the epistle to the Hebrews was originally written in the dialect of Palestine, from their belief (so universal in ancient times) of its having been addressed to some church, or to the churches, in that country. It was very natural to draw such a conclusion; for would not an epistle addressed to Hebrews, in all probability, be more acceptable if written in their own vernacular language? Moreover, Paul was well acquainted with that language, for he was brought up at Jerusalem, and " at the feet of Gamaliel;" and when he had visited there, he had addressed the Jewish multitude, who were excited against him, in their native tongue, Acts xxii. 1, 2. Why should it not be supposed, that if, as is probable, our epistle was originally directed to Palestine, it was written in the dialect of that country.

So the fathers above quoted evidently thought and reasoned; although other fathers have said nothing on this point, and do not appear to have coincided in opinion with those to which I have just referred. Among the moderns, also, several critics have undertaken to defend the same opinion; and particularly Michaelis, who has discussed the subject quite at length, in his introduction to this epistle.

I do not think it necessary minutely to examine his arguments. To my own mind they appear altogether unsatisfactory. Some of them are built on an exegesis most palpably erroneous, and which, if admitted, would deduce a very strange meaning from the words of the epistle. Yet, assuming such a meaning, he thence concludes, that the *original* writer must have expressed a different idea, and that the *translator* mistook his meaning. He then undertakes to conjecture what the original Hebrew must have been. In other cases, he deduces his arguments from considerations wholly *a priori*; as if these were admissible in a question of mere *fact*. He has not adduced a single instance of what he calls *wrong translation*, which wears the appearance of any considerable probability.

On the other hand, Bolton, a sharp-sighted critic, and well acquainted with the Aramean language, (who has gone through with the New Testament, and found almost every where marks, as he thinks, of translation from Aramean documents,) confesses, that, in respect to this epistle, he finds not a single vestige of incorrect translation from an Aramean original, and *no marks that there ever was such an original*. This testimony is of considerable importance in respect to the question before us: as it comes from a critic, who spent many years on the study of that which is most intimately connected with the very subject under consideration, viz. the detection of the Aramean originals of the various parts of the New Testament. Berth. p. 2976.

The principal *arguments* in favour of a Hebrew original, are deduced from two sources. First, that *Hebrews* are addressed in our epistle; to whom the Hebrew language would have been more acceptable and intelligible, and many of whom, indeed, could not understand Greek, certainly could not read it. Secondly, that the diversity of style in the epistle to the Hebrews is so great, when compared with that of Paul's epistles, that, unless we suppose the Greek costume did in fact come from another hand, we must be led to the conclusion, that Paul did not write it.

Both of these topics have been already discussed above. I merely add here, therefore, that in case the writer of the epistle designed it should have a wide circulation among the Jews, to write in Greek was altogether the most feasible method of accomplishing this. Besides, if Paul did address it to the church at Cesarea, it is altogether probable that he wrote in Greek, as Greek was the principal language of that city. Even if he did not, it was not necessary that he should write in Hebrew; for in every considerable place in Palestine, there were more or less who understood the Greek language. Whoever wishes to see this last position established beyond any reasonable doubt, may read Hug's Introduction to the N. Test. vol. II. pp. 32—50.

When Paul wrote to the *Romans*, he did not write in *Latin*; yet there was no difficulty in making his epistle understood, for the knowledge of Greek was very common at Rome. If Paul understood the Latin language, (which is no where affirmed, and he had not resided, when he wrote our epistle, in any of the countries where it was commonly used,) still he understood Greek so much better, that he would of course prefer writing in it.

For a similar reason, if no other could be given, one may regard it as more probable, that he would write the epistle to the Hebrews in the Greek language. At the time of writing it, he had been abroad twenty-five years at least, in Greek countries, and had been in Palestine, during all that period, only a few days. The Jews abroad, whom he every where saw, spoke *Greek*, not Hebrew. In Greek he preached and conversed. Is it any wonder, then, that after twenty-five years incessant labour of preaching, conversing, and writing in this language, he should have preferred writing in it? Indeed, can it be probable, that under circumstances like these, he still possessed an equal facility of writing in his native dialect of Palestine?

I cannot think it strange, therefore, that although the epistle to the Hebrews was in all probability directed to some part of Palestine, yet it was written by Paul in Greek, and not in Hebrew. But, whatever may be the estimation put upon arguments of this nature, there are *internal marks* of its having been originally composed in Greek, which cannot well be overlooked. Let us examine them.

Some of the arguments, produced by those who maintain that the original language of our epistle was Greek, it must be acknowledged, do not seem to be well founded. To such belongs the following.

" Instances of paronomasia occur in this epistle; which necessarily implies, that it was originally composed in its present language."

For example; Heb. v. 8, ἔμαθεν ἀφ' ὧν ἔπαθε. v. 14, πρὸς διάκρισιν καλοῦ τε καὶ κακοῦ. vii. 3, ἀπάτωρ, ἀμήτωρ. ix. 10, ἐπί βρώμασι καὶ πόμασι. xi. 37, ἐπρίσθησαν, ἐπειράσθησαν. xiii. 14, οὐ γὰρ ἔχομεν ὧδε μένουσαν πόλιν, ἀλλὰ τὴν μέλλουσαν ἐπιζητοῦμεν. vii. 22, κρείττονος διαθήκης γέγονε ἔγγυος Ἰησοῦς, comp. v. 19, ἐγγίζομεν τῷ Θεῷ. x. 34, τὴν ἁρπαγὴν τῶν ὑπαρχόντων ὑμῶν μετὰ χαρᾶς προσεδέξασθε, γινώσκοντες ἔχειν ἐν ἑαυτοῖς κρείττονα ὕπαρξιν ἐν οὐρανοῖς. See Eich. § 270. Bertholdt, p. 2987, who has only repeated the same things which Eichhorn had before said.

Of these instances, that only from x. 34 seems to betray any real marks of *design;* and even here, the marks are by no means of a decisive nature. Every one, who will examine any Greek writing whatever, may find in it more or less of apparent paronomasia, in the same way, without any difficulty; and this, where the author had no intention of exhibiting it. Whether an author really *designed* to exhibit paronomasia, or not, will in general be very apparent. I cannot perceive, that any one of the alleged paronomasias in question, really appears to be the effect of design. If they are altogether accidental, they may have occurred in the epistle to the Hebrews, even if its present language is merely that of a *translation.* In fact, even designed paronomasias may, not unfrequently, occur in a translation. The argument in favour of the Greek being the original language of the epistle to the Hebrews, built on such instances of paronomasia as the above, (where, in most cases, it is a mere homophony of like tenses or cases,) is too uncertain and too slender to be rested on, as a proper support of the opinion in question.

But there are better arguments than such, to prove that the epistle to the Hebrews was originally written in Greek. They may be derived, from the manner in which the quotations from the Old Testament are made and employed, in our epistle.

(1.) The author has, throughout, quoted the Sept. version, and followed it in nearly all cases, even where it differs considerably from the Hebrew. This, indeed, might be done to a certain extent, by a translator. For example; if Paul had appealed to the Hebrew Scriptures, and cited passages from them, the translator might have taken the corresponding passages in his Greek Bible. It might easily be supposed, that it would have been very natural for him to do so, in all cases where there was no considerable difference between the original Hebrew and the Greek version. But,

(2.) The writer of the epistle to the Hebrews has cited and employed the Septuagint version, in order to illustrate his positions, in cases where the Septuagint does not correspond with the original Hebrew. For example; Heb. i. 6, *Let all the angels of God worship him*, is quoted, in order to show that the Son of God is superior to the angels. If this be quoted, (as is more generally supposed,) from Ps. xcvii. 7, the context there appears to show, that the subject is, *the superiority of Jehovah to idol-gods*, not of Christ to the angels. Instead of " Let all the angels of God worship him," the Hebrew runs thus : " Worship him, all ye gods;" and so our English translation has it. If the quotation be made from Deut. xxxii. 43, (as some have supposed,) then is the argument still stronger; for in the original Hebrew there is not a vestige of the passage quoted; it is found only in the Septuagint. In either case, the force of the appeal seems to rest on the Septuagint version, and not on the original Hebrew. Of course, the writer must be supposed to have used that version, in his original composition, by all those who hold that he appeals, in this case, to a passage of the Old Testament.

But, as I have some doubts whether such an appeal is here made by the apostle, of course I cannot attribute much weight to this argument. See Comm. on Heb. i. 6.

(3.) The writer appeals, in Chap. ii., to Ps. viii., in order to prove that the Son of God must possess a human nature, which should be exalted above that of angels, and placed at the head of the creation. But the phrase in Hebrew, *Thou hast made him a little below the*

THE EPISTLE ORIGINALLY WRITTEN? 245

Elohim, is rendered by the Septuagint, *Thou hast made him for a little time*, [or, *a little*] *lower than the angels;* rendering אֱלֹהִים *angels*, which, to say the least, is an unusual sense of the word. Yet, on the sense of the version in the Septuagint, turns the force of this proof, that Christ was, in his human nature, superior to the angels.

(4.) In chap. vii., the writer has translated the appellations, *Melchisedek, king of Salem*, and told at length what they mean in Greek. It is possible, that such a thing might be done by a translator; but then the explanation, in this case, appears plainly to be interwoven with the discourse itself, and to be *a prima manu*.

(5.) In chap. ix. 16, 17. Christ is said, in reference to the *old* covenant under Moses, to be the mediator of a *new* and *better covenant*, בְּרִית, in Greek διαθήκη. But, from the double meaning of διαθήκη in Greek, viz. *covenant* and *testament*, the writer takes occasion, having mentioned the death of Jesus, to observe, that the new διαθήκη has received its full confirmation, viz. as a *testament*, by the death of the testator; and that he may the more effectually remove all offence at the death of Jesus, he goes on to say, that *a* διαθήκη, *testament*, (for now he uses the word in this sense,) *has no force while the testator is living*. Of course, the death of Jesus was necessary to ratify the *new* διαθήκη; and it did in fact ratify and establish it, to all intents and purposes.

Now the whole of this reasoning depends on the two-fold sense of the word διαθήκη, in Greek; for the original word בְּרִית, in Hebrew, never has the sense of *testament* or *will*.

The Greek word διαθήκη has, indeed, been adopted into the Rabbinic Hebrew, and sounds דְּיָתִיקִי. But that it belonged to the Hebrew language in Paul's day, there is no certain proof; and even if there were, בְּרִית must have been the only word to which he referred, for בְּרִית is an appropriate word to designate the Abrahamic and Mosaic dispensations, or the old covenant. Of course, the writer's illustration depends on the two-fold meaning of the *Greek* word διαθήκη; consequently, his language must have been Greek.

(6.) In chap. x. 3, seq. the writer undertakes to show, that the sacrifice of Christ was not only necessary, in order to make expiation for sin, but that it was predicted in the Psalms, that he should make such an offering. In proof of this, he quotes the Septuagint version, *A body hast thou prepared for me*, x. 54, viz. a body for an offering or expiatory sacrifice. Compare now Psalm xi. 7, where the Hebrew runs thus, אָזְנַיִם כָּרִיתָ לִּי, *mine ears hast thou opened*, or *bored*, i. e. thou hast made me obedient. But it is the Septuagint version which appears to give direct occasion for the specific allegation of the writer, viz. that Christ had made an offering of himself as a propitiatory sacrifice.

Other instances of a similar nature have been produced by critics, from our epistle; but as they are less striking, and may admit of some doubt, I have thought best to exclude them. These are sufficient to show, that as the very nature of the proof or argument, which the writer brings forward, depends, in some respects, on the form of the Septuagint version, or, to say the least, the *form* of the proof depends on this, so he must have written in Greek, and appealed to the Greek version; for it is improbable to the last degree, that if the epistle had been written in Hebrew, he would have appealed to any but the original Hebrew Scriptures, when addressing those who were acquainted with them.

Whatever difficulties the theologian or the interpreter may find, in reconciling these facts with the method of arguing which he may suppose appropriate to an inspired writer, it cannot alter the *facts themselves.* These are palpable, and not matters of conjecture. And admitting this, we are compelled to draw the conclusion, that THE ORIGINAL LANGUAGE OF OUR EPISTLE MUST HAVE BEEN GREEK.

I would add merely, that the vivid colouring and animation of the whole epistle, the impassioned and energetic expression of it, and its native, unconstrained appearance, all contribute to prove, that it was originally written in the same language in which it now appears.

§ 40. *Critical and Exegetical helps to the study of the Epistle.*

It is not my object to make out a copious catalogue of these: but only to notice those which are more particularly deserving of attention.

Ancient Greek Commentators.

Chysostom, Theodoret, and Theophylact, the Greek commentators on this epistle, are all deserving of an attentive perusal, in various respects. Philological, in the technical sense of this word, the reader must not expect to find them. Chrysostom is the most copious, flowing, and oratorical; Theodoret, the most brief and comprehensive; but Theophylact is by far the most agreeable, especially for beginners in the study of Greek commentary. He comprises all that is valuable in Chrysostom, and, for the most part, nearly in Chrysostom's words; while, at the same time, he has given to the whole, more ease, simplicity, and compactness. Seldom does he venture upon any new opinion of his own; and when he does, it is with great deference to his predecessors. The book deserves a republication at the present day, as a part of the apparatus requisite to the study of our epistle, and as one of the easiest and best means of introducing the young interpreter to an acquaintance with the Greek Commentators.

If a glossary should be added to such a book, containing the few words in Theophylact that are not found in our common Greek lexicons, and also the very good Latin translation which now accompanies the Greek of Theophylact, it would constitute an excellent book, for commencing the study and the knowledge of the original Greek fathers. Such an apparatus is already prepared, and the book only waits for patronage, in order to be published.

English Commentators.

Owen, Exposition of the Epistle to the Hebrews, with preliminary Exercitations, 7 vols. 8vo. Edinb. 1812-14.—This work is replete with remarks of a doctrinal and experimental nature. The philology of it will be less valued at the present day.

J. Pierce, Paraphrase and Notes on the Epistles of Paul, 4to. Lond. 1733. Some of the sentiments differ widely from those of Owen, and are such as ought to be examined with great caution; but the work, as a whole, exceeds any English commentary which I have read. The author has a great deal of acuteness, and is by no means wanting in regard to a tact for criticism.

The works of Sykes, Whitby, Doddridge, Macknight, Scott, Clark, and others, on this epistle, may profit some classes of readers, but they are not adapted to the higher purposes of philology.

Commentaries in Latin and German.

Among the older commentators, Erasmus, Grotius, Le Clerc, Drusius, J. Cappell, Limborch, and Wolfius, have distinguished themselves. The more recent works are the following.

J. B. Carpzovius, Exercitt. in Pauli Epist. ad Hebræos ex Philone Alexandrino, 8vo. Helmst. 1750.—The same author has also published, Uebersetzung des Briefs an die Hebräer, Helmst. 1795.

J. A. Cramer, Erklärung des Briefs an die Hebräer, 4to. Kopenhagen, 1757.

C. F. Schmidius, Observatt. super Epist. ad Hebræos, histor. crit. et theologicæ, 8vo. Lips, 1766.

§ 40. HELPS TO THE STUDY OF THE EPISTLE.

J. D. Michaelis, Erklärung des Briefs an die Hebräer, 4to. 2 edit, 1780.

S. F. N. Morus, Der Brief an die Hebräer uebersetzt, 8vo. Leip. 1786.

G. C. Storr, Pauli Brief an die Hebräer erläutert. 8vo. Tübingen, 1809.

J. A. Ernesti, Lectiones in Epist. ad Hebræos; illustrationes adjecit *G. J. Dindorf*, 8vo. Lips. 1795;—a book of real worth, in a critical respect, although not executed with much taste as to form and manner. I have found in it more to my purpose than in any other of the commentaries which I have consulted.

Heinrichs, in Nov. Test. Koppiano, Vol viii. This is a work, which exhibits some striking remarks, and no inconsiderable tact for exegesis. But the occasional extravagance of this writer's opinions, and the haste with which he throws off his works, are to be regretted; as he plainly possesses ability to go deeper into his subjects of inquiry.

D. Schulz, Der Brief an die Hebräer, Einleitung, Uebersetzung, und Anmerkungen, 8vo. Breslau, 1818.

The latest work is by *C. F. Boehme*, Epist. ad Heb. Latine vertit, atque commentario instruxit perpetuo. 8vo. Lips. 1825. See above, § 31.

Literature of the Epistle.

The introductions of Michaelis, Hænlein, Eichhorn, Hug, Bertholdt, and De Wette, exhibit the sum of what has been hitherto accomplished, in regard to this subject. Seyffarth and Schulz, in the works examined above, have also discussed the same subject; as have Ziegler, Noesselt, Weber, Lardner, and others. Wolfius, Storr, Schmidt, Cramer, and most other commentators, have touched, more or less, on the literary topics that pertain to the epistle. Lardner, Storr, Ziegler, Cramer, Eichhorn, Bertholdt, Hug, and Schulz, are most conspicuous among the class of writers now under consideration.

THE EPISTLE TO THE HEBREWS.

Dignity of Christ. His superiority over the angels.

I. God, who in ancient times spake often and in various ways to
2 the fathers by the prophets, hath in these last days spoken
to us by his Son; whom he hath appointed Lord of all things,
3 by whom also he made the worlds; (who, being the radiance
of his glory and the exact image of his substance, and controlling all things by his own powerful word,) after he had by
himself made expiation for our sins, sat down at the right
4 hand of the majesty on high, being exalted as much above
the angels, as he hath obtained a name more excellent than
they.
5 For to which of the angels said he, at any time, "Thou art
my Son, this day have I begotten thee?" And again, "I will
6 be his Father, and he shall be my Son?" Again also, when
he bringeth his first begotten into the world, he saith, "Let
all the angels of God worship him."
7 Moreover, of the angels it is said, "Who maketh his angels
8 winds, and his ministering servants a flame of fire." But of
the Son, "Thy throne, O God, is eternal; a sceptre of upright-
9 ness is the sceptre of thy kingdom. Thou hast loved righteousness, and hated iniquity; therefore, O God, thy God hath
anointed thee with the oil of gladness above thy fellows."
10 Also, "Thou, Lord, in the beginning, didst lay the foundations
11 of the earth, and the heavens are the work of thy hands: they
shall perish, but thou shalt endure; yea, they shall all wax
12 old like a garment, and as a vesture shalt thou fold them up,
and they shall decay; but thou art the same, and thy years
shall never cease."
13 Unto which of the angels, also, hath he ever said, "Sit thou
at my right hand, until I make thine enemies thy footstool?"
14 Are they not all ministering spirits, sent forth to assist those
who are to obtain salvation?

Exhortation diligently to seek the salvation proffered by the Lord of glory.

II. It behooveth us, therefore, the more abundantly to give
heed to the things which we have heard, lest at any time we

2 should slight them. For if the law communicated by angels was established, and every transgression and disobedience
3 received a just reward; how shall we escape, if we neglect so great salvation? which being first declared by the Lord, was afterwards confirmed unto us by those who heard [him;]
4 God also bearing witness with them, by signs, and wonders, and diverse miraculous powers, and communications of the Holy Spirit, according to his will.

Further declaration of Christ's superiority over the angels. Objections against this, drawn from his human nature, removed, by showing the elevation of that nature, and the important objects accomplished by assuming it.

5 Moreover, unto the angels hath he not put in subjection the world that was to come, of which we are now speaking.
6 But one, in a certain place, hath testified, saying, "What is man, that thou art mindful of him; or the son of man, that
7 thou dost regard him? [Yet] thou hast made him but little lower than the angels; thou hast crowned him with glory and honour, and hast set him over the works of thy hands. All things
8 hast thou put under his feet." Now, by putting all things in subjection to him, he left nothing which is not subject to him. For the present, indeed, we do not see all things yet subjected
9 to him; but we see Jesus, who was made but little lower than the angels, crowned with glory and honour on account of the suffering of death, when by the grace of God he had tasted
10 death for all. It became him, also, for whom are all things, and by whom are all things, to bestow, on account of sufferings, the highest honours upon him who is the Captain of their salvation, leading many sons to glory.
11 Furthermore, both he who maketh expiation, and they for whom expiation is made, are of one [nature;] for which cause
12 he is not ashamed to call them brethren, saying, "I will declare thy name to my brethren; in the midst of the congrega-
13 tion will I praise thee." And again, "I will put my trust in him." And again, "Behold, I, and the children which God
14 hath given me!" Since then the children are partakers of flesh and blood, himself also in like manner partook of them, in order that by his death he might subdue him who had a
15 deadly power, that is, the devil, and free those, who, through fear of condemnation, had, during their whole lives, been exposed to a state of bondage.
16 Besides, he doth not at all help the angels, but he helpeth
17 the seed of Abraham. Hence it was necessary, that in all respects he should be like to his brethren, so that he might be a merciful and faithful high priest as to things which pertain to God, in order to make atonement for the sins of the
18 people. For inasmuch as he himself suffered, being tempted, he is able to succour those who are tempted.

Comparison of Christ with Moses. Warning against disregarding his admonitions.

III. Wherefore, holy brethren, who have received the heavenly invitation, attentively consider Jesus, the apostle and high 2 priest whom we have acknowledged; who was faithful to him that appointed him, even as Moses [was] in all his house. 3 For he is worthy of more glory than Moses, inasmuch as the 4 builder is entitled to more honour than the house. (Now, every house is built by some one, and he who formed all things is 5 God.) Moses, however, was faithful in all his house as a servant, for the sake of testifying those things which were to 6 be declared: but Christ, as a Son, over his house; whose house we are, provided we hold fast unto the end our confidence and joyful hope.

7 Wherefore, as the Holy Spirit saith, "To-day, while ye 8 hear his voice, harden not your hearts, as in the provocation, 9 in the day of temptation in the wilderness, when your fathers tempted me, proved me, and saw my works forty years. 10 Wherefore I was angry with that generation, and said, They do always err in their hearts, and they have not acknowledged 11 my ways. So I sware in my wrath, They shall not enter into my rest."

12 Beware, brethren, lest there be in any of you an evil and unbelieving heart, so that he may apostatize from the living 13 God. But admonish one another continually, while it is called to-day, so that no one of you may become hardened by 14 sinful delusion. For we shall be made partakers of the blessings which Christ bestows, provided we hold fast even to the end our first confidence.

15 With regard to the saying, "To-day, while ye hear his voice, 16 harden not your hearts, as in the provocation;" who now were they, that when they heard did provoke? Nay, did not all, 17 who came out of Egypt under Moses? And with whom was he angry forty years? Was it not with those who sinned, 18 whose corpses fell in the wilderness? To whom did he swear, that they should not enter into his rest, except to those 19 who did not believe? We see, then, that they could not enter in, because of unbelief.

The rest promised to believers in ancient times is still proffered. The threatenings against unbelief remain in full force.

IV. Let us beware, therefore, since a promise is still left of entering into his rest, lest any one of you should come short 2 of it. For to us also blessings are proclaimed, as well as to them; the word, however, which they heard, did not profit them, not being connected with faith in those who heard it. 3 But we who believe do enter into the rest; as he says, "So I sware, in my wrath, [unbelievers] shall not enter into my rest;" namely, [rest from] the works which had been per- 4 formed, after the foundation of the world was laid. For [the

Scripture] speaketh, in a certain place, concerning the seventh day, in this manner, "And God rested, on the seventh day, 5 from all his works." And again, in this [manner,] "They 6 shall not enter into my rest." Since then it remaineth that some must enter into that [rest,] and they, to whom this blessing was formerly proclaimed, did not enter in because of unbelief, [it followeth that believers only can enter into it.] *

7 Again, he specifieth a particular day, TO-DAY, when speaking by David, so long a time afterwards; as it is said, "TO-8 DAY, while ye hear his voice, harden not your hearts." Now, if Joshua had given them rest, then he would not have spoken of another day.

9 Consequently, there remaineth a rest for the people of God.
10 He, moreover, who entereth into his [God's] rest, will also cease from his own works, as God did from his.
11 Let us strive, then, to enter into that rest, so that no 12 one may perish in like manner, through unbelief. For the threatening of God hath an active and mighty power, yea, it is sharper than any two-edged sword, piercing even to the dividing asunder of both life and spirit, and of the joints and mar-
13 row; he also judgeth the thoughts and purposes of the heart; nor is there any thing which can be concealed from his sight, but all is naked and exposed to the view of him, unto whom we must render our account.

Comparison of Christ with the Jewish high priest introduced. Reproof for ignorance of the higher doctrines of the Christian religion, followed by encouragement and exhortation.

14 MOREOVER, since we have a high priest who has passed through the heavens, Jesus the Son of God, let us hold
15 fast to our profession. For we have not a high priest, who is not able to sympathize with our weaknesses; but one who was tempted in all respects as we are, [yet] without sin.
16 Let us, therefore, approach the throne of grace with confidence that we may obtain mercy, and find favour, so as to be assisted in time of need.

V. Now every high priest, taken from among men, is appointed in behalf of men on account of things which pertain to God, that he may present both oblations and sacrifices for sin;
2 being able to shew kindness to the ignorant and the erring,
3 inasmuch as he himself is compassed with infirmity. On this account, also, he must present sin-offerings, as well for himself
4 as for the people. Moreover, no one assumeth for himself this honour, but he is called [thereto] of God, even as Aaron was.
5 In like manner, Christ also did not claim for himself the honour of being high priest; but he who said, "Thou art my

* Supplied from ver. 3.

Son, this day have I begotten thee," [bestowed this honour
6 upon him.] So also he saith, in another place, "Thou art a
priest for ever, after the order of Melchisedek."
7 The same, in the days of his incarnation, (having offered up
prayers and supplications, with strong cries and with tears,
unto him that was able to save him from death, and being
8 delivered from that which he feared,) although a Son, was
9 made acquainted with obedience in a state of suffering. Then,
when exalted to glory, he became the author of eternal salva-
10 tion, to all who obey him, being called of God, "A high
priest, after the order of Melchisedek."
11 Respecting him we have much to say, which it will be dif-
12 ficult to explain, since ye are dull of apprehension. For even
when ye ought to be able to teach, after [so long] a time, ye
have need to be taught again the first elements of the oracles
13 of God, and need milk rather than solid food. For every one,
who is a partaker of milk, is unskilled in the doctrines of reli-
14 gion; he is yet a child. But solid food is for those of mature
age, who have faculties exercised by practice for the distinguishing of both good and evil.

VI. Wherefore, leaving the first principles of Christian doctrine,
let us go on toward a mature state [of religious knowledge;]
not laying again the foundation, concerning repentance from
2 works which cause death, and faith towards God; [concerning]
the doctrine of baptisms, and the laying on of hands, and the
3 resurrection of the dead, and eternal judgment. And this will
4 we do, if God permit. For it is impossible, that they, who
have been once enlightened, and have tasted of the heavenly
5 gift, and been made partakers of the holy Spirit, and have
tasted the good word of God, and the miraculous powers of the
6 age which was to come, and have fallen away, should be again
renewed to repentance, since they have crucified for themselves
the Son of God, and openly exposed him to shame.
7 Now the earth, which drinketh in the rain that frequently
cometh upon it, and bringeth forth fruits useful to those for
8 whose sake it is tilled, receiveth blessings from God. But
that which bringeth forth thorns and briars, is reprobate, and
is near to a curse which will end in burning.
9 But, beloved, we confidently hope for better things concern-
10 ing you, even those connected with salvation, although we
thus speak. For God is not unkind, so that he will forget
your labour, and the love which ye have shown toward his
name, in having performed kind offices towards the saints, and
in still performing them.
11 Moreover, we are desirous that every one of you should
manifest the same diligence, for the sake of a full assurance of
hope, even to the end; so that ye may not be slothful, but
12 imitators of those who, through faith and patient expectation.

13 have come to the possession of promised blessings. For when
God made a promise to Abraham, seeing he could swear by no
14 greater, he sware by himself, saying, "I will greatly bless
15 thee, and exceedingly multiply thee." And so, having
16 patiently waited, he obtained the promised blessing. Now,
men swear by one who is greater, and the oath for confir-
17 mation [maketh] an end of all dispute among them. In like
manner, God, desirous of shewing more abundantly to the
heirs of promise the immutability of his purpose, interposed
18 by an oath; so that by two immutable things, concerning
which it is impossible for God to lie, we, who have sought for
a refuge, might be strongly persuaded to hold fast the hope
19 that is set before us, which we cleave to as an anchor of the
soul sure and firmly fixed, and which entereth within the veil,
20 whither Jesus our forerunner hath gone, being made high-
priest for ever, after the order of Melchisedek.

Comparison of Christ, as a priest, with Melchisedek. New order of things required by the appointment of such a priest; which appointment was made with the solemnity of an oath; and the office created by it was perpetual, allowing of no succession like that of the Jewish priests.

VII. Now this Melchisedek was king of Salem, and priest of the
most high God. The same met Abraham returning from the
2 slaughter of the kings, and blessed him. To him, also, Abraham gave a tenth part of all. By interpretation, [his name]
meaneth, first King of Righteousness; and then, he is also
3 King of Salem, which meaneth, King of Peace. Without
father, without mother, without genealogy; having neither beginning of days nor end of life, but being like to the Son of God;
he remaineth a high priest perpetually.
4 Consider, now, how great he must be, to whom Abraham
5 the patriarch gave a tenth part of the spoils! Even the sons
of Levi, who take the office of priests, have indeed a command
by the law to tithe the people, that is, their brethren, although
6 descended from the loins of Abraham; but he, whose descent
is not counted from them, tithed Abraham, and blessed him to
7 whom the promises were made. And beyond all controversy,
the inferior was blessed by the superior.
8 Here, also, men receive tithes who die; but there, one of
9 whom it is testified that he liveth. Yea, (if I may so speak,)
even Levi himself, who receiveth tithes, was tithed in Abra-
10 ham; for he was then in the loins of his ancestor when Mel-
cisedek met him.
11 Moreover, if there had been a perfect accomplishment of
what was needed, by the Levitical priesthood, (for the law
was given to the people, in connexion with this), what necessity was there still, that another priest should arise after the
order of Melchisedek, and not be named after the order of
12 Aaron? But if the priesthood be changed, there must needs

13 be also a change of the law. Now he, concerning whom these things are said, belonged to a different tribe, none of whom
14 served at the altar; for it is plain, that our Lord sprang from Judah, in respect to which tribe, Moses said nothing concern-
15 ing the priesthood. And still more manifest is it, [that the priesthood is changed,] if another priest hath arisen, like to
16 Melchisedek; who hath not been made so by a law of tempo-
17 rary obligation, but by an authority of endless duration. For [the Scripture] declareth, "Thou art a priest for ever, after the order of Melchisedek."
18 There is, also, a setting aside of the preceding law, because
19 it was weak and unavailing. For the law did not fully accomplish any thing; but the introduction of a better hope [doth], by which we draw near to God.
20 Furthermore, inasmuch as not without an oath [Jesus was made a priest], (for they are made priests without an oath, but he with an oath, by him who said to him, "The Lord hath sworn, and will not repent, Thou art a priest for ever, after the
22 order of Melchisedek,") by so much hath Jesus become the surety of a better covenant.
23 Those priests, moreover, are many, because they are not
24 suffered to continue by reason of death; but he, because he continueth for ever, hath a priesthood without any succession;
25 and on this account he is able always to save those who come unto God by him, since he ever liveth to interpose in their behalf.

The subject of Christ's qualifications for the office of a priest, (proposed in ch. v. 23, and briefly discussed in ch. v. 7—9), resumed. His superiority over the Jewish priests, in respect to these, exhibited.

26 Such a high priest, moreover, was needful for us, who is holy, harmless, undefiled, separate from sinners, and exalted
27 above the heavens; who hath not any daily necessity, like the high priest, to offer sacrifices, first for their own sins, and then for the sins of the people; for this he did, once for all,
28 when he offered up himself. Now the law maketh men high priests, who have infirmity; but the word of the oath, which was since the law, [maketh] the Son [high priest], who is exalted to glory for evermore.

Expiatory office of Christ as a priest. His functions, the dispensation under which they are performed, the place of exercising them, the manner and effects of them, compared with those of the Jewish priests.

VIII. The principal thing, however, among those of which we are speaking, is, that we have such a high priest, who is seated
2 on the right hand of the throne of Majesty in the heavens, a minister of the sanctuary, and of the true tabernacle which the Lord hath reared and not man.
3 Now every high priest is appointed, in order that he may present oblations and sacrifices; whence it becometh neces-

sary, that this one also should have something which he may
4 present. But if he were on earth, then he could not be a
priest, seeing there are priests who present oblations according to the law; (the same who perform service in [that sanctuary which is but] a mere copy of the heavenly one; for Moses, when about to build the tabernacle, was divinely admonished, "See now," said he, "that thou make all things
6 according to the pattern shewed thee in the mount.") But now, he hath obtained a service which is more excellent; as much more as the covenant is better of which he is mediator, and which is sanctioned by better promises.

7 Moreover, if that first covenant had been faultless, then
8 would no place have been sought for the second. But finding fault [with the first], he saith to them, "Behold the days are coming, saith the Lord, when I will make a new covenant
9 with the house of Israel and with the house of Judah; not according to the covenant which I made with their fathers, in the day when I took them by the hand, to bring them out of the land of Egypt; for they did not continue in my covenant,
10 and I rejected them, saith the Lord. But this is the covenant, which I will make with the house of Israel after those days, saith the Lord; I will impress my laws upon their minds, and engrave them upon their hearts; and I will be their God, and
11 they shall be my people. No one shall teach his fellow-citizen, nor any one his brother, saying, Know the Lord; for
12 all shall know me, from the least even to the greatest. For I will be merciful in respect to their iniquities, and their sins and their transgressions will I remember no more."
13 By saying, "a new [covenant]," he representeth the first as old; now that which hath become old, and is advancing in age, is nigh to dissolution.

IX. Moreover the first [covenant] had ordinances of service, and
2 a sanctuary of an earthly nature. For an outer tabernacle was prepared, in which was the candlestick, and the table, and the
3 shewbread, which is called, The holy place. And behind the
4 second veil was the tabernacle, which is called, The holy of holies, containing the golden censer, and the ark of the covenant overlaid with gold on every part, in which was the golden urn that contained the manna, and the rod of Aaron
5 which budded, and the tables of the covenant. Over it, also, were the cherubim of glory, overshadowing the mercy-seat. Of these things, it is not necessary, at present, particularly to speak.
6 Now, these being thus prepared, the priests performing the
7 services entered continually into the outer tabernacle. But into the inner one, only the high priest [entered], once in each year, not without blood, which he presented for himself
8 and for the sins of the people. By this the Holy Spirit signi-

fied, that the way to the most holy place was not yet open,
9 while the first tabernacle had a standing; which hath been a type down to the present time, in which both oblations and sacrifices are presented, that cannot fully accomplish what is
10 needed in regard to the conscience, for him who performeth the services; [and all the] ordinances pertaining to the flesh, had respect only to meats, and drinks, and divers ablutions,
11 enjoined until the time of reformation. But Christ being come, a high priest of future blessings, through a greater and more perfect tabernacle, not made with hands, that is, not of
12 this [material] creation, he entered once for all into the holy place, not with the blood of goats and of bullocks, but with
13 his own blood, procuring eternal redemption. Now if the blood of bulls and goats, and the ashes of a heifer sprinkling the unclean, cleanse in respect to the purification of the flesh,
14 how much more shall the blood of Christ, who by an eternal Spirit offered himself without spot to God, purify our conscience from works which cause death, so that we may serve the living God!
15 On this account, also, he is the mediator of a new covenant, so that, his death being a ransom for the sins [committed] under the former covenant, they who have been called might
16 receive the promised blessing of the eternal inheritance. For where there is a testament, it is necessary that the death of
17 the testator should take place; because a testament is valid in respect to those only who are dead, seeing it hath no force while the testator is living.
18 Hence, not even the first [covenant] was ratified without
19 blood. For when all the commandment, according to the law, had been read by Moses to all the people, taking the blood of bullocks and of goats, with water and scarlet wool and hyssop, he sprinkled both the book itself and all the people, saying,
20 "This is the blood of the covenant which God hath enjoined
21 upon you." The tabernacle, also, and likewise all the vessels for service, did he sprinkle in the same manner with blood.
22 Indeed, almost every thing is required by the law to be purified by blood; and without the shedding of blood there is no forgiveness.
23 Since, then, the likenesses of heavenly things must needs be purified in this manner, the heavenly things themselves
24 [must be purified] by better sacrifices than these. For Christ did not enter into a sanctuary made with hands, which is only a copy of the true one, but into heaven itself, that he might
25 thenceforth appear before God for us. Yet not that he might frequently make an offering of himself, like the high priest who entereth into the sanctuary every year with blood not his
26 own, (for then he must needs have often suffered, since the foundation of the world); but now, at the close of this age,

he hath once for all made his appearance, in order that he might remove the punishment due to sin, by the sacrifice of
27 himself. For since it is appointed unto men to die but once,
28 and after this [cometh] the judgment; so Christ also, after having once for all made an offering of himself to bear the sins of many, will appear, at his second [coming], without a sin-offering, for the salvation of those who wait for him.

X. Moreover, the law, which containeth a mere outline of future blessings, and not the complete image of these things, can never, by those yearly sacrifices which are continually offered, fully accomplish what is needed for those who approach
2 [the altar.] For if it could, then would not these offerings have ceased, because the worshippers, once for all made clean,
3 would no longer have been conscious of sins? On the contrary, by these [sacrifices] yearly remembrance is made of sin.
4 And truly, it is impossible that the blood of bulls and goats
5 should take away sin. Wherefore, [Christ,] entering into the world, saith, "Sacrifice and oblation thou desirest not, but a
6 body hast thou prepared for me; in whole burnt offerings and
7 [offerings] for sin thou hast no pleasure. Then said I, Lo! I come, O God, to do thy will; (in the volume of the book it is
8 written concerning me.") When he saith, in the first place, "Sacrifice and oblation, and whole burnt offerings and [offerings] for sin, thou desirest not, nor hast pleasure in them,"
9 (which are presented according to the law;) [and] then saith, "Lo! I come to do thy will;" he abolisheth the first, that he
10 may establish the second. By this will, expiation is made for us, through the offering of the body of Jesus Christ once for all.
11 Now every priest standeth, performing daily service, and oftentimes presenting the same sacrifices which can never take
12 away sin; but this one, having once offered a perpetual sacri-
13 fice for sin, sat down at the right hand of God, thenceforth
14 waiting until his enemies be made his footstool. By one offering, then, he hath fully accomplished, for ever, what was needed by those for whom expiation is made.
15 Moreover, the Holy Spirit also testifieth this to us; for after
16 saying, "This is the covenant which I will make with them, after those days, saith the Lord, I will write my laws upon
17 their hearts, and engrave them upon their minds," then [he
18 saith,] "Their sins and their iniquities will I remember no more." But where there is remission of these, there is no more offering for sin.

Exhortation to perseverance, from a consideration of the faithfulness of God, of the severe doom of apostates, and of the sufferings which the Hebrew Christians had already endured for the sake of religion.

19 Having then, brethren, free access to the sanctuary, by
20 the blood of Jesus, in a new and living way, which he hath

Joseph's sons, and bowed himself upon the top of his staff.
22 By faith Joseph, at the close of life, made mention of the departure of the children of Israel [from Egypt], and gave commandment respecting his own bones.
23 By faith Moses, after his birth, was concealed for three months by his parents, because they saw that he was a goodly child, and did not fear the king's commandment. By faith Moses, when arrived at mature age, refused to be called the
25 son of Pharaoh's daughter, choosing rather to suffer affliction with the people of God, than to enjoy the pleasures of sin for
26 a season; counting reproach, such as Christ endured, to be greater riches than all the treasures of Egypt; for he had
27 respect to a state of reward. By faith he left Egypt, not fearing the anger of the king; for he continued stedfast, as
28 one who seeth him that is invisible. By faith he observed the passover and the sprinkling of blood, so that he who destroyed the firstborn might not touch them.
29 By faith they passed through the Red Sea, as on dry land;
30 which the Egyptians assaying to do, were drowned. By faith the walls of Jericho fell down, after they had been compassed about for seven days.
31 By faith Rahab, the harlot, having entertained the spies in a friendly manner, perished not with the unbelieving.
32 And what shall I say more? For time would fail me, should I tell of Gideon, of Barak also, and Samson, and
33 Jephtha, of David too, and Samuel, and the prophets; who, through faith, subdued kingdoms, executed justice, obtained
34 promised blessings, stopped the mouths of lions, quenched the violence of fire, escaped the edge of the sword, were made strong from a state of infirmity, became mighty in war, over-
35 threw the armies of foreigners. Women recovered their dead by a resurrection. Some were tortured, not accepting a deliverance, in order that they might attain to a better resur-
36 rection. Others were tried by mockings and scourges, and
37 also by bonds and imprisonment. They were stoned, they were sawn asunder, they were tempted, they perished by the murderous sword, they went about in sheep-skins and goat-
38 skins, suffering want, afflicted, injuriously treated, (of whom the world was not worthy), wandering around in deserts and mountains, in caves also and dens of the earth.
39 All these, moreover, who are commended on account of
40 their faith, did not receive the promised blessing; God having provided some better thing for us, so that without us they could not obtain a full accomplishment of what was needed.

HEBREWS XII. 1—19.

Encouragement to persevere. Trials must not dishearten, for God sends them in kindness to his children. The gospel holds out more that is cheering and encouraging, than the law. The voice of its author must not be slighted.

XII. Since now we are encompassed by so great a multitude of witnesses, laying aside every incumbrance, and especially the sin which easily besetteth us, let us run with perseverance
2 the race which is set before us; looking unto Jesus, the author and perfecter of our faith, who, on account of the joy set before him, endured the cross, not regarding shame, and hath sat down at the right hand of the throne of God.
3 Consider, now, him who endured such opposition against himself from sinners, lest becoming discouraged in your minds
4 ye grow weary. Ye have not yet resisted unto blood, in your
5 struggle against sin. And have ye forgotten the exhortation, which is addressed to you as children, " My son, do not slight the chastenings of the Lord, nor be disheartened when reproved
6 by him; for whom the Lord loveth he chasteneth, and scourg-
7 eth every son whom he receiveth?" If ye endure chastisement, God is dealing with you as children; for what son is
8 there, whom his father does not chasten? But if ye are without chastisement, of which all [children] are partakers, then are ye bastards, and not sons.
9 Furthermore, we have had fathers of our flesh, who have chastened us, and we have yielded them reverence; shall we not much more yield subjection to the Father of [our] spirits,
10 that we may live? They, indeed, chastened us for a little while, according to their own pleasure; but he, for our good,
11 that we might be made partakers of his holiness. Now, all chastening seemeth for the present not to be matter of joy, but of grief; yet afterwards, it yieldeth the happy fruits of righteousness, to those who are exercised thereby.
12 Wherefore, "Strengthen the weak hands and the feeble
13 knees," and "Make plain the paths for your feet," so that what is lame may not be wrenched, but rather healed.
14 Follow after peace with all men, and holiness, without
15 which no man shall see the Lord. See to it, that no one fail of the favour of God; that no root of bitterness spring up and
16 trouble you, and many be defiled thereby. Let there be no fornicator, nor profane person, like Esau, who for one morsel
17 of meat sold his birthright. For ye know, that when he was afterwards desirous to obtain the blessing, it was refused; yea, he found no place for a change of mind [in his father,] although he sought for it with tears.
18 Moreover, ye are not come to the mount which could be touched, and to flaming fire, and thick clouds, and darkness,
19 and tempest; nor to the sound of the trumpet, and the voice of commands, the hearers of which refused that another word

20 should be added to them; (for they could not endure the admonition, " If even a beast touch the mountain, it shall be
21 stoned;" and—so terrible was the sight—even Moses said,
22 "I fear and tremble:") but ye are come to mount Zion; and to the city of the living God, the heavenly Jerusalem; and to an innumerable company, the joyful host of angels; and to
23 the assembly of the first-born, enrolled in heaven; and to the Judge, the God of all; and to the spirits of the just, who
24 have obtained their final reward; and to the mediator of the new covenant, Jesus; and to the blood of sprinkling, which speaketh better things than [the blood of] Abel.
25 Take heed, that ye turn not away from him, who speaketh to you; for if they did not escape who turned away from him who warned them on earth, much more shall we [not escape,]
26 if we slight him who [warneth us] from heaven. His voice then shook the earth; but now it is promised, saying, " Yet once more, I will shake not only the earth, but heaven also."
27 Now this " Yet once more," denotes a removing of the things which are shaken, as of created things, in order that the things which are not shaken may remain.
28 Wherefore, having obtained a kingdom which cannot be shaken, let us manifest gratitude, (by which we may serve
29 God acceptably,) with reverence and godly fear. For our " God is a consuming fire."

Various practical directions and cautions. Closes with affectionate requests and salutations.

XIII. LET brotherly love continue. Forget not hospitality; for
2 by this some have entertained angels unawares. Remember
3 those who are in bonds, as if ye yourselves were fellow-prisoners; those who are suffering evil, as being yourselves
4 yet in the body. Let marriage be honourable among all, and the bed undefiled; for whoremongers and adulterers God will
5 judge. Let your conduct be free from covetousness, and be contented with what ye possess. For he hath said, " I will never leave thee, nor forsake thee:" so that we may boldly
6 say, " The Lord is my helper, and I will not be afraid. What can man do to me?"
7 Remember your leaders, who have spoken unto you the word of God; and attentively considering the end of their
8 manner of life, imitate their faith. Jesus Christ is the same,
9 yesterday, to-day, and for ever. Be not carried hither and thither by diverse and strange doctrines; for it is good that the heart should be confirmed by grace, and not by meats, by which those have not been profited, who have been occupied
10 therewith. We have an altar, of which they have no right to eat, who render their service to the tabernacle.

11 Moreover, the bodies of those animals, whose blood was carried into the sanctuary as a sin-offering by the high priest,
12 were burned without the camp. Wherefore, Jesus also, that he might make expiation for the people by his own blood,
13 suffered without the gate. Let us, then, go forth to him
14 without the camp, bearing reproaches like his; for here we
15 have no abiding city, but are seeking for one yet future. By him, therefore, let us continually present to God the sacrifice of praise, that is, the fruit of our lips ascribing praise to his name.
16 Forget not kindness, also, and liberality; for with such
17 sacrifices God is well pleased. Obey your leaders, and be subject to them; for they watch over your souls, as those who must give an account. [So obey,] that they may do this with joy, and not with grief, for this would be unprofitable to you.
18 Pray for us; for we trust that we have a good conscience, being desirous in all things to demean ourselves uprightly.
19 I make this request, also, the more earnestly, in order that I may speedily be restored to you.
20 Now, may the God of peace, that raised from the dead our Lord Jesus, (who by the blood of an everlasting covenant has
21 become the great Shepherd of the sheep,) prepare you for every good work, that ye may do his will; working in you that which is well pleasing in his sight, through Jesus Christ, to whom be glory for ever and ever. Amen.
22 Moreover, I beseech you, brethren, to bear with this word of exhortation; for I have written briefly to you.
23 Know ye, that our brother Timothy is sent away; with whom if he return speedily, I shall visit you.
24 Salute all your leaders, and all the saints. They of Italy
25 salute you. Grace be with you all. Amen.

COMMENTARY.

GENERAL VIEW OF THE CONTENTS

OF THE

EPISTLE TO THE HEBREWS.

The writer of this epistle is a Hebrew, and addresses his Hebrew brethren, who had made a profession of the Christian religion. Nothing can be plainer, than that those addressed are considered as being in danger of apostacy from that religion. To warn them against this danger, is the principal object of our epistle. In order to do this, the writer proceeds to lay before them the aggravated guilt, and the awful doom, of those who make defection from Christianity; to direct their views towards that crown of glory which fadeth not away, and which is reserved in heaven for all who persevere, even to the end of life, in their fidelity to Christ; to put them on their guard against the various enticements of sin, which might allure them from the paths of Christian duty; and especially to guard them against relapsing into superstitious views respecting the importance and necessity of the ceremonial rites and sacrifices of the Levitical institutions, and against being induced by these to relax their confidence in Jesus, and in his atoning sacrifice.

It was these last sources of danger, to which the Hebrew Christians were particularly exposed. Nothing could well be more magnificent and imposing than the temple worship, as practised by the Jews at that time. The temple, built after their return from the captivity, was not indeed, so rich in ornament as that which Solomon had built. But had, at a vast expense, been greatly extended and beautified by Herod It was regarded by all Jews, as the peculiar dwelling-place of Jehovah— the only one in which he deigned to manifest himself on earth. The Jewish nation, also, habitually regarded themselves, as the only one to whom God had made a special revelation. The worship, practised in the temple, had been instituted by Moses, under divine guidance, and continued, with but partial interruptions, for about 1500 years. All the exterior of this worship was adapted to strike the eye, and impress the mind, of the beholder. The awfulness of the place in which it was celebrated; the magnificent costume of the priests; the spacious and lofty apartment in which they officiated; the solemn part which he who offered any sacrifice was himself called to perform; above all, the apprehension that full pardon for sin, and reconciliation to God, were obtained by the rites and offerings which the law prescribed; contributed to make deep and lasting impressions on the mind of all Hebrews, who seriously exercised their thoughts on the subject of religion, and paid their devotions in the temple. All their education, from the first dawning of the youthful mind, had a direct tendency to confirm and strengthen these impressions. Never was a nation more enthusiastically attached to its customs, rites, and country, than were the Jews. They looked abroad upon other nations, as outcasts from God, and unworthy of his paternal kindness and blessing.

The New Testament is full of evidence, adapted to show the correctness of this statement. The disputes which the extension of Christian privileges to the Gentiles occasioned among the first Jewish converts; the reluctance with which the former were admitted to participate in them; and the repeated, violent, and long-protracted opposition that was made to abandoning the peculiar rites of the Mosaic institutions; all contribute to evince, how deeply engraven upon the mind of every Jew was the impression, that the laws of Moses were never to be changed, and that the Messiah himself was rather to restore and modify, than to repeal them.

In such a state of mind had the Christian converts once been, whom the writer of our epistle addressed. What wonder, now, if they were exposed from this quarter to be shaken in their attachment to the new religion which they had professed, and which confessedly gave up all confidence in the religious rites of the Levitical institutions? Temptations from without also assailed them. Their unbelieving Hebrew brethren argued with them; opposed them; ridiculed them; made powerful appeals to all the feelings with which their birth, education, and former worship had inspired them; persecuted them; traduced them to heathen magistrates; and excommunicated them. They suffered the loss of property, and of liberty. Their lives were threatened. The coming of Christ, which they had supposed would speedily take place for their deliverance, was delayed. How could it be, that human frailty, joined with former prejudices and present sufferings, should not have a dangerous influence upon them?

In this state the apostle saw them to be, and set himself about the important and difficult work of correcting their errors, and encouraging their desponding minds. How was this to be done with the greatest probability of success? Plainly, arguments and considerations, of such a nature as were best adapted to meet the difficulties with which they were contending, were those to which he would most readily resort. And throughout the whole epistle, it is manifest that he has done this, with consummate skill, judgment, and force.

As the greatest of all the dangers to which the Hebrew converts were exposed, was that which resulted from their former religious attachments and prejudices, excited and augmented, as they daily were, by the efforts of their unbelieving Jewish brethren; so the writer of our epistle employs his principal force, in order to preclude or avert this danger. Other topics are subordinate with him. Although they are often touched upon, and with great skill and power, yet they are so interwoven with the main object before him, that they are in a measure concealed from the first view of a hasty reader.

The general plan of the epistle may be briefly represented. It consists in a comparison of the new dispensation with the old, and in pointing out the various grounds of preference which belong to the new. From this superiority of the new dispensation, various arguments are deduced, in order to shew the importance of cleaving to the Christian profession, instead of reverting back to Judaism, which could not now be the means of saving those who embraced it. Considerations of such a nature are repeated, as often as the comparisons introduced afford occasion for them. This accounts for the repetition of hortatory addresses, so often found in our epistle.

The Jews gloried in their dispensation, because angels had been employed as mediators of it, when the law was given at Sinai. In their view, this stamped a high and heavenly honour upon it. Our author does not attack their views of this subject, but he commences his epistle by shewing that Christ, the mediator and head of the new dispensation, as it regards his name, his rank, his dominion, his creative and eternal power, is superior to the angels, chap. i. 1—14. On this ground, then, Christianity may claim a precedence; and hence he exhorts them to give their most earnest attention to it, chap. ii. 1—4.

Nor can they object to the superiority of the Messiah, that he possessed a *human* nature, while the angels are spiritual and heavenly beings. For in human nature he is Lord of the universe, ch. ii. 5—10. It was this nature, too, which gave him a nearer and more endearing sympathy with his followers; and by taking this upon him, he was enabled to make an expiatory offering for sin by his death; so that he is now fitted not only to exercise compassion toward men, but to save them from the bondage of sin, and from its condemning power, ch. ii. 11—18.

Having thus disposed of this topic, he next proceeds to compare Jesus, the head of the new dispensation, with Moses, the head of the ancient one. Like Moses, he was set over the house of God, and entrusted with it, and was faithful to his trust. But the honour due to Jesus is as much more than that due to Moses, as the builder of a house is worthy of more honour than the house itself. Christ too was set over God's house as a *Son;* but Moses only as a *servant,* ch. iii. 1—6.

If now the Israelites of old were solemnly admonished to hearken to the precepts given under the Mosaic dispensation; then surely believers in Christ may be more solemnly urged, to beware of disobedience to his injunctions, ch. iii. 7—19. And this warning holds good, and is applicable in all respects, because the rest which was promised to believers in ancient times, and was lost through unbelief, is still proffered to all who believe in Jesus and persevere in their profession, and only to believers, ch. iv. 1—10. Awful commination is indeed still uttered against those who are guilty of apostasy, ch. iv. 11—13.

Thus much for the comparison of Christ with Moses. Next, the writer proceeds to compare Jesus, as a priest, with the Jewish priesthood, and particularly with the high priest, the most dignified of all who were invested with the sacerdotal office.

He first introduces Christ as a compassionate high priest, and exalted to the highest dignity in the heavens, ch. iv. 14—16. Next, he states the various things which are attached to the priesthood, as existing among the sons of Levi. (1.) A high priest must present oblations and sacrifices, ch. v. 1. (2.) He must be compassionate and sympathetic towards others, and especially so, as he is himself frail and erring, ch. v. 2, 3. (3.) He must be appointed of God to this office, ch. v. 4.

In all these respects, he now goes on to make a comparison of Jesus, the high priest of Christianity, and to shew his superiority. He shews,—

First, that Christ was divinely appointed a priest, and that of the highest order, ch. v. 5, 6.

Next, he shews that Christ our great high priest was compassed with human infirmity, like other priests, so that, like them, he was fitted to exercise compassionate sympathy, ch. v. 7, 8. But after he had suffered, he was raised to glory and became a high priest of the most exalted order, i. e. of the order of Melchisedek, ch. v. 9, 10.

The difficulty of the subject now suggested, affords an occasion for the writer to advert to the state of religious ignorance, in which those were whom he addressed, ch. v. 11—14; to exhort them to come out of it, and to warn them against the fearful danger that would result from not doing so, ch. vi. 1—8. To this he subjoins commendation as to some things, and powerful motives of encouragement, ch. vi. 9—20.

He now resumes the subject of Melchisedek; shews the superiority of his priesthood over that of the sons of Levi, ch. vii. 1—10; and then argues that Christ, who was a perpetual priest of the like order with Melchisedek, must of course be superior to the Jewish priests, ch. vii. 11—25.

Christ too, as high priest, differed in one important respect from other priests, viz. in that he needed no sacrifice for himself, as an erring, sinful man, like the sons of Levi, but was sinless and perfect, yea, even exalted to a state of supreme glory, ch. vii. 26—28.

The great object, however, at which the writer is going to aim in the sequel of his epistle, is, to shew that the high priest of Christianity officiates in heaven for his followers, ch viii 1, 2. The Jewish priests perform their functions in a temple, which is merely an image of the heavenly one, ch. viii. 3—6.

The new covenant, of which Jesus is mediator, is altogether superior, also, to the old, ch. viii. 6—13. The ordinances and apparatus of service attached to this, were all mere types of heavenly things, ch. ix. 1—10. The services themselves were imperfect, as to the end attained by them, since they accomplished nothing more than external purification; but the blood of Christ sanctifies internally, and procures eternal redemption and an everlasting inheritance, for all the chosen of God in every age of the world, ch. ix. 11—15.

The new *testament*, which gives an *inheritance* to the people of God, was sanctioned by the *death* of Jesus, ch. ix. 15. Such is the custom in regard to *testaments*, ch. ix. 16, 17. As a symbol of this, even the first covenant, (διαθήκη,) with all the apparatus attached to it, was sanctioned by blood, i. e. the emblem of death, ch. ix. 18—22. If the earthly sanctuary was thus consecrated, then the heavenly one must be so, by a sacrifice of a still higher nature, ch. ix. 23, 24. Sacrifices in the earthly temple must be *often* repeated; but the sacrifice of Christ did, *once for all*, accomplish the great purposes for which it was offered, ch. ix. 24—28.

Indeed, no legal sacrifices could make any real atonement for sin, ch. x. 1—4. Therefore Christ voluntarily proffered himself as a sin offering, entirely and for ever to effect this, ch. x. 5—18.

Thus is completed the comparison of Christ, and of his functions as a priest in the heavenly tabernacle, with the Jewish priests and their functions in the earthly tabernacle. In all respects, Jesus, the high priest of the Christian religion, appears greatly superior.

The writer now proceeds to various bold and powerful exhortations, mixed with awful warnings against defection from the Christian religion, ch. x. 19—31. He sets before them the effects of persevering faith, in the ancient patriarchs, prophets, and distinguished worthies, ch. xi. 1—40. This he follows up with continued exhortations, and encouragements, and warnings, ch. xii. 1—29; and then closes his epistle with divers practical directions, cautions, and salutations, ch. xiii. 1—25.

Such is the brief view of the course of thought and reasoning in our epistle. It is plain that there are three great points of comparison in it, which constitute the main object at which the writer aims, in order that he may show the superiority of Christianity over Judaism.

I. The superiority of Christ, the mediator of the new covenant, over angels who were employed as mediators, when the old covenant was established,—chap. i. ii.

II. The superiority of Christ, the head of the new dispensation, over Moses, the head of the old,—chap. iii. iv.

III. The superiority of Christ as high priest of the new dispensation, and of the services which he performs, over the priesthood of the Mosaic institution, and all the services which were appropriate to their office,— ch. v. 1; x. 18.

Exhortations, warnings, reproofs, and encouragements, are intermixed in some manner with the main discussions: e. g. ch. ii. 1—4; iii. 1; iii. 7—iv. 16; iv. 11—vi. 20; but from ch. x. 19 to the end of the epistle, nearly all is of the nature just described; so that about one half of the epistle is of a parenetical or hortatory nature.

In judging of the relevancy and importance of the subjects discussed in our epistle, it is very plain, that we are not to make up an opinion, deduced merely from viewing the present necessities and condition of Christians. We were not born Jews, nor educated as such. We have none of their prejudices, peculiar sympathies, temptations, and trials. What was adapted to them, in the days of Paul, and under the circumstances above described; nay, what was absolutely indispensable for their instruction, reproof, and confirmation, may, in many respects, be scarcely appropriate to us, in our condition and circumstances. Such is indeed the fact, in regard to many of the things introduced into the epistle to the Hebrews; as I shall have occasion hereafter repeatedly to notice. But who, that judges with any good degree of candour and fairness, would ever think of bringing it as an accusation against our author, that he has inserted in his epistle, that which was altogether appropriate to those whom he addressed, although it may not, and does not, have an equal bearing upon all times and nations? Surely, the last ground of just accusation which can be advanced against any writer, is, that " he has written in a manner peculiarly adapted to accomplish the end for which he wrote." In what a different plight would the world of authors be, if all of them were justly liable to such an imputation!

Of necessity, now, many things addressed to the Jews of Paul's day, are comparatively inapplicable to us. So far, however, as our circumstances agree with theirs in any respect, just so far the spirit of what was said to them will apply to us. So far as what was said to them was founded in general Christian truths and principles, just so far we may be instructed and guided by it. Consequently, as it must follow from these positions, the epistle, while it contains many things appropriate to the Hebrews of early times, also contains many which can never cease to interest the church of God, while Christianity exists in the world.

These general views may serve to aid the critical student, in commencing the exegetical study of our epistle. The more particular detail of what is here hinted, is reserved for the introductions to various parts of the epistle, which are inserted, *pro re natâ*, in the body of the commentary which follows.

COMMENTARY.

CONTENTS OF CHAPTERS I. 1—II. 4.

The object of the writer being to commend Christianity to those whom he addressed, in such a manner as to prevent defection from this religion; he begins by setting forth Christ as the author of the new revelation which God had made to men, ch. i. 1. He then touches upon the dignity of his office; he is Lord of the universe; which, indeed, he also created, ver. 2. He is the true image of God, and the representative of his glory and perfections to men; he is endowed with sovereign power; and having made atonement for the sins of men, he is exalted to the highest majesty in the heavens, ver. 3. This mediator of the new dispensation is exalted above angels, who were the mediators of the ancient one. His name, SON, is more exalted than theirs; for they have not been addressed, like him, with such an appellation, ver. 4, 5. He is the object of worship by the angels; while they are employed only as the swift and ready messengers of God, ver. 6, 7. The King Messiah has an eternal and righteous dominion; and is elevated, on account of his love of righteousness, to honour and happiness above all other kings, ver. 8, 9. Him, too, the sacred writer addresses, as the Creator of the heavens and the earth, and as immutable and imperishable, ver. 10—12. But no exaltation to such dominion is conferred upon angels, ver. 13; they are only ministerial agents, employed for the good of those who are to be heirs of the salvation which Christ bestows, ver. 14.

If such be the dignity and elevation of the Messiah, then, surely he may justly demand the attentive consideration of all which he addresses to his followers. Obedience to the ancient revelation was enforced by just and unavoidable penalties; how can the neglect of the new and more perfect one go unpunished? ch. ii. 1, 2. Especially must this be the case, since it was promulgated by Christ himself in person, and was confirmed, on the part of God, by a great variety of wondrous miracles, ver. 3, 4.

CHAP. I

Ἡ πρὸς Ἑβραίους ἐπίστολὴ. See, on this title, § 10. p. 35, seq.

1. Πολυμερῶς καὶ πολυτρόπως, literally *in various parts and in various ways*. Of the Greek commentators, some give a different sense to each of the words; e. g. Theodoret, πολυμερῶς—τὰς παντοδαπὰς οἰκονομίας σημαίνει, τὸ δὲ πολυτρόπως, τῶν θείων ὀπτασιῶν τὸ διάφορον, i. e. πολυμερῶς *signifies the various dispensations*, and πολυτρόπως *the diversity of divine visions*. Theophylact interprets the words in question, by διαφόρως

καὶ πολυειδῶς, *diversely, and in various ways*. But Chrysostom expresses the sense of both words, by διαφόρως simply. Modern commentators are divided in the same manner. The Greek idiom allows either mode of interpretation; and precedents may be found for each. See Schleusner on the words; and compare Clem. Alex. Strom. I. 4. p. 331; V. p. 667, ed. Potter. If the two words be construed separately, then πολυμερῶς should be interpreted as referring to the matter of ancient revelation, given in different parts and at different times, thus conveying the idea of the gradual development of truth in different ages and by different persons; and πολυτρόπως must be understood as indicating the *various ways in which these revelations were communicated*, i. e. by dreams, visions, symbols, Urim and Thummim, prophetic ecstacy, &c. But if both words are regarded, as being used only to designate with intensity the *variety* of ancient revelations, (and such a mode of phraseology is very common both in the Greek and Hebrew Scriptures,) then the whole may be paraphrased thus : " God, who in ancient times made communications, *in many different ways*, by the prophets to the fathers, hath," &c. The word πολυμερῶς does not, of itself, signify *sundry times;* but still, the idea of *various parts* or *portions*, which it does properly signify, may very naturally be understood as implying *diverse times* at which, or *occasions* on which, the different parts of revelation were communicated; or the idea of πολυμερῶς may be simply that of *repetition*, so that *often* would well communicate the sense of it. In this way I have ventured to translate it.

Of the two modes of interpreting these words, I rather prefer that which separates them, and gives a distinct meaning to each. The writer evidently designs to present an antithesis between the manner of the ancient and the Christian dispensation. This antithesis is rendered more striking, if we understand the first clause in the verse thus :* " God, who in ancient times made communications to the fathers by the prophets, in sundry parts and in various ways, has now made a revelation to us by his Son;" i. e. he has completed the whole revelation, which he intends to make under the new dispensation, by his *Son*, by his *Son only*, and not by a *long continued series* of prophets, as of old. The apostles, and other inspired writers of the New Testament, received their communications from the *Son*, who gave them the Holy Spirit, Matt. xi. 27, comp. John xiv. 26; xvi. 13; and facts shew, that the Christian revelation was completed, during that generation who were contemporary with the Saviour, when he dwelt on earth.

Πάλαι, *in ancient times;* for communications by prophets to the Jews had ceased, from the time of Malachi and his contemporaries, i. e. for the space of about four hundred years. Hence, the writer avoids using an expression which would imply, that revelations had been continued down to the time then present. By πάλαι, he evidently means to designate the whole time, during which communications of the Divine will were continued under the former dispensation.

Λαλήσας most commonly designates *oral communication*. But since the writer here affirms, that God had spoken (λαλήσας) πολυτρόπως, it must of course be understood (as indeed it is often used) to designate the more general idea of *communication made in any manner*, by visions, symbols, &c. as well as by voices.

Τοῖς πατράσιν, *ancestors;* see Wahl's Lex. We might naturally expect that ἡμῶν would be subjoined; but Paul commonly uses the word πατέρες in the sense just noted, without the pronoun annexed. See Rom. ix. 5; xi. 28; xv. 8.

'Εν τοῖς προφήταις, *by the prophets.* The use of ἐν with the dative, instead of διά with the genitive, is frequent in the New Testament; as any one may see in Wahl's Lexicon, ἐν no. 3. a. The *frequent* use of it, in this way, is a *Hebraism;* for ἐν corresponds to the Hebrew בְּ, which is employed with great latitude of signification, and in cases of the same nature as that in question ; e. g. Hosea i. 2, *the word of the Lord by Hosea,* בְּהוֹשֵׁעַ. But an occasional use of ἐν in a similar way, by native Greek writers, may also be found; e. g. Thucyd. VII. 11, *what has been done before, ye know,* ἐν ἄλλαις πολλαῖς ἐπιστολαῖς, *by many other letters.*

Προφήταις, in the language of the New Testament, means, not only those who predict future events, but *all who were employed by God, as the medium of making religious communications of any kind* to his people.

'Επ' ἐσχάτου τῶν ἡμερῶν, in many copies ἐπ' ἐσχάτων τῶν ἡμερῶν. The LXX. use both forms of expression, as a translation of the Hebrew אַחֲרִית הַיָּמִים; thus showing that they were regarded by them as *synonymes.* It is a matter of indifference, as to the *sense* of the text, which reading is adopted.

The meaning of the phrase is best understood, from a comparison of the corresponding expressions in Hebrew. In the Old Testament, אַחֲרִית הַיָּמִים, אַחֲרִית, אַחֲרֵי־כֵן, and יוֹם אַחֲרוֹן, are often employed *synonymously;* and all of them to designate the general idea of *here-*

after, at a future time, in the sequel. Whether this future time be more or less remote, depends entirely on the context, and scope of the passage. See Gen. xlix. 1. Numb. xxiv. 14. Deut. iv. 30. Prov. xxxi. 25. But אַחֲרִית הַיָּמִים, in particular, is used to denote *the future period in which the Messiah (ὁ ἐρχόμενος) was to appear;* Isa. ii. 2. Hos. iii. 5. Micah iv. 1. Joel iii. 1, [Eng. ii. 28,] אַחֲרֵי־כֵן. This phrase (as it would seem from the usage in these places) early passed into a kind of technical designation of the time of the Messiah, or rather of the new dispensation under him. Thus Rabbi Nachmanides, on Gen. xlix. 1, says, "All our doctors agree, that אַחֲרִית הַיָּמִים means, *the times of the Messiah.*" That such a use of the phrase in question, was already an established one, in the time of our Saviour, is abundantly evident, from the frequency with which αἱ ἔσχαται ἡμέραι is employed in the New Testament, to designate *the period of the Christian dispensation.* Like other appellations, acquired in a similar way, (comp. Luke vii. 20,) it continued to be employed, after the "last days," i. e. the Christian dispensation, had commenced; and it is employed to designate *any part of the time which this dispensation comprises:* being limited only by the context, in the same manner, as the Hebrew אַחֲרִית הַיָּמִים &c. as exhibited above. In John vi. 39, 40. 44. 54, and xi. 24, ἐσχάτη ἡμέρα is indeed used to denote the *end of time,* when the resurrection of the dead will take place. But, in each of these cases, ἀναστήσω or ἀνάστασις accompanies it, so as to save all doubt in respect to its meaning. In all other cases, it designates *the period of the new dispensation.* Many synonymous expressions are also employed, to designate the same idea: e. g. ὁ ἔσχατος καιρός, οἱ ἔσχατοι καιροί, ἡ ἐσχάτη ὥρα, and ὕστεροι καιροί.

The Jews, it is said, divided the periods of the world into הָעוֹלָם הַזֶּה, *the present age* or *world,* i. e. the period of the Mosaic dispensation, and הָעוֹלָם הַבָּא, *the age* or *world to come,* i. e. the time of the Messiah's reign. The former is called, in the New Testament, ὁ αἰὼν οὗτος, ὁ νῦν αἰὼν τοῦ κόσμου τούτου, ὁ αἰὼν ὁ ἐνεστώς, καιρὸς οὗτος, and ὁ αἰών: the latter, ὁ αἰὼν ὁ μέλλων—ἐρχόμενος—ἐκεῖνος, οἱ αἰῶνες ἐπερχόμενοι, ἡ οἰκουμένη ἡ μέλλουσα. This latter class of expressions, thus understood, are equivalent to the phrases ἔσχαται ἡμέραι, ἐσχατῶν ἡμερῶν, &c.

Such is the representation of Wahl, (on the word αἰών, in his Lexicon,) of Brettschneider (Lex.), and of other critics, in regard to this subject. But that it is too definitely made, and therefore not in all respects well founded, is quite clear from the very authority to which Wahl refers;

, e. Buxtorf. Lex. Chald. sub voc. עוֹלָם. The Rabbins certainly used עוֹלָם הַזֶּה for *mundus hic, mundus habitabilis;* also for *mundus medius,* i. e. the regions of the air, stars, firmament, &c.; and for *mundus supremus,* i. e. of angels and spirits. It is equally certain, that they employed עוֹלָם הַבָּא for *mundus post resurrectionem mortuorum, mundus animarum a corpore solutarum,* as well as for *the age of the Messiah.* Buxtorf merely says, " Quidam per עוֹלָם הַבָּא intelligent יְמוֹת הַמָּשִׁיחַ, *dies Messiae.*" It would seem, then, that Wahl and Brettschneider have made an excessive use of the supposed Rabbinic sense of the word αἰών.

Be this, however, as it may; from the Old Testament usage we may easily make out (as I have endeavoured to do,) the sense of ἐπ' ἐσχάτου τῶν ἡμερῶν. The phrase, in Heb. i. 1, appears to mean, *during the last dispensation,* or, *under the last period,* viz. that of the Messiah.

Τούτων, THESE *last days,* is as much to say, " The period in question has already commenced."

Ἡμῖν, *to us,* by a κοίνωσις, i. e, a figure of speech, or mode of speaking, in which the writer joins himself with those whom he addresses. The meaning is, *to Christians, to the church;* not excluding others, but intending still to designate, in this place, particularly himself and those to whom he wrote. So Luke uses ἡμῖν for *Christians,* in chap. i. 1, and Paul, in like manner, often, in his epistles.

Ἐν υἱῷ, i. e. διὰ τοῦ υἱοῦ. So Chrysostom and Theophylact; for ἐν here is used as above, in ἐν τοῖς προφήταις. That the article would be added to υἱῷ here, if the phrase was constructed according to the common usage of the Greek language, and of the New Testament writers, is quite obvious; although I find none of the modern commentators who take notice of it. In accordance with this principle, both Chrysostom and Theophylact supply it in their paraphrase, expressing the sense by διὰ τοῦ υἱοῦ. After all the *rules* which have been laid down respecting the insertion or omission of the article in Greek, and all the theories which have been advanced, he who investigates for himself, and is guided only by *facts,* will find not a little that is arbitrary in the *actual* use of it. The cases are certainly very numerous, where Greek writers insert or reject it at pleasure. What is this but an *arbitrary* use of it? Some very sensible remarks on this subject may be found, in Lawrence's Remarks on our English Version.

It is plain, in the present case, that υἱῷ is *monadic;* that it designates one individual peculiarly distinguished; and that the pronoun αὐτοῦ is omitted after it; on all which accounts, (according to *theory,*) the article should be added. But all the Codices of the New Testament agree in omitting it. The circumstance is in itself of but little importance; still, as it has an important bearing upon *theories* which respect the use of the article, it well deserves particular notice.

Perhaps υἱῷ, in this case, may be employed as a kind of *proper* name, (just as we now use it;) and on this account it omits the article, by a license usual in respect to proper names.

Some distinguished commentators have maintained, that the sentiment of Heb. i. 1, is in direct opposition to the opinion commonly received by the Christian fathers, and still very generally maintained, viz. that the Son of God made all the revelations to the ancient prophets; and that all the *theophanies*, mentioned in the Old Testament, are to be ascribed to the *Logos*. These commentators suppose their own views, in opposition to the sentiment of those fathers, to be confirmed by Heb. ii. 1—4; where the *aggravated* guilt of those who reject the gospel, which was revealed by the Son of God, is urged; and the writer grounds the fact of its *being aggravated* upon the assumption that the law, in ancient times, was spoken only by the mediation of angels. But still, though this reasoning seems to be satisfactory at first view, it should be remembered that the writer is there, as well as in Heb. i. 1, speaking of the Son of God as *incarnate*, as possessing our nature, and addressing us in it. In this manner he did not address the church, in ancient times; and the emphasis may lie upon this circumstance. Comp. John i. 14. For, that the *Logos*, or Christ in his divine nature, did make revelations to the ancient church, seems to be an obvious deduction from John xii. 41. 1 Cor. x. 9; x. 4, and other like passages.

2. Ὅν ἔθηκε κληρονόμον πάντων, *whom he has constituted lord of all*, i. e. of the universe. Ἔθηκε, *constituted, appointed, ordained;* see Wahl on τίθημι, no. 3. In the same sense the Greeks employ τίθημι.

Κληρονόμον, *lord, possessor*, in accordance with the Hebrew idiom. In classic Greek, κληρονόμος is (1.) *One who acquires any thing by lot;* (2.) *One who inherits any thing after the death of the possessor.* The Son *inherited* the universe in neither of these ways; consequently κληρονόμος here is employed in the manner of the Hebrew יָרַשׁ, which means, *to take into possession* in any manner, or simply *to acquire*. *To inherit* is only a secondary sense of יָרַשׁ. The Latins employed *haeres*, in a sense like that here assigned to κληρονόμος. Thus Justinian, Inst. II. 19. § ult., *Pro haerede gerere, est pro domino gerere;* veteres enim *haeredes pro dominis* appellabant. So Festus, *Haeres* apud antiquos pro *domino* ponebatur. Comp. Gal. iv. 1; Acts x. 46. ii. 36; Ps. lxxxix. 27 [28]; John xvii. 10; which confirm the interpretation here given, as to the correctness of the sentiment which it conveys.

'Δι οῦ, *by whom*. It is contended here διά is not limited to signify the *instrumental cause* (so called), but that it often designates the *principal cause*. This is true; see Wahl on διά, l. c. where both the classical and New Testament usage of διά, in this sense, is shewn. But there is still a *poosibility* of the sense which Grotius gives it here, viz. *on account of whom*; see Wahl, no. 2., and to the instances there adduced of διά used with the genitive, and signifying *on account of*, add Rom. v. 19, bis. viii. 3; and perhaps 2 Cor. ix. 13; and 2 Pet. i. 3, διά δόξης. In all these cases, however, διά does not properly denote the *final cause* or *end* for which a thing is done; but only a *motive* for doing it, an *instrument*, as it were, in bringing it about. To say, that the worlds were made *on account of the Son*, as the final end or object of them, would imply something more, or something different from saying, that they were made *by him*. The sense which Grotius puts upon διά cannot be defended by any examples sufficiently plain, and cogent enough to justify the admission of it.

Τοὺς αἰῶνας ἐποίησε, *he*, [i. e. Θεὸς] *made the worlds*, or *the universe*. So, beyond any reasonable doubt, αἰῶνες is to be understood in xi. 3, and in 1 Tim. i. 17. The singular (αἰών) is not employed to designate *world*. The classical use of αἰών is (1.) *Age, period of time*. (2.) *Age of man, time of life*. Αἰῶνας, then, is used here, (like עוֹלָם, עוֹלָמִים, in the Chaldee and the later Hebrew), for *world, worlds, universe*. Theodoret explains it as meaning *ages*; and so others have since done. But what is the sense of the assertion, that God made the *ages* by his Son? If we understand this of the common periods of the life of man; or (with Theodoret) of the ages of the world; or of the Jewish and Christian dispensations, with others; what is it to the writer's purpose to assert this, in a passage which is evidently designed to shew the *exalted pre-eminence* of the Son of God. As to the sentiment conveyed by the interpretation which I have adopted, viz. *he made the worlds*, it is confirmed by Eph. iii. 9. Col. i. 15—19. John i. 3, 10. 1 Cor. viii. 6. Heb. i. 10. See Excursus I. II.

3. Ὅς ὢν ἀπαύγασμα τῆς δόξης καὶ χαρακτὴρ τῆς ὑποστάσεως αὐτοῦ. The ancient Greek commentators, and after them most of the modern ones, have applied these words to the *divine* nature of Christ. An

examination of the imagery which they present is necessary, in order to develop their real meaning.

'Απαύγασμα means *radiance, light flowing from a luminous body*, and is a derivate of ἀπαυγάζω i. q. αὐγάζω, *to shine, to emit splendour*. Δόξα, in classical Greek, means (1.) *Opinion, sentiment, supposition, maxim.* (2.) *Fame, honour, reputation.* But in our text, it plainly means the same as the Hebrew כָּבוֹד often does, viz. *splendour, brightness*. Comp. Luke ii. 9; ix. 31. Acts xxii. 11; vii. 55. Matt. vi. 29. 1 Cor. xv. 41.

Χαρακτὴρ is properly *an engraving* or *stamping instrument*, or, *a person who engraves* or *stamps*. But it is very commonly employed for the *figure itself*, or *image engraved* or *stamped*, e. g. upon coins, stones, metal, wood, or wax. So our English version, *express image*, i. e. image expressed or stamped. Hence, because the resemblance between the figure enstamped, and the instrument by which it is enstamped, is so exact, χαρακτὴρ means also, *exact image, resemblance*, or *delineation*.

Ὑπόστασις, in the classical sense anciently attached to it, means, (1.) *Foundation, substratum, substructio*. (2.) *Steadfastness, courage*. (3.) *Purpose, resolution, determination*. (4.) *Substance, essence, being*. In the sense of *person*, it first began to be used by the Greek writers *after* the Arian controversy commenced. It was employed particularly in this way by Athanasius, in order that he might make a distinction between οὐσία and ὑπόστασις, while he maintained that the *persons* (πρόσωπα) in the Trinity were of one οὐσία, but yet were three ὑποστάσεις. The sense of *person*, then, being attached to this word long *after* the New Testament was written, it cannot be properly assigned to the word here. It plainly retains the more ancient meaning of *substance* or *essence*.

The nature of the imagery, presented by the two phrases in our verse, may be thus explained. If God be represented to us under the image of *splendour*, of *a luminary, the source of light;* then is Christ the *radiance of that splendour*, or *the light emitted from that luminary*. That is, as a luminous body becomes perceptible in consequence of the light radiated from it; so God has manifested or exhibited himself to us, in the person of his Son. To the same purpose, John says, "No man hath seen God at any time; the only begotten Son, who is in the bosom of the Father, he hath revealed him," John i. 18. So again, "He that hath seen me, hath seen the Father," ch. xiv. 9; and again,

"He that seeth me, seeth him that sent me," ch. xii. 45. In Col. i. 15, Christ is called "the image of the invisible God," i. e. he by whom the invisible God is, as it were, presented to our inspection. In him, God has exhibited to men the perfections of his character, i. e. has exhibited τὴν δόξαν αὐτοῦ, which word is figuratively used to designate the divine perfections. So 2 Cor. iv. 6, δόξης τοῦ Θεοῦ ἐν προσώπῳ 'Ιησοῦ Χριστοῦ, i. e. the divine perfections as displayed by Jesus Christ; a phrase of the like nature with that which I am endeavouring to explain.

Again: if God be represented under the image of ὑπόστασις, *substance, essence,* then is Christ the development of that substance to our view; he is the *image, representation,* or *delineation* of it. As an image upon a coin presents the exact lineaments of the stamp which made it; so does Christ present the χαρακτὴρ of the Father, he presents us with his likeness, i. e. reveals to us, in his person and work, just and proper views of the perfections of the Father. So, the old Syriac Version renders ὑπόστασις αὐτοῦ by ܩܢܘܡܗ, i e. his substance.

That both expressions are to be understood *figuratively,* is beyond all doubt; for God is not, in a *literal* sense, *splendour* or *a luminous substance;* nor is his ὑπόστασις, in itself considered, i. e. physically or metaphysically considered, capable of being represented to our senses.

In the opinion, that the verse now under consideration relates to the incarnate Messiah, and not to the Logos in his divine nature simply considered, I find that Scott and Beza concur, not to mention others of the most respectable commentat rs. See EXCURSUS III.

Φέρων . . . τῆς δυνάμεως αὐτοῦ, *sustaining,* i. e. guiding, managing, controlling, *the universe by his own powerful word.* So Chrysostom φέρων, τουτέστι κυβερνῶν, τὰ διαπίπτοντα συγκρατῶν, *governing, holding together that which is ready to fall asunder,* or *preserving that which is ready to perish.* So Paul says of Christ, as εἰκὼν τοῦ Θεοῦ, that *he is before all things* καὶ τὰ πάντα ἐν αὐτῷ συνέστηκε, Col. i. 17. Φέρων, thus employed, corresponds to the Hebrew נָשָׂא, as used in Isa. xlvi. 3; lxvi. 9, in the sense of *curo, conservo, to sustain and preserve,* as a mother does her child. The Greeks sometimes joined φέρειν and ἄγειν in the same phrase, in order to express the *administration of affairs.* Τὰ πάντα is a common expression in Greek for the *universe.*

Τῷ ῥήματι τῆς δυνάμεως αὐτοῦ, *his own powerful word.* Such a mode of expression is not, as Ernesti names it, properly a Hebraism; for it is very common in all languages, although more frequent in the Oriental than in the Occidental tongues. Αὐτοῦ, sc. ἑαυτοῦ (not αὐτοῦ) that is, *by his own* powerful word, viz. the word of the Son, and not by the word of God, as αὐτοῦ would mean. The meaning of the whole phrase is, " He directs and controls the universe by his omnipotent word." It seems to be evidently an expression of the like nature with " God said, Let there be light, and there was light," Gen. i. 3 ; also, " He spake, and it was done ; he commanded, and it stood fast," Psa. xxxiii. 9. In other terms, the Son has the universe at the control of his mere *word ;* an expression signifying omnipotent, irresistible control. But inasmuch as the universe was created by him (ver. 2,) it surely cannot appear strange that he who made it should control it.

Δι ἑαυτοῦ....τῶν ἁμαρτιῶν ἡμῶν, *having by himself made expiation for our sins.* Καθαρισμὸς usually means *purification ;* but in Hellenistic Greek, it is also employed for *expiation*; e. g. in Exod. xxix. 36, xxx. 10, the LXX. use it for the Hebrew הַכִּפּוּרִים, *atonement, expiation.* That καθαρισμὸν cannot be used here in the simple sense of *purification* by moral means, such as doctrine, &c. is evident from its being joined with δι ἑαυτοῦ ; which is explained in ch. ii. 14, by διὰ τοῦ θανατοῦ ; in ch. ix. 12, by διὰ τοῦ ἰδίου αἵματος ; and in ch. ix. 26, by διὰ τῆς θυσίας αὐτοῦ. This last expression I regard as the *full* form, expressing what is elliptically expressed in our text by δι ἑαυτοῦ.

After he had thus by the sacrifice of himself made expiation for sin, ἐκάθισεν ἐν δεξιᾷ τῆς μεγαλωσύνης ἐν ὑψηλοῖς ; *he sat down at the right of the majesty on high,* i. e. of God in the highest heavens, οὐρανοῖς being understood after ὑψηλοῖς ; or, *of supreme majesty ;* (see Wahl Lex. on οὐρανὸς.) The verb ἐκάθισε here corresponds to the Hebrew יָשַׁב, which, applied to God, and to kings, does not mean simply *to sit*, but *to sit enthroned, to sit on a throne ;* e. g. Ps. ii. 4, and often. *To sit on a throne,* or, *to sit at the right hand of one on a throne,* implies here, *commanding, ruling, judging.*

Μεγαλωσύνης, *majesty, magnificence,* גְּדוּלָה, גֹּדֶל, אַדֶּרֶת. Here it is the *abstract* (as grammarians say) used for the *concrete,* i. e. on the right hand of the *majestic One,* or the *magnificent One,* viz. לִימִין אֱלֹהֵי הַכָּבוֹד. So Liber Enochi, (Fabricii Cod. Pseudep. V. T. p. 187,) ἐνώπιον τῆς δόξης τῆς μεγαλωσύνης. See EXCURSUS IV.

4. Τοσούτῳ κρείττων .... ὄνομα, *being exalted as much above the angels, as he has obtained an appellation more honourable than they.* Κρείττων, *praestantior, augustior, of higher rank* or *place, eminentior.* Γενόμενος, *constituted, rendered,* &c. It is here applied to the elevation of the Son to the *mediatorial* throne, after his death. Διαφορώτερον,

more eminent, more distinguished; παρ᾽ αὐτοὺς, than they, i. e. the angels. Παρὰ, after the comparative degree, appears to be peculiar to this epistle. It makes of itself a comparative degree, as used in Rom. i. 25; xiv. 5. Heb. i. 9; ii. 7. Κεκληρονόμηκε, obtained, acquired, as in ver. 2. ῎Ονομα, either *name*, i. e. title, as υἰὸς, or *rank, dignity*. Commentators are divided in opinion, respecting which of these meanings should be preferred. But the argument, in the sequel, shows that the title, SON, is the ground on which the superiority of Christ over the angels is proved. If it be objected, that angels are also called *sons*: and men too; the answer is easy. No one *individal*, except Jesus, is ever called, by way of eminence, THE SON *of God*, i. e. the Messiah, or the King of Israel, John i. 49.

The appeal is here made to Jewish readers of the Old Testament, who applied Ps. ii. 7, and 2 Sam. vii. 14, to the Messiah. In *such* a sense as in these passages, namely, one that imported supreme dominion and authority, neither angels nor men were called *sons of God*. But Jesus bore this title, which, according to the Jewish Scriptures, was indicative of supreme dignity; and, consequently, he had an appellation of a more exalted nature than that of the angels, who are *servants*, (ch. i. 14,) not *lords*.

5. Τινὶ γὰρ.... γεγέννηκὰ σε, *for to which of the angels said he at any time, Thou art my Son; this day have I begotten thee?* Γεγέννηκὰ σε must of course be *figuratively* understood. But how? In Ps. ii. the context shews that the expression here quoted has reference to Christ *as king*, as constituted king or lord over all; see ver. 6, 8, &c. *To beget*, is metaphorical language suited to the name *Son;* but as *Son* here plainly means *Messiah*, or the *anointed king*, dropping the metaphor, we come of course to the meaning, *constituted, made, appointed*, or γενόμενος as above.

In regard to σήμερον, which has been often construed as meaning, *from eternity*, Theodoret has plainly expressed its true sense; οὐ τὴν αἰώνιον δηλοῖ γέννησιν, ἀλλὰ τὴν τῷ χρόνῳ συνεζευγμένην, *it does not express his eternal generation, but that which is connected with time.* For surely Christ was exalted to the mediatorial throne in time, i. e. after his resurrection; and such an exaltation is the subject of description, in the second Psalm. Such a view of the meaning the context also demands, where his *acquired* condition is the particular subject of comparison with the rank and condition of the angels. So Chrysostom, after quoting ver. 5, says, ταῦτα εἴρηται μὲν εἰς τὴν σάρκα, *this is spoken concerning his human nature*.

Ἐγὼ ἔσομαι .... εἰς υἱόν. In common Greek it would be, ἐγὼ ἔσομαι πατὴρ αὐτοῦ ...υἱὸς μου. The form of expression, αὐτῷ εἰς πατέρα, corresponds altogether to the Hebrew לִי לְאָב; and μοὶ εἰς υἱὸν to לְבֵן לִי, 2 Sam. vii. 14, whence the quotation is taken. The term *Son* seems here to designate one who should be entitled to all the rights and privileges of a Son; and in particular, one who should be an heir to the throne of his Father. This same figurative expression, *heirship, being heir*, the writer has applied to the Son in the context, ver. 2. 4. Now, as the angels are not entitled to *such* privileges, the appellation *Son*, (which implies a right to them in this case,) shows that he to whom it is applied, is elevated above the angels. And this is the position, which the argument in Heb. i. is designed to establish.

If we may credit Abarbanel, the ancient Jewish doctors held that the Messiah would be exalted above Abraham, Moses, and the angels. However this may be, the apostle, in applying this and the following quotations to the Messiah, must have supposed himself addressing those, who would readily concede that they ought to be thus applied. Otherwise, we cannot suppose that he could have regarded this mode of reasoning as at all efficacious, or adapted to convince those to whom he wrote.

Ver. 6. Ὅταν δὲ πάλιν .... λέγει, *again also, when he bringeth his first-begotten into the world, he saith;* a passage replete with difficulties. Does πάλιν qualify εἰσαγάγῃ? Or is it to be transposed thus, πάλιν δὲ, ὅταν, κ. τ. λ.? Many contend for this transposition; and Abresch cites what he calls similar instances of a metathesis, in Acts xiii. 27. 1 Cor. iv. 18; 2 Cor. vii. 6. These, however, come short of establishing his position. Admitting the transposition in question, we must translate πάλιν, κ. τ. λ. by *again,* i. e. in another passage of scripture, *when he introduces,* &c. But this transposition is unnecessary, even if the sense here given to πάλιν be retained; for we may translate equally well, *but when, in another place, he introduces,* &c. One might translate πάλιν here, (with Storr, Wahl, and others,) *on the other hand, on the contrary,* i. e. God speaks in quite a different way to the angels, when he introduces his first begotten into the world, viz. instead of calling them *sons,* he commands them *to worship his Son.* See Wahl's Lex. on πάλιν. So Schneider, πάλιν, *im Gegentheile, (ex adverso,)* specially in composites, as παλίμφημος, *contradictory,* &c. There is no ground for the sneer with which Schulz treats Storr's translation of πάλιν by *hingegen,* i. e. ἐξ ἐναντίας.

After all, however, I am more inclined to interpret πάλιν here as meaning *again*, i. e. something in addition to what had been already said or stated. But as the position, which the writer has given it, is somewhat different from that of the preceding καὶ πάλιν, (which *commences* the clause or assertion in which it stands), I suppose the writer means to convey the idea, by using δὲ πάλιν in the latter case, that what he is going to suggest is only additional matter, and not simply additional scriptural quotation. Certain it is, that, on other occasions, where he cites several texts of scripture continuously, he uses καὶ πάλιν in the same way before each citation; e. g. Heb. ii. 12, 13. [The assertions of our author, (according to the views which I have of the use of δὲ πάλιν here), would run thus, " God declares in the scripture, that he has begotten the Messiah his Son; and again, that he is his Father, and the Messiah his Son; and *God has also said*, (which shews the superiority of Christ over angels), that all the angels must worship him." In this way all is natural and easy.]

As another reason for translating as I have done, it may be added, that no direct antithesis (between the declarations, that God had begotten the Messiah his Son, and that the latter was the Son of God the Father, contained in ver. 5) is found in verse 6. This is a sufficient reason for avoiding here the translation which Storr, Wahl, and others, have given to πάλιν, viz. *ex adverso, hingegen*=ἐξ ἐναντίας. I have no doubt that πάλιν may have, and sometimes has, such a meaning; but it is unnecessary here, and on the whole, it is an improbable one

Εἰσαγάγῃ, κ. τ. λ. Does this mean *to introduce into the world*, in the same sense as we now speak of introducing one *to* the world, i. e. *announcing him to them?* This is the common mode of interpretation. But some interpret εἰσαγάγῃ by *commend, producere et conspicuum facere.* Others, (with Chrysostom and Theophylact), ὅταν ἐγχειρίσῃ αὐτῷ τὴν οἰκουμένην, *when he delivers the world into his hands,* i. e. makes him king over all; a sense which *introducing to the world,* or *into the world,* will hardly bear. None of these interpretations seem to accord with the *usus loquendi* of the New Testament. Εἰσαγαγεῖν εἰς τὴν οἰκουμένην and ἀποστέλλειν εἰς τὸν κόσμον, are plainly phrases of equivalent import; and the latter is repeatedly used concerning Christ, John iii. 17; x. 36, and employed to denote either his birth, or his appearing before the world in his public character. Such, too, is the Rabbinic usage of בָּא בָעוֹלָם Comp. Heb. x. 5. John xvi. 28; xviii. 37; i. 9. It is not, then, an introduction of the Son to the world by *prophecy,* as expressed in the

Old Testament, which is here spoken of; but an introduction in *fact*, i. e. his birth, or perhaps his entrance on his public office. It was at that time, as it would seem, that the angels received the command in question. Gregory Nyssen says, καθὸ τὸ κτιστὸν ἥνωσεν ἑαυτῷ, εἰσαχθῆναι λέγεται εἰς τὴν κτίσιν, *as he united that which was created with himself, he is said to be introduced into the creation;* cited by Theoph. in locum.

Καὶ προσκυνησάτωσαν αὐτῷ .... θεοῦ, *let all the angels of God worship him.* Compare with this, Luke i. 11, seq.; i. 26, seq.; in particular, ii. 8, seq.; where the angelic choir appear, and celebrate the birth of the Saviour. The καὶ here denotes, that the sentence quoted stood in connexion with something else which preceded it; but as this is not quoted also, the καὶ cannot well be translated.

If this exposition be admitted, (and it appears to be supported both by the *usus loquendi* of the New Testament, and by fact), then we need not be very solicitous, whether the passage in Deut. xxxii. 43 (Sept.), or in Ps. xcvii. 7, is here quoted by the writer; nor whether either of them is quoted. See EXCURSUS VI.

If I have rightly interpreted ver. 5 and 6, the meaning may be briefly expressed thus; " Prediction in the scripture assigned to the Son a rank above that of the angels, and occurrences at his birth demonstrate such to be the fact."

Ver. 7. Καὶ πρὸς μὲν .... πυρός, *moreover, with respect to the angels it is said, Who maketh his angels winds, and his ministering servants flaming fire;* i. e. who maketh his angels that serve him the ministers of his will, as the winds and the lightning are. The Hebrew אֵשׁ לֹהֵט, and Greek πυρὸς φλόγα, often mean *lightning;* as plainly they do here. The whole phrase is susceptible of another interpretation; viz. who making his angels winds, i. e. swift as the winds, and his servants lightning, i. e. rapid, or terrible, or resistless as the lightning. But this does not suit the design for which the apostle quotes it, so well as the first interpretation. His object is to shew, that the angels are employed simply in a *ministerial* capacity; while the *Son* is *Lord of all*. Our English version, which has rendered רוּחוֹת (Ps. civ. 4,) by *spirits*, gives an erroneous view of the meaning of the original.

Others construe the Hebrew original thus, *Who maketh the winds his messengers, and the lightnings his servants;* and they defend this by alleging, that the context in the Psalm shews the design of the writer to be, only to declare the glory of God as displayed in the *visible* creation:

and consequently, it is inapposite to suppose him here to be speaking of the *angels*, as an order of *invisible*, intelligent beings. But in Ps. civ. 1—3, the *invisible* as well as *visible* majesty of God is described; and it is natural that the writer should proceed, and augment the force of his description, by introducing the angels as the ministering servants of the Deity. Besides, the Hebrew does not allow us properly to translate, *Who maketh the winds his angels* or *messengers*. In order to mean this, the Hebrew must be written עֹשֶׂה רוּחוֹת מַלְאָכָיו, and not (as now) עֹשֶׂה מַלְאָכָיו רוּחוֹת. See Heb. Gram. sect. 197, 3, and comp. in Ps. civ. 3, הַשָּׂם עָבִים רְכוּבוֹ, which surely cannot be rendered, be rendered, "Who maketh his chariot clouds."

As to λέγει, in this verse, it is clear that the nominative cannot be Ѳεὸς, for then the quotation would be in the *first* person, as it is in ver. 5, above. The nominative, beyond all reasonable doubt, is ἡ γραφὴ, or ὁ νόμος. I have rendered λέγει in the passive voice, merely to avoid expressing the nominative, since the writer has not expressed it. To the same purpose Storr and Schulz, *heisst es, it is said*. So the usual appeal in the Mishna, נֶאֱמַר. Compare also φησὶ, in 1 Cor. vi. 16. The quotation, in our verse, is from Ps. civ. 4.

Ver. 8, 9. Πρὸς δὲ τὸν υἱὸν .... αἰώνιος, *but respecting the Son,* [*he saith*], *Thy throne, O God, is eternal*. Θρόνος is plainly the emblem of *dominion;* because kings, when acting in their capacity as rulers, were accustomed to sit on thrones. Ὁ Ѳεὸς is not the *nominative* case, as some have maintained, but the *vocative*. It is the usual vocative, and nearly the only form of it, throughout the Septuagint; e. g. Ps. iii. 7; iv. 1; v. 10; vii. 1, et passim. The Attics, moreover, frequently retain the form of the nominative, in the vocative of the second declension. Buttman's Gram. sect. 33, n. 2. To translate the phrase by *God is thy throne*, would be to introduce a mode of expression foreign to the *usus loquendi* of the Scriptures; for where is God ever said to be the *throne of his creatures?* And what could be the sense of such an expression? *Throne* is the emblem of *dominion*, not of *support*. So Theoph. Ѳρόνος γὰρ .... ὁ βασιλείας σύμβολον. Figuratively used, as here, it is of the same import as *sceptre,* ῥάβδος. Gesenius renders the phrase, *thy God's throne is eternal*, i. e. the throne which God gives thee. But this is doing violence to כִּסְאֲךָ אֱלֹהִים, which, to support his rendering, should be כִּסֵּא אֱלֹהֶיךָ, the pronoun following the second of two nouns in regimen, according to the usual custom, Heb. Gram. sect. 185, 1.

Ῥάβδος εὐθύτητος .... σου, *a sceptre of justice is the sceptre of thy kingdom*, or, *thy reign is just*. The former clause designates the perpetuity of the Son's reign; the present one, its equitable nature. It is quite plain, too, that the two clauses are a poetic parallelism, as they belong to Ps. xlv. 7; and also that the subject of both clauses is the ame, viz. the dominion or reign of the Son or Messiah.

Ἠγάπησας ... ἀνομία, *thou hast loved righteousness and hated iniquity*, i. e. thou hast administered the affairs of thy government in a manner altogether just; or, thine equity is highly conspicuous. Such a negative form of expression (καὶ ἐμίσησας ἀνομίαν,) following an affirmative one, is very common in the Scriptures, and is designed to give intensity to the affirmative assertion which precedes it. Comp. John i. 3, 20. et al. sæpe.

Διὰ τοῦτο .... ἀγαλλιάσεως, *because of this, O God, thy God has anointed thee with the oil of gladness*. But the phrase is equally susceptible of the rendering, *God, thy God, has anointed thee*, &c.; and this without any alteration of the general sense of the passage. Theophylact, however, thought otherwise; for he says " ὁ θεὸς, ἀντὶ τοῦ ὦ θεὲ ἐστι, as our enemy Symmachus (here a credible witness) affirms, who renders the Hebrew thus, θεὲ, ὁ θεός σου."

Ἔλαιον ἀγαλλιάσεως, i. e. κατ' ἔλαιον. Kings were anointed with oil, in order to consecrate them to their office; see Ps. ii. 6. 1 Sam. x. 1; xvi. 13. But perfumed oil, or precious ointment, was often employed also on festive occasions; and honoured guests at an entertainment were often bedewed with it. That ἔλαιον ἀγαλλιάσεως here does not mean the *oil of consecration to office*, is plain, from the consideration, that the administration of the kingly office is described, in the preceding context, as having already existed. The meaning then must be, " God has exalted his *Son*, with honor greater than that bestowed on kings," or, " bestowed a higher joy on him than on *other kings*."

Παρὰ τοὺς μετόχους σου, lit. *in comparison with thine associates*, i. e. in office, viz. kings. God has bestowed a higher reward, a greater honor, on the king Messiah, than on any other kings.

Thus much for the *words*. The general *sentiment* remains to be stated. The words are quoted from Ps. xlv. 6, 7. That this whole psalm relates to the Messiah, has been generally believed by Jewish and Christian commentators; and it is at last acknowledged by Rosenmüller, in the second edition of his *Comm. in Psalmos*. All other explanations seem liable to insuperable difficulties; and this, one may hope, will soon be universally felt and acknowledged.

That the whole Psalm relates to the Messiah, however, as *mediatorial king*, can scarcely be doubted by any one who compares together all its different parts. The king is called אֱלֹהִים, Θεός. Does the word Θεός here denote the *divine*, or the *kingly* nature or condition of the Messiah? Most interpreters, who admit the doctrine of the Saviour's divine nature, contend for the first of these senses; as I have myself once done, in a former publication. But further examination has led me to believe, that there are grounds to doubt of such an application of the word Θεός, in this passage. The king, here called Θεός, has for himself a Θεός; " *thy God* hath anointed *thee*." The same king has *associates* (μετόχους,) i. e. others who, in some respects, are in a similar condition or office. As *divine*, who are μέτοχοι with the Saviour? Besides, his equity, his government, his state, as described in Ps. xlv. are all such as belong to the *King Messiah*. Now, as *Elohim* is a title sometimes given to kings or magistrates, as one may see in Ps. lxxxii. 1, 6; comp. John x. 35, (in Ex. vii. 1; and iv. 16, it is a different case,) although no one individual king or magistrate is ever called simply *Elohim*, may not this title be applied, in a sense altogether *peculiar* and *pre-eminent*, to the Messiah as king; designating his great superiority over all other kings, and distinguishing him as σύνθρονος with God, as " King of kings, and Lord of lords?" Rev. xvii. 14; Comp. Heb. i. 3, and the note on ἐκάθισεν ἐν δεξιᾷ, κ. τ. λ. Such an explanation, to say the least, removes some of the difficulties which attend the usual one; while the following verses leave no just room to doubt what was the opinion of the writer of our epistle, in regard to the divine nature of the Messiah.

The *perpetuity* of the kingdom mentioned here, may be the same as that in Luke i. 33; with which is to be compared 1 Cor. xv. 24—28. Indeed, it must be such, allowing the kingdom of the Messiah to be the one which is here meant.

Ver. 10. Καὶ, σὺ κατ' ἀρχὰς . . . . ἐθεμελίωσας, also, *Thou, Lord, in the beginning didst lay the foundation of the earth*. This verse is, by construction, necessarily connected with the preceding ones; ver. 7, καὶ πρὸς μὲν τοὺς ἀγγέλους λέγει—ver. 8, πρὸς δὲ τὸν υἱὸν [λέγει] ver. 10. καὶ [i. e. πρὸς τὸν υἱὸν λέγει.] An address to Jehovah here, considered simply as creator, is utterly irrelevant to the scope of the writer, and to the object which he evidently has in view. Both the grammatical construction, and the plain design of the passage, unite in declaring this.

U

Κατ' ἀρχὰς, in the Hebrew, Ps. cii. 25, it is לְפָנִים, *of old, formerly,* equivalent to בְּרֵאשִׁית in Gen. i. 1. Κύριε in the New Testament and Septuagint, corresponds both to יְהוָֹה and אֵל or אֱלֹהִים, in the Hebrew. Here it corresponds to אֵל, in Ps. cii. 24. Ἐθεμελίωσας, *thou hast laid the foundation*; θεμελιόω, applied to a building, has this sense. But here it is, of course, applied in a figurative manner, to designate the original and primary act of creation (so to speak); viz. that act which may be compared to what a workman does, when he lays the foundation of a building. The Son, therefore, did not merely arrange or set in order the materials of creation already brought into being, but laid the foundation of the universe, i. e. performed the original act or first work, that of bringing it into being.

Ἔργα τῶν χειρῶν σου מַעֲשֵׂה יָדֶיךָ, *the work of thy hands*, i. q. thy work. The phrase is borrowed from the fact, that *hands* are the instruments by which men usually perform any operation; and this is, like other human operations and affections, figuratively transferred to God. Οἱ οὐρανοὶ means, all parts of the creation except the earth; see Gen. i. 1. The Hebrews designated the sun, moon, and stars, i. e. all the visible creation besides the earth, by the word שָׁמַיִם, *heavens*.

Ver. 11. Αὐτοὶ, *they*, i. e. the heavens and the earth. Σὺ δὲ διαμένεις, (Hebrew תַּעֲמֹד,) *thou shalt continue, be permanent, stand fast*. It is the opposite of ἀπολοῦνται. Παλαιωθήσονται, *shall wax old*, a word which, applied to a garment (the image here used,) means, *to go into a state of decay*, or *desuetude, to become unfit for use*. Hence the metaphorical language that follows.

Ver. 12. Καὶ ὡσεὶ . . . . αὐτοὺς, *and as a vesture shalt thou fold them up*. Ἑλίξεις, means, *to fold up, to roll together*. The heavens are often represented as an *expanse* (רָקִיעַ) and *rolling them up*, is, of course, *to remove* them. The language, however, in the case before us, is borrowed from the custom of *folding up* and *laying aside* garments which have become unfit for use. The Hebrew word (for which ἑλίξεις is put) is תַּחֲלִיף, *thou shalt change, remove*. Ἀλλαγήσονται, *they shall decay, they shall be changed*, i. e. removed, taken away, or *shall pass away*, Hebrew יַחֲלֹפוּ Ps. cii. 26, Comp. 2 Pet. iii. 10; Is. li. 6; also xxxiv. 4, where the image is fully presented. Σὺ δὲ ὁ αὐτὸς εἶ, (Hebrew וְאַתָּה הוּא,) *thou art he*, viz, who liveth for ever, *thou art always the same*. So the sequel leads us to interpret this. Τὰ ἔτη σου οὐκ ἐκλείψουσι, *thy years shall never cease or fail*, i. e. shall never come to an end.

This would be true, if it was spoken merely with reference to the future, and should be construed as having respect only to eternity *a parte post*, as it is technically called, i. e. eternity to come. But as it stands here, in connexion with having created the heavens and the earth, κατ' αρχὰς, it can hardly be understood to mean less than absolute eternity, or eternity *a parte ante et a parte post*. See Excursus VII.

Ver. 13. Πρὸς τίνα δὲ τῶν ἀγγέλων . . . . δεξιῶν μου, *unto which of the angels, also, has he ever said, sit at my right hand*. That is, where is any example of his addressing any one of the angels, and asking him *to sit at his right hand*, i. e. to be σύνθρονος with him? See on δεξιᾷ μεγαλοσύνης, under ver. 3, above.

Ἕως ἂν θῶ . . . . ποδῶν σου, *until I shall make thine enemies thy footstool*, i. e. reduce them to the most entire subjection. These words are quoted from Ps. cx. 1, (Sept. cix. 1,) and are applied to the Messiah. *To make enemies a footstool*, is an expression borrowed from the custom, in ancient times, of treading upon the necks of captives and captive kings, on the occasion of celebrating a triumph over them, and in token of their complete prostration and subjection; see Joshua x. 24, and so often in Homer. *Enemies* signify all such as are opposed to the doctrines or duties of the Christian religion. In Ps. cx. 1, the Messiah is invited *to sit at the right hand of God*, (i. e. at his right hand on his throne, comp. Rev. iii. 21,) *until* (עַד, ἕως ἂν) *his enemies should be utterly subdued*. But what follows this period, when they shall have been thus subdued? The apostle has told us. It is the *mediatorial* throne to which the Messiah is exalted; it is to him as *constituted* king, that his enemies are to be brought in subjection; and when this is accomplished, the *mediatorial* throne and reign, *as such*, are to cease. So 1 Cor. xv. 24—28, seems to assure us.

Ver. 14. How different the station and employment of angels from that of the Messiah! He is σύνθρονος with God, and commands the universe; they are spirits employed merely as ministers to execute his will. Are they not all λειτουργικὰ πνεύματα? Comp. 1 Kings xxii. 19; Zech. iii. 5—7. Dan. vii. 10. Is. vi. 1. Luke i. 19. By the Rabbins, the angels are frequently named מַלְאֲכֵי דְשֵׁירוּתָא, *angeli ministerii*. Εἰς διακονίαν, *for ministering, in order to serve*, i. e. assist. Διακονία means any kind *of service* or *assistance* whatever. It is here said to be performed, διὰ τοὺς μέλλοντας κληρονομεῖν σωτηρίαν, *on account of those who are to obtain salvation*, i. e. on account of Christians who are the heirs of future glory or happiness, or, who will obtain it.

Whatever may be the opinion of some modern critics, in regard to the real existence of angels as intelligent beings, it appears quite clear that the writer of our epistle regarded them as such. To have instituted a comparison between the Son of God, on the one hand, and mere *abstract qualities* or *imaginary beings*, on the other, would not seem to be very apposite, at least not apposite to any serious purpose. And if the writer looked upon angels as only *imaginary* beings, or personifications of qualities, with what propriety or consistency could he represent them as worshipping the Son of God, or as ministering to the saints? But Ps. cii. 3, is first erroneously translated, *He maketh the wind his angels, and flaming fire his servants*, λειτουργοὺς αὐτοῦ, and it is then used as a proof that the *elements* themselves are called *angels*. Hence it is concluded, that it is unnecessary to suppose angels to be an order of *real, intelligent beings*. But as this translation is not well grounded, (see on ver. 7,) any such conclusion built upon it cannot be stable. That the sacred writers every where regard angels, and speak of them, as intelligent beings, having a *real* existence, appears so plain, that it would seem as if no one who is not strongly wedded to his own *a priori* and philosophical reasoning, could venture to deny it.

CHAP. II.

Ver. 1. Διὰ τοῦτο *on this account, therefore*, i. e. since Christ who is at the head of the new dispensation, is so much exalted above the angels who were the mediators of the old (see ver. 2,) *it becomes us*, &c. Ἡμᾶς, *us* by κοίνωσις, i. e. a method of speaking in which the writer includes himself with those whom he addresses. See Heb. i. 1; ii. 3; iii. 1, 14; iv. 2, &c. See also similar cases in 1 Cor. x. 8, 9. 2 Cor. vii. 1. Acts vi. 17, et alibi.

Προσέχειν is elliptical, (προσέχειν τὸν νοῦν is the full expression,) and means, *attendere, to give heed to*. Abresch thinks it is here equivalent to ἀντέχεσθαι, *retinere, tenaciter adhaerere;* which Dindorf also favours. But evidently this is unnecessary, inasmuch as περισσοτέρως is connected with it, and designates the *intensity* of mind, with which attention should be paid to the things that the Son of God reveals. Ἀκουσθεῖσι, *things heard*, are the truths and doctrines of the Christian religion, which had been declared to them, see ver. 3, 4.

Παραῤῥυῶμεν, a long-contested and difficult word. Two senses have been principally contended for; (1.) *to fall, to stumble*, or *to perish*. This latter sense Chrysostom and Theophylact give it; παραῤῥυῶμεν, τουτέστι, ἀπολώμεθα, ἐκπέσωμεν. Both illustrate it by the proverbial saying, addressed to a child, υἱὲ, μὴ παραρρυῇς, Prov. iii. 21, in order to guard him against stumbling. In like manner, Theodoret represents the word as spoken here, ἵνα μή τινα ὄλισθον ὑπομείνωμεν, so that we may not suffer a lapse, or may not stumble, fall. So Suidas explains it by παραπέσωμεν; Hesych. by ἐκπέσωμεν; Lex. Cyrilli, μὴ παραρρυῇς, μὴ ἐκπέσῃς, μὴ παρασύρῃς. The Syriac and Arabic interpreters have rendered it, *that we may not fall*. Alberti and Matthiae, with many modern critics, assign to it the same sense. The idea connected with *stumbling, falling*, by this class of commentators, is not that of *transgression*, but of *punishment*, of *destruction*, as is evident from the whole of their illustrations, when compared each with himself and with the others.

But, although this view of the word has been often given, none of the passages adduced from the Greek writers, and alleged to justify it, seem adequate for this purpose. Wetstein has collected a large number of passages, which contain the word in question. But most of them are only such as designate the well-known senses of the word παραρρύω, viz. *to flow, to flow by*; as, τῷ παρὰ πόλιν παραρρέοντι ποταμῷ (Plutarch;) πιεῖν ἀπὸ τοῦ παραρρέοντος ποταμοῦ (Xen.;) *to flow into*, as παραρρυεὶς . . . . εἰς τὸ στόμα ἱδρώς (Galen;) in all which cases the word is applied to the flowing of *liquids*; *to flow out*, as εἴ τις ἀφροδίσιος λόγος παραρρυῇ (Ælian.) In some cases the word is figuratively applied to locomotion in men; as παραρρυεὶς γὰρ ἄνθρωπος εἰς τὸν νεὼν [ναὸν] τοῦ Ἀσκληπιοῦ (Plutarch.) None of these instances justify the sense of *perishing, falling into ruin*.

2. The other sense contended for is, that of *suffering to flow from the mind* or *memory*, i. e. *to forget*. That παραρρυεῖν is frequently applied to things that glide or pass away from the mind, is well established. E. g. " Many, who seem to be believers, ... need, for the sake of remembering, ... examples drawn from objects of sense . . . . ἵνα μὴ τέλεον παραρρυῇ, *so that they will not entirely escape*, i. e. from the mind, Origen contra Celsum, p. 393." " That τὰ καλὰ may not be merely temporary, καὶ μὴ παραρρυῇ λήθης βυθοῖς ἀμαυρουμένα, *and may not escape* [flow away,] *being obscured in the abysses of forgetfulness*, Greg. Nazianz." So Lucian, εἴ τι ἐν τῷ ποιήσεως δρόμῳ παραρρυὲν λάθῃ, *if any thing flowing away* [escaping] *in the poetic course is forgotten*, Diss. cum Hesiod. 5. So in Latin, " frustra docemur, si quidquid audimus praeterfluat [παραρρυεῖ,] Quinctil. XI. 2." " It cannot enter into the mind of the judge, ante enim praeterlabitur quam percepta

est, for *it glides away* before it is apprehended," Cicero de Orat II. 25.

But in all these cases, παραρρυῶ is applied only to *things*, and not to *persons.* That a thing παραρρυῇ, *should escape* from me, and that *I* should be said παραρρυεῖν in respect to that thing, are two very different expressions; and consequently, all the instances above, which have been adduced by learned critics, do not meet the difficulty of the case. Παραρρυῶμεν is applied, in our text, to *persons*, not (as here) to *things.*

In the classics, I have been able to find no example, which is in point for our case. The Septuagint have used the word but once, Prov. iii. 21, υἱὲ μὴ παραρρυῇς, τήρησον δὲ ἐμὴν βουλὴν καὶ ἔννοιαν, *Son, do not pass by* [neglect,] *but keep my counsel and advice.* This is the very proverb to which Chrysostom and Theophylact appeal, as an illustration of the word in question ; but the true sense of this word, in Prov. iii. 21, they do not seem to have apprehended. Παραρρυῇς here plainly does not mean to *perish, to fall*, but it is the antithesis of τήρησον, *keep, attend to, practise,* and consequently means, *to pass by, to neglect, to transgress.* In like manner, Clemens Alex., speaking of women, says, " They are bound by virtuous modesty, ἵνα μὴ παραρρυῶσι τῆς ἀληθείας διὰ χαυνοτητα, *not to neglect* [pass by, transgress] the truth on account of effeminate weakness, Pedagog." III. p. 246. These two instances seem to meet the wants of our case, as παραρρυῶ is here applied to *persons.*

The sense which our passage demands, is better made out by following these examples, than in any other way. The writer of our epistle does not design to say, in ch. ii. 1, *Take heed, or you will perish:* for he speaks of *punishment* immediately after, in ch. ii. 2. The explanation of Chrysostom, then, and of the great number of critics who have followed him, is rendered improbable by the nature of the context, and it is unsupported by any classic example in point. The other explanation, *lest we should let them slip, lest we should not retain them, lest they should glide away,* is an approximation to the right meaning of the word. Plainly, μὴ παραρρυῶμεν, here applied to *persons*, means, *lest we should pass by,* viz. the things which we have heard, *lest we should neglect them, lest we should transgress,* [pass beyond] *them;* for so the writer himself has explained it, in the context. *For if,* says he, *every* παράβασις *and* παρακοὴ *received a due reward* [under the law of Moses,] *how shall we escape punishment,* ἀμελήσαντες, *having neglected so great salvation.* That ἀμελήσαντες here refers to the same thing which is designated by παραρρυῷμεν, is quite clear; for, first, the writer exhorts them "to attend diligently to what they had heard, lest they should *pass by* or *neglect* it;" and then he says, "If they *do neglect* it (ἀμελήσαντες,) punishment will be the certain consequence, a punishment more severe than that inflicted on transgressors under the law."

The same sentiment is obtained, if we compare παραρρυῶμεν with the preceding περισσοτέρως . . . προσέχειν, of which it is plainly the opposite or antithesis. Now as προσέχειν means, *to attend diligently, to give heed,* so παραρρυῶμεν must mean, (as its antithesis,) *not to attend diligently,* i. e. *to treat with neglect, to be* ἀμελήσαντες, as it is expressed in the following verse. In a word, the sentiment is, "*diligent* attention to the truths of the gospel is necessary to guard us against *neglect* or *transgressions;* which neglect is followed by certain and aggravated condemnation."

If an apology be due for dwelling so long on the verbal criticism of this word, it is, that the word has been so long contested, and so unsatisfactorily illustrated.

Ver. 2. Εἰ γὰρ ὁ δι᾽ ἀγγέλων λαληθεὶς λόγος, *if the communication* [revelation] *made by angels.* The *Jewish law* is undoubtedly the λόγος δι᾽ ἀγγέλων λαμηθεὶς, in this case. The meaning is, that angels were present, and assisted, at the giving of the law. See Excursus VIII.

Ἐγένετο βέβαιος, *was ratified, was made firm and stable,* i. e. its threatenings and promises were exactly fulfilled; nothing which the law declared was null, or failed of being carried into execution. Comp. Rom. iv. 16. Heb. ix. 17. 2 Pet. i. 19.

Καὶ πᾶσα παράβασις καὶ παρακοὴ, *every transgression and act of disobedience.* The words are nearly, or quite synonymous by usage, both of them being employed in a secondary or derived sense. Παράβασις, (from παραβαίνω,) literally, *going beyond, passing by* any thing, is here applied to a *moral* action. So παρακοὴ comes from παρακούω, which means, first, *to hear in a careless or negligent manner;* and secondly, *to disobey,* i. e. it is the opposite of ἀκούω, *to hear,* and *to obey.* Παράβασις καὶ παρακοὴ taken together mean, *every kind of transgression,* or, *every kind of offence, against the law.*

Ἔνδικον μισθαποδοσίαν, *just retribution,* or *condign punishment.* Μισθαποδοσία designates the reward of retributive justice, i. e. punishment, as well as the reward for virtuous conduct; and this, in heathen as well as sacred writers.

296 COMMENTARY ON HEB. II. 4.

Ver. 3. Πῶς ἡμεῖς ἐκφευξόμεθα, *how shall we escape?* viz. escape the μισθαποδοσίαν reserved for transgressors. Comp. Heb. xii. 25. So Rom. ii. 3, ἐκφεύγειν τὸ κρίμα τοῦ Θεοῦ. So Æsch. Eumen. v. 756, ἐκφεύγειν αἵματος δίκην. Τηλικαύτης σωτηρίας, i. e. the Christian religion; for so the word σωτηρίας sometimes signifies. Comp. Jude ver. 3, perhaps Rom. xi. 11, and Heb. vi. 9. The full phrase would seem to be ὁ λόγος τῆς σωτηρίας, which is found in Acts xiii. 26. It is, however, the Christian religion, with all its promised blessings and tremendous threats, which is here designated by σωτηρία. How can we escape with impunity, *if we neglect* (ἀμελήσαντες) them? Ἀμελήσαντες here means more than simple *neglect*; it is plainly emphatic in this connexion, and means, *to treat with utter disregard* or *contempt*, such, namely, as would be implied in apostacy.

Ἥτις ἀρχὴν λαβοῦσα λαλεῖσθαι, equivalent to ἐν ἀρχῇ λαληθεῖσα, *which was at first declared* or *published*. The Greeks often use the phrase ἀρχὴν λαβὼν, for, *at first*, or *taking its rise, commencing its origin*. Τοῦ Κυρίου, viz. Christ.

Ὑπὸ τῶν ἀκουσάντων εἰς ἡμᾶς ἐβεβαιώθη, *was confirmed unto us by those who heard* [him,] i. e. the Lord, or, *by those who heard* [it,] i.e. the gospel, σωτηρίαν. Ἐβεβαιώθη here means *delivered* or *declared with confirmation to us*, i. e. Christians. So Theophylact, διεπορθμεύθη εἰς ἡμᾶς βεβαίως καὶ πιστῶς, *was propagated to us surely and faithfully*. Because the writer here says εἰς ἡμᾶς, some critics draw the conclusion that Paul could not have been the author of this epistle, since he received the gospel immediately from Christ himself, Gal. i. 12, and not from those who heard the Saviour declare it. But who that reads his writings with care, can fail to observe how often he employs κοίνωσις, when addressing Christians? Cicero says, in one of his orations, Νος *perdimus rempublicam.* Shall we conclude that he did not write the oration, because he did not himself destroy the republic? See on ἡμᾶς, under ver. 1, and also Introduction, § 27, No. 17.

Ver. 4. Συνεπιμαρτυροῦντος τοῦ Θεοῦ σημείοις τε καὶ τέρασι, *God attesting, being co-witness*, viz. to the truth of what was preached, *by various wonderful events*, Σημεῖον, as used often in the New Testament and in the Septuagint, means, *any extraordinary sign,* or *miraculous event,* designed to show the certainty that something which had been promised or predicted should take place, or that a prophet was what he professed to be. Τέρας, *portentum, prodigium, miracle,* has nearly the same meaning, and is very commonly joined with σημεῖον, in the New Testament. Both connected, mean, *various extraordinary events* or *prodigies,* designed to confirm, establish, or render credible, any prediction or declaration of Christ, or of his messengers. Heathen writers sometimes employ both words in connexion; e. g. Ælian, Var. Hist. XII. 57. The corresponding Hebrew phrase is, אֹתוֹת וּמוֹפְתִים, *signs and wonders,* i. e. wonderful signs or proofs of any thing. Such the people of God often required, and such were often given. See Gen. xv. 8—18; xxiv. 12—27. Judges vi. 17. 21. 36—40. 2 Kings, xix. 29. Isa. xxxviii. 7, 8; vii. 14—16, et alibi. Comp. Matt. xii. 38. xvi. 1—3.

Καὶ ποικίλαις δυνάμεσι, *and various miraculous powers.* Sometimes δύναμις is put for *miracle,* as Matt. vii. 22; xi. 20, 21. 23, et alibi. But as σημείοις και τερασι denote *miraculous events,* in our verse, I understand δυνάμεσι as referring here to the *miraculous powers* which were imparted to the primitive teachers of the Christian religion. In such a sense the word is employed, in Mark vi. 14. Acts vi. 8; x. 38. The Septuagint do not employ this word to translate either אוֹת or מוֹפְתִים, but always use σημεῖον and τέρατα.

What follows, is connected with the phrase just explained; viz. καὶ πνεύματος ἁγίου μερισμοῖς, literally, *and distributions of the Holy Spirit,* i. e. the imparting of divine influence; which refers particularly to the species of this influence, which consisted in the power of working miracles. See 1 Cor. xii. 6—11. Comp. also John vii. 39. Acts i. 5. 8; ii. 4. 17, 18. 33; v. 32; viii. 15—19; x. 44—47; xix. 1—6.

Ποικίλαις δυνάμεσι . . . . καὶ μερισμοῖς, if considered as a Hendyadis (ἓν διὰ δυοῖν,) may be thus rendered, *various miraculous powers, imparted by divine influence.* But I rather prefer the rendering which I have given it in the version, as μερισμοὶς probably designates the additional gifts of the Spirit, other than miraculous power.

Κατὰ τὴν αὐτοῦ θέλησιν, *as it seemed good in his* [God's] *sight, as he pleased;* or, *as the Holy Spirit pleased,* which last is favoured by 1 Cor. xii. 6—11.

The sum of the whole warning (ver. 1—4) is, " Beware that ye do not slight the gospel, whose threatenings are more to be dreaded than those of the law; inasmuch as the gospel is a revelation of a higher nature, and has been confirmed by more striking and more abundant miracles, wrought by divine power."

The writer, after having thus stopped for a moment to warn his readers against the consequences of defection from Christianity, returns to his subject, viz. the comparison of Christ with the angels. Having established, by appeals to the Old Testament (i. 5—14,) the superiority of the former over the latter, in several points of view; he now proceeds to show, that the new or Christian dispensation was not ordered or arranged (like the Mosaic one) by angels, but that the Son of Man, the Messiah, was, in his human nature, placed at the head of it. Now, as the Jews, one and all, conceded that the dispensation of the Messiah would be of a higher order than that of Moses, proof that Jesus was the sole mediator or head of the new dispensation, and that angels were not employed as mediators or *internuntii* in it, would satisfy them that Jesus was superior to the angels; since the place which he holds in the *new* economy, is higher than that which they had under the *old*, because the new economy itself is of a higher nature than the old. At the same time, an objection which a Jew, weak in Christian faith and strong in his attachment to the Mosaic institutions, would very naturally feel, is met, and tacitly answered by the apostle, in what follows. The unbelieving Jews, doubtless, urged upon those who professed an attachment to Christianity, the seeming absurdity of renouncing their subjection to a dispensation of which angels were the mediators, and of acknowledging a subjection to one of which the professed head and mediator appeared in our nature. The history of the objections made by the unbelieving Jews, to the claims of Jesus as being the Son of God (John x. 30—39, et alibi,) shows how very repulsive it was to their feelings, that one to all appearance like a man, and made up of flesh and blood in the same manner as themselves, should advance a claim to the exalted honours of a superior and divine nature. The sects of the Nazarenes and Ebionites, which arose even in the apostolic age, from professed Jewish Christians in Palestine, show how prone the Jewish Christians were, to feel doubts and difficulties about the claims of Jesus to a nature higher than the human, and to which divine honours were due.

No wonder, then, that the apostle found it necessary to meet, in our epistle, those doubts and difficulties with regard to the superior nature of the Christian dispensation, which were urged upon the minds of Jewish converts by the unbelieving Jews, who regarded Christ as a mere man. We shall see, however, that our author disposes of this difficulty, so as to further the great purpose of his general argument.

He concedes the fact entirely, that Jesus had a nature truly and properly human, ver. 6—18. But instead of granting that this proves the new dispensation to be inferior to that of Moses, he proceeds to adduce evidence from the Old Testament Scriptures, to show that man, or the human nature in the person of the Messiah, should be made Lord of the universe. Consequently, in this nature, Jesus the Messiah is superior to the angels. Of course, the possession by Jesus of a nature truly and properly human, does not at all prove either his inferiority, or the inferiority of the dispensation of which he is the head (ver. 6—9;) which meets an objection strongly urged upon the Hebrew Christians by their unbelieving brethren.

Nay, more; it was becoming that God should exalt Jesus, in consequence of his obedience unto death; a death necessary for the salvation of Jew and Gentile, ver. 9, 10. To suffer this death, he must needs take on him a nature like ours; and, as his object was the salvation of *men* (and not of *angelic beings*,) so he participated in the nature of men, in order that by *experience* he might know their sufferings, temptations, and trials, and thus be prepared, in a peculiar manner and in their own nature, to be compassionate, faithful, and ready to succour them, ver. 11—18.

The sum of the whole is: " The possession of a human nature by Jesus, is far from being a reason, why the ancient dispensation (of which angels were the *internuntii*) is preferable to the new one; for (1.) This very nature is exalted far above the angels. (2.) Without participating in this nature, Jesus could not have made expiation for sin by his death. And (3.) The possession of such a nature did contribute, in a peculiar and endearing manner, to constitute him such a Saviour as men could approach with the greatest boldness and confidence, in all their wants and all their woes."

Such appears to be the course of reasoning and thought, in Heb. ii. The words and phrases remain to be explained.

Ver. 5. Τὴν οἰκουμένην τὴν μέλλουσαν, equivalent to ὁ αἰὼν ὁ μέλλων, i. e. *the Christian dispensation*, the world as it will be in future, ὁ μέλλων, i. e. the world under the reign of Christ. See Wahl, on the word αἰών. The addition of the writer, περὶ ἧς λαλοῦμεν, shows that such is the sense of the phrase; for it is *Christianity*, to which he had just been urging the Hebrews to pay the strictest regard.

Ver. 6. Διεμαρτύρατο δέ που τὶς, *one in a certain place*, i. e. passage of Scripture, *bears this testimony*. The writer speaks to those who were supposed to be familiar with the Jewish Scriptures, and who needed only a reference to them, by quoting some of the words which any passage contained, in order that they might be found. For a Hebrew to acknowledge the *authority* of his own Scriptures, might be expected as a matter of course. The passage quoted here in Ps. viii. 4—6, exactly according to the version of the LXX.

Τί ἐστιν ἄνθρωπος, ὅτι μιμνήσκῃ οὑτοῦ; *what is man, that thou shouldest kindly remember him?* The secondary sense of μιμνήσκω is, *to remember with affection, to treat with kindness.* So the Heb. זָכַר; and so μιμνήσκεσθε, in Heb xiii. 3.

Ἢ υἱὸς ἀνθρώπου, ὅτι ἐπισκέπτῃ αὐτόν, *or the son of man that thou shouldest regard him!* The phrase υἱὸς ἀνθρώπου, is equivalent to ἄνθρωπος: just as in Hebrew, בֶּן אָדָם is equivalent to אָדָם. The subject is evidently the same as in the preceding clause, and υἱὸς ἀνθρώπου is employed merely for the sake of giving variety to the mode of expression. Ἐπισκέπτομαι, *to visit*, is usually, *to inspect*, or *look upon favourably, to watch over one* for his good, *to succour* him, *to assist* him. See Matt. xxv. 36. Luke i. 68. James i. 27. In the New Testament, it is used only in a sense which designates *inspecting with an eye of favour*.

But in the Septuagint it is also used for, *visiting in order to punish*; as is the Hebrew פָּקַד, e. g. Ex. xxxii. 34; xxxiv 7, et alibi. Our English word *regard* (taken in a good sense,) answers well to ἐπισκέπτομαι. The *classical* use of the word sometimes, though rarely, accords with the sense in which it is here employed.

Ver. 7. Ἠλάττωσας αὐτὸν βραχύ τι παρ ἀγγέλους, *thou hast made him but little inferior to the angels*. Παρὰ here means, *in comparison with;* as in ch. i. 4, παρ αὐτούς. Βραχύ τι may signify either *a little time*, or *a little in respect to degree* or *rank* : in which last case, it would be equivalent here to our English word *somewhat*. In the Septuagint it is employed in both these senses; as is also the Hebrew word מְעַט which, is here rendered by βραχὺ τι. In Ps. viii. 6, מְעַט seems pretty plainly to refer to *inferiority of rank* or *station*, and not to *time*. But in our text, most recent commentators have maintained that it refers to *time;* and consequently, that the apostle has merely *accommodated* the passage in Ps. viii. to an expression of his own views. But such a mode of interpretation is, at least, unnecessary here. The object which the writer of our epistle has in view, is not to prove how little time Christ appeared in our nature; but that, although he did possess a nature truly human, still, in this nature he was exalted above the angels. Ἠλάττωσας αὐτὸν βραχὺ τι παρ ἀγγέλους, then, simply designates the *condition of man*, as being in itself but little inferior to that of the angels. Man is made in the image of God, Gen. i. 26, 27; ix. 6. It is plainly the *dignity* of man which the Psalmist intends to describe, when he says, וַתְּחַסְּרֵהוּ מְעַט מֵאֱלֹהִים. To such a view of his design, the context of this passage in Ps. viii. leads us. The Psalmist looks abroad, and surveys the heavens in all their splendour and glory, and then, with deep sensations of his own comparative insignificance, he exclaims, " What is man! that thou shouldest be mindful of him! or the son of man, that thou shouldest regard him! Yet, [וְ *but, yet*] thou hast made him but little inferior (וַתְּחַסְּרֵהוּ מְעַט) to the angels, thou hast crowned him," &c. The nature of the case, and the nature of poetic parallelism, here require such an interpretation of the passage in the original Psalm.

But the very same interpretation of it is altogether apposite to the purpose of the writer, in Heb. ii. 1. What is his design? To prove that Christ, in his human nature, is exalted above the angels. How does he undertake to prove this? First, by showing that this nature itself is made but little inferior to that of the angels, ἠλάττωσας αὐτὸν βραχύ τι παρ ἀγγέλους; and next, that it has been exalted to the empire of the world

"Thou hast crowned him with glory and honour, and set him over the work of thy hands."

But suppose, now, that we should render βραχὺ τι, *for a little while ;* what object, which the writer designs to accomplish, is accomplished by such an assertion? It would not contain any proof of the *dignity* of Christ in his human nature, but merely of *temporary inferiority,* i. e. inferiority during the time of his incarnation. Clearly it is not the present object of the writer to prove this. Much more to the purpose does he appear to reason, when we understand him as using βραχὺ τι, in the same sense as מְעַט is used by the Psalmist. The passage thus understood, renders the vindications (attempted by many) of the *liberties,* which the writer is alleged to have taken with Ps. viii. 6, quite unnecessary.

Παρ ἀγγέλους, in the Hebrew מֵאֱלֹהִים. On the subject of rendering אֱלֹהִים, ἀγγέλοι, see on ch. i. 6. If we insist that the *usual* meaning of the Hebrew word *Elohim* should be retained, the argument would be still stronger, to prove the dignity of the Messiah in his human nature. *Thou hast made him but little inferior to Elohim,* would represent him at least, as ἰσάγγελος, if not above, the angels. See Gen. i. 26, 27, from which the language here, and in the sequel, appears to be borrowed.

But how could the apostle use παρ ἀγγελους, as conveying the sense of מֵאֱלֹהִים? In answer to this, we may say, (1.) It conveys no meaning that is untrue. If man is but little below Elohim, surely he is not much inferior to the angels. (2.) As angels are here compared by the writer with man, or rather, the angelic with the human nature in the person of the Saviour, the passage, as it stands in the Septuagint, and as the apostle has quoted it, is apposite to his purpose; although it claims, in fact, *less* for the argument, than would be claimed, by insisting that the word אֱלֹהִים should be interpreted as usual. As the writer was addressing those who used the Septuagint version of the Scriptures, nothing could be more natural than to quote that version as it should, unless it conveyed an idea that was essentially erroneous. This is just what we do, every day, with our English version of the Scriptures, without suspecting that we are violating any rule of propriety.

Besides the LXX. the Chaldee has rendered מֵאֱלֹהִים by מִמַלְאֲכַיָּא, i. e. παρ ἀγγέλους. With this rendering Aben Ezra agrees; as do Mendelsohn, Michaelis, Dathe, and others. But, as the writer seems to refer, in Ps. viii. 6—9, to Gen. i. 26—28, the probability that

אֱלֹהִים in Ps. viii. 6, means, *God*, i. e. that the author of the Psalm originally meant to convey this idea when he used it, is pretty strong. Still the apostle, by using the version of the LXX, παρ ἀγγέλους, has, as I have already said, assumed less in the argument, than the original would have given him; and at the same time, he has taken a version, which in its present shape is exactly apposite to his purpose, i. e. to show, that if a comparison of Christ with the angels be made, it will be seen, that during his humiliation he was but little inferior to them, while in his exaltation in the human nature, he is far above them.

Δόξῃ καὶ τιμῇ ἐστεφάνωσας αὐτόν, *thou hast crowned him with glory and honour*, or, *with exalted honour*. Δόξῃ καὶ τιμῇ are nearly equivalent or synonymous; and two synonymous nouns, thus constructed, are expressive of intensity, agreeably to the well-known usage of the Hebrew language, from which this idiom is borrowed. In the original, וְכָבוֹד וְהָדָר תְּעַטְּרֵהוּ, which is very literally rendered in the Greek.

But what is the *exalted honour* conferred upon the human nature of Jesus? Καὶ κατέστησας αὐτὸν ἐπὶ τὰ ἔργα τῶν χειρῶν σου, *thou hast set him over the works of thy hands*, i. e. thou hast given him dominion over the creation. Ἔργα τῶν χειρῶν σου means simply, *the works which thou hast made*, i. e. thy works. The form of expression is borrowed from the mode of human operations, in which *hands* are the most conspicuous instrument. Καθίστημι, *sisto, colloco, statuo.* It should be noted, however, that this clause is omitted in some Codices of good authority; such as B. D. and several others.

Ver. 8. Πάντα ὑπέταξας ὑποκάτω τῶν ποδῶν αὐτοῦ, *thou hast subjected all things to him*, i. e. given him universal dominion. The phrase, *to put under one's feet*, denotes, to put in a state of complete, entire subjection. See Excursus IX.

The writer proceeds to comment on the quotation just made. Ἐν γὰρ τῷ ὑποτάξαι αὐτῷ τὰ πάντα, οὐδὲν ἀφῆκεν αὐτῷ ἀνυπότακτον, i. e. the expression is one of universality, it makes no exception, but only God himself; comp. 1 Cor. xv. 27.

Νῦν δὲ οὔπω ὁρῶμεν αὐτῷ τὰ πάντα ὑποτεταγμένα, *at present, indeed, we do not see all things yet subjected to him.* Ὑποτεταγμένα, *subject to his ordering, arrangement* or *disposal*. In other words, 'This prophecy of the Psalmist is not, as yet, wholly fulfilled; but so much of it has been accomplished, that we may regard it as a pledge, that a fulfilment of the rest will certainly follow.' So the sequel.

Ver. 9. Τὸν δὲ βραχύ τι . . . γεύσηται θανάτου, *but we see Jesus, who was made but little inferior to the angels, crowned with glory and honour on account of the suffering of death, after that he had, by the grace of God, tasted of death for all,* i. e. for Jew and Gentile. So I understand this much controverted and somewhat difficult passage. Two objections against the superiority of Christ over angels, were very naturally urged by the unbelieving Jews upon the believing ones. (1.) Christ was a man. (2.) He suffered an ignominious death. To the first, the apostle replied in the quotation which precedes, and on which he is commenting. But in doing this, he also suggests the consideration, that the death of Jesus, so far from proving his condition to be inferior to that of the angels, was immediately connected with his exaltation to glory, and with the salvation of the world.

It would be tedious to recount all the various interpretations which have been given to particular parts of the ninth verse. I limit myself merely to stating the reasons of the interpretation which I have given.

Δόξῃ καὶ τιμῇ ἐστεφανωμένον, *crowned with the highest honour,* διὰ τὸ πάθημα τοῦ θανάτου, *on account of his suffering death.* See the same sentiment in Phil. ii. 8—11; Heb. xii. 2. Compare John xvii. 4, 5; Heb. v. 7—9; Eph. i. 20—23; Rev. iii. 21.

Ὅπως, the great mass of commentators have translated, *ut, eum in finem ut, unde sequitur ut,* &c. But how was Christ crowned with glory and honour, that he might taste death? To avoid this difficulty, most of them transpose the clause, ὅπως χάριτι, κ. τ. λ. so as to connect it with the first clause of the verse, and translate thus, *Jesus, made for a little time lower than the angels, in order that* [ut, ut sic] *he might taste of death,* &c. But the apostle's object here, is not to show simply that Jesus possessed a nature in which he might taste of death; but that the suffering of death in it, (a fact conceded by all,) is no reason why he should be deemed inferior to the angels. Consequently the turn given to the passage, by the above transposition and explanation, is inapposite to the purpose of the writer.

That ὅπως generally means, *that, so that, in order that,* &c.; particularly, that it has this meaning in most instances where it occurs in the New Testament, there can be no reasonable doubt. But ὅπως also means, *cum, quando, postquam, when, after, after that.* So it means, plainly, in Acts iii. 19, although Wahl has overlooked the passage. So also in Herod. i. 17. Aristoph. Nub. 61. Soph. Œdip. Col. 1638. Homer. Il. XII. 208. Odys. III. 373; XXII. 22. Eurip. Phœnis. 1155.

1464. This sense also Hoogeveen, Zeunius, Ernesti, Schleusner, and Schneider, assign to it. Ὅπως is construed, more usually, with the future indicative, or with the subjunctive first or second aorist, in case these tenses are found in any verb. In the instances before us, it is followed by γεύσηται, in the subjunctive first aorist, middle voice. It may then be rendered by the *past* time, (as I have translated it;) just as in the cases where the formula ὅπως πληρωθῇ occurs, it is often rendered, or should be rendered, *so that there was an accomplishment.* The only difference in the latter case is, that the voice is passive; which, however, does not affect the question about the mode of rendering the tense.

This method of interpreting the verse frees us from the very great embarrassments, which are presented by most of the others; and the sentiment becomes plain and apposite. " Jesus did indeed take on him our nature, and suffer in it; but his sufferings were the means of advancing him to supreme dignity, after he had by them procured salvation for the human race, ὑπὲρ παντός. So long, then, as the highest glory was consequent upon the sufferings of Jesus, and the salvation of Jew and Gentile was accomplished by it, surely the death of Christ can never prove that he is inferior to the angels." In this way, all the reasoning of the writer seems to be apposite to his purpose.

Χάριτι Θεοῦ means, *by the goodness, kindness, mercy of God.* Ὑπὲρ παντός means, *all men without distinction,* i. e. both Jew and Gentile. The same view is often given of the death of Christ. See John iii. 14—17; iv. 42; xii. 32. 1 John ii. 2; iv. 14. 1 Tim. ii. 3, 4. Tit. ii. 11. 2 Pet. iii. 7. Compare Rom. iii. 29, 30; x. 11—13. In all these and the like cases, the words *all*, and *all men,* evidently mean, Jew and Gentile. They are opposed to the Jewish idea, that the Messiah was connected appropriately and exclusively with the Jews, and that the blessings of the kingdom were appropriately, if not exclusively, theirs. The sacred writers mean to declare, by such expressions, that Christ died really and truly as well, and as much, for the Gentiles as for the Jews; that there is no difference at all in regard to the privileges of any one who may belong to his kingdom; and that all men, without exception, have equal and free access to it. But the considerate interpreter, who understands the nature of this idiom, will never think of seeking, in expressions of this kind, proof of the final salvation of *every individual* of the human race. Nor do they, when strictly scanned by the *usus loquendi* of the New Testament, decide directly against the views of those who advocate what is called a *particular redemption*. The question, in all these phrases, evidently respects the *offer* of salvation, the opportunity to acquire it through a Redeemer; not the actual application of promises, the fulfilment of which is connected only with repentance and faith. But whether such an offer can be made with sincerity to those who are reprobates, (and whom the Saviour knows are and will be such,) consistently with the grounds which the advocates for particular redemption maintain, is a question for the theologian, rather than the commentator, to discuss.

Γεύσηται θανάτου, *taste of death,* i. e. *experience death, suffer it.* So the Hebrew writers use the word טָעַם for *experience;* and classic Greek authors, the word γεύομαι in the same sense. E. g. Ps. xxxiv. 9. Sibyll. Orac. I. p. 164, 'Αδὰμ γευσάμενος θανάτου. Eunapius de Porphyrio, " *Porphyry* praised the spell of purity, καὶ διὰ πείρας γευσάμενος, *and first tried* [tasted] *it himself.*" Philo (de vita Mosis, p. 632,) ἡ διάνοια τῶν γευσαμένων ὁσιότητος, *the mind of those who have experienced* [tasted] *holiness.*

Ver. 10. "Επρεπε γὰρ αὐτῷ δἰ ὃν τὰ πάντα καὶ δἰ οὗ τὰ πάντα, *it became him, for whom all things* [were made,] *and by whom all things* [were made;] i. e. it became the supreme Lord and Creator of all things. The writer leaves his readers to feel and acknowledge the truth of this assertion, without stopping to offer proof of its correctness. The force of the appeal seems to lie in the tacit acknowledgment of all, that reward is properly consequent upon trial and approbation, and is not to be bestowed without them. Now, as Christ possessed a nature truly human, and as all men are, by the universal arrangement of a wise and overruling providence, subjected to trial; so it was proper or becoming in God, that Jesus should be subjected to trial in our nature, before he was advanced in it to glory.

Πολλοὺς υἱοὺς ἀγαγόντα, κ. τ. λ. This part of the verse contains an involved construction of the words, in respect to their order. The arrangement of the sense I take to be as follows: "Επρεπε γὰρ αὐτῷ .... διὰ παθημάτων τελειῶσαι τὸν ἀρχηγὸν τῆς σωτηρίας αὐτῶν, ἀγαγόντα πολλοὺς υἱοὺς εἰς δόξαν. *It became him,* τελειῶσαι τὸν ἀρχηγὸν. The word τέλειος means *full grown, of mature age,* either literally, or figuratively. In the latter sense it is employed in 1 Cor. ii. 6; *however, we speak the doctrines of wisdom,* ἐν τοῖς τελείοις. So Heb. v. 14, comprehending, as it were, both the above senses, where it is opposed to νήπιος. See also 1 Cor. xiv. 20. Eph. iv. 3, et alibi. Τέλειος also means *mature* in

x

a moral sense, i. e. *integer, just, free from vices, perfect*. It is also, very naturally, used in a secondary sense, to denote a *consummation* or *maturity* of our nature and happiness in a better world; e. g. 1 Cor. xiii. 10. Hence the verb τελειόω, formed from the adjective τέλειος, is often used to designate, *exaltation to a state of reward or happiness in a future world*. Among the Greeks, this verb was employed to designate the condition of those who, having run in the stadium, and proved to be victorious in the contest, were proclaimed as successful ἀγωνισαὶ, and had the honours and rewards of victory bestowed upon them. (So τέλος is used by the Greeks for *reward*, i. e. *consummation*; see Schleusner on τελειόω.) Such persons were τετελειωμένοι. In a sense like this is τελειόω usually employed, with reference to Jesus, throughout the epistle to the Hebrews. E. g. ch. v. 9, τελειωθεὶς, *being advanced to a state of glory*; vii. 28, τετελειωμένον, id. The same sense the word has, in the verse under examination. In ver. 9, the writer had said, that, *on account of the suffering of death, Jesus was δόξῃ καὶ τιμῇ ἐστεφανωμένον*. Here he says, διὰ παθημάτων τελειῶσαι, *on account of sufferings to exalt to glory*, or, *to bestow the highest honours*. As the writer evidently says this, in commenting on the preceding expression, it is plain that διὰ παθημάτων τελειῶσαι is merely an equivalent for διὰ τὸ πάθημα τοῦ θανάτου δόξῃ καὶ τιμῇ ἐστεφανωμένον. So Theophylact; " τελείωσις here means, δόξαν ἣν ἐδοξάσθη."

Τὸν ἀρχηγὸν σωτηρίας αὐτῶν, *auctor salutis, the author of salvation;* so it is usually interpreted. So Chrysostom, αἴτιος, ὁ τὴν σωτηρίαν τεκὼν. Probably the phrase, ἀρχηγὸς σωτηρίας αὐτῶν, may mean here, the same as ἀρχηγὸν καὶ σωτῆρα in Acts v. 31, i. e. *their Prince and Saviour*. In Acts iii. 15, ἀρχηγὸν τῆς ζωῆς is applied to Jesus; and in Heb. xii. 2, ἀρχηγὸν τῆς πίστεως; which would rather favour the first interpretation. The sense, however, seems to be substantially expressed, if we render, *on account of sufferings, to exalt to a state of glory their Prince and Saviour*. Thus understood, the passage contains admirable matter of exhortation to the Hebrew Christians, to persevere in their adherence to Christianity, amid all their trials and sufferings; for Jesus their Prince and Saviour himself suffered, and was exalted to glory by his sufferings. If Jesus himself, then, exalted as he was, endured suffering, how could they expect to be exempt from it? Yet, if they persevered in their adherence to him, like him they would be τετελειωμένοι.

Ver. 11. Ὅ,τε γὰρ ἁγιάζων καὶ οἱ ἁγιαζόμενοι ἐξ ἑνὸς πάντες. The word ἁγιάζω seems not to have been well understood here, by most commentators, and requires, in order to explain the sense in which it is used in our epistle, a particular investigation. Ἁγιάζω corresponds to the Hebrew קָדֵשׁ הִקְדִּישׁ, which often means, *to consecrate to God as an offering* ; e. g. Lev. xxii. 2, מִקְדָּשִׁים לִי, Sept. ἁγιάζουσί μοι ; chap. xxii. 3, יַקְדִּישׁוּ, Sept. ἁγιάζωσι ; Exod. xiii. 2, קַדֶּשׁ לִי, Sept. ἁγίασον μοι, et alibi. The verb קָדַשׁ also means, by a natural association of ideas, *to expiate, to make atonement for* ; e. g. Job i. 5, יְקַדֵּשׁ, *he made atonement for them,* where, however, the Sept. has ἐκαθάριζεν αὐτούς ; so Exod. xix. 10, 14, and Josh. vii. 13, according to Gesenius, where the Sept. has ἅγνισον, ἡγίασε, and ἁγίασον. Comp. also Ezek. xliv. 19. The verb ἁγιάζω also corresponds, in the Septuagint, to the Hebrew כִּפֶּר, which is the appropriate word to designate *the making of an atonement, to expiate ;* e. g. Exod. xxix. 33, *they shall eat those things,* אֲשֶׁר כֻּפַּר בָּם, *with which expiation was made,* Sept. ἐν οἷς ἡγιάσθησαν ἐν αὐτοῖς ; Exod. xxix. 36, *and thou shalt purify the altar,* בְּכַפֶּרְךָ עָלָיו, *when thou makest an expiatory sacrifice upon it,* Sept. ἐν τῷ ἁγιάζειν σε ἐπ᾽ αὐτῷ. From the *usus loquendi* of the Hebrew and the Sept. it is plain, then, that ἁγιάζω may mean *to make expiation, to atone.*

Our epistle presents some plain instances of the use of ἁγιάζω in this sense. Eg. ch. x. 10, *according to which will* ἡγιασμένοι ἐσμεν, *we are atoned for,* i. e. expiation is made for us. How ? The writer immediately subjoins, διὰ τῆς προσφορᾶς τοῦ σώματος Ἰησοῦ Χριστοῦ ἐφάπαξ ; which necessarily refers ἡγιασμένοι to the *propitiatory offering* of Christ ; and consequently it has the sense which I have given to it. So ch. xiii. 11, 12, " For the bodies of those animals, whose blood was carried into the sanctuary by the high priest, as a sin-offering, were burned without the camp ; wherefore Jesus, ἵνα ἁγιάσῃ the people with his own blood, suffered without the gate ;" where ἁγιάσῃ plainly means, *to make expiation for, to atone for.* Both of these passages compare well with that under consideration ; and all three predicate ἁγιασμὸς of the sufferings and death of Christ ; for in our context, in the very next preceding clause, the writer has spoken of Christ as τετελειωμένον διὰ παθημάτων ; and he had just declared, that " Jesus, by the grace of God, *had tasted of death for all men.*"

We may then render ὅ,τε ἁγιάζων καὶ οἱ ἁγιαζόμενοι, *both he who makes expiation for sin, and they for whom expiation is made,* אֲשֶׁר כֻּפַּר לָהֶם. The *usus loquendi* of the epistle seems not merely to justify, but to demand, this interpretation.

'Εξ ἑνὸς πάντες, i. e. have God for their common father. So most commentators. Some say, " Have Adam for their father ;" others, " Abraham." The context leads me to doubt whether any of these interpretations is correct. Ver. 14, et seq. very plainly refers to a community of nature, and states the grounds or reason why such a community existed. 'Εξ ἑνὸς then means, that Christ, and those for whom he atoned by his sufferings, were ἐξ ἑνὸς γενοῦς, i. e. possessed in common of the same nature, see ver. 14. The reasoning of the writer, when the words are thus understood, is altogether apposite. It seems to be this : " That Christ had a nature truly human, is no objection to regarding him as a Saviour exalted above the angels, and altogether adapted to the wants and woes of the human race. In the human nature he suffered, and was advanced to glory ; in it he made atonement for men ; in it he sustains a most endearing relation to those for whom he made expiation, he sympathizes with them, ver. 17, 18, and they are united to him as brethren having one common nature, ἐξ ἑνὸς πάντες, κ. τ. λ. ver. 11—13.

Δι ἣν αἰτίαν . . . . καλεῖν, on account of which, i. e. because he possesses the same nature in common with them, *he disdains not to call them his brethren.* Οὐκ ἐπαισχύνεται, Chrysostom says, is used with regard to a person of higher rank, who condescends to associate with those of a lower standing. But if Christ were *merely* a man, and nothing more, where (we may ask with Abresch) would be either the great condescension, or particular kindness, manifested in calling men his brethren? If, however, he possessed a higher nature, if ἐκένωσε ἑαυτὸν, μορφὴν δούλου λαβὼν, Phil. ii. 7 ; if ἐταπείνωσε ἑαυτὸν, Phil. ii. 8 ; then was it an act of peculiar kindness and condescension in him, to call men his *brethren.* It is this high privilege, to which men have attained, that the apostle is endeavouring to establish and illustrate ; and all this affords additional reason not to think diminutively of Jesus, as possessing a human nature.

Having introduced the proposition, that " Christ, possessing a nature truly human, regards men as his brethren ;" the writer appeals, as is usual with him, to the Old Testament, in confirmation of this sentiment, and to show the Hebrews, that it is no new doctrine respecting the Messiah which he inculcates.

Ver. 12. Λέγων, *saying,* i. e. since he (Christ) says : ἀπαγγελῶ, κ. τ. λ. The passage is quoted from Ps. xxii. 22 [xxi. 22,] where, for the Hebrew אֲסַפְּרָה, the LXX. have διηγήσομαι ; instead of which, our text employs its equivalent or synonyme, ἀπαγγελῶ. Such departures from the Septuagint are very common, in the New Testament quotations.

That the twenty-second Psalm relates to the Messiah, the Jews themselves confess, (see Dindorf in loc.;) and the history of his death seems, indeed, to be a kind of practical commentary upon it. I can find nothing in the Psalm which forbids the application of it to the Messiah; although I can find enough to satisfy me that it is quite inapplicable to David. The general conversion of the nations to God (ver. 27—32) accords well with the gospel dispensation, but not with the Jewish; which from its very nature could not be a *universal* religion; for how could all nations, from the extremities of the earth, ever go up three times in a year to Jerusalem, to worship and to offer sacrifice there? And can it be rationally supposed, that David uttered such words as those to which I have just adverted, in reference merely to Judaism?

The whole object of the present quotation is merely to show, that Christ is exhibited in the Jewish Scriptures, as having recognized men as his brethren, ἀδελφοὺς.

Ἐν μέσῳ ἐκκλησίας ὑμνήσω σε, *among the assembly will I praise thee,* i. e. in or among the assembly of my brethren, of men, will I celebrate thy praise. In the Hebrew, the words לְאֶחָי and בְּתוֹךְ קָהָל correspond to each other, and are equivalent, as to the subjects comprised in them. The first part only of the apostle's quotation, is directly to the point which he is labouring to illustrate and confirm; the second part, (as in many like cases,) is cited principally because of the intimate connexion which exists between it and the preceding parallelism, and because the memory of those whom he addressed would be assisted, by a quotation at large of the whole verse.

Ver. 13. Καὶ πάλιν, *again the Scripture says,* ἐγὼ ἔσομαι πεποιθὼς ἐπ' αὐτῷ, *I confide in him,* or, *I will confide in him.* But whence is this quoted? In Ps. xviii. 3., the Hebrew has אֶחֱסֶה בּוֹ which the LXX. render, ἐλπιῶ αὐτῷ; in 2 Sam. xxii. 3, the same Hebrew words occur, which they render according to the phraseology of our text, πεποιθὼς ἔσομαι ἐπ' αὐτῷ. Some critics have defended the opinion, that the quotation of the apostle is from one of these passages. But as it is plain, not only that the Messiah is not described or alluded to in these passages, but also that the Jews have never been accustomed to interpret them as referring to him; so there is surely no need of defending this position, if another passage as apposite as these can be found, which is less exceptionable in regard to its application. Critics are pretty generally agreed, therefore, that Isa. viii. 17, is quoted, the Hebrew of which is וְקִוֵּיתִי לוֹ, the Septuagint version of which is the same as our quotation. This, considered in connexion with the quotation immediately following, (which is taken from Isa. viii. 18,) renders it altogether probable, that the writer had this place of scripture, rather than either of the others, in his mind, when he made the two quotations in question. The Hebrew וְקִוֵּיתִי לוֹ, may be rendered, *I will wait for him*, or, *I will trust in him*. The latter is adopted by the Septuagint, and by the apostle.

Καὶ πάλιν ἰδοὺ, κ. τ. λ. has been adduced as an argument that the passage quoted here must be from a different part of scripture, and not from the same with that of the quotation immediately preceding. But this does not follow; for in this same epistle, ch. x. 30, a quotation is made from Deut. xxxii. 35, and another from Deut. xxxii. 36, with καὶ πάλιν between them as here. In such a case, καὶ πάλιν is to be rendered, *and further*, or, *and moreover*.

The argument in this case appears to be this. 'Men exercise trust or confidence in God. This is predicated of them as dependent, and possessing a feeble nature. The same thing is predicated of the Messiah; and consequently he possesses a nature like theirs, and therefore they are his brethren; ἐξ ἑνὸς πάντες.' See Excursus X.

Ver. 14. Κεκοινώνηκε σαρκὸς καὶ αἵματος, *participated in flesh and blood*, i. e. possessed a human nature, a body made up of flesh and blood. See 1 Cor. xv. 50. Eph. vi. 12; and comp. Matt. xvi. 17. Gal. i. 16. Sirach xiv. 18. *The children*, παιδία, here mentioned, are the same that are described in the preceding verse, viz. the disciples, the spiritual children of the Messiah.

Καὶ αὐτὸς παραπλησίως μετέσχε τῶν αὐτῶν. Here μετέσχε is a synonyme of κεκοινώνηκε, *participated in*. Παραπλησίως is equivalent to ὁμοίως, *in the same manner as, as well as*. The Docetæ exchanged παραπλησίως here for ὁμοίως, and then construed ὁμοίως as indicating only an *appearance* similar to flesh and blood; in opposition to whom the Christian fathers maintained that παραπλησίως signified οὐ δοκητῶς ἀλλ' ἀληθινῶς, οὐ φανταστικῶς ἀλλ' ὄντως.

Τῶν αὐτῶν, i. e. σαρκὸς καὶ αἵματος. The meaning is, that Christ had a natural body, truly corporeal and mortal. With this he was endowed, in order that he might suffer death in it, and by that death vanquish the spiritual enemy of mankind, the great adversary of souls.

"Ινα διὰ θανάτου . . . τὸν διάβολον, *that by his death he might subdue him who has a deadly power, that is, the devil.* Καταργέω is scarcely used by Greek writers, and, when it is employed, it has the sense of *delaying, rendering inactive, hindering,* i. q. ἐμποδίζειν, which is used to explain it, by the Scholiast on Eurip. Phœniss. 760. In this sense, it is often used in the Apocrypha. In the New Testament, the use of the word is not unfrequent; but with some latitude of signification, as may be seen by the lexicons. Here it means, *to render inefficacious,* or, *to subdue,* viz. Satan, the spiritual enemy of man, who has *a deadly power;* comp. 1 Cor. xv. 24—26. 2 Tim. i. 10. I understand τὸν τὸ κράτος τοῦ θανάτου ἔχοντα, in this plain and simple manner; which renders all the speculations, about the power of the devil to inflict the sentence of *natural death* upon men, unnecessary; and equally so, all the efforts to show what the Rabbins have taught about Sammael, the angel of death, מַלְאַךְ הַמָּוֶת. That a deadly power, i. e. a power of leading men to sin, and consequently of bringing them under sentence of spiritual death, is ascribed to Satan in the New Testament, is sufficiently plain: see John xvi. 11; xii. 31; xiv. 30. Eph. ii. 2; vi. 12. Col. ii. 15. 2 Cor. iv. 4; et alibi. In 1 John iii. 8, is a passage altogether of the same tenour as ours. *To render null the deadly power of Satan,* is to prevent the effects of it as bringing men to incur the sentence of spiritual death, i. e. to redeem them from the effects of such a sentence, or to redeem them from the curse of the law, Gal. iii. 13; comp. Rom. v. 9. seq. 1 Thess. i. 10. Even the temporal consequences of death are removed by Christ, 1 Cor. xv. 26. 45. 52, seq. Thus interpreted, we have a plain sense of the passage, and one analogous to numerous other parts of the Scriptures.

Ver. 15. Καὶ ἀπαλλάξῃ τουτοὺς . . . δουλείας, *and free those* [from condemnation,] *who, during their whole lives, though fear of condemnation, had been exposed to a state of bondage.* Ἀπαλλάξῃ means primarily, *to remove, to depel, to depart.* But here, (as sometimes in classic authors,) it means, *to free, to liberate.* So Theophylact, ἐλευθηρῶσαι. It may be questionable, whether it is connected with θάνατος understood, or with δουλεία. Either way of construing it would make good sense, and be apposite to the design of the writer. I have preferred to connect it with θάνατος, because of the sentiment, in the preceding verse, which respects the θάνατον inflicted by Satan, i. e. the condemning sentence of the law incurred in consequence of sin, committed through the wiles or temptation of Satan.

Φόβῳ θανάτου, I understand as referring to the fear of that condemnation or punishment, to which sin exposes men; not to the fear of natural death; an evil from which no precaution can deliver us, and which Christians as well as others must suffer, notwithstanding the death of Christ. But the death of Christ has freed them from suffering that condemnation or punishment which they feared, in a future life. This seems to be the obvious meaning of the writer; although it has been generally overlooked.

Διὰ παντὸς τοῦ ζῆν, i. q. διὰ πάσης τῆς ζωῆς, the infinitive mode being here used, as it often is in the Greek classics, as a mere noun. But it is not the usage of the older Greek writers, to put the infinitive *nominascens* after an adjective, as here. We may, therefore, understand χρόνου as implied after παντὸς The later Greek, however, affords examples like ours; e. g. τὸ ἀδιάκριτον ζῆν, τὸ ἀληθινὸν ζῆν, ἐκ τοῦ προκειμένου ζῆν, Ignat. Ep. ad. Trall.

Ἔνοχοι ἦσαν δουλείας, *had been subjected*, [obnoxious, exposed] *to servitude*, i. e. subject to a depressed and miserable condition, like that of slaves under a tyrannical master. Ἔνοχος comes from ἐνέχομαι, *adstringor*, and so means, *adstrictus*, *alligatus*. It usually governs the dative, as Matt. v. 21, 22, bis; and thus in classic writers. But it also governs the genitive, as here; e. g. Matt. xxvi. 66. Mark iii. 29; xiv. 64. 1 Cor. xi. 27. James ii. 10. Δουλείας means, the servile and depressed condition of those who are exercised with the fear of death, i. e. of future misery. It is the death of Christ which delivers them from the condemnation, the anticipation or fear of which had often, during their lives, depressed them, or made them unhappy. Comp. John viii. 32, 35, where, however, the δουλεία referred to is the servitude of sin. Here it is the condition, into which the fear of future condemnation casts Christians.

The deliverance spoken of, is accomplished by anticipation here, Rom. viii. 14, 17; but fully and finally, in another world, where the pious are admitted to a state of confirmed happiness. Διὰ παντος τοῦ ζῆν ἔνοχοι ἦσαν δουλείας, does not necessarily imply, that *the whole time of life* had been actually occupied with a state of fear and depression, δουλείας; but that during the whole of it, those who are delivered had been, more or less, *exposed* to agitation by fears of this nature. From the object of such fears Christ delivers, or will deliver, them; and this is the simple sentiment of the text.

Ver. 16. Οὐ γὰρ δήπου ἀγγέλων ἐπιλαμβάνεται, *besides, he did not extend aid at all to the angels;* another reason why he took on him a nature that was human. He came to the aid of *man;* he became like him, so as the more intimately to sympathize with him, and to help him. Δήπου, *profecto, omnimodo, certe,* strengthens the affirmation, i. e. gives intensity to it. Ἐπιλαμβάνεται, lit. *to grasp,* or, *to take hold of with the hand.* Hence, figuratively, (1.) *To assert one's right* to a thing; to *lay hold of it* as one's own; and (2.) *To aid, help, succour, to take hold of* when falling, or in danger. In the Septuagint, it answers to the Hebrew חָזַק, אָחַז; תָּפַשׂ. The Christian fathers have applied it to the assumption of an angelic nature, which they suppose the writer here denies. But the *usus loquendi* is against this; and the context also. For the apostle had just asserted above, that Jesus took on him a nature *human;* and it would be mere repetition of the same sentiment here, if we construe ver. 16 as meaning thus: "He did not assume the angelic nature, but that of the seed of Abraham." But if the argument be, that "Jesus assumed the human nature, because he was *to aid* men and not angels," then the sixteenth verse contains a reason why the Saviour did and should take on him the nature of man; viz. that it was altogether accordant with the great object of his mission.

Σπέρματος Ἀβραὰμ, *progeny of Abraham.* In such a sense, profane as well as sacred writers use σπέρμα. Is it the *natural* or *spiritual* seed of Abraham, which is here meant? Either will make good sense, and agree with the object of the writer. *Believers* are the children of Abraham, Gal. iii. 7; and Gentiles as well as Jews, Rom. iv. 12—18; ix. 7, 8; iii. 29, 30. So, the assertion that Christ died, ὑπὲρ παντὸς, (ver. 9,) does not disagree with the assertion that he helped the seed of Abraham, who are both Jews and Gentiles. But, although this interpretation may be sufficiently justified to render it worthy of acceptation, I am inclined to believe, that it does not give the original sense of the writer. He is addressing *Jews.* He says, "Christ had a human nature; this it behoved him to possess, for he came to help the seed of Abraham, i. e. those who, being descended from Abraham, possessed a nature that was human." His assertion extends merely to such as he was addressing. But surely this would not imply a denial that he helped any others, who were possessed of the same nature. So far is it from this, that it implies the contrary; for the amount of the assertion is, "He came to help those who possessed a nature such as that which he had assumed."

Ver. 17. Ὅθεν, an illative particle, *whence*, i. e. because he was to help the seed of Abraham. Ὤφειλε......ὁμοιωθῆναι, *he must needs be made like unto his brethren*, i. e. to men, ver. 10—12. Κατὰ πάντα, i. e. in all things requisite to constitute a nature truly human. The meaning is, that he should be wanting in none of the innocent infirmities, and in none of the sympathies, of man's nature. To deduce more than this from the expression now in question, would be to do what the writer plainly never designed should be done.

But why? Ἵνα ἐλεήμων γένηται καὶ πιστὸς ἀρχιερεὺς, *that he might be a compassionate and faithful high priest.* Ἐλεήμων, *merciful, sympathizing with those who are in distress.* As those are best adapted to do this, who have themselves been sufferers; so Jesus took on him our nature, in order that he might suffer in it. Πιστὸς is either *faithful*, or, *worthy of trust* or *confidence*. In the former sense I take it here. Jesus assumed our nature, that he might qualify himself in a peculiar manner to exercise compassion toward us; and that he might discharge with fidelity the duty laid upon him as our high-priest. A priest to offer sacrifice for us, must be homogeneous with us. Such a priest was Jesus, faithful in discharging the duties of his office. What were those duties? They were τὰ πρὸς τὸν Θεὸν, *things which had respect to God*, i. e. services of a religious nature. The phrase πιστὸς......τὰ πρὸς τὸν Θεὸν, is elliptical. In full, it would be thus: κατὰ τὰ πράγματα τὰ πρὸς τὸν Θεὸν, *faithful as to things*, &c.

But what things were these? Ἱλάσκεσθαι τὰς ἁμαρτίας τοῦ λαοῦ. The common expression is, ἐξιλάσασθαι περί τινος; as in Lev. iv. 20. 26. 31. 35; or, ἐξιλάσασθι περὶ τῆς ἁμαρτίας τινὸς, Lev. v. 13; iv. 35. But ἐξιλάσασθαι ἁμαρτίας also occurs, Dan. ix. 24. 1 Sam. iii. 14. Sirach xxviii. 5. Ἱλάσκομαι means, *to render propitious, to appease*. But this sense it can have directly only when the *person* appeased is expressed, or understood, after the verb. Hence ἱλάσκεσθαι ἁμαρτίας must mean the same as כִּפֶּר חַטָּאת, *to make appeasement for sin, to cover sin, to make atonement for it.* The Septuagint sometimes translate כִּפֶּר by ἱλάσκομαι. Christ, then, as high-priest, was faithful to perform the peculiar duty of that office, which was, on the great day of atonement, to make a propitiatory sacrifice for the sins of the people. How he did this, is shewn in the sequel of the epistle. Here, only so much is asserted, as was requisite to enforce the considerations which the writer had immediately in view.

Ver. 18. Ἐν ᾧ γὰρ, *for since*, i. q. ὅτι γὰρ, Hebrew בַּאֲשֶׁר, *because that, inasmuch as*. Πέπονθεν αὐτὸς πειρασθεὶς, *he himself suffered when exercised with trials*. Πειράζω means *to try, to put to the proof*, in order to ascertain the disposition purpose, capacity, &c. of any one. This trial may be, (1.) For a good purpose ; by subjecting one to any evils or dangers, as God tried (נִסָּה) Abraham, Gen. xxii. 1 ; or, by placing him in circumstances either prosperous or adverse, that are of a peculiar nature, as God did Israel, Exod. xvi. 4. Judg. ii. 22. Trial may be, (2.) For an evil purpose ; as the Pharisees ἐπείρασαν Ἰησοῦν, by proposing to him ensnaring and subtile questions, Matt. xix. 3, seq. ; xxii. 18, 35, et sæpe ; or, by laying before any one inducements to sin, as Satan does before the minds of men, 1 Cor. vii. 5. 1 Thess. iii. 5 ; comp. James i. 13, 14. In both of these senses, Christ was tried. " It pleased the Lord to bruise him, and to put him to grief," Isa. liii. 10 ; and, " It became him, for whom and by whom are all things, to advance to glory our Prince and Saviour," διὰ παθημάτων, Heb. ii. 10. The same Saviour was solicited by Satan to sin, Matt. iv. 1, 3. Mark i. 13. Luke iv. 2. Understood in either way, then, the Saviour was tempted in like manner as we are, (κατὰ πάντα, καθ' ὁμοιότητα, Heb. iv. 15,) though without sin. That he did not yield to any excitement to sin, was owing to the strength of his virtue and holiness, not to the weakness of the temptation in itself considered. Temptation, in the second sense, is that which is presented to the mind as an inducement to sin, and does not relate to the actual state of the mind or person to which it is presented. Men tempt God ; they tempt Christ ; and so did Satan ; but there never was any disposition in Christ to yield to it.

There are two or three cases, however, in which the word πειράζω seems to denote yielding to sin, i. e. having the effect of πειρασμὸς produced upon one ; e. g. Gal. vi. 1, perhaps James i. 14 ; comp. ἀπείραστος, *not induced to sin*, in James i. 13. But this is an *unusual* sense of the word πειράζω and altogether inapplicable to the Saviour, who was " separate from sinners," Heb. vii. 26. Christ then, πειρασθεὶς, *being proved*, both by sufferings and by solicitations to sin, δύναται τοῖς πειραζομένοις βοηθῆσαι, is fitted in a peculiar manner to succour those who undergo either kind of trial. He is not only possessed of a merciful regard for them, (ver. 17,) but he has direct and immediate sympathy with them, the result of his own personal feeling and experience. Wonderful condescension of redeeming love ! Here lies the great mystery of godliness, God made manifest in the flesh. And while Jesus sits on the throne of the universe, Lord over all, the Christian is reminded, that he does this in his nature, as his *brother*, ver. 11. In the person of Jesus, man is exalted above the angels ; yea, he himself is to attain a rank superior to theirs ; for while Jesus passed them by, (ver. 16,) he laid down his life for us, in order to exalt us above them, 1 Cor. vi. 3. Deeper and deeper still becomes the mystery. The debt of gratitude appears boundless, when viewed in this light ; the baseness of our ingratitude and disobedience as boundless too ; and all that we can do is to lie down in the dust, overwhelmed with a sense of them, exclaiming at the same time with the prophet, " Who is like unto thee ? A God forgiving iniquity, and passing by the offences of thine heritage !"

Next to the consideration, that the " law was διαταγεὶς δι' ἀγγέλων," the grounds of its pre-eminence in the estimation of the Jews were, the exalted character of Moses, and the dignity and offices of the high-priest, who was the instrument of reconciling the people to God, when they had lost his favour by sinning. In respect to both these points, the apostle undertakes to show that the gospel has a preference, because that Jesus is superior. If he be compared with Moses as שלוח, ἀπόστολος, *curator ædis sacræ*, (οἴκου, ver. 2, 3 ;) he will be found to excel him. If he be compared with the high priest, his superiority, in every respect, is equally visible. The first comparison is made in ch. iii. 2—6, and the warning against defection from the gospel that immediately follows it, is continued through ch. iii. 7—19, to iv. 13. The writer then proceeds with the comparison of Christ as high priest, and extends it through the remainder of the doctrinal part of the epistle.

CHAPTER III.

Ver. 1. Ὅθεν, *whence*, i. q. διὰ τοῦτο, by which Chrysostom expresses the sense of it. It refers to *place*, in common usage ; but it is also *illative*, particularly in our epistle.

The manner in which the writer makes his transition here, from one topic to another, is deserving of notice. He had just been showing how and why Christ was a " merciful and faithful high priest, and able to succour all who are tempted." He now adds, ὅθεν, i. e. allowing these things to be true, it follows, that we are under peculiar obligation to contemplate and well examine the Saviour's character, before we venture to reject him. But in making this suggestion, the writer at the same moment introduces new topics for discussion, viz.

the comparison of Christ with Moses, and with the high-priest under the Jewish dispensation. The transition is almost insensible, as it is actually introduced under the form of a deduction from the preceding discussion.

'Ἀδελφοὶ, as applied by Christians to each other, means, *one of the same faith* or *profession*, with the adjunct idea of *possessing a friendly, brotherly feeling*, Acts ix. 30; xi. 29. 1 Cor. v. 11, al. "Ἅγιοι, *consecrated, devoted*, i. e. to Christ, *set apart* as Christians. So I understand this appellation. *Holy*, in the sense of possessing internal purity, the apostle did not mean to affirm that all were, whom he addressed; for surely, when the ancient prophets called the whole Jewish nation קְדֹשִׁים (ἅγιοι), or עַם קָדוֹשׁ (λαὸς ἅγιος), they did not mean to assert that every individual among them was *spiritually* sanctified. But to remind his brethren, (brethren in a double sense here, as they were also the writer's kindred according to the flesh), that they had been *consecrated* to Christ, and *set apart* as his disciples, was altogether adapted to prepare them for the exhortation to fidelity which ensues. In a like sense, the ancient prophets called the whole body of the Jewish nation *holy*, קָדוֹשׁ.

Κλήσεως ἐπουρανίου μέτοχοι, lit. *partakers of the heavenly invitation*. Κλῆσις is the invitation given on the part of God and Christ to men, to come and partake of the blessings proffered by the Christian religion. It does not appear, however, to designate the offers of the gospel, generally considered, and in reference to all men without discrimination; for it is applied in the New Testament only to those who by profession are Christians. Κλῆσις, then, is the *proffer* of blessings to such; the *invitation* given to all the professed friends of the Christian religion, to accept the favours which the Redeemer is ready to bestow, in case of their obedience. The epithet ἐπουρανίου may mean, in this case, that the blessings proffered are of a *celestial nature*. So Wahl and others, who compare the phrase with τῆς ἄνω κλήσεως, Phil. iii. 14. Thus interpreted, the implication of the passage would be, that the proffered blessings of the gospel were ἐπουράνια, in distinction from those offered under the law, i. e. they are of a higher, more spiritual, more sublime nature. But ἐπουρανίου may also mean, that the κλῆσις was given from heaven, i. e. by one from heaven, viz. Christ; comp. ch. xii. 25, and ii. 3. Understood in either way, it is apposite to the purpose of the writer, and well adapted to urge upon his readers their obligation to adhere to the Christian religion.

Κατανοήσατε, *observe well, consider attentively, perpendite,* ad *animum revocate;* and this, in order that they might not be tempted to swerve from their fidelity to Christ, out of excessive regard to the Mosaic institutes; for Christ, as the writer proceeds to show, was in all respects superior to Moses.

Τὸν ἀπόστολον ... ἡμῶν, *the apostle and high priest of our religion.* The appellation ἀπόστολον, (which is a ἅπαξ λεγόμενον as applied to Christ,) has given rise to much philological and critical discussion. The word itself may convey two ideas, nearly related, but not identical. (1.) Ἀπόστολος is equivalent to ὁ ἀπεσταλμένος; as Thomas Magister explains it, quoting Demosthenes as employing it, in this manner. It means, then, *any messenger, any person commissioned or sent to perform duties of any kind for another,* and particularly to make known his will, desire, or command; in which sense it is commonly employed by the New Testament writers. (2.) The Jews applied the term שָׁלִיחַ, (from שָׁלַח *mittere*), to the *minister of the synagogue,* i. e. the person who presided over it, and directed all its officers and affairs, the curator of all its concerns, *ædituus, negotii, ædis sacræ curator.* See Buxtorf Lex. Chald. verbum שְׁלִיחַ, and Vitringa de Vet. Synag. Lib. III. p. ii. c. 2. In either of these senses it may be understood, in the passage under consideration. Interpreted agreeably to the first sense of ἀπόστολος, the meaning would be, that Christ is the messenger of God to men, in order to communicate his will, and to accomplish the business to be done for the establishment of the new dispensation. But the particular reason why he is called ἀπόστολος here, lies, probably, in the comparison which the writer is about to make of Jesus, the head of the new dispensation, with Moses the head of the old. When Moses received a divine commission to become the leader and head of the Israelites, God says to him, שְׁלַחְתִּיךָ, *I have sent thee;* which idea is frequently repeated, Exod. iii. 10. 12. 14, 15. Moses then was שָׁלִיחַ, ἀπόστολος, in respect to this important business. Jesus, in like manner, was sent on an errand of the like kind, but of still greater importance. He was *sent* by the Father for this purpose, John iii. 34; v. 36, 37; vi. 29; x. 36, al. Now, as the writer was just about to make a comparison between Christ and Moses, it was very natural that he should call Christ ἀπόστολον, i. e. *one sent* or *commissioned of God,* because Moses was thus *sent;* as the passages above cited prove.

We might acquiesce in this explanation, as most interpreters have done, were it not that one still better may be found, in the supposition that ἀπόστολος is here employed in the second or Jewish sense, explained above. The apostle proceeds immediately to speak of Moses and of Christ as presiding over, and administering the affairs of, the οἶκος, committed respectively to them (ver. 2—4;) i. e. each was a שְׁלִיחַ הַצִּבּוּר, ἄγγελος ἐκκλησίας, curator, ædis sacræ, ἀπόστολος in the *Jewish* sense. This certainly gives a meaning more apposite to the context, and, indeed, a sense which, in connexion with it, seems to be a necessary one. The general idea of being *sent* of God, or *divinely commissioned*, is retained; inasmuch as Moses was thus sent and commissioned, and with him the comparison is made. The meaning then is, that if the *curator ædis sacræ et novæ* be compared with the *curator ædis sacræ et antiquæ*, the result will be such as the sequel discloses.

Καὶ ἀρχιερέα, *high priest*. Two reasons may be given for this appellation: the one, that in Ps. cx. 4, the Messiah is so named; the other, that the writer means to compare him, in the sequel, as making atonement for men by the propitiatory sacrifice which he offered, with the high priest of the Jews who made expiation for the people. The latter I regard as the principal reason of the appellation here.

Τῆς ὁμολογίας ἡμῶν, *of our profession*, or *confession;* i. e. the apostle and high priest whom we have confessed or acknowledged as ours. This they had done, when they became Christians. Ὁμολογίας is used here as an adjective or participle; and the phrase is equivalent to ἀπόστολον ἡμῶν καὶ ἀρχιερέα ὁμολογούμενον, i. e. the apostle and high priest τῆς πίστεως ἡμῶν (as Chrysostom paraphrases it,) in whom we have believed, or whom we have acknowledged as ours. Comp. 2 Cor. ix. 13, τῇ ὑποταγῇ τῆς ὁμολογίας ὑμῶν, *your professed subjection;* Heb. x. 23; v. 14.

Others take ὁμολογίας in the sense of *covenant*, בְּרִית, which the word sometimes has in profane writers; see Schleus. Lex. in verbum. This sense of the word would not be inapposite here, inasmuch as it would convey the idea of an *engagement* or *covenant* made with Christ, by those whom the apostle is addressing. But as this use of the word is not found in the New Testament, it would hardly be proper to admit it here.

The writer now proceeds to show the reason why the Hebrews ought attentively to regard Jesus, in respect to the two great points of comparison which he had hinted at, by applying to him the epithets ἀπόστολος and ἀρχιερεύς.

Ver. 2. Πιστὸν, *faithful*, i. e. he fully and truly performed the duties of his station. See ch. ii. 17, where, in like manner, he is called πιστὸς ἀρχιερεὺς. Others interpret πιστὸς, *entrusted with*, or, *worthy of trust;* a sense, indeed, which the word sometimes has ; but it is not so apposite here. Τῷ ποιήσαντι αὐτὸν, *to him who constituted* or *appointed him*, viz. ἀπόστολον ; to him who sent him, John x. 36 ; to him who made him שִׁלְיָה, *curator ædis sacræ*. So ἐποίησε, Mark iii. 14.

Τῷ οἴκῳ αὐτοῦ, *his house*, i. e. family, meaning the Jewish nation, or, his worshipping people. Οἶκοι evidently does not mean *temple* here, for that was not built in the time of Moses ; nor does it mean *tabernacle*, for over that Aaron presided, and not Moses. It means, then, the *spiritual house* committed to Moses, i. e. the Jewish nation who were to be guided, regulated, and instructed, in spiritual things, by the revelations which he gave them. So Chrysostom, who substitutes λαὸν as an explanation of οἶκον. So in English, we use *house* for *family*, and *church* (οἶκος θεοῦ) for *the worshippers* in it. It is, moreover, only in this way, that a comparison can be made between Moses and Christ ; as the latter was not the minister of any *literal house*, but *curator ædis Dei sacræ et spiritualis*. Comp. 1 Tim. iii. 15. 1 Pet. ii. 5. οἶκος πνευματικὸς. Eph. ii. 20—22. Heb. iii. 6.

The sentiment of ver. 2, is, that with regard to *fidelity* in discharging the duties of his office, as head of the new dispensation, Christ yields not in any respect to Moses, who (as the Scripture testifies, Num. xii. 7,) was faithful in respect to all his duties toward the people of God, that were committed to his care. In *this* respect there is no inferiority. In *another* respect, however, Christ may justly claim great superiority over Moses, as the writer now goes on to show.

Ver. 3. Δόξης, *honour, dignity, regard ;* governed in the genitive by ἠξίωται. Ἠξίωται, *is worthy, deserves, is counted worthy*. Ἀξιόω also means, not unfrequently, *to obtain, to acquire ;* e. g. οἱ καταξιωθέντες τῆς τοῦ πνεύματος χάριτος, *those who have obtained the grace of the Spirit*, Chrysostom, I. p. 730. Τῆς ἐπιγνώσεως τοῦ ὄντος μὴ καταξιούμενος, *not having obtained a knowledge of what is real*, Basil I. p. 515. In a similar way, it is also used in the classics ; as τῶν μεγίστων ἀξιούμενος, *having obtained the greatest honours*, Lys. Orat. p. 101. ed. Taylor. But still, this is not the usual sense of the word ; nor does it so well fit the passage under consideration, as the other and usual meaning, although many commentators have preferred it. Δόξη παρὰ Μωϋσῆν, *glory in comparison with Moses*, as in Hebrew כָּבוֹד מִמֹּשֶׁה. See on ch. i. 4, 9, where παρὰ is employed in the same way.

Καθ' ὅσον may signify, *in proportion as, as much as*, and may have relation here to πλείονος in the first member of the verse. The usual Greek method of expression in such cases is τόσῳ....ὅσῳ, &c. But I prefer the sense given in the version, because the nature of the proposition seems to require it. So Schulz, Eng. Version, alii.

Πλείονα τιμὴν, κ. τ. λ. *he who builds a house, has more honour than the house*; i. e. the difference between the honour due to Moses and that due to Christ, is as great as between the honour due to the founder of a house [family] and that which should be paid to the family which he founds; or, between the honour due to the architect that framed a building, and that due to the building itself. It is difficult to say in which of these senses the writer meant that the words should be taken. Either fits his purpose. Either is designed to show that Christ, at the same time that he is the head of the new spiritual house, is also the founder of it; while Moses, who was at the head of the ancient spiritual house, was himself only one of the household. As a steward or overseer of a house, while he is curator of all in the house, is still but a servant; so Moses, as is asserted in ver. 5, was but a servant; while Christ, who was curator, was also *son*, and therefore " heir and lord of all." The point of comparison between Moses and Christ, in which the latter appears to have a decided preference, is not the being at the head of God's house or family, (for such an office Moses sustained ;) but it consists in this, viz. that while Moses was *curator*, he was also θεράπων; but while Christ was *curator*, he was at the same time υἱὸς, and κατασκευάστης οἴκου.

Κατασκευάζω means, *to furnish, to fit up, to make ready*, i. e. for use ; also, *to construct, prepare, build, condere, exstruere*. In some cases it seems to combine the idea of *constructing* and *furnishing*, both of which indeed are included under the general idea of *preparing* or *making ready for use*; e. g. Heb. ix. 2—6. The LXX. sometimes used this word, in order to translate e. g. עָשָׂה, in Prov. xxiii. 5. 2 Chron. xxxii. 5; sometimes they employed it as corresponding to בָּרָא, as in Isa. xl. 28 ; xliii. 7. So the book of Wisdom ix. 2, " By thy wisdom κατασκευάσας τὸν ἄνθρωπον, *thou hast created* [formed] *man*." In our text, κατασκευάσας αὐτὸν, scil. οἶκον, is equivalent to the Latin, *condere domum*. But as οἶκος here means, *family, household*, so κατασκευάσας must be taken in a sense that will correspond to this, viz. that of *establishing, instituting, founding ;* which is evidently the meaning of the phrase.

Others render the last clause of the verse thus: *inasmuch as he who founded the household hath greater honour from the house,* understanding τιμὴν οἴκου to be the honour which the house renders, and thus making οἴκου dependent on τιμὴν instead of πλείονα. Storr translates the whole verse thus: *For Christ hath a preference above Moses, the greater, in proportion as this house is more highly estimated by its founder.* But these methods of rendering, (to say nothing of the improbable and forced construction which they give to the language of the verse,) would constrain us to lose sight of the *apodosis,* which the latter part of the verse evidently contains. " Christ," says the apostle, " has more glory than Moses." How? or, how much more? The answer is: " As much more as is due to the founder of a family, [or, to the architect of a building,] above that which is to be paid to the family itself, [or, to the edifice which is reared."] In other words, Christ is to be honoured as the *head* and *founder* of the οἶκος which has been erected; Moses, only as the *head;* for he himself was still a part of the οἶκος itself, ὡς θεράπων, ver. 5. Interpreted in any other way, the whole force of the comparison seems to vanish. In this way it is (to say the least) intelligible, if not quite simple. If the reader wishes to see the endless discrepancies among critics about this and the following verse, he may consult Wolfii Curæ Philol., or Dindorf's edition of *Ernesti in Ep. ad Hebræos.*

Ver. 4. This verse has been a kind of *offendiculum criticorum* in past ages, and has never yet, in any commentary which I have seen, been satisfactorily illustrated. The difficulty lies, not in the simple sentiment of the verse by itself considered, (for there is none in this respect;) nor in the words, which in themselves are not obscure; but in discovering and explaining the connexion in which this verse stands with the context, and how it modifies or affects it. If the verse be entirely omitted, and the third verse be immediately connected with the fifth, there seems to be nothing wanting, nothing omitted that is at all requisite to finish the comparison which the writer is making. Nay, on account of the difficulty which adheres to the fourth verse, the mind is greatly relieved by the omission of it; and little is then presented, which raises doubts or scruples about the object of the writer. There is no evidence, however, that the verse in question is a mere gloss; at least, none from manuscripts or versions that is of any value. We must receive it, then, as a part of the text, the integrity of which (however difficult the passage may be) cannot be made to depend on our ability to explain it

Πᾶς γὰρ οἶκος .... Θεὸς, I translate thus: *every house must have some builder, or, is built by some one; and he who formed all things is God.* But what are the *all things* (τὰ πάντα) which are *formed* or *built?* The universe? Or all οἶκοι, all *dispensations*, viz. both the Jewish and Christian? The context seems to demand the latter meaning. The former has common usage in its favour. Is it appropriate to construe it agreeably to this usage? It is directly to the writer's purpose, if he can show, that every dispensation must of necessity have some founder, and that this founder was Christ. But how is this shown? To say that God, simply considered, was *the author of all things*, would not be to show that Christ was the founder of the Jewish and Christian οἶκοι. Indeed, I can see no possible connexion of this proposition with the object which the writer has in view. Nor can I see how Christ is shown by him to be a *founder* at all, unless I understand him to assert this to be the fact, because Christ is divine, or is Θεὸς. The argument would then stand thus: "God is the author of all things, (and, by consequence, of the Jewish and Christian οἶκοι) Christ is God; of course he must be regarded as the original author or founder of these dispensations." The fact itself that Christ is Θεὸς, the writer surely could not hesitate to assert, after what he has said, ch. i. 8—12. John i. 1, asserts the same thing; as Paul also does, in Rom. ix. 5, and in other places. I must regard the expression here, as predicated on what the writer had said in ch. i. respecting the Son. The amount, then, of the reasoning seems to be: "Consider that Christ, as Θεὸς and the former of all things, must be the *author* too of the Jewish and Christian dispensations; which shows that a glory belongs to him, not only in his mediatorial office, and as being at the head of the new dispensation, but also as the founder both of this and the Jewish dispensation, in his divine character; while Moses is to be honoured only as the head of the Jewish dispensation, in the quality of a commissioned superintendent, but not as author and founder."

All other methods of constructing this passage fail of making it contribute to the writer's purpose; and this is, with me, an insuperable objection against them. To make Θεὸς, in ver. 4, refer simply to God the Father, is, at least, making the apostle say something very different from what contributes to his purpose, if it be not at variance with it. I propose this exegesis, however, only as being that which, after repeated investigations, I have felt myself constrained to adopt by the reasoning in the context, and the design of the writer; not as one so indubitably clear as to admit of no specious objection. The whole passage is so obscure, that no one can reasonably expect, as yet, a very convincing interpretation of it. If probability can be attained, it is as much as can be fairly demanded, at present.

Ver. 5. 'Εν ὅλῳ τῷ οἴκῳ αὐτοῦ, *in all his house;* not ἐπὶ τὸν οἶκον αὐτοῦ, *over his house*, as it is expressed in the following verse, where the writer speaks of Christ. I think the writer means here to make a distinction, by these different modes of expression, between the relation of Moses to the house in which he was θεράπων, and that of Christ to the house over which he was as υἱὸς. The former was ἐν τῷ οἴκῳ, *in the house*, i. e. he himself belonged to the family of God, was simply a member of it in the capacity of θεράπων; while the latter was ἐπὶ τὸν οἶκον, *over the house*, i. e. lord of the house, founder and proprietor of it.

Αὐτοῦ, HIS, i. e. God's house, both in ver. 2, and here. *God's household* means, those who profess to be his worshippers, to belong to him. In both cases, αὐτοῦ might refer to Christ, were it not that in Numb. xii. 7, (from which the passage is quoted) the language is, *my house*, בֵּיתִי; and it is *God* who says this. The sense, however, would not be materially changed, by referring αὐτοῦ to Christ. The scope of the sentence does not depend on this; for whether you say οἶκος αὐτοῦ is the family of God, or of Christ, the same persons are designated by the word οἶκος, in both cases.

Θεράπων, according to general usage, differs from δοῦλος and οἰκέτης, being a more honourable appellation. E. g. the correlate of δοῦλος and οἰκέτης is δεσπότης; but θεράπων is related to πατὴρ, κύριος, or βασιλεύς. In English, we should call the former a *servant*, or *a slave;* the latter, *an assistant, an usher, a helper,* &c. The Heb. עֶבֶד, however, means *servants* of every, or any rank. But עֶבֶד יְהֹוָה, *servant of Jehovah*, is always an appellation of honour. In the East, courtiers of the highest rank pride themselves in the appellation of *king's servants*. The word θεράπων is very happily applied by the LXX., and after them in the present case by our author, to Moses; who was a servant of Jehovah, in a highly honourable sense. Comp. Josh. i. 1, 2. After all, the θεράπων is inferior to the πατὴρ or κύριος of a family. Moses, therefore, was inferior to Christ, who was κύριος οἴκου θεοῦ.

Εἰς μαρτύριον τῶν λαληθησομένων, *for testimony to those things which were to be declared,* i. e. to make disclosures to the Israelites of those things which were to be revealed, under the ancient dispensation, or during the Mosaic period. The meaning is, that Moses was a θεράπων of God, for delivering to the people the ancient oracles. Μαρτύριον may signify either *instruction*, or *declaration, publication ;* just as μαρτυρέω signifies, in the New Testament, both *docere, instituere,* and *declarare, notum facere ;* as may be seen in the lexicons. Λαλη-θησομένων may also mean, either *things to be announced, published,* or, *things to be inculcated, taught.* The sense will not be materially altered by either method of translation. The meaning will still be, simply, that Moses was to be the instrument of delivering to the people divine communications, or, he was to teach them in matters of religion.

Ver. 6. Χριστὸς δὲ . . . ἐσμεν ἡμεῖς, *but Christ as a Son, over his house, whose house we are,* i, e. to whose family we belong, we who have made a Christian profession ; meaning himself, and those whom he addressed. This is as much as to say, " We now belong not to the house over which Moses was placed ; but to that which Christ governs or administers." Αὐτοῦ, *his,* i. e. God's, our English translators have rendered as if written αὐτοῦ, sc. ἑαυτοῦ, *his own ;* so Beza, Vogel, Erasmus, Heinrichs, and others. But Stephens, Mill, Bengel, Wetstein, Griesbach, Knapp, and Tittmann read αὐτοῦ, as I have translated.

The writer adds, however, that we really belong to the house which Christ governs, ἐάνπερ τὴν παρρησίαν . . . κατάσχωμεν, *provided we hold fast unto the end our confidence and joyful hope.* Παρρησία means originally, *the liberty of speaking boldly*, without fear or restraint, and comes etymologically from παρὰ and ῥῆσις. The secondary sense is *boldness, confidence.* Καύχημα primarily means, *gloriatio, the act of glorying,* or, *that in which we glory* or *joy ;* secondarily, it means, *joy, glory,* &c. I take the phrase as a Hendiadys. Ἐλπίδος is the subject, and καύχημα qualifies it ; as is often the case with similar constructions, in many parts of the sacred writings ; e. g. 1 Tim. vi. 17. Philem. 6. Rom. vi. 4. Col. ii. 5. 2 Cor. iv. 7. Gal. ii. 14 ; where the genitive (as in the instance before us,) is the *principal* noun, and the other noun joined with it (whatever case it may be in,) serves only in the office of an adjective. More usually, indeed, the noun in the *genitive* serves the office of an adjective, both in Hebrew and in Hebrew Greek. But the above cases show, that the noun which *precedes* the genitive, not unfrequently serves the same end ; and such too is the case in Hebrew, as may be seen in Heb. Gram. § 161. *b.*

The *confidence and joyful hope* here mentioned, is that which the Christian religion inspires. This must be held βεβαίαν, *firm, steadfast*. Βεβαίαν here agrees, in respect to grammatical construction, with παρρησίαν, the remoter noun in the preceding phrase, (as is frequently the fact in such cases,) but it is related to the *whole* phrase, in regard to its meaning. Εἰς τέλους, *to the end*, i. e. of life ; in other words, " We must persevere, to the last, in maintaining our Christian profession ; we must never abandon the confident and joyful hope which it inspires, if we mean to be considered as belonging to the family of Christ."

Ver. 7. Διὸ, *wherefore*, i. e. because Christ is superior to Moses, and has higher claims upon us, hearken, Christian brethren, to the admonitions which I give you, in the words with which the Israelites of old were warned.

Καθὼς λέγει τὸ πνεῦμα τὸ ἅγιον, i. e. as the divine word, given by the influence of the Holy Spirit, saith : compare Acts i. 16 ; xxviii. 25. This is one of the various ways of appealing to the scripture, which was usual in the time of the apostles ; and which is still practised by our churches. It involves the idea, that the Holy Scriptures are given by divine inspiration—are θεόπνευστοι.

Σήμερον, *to-day*, *now*, *at present*, like the Hebrew הַיּוֹם, to which it corresponds. Ἐὰν τῆς φωνῆς αὐτοῦ ἀκούσητε, *when* or *whilst ye hear his voice*. Ἐὰν, *when*, like the Hebrew אִם, to which it corresponds : compare John vi. 62 ; xii. 32 ; xiii. 20 ; xiv. 3. So Sept. for אִם, Prov. iii. 24. Isa. xxiv. 13, et alibi. Τῆς φωνῆς αὐτοῦ, i. e. his warning voice, his admonition.

Ver. 8. Μὴ σκληρύνητε τὰς καρδίας ὑμῶν. *To harden the heart*, is to make it insensible. In this case, to harden the heart, is to remain insensible to divine admonition, to neglect it, to act in a contumacious manner. The form σκληρύνω is of the later Greek. The classical writers used σκληροῦν, and this in a *physical* sense only, not in a *moral* one.

Παραπικρασμῷ corresponds here to the Hebrew מְרִיבָה, *strife, contention*. It is not a classic word ; but it is employed by the Septuagint. The meaning of it is *exacerbation, provocation, embittering*, from πικραίνω, *to be bitter, to embitter*. It is here applied to designate the act of the Israelites, who provoked the displeasure of God ; in particular, to their unbelief and murmuring at Massah or Meribah, Exod. xvii. 7, and afterwards at other places.

Κατὰ τὴν ἡμέραν τοῦ πειρασμοῦ ἐν τῇ ἐρήμῳ, *when they tempted* [God] *in the desert*. Κατὰ τὴν ἡμέραν, Hebrew כְּיוֹם (for כְּבְיוֹם) *as in the day that, when.* Πειρασμοῦ, *of temptation,* i. e. their unbelief and murmuring put the patience of God to a trial, (speaking after the manner of men.) Πειράζω means, *to solicit to do evil,* but also, *to prove, to assay.* When the scriptures speak of men as *tempting* God, the meaning is, that men do that which puts the divine patience, forbearance, goodness, &c. to a trial, i. e. make it difficult, as it were, to preserve a strict regard to these. Dindorf is mistaken, when he asserts, on this passage, that πειράζω is never used by the Greek writers in the sense of *enticing to sin;* for πειρᾶν (i. q. πειράζειν) γυναῖκα is a very common phrase, in the best Greek writers.

Ver. 9. Οὗ, *when, adverb,* i. q. ὅπου, as Œcumenius remarks. Οἱ πατέρες ὑμῶν, i. e. the ancient Israelites. 'Επείρασάν με . . . ἐδοκίμασάν με, *tried and proved me,* i. e. put me to a thorough trial; the repetition of a synonymous word merely denoting intensity.

Καὶ εἶδον, *although they saw.* So καὶ in John iii. 32; xiv. 32; xvii. 25. Rev. iii. 1, et al. In the same manner the Hebrew וְ, Gen. xviii. 27. Mal. ii. 14, et al. Τεσσαράκοντα ἔτη is joined (in the Hebrew) with the following verse, *forty years was I grieved,* &c. But this depends on the punctuation system of the Masorites, which the apostle has not followed. In regard to the sense, it matters not with which verb it is joined. If they tempted God forty years, he was grieved by their conduct during the same time; and if he was grieved by them for that time, it was because they tempted him.

Ver. 10. Διὸ, *wherefore,* i. e. because they tempted me, &c. This word is not in the Hebrew nor Septuagint. The writer has added it to the quotation, in order to render the sense of it more impressive or explicit.

Προσώχθισα, *I was indignant, offended at.* The word is Hellenistic. The Greeks use ὀχθέω and ὀχθίζω. According to etymology, it consists of πρὸς, *to, against, upon,* and ὄχθη, *bank, shore.* It is applied primarily to a ship infringing upon the shore, or, as we say, running aground. It answers to the Hebrew קוּט, מָאַס, קוּץ, &c.

Τῇ γενεᾷ ἐκείνῃ, *the men of that age,* or, as we say in English, *the generation then upon the stage.*

'Αεὶ πλανῶνται τῇ καρδίᾳ, the corresponding Heb. is, עַם תֹּעֵי לֵבָב הֵם *a people of erring heart are they,* the word ἀεὶ having nothing in the original which corresponds to it. Still, the sense of the Hebrew is tantamount to what the apostle (with the Septuagint) has expressed in the Greek. *To err in heart* may mean, either to err in judgment, or in disposition, intention; for the Hebrew לֵבָב, לֵב, and after it the Greek καρδία, means, either, *animus, judicium*, or, *mens, cogitatio, desiderium*. I understand καρδία here, as used according to the Hebrew idiom (in which it is often pleonastic, at least it seems so to us,) so that the phrase imports simply, *They always err*, i. e. they are continually departing from the right way.

Αὐτοὶ δὲ οὐκ ἔγνωσαν τὰς ὁδούς μου, *neither* (δὲ οὐκ means, *neither have they approved my doings*. Γινώσκω (like the Hebrew יָדַע, Ps. i. 6; xxxvi. 11,) means, *to approve, to like, to be pleased with*, Matt. vii. 23. John x. 14, 15. 27. 2 Tim. ii. 19. 'Οδὸς corresponds to the Hebrew דֶּרֶךְ, which means, *counsel, design, purpose*, also *operation, manner of conducting or acting towards any one*. In this last sense I take the word to be employed here. The meaning is, the Israelites had been discontented with the manner in which God had dealt with them in the wilderness; they disapproved of his manner of treating them. See, for an illustration of this, Deut. viii. 2—5; iv. 32—37; and particularly xxix. 2—4.

Ver. 11. 'Ως, *so that*, a conjunction; see Wahl on ὡς, II. 2. 'Εν τῇ ὀργῇ μου, *in my indignation*, viz. that which their unbelief and contumacy had excited. Compare παραπικρασμῷ in ver. 8, which means the provocation given by the Israelites.

Εἰ εἰσελεύσονται, *they shall not enter*. Εἰ borrows its *negative* meaning from the Hebrew אִם, to which it corresponds. The Hebrews used אִם, in the latter clause of an oath which ran thus: *God do so to me*, IF (אִם) *I do thus*, &c. See the full form in 1 Sam. iii. 17. 2 Sam. iii. 35. 2 Kings vi. 31. The former part of this oath was sometimes omitted, and אִם had then the force of a strong negative; see 2 Sam. xi. 11. 1 Sam. xiv. 45, alibi; vide Ges. Heb. Lex. under אִם, No. 6. So in Ps xcv. 11, אִם יְבֹאוּן contains a strong negative; which the Septuagint (and our author after them) have rendered εἰ εἰσελεύσονται.

The passage exhibits God as speaking after the manner of men, and as affected, like them, with feelings of indignation. The idea conveyed by such expressions plainly is, that God, as a measure of justice to the Israelites for their wickedness, gave solemn assurance that they should not enter into his rest.

Εἰς τὴν κατάπαυσίν μου, Hebrew, מְנוּחָתִי, *my rest*, means, *such rest as I enjoy*, or such as I have prepared or provided. See more on the subject of this rest in the commentary on Chap. IV.

Ver. 12. Μήποτε ἔσται . . . . ἀπιστίας, *lest there be in any of you an* evil and unbelieving heart. Ἀπιστίας, of unbelief, is here used as an adjective to qualify καρδία, according to an idiom very common both in the Old and New Testament.

Ἐν τῷ ἀποστῆναι ἀπὸ Θεοῦ ζῶντος, in apostatizing from the living God; or rather, so that he may apostatize, &c. Ἀποστῆναι is to revolt, to apostatize, to make defection from. Θεοῦ ζῶντος, living God, either in opposition to idols, which had no life, as in Acts xiv. 15. 1 Thess. i. 9. 1 Tim. iv. 10; or, living may mean immortal, eternal, as probably it does in Heb. ix. 14; x. 31; xii. 22. 1 Pet. i. 23, and often in the Old Testament. Thus perennial water is called ζῶν, John iv. 11; vii. 38. So the commentators and lexicographers. Perhaps, after all, ζῶν in such cases may mean, the author, or giver of life : compare John vi. 51, 57 ; ch. vii. 38.

The sense of the passage taken together is, " Beware, brethren, of an unbelieving and evil heart, such as the Israelites possessed, lest, like them, you apostatize from the living God," i. e. lest you apostatize from the religion of Christ, which he has required you to receive and to maintain, and thus perish like ancient Israel who revolted from God.

Ver. 13. Ἀλλὰ παρακαλεῖτε ἑαυτοὺς, but admonish one another, Ἑαυτοὶ, in the New Testament and in the classics, is often used as the equivalent of ἀλλήλοι; and so I understand it here.

Καθ' ἑκάστην ἡμέραν, every day, i. e. constantly, habitually, Ἄχρις οὗ τὸ σήμερον καλεῖται, either [καιροῦ] οὗ, κ. τ. λ., or οὗ may be the adverb of time, as in ver. 9. Καλεῖται, like the Heb. נִקְרָא קָרָא, is. See Wahl's Lexicon, and Gesenius. The meaning is, daily, while you have opportunity, admonish one another. In τὸ σήμερον, the article is joined, (as it often is,) with an adverb which expresses the sense of a noun; constructio ad sensum.

Ἵνα μὴ σκληρυνθῇ τις . . . . ἁμαρτίας, so that no one may be hardened by sinful delusion. Ἀπάτῃ τῆς ἁμαρτίας means, the sinful delusion which false teachers or Judaizing zealots might occasion; or, that delusion into which they might be led, by their oppressive condition arising from persecution, or by any allurements of a worldly nature; so that they would become insensible to the warnings which they had received, and might abandon their Christian profession. This would be a delusion indeed, and be highly sinful. Mutual daily admonition, the apostle intimates, would tend to prevent this evil.

Ver. 14. Μέτοχοι γὰρ τοῦ Χριστοῦ γεγόναμεν, we are, or we shall be, partakers of the blessings which Christ bestows. That Χριστὸς is sometimes put for the Christian religion, and sometimes for the blessings which are proffered by it, may be seen in the lexicons.

'Εάνπερ τὴν αρχὴν .... κατάσχωμεν, *if we hold fast, unto the end, our former confidence.* Τὴν ἀρχὴν τῆς ὑποστάσεως, i. q. τὴν πρώτην πίστιν, 1 Tim. v. 12. The sentiment is, Continue, to the end of life, to exercise confidence in Christ, and you shall obtain the reward which he has promised; see μέχρι τέλους, in ver. 6, above.

Ver. 15. 'Εν τῷ λέγεσθαι *in respect to what is said,* or, *in regard to the declaration,* viz. the declaration which follows, or the quotation of what had before been cited. 'Εν τῷ λέγεσθαι is equivalent to ἐν τῷ λέγειν, ch. viii. 13, or to κατὰ τὸ λεγόμενον. The design of this expression is, merely to remind the reader of what had just been cited from the Old Testament, a part only of which is now repeated, and the rest is left to be supplied by the reader's recollection.

Σήμερον ἐὰν, κ. τ. λ. *now, while* (see ἐάν, ver. 7,) *you hear his voice,* &c.

Ver. 16. Τίνες γαρ ἀκούσαντες παρεπίκραιναν; so, with Greisbach, Knapp, Tittmann, and others, I prefer to accent and punctuate this clause. The common editions have τινὲς, (accented on the ultimate,) and meaning *some,* instead of τίνες, the *interrogative,* meaning *who?* They also omit the interrogation point after παρεπίκραιναν. According to this last mode of exhibiting the text, it must be rendered, (as in our English version,) *For some, when they had heard, did provoke: howbeit, not all that came out of Egypt by Moses;* which is altogether inapposite to the design of the apostle. The true rendering I take to be, *Who now were they, that when they heard did provoke* [the Lord?] Or, *Who, let me ask,* (see on γὰρ, Wahl, no. 1, b. β.) *were they,* &c. The design of this and the following questions is, to lead the minds of the readers to consider the specific sin, viz. unbelief, which occasioned the ruin of the ancient Israelites, and which would involve their posterity in the like condemnation.

'Αλλ' οὐ πάντες.... Μωϋσέως, *rather, were they not all who came out of Egypt by Moses?* 'Αλλὰ, *rather,* or, *nay.* The same form occurs in Luke xvii. 8 : " Who of you, having a servant ploughing, or tending sheep, will say to him when he returns from the field, Come and sit down immediately at the table? *Will he not rather say,* or, *nay, will he not say, to him,* (ἀλλ' οὐχὶ ἐρεῖ αὐτῷ,) *prepare my supper?*" &c. The force of ἀλλὰ, in our text, it is not difficult to perceive. The writer first asks, " Who now were those, that when they had heard divine warnings still provoked the Lord?" He then, as though the question in this form were almost superfluous, immediately adds, "*Might I not rather ask*, or, *nay, might I not ask*, Did not all who came out of Egypt do this?" He means to intimate by this, that the number who embrace error cannot sanction it; nor can unanimity in unbelief render it any more excusable. Consequently, that the great body of the Jews rejected the Messiah at the time then present, and urged the Christian converts to do the same, would be no excuse for apostasy. Πάντες is not to be taken in the strict metaphysical or mathematical sense here, any more than in multitudes of other places; e. g. "*All* Judea went out to John to be baptized, confessing their sins," Matt. iii. 5, 6; "*all* men came to Jesus to be baptized of him," John iii. 26; and so often. Of the adults, only Caleb and Joshua among the Israelites are excepted, as not having taken part in the murmurings against the Lord, Numb. xiv. 30. Of course, there could be no scruples in the apostle's mind about applying the word πάντες in this case, just as it is applied in a multitude of others, viz. to designate *great multitudes*, or *the great majority*.

Διὰ Μωϋσεως, *by Moses*, means under his guidance, by his instrumentality.

Ver. 17. Τίσι δὲ....ἔτη, *and with whom was he indignant for forty years?* Above, in the quotation, ver. 10, *forty years* is connected with εἶδον τὰ ἔργα μου. But the sense of the whole passage is not materially changed, by the manner of expression in ver. 17. It is true, that the Israelites saw the works of the Lord for forty years, and that he expressed his indignation against them during that time, until the generation who had rebelled were destroyed.

Οὐχὶ τοῖς ἁμαρτήσασι; *was it not with those who had sinned?* Ernesti and Dindorf labour to show, that ἁμαρτάνω means the same here as ἀπειθέω. Doubtless, it includes the sin of *unbelief;* but it is of itself more generic than ἀπειθέω, and includes various sins of the Israelites, such as rebellion, murmurings, &c. the consequence of unbelief.

Τὰ κῶλα, lit. *members*, such as arms, legs. It is here put, however, by synecdoche, for the *whole body*, and corresponds to the Hebrew פְּגָרִים, *corpses*, in Numb. xiv. 29, 32; to which passages the apostle here refers. Ἔπεσε in Greek, and the corresponding Hebrew נָפַל, are both used to designate the *prostrate condition of dead bodies, or the falling down dead.* The whole phrase may be thus paraphrased, "Who perished in the desert."

Ver. 18. Τίσι δὲ ὤμοσε....κατάπαυσιν αὐτοῦ; *to whom did he swear*, (see Numb. xiv. 23. 28—30. Deut. i. 34, 35,) *that they should not enter into his rest, except to those who disbelieved?*

In Numb. iv. 23. 28—30, is an account of an oath, on the part of Jehovah, that the rebellious Israelites should not enter into *the land*, which he had sworn to their fathers should be given to them, i. e. in case they were obedient. In Deut. i. 34, 35, there is another mention of a like oath, viz. that they should not enter into *the goodly land*, pledged by oath to their fathers. But in neither case is the word *rest* employed. The reasoning of the apostle, however, in the chapter before us, would lead us to suppose, that the manner in which the unbelieving Jews were declared, in the above passages, to be excluded from *the goodly land*, and the *reasons* stated for that exclusion, necessarily implied exclusion from the heavenly Canaan also, or, from *the rest of God*.

Ver. 19. Καὶ βλέπομεν....δι᾽ ἀπιστίαν, *we see, then, that they could not enter in, because of unbelief.* Καὶ, *then*, in the apodosis of a sentence, or in a connected series of reasoning, as here. See Wahl on καὶ, II. 2 ; and compare Gesen. Heb. Lex. on וְ, No. 5.

The writer having thus appealed, for the sake of warning, to the example and consequences of unbelief among the Israelites of old in the wilderness, proceeds now further to confirm the application of what he had been saying to those whom he addressed, and to remove objections which might be raised against this application. Two objections, he seems to apprehend, might probably be raised against the use which he had made of the citation from the Old Testament: the one, that the rest there spoken of meant only, *a rest in the land of Canaan*, or, the quiet possession of the promised earthly inheritance; the other, that the ancient Israelites were excluded from the promised rest, on account of murmuring and rebellion, crimes not charged upon those whom the apostle addressed. The writer has deemed it expedient, and it was proper, that both of these objections to the use which he had made of the Old Testament Scriptures should be removed, before he proceeded further with his main design.

In chap. iv. 1, he brings forward the assertion, that the promise of entering into the rest of God still remains, addressed to the Hebrew Christians, as it was to the Israelites of old. In ver. 2, he proceeds to repeat the idea, (for the sake of deeply impressing it,) that blessings are announced to us (to Christians) in like manner as to the ancient Hebrews; and he now adds, that *they* failed to obtain the proffered blessings *through unbelief*. These declarations involve two propositions; the first, that the blessings in question must be of a spiritual nature; the second, that unbelief is the great cause of that sin which excludes from the enjoyment of them. The last of these propositions he does not *formally* labour to establish, as he does the other; because the evidence of it is involved in the quotation which he had made in ch. ii. 7—11 ; for it is there affirmed, that after all which the Israelites had seen of the works of God for forty years in the desert, they still tempted and provoked him, i. e. they gave no credit to all the testimonies which he had set before them of his fidelity toward his promises, and of his love and pity for them; *nor did they believe* his comminations against the disobedient. Consequently, they were excluded, by this *unbelief*, from his rest.

But what is the *rest* in question? Is it quiet possession of the land of Canaan? No, says the apostle. Believers *now* enter into the rest (ver. 3,) i. e. the same kind of rest as was anciently proffered. Moreover, God calls it κατάπαυσίν μου, MY *rest*, i. e. (adds he) such rest as God enjoyed, after he had completed the creation of the world ; consequently *spiritual, heavenly* rest. This is plain, (as he goes on to show in ver. 4,) from what the Scripture says, Gen. ii. 2, concerning the *rest of God*. Again, it is involved in the very form of expression, in Ps. xcv. 11, viz. MY *rest*, ver. 5.

"Now," continues he, (ver. 6,) " as some must enter into the rest in question," (for surely God would not provide and proffer a rest altogether in vain; "and since they, to whom it was offered, lost it through *unbelief*—[it follows that *believers* only can attain to it."] But this last idea, the author has not *expressed*. He has left the reader to supply it; as he may do without any difficulty, from what the writer had already said in ver. 2, 3. The illustration and confirmation of this truth, is plainly one of the objects which the writer has in view (as was stated above:) and while ver. 3—5 show that the rest spoken of is of a *heavenly* nature ; the object of ver. 6. is, to intimate that *unbelief* was the sin which excluded from it.

But lest there might be some doubt about the nature of the *rest* to which the ancient Scriptures refer, the writer resumes the argument respecting the nature of it, and adduces other considerations, to show that it must be spiritual and heavenly.

"Moreover," says he, (ver. 7,) " David himself, (who lived nearly five centuries after the land of promise had been occupied by the Israelites)—David speaks of a definite time, then present, in which he warns his cotemporaries against losing the *rest* which God had promised to the believing and obedient; (a rest of the same nature as that from which the Israelites of old had been excluded, as may be seen in Ps. xcv.)" "Now," (adds he,) "If Joshua, who gave Israel possession of the land of Canaan, had given them the *rest* to which the scripture refers when it speaks of *God's rest*, then the Psalmist could not have spoken, so many centuries afterwards, of a rest that was still proffered to Israel, and from which the unbelieving would be excluded, ver. 9." "Hence," he concludes, " it is evident, since the rest which is spoken of is not of a temporal nature, but of a spiritual enduring nature, that there remains a rest for the people of God, i. e. believers."

That the main object of the writer, in chap. iv. 1—9, is to prove the spiritual and abiding nature of the proffered rest, is stated so explicitly in ver. 10, that there can be no reasonable doubt left in respect to his intention; "For," says he, "he who enters into his [God's] rest, rests from his own labours, as God did from his."

That is, he who attains to the rest proffered to Israel in the time of David, and to the more ancient Israelites in the wilderness, attains to a rest like that of God (described in Gen. ii. 2;) i. e. he will rest from the toils, and trials, and sorrows of a probationary state, and enjoy a happiness heavenly and divine in a better world above.

The writer then proceeds, in his usual manner, to close the topic by adding exhortations diligently to seek the rest in question, and awful warnings against incurring, by unbelief, the righteous indignation of that holy and omnipotent Judge, unto whom their account must be rendered, ver. 11—13.

In regard to the views of our author, relative to the subject of the *rest* which is proffered in the Old Testament to all who are believing and obedient, they, doubtless, differ very much from many commentators and critics of the present day, who are distinguished for their literary attainments. But it will not follow from this, that they are erroneous. Certain it is, that all the writers of the New Testament had similar views, respecting the spiritual nature of some of the promises contained in the Jewish Scriptures. I cannot, therefore, regard the passage which we have just considered, as a mere *accommodation* (a somewhat forced one too) of promises and threatenings addressed to Israel of old, that had respect only to the land of Canaan; nor as a mere *fanciful* application of things ancient, to the Hebrews whom our author is addressing. I cannot help believing, at all events, that *he* regarded the rest spoken of in Ps. xcv. 11, and Gen. ii. 2, as spiritual and heavenly rest. Consequently, an appeal to the examples contained in the Old Testament, is more to the point, and more forcible, when thus understood, than it would be in any other mode of explaining the views and design of the writer.

As to the *mode of reasoning*, in order to establish the positions which the writer has in view, it is quite different, indeed, from that to which we now resort, who have the whole of the New Testament in our hands, in which "life and immortality are brought [so fully] to light." *We* need to take but very little pains, in order to prove that promises of *rest* in a *future* world, promises respecting a spiritual and heavenly country, are made to Christians. But we must remember, while we are labouring to understand the reasoning of Paul in the chapter before us, that the Hebrews whom he addressed had no New Testament; for some of it was not yet written, and none of it had acquired a general circulation among the Christian churches. This is the reason why Paul, in all his epistles, whenever he has occasion to quote scripture, uniformly quotes the Old Testament only. How could he appeal to the New Testament, which was, when he wrote our epistle, only in a forming state, and was not completed until after his death? Indeed, it was not embodied in its present form, and generally circulated among the Christian churches, until nearly a century after the death of Paul.

This may suffice to show why Paul appeals to the Old Testament, and not to the New, when he designs to establish any thing from the sacred oracles. Every one, moreover, who believes with Paul that the "gospel has brought life and immortality to light," will of course suppose it to be more difficult, to establish promises of *rest* in *a future world* from the Old Testament than from the New. Hence, he may be less forcibly struck with the argument of Paul, in Heb. iv. to prove a promise of future happiness to believers, than he will with many an argument which his own mind will supply from the New Testament. And with good reason. The New Testament does afford arguments far more explicit and convincing than the Old; and of course more powerful arguments than those which Paul deduces, in our chapter, from the Old. But this is no fault in the writer of our epistle. It is merely a result of the circumstances in which he, and those whom he addressed, were placed. He had asserted, in writing to them, that a promise of the same nature was proffered to Christians, as was proffered to the ancient Israelites, ch. iv. 1, 2. The consequence he deduces from this is, that as unbelief with respect to this promise occasioned their ruin, so the like unbelief would now produce the like consequences. Nothing could be better adapted to his purpose, when writing to the Hebrews, than to produce an example of the consequences of unbelief, that was taken from their own progenitors, and recorded in their own Scriptures, which they acknowledged as the word of God. To the New Testament he could not appeal, for it was not then in their hands. To the Old Testament Scriptures, then, he chooses (and for the best of reasons) to make the appeal, in establishing the assertion he had made, that a promise of entering into the rest of God was still left; that the proffered blessing was announced to Christians in the same manner as to God's ancient people, ch. iv. 1, 2; and that it would be conferred only on those who remained firm in their belief.

The whole argument is, indeed, in some sense, *argumentum ad hominem*. It is appropriate to the time, to the circumstances in which the apostle wrote, and to the people whom he addressed. But who can, with any propriety, make it a matter of accusation against the writer, that he consulted the good of those whom he addressed, by arguing with them in a manner that was most appropriate to their condition? Did not their Saviour constantly do the same? And ought we not to follow his example?

It is indeed true, that the views of the apostle, in respect to what is revealed in the Old Testament with regard to a future state, were plainly very different from those of many commentators and critics, who represent the Jews, God's chosen people, and favoured with the light of revelation, as more profoundly ignorant of the doctrine of immortality, and of future rewards and punishments, than any of their heathen neighbours; a thing as improbable in itself, as it is contrary to the reasoning of the apostle, on which I have been commenting. Nor is it at all necessary to maintain, with most of the recent commentators, that Paul *allegorizes* the *rest of Canaan* here, in such a way as to accommodate himself to the spirit of the age in which he lived, and the taste of the Jews who were his cotemporaries. So far am I from embracing this view of the subject, that I am quite persuaded, he has designedly undertaken to show, that the interpretation his cotemporaries put upon the passage which respects *exclusion from the rest of God*, was an erroneous one. Plainly he labours to show, that *rest in the land of Canaan* could NOT possibly have been meant by the Psalmist. Where then is the *allegorizing* of the apostle here, of which so much has been said? Who can say confidently, against the reasoning and the decision of Paul, that the rest of which David spake, was not *spiritual?* I content myself, whatever others may do, with the exegesis of the apostle; and do fully believe that he is in the right.

If he is correct in his views, then it follows, that the future punishment of the unbelieving Israelites is clearly intimated, by the exclusion from spiritual, or heavenly rest which is threatened. This is a necessary inference from the reasoning and conclusions of the apostle.

CHAPTER IV.

Ver. 1. Φωβηθῶμεν, *let us beware,* lit. *let us be afraid of.* As fear, however, in its *literal* sense, is not applicable in this case, the exact shade of meaning is, *caveamus, let us beware.*

Καταλειπομένης ἐπαγγελίας, *a promise being still left.* Καταλείπω, according to both sacred and classic usage, may mean, *to forsake, desert, neglect;* e. g. in Acts vi. 2. 2 Pet. ii. 15, et al. In this sense many critics have understood it, in the passage now in question. The sense then would be, "Let us beware, lest by neglect of the promise made to us," &c. But I much prefer the other sense of the word, i. e. *to leave behind,* and (passively) *to be left behind, to remain, to be still extant;* e. g. in Acts xxiv. 27. Luke xx. 31. Mark xii. 19, al. and especially comp. ver. 9, below. The meaning then is, that the promise, which was implicitly made to believers among the ancient people of God, is still in being, and is made to us, i. e. to Christians. This the next verse so directly asserts, as to render the interpretation just given nearly certain.

Ἐπαγγελίας *declaration, annunciation, promise,* i. e. annunciation of the reward offered to the believing, or faithful.

Μήποτε . . . . δοκῇ τις ἐξ ὑμῶν ὑστερηκέναι, *lest . . . . any one of you may fail of obtaining it.* By sacred and classical usage, δοκέω is frequently joined with other verbs, without making any *essential* addition to the sense of them; i. e. it is said to be used *pleonastically;* by which, however, can be meant only, that it is incapable of being precisely rendered into our own language, and *apparently* adds nothing to the sense of a phrase. But this is not exactly true of δοκέω. In many cases, it is plainly designed to soften the expression to which it is attached; e. g. 1 Cor. vii. 40, Paul says, δοκῶ δὲ κἀγὼ πνεῦμα Θεοῦ ἔχειν, *I seem to myself to possess the Spirit of God;* a modest way of asserting the fact, instead of speaking categorically. In a similar way δοκέω is employed, in 1 Cor. xiv. 37; x. 12, ὁ δοκῶν ἑστάναι, he *who seems to himself to*

COMMENTARY ON HEB. IV. 2. 337

stand; ch. iii. 18; iv. 9. In a few cases, it is difficult to distinguish what addition is made to the phrase, by the use of δοκέω: e. g. Luke xxii. 24, τίς αὐτῶν δοκεῖ εἶναι μείζων, i. q. τίς εἴη. So Luke viii. 18, ὁ δοκεῖ ἔχειν is expressed, in Luke xix. 25, by ὁ ἔχει. 1 Cor. xi. 16, εἰ δέ τις δοκεῖ φιλόνεικος εἶναι. There can scarcely be a doubt, however, that in all cases, the Greeks designed to give some colouring to a sentence, by employing it. It would often seem to be something near to our *may, might, can, could,* &c. when used to soften forms of expression that might have been categorical. So Theophylact understood it, in our phrase. The words δοκεῖ τις ὑπερηκέναι, he thus explains: τουτέστι, μήπως ὑστερήσῃ, lest he may come short—and fail to enter into the promised rest. *The writer uses a mild and gentle address,* not saying μὴ ὑστερήσῃ, but μὴ δοκῇ ὑστερηκέναι. Theophylact in loc." This, I apprehend, is hitting the exact force of the phrase here; an imperfect view of which is given in the lexicons.

Ἐξ ὑμῶν, in some manuscripts and fathers, ἡμῶν: which would better accord with the usual κοίνωσις of the writer; e. g. ch. i. 1; ii. 1. 3; iii. 1. 6. 19. al. But it is not an unusual thing for Paul to change or intermingle different persons, in the same passage; e. g. Rom. xiv. 13. Heb. x. 24, 25.

Ὑστερέω lit. means, *to come afterwards, to come late.* In the secondary sense it means, *to fail, to come short of;* as he must fail of obtaining a thing, who comes too late for it. If the exhortation here be regarded as having a special reference to the *time* (σήμερον) when the offers of rest are made, μήποτε . . . ὑστερηκέναι may be rendered happily, as in Wahl, *lest . . . ye come too late,* i. e. after σήμερον. But I prefer the more simple method; *lest . . . ye fail of obtaining the promised blessing.*

Ver. 2. Καὶ γάρ ἐσμεν εὐαγγελισμένοι, *for to us also are blessings announced,* or, *we are evangelized,* i. e. the promise of blessings is declared or made known to us, *as well as to them.* Εὐαγγελίζω is used classically in the same sense, i. e. *to announce joyful tidings, to proclaim proffered good.* The proffered blessing, implied in the text, is *the rest* of which the writer had been speaking, and of which he continues to speak.

Ἀλλ' οὐκ ὠφέλησεν ὁ λόγος τῆς ἀκοῆς, *the promise or declaration which they heard,* [or *which was proclaimed,*] *was of no benefit to them.* Ὁ λόγος τῆς ἀκοῆς may be equivalent to ὁ ἀκουσθεὶς λόγος, i. e. the word heard by them; or it may be like the Hebrew דְּבַר שְׁמוּעָה

z

word of annunciation or *report,* i. e. word announced or reported. The sense is not materially changed, whichever of these interpretations is adopted.

Συγκεκραμένος . . . ἀκούσασι, *not being joined with faith in them that heard it,* or, *not being united to faith,* i. e. faith not accompanying it, or associating with it. Συγκεκραμένος is explained, by many commentators, as being tropically employed here; and the metaphor, they allege, is taken from food, which, when digested, unites with the corporeal system, and becomes aliment to it. So here, the *word,* if duly received, would have incorporated itself, so to speak, with the internal, spiritual man; but as it was not received, it did not so incorporate itself. But this is not so simple and easy a mode of explanation, as that given in the above translation.

Many manuscripts and editions read συγκεκραμένους and some συγκεκερασμένους; which some critics and interpreters prefer. But it is difficult, if not impossible, to make any tolerable sense of these readings. The common one is much preferable.

Τοῖς ἀκούσασι —equivalent here to the genitive τῶν ἀκουσάντων. The meaning is, that the λόγος was not associated with the faith of *those who heard it.* The Hebrews usually designate possession, by the dative with לְ; e. g. *the Song of songs,* אֲשֶׁר לִשְׁלֹמֹה *which is Solomon's.* So, frequently, in Greek; e. g. οἱ πατὴρ *his father,* Pind. Olymp. i. 91. *Neither do thy children* [σοί τέκνα] *see the light,* Eurip. Phœniss. 1563. *Men are one* κτημάτων τοῖς θεοῖς, *of the possessions of the gods,* Plato, Phæd. See Matt. Gr. Gram. § 392. g. 1. et seq. In all such cases, there is an ellipsis of a pronoun relating to the object possessed, and of the verb of existence, which governs the dative when it signifies possession or property; e. g. κτημάτων [ἅ ἐςι] τοῖς θεοῖς.

The sense of the whole verse is simply this; " a promise of rest is made to Christians now, as well as to God's ancient people. But they received no advantage from it, because of unbelief;" the implication is φοβηθῶμεν, (as he had just said,) μή τις δοκῇ, κ. τ. λ, that is, guard well, then, against unbelief.

Ver. 3. Εἰσερχόμεθα γὰρ . . . πιςεύσαντες, *but we who believe do enter into the rest,* viz. God's rest. Γὰρ, *but;* for plainly εἰσερχόμεθα γὰρ is put in distinction from the preceding ἀλλ' οὐκ ὠφέλησε, to which the writer subjoins, *but* (γὰρ) *we who do believe, are profited by* it, &c. It may also be rendered, nearly to the same purpose, *still,* or, *yet* (γὰρ,) *we who do believe, &c.* provided the preceding ἀλλ' be translated, *although*. The sentiment of the two clauses is either this; " Be it that the unbelievers reaped no advantage from the rest proffered to them, yet we who are believers do enter into that rest ;" which the writer then proceeds to prove : or it may be stated in another form, thus, " An offer of rest is made to us, as well as to them; *but* (ἀλλ') unbelief excluded them from that rest; we, *then* (γὰρ,) who believe shall be admitted to it." That is, if our character be the opposite of theirs, then will our lot be the opposite also.

Εἰσερχόμεθα in the *present* tense, appears to have created difficulty in the minds of some critics, who have changed it into εἰσελευσόμεθα (future tense.) But how needless this change is, every one conversant with the idiom of the bible may easily judge; in which the *present* tense is very often used as a *universal* tense, embracing time past, present, and future. In Hebrew, it is very common to use the *present* participle, for the same purposes as the Latins use their future in *rus*.

Καθὼς εἴρηκεν·, κ. τ. λ. that is, a solemn asseveration that *unbelievers* should *not* enter into his rest, implies, of course, that *believers* should enter into it. See on ch. iii. 11.

Καίτοι τῶν ἔργων . . . . γενηθέντων, *namely* [rest from] *the works that were done after the world was founded*. Καίτοι is a particle, the meaning of which has been much controverted here. There is no doubt, that it sometimes has the meaning of *although*, which our English version has here given to it. But I am unable to make any sense of the passage, under consideration, if καίτοι be thus translated. Nor does καίτοι seem originally to mean, *although*. Its principal signification is, *et quidem, et sane*. So Xenophon (Cyrop. III.,) καίτοι, εἴτι ἐκείνους μὲν φοβερωτέρους ποιήσομεν, κ. τ. λ. *and truly, if we shall make them somewhat more timid, &c.* Thucyd. IV. 60, καίτοι, γνῶναι χρὴ, κ. τ. λ. *and truly, we ought to know*. Aristoph. Plut. 1179, καίτοι τότε, ὅτι εἶχον οὐδέν, *and indeed then, when they possessed nothing*. " Adhibetur," says Hoogeveen, " cum sequitur aliquid nova attentione dignum ;" and again, " Quartus usus est, *si dictum exemplo confirmatur*," (Hoogev. Doctrina Part. Græc. ed Schütz. vocab. καίτοι;) which is the very case in question. For here the writer gives the example of God's rest after the creation, in order to explain what is the meaning of MY *rest*. I have given the sense, by rendering καίτοι, *namely*, which is equivalent in many cases to *et quidem et sane*. So Devarius (de Partic. Ling. Græc.) explains καίτοι ; and after him Carpzoff, (Comm. in loc. nostrum.) The latter says, "Devarius evicit, eam (καίτοι) simpliciter ad exponendam aliquam sententiam poni." The sense will be substantially the same, if καίτοι be rendered, *and truly, and indeed* ; but the other mode of translating is more explicit, and makes the connexion more facile.

Τῶν ἔργων [rest from] *the works.* That κατάπαυσιν is to be understood, before ἔρχων is clear from ver. 4 and 10, where the same sentiment is repeated. The ellipsis may be either [κατάπαυσιν] τῶν ἔργων, or, [κατάπαυσιν ἀπὸ] τῶν ἔργων; more probably the latter, for ἀπὸ is supplied after the verb κατέπαυσε, both in ver. 4 and 10. 'Απὸ, however, is not absolutely *necessary* here, as nothing is more common than the genitive case, without any preposition, to mean *in respect to, in regard to;* e. g. ἐγγύτατα αὐτῷ εἰμι γένους, *I am very nearly allied to him,* IN REGARD TO *descent;* ἄπαις ἀρρένων παίδων, *childless* IN REGARD TO *males;* see Buttman's Gram. § 119. 6. 1. Matthiæ, § 315.

'Απὸ καταβολῆς κόσμου γενηθέντων, *done,* i. e. completed or performed, *when the world was founded.* 'Απὸ καταβολῆς, *at* or *after the foundation,* i. e. beginning ; in a sense, like ἀπὸ ἀρχῆς, *at first,* in Matt. xix. 4 ; and in Luke xii'. 25, ἀφ' οὗ means *when.* Josephus uses καταβολή for *beginning;* e. g. Lib. II. 17, Bell. Jud. he says, "This was καταβολὴ πολέμου, *the beginning of the war,*" viz. with the Romans.

By rendering ἀπὸ, *after,* I follow the more usual sense of the word. The nature of the image I take to be this. The *foundation* (καταβολὴ) of a building is merely its commencement, a state or condition preparatory to the completion of the superstructure. So here, the καταβολὴ *founding* of the earth, was the act described in Gen. i. 1. The completion of the building (so to speak) followed, during the work of the six days which succeeded. These were the ἔργων γενεθέντων which our author mentions here, and these were the works from which God rested, after they were completed. That ἀπὸ, joined with nouns designating time, may mean *after, since,* every lexicon will show.

Ver. 4. The writer now proceeds to cite a passage of scripture, in order to show that God did enjoy such a rest as he had spoken of. Εἴρηκε γὰρ, *for* [the scripture] *says,* or, [the Holy Ghost] *says;* the usual mode of appealing to the Old Testament.

Ποὺ *in a certain place* or *passage.* Chapter and verse are no where cited in the New Testament; and very rarely is any particular book named, unless, indeed, it bears the same name as its author. An appeal to Scripture, by merely saying πού, shows that the writer must have supposed his readers to be familiar with the contents of the Jewish Scriptures. The passage cited may be found in Gen. ii. 2. Κατέπαυσεν ὁ Θεὸς. The *rest* here spoken of, is of course to be considered as described ἀνθρωποπαθῶς, i. e. in accommodation to the capacities of men. It surely does not imply, that God was *wearied* by his work of creation ; but that he simply ceased from it, and enjoyed a holy and delightful quiet, in the pleasing contemplation of the works which had been accomplished. Compare Gen. i. 4. 10. 18. 25. 31.

Ver. 5. Such, then, was the rest of God, of which the scripture speaks. To such rest, the apostle says, the writer of the ninety-fifth Psalm refers. Καὶ ἐν τούτῳ πάλιν, *again in this passage also*, viz. in the passage which he had already quoted from Ps. xcv. 11, i. e. the passage which he is now going to mention, the Scripture represents God as saying, MY rest, i. e. such rest as I have, or, such as I enjoy. In other words, both Gen. ii. 2, and Ps. xcv. 11, speak of a *holy, spiritual rest*, since they speak of a rest which God himself enjoys.

Ver. 6. Ἐπεὶ οὖν ἀπολείπεται .... δι ἀπείθειαν, *since then it remains, that some must enter into that* [rest], *and* [since] *they to whom the promise was formerly announced, did not enter in, because of unbelief ;* [it follows that believers only can enter in], compare ver. 3 ; or, [it follows, that a rest remains for believers], compare ver. 9.

This seems to be a continuation of the subject in ver. 3. There the writer says, " Believers enter into the rest of God." How is this ·proved ? " Because he has sworn, that *unbelievers* shall not enter into it ;" which necessarily implies that *believers* shall enter into it. Then, after delaying a moment, in order to show what the nature of the rest in question is, viz. that it is *God's rest*, i. e. such rest as God enjoyed after the work of creation was completed, (ver. 3—5,) the author resumes the consideration of the proposition advanced in the first part of ver. 3, and avers, that, as some must enter God's rest, (for God could not be supposed to have provided one in vain ;) and as *unbelievers* cannot enter in ; so it is necessarily implied, that *believers*, and they only, will enjoy the rest in question. See the illustration of the reasoning prefixed to ch. iv. in the preceding pages.

Others construe the verse in this manner : " Since, then, some must enter into his rest, and unbelievers of former days did not enter in ; therefore he defines again (πάλιν) a *particular day*," &c. constructing ver. 6 and 7 as one connected sentence. But this makes the sentence very much involved, and obscures the design of the writer. His object certainly is, to show that the rest proffered in ancient times, in the ninety-fifth Psalm, still remains for the people of God; see ver. 9, 10. But how can this be proved by merely showing that David speaks of a definite time, when he wrote the ninety-fifth Psalm, in which the offer of rest was *then* made ? On the other hand, I understand it to be the particular object of the writer, in ver. 7, seq. to exhibit further proof, that the proffered rest is of a *spiritual* nature, and therefore not to be limited by assigning to it a merely *temporal* sense. See the preceding illustration, referred to above.

Ver. 7. Πάλιν τινὰ ὁρίζει ἡμέραν .... καρδίας ὑμῶν, *again he specifies a particular day*, TO-DAY, *when speaking by David, so long a time afterwards; as it is said, " To-day, whilst ye hear his voice, harden not your hearts."* See above, on ch. iii. 7, 8, particularly ver. 18. The reasoning stands thus : " In David's time, nearly five hundred years after unbelievers in the wilderness were threatened with exclusion from the promised inheritance, the Psalmist makes use of the commination which has been quoted, in order to deter those whom he addressed, from hardening their hearts as the ancient Israelites did, and so losing the rest as they did, which God had proffered to the obedient and believing." This rest, then, could not be merely *the land of Canaan*, (as the Jews of Paul's time understood it to be,) for this both believers and unbelievers, living in the time of the Psalmist, already enjoyed. Consequently, the *rest* spoken of by the Psalmist was of a *spiritual* nature, pertaining only to believers. All this is plainly implied in—

Ver. 8. Εἰ γὰρ αὐτοὺς Ἰησοῦς .τ.. ἡμέρας, *now, if Joshua had given them rest*, i. e. the rest of God, of which the Scripture speaks, *then he* [David] *would not have spoken of another time*, viz. when rest was to be given, or to be obtained. That is, " If the *rest of God* be only the rest of Israel in Canaan, or the quiet possession of the promised land, then the Psalmist could not have spoken of it as still proffered, in his time, after it had been in fact given to Israel by Joshua, nearly five centuries before. The *other time*, here spoken of, is the same which is designated by the word σήμερον in the quotation ; which implies a time different from that, and subsequent to that, in which the Israelites obtained the rest of Canaan.

That Ἰησοῦς means *Joshua* here, there can be no doubt ; for the object of the writer is to prove, that Jesus *does* bestow the rest spoken of, viz. that which the Ἰησοῦς here named did *not* bestow. Κατέπαυσε, *caused to rest,* exactly as the Hiphil conj. in Hebrew is used ; e. g. הֵנִיחַ (from נוּחַ)in Deut xii. 10, in the same sense as κατέπαυσε here.

Ver. 9. ῎Αρα ἀπολείπεται . . . τοῦ Θεοῦ, *consequently, there remaineth a rest for the people of God,* i. e. for believers see ver. 3. Here the object of the preceding argument is plainly developed ; so plainly, that we are not left at liberty to doubt concerning it. Here is fully *expressed,* what is plainly *implied* in ver. 6, although in an elliptical manner, as has been already noticed. Such a manner is not unfrequent with Paul. Compare Rom. v. 12 with v. 18, 19. See Intr § 22. 3.

Σαββατισμὸς, (Heb. שַׁבָּת, שַׁבָּתוֹן *rest, sabbatism,) holy, religious, spiritual rest.* Σαββατισμὸς is a mere Hebrew word with a Greek ending ; and it is here employed as equivalent to κατάπαυσις, but with special reference to the Hebrew expression יִשְׁבֹּת (from שָׁבַת) in Gen. ii. 2, which there describes the *rest* of God. The Hebrew שַׁבָּתוֹן is a kind of intensive noun, formed from שָׁבַת, and means, *sabbath by way of eminence.* Σαββατισμὸς, which stands for שַׁבָּתוֹן, seems to be a word coined by the writer purposely for the occasion, and is very appropriate to his design.

That believers do enter into the *rest of God,* i. e. a rest like his, is further shewn by—

Ver. 10. ῾Ο γὰρ εἰσελθὼν . . . ὁ Θεὸς, *he who enters into his* [God's] *rest, he will also cease from his own labours, as God did from his.* As God ceased from his work on the seventh day, and enjoyed holy delight in the contemplation of what he had done, (see on ver. 4. above,) so the believer, in a future world, will cease from all his toils and sufferings here, and look back with holy delight on the struggles through which he has past and the labours which he has performed, for the sake of the Christian cause. Or, as God enjoys a most pure and perfect rest or happiness in heaven ; so the believer will enjoy a similar happiness there.

There surely is no more difficulty in calling that rest, which is promised to believers, *the rest of God,* than there is in saying, that man " was formed in his image ;" that Christians " are made partakers of the divine nature ;" or that " we shall be like him, when we shall see him as he is." *The rest of God,* is rest like that which God enjoys. And it deserves to be noticed, that the writer, in order to illustrate the nature of this rest, has chosen the description of it, as following the work of creation, in order to make a comparison between it and that rest which believers will have, when all their toils and sufferings are ended. This was well adapted to take hold of the minds of those to whom he was writing, and who were exposed to many hardships and trials.

Having now shown that there is a promise of spiritual rest to believers, implied in what the Jewish Scriptures say, the apostle repeats the caution, which lay so near his heart, against unbelief in the Saviour, and the consequences of it.

Ver. 11. Σπουδάσωμεν οὖν . . . ἀπειθείας, *let us earnestly endeavour then, to enter into that rest,* [the rest of God,] *lest any one should perish, in like manner, through unbelief.* Ἐν τῷ αὐτῷ ὑποδείγματι, *after the same example, after the like manner,* viz. as they (the Israelites) perished. Πέσῃ is often used in this way, in an *intransitive* sense. Ἀπειθείας I take to be the genitive (as grammarians say) of *means, instrument,* &c.

The awful nature of the commination, that unbelievers should not enter into the *rest of God,* the writer now describes, in order to leave a deep impression on the minds of his readers, and to guard them more effectually against unbelief and apostacy.

Ver. 12. Ζῶν γάρ . . . ἐνεργής, *for the declaration of God has an active and mighty power,* or, *is enduring and powerful,* i. e. has an efficiency that never ceases. The meaning according to the latter interpretation is, that the commination, uttered in ancient days, against unbelievers, (and which had been repeated above by the writer) has abated nothing from its force or efficacy, down to the present time; it still lives; unbelievers are still subject to its power. In defence of this interpretation, it might be said that ζῶν is applied here to the *divine word,* i. e. commination, in a manner like that in which it is applied to God in the phrase אֵל חַי, Θεὸς ζῶν, often used in the Scriptures, which designates him as *eternal, immortal, never dying, endowed with unfailing life,* in opposition to idols destitute of a living principle, and made of perishable materials. It is evident, too, that the sense of *perpetual* or *perennial,* may be considered as appropriate to the passage before us.

But others interpret ζῶν as meaning *active,* a sense which is common to this word, and to the Hebrew חַי. I understand both terms as conveying the idea of *active and mighty energy;* which is altogether appropriate to the writer's purpose, whose object it is to persuade his hearers, that the commination uttered against the unbelievers of former days, and which is still in force, has a dreadful power, at which they ought to shudder.

Καὶ τομώτερος . . . . δίστομον, *and sharper than any two-edged sword*, i. e. it has a more effective power to inflict wounds, than a sword with two edges. The efficacy of divine commination is often compared to a sharp sword. E. g. the Son of man is represented by John, as having, when he appeared to him in vision, a sharp two-edged sword issuing from his mouth, i. e. his words cut as it were like a sharp sword, or his reproof, commination, wounded deeply, Rev. i. 16; ii. 12, 16; xix. 15, 21. Compare also Isa. xlix. 2; xi. 4, in which last passage the expression is, *with the rod of his mouth*, and in the parallel στίχος, *with the breath of his lips*, [with his words] *shall he slay the wicked.* Language then of reproof, of severe threats or commination, or of condemnation, is by the sacred writers called the *sword* or *rod of the mouth*. So in our verse, the divine commination is represented as terribly efficacious, by resorting to the same species of imagery in order to make a comparison.

Καὶ διϊκνούμενος . . . . πνεύματος. The writer continues the description of the efficacy of the divine threatening, by carrying on still further the description of the effects produced by a sharp sword upon the natural body. *Piercing even so as to separate life and spirit.* Ψυχὴ, when used as here, in distinction from πνεῦμα, means the *animal* soul or principle of *animal* life in man; as πνεῦμα in such a case means, the *rational* or *intellectual* soul, the *immaterial* principle within man. See 1 Thess. v. 23, where σῶμα is added, in order to designate the merely *physical* or *corporeal* part of the human system. In the phrase under consideration, *piercing so as to divide* [or separate] *life and spirit*, plainly means inflicting a wound so deep as shall prove deadly; for that which separates the soul from the system endowed with animal life, is of course deadly. We may paraphrase both expressions thus; *a sharp sword that inflicts deadly wounds.*

Ἁρμῶν τε καὶ μυελῶν, [piercing so as to divide] *joints and marrow*, i. e. so as to divide the joints or limbs from the body, (which was often done in the severer kinds of punishment;) and so as to pierce through the very bone to the marrow, or to separate the marrow from the bone, by perforating it; a tremendous image of the sharpness of the sword and the effects it produces. The sense is, that the divine commination is of *most deadly* punitive efficacy.

Καὶ κριτικὸς . . . . καρδίας, *he also judges* [takes cognizance of] *the desires and purposes of the heart*, i. e. Θεὸς κριτικὸς ἐστι. That κριτικὸς, *aptus ad judicandum*, here applies to God, and not to λόγος, seems evident. That there is a transition to Θεὸς is quite evident from ver. 13, where ἐνώπιον αὐτοῦ, ὀφθαλμοῖς αὐτοῦ, and πρὸς ὅν, one cannot well doubt, are to be applied to God. There is, then, a transition somewhere to Θεὸς; and the nature of the case shows, that the appropriate place for it is at καὶ κριτικὸς. In the preceding part of the verse, λόγος Θεοῦ, *divine commination*, is represented (very forcibly and properly) as *punitive*. This idea is consummated by the phrase which ends with μυελῶν; and as Θεὸς comes in as the subject of discourse, in the sequel, (at least in ver. 13,) I see no place so apposite for its introduction, as at καὶ κριτικὸς. Indeed, there can be no other; for, unless it comes in here, we must carry λόγος Θεοῦ, as the subject, through the whole paragraph; which does not seem to me to be the design of the writer.

God is here represented as one who scans the whole of man's internal character, and sits in judgment upon it. Consequently, as the writer intimates, no secret act or purposes of unbelief, or defection from the Christian cause, will remain unnoticed or unpunished. Ἐνθύμησις and ἔννοια are nearly allied in meaning. They are both employed here, merely for the purpose of designating *universality*, i. e. the whole of men's internal thoughts and purposes.

Ver. 13. Καὶ οὐκ ἔστι .... αὐτοῦ, *yea, nothing is concealed from the view of him* [i. e. of God.] Κτίσις means *any created thing;* literally, *act of creation*, but it follows the Hebrew בְּרִיאָה. Οὐ κτίσις means, *no thing*, לֹא כֹל = οὐδὲν, or לֹא בְּרִיאָה.

Πάντα .... τετραχηλισμένα, *but all things are naked and exposed to the view of him, to whom we are accountable*. Τραχηλίζω is best explained here, in the sense which the Greek classical writers attach to it. It means, (1.) To lay bare and bend back the neck, so as to expose the throat, in order to its being cut open or dissevered. Hence, (2.) *To expose, to lay open;* which is the idea of the word in the phrase before us; as it is given in the translation above. Ὀφθαλμοῖς, *eyes*, i. e. *sight, view, cognizance;* for it is often used in this way.

Πρὸς ὃν ἡμῖν ὁ λόγος, literally, *with whom,* [before whom, in whose power, or, at whose disposal,] *is our account*. The sense of *account*, λόγος often has. The common way of rendering λόγος here, is, *concern, dealing, business*. This sense the word will bear; but it is less in conformity with the *usus loquendi*, and less apposite to the design of the writer. Chrysostom understands it as I have translated it. And so the preceding clause requires it to be rendered ; for this speaks of God, (or λόγος, if you please) as κριτικὸς, i. e. *aptus ad judicandum ;* the clause, now under consideration, represents men as actually accountable to him who is the omniscient Judge.

View of the Contents of HEB. iv. 14.—x. 18.

The writer now proceeds to the consideration of a subject, at which he had merely hinted in ch. iii. 1. ; where he calls Christ the ἀρχιερέα of the Christian religion. As ἀπόστολος (שליח הצבור,) *præfectus domo Dei,* he had already compared him with Moses, ch. iii. 2—6 ; and then built upon the result of this comparison, the very solemn and affectionate warning against unbelief which follows, ch. iii. 7—19. For the encouragement of the Hebrew Christians, he had also taken occasion, (after having spoken of *unbelievers* as excluded from the *rest* of God,) to represent the promises still held out to *believers,* of enjoying that rest. Such was the case, under the ancient dispensation, and such, he argues, is still the case; "there remains a σαββατισμὸς for the people of God." He then, as we have seen, concludes the subject, as usual with an exhortation ; in which he calls on them not to fail of this rest, ch. iv. 11 ; nor to incur the awful penalty attached to unbelief, ch. iv. 11—13.

Having thus completed the comparison of Christ as ἀπόστολος with Moses, and drawn from the result of it those practical deductions at which our epistle everywhere aims ; the writer now proceeds to compare Christ, as ἀρχιερεὺς, with the Levitical order of priesthood ; which comparison, with its various subordinate parts, and the occasional warnings and comminations that now and then are intermixed, extends to ch. x. 18.; which is the end of what may be called the *doctrinal* part of our epistle.

The mind of the writer plainly appears to have been more intensely engaged with comparing Christ's priesthood to that of Aaron and the Levites, than with any other subject in his epistle. The comparison, for example, of Christ with the angels, in ch. i. is short; the comparison of him with Moses, in ch. iii. still shorter. But the comparison of the Aaronical priesthood, as to dignity, duties, offices, and utility, with that of Christ, and of their functions with his, makes up, in fact, the body of our epistle. It is natural to inquire, why this should be so ; and the obvious answer seems to be, " Because the writer regarded this part of the Saviour's office and work, as being, in a comparative sense, by far the most important. As a *priest* he made atonement for sin by the sacrifice of himself; in regard to which, no angel, no prophet, no teacher, no Aaronical priest, could bear a comparison with him. The most prominent part of all his character, as a Saviour of sinners, is, that he is " the Lamb of God, which taketh away the sins of the world."

VIEW OF THE CONTENTS OF HEB. IV. 14.—X. 18.

Nothing could be more inappropriate, than the division of chapters made, in some cases, in our epistle. Ch. iii. most plainly ought to be united with ch. iv. 1—13; thus comprising all that properly belongs to one and the same subject. Ch. iv. ought to begin at ch. iv. 14, and to terminate with the end of ch. v. where there is a transition from doctrine to exhortation.

In regard to the course and method of argument, pursued through this leading portion of our epistle, (viz. from ch. iv. 14, to ch. x. 18,) in which a comparison between the Aaronical priesthood and that of Christ is made, and where all that is connected with the office, and person, and duty of priests is also drawn into the comparison; I have been able to find no satisfactory elucidation of it, in any commentator or critic whom I have perused. After attentive study of this whole passage, often repeated, it seems to me that the method of the writer is capable of being intelligibly stated; and I shall now venture upon the experiment.

The apostle introduces the topic, (to which he had adverted in ch. iii. 1, by calling Christ the ἀρχιερὰ τῆς ὁμολογίας ἡμῶν,) by calling Jesus ἀρχιερὰ μέγαν, and exhorting the Hebrews to hold fast the profession (ὁμολογίας) which they had made, ch. iv. 14. He again hints, very briefly, an encouragement to persevere, although subjected to trials and afflictions, because of the sympathy that the Saviour would feel for them, as having possessed a nature like theirs, exposed to trial and suffering, ch. iv. 15, 16. But as he had already dwelt at large on this topic (ch. ii. 16—18,) he merely adverts to it here, and passes on to suggest the points of comparison between the Levitical priesthood and that of Christ.

(1.) Every priest is appointed in behalf of men, in order that he may superintend and direct the concerns which men have with God, and may present their oblations and sacrifices before him, ch. v. 1.

(2.) Every priest, being himself "compassed with infirmity," is prepared by his own experience to sympathize with others in like condition; and because of his own sins and imperfections, it becomes his duty to offer expiatory sacrifices for himself as well as for them, ch. v. 2, 3.

(3.) No priest appoints himself to the sacred office; his appointment is by divine direction, ch. v. 4.

In making a comparison of Christ, as high-priest, with the Aaronical priests, in regard to the points here stated, the apostle inverts the order in which they are brought forward, and shows:

(1.) That Christ was constituted high priest by Divine appointment. This he proves in ver. 5, 6, by quotations from the second Psalm, and also from Ps. cx. 4.

(2.) He then passes to the *second* topic of comparison, viz. the infirmity of the nature which Christ, our great high priest, possessed; and which qualified him, in a peculiar manner, to sympathize with the infirmities of his people. He represents Christ as having, during his incarnate state, uttered vehement supplications on account of his trials and distresses, and as experiencing, like other men, deliverance from them, ch. v. 7. Even though he was clothed with the dignity of the Son of God, he acquired a practical knowledge of what it is to obey in the midst of sufferings, ch. v. 8. Thus was he fitted μετριοπαθεῖν τοῖς ἀγνοοῦσι; and having thus obeyed and suffered, in consequence thereof, he was exalted to glory (τελειωθεὶς,) where, as *kingly* high priest, after the order of Melchisedek, he is an all-sufficient Saviour to those who believe and obey him, ch. v. 9, 10.

As one of the proofs that Christ was exalted to be an all-sufficient Saviour, the writer has again, ver. 10, produced the passage, which asserts him to be a priest for ever, after the order of Melchisedek, i. e. a kingly priest, whose office is not of limited extent, or temporary duration. But having thus introduced a topic attended with difficulty, and demanding an enlightened knowledge of the Scriptures and of the nature of Christianity, in order to be rightly and fully comprehended, the apostle stops short in the prosecution of his subject, in order to admonish those whom he was addressing, with regard to the little progress which they had made, in such knowledge as would render them adequate fully to comprehend the discussion concerning the topic in question, in which he was about to engage. His reproof for their comparative ignorance, he pursues through ch. v. 11—14. In ch. vi. 1—3, he warns them against the awful danger which would result from stopping short or turning back in their course, in order that he might thus excite them to more diligence and exertion, respecting religious improvement. Notwithstanding the seeming severity of his remarks in regard to his topic, he assures them that he has an affectionate confidence in their good estate, ch. vi. 9; and this, because God will have regard to the benevolent character which they had before exhibited, ch. vi. 10. He then exhorts them to press forward in their Christian course, ch. vi. 11; and assures them, that the promise and oath of God are pledged, that believers who persevere shall attain to salvation, ch. vi. 13—19.

After this digression, (if that may be called digression which is so directly concerned with the main object of the writer,) he proceeds to descant upon the topic of Christ's priesthood, as instituted by God, and compared with that of Melchisedek, which had been brought to view by the text of scripture cited in ch. v. 6, 10.

In order to do this so as to make a strong impression, he begins by giving an account of the dignity of Melchisedek. He was king of Salem, and priest of the most high God; his superiority was acknowledged by Abraham, when he paid him a tithe of the spoils which he had taken, ch. vii. 1, 2. The same Melchisedek was not descended from priests, (and therefore his office did not fall to him by the mere right of succession, but was the special appointment of God;) he has no genealogy assigned him in the sacred writings, nor any limited term mentioned in which his priesthood began or expired; like Christ's priesthood, his is unlimited, ch. vii. 3. Abraham himself, exalted as this patriarch was, acknowledged the superiority of Melchisedek; and the Levitical priests, descended from him, did, as it were, acknowledge the same by their progenitor who paid this homage, and to whom they must be counted inferior, ch. vii. 4—7. Besides, the Levitical priests, who receive tithes, hold their office only for a limited duration; while Melchisedek is a priest for an unlimited time, ch. vii. 8. Indeed, (if one may venture so to express himself,) the Levites themselves paid tithes to Melchisedek, through Abraham their progenitor, ch. vii. 9, 10.

Thus much for the superiority of Melchisedek over the Levitical priests. The conclusion, in this case, is left to be supplied by the reader's mind, after the manner in which Paul often writes. The reasoning is thus: " Christ is a priest, after the order of Melchisedek; Melchisedek is superior to the Aaronical priests; consequently, Christ, as a priest, is superior to them."

The writer next proceeds to another topic of great importance, and which very naturally connected itself with the consideration of Christ's priesthood, as compared with that of Melchisedek. If, says, he, the Levitical priesthood was adequate for all the purposes of atonement, and for the purification of the consciences of sinners, then, what necessity that the appointment of another priest should be made, as is predicted in Ps. cx. 4. Heb. vii. 11. Now, another order of priesthood necessarily demands a change of former institutions, ch. vii. 12; and that another order is necessary, follows from the fact, that Christ (the priest after the new order) was to spring from the tribe of Judah, ch. vii. 13. Still more evident must it be, that the order would be different, because the new priestly office is to be *perpetual*, ch. vii. 15—17. Consequently, the old order of things gives place to a new and better one, ch. vii. 18, 19.

Besides, the new priest is appointed by the solemnity of an oath, while the Aaronical priests were not, ch.vii.20,21;consequently, we must suppose the new order of things to be superior, ch. vii. 22. This superiority appears specially in the fact, that the priesthood of Christ is perpetual, while that of the Levites was constantly changing by succession, ch. vii. 23, 24. Christ, therefore, is an adequate and *never-failing* helper, to all who come unto God through him, ch. vii. 25.

It is thus that the apostle illustrates, enlarges, and confirms his views, respecting the subject introduced in ch. v. 6, 10, by a quotation from Ps. cx. 4, respecting the priesthood of Christ. The amount of the argument is, that by the oath of God, Christ was appointed to his priesthood, while the Aaronical priests were appointed without such a solemnity; that the priesthood itself, being of the order of Melchisedek, i. e. not by descent, not limited, not temporary, and of higher dignity than that of Aaron, Christ must be regarded as altogether superior to the order of Jewish priests. The inference of course is, that the Hebrews ought not to forsake him who was a superior priest, in order to attach themselves to those who were inferior ones.

Having thus completed what he had to say, respecting the comparison of Christ and Melchisedek as priests, (all of which is employed to the advantage of the cause which he is advocating) the writer resumes the topic which he had begun in ch. v. 7, 8, viz. that of Christ's sympathy with those " who are compassed with infirmity." He had already suggested there, that Christ possessed all the common sympathies and innocent infirmities of our nature, in common with other priests. But not to leave it uncertain, whether in *all* respects Jesus was " compassed with such infirmities" as the Jewish priests, he now proceeds to point out one important difference, viz. that the high priest of the new dispensation is altogether superior to the priests of the old, in regard to the moral purity and perfection of his character. He is holy, and altogether sinless, ch. vii. 26; and therefore needs not, like them, to offer any sacrifice on his own account, ver. 27; for he has no such infirmity as renders this at all necessary, since he is priest in a state of perfection and glorious exaltation, ver. 28.

Having thus shown the superiority of Christ over the Levitical priests, in respect to the second particular, viz. *the qualifications for sympathizing with erring men*, the writer next proceeds to the most important topic of all, viz. *the office of Christ, as a priest, in directing the concerns of men with God, and in presenting a propitiatory sacrifice for them.*

He begins by averring, that the principal thing, (κεφάλαιον,) in respect to the matters which he is discussing, is the priesthood of Christ in the heavenly sanctuary, ch. viii. 1, 2. He then re-introduces the topic, which he had before stated in ch. v. 1 Taking for granted the truth of the sentiment there stated, he now draws the inference from it, that Christ (being a priest) must also have an offering to present, ch. viii. 1—3. But if Christ were on earth, he could not be a priest; for priests, whose office it is to perform duty in the *earthly* sanctuary, are already constituted by divine appointment, ver. 4; and these perform their office in a temple that is merely a copy or resemblance of the heavenly one, ver. 5. Christ's ministry is as much superior to theirs, as the new covenant is to the old one, ver. 6; and the Scripture itself predicts, that the old covenant should be abolished, and the new one introduced in its stead, ver. 7—13. Of course, the new covenant must be superior; and Christ, who ministers in the heavenly temple, must be superior to those who serve merely in the earthly one.

Next, the writer proceeds to consider the manner and design of the sacerdotal service, and the ends which could be accomplished by it.

The earthly temple consisted of various apartments, and contained a variety of utensils, ch. ix. 1—5. The priests performed daily service in the outer temple, ver. 6; while the high priest entered the inner one (where God dwelt) only *once* in each year, when he presented the blood of the great atoning sacrifice, ver. 7. A permission to enter only so seldom into the inner sanctuary, showed that free access to God, at all times and places, was not yet disclosed, while the first dispensation lasted, ver. 8. Indeed, these rites, with all their appurtenances, were merely a symbol of what was to be effected under the gospel, ver. 9, 10.

Christ, on the other hand, the heavenly high priest, entered the eternal sanctuary with his own blood, procuring everlasting redemption for sinners, ver. 11, 12. The blood of bulls and goats, presented by the Jewish high priest, effected nothing more than ceremonial, external purification, ver. 13; while the blood of Christ purifies the conscience, and renders the worshipper truly acceptable to God, ver. 14.

Such is the efficacy of the propitiatory sacrifice made by the death of Christ, that it extends back to the sins of former ages; so that all who are called of God to partake of the blessings of the gospel, attain, through *his death*, to a heavenly *inheritance*, ver. 15.

The mention of Christ's *death* here, in connexion with the assurance effected by it of a heavenly *inheritance* for believers, affords occasion to the writer to compare the new διαθήκη ratified by the death of Christ, with the διαθήκαι which are ratified by the death of testators. The Greek word διαθήκη not only answers to ברית, but also means such an arrangement as is made by a man's *last will* or *testament*, and is employed, not unfrequently, in this latter sense. Hence, our author, after asserting (ver. 15) that Christ's *death* made sure an *inheritance* to believers, falls very naturally upon comparing the διαθήκη thus ratified by the death of Jesus, with the διαθήκαι ratified by the death of their respective testators. Such, says he, is the custom among men, in regard to *testaments*, that the death of the testators must supervene, in order to give them full effect and confirmation, ver. 16, 17. Even the first διαθήκη, (ברית,) although it could not be so appropriately called a *testament*, was sanctioned in a manner not unlike that in which the new διαθήκη is sanctioned; for *blood* (the emblem of death) was applied to almost every thing which pertained to the ancient covenant or διαθήκη, in order either to ratify, or to consecrate it, ver. 18—22. Now, since this was so extensively done in regard to things here, which are mere resemblances or types of heavenly things, these heavenly things themselves, being of a nature so much more exalted, must be consecrated by a corresponding sacrifice, of a higher nature than any offered in the earthly temple, ver. 23. For it is in the heavenly temple that Christ discharges the functions of his priestly office, ver. 24; yet not, like the Jewish priests, repeating expiatory offerings frequently but once for all performing this sacred rite, ver. 25, 26. As men die but once, and Christ in his human nature, and by dying in it, made an expiatory offering, so he could make this but once; therefore, when he shall make his second appearance, it will not be to repeat his sin-offering, but for the deliverance of all who wait for his coming, ver. 27, 28.

Having thus compared various particulars, which have respect to the priesthood of the descendants of Aaron, to those which relate to the priesthood of Jesus; the writer comes, last of all, to treat more fully of the inefficacy of the Jewish sacrifices, and of the perfect and everlasting efficacy of that propitiatory offering which was made by the high priest of the heavenly sanctuary. He had, indeed, already hinted at this, several times, in the preceding parts of his epistle, e. g. ch. vii. 11, 19; ch. viii. 7, 13; ch. ix. 8—10; ch. ix. 13, 14; but as it was the most important topic of all, and the most difficult to be urged on the minds of Jews, he reserved it until the last, in order that he might give it a more ample discussion.

He begins by declaring, that the rites of the law were designed to be *typical*, and that the yearly sacrifices which were offered under it, never could quiet and purify the consciences of men, ch. x. 1; otherwise, the offerings need not have been continually repeated, ver. 2. The remembrance of sin is constantly renewed by them, ver. 3. Indeed, it is plainly impossible that the blood of bulls and goats should take away sin, i. e. remove the penalty of it, or lessen its power, ver. 4. In accordance with this sentiment, the Scripture (Ps. xl.) represents the Saviour, when entering upon his work, as saying, that sacrifices and offerings are of no value in the sight of God, ver. 5, 6. The Messiah represents himself as doing what God requires, viz. what God requires in order that he may exercise his clemency, ver. 7. Of course (so our author reasons) sacrifices and offerings are rejected, in respect to making real propitiation, while the "obedience of Christ unto death" is accepted instead of them, ver. 8, 9. This sacrifice is truly efficacious for moral purposes, ver. 10. The Jewish priests repeated continually their sacrifices; but the offering of Christ, *once* made, is of everlasting efficacy, ver. 11, 12. Having once made this, he may expect the cause, on account of which it was made, victorious, ver. 13; for *one* offering, *once* made by Jesus, is all-sufficient; its effects are never to cease, ver. 14. To such an efficacy of Christ's offering, the Holy Spirit has testified in the Scriptures, by declaring, that under the *new* covenant sin should be forgiven, and iniquity no more remembered, ver. 15—17. Consequently, offering for sin needs not to be repeated, after pardon is actually obtained, ver. 18.

With this consideration, the author closes the comparison of Jesus, as a priest, with the Jewish priests under the Levitical dispensation. This comparison in all its parts, however, occupies the greater portion of his epistle, viz. from ch. iv. 14, to ch. x. 18. He then proceeds to exhortations, warnings, and various arguments drawn from different sources, in order to urge upon his Hebrew brethren the importance of persevering in the Christian faith.

The writer of our epistle has sometimes been charged with being discursive, and with having very little connexion in the series of his reasoning. If the charge of *discursiveness* means, that he often stops short in his course of argument, in order to warn those whom he was addressing, against danger, and to expostulate with them, this is certainly true in a remarkable degree. But this is the ultimate and highest end, which the writer himself had in view. If he has practised digression, it is digression exceedingly to his purpose, and altogether consonant with the unconstrained nature of epistolary address.

In respect to an alleged want of connexion in the author's reasoning, the analysis already presented is the best answer which I can give to this charge. The method of reasoning seems, indeed, to have been too commonly overlooked, or to have been only partially discerned, in the commentaries to which I have had access; but I cannot help thinking that there is a connexion, which can be clearly and satisfactorily traced, throughout the whole. If I have succeeded in attempting to trace it, then the student will be aided in forming his views, with respect to the relation that one part of our epistle bears to another, in that portion of it which has now been analysed.

If the question be asked, why the apostle should resort to comparisons of this nature, in order to illustrate the office of Christ, or, rather, the virtue and efficacy of his mediation and redemption; the answer plainly is, A regard to the condition and feelings of those whom he addressed, led him to do so. The Jews of that day regarded the office of high priest as the most honourable of all offices then sustained. The authority and dignity of this office were very great, in earlier times, under the Jewish kings. But after the captivity, the offices of king and high priest were frequently united in the same person. This, of course, would tend to elevate the esteem in which the Jews held the rank of high priest. When the Romans reduced Judea to a tributary province, the *civil* power was transferred to the procurator sent there by them; but the *ecclesiastical* power still remained in the hands of the high priest, who was supreme judge of the land, and president of the Sanhedrim. The high priest, was, moreover, the only person who could enter the most holy place, on the great day of national expiation, and make atonement for the people. On all these accounts, the Jews cherished the greatest degree of reverence for this office. They looked upon it as their glory, and expected from the functions of it, pardon for sin, and acceptance with God. How difficult it was to wean them from these views, even those of them who had embraced Christianity, the Acts of the Apostles, and almost all the apostolic epistles, abundantly testify. But this must necessarily be done, however difficult, if Christianity was to be fully admitted and practised by them.

There can be no doubt, that the unbelieving Jews would urge with all their power, upon the new converts to Christianity, the views and feelings which the latter had once possessed in common with them, with regard to this subject. It entered into the very essence of Judaism, that such views and feelings should be cherished; and this was a trait which distinguished the Jews, in a peculiar manner, from other nations. The apostle, in addressing the Hebrew Christians, had to contend with such arguments as the adversaries of Christianity among the Jews would bring, in order to shake the constancy of the new converts. The splendour and the supposed importance of the Jewish high-priesthood, however, was, after all, a thing which Jewish Christians must be brought to renounce. How could they, educated as they had been, do this? To satisfy their minds on this subject, the apostle presents a comparison of this office in all its various respects, with the office of high priest, as sustained by Christ; and he shows that, instead of giving up any thing, by embracing the new religion, they would only exchange a high priest who was imperfect, who offered sacrifices that effected a purification only external, and of mere temporary efficacy, who officiated in a temple made with hands—all the mere type or symbol of something that was of a spiritual and more exalted nature—all this they would exchange, by embracing and adhering to the Christian religion, for a high priest without sin, whose sacrifice "purged the conscience from dead works," and had an "everlasting efficacy;" which was offered too in a temple not made with hands, of which the Jewish temple, with all its splendour and solemn pomp, was only a mere image. Could any thing, now, be better adapted to fortify the minds of those to whom he wrote, in their Christian profession, and to wean them from their old prejudices? And is it not allowable, that an apostle should reason in a manner best adapted to the condition and feelings of those whom he addresses?

I am aware that much has been said by recent commentators, on arguing κατ' ἄνθρωπον, or in a way of *accommodation*, in our epistle; and that all the comparisons made in it, between things and persons, under the law and under the gospel, have been ranked with this class of reasoning or argument. For those who do not acknowledge the divine origin of the Jewish religion, nor that any of its rites, sacrifices or persons, were symbolical of anything belonging to Christianity, such a mode of explanation may be necessary. But for those who believe, with the writer of our epistle, that the Jewish religion was of God, and that the ancient Scriptures have revealed a Messiah; very little, if any, of arguing merely in the way of accommodation, in our epistle, needs to be admitted. Does not the one hundred-and-tenth Psalm call Christ a *high priest?* And did not the Jews of Paul's day admit (as well as

Paul himself) that this Psalm had respect to the Messiah? Undoubtedly they did. Where then is the *accommodation* of the writer to the mere prejudices of those whom he addressed, when it is evident that both he and they entertained an opinion in common, with regard to the exegesis of the one hundred-and-tenth Psalm? Of course, both admitted that Christ was to be a high priest. But how? Why? Not of the ordinary kind; for he did not descend from Aaron. Not to make an expiation which should merely pertain to external purification; but to make an expiation which should purge " the conscience from dead works," and which should procure the pardon of sin with God, and " bring in everlasting redemption for his people."

It is not, then, merely to satisfy the Jew, that he need relinquish nothing of his regard for the excellence and importance of the office of high priest, by embracing Christianity, and that he has exchanged a less splendid office of priest under Judaism, for a more splendid one under Christianity, that Paul dwells so long on the virtues and dignity of Christ's office as high priest. No doubt, he had this object in his eye, as I have already stated, when he entered upon the consideration of this topic. But why does he dwell on it so much longer than he does on the comparison of Christ with Moses? Not because the Jews exalted the high priest above Moses, for this surely they did not. It was because Christ, in the office of high priest, performed that peculiar duty, which, of all others, made him what he was, the SAVIOUR of *sinners, the* REDEEMER *of lost men;* because, as *priest,* he offered an *expiatory sacrifice,* which takes away the sins of the world, and makes him the propitiation for their offences. I am entirely unable to explain the copiousness of our epistle on this point, if this be not the reason of it. And if this be admitted, then there is reason enough why the apostle should dwell so long upon it.

I know of no part of the Scriptures which explains the nature and object of the Jewish ritual in a manner so spiritual, so satisfactory, so clear, so worthily of God, and so profitably to us, as ch. v—x. of the epistle to the Hebrews. As a key to the Old Testament, these chapters deserve the most attentive and thorough study of all who wish to understand the Bible. As a statement and vindication of the great work of Christ, and the atonement which he made by his blood for sin, they stand in the very first rank of all the scripture writings. As adapted to the wants and condition of those whom the apostle addressed, they are a consummate specimen of skilful argument, and of powerful persuasion and remonstrance.

Ver. 14. "Εχοντες οὖν ἀρχιερέα μέγαν; *moreover, since we have a great High-priest.* So the words, literally construed, seem to mean. But it is doubtful whether this translation conveys the exact shade of meaning which should be attached to the original. In the apostle's day, ἀρχιερεὺς no longer designated merely one man, the single head of the whole priesthood, but it was applied also to his deputy (סָגָן;) to those who had quitted the office of the high-priesthood (exauctorati;) and also to the priests, at the head of each of the twenty-four classes of the priesthood. The word ἀρχιερεύς, of itself, then, without any adjunct, did not in the time of Paul, designate the *high-priest* by way of eminence, who was the only person that could enter the most holy place, and make atonement for sin. Hence the apostle says, not simply ἀρχιερεύς, but ἀρχιερεὺς μέγας; which designates a specific individual. This corresponds exactly to the idea conveyed by the Hebrew כֹּהֵן גָּדוֹל, which was applied only to him who was actually *Pontifex Maximus*.

Διεληλυθότα τοὺς οὐρανούς, *passed through the heavens.* Wahl and others, *passed into the heavens;* interpreting διεληλυθότα as equivalent to εἰσερχόμενον, *entered into.* But they seem to me plainly to have mistaken the force of the writer's expression here. According to the Hebrew idiom, God dwells above the visible firmament, שָׁמַיִם, οὐρανοί. *Through* this Jesus passed, when he ascended to take his " seat at the right hand of the majesty on high," ch. i. 3. There is a plain allusion, too, to the high-priest of the Jews, who, once in a year, went into the most holy place, *passing through* the veil, which screened the residence of divine majesty from the view of men, ch. ix. 7, 8. So, our great high-priest has passed through the heavens, into the immediate presence of God, into the " holy of holies" in the upper world. This explanation, which Bengel and Owen defend, I must think to be the right one; although Ernesti ventures to call it *stulta animadversio*.

Ἰησοῦν τὸν υἱὸν τοῦ θεοῦ is added, to show whom he means by ἀρχιερέα. Κρατῶμεν τῆς ὁμολογίας *let us firmly hold* [tenaciously adhere to] *the religion which we have professed,* viz. Christianity. Κρατέω takes either the accusative or genitive after it.

To encourage them to follow this advice, the writer sets before them the assistance which they may expect, in their efforts so to do.

Ver. 15. Οὐ γὰρ . . . . ἀσθενείαις ἡμῶν, *for we have not a high priest who is incapable of sympathizing with our weaknesses.* The form of the expression is negative; a mode of expression frequently employed by the sacred writers. When the negative form is thus employed, it is of the same meaning as an affirmative assertion would be, i. e. it is the same in this case, as if the author had said, " We have a high priest, who will sympathize with our weaknesses." So, " John confessed, and denied not, but confessed," &c. John i. 20. In most cases, however, there is some *intensity* of colouring designed to be given, when this negative form of expression is chosen, in preference to simple affirmation.

Πεπειρασμένον, see on ch. ii. 18. Κατὰ πάντα, *in all respects;* not to be metaphysically or mathematically taken. The meaning is, that he, like us, was subjected to trial by suffering on account of the truth; he, like us, was solicited to sin, e. g. when Satan tempted him, and often when the Scribes and Pharisees tempted him. Καθ' ὁμοιότητα, scil. ἡμῶν, i. e. *who was tempted like us;* παραπλησίως ἡμῶν, says Theophylact; ὁμοίως ἡμῖν, Origen. This surely does not imply, that temptations had, in all respects, the same influence upon him as upon us; but only, that he was exposed to be attacked by them, in like manner as we are. He possessed a nature truly human, ch. ii. 14. 17; he was, therefore, susceptible of being excited by the power of temptations, although he never yielded to them. So the writer:

Χωρὶς ἁμαρτίας, *without sin ;* i. e. although assailed by temptations of every kind, he never yielded, in any case, to their influence. He remained sinless. But why is this here asserted? Principally, I apprehend, to guard against any mistake, in respect to what the writer had just said. To show the Hebrews, that they might depend on the sympathy and compassion of their high priest, (compare ch. ii. 17, 18,) to help them, in all the trials and difficulties to which an unshaken adherence to Christianity would subject them, he declares that Jesus was himself subject to the like trials, in all respects. But when he had so said, as if fearing they might draw the conclusion, that in in some cases, at least, he was (like others) overcome by them, the author immediately adds, χωρὶς ἁμαρτίας. It may be, that the expression implies an exhortation thus, viz. " Jesus when tried did not sin ; Christian brethren, follow his example." I prefer, however, the former explanation.

Ver. 16. *Let us, then, approach the throne of grace,* μετὰ παρρησίας, *with freedom of speech ;* i. e. since we have such a sympathizing, compassionate high priest, to offer our supplication to God, and to help us, let us go to God with confidence that we shall receive the aid that we need. " Ask, and ye shall receive." Τῷ θρόνῳ τῆς χάριτος has reference to *the mercy-seat,* in the temple, on which God is represented as sitting enthroned. There he heard the supplications of his people, presented by the high priest; there he accepted their oblations; and from thence he dispensed to them the blessings which they needed. Christians may now approach the mercy-seat in heaven, by their high priest, and may come, μετὰ παρρησίας, *with confidence.*

Ἵνα λάβωμεν ἔλεον, *that we may obtain mercy,* i. e. that compassion may be exercised towards Christians, in their afflictions and trials. Καὶ χάριν εὕρωμεν . . . . βοήθειαν, *and find favour in respect to timely assistance.* Χάριν does not differ much here, from ἔλεον, except that it is a word of a more generic nature. The sentiment is, *be helped opportunely*; i. e. now, when we are persecuted and sorely pressed by trials, we may obtain that aid which such seasons require. This is exactly the idea conveyed by εὔκαιρον βοήθειαν, *auxilium opportunum*. Literally the Greek runs thus, *And find grace, with respect to opportune assistance*.

CHAPTER V.

Ver. 1. 'Εξ ἀνθρώπων λαμβανόμενος, *selected, taken from men*. So λαβεῖν, in Acts xv. 14. In a similar sense, לָקַח is often used in Hebrew; and λαμβάνω, not unfrequently, in the classics. The meaning is, that priests, appointed according to the usages of the Levitical law, are appointed to have the oversight of the religious concerns of the people, specially to make their oblations and sacrifices.

Ὑπὲρ ἀνθρώπων καθίσταται τὰ πρὸς τὸν Θεόν, *is constituted for the benefit of men, in relation to their concerns with God*. Καθίσταται is often employed to designate an appointment to office of any kind; e. g. Matt. xxiv. 45. Luke xii. 14, et al. So, also, it is used by heathen writers. Ὑπὲρ, *for the benefit of, for the sake of, on account of*; a frequent use of the word. Τὰ πρὸς τὸν Θεόν, for κατὰ τὰ, κ. τ. λ. there being an ellipsis of the preposition, which is very common in such cases. The idea is, " In respect to their religious concerns; in regard to business which they have to transact with God;" particularly,

"Ἵνα προσφέρῃ . . . . ἁμαρτιῶν, *that he may offer* [to God] *both oblations and sacrifices for sin*. Δῶρα I take here to mean, the various kinds of *thank-offerings*, &c. that were to be presented to God, agreeably to the ritual established by Moses; and θυσίας, the various *sin* and *trespass offerings*, that were made with slain beasts. To the act of *slaying* θυσίας refers, as it is derived from θύω, *to kill*. In all these, and the like concerns, the high priest was to act the part of an *internuntius*, a mediator, between God and men; i. e. he was to aid men in regard to their spiritual or religious concerns. It should be remarked, however, that δῶρα sometimes includes the idea of sacrifices, e. g. ch. viii. 4, compare ch. viii. 3. Yet, where both δῶρα and θυσία are employed, they are not to be regarded as synonymes. Both are employed to designate the *universality* of the idea intended, i. e. (in this case) offerings of every kind.

Ver. 2. Μετριοπαθεῖν δυναμενος, *one who can exercise gentleness* or *moderation*. This classic or philosophic use of the word μετριοπαθεῖν may be briefly explained. The Stoics maintained that a man should be ἀπαθὴς, i. e. not subject to passions, such as anger, fear, hope, joy, &c. The Platonists, on the other hand, averred, that *a wise man* should be μετριοπαθὴς, *moderate in his affections*, and not ἀπαθὴς. The leading sense, then, of the word μετριοπαθεῖν, is *to be moderate in our feelings or passions*. In our text, the connexion shows us, that this moderation or gentleness was to be exercised by the high priest, τοῖς ἀγνοοῦσι καὶ πλανωμένοις, *toward those who were ignorant and erring*. In other words, he was to be lenient towards offenders, to treat them with gentleness and moderation, with kindness, and not with severity. The comparison of Christ as a priest, in respect to this point, is presented in ch. v. 7—9, and ch. vii. 26—28.

Ἀγνοοῦσι καὶ πλανωμένοις some have construed as a Hendiadys, and rendered the phrase thus: *those who ignorantly offend*, or, *who offend through ignorance*. But surely the indulgence of the high priest on earth was not limited merely to this class of offenders, much less is the clemency of our great high priest in the heavens so limited. Ἀγνοέω is repeatedly used by the LXX. as a translation of the Hebrew שָׁגָה, שָׁגַג, אָשֵׁם, which signify, *to err, to commit sin, to render one's self guilty*. So Sirac. ch. v. 18, *in a great or little thing*, μὴ ἀγνόει, *sin not*. So Polyb. V. 11. 5, πολεμεῖν τοῖς ἀγνοήσασι, *to make war on those who have been faulty*. But if any should think it preferable, in our verse, to retain the common sense of *ignorance*, then plainly it must be construed of voluntary criminal ignorance; and, in such a case, πλανωμένοις designates those who commit offences in consequence of such ignorance. But I prefer the other rendering, which makes ἀγνοοῦσι καὶ πλανωμένοις to be an accumulation of descriptive words, in order to designate offenders of various kinds. This comports better too with *fact*, either in relation to the office of the Levitical priest in the earthly sanctuary, or to that of Jesus in the heavenly one.

Ἐπεὶ καὶ . . . ἀσθένειαν, *since he himself is compassed wich infirmity*, i. e. he is himself an offender, or, he is exposed by his weaknesses to commit the like sins with those whose offerings he is called to present to God. Περίκειται, in the passive, is construed with an accusative after it. Ἀσθένεια means here, *moral infirmity*, or *weakness*, not natural frailty of the *physical* system. The meaning is, that the high priest, "haud ignarus mali, miseris succurrere discit."

Ver. 3. Καὶ διὰ ταύτην . . . ἁμαρτιῶν, *and on this account,* [viz. because he is himself a sinner,] *he must present sin-offerings, as well for himself as for the people.* Προσφερεῖν, i. e. πρόσφοραν vel θυσίαν, Hebrew הֶעֱלָה עֹלָה. Προσφέρω is the common word employed to denote the presentation of an offering, gift, or sacrifice to God, and corresponds to the Hebrew עָלָה, or rather, הֶעֱלָה in Hiphil. See the superiority of Christ represented, in respect to the point here suggested, in ch. vii. 26—28.

Ver. 4. Καὶ οὐκ ἑαυτῷ . . . 'Ααρών, *moreover, no one can assume the honour* [of the high priesthood] *to himself, but he is appointed by God, even as Aaron was.* Καλούμενος, i. e. δεῖ καλούμενος εἶναι.

Ver. 5. Οὕτω καὶ . . . ἀρχιερέα, *accordingly, Christ did not claim for himself the honour of being high priest,* or, Christ *did not exalt himself to the honour of being high priest.* Δοξάζειν, *to exalt, to claim honour for,* John viii. 54. Rom. xi. 13.

'Αλλ' ὁ λαλήσας . . . γεγέννηκά σε, *but he who said to him, Thou art my son, this day have I begotten thee,* ἐδόξασεν αὐτὸν, *exalted him.*] So the ellipsis must be supplied. The meaning is, exalted him to the office of high priest ; i. e. the *Father* bestowed this honour upon the Son, see on ch. i. 5 ; or, in other words, he was *divinely appointed.*

Ver. 6. Καθὼς καὶ ἐν ἑτέρῳ λέγει, *so also he declares in another passage* [of scripture.] The declaration is, that the *Father* constituted the Son a priest ; for the writer had affirmed, in ver. 4, that a priest must be divinely constituted. The quotation is from Ps. cx. 4 ; a Psalm which, as I have before remarked, not only the apostle and most Christian commentators, but even the Jewish rabbies in general, agree, has relation to the Messiah.

Σὺ ἱερεὺς . . . Μελχισεδέκ, *thou art a priest for ever, after the order of Melchisedek.* Ἱερεὺς designates here a priest *generically* considered. The Psalmist, and after him the apostle, does not say, ἀρχιερεὺς, because the sequel shows that the personage referred to must be of the highest order of priests, viz. of the same order with that of Melchisedek.

Κατὰ τὴν τάξιν, Hebrew עַל דִּבְרָתִי, i. e. עַל דִּבְרַת, for י is paragogic here. This Hebrew phrase commonly means, *on account of; for the sake of;* but such a meaning would be wholly inapposite in Ps. cx. 4. The sense of it, as there employed, plainly is similar to that of דָּבָר in Deut. xv. 9 ; xix. 4. 1 Kings ix. 15, viz. *manner, order, arrangement, kind.* So the classic sense of τάξις is, *order, arrangement, place, office, rank.* The simple meaning is, "Thou art a priest, of an order or rank like that of Melchisedek."

When in ver. 10, the writer repeats the quotation here made, he uses ἀρχιερεὺς instead of ἱερεὺς, the word employed in his first quotation. The object of the quotation in ver. 6, is simply to prove, that the office of high priest was conferred on Christ by Divine appointment; comp. ver. 4. and 6. The particulars of the comparison, in respect to the priesthood of Christ and Melchisedek, are not immediately brought into view, but suspended until the writer has introduced other considerations relative to Christ as a priest, ch. v. 7—9. and given vent to his feelings of concern for those whom he was addressing, by suggesting various considerations, adapted to reprove, ch. v. 11—14; to warn, ch. vi. 1—9; as well as to excite and animate them, ch. vi. 10—20.

In regard to κατὰ τὸν αἰῶνα, it is to be taken in a qualified sense here, as often elsewhere, e. g. compare Luke i. 33, with 1 Cor. xv. 24—28. The priesthood of Christ will doubtless continue no longer than his mediatorial reign; for when his reign as mediator ceases, his whole work both as mediator and as priest will have been accomplished.

In respect to the application of Ps. cx. to the Messiah, see Matt. xxii. 41—45. certain it is, from this passage, that Jesus considered and treated this Psalm as applying to himself.

The three following verses I take to be a comment on ch. v. 2; or, to express my meaning more fully, a comparison of Christ, as a priest, which the Jewish priests, who being themselves compassed with infirmity, were taught by experience μετριοπαθεῖν τοῖς ἀγνοοῦσι καὶ πλανωμένοις. It is, however, only the infirmities of one exposed to *suffering*, that are brought to view here. These Christ possessed in full, so that he could, like other priests, sympathize with those who are tempted, and tried by suffering. None of his disciples are tried more severely than he was.

The writer, however, does not complete this topic here. He breaks off, in order to pursue the course of thought to which the introduction of Melchisedek's priesthood led him, and for the sake of inserting practical warning, reproof, and exhortation, ch. v. 11.—vii. 55; and in ch. vii. 26, he resumes the consideration of the topic thus interrupted, and shows, that as to *sinful infirmities*, Christ was not to be compared with the Jewish priests; for he had none of them. Thus, while, like other priests, he was fitted to exercise compassion on those who are suffering and are tempted, he was altogether superior to them in the moral perfection of his own character. He needed no sin-offering for himself, (compare ch. v. 4;) but was high priest in a state, where he was εἰς τὸν αἰῶνα τετελειωμένον, ch. vii. 26—28.

Ver. 7. Ὅς ἐν ταῖς ἡμέραις τῆς σαρκὸς αὐτοῦ, *who, during the time of his incarnation*. Ἡμέραι, like the Hebrew יָמִים, means, *time, season.* Τῆς σαρκὸς I understand, as designating the condition of the Logos incarnate, or ἐν σαρκὶ; compare John i. 1. 14. 1 Tim. iii. 16. The whole expression designates the period of the Saviour's humiliation, when " he was tempted in all points as we are," ch. iv. 15.

Δεήσεις καὶ ἱκετηρίας . . . προσενέγκας, *offered up prayers and supplications*. These two words are often joined, by profane writers ; e. g. ἱκετηρίας πολλὰς καὶ δεήσεις ποιούμενοι, Isoc. de Pace. Χωρὶς δὲ ἱκετηρίας καὶ δεήσεως, Philo de Cherub. p. 116. So also Lucian and Plutarch. Some critics have referred δεήσεις to prayers proceeding from a *sense of need ;* and ἱκετηρίας to *submissive intercession*. But although, in some cases, the words may be thus employed, they are generally used as synonymous, or nearly so. The conjunction of both these synonymes denotes *intensive supplication* or *intercession ;* a mode of expressing intensity, which is very frequent in the sacred writings.

Πρὸς τον δυνάμενον σώζειν αὐτὸν ἐκ θανάτου, i. e. to the sovereign Lord of life and death, the " God in whose hands our breath is, and whose are all our ways :" a periphrasis, in this case, which means, God who is possessed of *supreme* power, or, the sovereign Lord of life and death.

Μετὰ κραυγῆς ἰσχυρᾶς καὶ δακρύων, *voce altâ et lacrymis, with loud cries, and with tears* or *weeping*. See Luke xxii. 41—44. Matt. xxvi. 38, 39 ; xxvii. 46. Mark xv. 34—36. Compare Luke xii. 50. John xii. 27, 28. Κραυγῆς ἰσχυρᾶς denotes the intensity of the voice, as raised high by agonizing supplication, Luke xxii. 44. The evangelists do not mention the weeping of the Saviour; but who can doubt that he did weep, when he prayed in such an agony, that he sweat as it were drops of blood ? Luke xxii. 14.

Καὶ εἰσακουσθεὶς ἀπὸ τῆς εὐλαβείας, *and was heard in respect to that which he feared*, or *was delivered from that which he feared*. The classic sense of εὐλάβεια is, *fear, dread ;* and this is the sense in which it is commonly employed in the Septuagint. But as the Hebrew words יִרְאָה and יָרֵא mean, *reverence* and *to revere*, as well as *fear*, and *to fear*, or *to dread*, so the Greek εὐλάβεια, εὐλαβὴς, εὐλαβέω, are sometimes employed to designate the idea of *reverence*, and consequently (like יִרְאַת יְהוָה) of *piety, devotion, religion*. But the usual classic sense of the word is to be preferred, in our verse, viz. *fear*, or *object of dread*, like the Hebrew מוֹרָא. Εἰσακούω and ἐπακούω are frequently employed, in the Septuagint, in order to translate the Hebrew verb עָנָה; and עָנָה very often means, *to answer a prayer* or *request*. To answer a request for deliverance, is *to deliver* or *save from*. This sense the verb עָנָה sometimes has; e. g. Ps. xxii. 22, *from the horns of the wild bull* עֲנִיתָנִי, *deliver me*, (the preceding parallelism has הוֹשִׁיעֵנִי *save me ;*) Job xxxv. 12, *from the pride of the wicked* לֹא יַעֲנֶה, *he* [God] *will not deliver*. So Ps. cxviii. 5 et al. We may render εἰσακουσθεὶς, then, *was delivered*. Still, this is not absolutely necessary, inasmuch as *he was heard in respect to the object of fear*, gives the same sense, viz. from that which he dreaded Christ was delivered, or, his entreaties were listened to in respect to that which he dreaded. Ἀπὸ, like the Hebrew מִן, מִ, is sometimes employed in the sense of, *quod attinet ad*, so that it accords with the general meaning of περὶ; e. g. in Acts xvii. 2. See Schleusner Lex. ἀπὸ, No. 18, Gesen. Heb. Lex. מִן No. 4. If εἰσακουσ-θεὶς be translated (as the Hebrew עָנָה in some cases should be rendered,) *was delivered*, then the usual sense of ἀπὸ is perfectly appropriate; and, on this account, I have thought such a translation to be preferable, and made it accordingly. See Excursus XI.

Ver. 8. Καίπερ ὢν υἱὸς .... ὑπακοὴν, *although a Son, yet did he learn obedience by suffering ;* i. e. although he was God's only and well-beloved Son, a personage of such exalted dignity, yet was he put to the trial of obedience in the midst of sufferings ; or, he was subjected to learn experimentally, what it is to obey in the midst of sufferings. So I interpret this somewhat difficult and much agitated verse. I cannot suppose the object of the writer to be, an assertion that Christ did not understand the nature of obedience or recognize the duty of it, before he suffered ; but that it pleased God to exalt him to glory, in the way of obedience rendered by suffering as well as by action. Such is the sentiment in ch. ii. 10. Of such an obedience our epistle speaks, in ch. x. 7, quoted from Ps. xl. 8, 9 ; and such is that mentioned in Phil. ii. 8, *obedience unto death, even the death of the cross*, which, in the sequel, is asserted to be the special ground of Christ's exaltation to the throne of the universe. To mention such an obedience here, is altogether apposite to the apostle's design ; which was, fully to impress on the Hebrews the sympathizing and compassionate nature of the Saviour, and his fitness to succour those who were under sufferings and trials ; compare ii. 17, 18 ; iv. 15, 16. The same is implied in ch. v. 1, 2.

Ver. 9. Καὶ τελειωθεὶς .... αἰωνίου, *then, when exalted to glory, he became the author of eternal salvation* [he procured salvation] *for all those who obey him.* For τελειωθεὶς, see on ch. ii. 10, where is the same sentiment as here ; and where Christ, who is here said to be αἴτιος σωτηρίας, is called τὸν ἀρχηγὸν τῆς σωτηρίας, which has the same meaning. As to ch. ii. 10, the whole of the preceding context there, is occupied with showing the exaltation or kingly dignity of Christ; and to this state of exaltation τελειωθεὶς undoubtedly refers here. There is also conveyed, by ver. 9, an intimation that Christ's very sufferings stand in an intimate and necessary connexion with his exaltation to the kingly office, so that he is a *kingly* priest, as Melchisedek also was. There is evidently no necessity, however, of including ver. 7—9 in parenthesis, as many commentators have done; nor of regarding them as an interruption of the apostle's discourse. The fact is, as we have seen in the illustration above, that a new topic or head is introduced by them, which is broken off in the manner of Paul, in ch. v. 11, and resumed in ch. vii. 26.

Ver. 10. Προσαγορευθεὶς .... Μελχιζεδέκ, *being called by God,* [as I was saying,] *a high priest, after the order of Melchisedek.* Προσαγορεύω means, *to name, to salute by calling a name, to greet.* The meaning is, that Christ is greeted, or saluted, by the name or appellation, ἀρχιερεὺς, כֹּהֵן. In the Septuagint, Ps. cix. 4, [cx. 4,] and above, in ver. 6, it is ἱερεὺς. But the Hebrew כֹּהֵן means either ἀρχιερεὺς, or ἱερεὺς; see Lev. iv. 16, et al.; so that the apostle might render the original, in Ps. cx. 4, by either Greek word, as he has done.

Having thus introduced the subject of Christ's exaltation as priest, the nature of the comparison introduced, viz. the comparison of Christ's priesthood with that of Melchisedek, occasions the writer to stop short, in order to comment on this, and also to give utterance, in the first place, to his emotions of concern for those whom he addressed. The difficulty and obscurity of the subject which he is about to discuss, are, in his view, occasioned principally by the low state of religious knowledge in those whom he addresses. This he tells them very plainly, in order to reprove them for the little progress they had made in Christian knowledge, as well as to guard them against objecting to what he is about to advance.

Ver. 11. Περὶ οὗ πολὺς ἡμῖν ὁ λόγος .... λέγειν, *respecting whom we have much to say.* So Lysias in Panoe. πολὺς ἂν εἴη μοι λόγος διηγεῖσθαι. Dionys. Harlicar. I. 23. περὶ ὧν πολὺς ἂν εἴη λόγος.

Καὶ δυσερμήνευτος, *and difficult of explanation,* from δὺς and ἑρμηνεύω

Critics frequently couple the word λέγειν, which follows, with ἐυσερμή-
νευτος; but the example above, from Lysias, shows that it should be
associated with the former clause of the verse. The grammatical construction, or arrangement, I take to be this: περὶ οὗ [τὸ] λέγειν, πολὺς
ἡμῖν, [εἴη] ὁ λόγος; the infinitive λέγειν being used as a noun in the
nominative, or as the subject of the sentence, according to a common
usage.

Ἐπεὶ νωθροὶ γεγόνατε ταῖς ἀκοαῖς, *since ye are dull of apprehension*,
or, *slow in understanding*. Ταῖς ἀκοαῖς, lit. *in hearing*. But ἀκούω, *to
hear*, means often *to perceive, to understand*, like the Hebrew שָׁמַע.

The reason why they are so dull in respect to understanding religious
subjects, is next suggested by the writer; doubtless with the design
of reproving those whom he addresses, for their neglect to make a
suitable progress in Christian knowledge.

Ver. 12. Καὶ γὰρ ὀφείλοντες .... χρόνον, *for when ye ought to be even
capable of teaching, as it respects the length of time*, viz. since ye made
a profession of the Christian religion. The writer, doubtless, does not
mean to say, that the whole church whom he addressed should actually
be teachers; but that they ought to have made advances enough in the
knowledge of spiritual subjects, to be *able to teach* in them; or, in other
words, ought to have made very considerable acquisitions in religious
knowledge, considering the length of time that had elapsed since they
professed to be Christians. Διὰ, *after*, so before words signifying *time*;
e. g. Matt. xxvi. 61. Mark xiv. 58; ii. 1. Acts xxiv. 17. Gal. ii. 1.

Πάλιν χρείαν ἔχετε .... τοῦ Θεοῦ, *ye have need that one should
again teach you the very rudiments of divine doctrine*. Στοιχεῖα, *elements* or *rudiments* of any science. Στοιχεῖα τῆς ἀρχῆς, *the rudiments of
the beginning*, is the same as Horace's *elementa prima*, Serm. I. The
idea is expressed by the phrase, *very rudiments* or *first elements*, *elementa prima*. Τῶν λογίων τοῦ Θεοῦ, I should refer particularly to those
parts of the Old Testament, which have a respect to the Christian
religion, and especially to the Messiah, were it not that in ch. vi. 1—3,
the writer has shown that he means the rudiments of *Christian doctrine*
in its *appropriate* sense. Λογίων Θεοῦ then must mean here, *doctrines* or
communications of God, viz. which God has revealed under the gospel,
i. e. divine doctrine, or doctrines of divine original.

This feeble, imperfect, spiritual condition, the writer now describes
by a very appropriate figure, taken from the aliment and condition of
young children.

Καὶ γεγόνατε χρείαν . . . . τροφῆς, *and ye have become* [like] *those who need milk, and not solid nourishment;* literally, ye have become those who need, &c. But the particle of similitude is, in such cases, very often omitted in the Old Testament and in the New. The meaning is, " Ye have in spiritual things become as children are in regard to food, i. e. unable to bear or to digest any thing but the most light and simple nourishment; ye cannot understand or bear the higher and more difficult doctrines, ye cannot properly apprehend them when they are proposed to you." Τροφὴ, *nourishment, any kind of food*, not *meat* only.

Ver. 13. Πᾶς γὰρ ὁ μετέχων . . . . νήπιος γὰρ ἐστι, *now, every one who partakes of milk, is unskilled in the doctrine of salvation, for he is a child.* Ἄπειρος, *inexpers, ineptus ad aliquam rem*, that is, one who has not that skill or experience in regard to any thing, which is requisite to a due apprehension and consideration of it. The sentiment is, " As he, who must be fed with milk, is yet a child; so ye, who can bear only the lighter kinds of spiritual nourishment, are yet νήπιοι in religion." Λόγου δικαιοσύνης, *doctrine of salvation*, i. e. the gospel, or the Christian religion. The Hebrew צֶדֶק and צְדָקָה are often equivalent to מִשְׁפָּט, *statute, ordinance, rule of life*. It is evident, here, that δικαιοσύνης means, *what the Christian religion sanctions* or *ordains*. See Schleusner on δικαιοσύνη, No. 9. Or, δικαιοσύνη may be here rendered, *grace, favour*, i. e. the gospel which reveals grace, favour, pardon.

Ver. 14. Τελείων δέ ἐστιν ἡ στερεὰ τροφὴ, *but solid food is for those of mature age*. Τελείων, *adult, grown up, having attained completion in a physical respect*. See on ch. ii. 10; v. 9.

Τῶν διὰ τὴν ἕξιν . . . . κακοῦ, *who possess organs of sense, exercised by practice, for distinguishing between good and evil*. The metaphor here, as in the preceding verse, is of a mixed nature; the latter clause being appropriate to moral τέλειοι. The meaning is, that *solid food*, which is an image of the more difficult part of gospel doctrines, is appropriate to *full-grown* men, i. e. to Christians who have come to a maturer state, and who by experience in matters of religion, and frequent reflection upon them, have made advances so as to be able to distinguish what is right and what is wrong respecting them. Ἀισθητήρια here means the *internal senses* of Christians, their moral powers or faculties of distinguishing and judging; although the term itself, in its *literal* acceptation, designates the *external organs of sense*. Διάκρισιν καλοῦ καὶ κακοῦ is borrowed from the Hebrew יָדַע טוֹב וָרָע. See Gen. ii. 17;

Deut. i. 39 ; and compare Isa. vii. 15, 16 ; Jonah iv. 11. It is applied, by the Hebrews, to designate a more mature and advanced state of knowledge in respect to any thing, and not simply to the mere perceiving of a difference between the moral nature of good and evil. So in the verse before us ; we cannot suppose the writer to mean, that the Hebrews were not yet τέλειοι in such a sense as to be able to discern the difference between good and evil, simply considered. He evidently means, that they were in such a state, as not readily to discern what was true or false, in respect to the more difficult doctrines of the Christian religion ; they were not as yet capable of rightly understanding and estimating them. From this state, it was their duty speedily to extricate themselves ; as the writer proceeds to exhort them to do.

CHAPTER VI.

Ver. 1. Διὸ ἀφέντες .... φερώμεθα, *wherefore, leaving the first rudiments of Christian doctrine, let us proceed to a more advanced state* [of knowledge.] Διὸ I interpret here in the usual sense. I understand the reasoning of the apostle thus : " Wherefore, i. e. since τέλειοι only are capable of στερεὰ τροφὴ, *solid food*, viz. of receiving, digesting, and duly appropriating the higher and more difficult doctrines of Christianity, and since ye are yet but νήπιοι, although ye ought to be *advanced* in Christian knowledge, if regard be had to the long time that ye have professed the Christian religion, ch. v. 12—14 ; διὸ, *therefore*, it becomes you to quit this state of immaturity, this νηπιότητα, and advance to a maturer state, to a τελειότητα." The reasoning is plain, when thus understood, and the connexion palpable. The word ἀφέντες is capable of the signification given to it by this method of interpretation. Ἀφίημι signifies, among other things, *relinquo, abeo, discedo, relinquo post me, &c.* and is frequently applied to quitting a thing, for the sake of going to some different place, or of engaging in a different employment ; e. g. Matt. iv. 20, 22 ; v. 24 ; xviii. 12 ; xix. 27 ; John x. 12. The meaning here, I take to be this, " Quitting the mere initial stage of pupillage, advance forward to a maturer state of instruction and knowledge ;" or, " Make such advances, that it shall be unnecessary to repeat *elementary* instruction in the principles of Christianity," ver. 2, 3

Others (and most commentators) understand ἀφέντες here in the sense of *omitting*, and apply it to the apostle in the following way : " Omitting now to insist on the first elements of Christian doctrine, let me proceed to the consideration of the more difficult principles of religion, not discussing, at present, the subject of repentance, baptism, &c.; which I will do, (i. e. I will discuss the higher principles,) if God permit ;" or, (as some interpret this last clause,) " Which [first rudiments] I shall discuss by and by, *Deo volente ;*" referring καὶ τοῦτο ποιήσομεν to the *discussion* of the doctrines just mentioned.

But a difficulty in admitting this interpretation, lies in the context which follows. According to the method of interpretation just proposed, the reasoning would be thus : " Omitting now all discussion respecting the first rudiments of Christian doctrine, I will proceed to disclose the more abstruse principles of the same; *for it is impossible* (ἀδύνατον γὰρ) that apostates should be again renewed to repentance." Is there any coherence in such reasoning ? If there be, it is, at least, very difficult to see it. But does the other method proposed, relieve the difficulty? Let us see. It stands thus : " Christian brethren, who ought by this time to be qualified, by your knowledge of religion, to become teachers of it, quit the state of ignorance in which you are. Let it not be necessary any more to teach you the first rudiments of Christian doctrine. Such progress we *must* make, *Deo volente.* Stationary we cannot remain ; we must either advance or recede. But guard well, I beseech you, against receding; ἀδύνατον γὰρ, &c. ver. 4—8."

Two things, at least, must be admitted. The one, that the apostle taxes them with negligence in regard to an enlarged acquaintance with religious doctrine ; the other, that he cautions them against the awful consequences of apostacy. Now, does it not follow, that he considers the state of comparative ignorance in which they were, as exposing them in a peculiar manner to apostatize ; and consequently, that he connects the danger of apostacy with reproof in regard to religious ignorance, so as to rouse them to more effort, in order to acquire a better acquaintance with the grounds and principles of Christianity ? And is not all this founded in the nature of things, as they have always existed ? Are not the ignorant most easily led away by impostors and heretical teachers ? The men who have prohibited the use of the Scriptures by the people at large, and who labour to suppress the diffusion of general knowledge, in order that the mass of the people may be kept in ignorance, and so be moulded by them at their will, have well understood the principle to which I have alluded.

The caution of the apostle, then, I consider as amounting to this: " Guard well against ignorance of Christian doctrines, for lapse is easy to the ignorant, and recovery exceedingly difficult, or impossible." I cannot, therefore, follow the usual method of expounding either the verse before us, or the subsequent context.

Φερώμεθα, the middle voice of φέρω, of signifies *to go, to come, to travel, to move* in any manner, or in any direction. Here φερώμεθα means, *to advance, to go forward*.

Μὴ πάλιν θεμέλιον καταβαλλόμενοι μετανοίας, *not again laying the foundation with respect to repentance;* not again commencing, (as we once have done,) with the first elements of Christian doctrine, e. g. the subject of repentance, &c. Μετανοίας here means the subject or doctrine of μετάνοια, see ver. 2. The genitive βαπτισμῶν διδαχῆς, designates, in this case, the relation signified by *in respect to;* which is a very common use of the genitive; see Buttmann's Grammar, § 119. 6. 1. It is plain, that the writer does not here speak of repentance as an *act*, but as a *doctrine* or subject of consideration ; and so of the other subjects mentioned in the sequel. That *repentance* was inculcated as an *initial* doctrine and duty of Christianity, may be seen by consulting the following passages, Matt. iv. 17. Mark i. 15. Acts ii. 38. xvii. 30, and others of the same kind.

Ἀπὸ νεκρῶν ἔργων, *from deadly works,* i. e. in respect to works which cause death, misery, or condemnation. Compare ch. ix. 14, and τοῦ θανάτου in ch. ii. 14. Or νεκρὸς may be interpreted as meaning *sinful, vicious:* as in Eph. v. 14. Rom. vi. 13; ch. xi. 15. Rev. iii. 1. It is not important which of these senses is adopted. The one implies the other.

Καὶ πίστεως ἐπὶ Θεὸν, *faith in God,* or, in respect to him. That this is an elementary principle of Christianity, is evident from the nature of the thing, as well as from Mark xi. 22. John xiv. 1. Heb. xi. 6, and many other passages of the New Testament. Here, however, *by faith in God,* is to be understood, faith in the declarations which God has made to men respecting his Son, the Saviour of the world. Compare Acts xvi. 31.

Ver. 2. Βαπτισμῶν διδαχῆς, *the doctrine of baptisms.* Here the word διδαχῆς is supplied by the writer; and I regard it as *implied* before the preceding μετανοίας and πίστεως. Some interpreters, however, point the text thus, βαπτισμῶν, διδαχῆς, i. e. *of baptisms*, of [elementary] *instruction;* which is too improbable to need discussion. The only difficulty lies in the plural word βαπτισμῶν; since we know of only *one* Christian baptism. Hence, Schleusner, and many other critics, refer βαπτισμὸς only to the ceremonial washings of the Jews, in all the cases where it occurs; and they suppose that βάπτισμα is the only appropriate term, with which the rite of Christian baptism is designated. But what has the apostle to do here with Jewish ceremonial rites, as the first elements of *Christian doctrine?* Plainly nothing; so that this exegesis cannot be admitted.

Another and better explanation is, that βαπτισμῶν does not differ, in any important respect, from βαπτισμοῦ. So, in John i. 13, stands the plural αἱμάτων; in 1 Cor. vii. 2, τὰς πορνείας; in 2 Cor. vii. 3, καρδίαις; all instead of the singular, in each case. See many like cases, in Glass. Philol. Sac. I. p. 62, seq. So the plural number of verbs is often employed when the subject is *indefinite*, and of the *singular number;* e. g. Mark v. 35; compare Luke viii. 49. Compare also Heb. ix. 17, ἐπὶ νεκροῖς. Storr supposes βαπτισμῶν to be used here in a kind of distributive sense, as the Hebrew plural often is; so that the sentiment is, " the doctrine that every believer must be baptized." But however this may be, it is clear that no stress can be laid upon the use of the *plural*, as there are so many examples where it means no more than the singular would do. Moreover, the Syriac version has the singular here. In regard to the *doctrine of baptism* being an *elementary* doctrine, there can be no difficulty. The rite itself was an *initiatory* one, for all who professed to be Christians.

Ἐπιθέσεως τε χειρῶν *imposition of hands.* It is a very palpable mistake, into which many Christians fall, who are not well acquainted with the rites of the primitive church, to suppose that *imposition of hands* was practised only in the case of ordaining persons to the holy ministry. It was common for the apostles to bestow extraordinary gifts upon converts to Christianity, immediately after their baptism, by the imposition of hands. See Acts ii. 38, λήψεσθε τὴν δωρεὰν τοῦ ἁγίου πνεύματος; compare Acts viii. 14—19; xix. 1—6. Hence, ἐπιθέσεως χειρῶν is reckoned as one of the things, the knowledge of which was communicated at an early stage of the Christian profession.

Ἀναστάσεως τε νεκρῶν, *of the resurrection of the dead.* Storr, and others, understand this here only of the resurrection of the pious. But I apprehend the sense is general; as in John v. 28, 29. Compare Matt.

xxii. 31; Acts iv. 2. A *general* resurrection of the *bodies* of men, is a doctrine which, if not left undecided by the Old Testament, is at least left in obscurity. The Jews, of the apostle's time, were divided in their opinion respecting it. Hence, it was insisted on with great earnestness by Christian preachers, as belonging to the peculiar and elementary doctrines of Christianity. It was connected, by them, with the account which every man is to render of himself to God; and such an accountability is a *fundamental* doctrine of the Christian religion.

Καὶ κρίματος αἰωνίου, *and of a judgment, the consequences of which are eternal.* In such a sense is λύτρωσις said to be αἰωνία, in ch. ix. 12; and διαθήκη to be αἰωνία in ch. xiii. 20. Both the *resurrection* and the *judgment*, in this case, pertain to the righteous and to the wicked. It is the *general* doctrine of a resurrection, and of responsibility and reward at the tribunal of God, which the writer means to describe. These doctrines were among those that were first preached, when men were to be instructed in the elements of Christianity. See Acts xvii. 31; x. 42. Rom. ii. 16. Matt. xxv. 31, seq. In regard to the *eternal* consequences of judgment, see Matt. xxv. 46. John v. 29. Dan. xii. 2. 2 Thess. i. 9. Matt. xviii. 8. Mark ix. 45. 48.

Ver. 3. Καὶ τοῦτο .... ὁ Θεὸς, *and this will we do, if God permit;* i. e. we will advance in Christian knowledge, go on, ἐπὶ τελειότητα, should God be pleased to spare our lives, and afford us continued opportunity of so doing. The frequency with which the writer of this epistle uses the first person plural (κοίνωσις) is worthy of remark. It gives a more delicate cast to his reproofs, and to his comminations.

Ver. 4. Ἀδύνατον γὰρ, *for it is impossible,* i. e. we will go forward in the attainment of what belongs to Christians, and not recede; for it is *impossible*, viz. that those who recede and apostatize, should be recovered from their lapse; as the sequel avers. But does ἀδύνατον here imply *absolute impossibility*, or only *great difficulty?* The latter, Storr and many other critics reply. To vindicate this sentiment, they appeal to Mark x. 25. 27, and to the parallel passages in the other evangelists. But this appeal is not satisfactory. In Matt. xix. 23, seq.; Mark x. 23, seq.; and Luke xviii. 24, seq., (all relating to the same occurrence,) Jesus is represented as saying, "πῶς δυσκόλως, shall a rich man enter into the kingdom of God!" He then adds, "It is easier for a camel to go through the eye of a needle, than for a rich man to enter into the kingdom of God!" His disciples are astonished at this, and ask, "*How is it possible that* any one [any rich man] can be saved?" τὶς ἄρα δύναται σωθῆναι; Jesus replies, " With men this is ἀδύνατον; but with God all things are δύνατα." Surely he does not mean merely, that this is *very difficult* with men, but, that it is *beyond their power* to accomplish it. The other examples of the use of this word in the New Testament, are not at all adapted to favour the exegesis of Storr; e. g. Acts xiv. 8. Rom. viii. 3; xv. 1, where the word, however, is figuratively employed. But, if the writer of the epistle to the Hebrews is to be compared with himself, then is it quite certain, that ἀδύνατον will not bear the qualified sense which Storr puts upon it. Compare Heb. vi. 18; x. 4; xi. 6; all clear cases of *absolute impossibility*, not of mere *relative difficulty*. These are all the instances in which the word is found in the New Testament. Nor will a resort to *classic* usage any better defend the interpretation of Storr.

Besides, if it could be shown, that such a qualified sense were agreeable to the *usus loquendi* in some cases, and therefore *possible*, a comparison with Heb. x. 26—31, would destroy all appearance of *probability* that such a sense is to be admitted here. If there " remains no more sacrifice for sin," (Heb. x. 26,) for those who have apostatized, then is there no hope of salvation for them; as is clear from Heb. x. 28—31. Moreover, to say merely, that it is *very difficult* to recover the lapsed Christians of whom the apostle is going to speak, would be at variance with the imagery employed to describe them, and the fate that awaits them, in ver. 7, 8. For all these reasons, such an explanation of ἀδύνατον cannot be admitted.

Τοὺς ἅπαξ φωτισθέντας, *those who have been once enlightened*, i. e. instructed in the principles of Christianity. So φωτίζω, in John i. 9. Eph. iii. 9. Heb. x. 32. In all the other passages of the New Testament where this word occurs, it is employed in the sense of *shining upon, throwing light upon, disclosing*. It does not, in itself considered, imply *saving illumination*, but illumination or instruction simply, as to the principles of the Christian religion.

Γευσαμένους τε τῆς δωρεᾶς ἐπουρανίου, *and have tasted of the heavenly gift*. Γευσαμένους, *tasted*, does not mean, *extremis labiis leviter degustare*, merely *to sip*, or simply *to apply for once to the palate*, so as just to perceive the taste of a thing; but it means, *the full enjoyment, perception*, or *experience* of a thing. When the Greek writers wish to communicate the former idea, they add χείλεσιν ἄκροις to the phrase; e. g. " They are witnesses, οἱ μὴ χείλεσιν ἄκροις γευσάμενοι τῆς φιλοσοφίας ἀλλὰ . . ἐςιαθέντες, *who have not only tasted with* the *extreme part of the lips* [sipped] *philosophy, but . . . feasted upon it,* Philo. Lib. I. de Monarchia, p. 816. So Chrysostom, ἄκροις τοῖς χείλεσιν γεύσασθαι, Hom. on Johan. v. 19. But when a *full* experience or perception of any thing is meant, γεύομαι is used simply; e. g. οἱ γευσάμενοι τῆς ἀρετῆς, Philo de Abraham. Oper. I. p. 14. So τοῦ ἀθανάτου γνώσεως γεύσασθαι, Clem. Rom. I. 38.

In the New Testament, θανάτου γεύεσθαι is, *to experience death;* e. g. Matt. xvi. 28. Mark ix. 1. Luke ix. 27. John viii. 52. Heb. ii. 9. Compare also Luke xiv. 24. 1 Pet. ii. 3. So Herod. VI. 5, γεύεσ͂αι ἐλευθερίας, *to experience* [to enjoy] *freedom.* Pindar. Nem. Od. V. 596, πόνων γεύεσθαι, *to undergo toils.* Soph. Trach. 1108, ἄλλων τε μόχθων μυρίων ἐγευσάμην, *I have suffered a thousand other evils.* So the Hebrew טָעַם Prov. xxxi. 18. Ps. xxxiv. 9.

But what is the *heavenly gift,* which they have enjoyed, or the benefits of which they have experienced? Some have explained it as being Christ himself, by comparing it with John iv. 10. But it is doubtful whether δωρεὰν here means Christ. It is more probable, that it means *beneficium,* i. e. the kindness or favour which God bestowed, in vouchsafing an opportunity to the Samaritan woman, to converse with the Saviour.

Others have represented δωρεὰν as being the extraordinary gift of the Holy Spirit to Christians, in the primitive age of Christianity; and they have compared the phrase here with πνεῦμα ἅγιον in Acts viii. 19, which means the special gifts of the Spirit, and which in ch. viii. 20, is called τὴν δωρεὰν τοῦ Θεοῦ. But the objection to this is, that the sequel of our text contains a *repetition* of the same idea, once at least, if not twice.

For these reasons, I prefer the interpretation which makes δωρεᾶς ἐπουράνιον the same here as κλήσεως ἐπουρανίου in ch. iii. 1, i. e. the proffered blessings or privileges of the gospel. The sense is then plain and facile: (1.) They had been instructed in the elementary doctrines of Christianity, φωτισθέντας. (2.) They had enjoyed the privileges or benefits of living under a Christian dispensation, i. e. the means of grace which the gospel afforded; and this is truly δωρεὰ ἐπουρανιὸς. I much prefer this mode of interpretation to any of the others.

Καὶ μετόχους γενηθέντας πνεύματος ἁγίου, *and have been made partakers of the Holy Spirit.* I understand this of the extraordinary gifts and influences of the Spirit, which the primitive Christians enjoyed, and which were often bestowed by the imposition of the apostles' hands. See above, on ἐπιθέσεως τε χειρῶν, in ver 2. Γενηθέντας is a more unusual word, in such a connexion as the present, than γενομένους ; but still, there are sufficient examples to show, that occasional custom sanctions the use of it in such cases as the present.

Ver 5. Καὶ καλὸν γευσαμένους Θεοῦ ῥῆμα, *and have tasted the good word of God*, i. e. enjoyed the consolations administered, or the hopes excited, by the divine promises which the gospel proffers. Γευσαμένους (as above) *experienced, known by experience*. Above, it is construed with the genitive after it ; here with the accusative ; both according to Greek usage, although the former method predominates.

Καλὸν .... Θεοῦ ῥῆμα, *the divine promise*, i. e. of good. So דְּבַר טוֹב means, in Jer. xxix. 10; xxxiii. 14; also in Joshua xxi. 45; xxiii. 14, 15, in which last verse it is opposed to דְּבָר רָע, *promise of evil, commination*. Καλὸν ῥῆμα means, *the word which respects good*, i. e. the promise of blessings or favours. So Paul calls the gospel, ἐπαγγελίαν Θεοῦ ἐν Χριστῷ, 2 Cor. i. 20. I prefer this simple method of explanation to all others. The gradation, moreover, of the discourse is more perceptible, than if ῥῆμα be here construed as indicating merely εὐαγγέλιον, which would make the whole clause to signify nearly, if not exactly, the same as ἅπαξ φωτισθέντας.

Δυνάμεις τε μέλλοντος αἰῶνος, *and the miracles of the gospel dispensation*. The sense here given to δυνάμεις is frequently in the New Testament; see Matt. vii. 22 ; xi. 20, 21, 23 ; xiii. 58. Mark vi. 5. Luke x. 13. Acts ii. 22, al. I apprehend that the writer refers here to those extraordinary, miraculous occurrences, which took place in confirmation of Christianity; viz. such as are adverted to in ch. ii. 4. The phrase, δυνάμεις μέλλοντος αἰῶνος, differs from the preceding μετόχους .... πνεύματος ἁγίου, in this respect, viz. that the latter relates to the *special* gifts and influences of the Spirit, bestowed *in general* upon the primitive disciples; while the former refers particularly to miracles of the *highest* order, which afforded peculiar proof that Christianity was a divine religion, and which are appealed to as such in ch. ii. 4. In regard to μέλλοντος αἰῶνος, see on οἰκουμένην μέλλουσαν, in ch. ii. 5.

Thus interpreted, there is a regular gradation in the whole passage. (1.) They had been taught the principles or doctrines of Christianity. (2.) They had enjoyed the privileges or means of grace, which the new religion afforded. (3.) They had experienced, in general, various gifts and graces bestowed by the Spirit. (4.) They had cherished the hopes which the promises of the gospel inspire. (5.) They had witnessed, (and perhaps he means to say, that some of them had experienced,) those special miraculous powers, by which the gospel was fully shown to be a religion from God; compare ch. ii. 4. Thus they had the *fullest* evidence, internal and external, of the divine origin and nature of the Christian religion. Consequently, if they apostatized from it, there remained no hope of their recovery.

Ver. 6. Καὶ παραπεσόντας, *and have fallen away, have made defection from*, viz. from the gospel, or from all the experience and evidence before mentioned ; παραπίπτω governing the genitive. The connexion stands thus, 'Αδύνατον γὰρ τοὺς ἅπαξ φωτισθέντας . . . . γευσαμένους τε . . . . καὶ γενηθέντας . . . . καὶ γευσαμένους . . . . καὶ παραπεσόντας. In compound verbs, παρὰ is often taken to denote *deterioration;* e. g. παραφρωνεῖν, *desipere;* παραλογίζεσθαι, *male ratiocinari;* παραρυθμίζειν, *deformare;* so παραπίπτειν, *deficere ab.* The *falling away* or *defection*, which is here meant, is a renunciation of Christianity, and a return to Judaism. This implies, of course, a return to a state of active enmity and hostility to the Christian religion.

Πάλιν ἀνακαινίζειν εἰς μετάνοιαν, *again to be renewed by repentance.* Πάλιν belongs to ἀνακαινίζειν, not only by common usage in respect to the position of the adverb when placed immediately before the verb which it qualifies, but the sense here requires it. The writer does not mean to say, " Those who have a second time fallen away ; but, that *those who fall away cannot be again*, or *a second time, brought to repentance.* Drusius, Cappell, Abresch, and others, take ἀνακαινίζειν here in the passive sense, as equivalent to ἀνακαινίζεσθαι ; and construe it, in connexion with what precedes, in this manner ; " It is impossible for those who have been once instructed, &c. *to be renewed* to repentance." The simple grammatical construction of ἀνακαινίζειν, as it now stands in the *active* voice, is thus ; " It is impossible again *to renew* by repentance those who have been once instructed," &c. If the latter method of construeing the sentence be adopted, who is the subject of the verb ἀνακαινίζειν? i. e. who is the agent that is to produce this renovation ? Is it God, i. e. the Holy Spirit, or Paul, or others? Brettschneider (Lex.) understands the word in an *active* sense, and supposes that Christian teachers are the agents to whom the writer refers. Storr renders it indefinitely, " Man kann unmöglich wieder bessern," *one cannot possibly produce another amendment.* But, instead of saying *one cannot*, in this case, I should prefer understanding ἀνακαινίζειν in an *impersonal* sense, and rendering it in English by our passive verb: since many verbs used impersonally convey a passive sense. See Heb. Gram. § 190. 2. note 1, 2. There is still another construction which may be made of the passage, and which is a very common Greek one; viz. πάλιν ἀνακαινίζειν τοὺς ἅπαξ φωτισθέντας .... καὶ παραπεσόντας, ἀδύνατον, *to renew*, or, *the renewal of, persons once instructed* .... *and who have apostatized, is impossible.* In this case, the infinitive ἀνακαινίζειν is used as a noun, and makes the *subject* of the proposition. This would afford the same sense as that which was last suggested above.

Εἰς μετάνοιαν, *by repentance;* so Chrysostom, Erasmus, and others. Εἰς, with the accusative, often signifies the *instrument* or *means*. If it be construed otherwise, (as in the version which I have made,) the sense will be " To renew them, so that they will repent." See EXCURSUS XII.

᾿Ανασταυροῦντας ἑαυτοῖς τὸν υἱὸν τοῦ Θεοῦ, *since they have crucified for themselves the Son of God*. Chrysostom construes ἀνασταυροῦντας as meaning πάλιν σταυροῦντας; and so our English translators, and many others. But this is not conformable to common Greek usage. ᾿Ανὰ, in composition, merely augments the intensity of a verb, if, indeed, it produces any effect upon its signification; for oftentimes it does not, e. g. ἀναζητεῖν, ἀνακρίνειν, ἀναθεωρεῖν, ἀναπληρόειν, &c. That the word in question is to be *figuratively* taken, is plain from the nature of the case. Actual *physical* crucifixion is out of the question. It means, then, *to treat with the greatest ignominy and contempt*.

But what does ἑαυτοῖς mean? It is susceptible of two interpretations. (1.) As *dativus incommodi*, i. e. *to their own hurt, shame, &c.* So Storr. See Winer's New. Test. Gram. § 24. 2. *b*. (2.) It may be constructed as Hebrew pronouns in the dative frequently are, viz. as *pleonastic;* e. g. לֶךְ־לְךָ, *go for thyself*, i. e. go; נָס לוֹ, *he has fled for himself*, i. e. he has fled; Heb. Gram. § 210. 3. I incline to the latter mode of explanation. Perhaps the shade of idea is, " Crucifying, so far as they are concerned," or, " Themselves being concerned in the transaction of crucifying."

Καὶ παραδειγματίζοντας, *and exposed him to public shame;* compare Matt. i. 19. By renouncing their adherence to Christianity, they would openly declare their belief that Christ was only an impostor, and, of course, that he suffered justly as a malefactor. By returning again to Judaism, they would approve of what the Jews had done; and thus they would, as it were, crucify Christ, and expose him to be treated by unbelievers with scorn and contumely. Every one knows, that an apostate from a good cause gives new occasion, by the act of apostacy, for the enemies of that cause to utter all the malignity of their hearts against it. In this sense, apostates expose the Saviour to public infamy, when they renounce all regard for him, and join with those who view him as an impostor and a malefactor.

The two participles, ἀνασταυροῦντας .... καὶ παραδειγματίζοντας, I regard, as grammatically connected with the preceding ones thus: τοὺς ἅπαξ φωτισθέντας .... καὶ παραπεσόντας .... ἀνασταυροῦντας .... καὶ παραδειγματίζοντας; the two latter words being in *apposition* with the preceding participles, and added for the sake of giving intensity to the whole description. On this account, καὶ is omitted before ἀνασταυροῦντας.

Ver. 7. Γῆ γὰρ .... ὑετὸν, *now the earth, which drinketh in the rain that frequently comes upon it.* Γῆ is used for *land cultivated* or *uncultivated*. Here it designates the former, as is evident from the sequel of the sentence. The image of the earth being *thirsty*, and *drinking in* the showers, is common in many languages.

Καὶ τίκτουσα βοτάνην, *and produceth fruits*. Τίκτουσα is often applied, by classical writers, to the production of fruits. Βοτάνην, like the Hebrew עֵשֶׂב, means, *any kind of grain, any produce of vegetation*, which is fitted for the service of man. But this use is Hebraistic. By classic usage, βοτάνη means, *herbage*, or *vegetation*, not including bread-corn.

Εὔθετον ἐκείνοις δἰ οὓς γεωργεῖται, *useful to those on account of whom it is cultivated*. Εὔθετον means, in its primary sense, *well situated, well located;* e. g. it is applied to a convenient harbour for ships, &c. *Useful, appropriate*, &c. are secondary meanings, which the word frequently has. Δἰ οὓς, *on account of whom*. That this is the *usual* signification of διὰ with the accusative, all will acknowledge; and as the sense demands no departure here from the usual construction, it is better to retain it, than to translate *by whom*.

Μεταλαμβάνει εὐλογίας ἀπὸ τοῦ Θεοῦ, literally, *receiveth blessings from God*. But what is the meaning of this? Is it, that the earth is, when thus fruitful, contemplated with satisfaction or complacency by its Creator? Or, does it mean, "The earth which thus produces useful fruits, is rendered still more fruitful by Divine beneficence?" The latter seems better to accord with the Hebrew idiom. E. g. when Jacob approaches Isaac, clad in Esau's perfumed garments, Isaac says, *The odour of my son, is like the odour of a field which God has blessed,*

i. e. of a fruitful field, with blossoming herbage. So, on the contrary the *curse* of the earth, in Gen. iii. 17, is explained in ver. 18, by adding, " Thorns and thistles shall it bring forth unto thee." In Mark xi. 14, our Saviour says of the *barren* fig-tree, " Let no one ever henceforth eat any fruit of thee;" to which Peter afterwards alluding, says, " Lo! the fig-tree which thou didst *curse*," Mark xi. 21. In 2 Cor. ix. 6, Paul says, " He who soweth, ἐπ' εὐλογίαις, *bountifully*, shall reap, ἐπ' εὐλογίαις, *bountifully*." Agreeably to this idiom, the phrase in question might be explained, *is rendered still more fertile*, or. *productive, by God*. But, although most commentators of note have adopted such an interpretation, I hesitate to receive it; and this, because the metaphor thus explained does not seem well adapted to the object for which it is used. The image of the *fruitful* earth is designed to signify, " Christians who bring forth fruits under divine cultivation." Supposing, then, that such Christians are here designated, (as plainly is the case,) does the writer mean merely to say, in addition, that they will be rendered still more fruitful in good works? Or does he mean to say, that when they thrive under the cultivation which they enjoy, they will obtain divine approbation and complacency? I incline to the latter interpretation, as tending more directly to exhibit the object which the apostle has in view.

Moreover, the antithesis, in ver. 8, presents the image of displeasure, of punishment. Consequently, the image of complacency, of reward, is presented in ver. 7. I should, then, rather interpret the phrase, *receiveth blessings from God*, as referring to the complacency or approbation with which God regards the fruitful earth. The sense is similar to that in which he is said, in Gen. i., to have regarded all the works of his hands, and considered them as *good*. The increased fruitfulness of the earth would, indeed, be the *consequence* of the divine blessing; and may, by metonymy, be taken for the blessing itself. But the other method of exegesis seems more simple. I might say, perhaps, that it is rendered almost certain by ver. 8, where the earth, which brings forth thorns and thistles, is considered merely as κατάρας ἐγγὺς, *nigh to a curse*, i. e. in danger of one. Yet, if commentators have rightly construed, εὐλογίας, in ver. 7, as meaning *fruitfulness*, then κατάρα, in ver. 8, must mean *barrenness*. But the land is *already* barren, which produces only thorns and briars; consequently it is not merely *nigh to barrenness* as a curse to come. As then the antithesis of εὐλογίας (viz. κατάρα) does not mean *barrenness*, so εὐλογίας does not mean *fruitfulness*.

Ver. 8. Ἐκφέρουσα δὲ [sc. ἡ γῆ] .... ἐγγὺς, *but the earth, which bringeth forth thorns and briars, is useless, and near to utter rejection, which will end in burning.* Κατάρα, exsecratio, maledictio, extrema atque dirissima devotio. Such barren ground, producing nothing but thorns and briars, is not only useless to the owners, but is given up or devoted by them to be overrun with fire, and to have all its worthless productions consumed. The explanation of this phrase in our lexicons, and in most of the commentaries, seems to me plainly incongruous, as I have just hinted above. Is not the earth which produces nothing but thorns and briars, already *barren*? How then can this earth be merely κατάρας ἐγγὺς, i. e. (as they explain it) only *near to barrenness?* The method of interpretation above proposed, avoids this incongruity, and adopts a more easy and natural explanation. Such earth is (1.) Useless, ἀδόκιμος, *deserving reprobation.* (2.) An object of execration, or nigh to be given up to the flames, which at last will consume all its worthless productions; i. e. when the owner of such barren ground has made the experiment long enough to see what its qualities are, (ἐδοκίμασε,) and finds it to be barren, then he considers it as ἀδόκιμος, *proved to be worthless after trial, to be condemned,* and determines speedily to abandon it (κατάρας ἐγγὺς,) and to subject it to the flames. Ἧς τὸ τέλος εἰς καῦσιν, *which* [κατάρα] *will end in* [will be accomplished or completed by] *burning.* Εἰς καῦσιν is a Hebraism, corresponding to the use of the infinitive *nominascens,* with the prefix לְ, Heb. Gram. sec. 200. 3. So Isa. xliv. 15, לְבָעֵר ...... וְהָיָה, LXX. ἵνα ᾖ .... εἰς καῦσιν· *and it shall be burned.* This mode of interpretation represents the *execration* of barren land, (κατάρα,) as ending in καῦσις; which agrees with fact.

Others refer ἧς to γῆ, i. e. the end of which land is burning. But I prefer the grammatical antecedent, κατάρα.

Thus construed, the whole affords a very striking image of the condition of the Hebrews. " You," the writer says, " are enjoying abundant means of spiritual improvement. If you act in a manner worthy of such privileges, God will approve and bless. But if you disobey the gospel, and become wholly unfruitful in respect to Christian graces, then you are exposed to final rejection and endless punishment. The doom of all apostates is near, and the sequel will be tremendous."

But lest what he had now said might wear the appearance of too much severity, and seem to imply a great degree of distrust, or want of confidence, in respect to those whom he addressed, the writer proceeds to show what is the real state of his feelings towards them, and that he has, out of affection for them, and solicitude for their highest welfare, so plainly and fully set before them the danger to which they were exposed.

Ver. 9. Πεπείσμεθα δὲ . . . λαλοῦμεν, *but we confidently hope for better things respecting you, beloved, even those connected with salvation, although we thus speak.* Κρείττονα [i. e. πράγματα] I understand as referring to what had just been said, in which the conduct and the doom of apostates had been represented. Πεπείσμεθα κρείττονα then means, "I confidently hope that you will neither imitate the conduct, nor undergo the doom, of apostates, whose end is εἰς καῦσιν."

Ἐχόμενα σωτηρίας, literally, *near to, conjoined with, salvation.* The form of expression appears as if it were designed to correspond with the preceding κατάρας ἐγγὺς ; i. e. as apostates are κατάρας ἐγγύες, so those who persevere in maintaining the true religion are ἐχόμενοι σωτηρίας ; i. e. their salvation is at hand, their time of deliverance from trials, and their season of reward is certain, and will not be long protracted. To refer σωτηρίας here merely to the *temporal* safety of believing Hebrews, seems to me very foreign to the object of the writer; although some critics of note have done this.

Ver. 10. Οὐ γὰρ ἄδικος ὁ Θεὸς, *for God is not unkind,* or, *God is kind.* The apposite of ἄδικος, is δίκαιος, which, among other meanings, not unfrequently bears that of *kind, benevolent, indulgent, merciful ;* see Matt. i. 19. John xvii. 25. 1 John i. 9. So in Hebrew, צַדִּיק and צְדָקָה often mean, *kind, kindness, merciful, mercy,* &c. Ἄδικος therefore, may mean *unkind, unmerciful,* &c. ; and this sense of the word is most appropriate to the passage.

Τοῦ ἔργου ὑμῶν, καὶ τῆς ἀγάπης. Many codices, and most editions, read τοῦ ἔργου ὑμῶν καὶ τοῦ κόπου τῆς ἀγάπης. But Griesbach, Knapp, and Tittmann, omit τοῦ κόπου ; which, however, is defended and received by many critics of good reputation. Ἔργον and κόπος are not unfrequently joined by the sacred writers ; e. g. 1 Thess. i. 3. Rev ii. 2. xiv. 13. But the weight of authority appears to be against the genuineness of κόπου here.

Instead of putting a comma after ὑμῶν, we may point the phrase thus, τοῦ ἔργου ὑμῶν καὶ τῆς ἀγάπης : regarding τῆς ἀγάπης as sustaining the place of an adjective in respect to ἔργου. Such constructions are very common in the sacred writings, i. e. Hendiadys. The translation would then be, *your benevolent labour ;* or (if this be more agreeable) *your labour and benevolence, which ye have exhibited.* But, on the whole, I rather prefer making ἔργον refer to the *efforts* which the Hebrew Christians had made, and ἀγάπη to the state of mind toward God which they had cherished. I have translated accordingly. Εἰς τὸ ὄνομα αὐτοῦ, *toward him,* i. e. toward God, or toward Christ. So ὄνομα is often used for person; e. g. Matt. vi. 9. John xvii. 26. Acts x. 43. John xx. 31. Acts iv. 10. So שֵׁם *name* in Hebrew, Exod. xxiii. 21. 1 Kings viii. 29; iii. 2. Ps. xx. 1, et. al. sæpe.

Διακονήσαντες . . . διακονοῦντες, *having performed kind offices to Christians, and in still performing them.* Διακονέω signifies, not merely to supply the wants of others by pecuniary aid, and by alms, but also to assist them in any way by offices of humanity and kindness. In this enlarged sense, it seems natural to understand it here. Ἁγίοις, *Christians,* i. e. those who were *consecrated* to God, or to Christ ; compare ch. iii. 1.

Ver. 11. Τὴν αὐτὴν ἐνδείκνυσθαι σπουδὴν . . . τέλους, *may exhibit the same diligence, for the sake of a full assurance of hope even to the end,* i. e. the end of life, or the end of their probationary state ; compare ch. iii. 6. Σπουδὴν, *strenuous endeavour, diligent exertion, sedulity.* The meaning is, " I wish you to continue active and benevolent efforts, such as you have already made, even to the end of your Christian course, so as to acquire, or to preserve, the full assurance of Christian hope. Πληροφορία and πληροφορέω are New Testament and ecclesiastical words, not employed by the classics. Πληροφορία is a *full burden* or *lading.* If applied to a fruit tree, it would designate the fulness or large burden of the fruit; applied to the lading of a vessel, it would denote the fulness of the cargo. Phavorinus explains πληροφόρησον by πλήρωσον : and, in like manner, πληροφορίαν here does not appear to differ from πλήρωμα or πλήρωσιν. The meaning of the writer is, " I desire that your diligence in good works should be persevered in, so that you may continue to cherish a full or confident hope, viz. of salvation even to the end of life." In this way, they would be most effectually guarded against apostacy ; for he who, on true grounds, cherishes the hope, which the Christian religion encourages, of future glory and reward, will hardly be tempted to abandon his religion, and exchange it for another.

Ver. 12. Ἵνα μὴ νωθροὶ γένησθε, *that ye may not be remiss,* viz. in the discharge of your Christian duties. Νωθροὶ, *tardi, segnes,* is applied either to body or mind, to external actions or internal conceptions.

Μιμηταὶ δὲ τῶν διὰ πίστεως . . . ἐπαγγελίας, *but imitators of those, who through faith and patient expectation have entered on the possession of promised blessings,* i. e. who, after continued belief (πίςεως) in the existence of those blessings, and patient waiting (μακροθυμίας) until the time of trial is finished for the possession of them, have at last realized the object of all their faith and patient expectation. Πίστις means here, belief in the reality of proffered future blessedness, (see Heb. xi. 1, 2, seq. ;) and μακροθυμία the patient waiting for it, amid all the troubles and trials of life. Some make a Hendiadys of the two words πίστεως and μακροθυμίας, and render them *patient faith.* I prefer the other method of explanation, as communicating a fuller meaning of the apostle's words.

Κληρονομούντων τὰς ἐπάγγελίας. Κληρονομέω, *to acquire, to obtain possession of,* see on ch. i. 4. Ἐπαγγελίας in the plural, in order to indicate promises of various kinds, both in respect to temporal and spiritual good, the proffered blessings which the ancient worthies did at last enjoy.

How directly it was to the writer's purpose, to exhort the Hebrews to persevering faith, and patient waiting for future blessings proffered by the Christian religion, is too evident to need any illustration. Such a course would be directly opposite to that abandonment of faith and discouragement of mind, which led directly to apostacy.

Ver. 13. Τῷ γὰρ Ἀβραὰμ . . . Θεὸς, *when, for example God had made a promise to Abraham.* Γὰρ, introduced in such a connexion, i. e. between the proposal of a doctrine or encouragement, and the relation of a fact which is to illustrate it, may well be explained by the phrase, *for example;* as it conveys the same idea in Greek, which these words do in English.

Ἐπεὶ κατ' οὐδενὸς . . . ἑαυτοῦ, *seeing he could swear by no greater, he sware by himself.* Εἶχε, *could, poterat.* Compare Mark xiv. 8. Luke vii. 42 ; xii. 4 ; xiv. 14 ; John xiv. 30 ; Lucian, Dial. Mort. 21. 2, " Concerning all these things, εἰπεῖν ἂν ἔχοιμι, *I could speak.*" Elian. Var. Hist. I. 25, " I honour thee ὄπητε καὶ ὅπως ἔχω, in whatever way, and whenever *I can.*"

Κατ' οὐδενὸς. The genitive, with κατὰ before it, usually follows the verb ὄμνυμι, when the object is designated by which a person swears. So Æsop. Fab. 68, ἡ μὲν σῦς ὤμνυε κατὰ τῆς Ἀφροδίτης, *sware by Venus.* The accusative with κατὰ, or the dative with ἐν, may also be used.

"Ὤμοσε καθ' ἑαυτοῦ, Hebrew בִּי נִשְׁבַּעְתִּי, Gen. xxii. 16. The formula of an oath of this kind, is found in Num. xiv. 21, חַי אָנִי. So in Num. xiv. 28, חַי אָנִי נְאֻם יְהוָֹה; and in Deut. xxxii. 40, חַי אָנֹכִי לְעֹלָם, *I live for ever.*

Ver. 14. Λέγων ἢ μὴν . . . πληθυνῶ σε, *saying, I will greatly bless thee, and exceedingly multiply thee,* i. e. I will give thee a numerous offspring. In Gen. xxii. 17, which is quoted here, instead of simply πληθυνῶ σε, the Hebrew runs thus, אַרְבֶּה אֶת־זַרְעֲךָ וְהַרְבָּה, *I will greatly multiply thy seed;* but in Gen. xvii. 2, it is אַרְבֶּה אוֹתְךָ בִּמְאֹד מְאֹד *I will multiply thee.* The apostle appears to unite both expressions, in the quotation before us. The obvious idea of both passages is, " I will give thee a very numerous posterity."

Μὴν, *certo, profecto,* i. q. ὄντως. Εὐλογῶν εὐλογήσω . . . πληθύνων πληθυνῶ. Such a re-duplication is very common in Hebrew, where, for the most part, it denotes *intensity,* Heb. Gram . § 199. 2. The *frequency* of it, in the Hellenistic writers, is Hebraism; but the formula itself is not without many examples in the Greek writers. E. g. Lucian. Dial. Menel. sub fine, ἰδῶν εἶδον. Xen. Cyrop. V. πείθων ἔπεισε. VIII. ὑπακούων ὑπήκουσα. Polyb. εὐχόμενος ηὔξατο τοῖς θεοῖς. Herod. IV. 23, καταφεύγως καταφεύγῃ. Diod. Sic. tom. I. p. 717, καταπέμψας ἔπεμψε. That *intensity* is designed in our text, is clear from consulting the context in Gen. xxii. and xvii.

Πληθυνῶ is found in what is usually called the *second future circumflex.* But verbs in λ, μ, ν, ρ, have no other future; see Buttmann, Gram. § 86. 8.

Ver. 15. Καὶ οὕτω μακροθυμήσας . . . . ἐπαγγελίας, *and so having patiently waited, he obtained the promised blessing.* Καὶ οὕτω, may be construed as equivalent to καὶ τότε, vel καὶ ἔπειτα, *and then,* and *afterwards.* So οὕτω in Acts vii. 8; xx. 11. Rom. xi. 26. Thess. iv. 17. Rev. xi. 5. Schneider (Lex.,) οὕτω, *folglich, sonach.* Schleusner (Lex.,) οὕτω, *sic tandem tum demum, deinceps etiam.* But I rather prefer the sense of *so* here, which means, *in accordance with the promises just recited.* Ἐπέτυχε τῆς ἐπαγγελίας, the noun being in the genitive; for ἐπιτυγχάνω governs either the genitive or accusative; see Matt. Gr. Gram. § 363. 5.

But what was the promised blessing which he obtained? The same, I reply, which the preceding context designates, viz. the blessing of a posterity, which should become numerous. When Abraham was called by God out of Haran, and the promise of a numerous posterity made to him, he was seventy-five years old, Gen. xii. 1—4. Twenty-four years elapsed after this, while he was a sojurner in a strange land without any fixed place of abode, before the manner in which this promise would be fulfilled was revealed to him, Gen. xvii. 1—16. It was only when he was an hundred years old, that the promised blessing of a son, from whom should spring a great nation, was obtained, Gen. xxi. 1—5. The preternatural birth of such a son, was deemed by Abraham a sufficient pledge, on the part of God, that all which he had promised respecting him would be fulfilled, Gen. xxii. 15—18. Heb. xi. 8—12, 17—19. Rom. iv. 17—22. Other blessings, besides that of a numerous posterity, were connected with the birth of Isaac and the faith of Abraham, Gen. xxii. latter part of ver. 17, with ver. 18. These blessings Abraham did not obtain, indeed, by *actual* possession; but by *anticipation, confident hope*, and *unwavering faith* in the promises of God; compare John viii. 56. In our text, however, the apostle refers to the promised blessing of a son, which, after long waiting, Araham obtained.

Ver. 16. "Ἄνθρωποι μὲν γὰρ . . . ὀμνύουσι, *now men swear by one who is superior*, i. e. men appeal to God, when taking an oath, as a witness of their sincerity, and as an avenger of falsehood and perjury.

Καὶ πάσης αὐτοῖς . . . ὁ ὅρκος, *and the oath for confirmation makes an end of all dispute among them;* i. e. an oath, that contesting parties will abide by terms of amity and concord agreed upon, puts an end to the disputes which had existed, the parties relying upon an engagement of a nature so solemn. An oath, then, is the highest pledge of fidelity which men can give. Αὐτοὶς is the dative after ἀντιλογίας, viz. ἀντιλογίας [ἥ ἐστι] αὐτοὶς.

Such is the custom of men, when ἀντιλογία, *contradiction, question, calling in question, dispute*, is to be quieted. God has condescended to act in a similar way, for our encouragement, and to confirm our belief in his promises.

Ver. 17. Ἐν ᾧ περισσότερον . . . . τῆς ἐπαγγελίας, *on account of which*, (i. e. because an oath removes all dispute or doubt,) *God, desirous of showing those to whom the promises are made*. Ἐν ᾧ, *on account of this*, see Wahl on ἐν, No. 5. Περισσότερον, *abundantly, modo, eximio, insigniter*. Ἐπιδεῖξαι, *to demonstrate, to exhibit so as to prove*. Κληρονόμοις, i. e. Christians; compare ch. iv. 1, 3, and 9.

Τὸ ἀμετάθετον τῆς βουλῆς αὐτοῦ, *the immutability of his purpose*, or, *of his decree;* for the *will* of God is the decree of God.

Ἐμεσίτευσεν ὅρκῳ, *interposed by an oath.* Μεσιτεύω means, according to classical usage, *to act the part of a mediator, to be an internuntius, conciliator,* between two parties. But here, this sense is impossible. God is not a mediator between himself and the heirs of the promise. The sense of *interposing,* then, becomes a necessary one. So the Vulgate, *interposuit jusjurandum.* He made a μεσίτην (so to speak) by an oath, interposed between himself and the heirs of promise ; i. e. he made an oath the means of removing all doubt or question, on their part, whether he would faithfully perform what he had promised.

Ver. 18. "Ινα διὰ δύο πραγμάτων .... Θεὸν, *so that by two immutable things, in regard to which it is impossible that God should prove faithless;* i. e. since men's doubts are removed by appeal to an oath, God, in condescension to their weakness, has also made confirmation of his promises by an oath, so that there might be no possible ground of doubt. But what are the *two immutable things?* His promise and his oath, answer almost all the commentators and critics. But there is room to doubt the correctness of this interpretation. The apostle in the preceding context has mentioned two oaths of God, which have respect to the salvation of believers. The one is in the context immediately preceding, ver. 13 ; which, in Gen xxii. 15—18, stands connected with the promise of a blessing to all nations, (ver. 18,) through the seed of Abraham, i. e. through the Messiah. The other is implied in Heb. iii. 11 ; where the oath that unbelievers shall be excluded from the rest of God, implies, of course, an assurance of the same nature, that believers shall be admitted to it ; compare ch. iv. 5, 6. Perhaps, however, the second oath is that by which the Messiah is constituted a High-priest, after the order of Melchisedek, Ps. cx. 4 ; and which had been twice adverted to by the writer, in the preceding part of his epistle, ch. v. 6, 10. This would best agree with the sequel, in ch. vi. 20, where the writer recurs to the order of Christ's high-priesthood, and thus shows that it was at that time in his mind. Here, then, are the two *immutable things,* in which believers may confide ; viz. *First,* The oath that Abraham should have a Son, (the Messiah,) in whom all nations should be blessed, Gen. xxii. 18. *Secondly,* The oath that this Son should be High-priest for ever, after the order of Melchisedek, Ps. cx. 4. These two oaths it is impossible God should disregard ; and the salvation of believers, therefore, is adequately and surely provided for.

In this opinion, I find that Storr, for substance, agrees.

On the other hand, to represent the promise and the oath to confirm the same, as the *two immutable things,* seems to be inapposite ; for the writer here states, that what is sworn to, even among men, must be regarded as fixed or established. The more surely, what God has once solemnly declared can never be annulled. The *two* things, then, which are immutable, are the two different oaths, viz. that in Gen, xxii. 15—18, and that in Ps. cx. 4 ; to which the writer had repeatedly adverted.

Ἰσχυρὰν παράκλησιν . . . ἐλπίδος, *we, who have sought a refuge, might have strong persuasion to hold fast the hope which is set before us.* That is, God has made adequate provision for the salvation of all who prove faithful to the cause of Christ; and he has secured it by oaths, made at different times, and on diverse occasions. The certainty, then, of obtaining the reward promised to fidelity, constitutes a powerful motive to persevere, for all those who have sought a refuge from the power and penalty of sin, in the religion of Jesus. Παράκλησιν, in the sense of *comfort, consolation*, is common in the New Testament; but, according to the classical use of the word, it means, *excitement, exhortation, persuasion*, &c. This latter use of the word is common also to the New Testament writers ; and in this sense I understand it, in the verse before us. *Consolation* is not so appropriate to the writer's object here, as *excitement, (Anregung,* Schneider.) *persuasion.*

Ἰσχυρὰν means *powerful*, i. e. having great force, proffering strong motives.

Οἱ καταφυγόντες, *we, who seek a refuge*. Καταφεύγω means, *to flee toward, to flee to, to flee under,* viz. a place of refuge, an asylum ; which latter is generally designated after the verb. But here, οἱ καταφυγόντες seems to be employed as a periphrasis, in order to designate Christians who are seeking a refuge from sin and sorrow. In like manner, σωζομένους is employed in Acts ii. 47.

Κρατῆσαι, *to hold fast, to take firm hold of, to grasp with tenacity,* Hebrews חֲזַק. Ἐλπίδος, *hope,* here means the objects of hope, i. e. the objects of Christian hope, for which Christians hope, or which they expect; just as ἐπαγγελία, above, means, *the objects promised, the things promised ;* and so, often, in respect to many other words of a similar nature. Προκειμένης, *proposed, set forth,* is a word which was employed in respect to the ἆθλον or *prize of victory,* in the Grecian games. This was said προκεῖσθαι, *to be proposed* or *set before* the competitors. So, in our text, the *object of hope,* viz. future happiness and glory, deliverance from sin and sorrow, is *set before* all Christians, who are καταφυγόντες, *seeking a refuge* from their guilt and miseries. And the repeated oath of God assures them, that such a refuge is to be found, and also affords a powerful excitement to seek it.

Ver. 19. Ἦν ὡς ἄγκυραν . . . βεβαίαν, *which we have as an anchor of the soul unfailing and firmly fixed*; i. e. which hope we are in possession of, ἔχομεν, and it will prove to us, in our troubles and distresses, what an anchor of sound materials and firmly fixed will be to a ship in a tempest; i. e. it will keep us from " making shipwreck of the faith." Many commentators refer ἣν to παράκλησιν ; but it seems to me quite contrary to the manifest object of the passage. Hope is often represented under the emblem of an anchor, among the heathen writers. Ἀσφαλῆ means, *that which will not fail*, i. e. like an anchor of good materials, which will not give way. Βεβαίαν means *firmly fixed*, i. e. having a tenacious hold, which cannot be slipped.

Καὶ εἰσερχομένην . . . καταπετάσματος, *and which enters into that within the veil*, i. e. which *hope* enters into the inner sanctuary, the *sanctum sanctorum*, where God dwells. Others refer εἰσερχομένην, to ἄγκυραν. The meaning, as I explain the passage, is, that the *objects of hope* are in heaven, where God dwells. The apartment within the veil of the temple at Jerusalem, was that in which the ark of the covenant was placed, and also the cherubim that shadowed the mercy-seat. There the glory of God appeared. This inner sanctuary was an emblem of heaven ; see Heb. ix. 1—11. 23 ; x. 1. The phrase ἐσώτερον τοῦ καταπετάσματος, here designates an image of heaven.

The sentiment of the writer, then, is as follows : " Hold fast the objects of your Christian hope. These will keep you steady in adherence to your holy religion, and preserve you, like an anchor, from making shipwreck of the faith. These objects of hope are heavenly in their nature, ἡ ἐλπὶς .... εἰσερχομένη εἰς τὸ ἐσώτερον τοῦ καταπετάσματος. Consequently, these objects are immutable, and so ἀσφαλεῖς καὶ βέβαιοι, like a good anchor."

Ὅπου πρόδρομος .... Ἰησοῦς, *whither Jesus our precursor has gone, on our account*. Πρόδρομος .... εἰσῆλθεν, I take to mean simply, that Jesus has *first* led the way into the heavenly sanctuary. So Æschylus, Her. ad Theb. v. 217, πρόδρομος ἦλθε, i. q. προῆλθε. Theodoret makes an appropriate remark on this passage. " The writer designs to increase their confidence by calling Jesus πρόδρομος ; for if he is their *precursor*, and has gone thither on their account, then ought Christians to follow after him, so as to attain the end of their course, Theod. in loc."

The expression in the latter part of ver. 19, εἰσερχομένη εἰς τὸ ἐσώτερον τοῦ καταπετάσματος, seems to have been purposely chosen as a periphrasis of the heavenly sanctuary, in order to direct the minds of the Hebrews to the *priesthood* of Christ; of which the writer now proceeds to treat, after having suspended the consideration of it from ch. v. 11, to ch. vi. 19, in order to introduce matter of warning and encouragement. It was lawful for the high priest only to enter, through the veil, into the inner sanctuary. So Jesus, as high-priest of the new dispensation, entered the eternal sanctuary above, making expiation of perpetual efficacy for sinners, Heb. ix. 11, 12, 22—26.

Having just reproved them for the little progress which they had made in Christian knowledge, ch. v. 11.—ch. vi. 3; warned them against the dreadful consequences of abandoning the Christian religion, ch. vi. 4—8: and encouraged them to hold fast their faith and hope even to the end, as they had the example of Abraham, and the oath of God to assure them of an adequate reward, ch. vi. 9—19; the writer now returns to make the comparison of Christ as high-priest, with Melchisedek, whose name, in connexion with that of Christ, had been already more than once introduced, ch. v. 6, and 10. This subject he pursues to the end of ch. vii. 25; where he resumes the topic broken off at ch. v. 10, and completes what he had to say concerning it, ch. vii. 26—28.

CHAPTER VII.

Ver. 1. Οὗτος γὰρ ὁ Μελχιζεδέκ, *now this Melchisedek*, i. e. the Melchisedek whom I have already named.

Βασιλεὺς Σαλήμ. Nearly all the Greek and Latin fathers held this place to be the same as *Jerusalem*. So Ps. lxxvi. 2, [3.] "In *Salem* is his tabernacle." Compare Gen. xiv. 18. The Σαλείμ, mentioned in John iii. 23, was probably a different place from that which our text names; if, indeed, Σαλήμ is meant by our author to designate a *place* at all. Is it not rather an appellative? See the writer's own interpretation, ver. 2.

Ἱερεὺς τοῦ Θεοῦ τοῦ ὑψίστου, Hebrew כֹּהֵן לְאֵל עֶלְיוֹן, Gen. xiv. 18. It was common, among the ancients, for a king to be priest also; thus uniting the two highest honours among men, in his own person. The Jewish kings did not do thus, so long as the race of David was upon the throne; because the priesthood was confined to the tribe of Levi. But the Maccabees did it; Joseph. Antiq. XIII. 19, compare Macc. in the

Apocrypha. Among foreign nations, this was very common. In reference to this double honour, Peter calls Christians βασίλειον ἱεράτευμα, 1 Pet. ii. 9 ; and John, in Rev. i. 6, says, that Christ has made for his followers a βασιλείαν, and constituted them ἱερεῖς τῷ Θεῷ.

How highly the Jews of the apostle's day estimated the *honour* of priesthood, may be seen from Philo ; who says, " The law of kingly office applies to priests εἰς σεμνότητα καὶ τιμὴν, *in regard to dignity and honour*, de Legat. ad Caium, p. 832." In the same book, he represents the Jewish people as regarding " the high priesthood to be as much above the kingly office, as God is more exalted than men." All this serves to show, that the apostle, by exhibiting and proving the priesthood of Christ, not only pointed out the way in which pardon of sin had been effected, but also contributed much towards causing the Messiah to be honoured, in the view of the Hebrews.

In calling Melchisedek *a priest of the most high God*, the scripture designs to exhibit him as a true priest of the true God, maker and lord of heaven and earth, Gen. xiv. 19, 22.

Ὁ συναντήσας . . . εὐλογήσας αὐτὸν, *who met Abraham returning from the slaughter of the* [confederate] *kings, and blessed him ;* see Gen. xiv. 17—20.

Ver. 2. Ὥι καὶ δεκάτην . . . Ἀβραὰμ, *to whom also Abraham gave a tenth part of all*, viz. a tenth ἀπὸ πάντων τῶν ἀκροθινίων, *of all the spoils* (see ver. 4,) which he had taken from the confederate kings whom he had discomfited, Gen. xiv. 14—16. 20. Δεκάτην agrees with μοῖραν understood.

Πρῶτον μὲν ἑρμενευόμενος, βασιλεὺς δικαιοσύνης, *by interpretation,* [his name] *means, first, righteous king*. Βασιλεὺς δικαιοσύνης resembles the formulas, *God of mercy, God of glory, &c.* instead of *merciful God, glorious God*, &c. which are common indeed in all languages, but more especially in the Hebrew. In fact, the sense put upon βασιλεὺς δικαιοσύνης, in the translation, is the only one that can be put upon it; for what is a *king of righteousness*, in any other sense ? The phrase, king of a nation or people, or of living beings, we understand ; but what a king of an *abstract* existence is, which belongs solely to *mental* conception, it would be difficult to understand.

Ἔπειτα δὲ καὶ βασιλεὺς . . . εἰρήνης, *and then he is a king of Salem, which means, king of peace.*

Ver. 3. Ἀπάτωρ, ἀμήτωρ, *having neither father nor mother*, i. e. recorded in the sacred genealogies ; or, perhaps, whose father and mother were not of kingly rank. These words were applied *literally*, by the Greeks, to some of their gods; then *figuratively*, to those who were orphans, and to those whose parents were obscure and of low origin. Thus Livy, IV. 3, nullo patre natus," respecting a person of ignoble descent. So Horace, Serm. I. 6. 10, " nullis majoribus natos." Philo calls Sarah, ἀμήτορα, probably, because her mother is not mentioned in the sacred records. And in such a sense, the apostle appears to call Melchisedek, ἀπάτωρ and ἀμήτωρ. The explanation of these terms is to be found, (as one will easily believe,) in the word ἀγενεαλόγητος, *without any genealogy*, viz. of whose genealogy no mention is made in scripture.

The Arabians say of a man, who has by his own efforts procured an exalted place of honour, and who is descended from ignoble parents, لا له اب, *he has no father*, i. e. he is not named from his father, or derives not his titles and honours from his father. Michaëlis prefers the explanation which this idiom would afford, in respect to the passage under examination. But the other seems preferable, on account of the explanation which the writer himself has made, by adding, ἀγενεαλόγητος. See Schleusner and Wahl, on ἀπάτωρ and ἀμήτωρ.

Μήτε ἀρχὴν . . . ἔχων, *having neither beginning of days, nor end of life*, i. e. either, " Whose time of birth or death is not related ;" or rather, " Who, as a high priest, has no limited time assigned for the commencement and expiration of his office :" for so the Levitical clause leads us to interpret this expression. The Levitical priests were limited in their service; see Numb. iv. 3. 23. 35. 43. 47. (compare Numb. viii. 24, 25.) Ζωῆς, according to the latter mode of interpretation, refers to the life of Melchisedek as priest, i. e. the time of his priesthood. Ζωὴ is often equivalent in sense to καιρὸς ζωῆς, the season or time which one lives. The meaning of the writer then is, that Melchisedek's priesthood was limited to no definite time, i. e. he was *sacerdos perpetuus*, a priest without limitation of office. So the Latins say, *Dictator perpetuus*, &c.

Ἀφωμοιωμένος δὲ .... διηνεκὲς, *being like to the Son of God, remaineth a priest perpetually*. The sacred writer, in Ps. cx. 4, says of the Messiah, that he is כֹּהֵן לְעוֹלָם, Septuagint, ἱερεὺς εἰς τὸν αἰῶνα, i. q. εἰς τὸ διηνεκὲς ; and then adds, " after the order of Melchisedek." First, then, Christ is asserted by the Psalmist to be a *perpetual* priest; and next, to confirm or explain this assertion, it is added, that he is so, according to the order of Melchisedek. The implication is, of course, that Melchisedek is *perpetual* priest; for this is a special point of the comparison. The apostle means to say, in our text, that inasmuch as Melchisedek is understood to have a perpetual priesthood, and since the priesthood of the Son of God is affirmed, in the hundred-and-tenth Psalm, to be like his; so it follows, of course, that the priesthood of Christ is understood to be perpetual, or that Melchisedek, in regard to his priesthood, was like to, or could be compared with, the Son of God.

In respect to the object of this assertion, I apprehend nothing more is intended, than that the priesthood of Christ and Melchisedek was not, like that of the sons of Aaron, limited to any *definite* period. In the *absolute* sense, εἰς τὸ διηνεκὲς clearly is not to be understood. Melchisedek's priesthood terminated with his life; so Christ's priestly and kingly office both will cease, when the work of redemption is fully accomplished, 1 Cor. xv. 24—28. But in neither case is there any statute, which limits the specific time of accession to office, and of egress from it. Of course, the order of Christ's priesthood, and that of Melchisedek, differed greatly in this respect from that of the sons of Aaron, and was, as the writer goes on to declare, greatly superior to it. *Dictator perpetuus* among the Romans, for example, was surely a higher, or at least, a more honorable office, than that of ordinary dictator!

Our English version of ἀφωμοιωμένος, *made like to,* does not seem to give the true sense of the passage. The apostle is not labouring to show that Melchisedek, in respect to his priesthood, was *made like to* Christ; but *vice versa.* He is seeking to illustrate and establish the perpetuity of Christ's priesthood, by comparing it with the well-known priesthood of Melchisedek. Hence, to say that Melchisedek was *made like to the Son of God,* is a ὕστερον πρότερον; for Ps. xc. 4, compares the Son of God as priest, to Melchisedek. This, too, is the order of nature and propriety; for the priesthood of Melchisedek *preceded* that of Christ; it was something with which the Hebrews were already acquainted, inasmuch as their Scriptures had repeatedly spoken of it. Of course, the apostle, in aiming to illustrate and establish the priesthood of Christ, (a priesthood that was recent, and not well understood by the Hebrews,) would very naturally pursue the method of comparison offered to his view in Ps. cx. 4, i. e. a comparison of Christ's priesthood to that of Melchisedek. Ἀφωμοιωμένος means then, not *made like to,* but *like to,* possibly, *likened to,* i. e. *being compared to.*

The whole passage, from ὁ συναντήσας in ver. 1, to τῷ υἱῷ τοῦ Θεοῦ, in ver 3, is plainly a *parenthetic* explanation, (a very common occurrence in the writings of Paul,) thrown in for the sake of suggesting to the reader's mind some considerations respecting the character and dignity of Melchisedek, which would be very very useful, in regard to a right understanding of the comparison that was to be made out in the sequel. Οὗτος γὰρ ὁ Μελχιζεδὲκ, &c. in ver, 1, is the immediate nominative to μένει ἱερεὺς εἰς τὸ διηνεκὲς, in ver. 3. The construction of the whole sentence is thus; "This Melchisedek, king of Salem, priest . . . (who met Abraham . . . and blessed him . . . whose name means, first, *righteous king*, and secondly, *peaceful king* . . . of a descent no where recorded, having a priestly office not limited, and being in respect to his priesthood like to the Son of God,) is a perpetual priest." If it be objected, that the participles ἑρμενευόμενος, ἔχων and ἀφωμοιωμένος have not, like συναντήσας, the article before them, and therefore cannot be arranged in such a construction; the answer is, that nouns, participles, and adjectives, put in *apposition*, either take or omit the article, at the pleasure of the writer. E. g. ὁ Μελχισεδὲκ—βασιλεύς . . . . ἱερεὺς, in apposition. Then ὁ συναντήσας . . . εὐλογήσας . . . ἑρμενευόμενος . . . ἀπάτωρ, ἀμήτωρ ἀγενεαλόγητος . . . ἔχων . . . ἀφωμοιωμένος—all in apposition with ὁ συναντήσας; a mode of using adjectives and participles by no means unusual. See Gersdorf, Beiträge, &c. Th. V. Ueber die Stellung der Adjectiven, &c. In the translation, I have, for the sake of perspicuity, broken up the involved construction of the original, and made several simple sentences. See Excursus XIII.

Ver. 4. Θεωρεῖτε δὲ . . . πατριάρχης, *consider now how great a personage this must be, to whom the patriarch Abraham gave a tithe of the spoils.* Θεωρεῖτε, *see, perceive, consider.* Πηλίκος, *of what exalted rank.* Ἀκροθινίων, in its literal sense, means, *summitas acervi frumenti, the top part of a heap of grain.* It was usual to offer the *primitiæ* or *first fruits* to God. But as offerings were made to their gods, by the Greeks, from spoils taken in war, ἀκροθίνια came at last to signify in the Greek language, *any kind of spoils*, from which an offering for the gods was taken. The Latins called such offerings, *manubiæ.* The word ἀκροθινίων has the *general* sense of *spoils* here, and evidently refers to the spoils which Abraham had taken from the confederate kings, Gen. xiv. 16.

The object of the apostle, in mentioning the circumstance here adverted to, plainly is, to exalt the dignity of Melchisedek. The high reverence which the Jews had for Abraham is well known. If now it could be shown to the Hebrews, that Melchisedek was superior to Abraham, then the superiority of Christ, who is like to Melchisedek, is also shown. Moreover, since the patriarch or head of a nation was reckoned in the East as excelling in dignity all his descendants; so, if Melchisedek's dignity exceeded that of Abraham; it would follow, that it exceeded that of all his descendants—among whom were the Levitical priests. It is for the sake of establishing this last point, that the comparison of Melchisedek with Abraham is introduced in ver. 4; as the sequel plainly shows. This being established, it would follow, that Christ's priesthood, (which was like that of Melchisedek,) was superior to the Aaronical priesthood; which is the point that the writer designs to illustrate and establish.

Ver 5. Καὶ οἱ μὲν , . . λαμβάνοντες, *moreover, the sons of Levi, who obtain* the *office of the priesthood,* i. e. who are constituted priests. *All* the sons of Levi were not properly priests; but only the descendants of Aaron. Hence, the writer adds, τὴν ἱερατείαν λαμβάνοντες. It was true, indeed, that the whole tribe of Levi had a right to tithes; Numb. xviii. 28—30; Deut. xiv. 22. 27—29. But it is not material to the writer's object here, to mention this. He is concerned merely with the priests; who, as descendants of Levi, were of course entitled to tithes. If he could show that the priests, the most honoured part of the Levites, who were legally entitled to receive tithes from the other descendants of Abraham, were still inferior to Melchisedek; then would he show that the priesthood of Christ was of an order superior to theirs. The payment of tithes is an acknowledgment of superiority, in regard to the rank of the person who receives them. If Abraham, then, paid tithes to Melchisedek, he acknowledged him as superior in respect to rank.

Ἐντολὴν ἔχουσιν .... νόμον, *have, by the law, a commission to tithe the people.* See the passages of the law just referred to. Ἐντολὴν, *direction, mandate,* a *precept* that gives liberty or confers a right to do any thing.

Τοῦτ' ἔστι .... Ἀβραὰμ, *that is, their own brethren, although descendants from Abraham.* Ἐξεληλυθότας ἐκ τῆς ὀσφύος, a Hebraistic mode of expression; e. g. Gen. xxxv. 11, *kings* מֵחֲלָצֶיךָ יֵצֵאוּ; Gen. xlvi. 26, יֹצְאֵי יְרֵכוֹ, Ex. i. 5, et al. The Greeks used γεννᾶσθαι ὑπό τινος, in such cases. The meaning of the passage is, the priests of the tribe of Levi, although descended in common with the other tribes from Abraham, yet have been elevated to a rank above them, and receive the tribute of *acknowledged elevation,* in the tithes which are paid them by the others.

But why should the elevation of the priests above their brethren be introduced here ? I answer, in order to show that the most honored part of the sons of Levi, the most honored tribe, were of a rank inferior to Melchisedek ; consequently, their priesthood was of an order inferior to that of Christ.

Ver. 6, Ὁ δὲ μὴ γενεαλογούμενος ἐξ αὐτῶν, *but he whose descent is not reckoned from them;* a periphrasis, by which Melchisedek is described, and, at the same time, additional intimation is given, that he was of an order of priests different from that of the Levites.

Δεδεκάτωκε .... εὐλόγηκε, *tithed* [received tithes from] *Abraham, and blessed him to whom the promises were made.* Δεδεκάτωκε is a Hellenistic word, being found only in the Septuagint and New Testament. The meaning is, that Melchisedek received from Abraham a *tenth* of the spoils ; which was the same ratio with the tithes received by the Levitical priesthood. Καὶ τὸν ἔχοντα τὰς ἐπαγγελίας εὐλόγηκε, a periphrasis designating Abraham, to whom God had made promises of great blessings : compare Heb. vi. 12—15.

Ver. 7. Χωρὶς δὲ πάσης .... εὐλογεῖται, *and beyond all controversy, the inferior was blessed by the superior.* Ἀντιλογίας, *gainsaying, dispute, doubt,* compare ch. vi. 16. Ἔλαττον here means merely *inferiority in point of rank, office,* or *station;* not inferiority in regard to moral or religious character, which it is not the writer's object to bring into view, as it is not to his present purpose. Melchisedek was both king and priest : Abraham was neither ; at least he is not called by either appellation. He was, indeed, an *Emir,* i. e. the head of a company of migratory shepherds, (Nomades,) and had a large number of dependants ; as may be seen in Gen. xiv. 14. Abraham is also called נָבִיא, *prophet,* Gen. xx. 7 ; but he is not called כֹּהֵן, although he repeatedly offered sacrifices ; nor do the Scriptures call him מֶלֶךְ, *king*.

Κρείττονος is the antithesis or correlate of ἔλαττον, and therefore means *superior.* Both adjectives are of the *neuter* gender, as is manifest from ἔλαττον ; but this gender in adjectives is employed to denote *abstract quality,* i. e. it is used in the same way as abstract nouns ; which are very frequently employed, by the sacred writers, instead of concrete ones. E. g. Christ is the *way,* the *truth,* and *life,* i. e. he is the guide, the instructor, and the author of life, to men. So here, the literal rendering would be, *inferiority is blessed by superiority,* i. e. **the inferior person is blessed by the superior one.**

The apostle takes this as a position which will be granted by the Hebrews, from the simple consideration, that Abraham, by paying tithes to Melchisedek, of course acknowledged his own inferior rank.

Ver. 8. Καὶ ὧδε μὲν . . . λαμβάνουσι, *here, also, men receive tithes who die; but there, one of whom it is testified that he lives.* A very difficult verse, about which there has been no small controversy. The *literal* sense of the words would make nothing for the writer's purpose. Of the *natural* life of men he is not speaking; but of the duration of the priestly office. Ὧδε means, *in respect to the Levites;* ἐκεῖ, *in regard to Melchisedek*. Ὧδε and ἐκεῖ may also be literally rendered, *in this place,* and, *in that place;* which gives the meaning just proposed. But what is ἀποθνήσκοντες? Is it the *natural* death of the body? But, in this respect, the Levites differed not from the king of Salem; both were mortals. In another world, too, they live as well as he, i. e. both are immortal also. Ζῇ, therefore, cannot refer simply to living in another world. Nor is there any ground for supposing the apostle means to assert, that Melchisedek's high priesthood continues in heaven; as some have imagined. There is no intimation in Scripture of any such thing, in regard to any one but Jesus. I must therefore understand ἀποθνήσκοντες as being used figuratively here, in order to denote the *brief* and *mutable* condition of the Levitical priesthood. The figurative use of θνήσκω and ἀποθνήσκω, in the New Testament, is very common; although no instance occurs, perhaps, where it has the same shade of meaning which it appears to have here. Schleusner, however, gives to θνήσκω, in 1 Tim. v. 6, the same sense, viz. *qui officio suo non fungitur.* But in the verse before us, he construes ἀποθνήσκοντες as meaning, *mortales,* and ζῇ as applying to *Christ,* not to Melchisedek; most plainly against the context that follows.

The word ζῇ seems to me, plainly, not to mean here, either *natural life,* or *future immortality,* but an enduring, unlimited time of priesthood; and to designate the same idea as μένει ἱερεὺς εἰς τὸ διηνεκὲς, in ver. 3. A sense like this, viz. that of *duration, perennitas,* the word ζάω often has. If this be correct, then its correlate, ἀποθνήσκοντες must of course have the sense of *short-lived,* or *deceasing,* viz. as to office, or the priesthood. In this way, and in this only, can I make out any tolerable sense of the passage, consistently with the context. Nothing can be plainer, than that the object of the writer is to show the perpetuity of Melchisedek's priesthood, and not that of his *natural* life; and by consequence, he would also make out the perpetuity of Christ's priesthood.

To construe ἀποθνήσκοντες, then, as referring to *physical* mortality, and ζῇ as having respect to *physical* or *natural* life, is to quit the subject under the consideration of the writer, and resort to one which is altogether inapposite to his purpose. That ζάω and ζωή, moreover, often denote *perpetuity, perennitas*, the reader may readily see by consulting Wahl's Lex. ζάω, No. 2, β, and ζωὴ, No 1, γ. The word ἀποθνήσκοντες, then, by the force of *antithesis*, denotes, the reverse of this; and *perennity*, here, is not ascribed to *natural life*, but to the *priesthood*.

Ver. 9. Καὶ, ὡς ἔπος εἰπεῖν . . . δεδεκάτωται, *yea, even Levi, who received tithes, was (if I may be allowed the expression) himself tithed, through Abraham*. Ὡς ἔπος εἰπεῖν is very common, in the best Greek writers. It is a μείλιγμα, *softening down*, of an expression, which a writer supposes his readers may deem to be too strong, or which may have the appearance of excess or severity. It amounts to an indirect apology, for employing an unusual or unexpected assertion or phrase. It is very happily introduced here; as the subject itself is one which the writer did not intend to urge as capable of being scanned with metaphysical exactness, but only as bearing a popular mode of explanation.

Καὶ, *verily truly, imo, vero, profecto;* See Wahl, Lex. καὶ, 2. b. β. Brettschneider, Lex. καὶ. 5, 6.

Ver. 10. Ἔτι γὰρ ἐν τῇ ὀσφύι . . . Μελχισεδέκ, *for he was then in the loins of his father, when Melchisedek met him*. Ἔτι *etiam, nunc, even now, already*, or, *etiam tunc, even then, then*. The meaning of the writer is, that at the time then present, viz. when Melchisedek met Abraham, Levi was ἐν τῇ ὀσφύϊ πατρός. Our English version, " He was yet in the loins of his father, gives a sense quite different from that of the writer; for the meaning of this must be, " he was yet to be begotten," i. e. he was not yet born. But the apostle designs to say, and it is appropriate to his object to say, that even then, when Melchisedek met Abraham, Levi already (in a certain sense) existed, and, through Abraham, paid tithes to the king of Salem, i. e. acknowledged inferiority compared with him. This is the very point which the writer is labouring to illustrate. See Excursus XIV.

Ver. 11. Εἰ μὲν οὖν τελείωσις . . . . . . ἦν, *further, if perfection were* [attainable] *by the Levitical priesthood* Μὲν οὖν, or, μενοῦν, *moreover, further*. Μὲν οὖν are often used as a continuative particle, merely indicating that the writer is advancing to another topic or paragraph. Οὖν is illative, in a general way; but when joined with μὲν, it should not, usually, be separately translated. That a new topic is begun here, will be plain to every considerate reader.

Τελείωσις, a word very variously understood and translated. Some render it, *accomplishment*, viz. of the design of the priesthood; others, *sanctification*; others, *consummate happiness*; others, *moral rectitude* or *perfection*. It is best explained by a reference to corresponding passages in the sequel. In ch. ix. 9, it is said, that "the Levitical sacrifices could not τελειῶσαι the person who offered them;" which (if we compare ch. ix. 14) appears plainly to mean, "to take away the burden of guilt, and to render pure or holy the minds of the worshippers." Again, in ch. x. 1, it is affirmed of the sacrifices, that "they could not τελειῶσαι those who approached the altar," i. e. those who offered them; and by comparing ch. x. 2—4 with this, it is plain the writer means to say, that "the sacrifices could not bestow peace of conscience—could not take away the burden of sin from the mind of the worshipper; but they left him filled with apprehensions, that the penalty of the divine law might still be executed upon him." Here, then, is plainly the τελείωσις, which the Levitical priesthood could not effect. It could neither purify the mind or soul of the worshipper, nor free him from the burden of his sins, or from the apprehension that they might be punished. Christ did both; and this is the τελείωσις here spoken of, which he accomplished, and which the law could not accomplish. Chap. x. 3. 14. is very direct to this purpose. The writer, then, has explained τελείωσις, by the sequel of his epistle; and in a manner altogether accordant with the object of his reasoning here.

Ὁ λαὸς γὰρ επ' αὐτῇ νενομοθέτητο, *(for the people received the law in connexion with this.)* This circumstance is evidently to be placed in a parenthesis. Νενομοθέτητο, *were subjected to the law, were put under the law.* Such a construction in the passive voice is peculiar; compare Rom. iii. 4. Επ' αὐτῇ, *on this condition, connected with this*, or, *under these circumstances;* compare Wahl on ἐπὶ II. 4, b. The meaning is, that the Levitical priesthood and the Mosaic law are closely and inseparably linked together, so that if one is changed, the other must of necessity be; as the writer proceeds to show in the sequel.

Τὶς ἔτι χρεία ...... λέγεσθαι, *what need was there, any more, that another priest should arise after the order of Melchisedek, and not be called after the order of Aaron?* That is, "if the Levitical priesthood, and the law connected with it, accomplished all, in respect to purification from sin, and the giving of quiet to the conscience, which was needed then why should the Psalmist speak of a priest, who was of an order different from that of Aaron, and who was yet to arise?" This would be unnecessary, if the priesthood of Aaron were adequate to the great purposes of salvation. "Ἔτι *any more, any longer.*

Ver. 12. Μετατιθεμένης γὰρ .... γίνεται, *but in case the priesthood is changed, there must needs be also a change of the law.* Μετατίθημι means, *to transfer, to translate.* This sense corresponds sufficiently well with the intention of the writer, whose design is to show, that the priesthood of the ancient dispensation had been *transferred* to Christ, although on conditions very different from those formerly attached to it; and that Christ not only was a priest in fact, but that his priesthood, coming in the place of the other ancient priesthood, superseded it. Νόμου here means, the Jewish dispensation, the Mosaic law. The change spoken of in respect to this, has reference to the fact, that all its ritual observances and its priesthood, (which were inseparably connected,) must be laid aside together, under the new dispensation. As Christ's priesthood differed from that of the Levites, so must the law, by which it is regulated, differ from that which regulated the Aaronical priesthood.

This conclusion is in itself so obvious, that the writer does not deem it necessary to produce any formal arguments here to establish it. He proceeds to show, that the priesthood itself is changed, by adducing facts and declarations recorded in the Old Testament. (1.) Christ sprang from the tribe of Judah, ver. 13, 14. (2.) He was to be a priest of the order of Melchisedek, ver. 15—17. Consequently, the law, which was necessarily connected with the Levitical priesthood, must also be changed.

Ver. 13. Ἐφ ὃν γὰρ ...... θυσιαστηρίῳ, *now he, concerning whom these things are said, belonged to a different tribe, none of whom served at the altar.* Γὰρ here connects the illustration or proof with the proposition in ver. 12. It may, however, be translated *but*, with nearly the same effect. The reasoning, then, would stand thus : " If the priesthood be changed, the law must also be changed ; but the priesthood is changed, [i. e. Christ, who is appointed to the priesthood, sprung from the tribe of Judah ;] therefore, the law is laid aside :" compare ver. 18. and seq.

Προσέσχηκε. Προσέχω means, *to give heed, to apply the mind to,* τὸν νοῦν being understood ; also, *to give one's care to, to serve.*

Ver. 14. Πρόδηλον γὰρ ...... ἐλάλησε, *for it is quite manifest that* our Lord sprang from Judah, in respect to which tribe, Moses said nothing concerning the priesthood, i. e. he gave the priest's office to the sons of Levi, Numb. xviii. 6, and not to the tribe of Judah. The reader is left to supply, at the end of the verse, the conclusion of the syllogism, (which Paul very frequently omits,) viz. μετατίθεται οὖν ἡ ἱερωσύνη, *consequently the priesthood is changed*; i. e. since Christ is high-priest, who was of the tribe of Judah, it follows, of course, that there must be a change in the priesthood; for none but Levites, under the ancient dispensation, could be priests.

Ver. 15. Καὶ περισσότερον ἔτι ...... ἕτερος, *and still more evident is it.* [viz. that the priesthood must be changed] *if another priest has arisen, like to Melchisedek.* Between δῆλον, πρόδηλον, and κατάδηλον, there is no important difference of signification. The two latter seem naturally to render the word somewhat more intensive. 'Ἀνίσταται, *is risen up*, viz. the high-priest in question, *has already arisen* or made his appearance, *is already extant*.

Καθ' ὁμοιότητα, *according to the likeness, in the similitude*, i. e. like, resembling: in a sense like that of κατὰ τάξιν, in ch. v. 6. 10; vi. 20; vii. 11, Hebrew, עַל־דִּבְרָתִי, Ps. cx. 4. Compare ἀφωμοιωμένος in ch. vii. 3.

Ver. 16. Ὃς οὐ κατὰ νόμον ...... ἀκαταλύτου, *who was not made* [a priest] *by an ordinance of temporary obligation, but by an authority of endless duration*; i. e. he was not made a priest under the Mosaic law, which was to be set aside, ver. 12. 18, seq.; but by the oath of God, which is immutable; compare ver. 20—24, and 28.

Σαρκικῆς, *fleshly;* hence, secondarily, *frail, infirm, short-lived, temporary, quicquid caducum*. So the Hebrew בָּשָׂר, Gen. vi. 3. Ps. lvi. 5; lxxviii. 39. Job x. 4. Isa. xxxi. 3; compare also ἀσθενὲς and ἀνωφελὲς, in ver. 18. 'Ἐντολῆς means here, the *precept* or *command* respecting the appointment of priests, contained in the νόμος, i. e. Mosaic law. 'Ἐντολῆς σαρκικῆς is, then, *preceptum caducum, a temporary command, an obligation of a temporary, perishable nature.* So ver. 12 and 18 require us to interpret the passage.

Δύναμιν, *authority, authoritative appointment.* So Acts iv. 7, ἐν ποίᾳ δυνάμει; *by what authority?* see also 1 Cor. v. 4. Ζωῆς, *perennitas, perpetuity;* see on ver. 8, above. 'Ἀκαταλύτου, *quod destrui nequit, indissoluble*, hence *immutable, imperishable, perpetual.* As it is the antithesis of σαρκικῆς, the meaning of σαρκικῆς must be that which is given above.

That this interpretation of the whole verse is well grounded, follows plainly from the succeeding verse, (ver. 17,) which is adduced simply to prove the *perpetuity* of Christ's priesthood.

Ver. 17. Μαρτυρεῖ γὰρ, viz. ἡ γραφὴ, or τὸ πνεῦμα τὸ ἅγιον. The nominative, in such cases, would of course be supplied by the readers of the epistle. In the writings of the Mishnical doctors, the usual mode of appeal to the Scriptures is, שֶׁנֶּאֱמַר, i. e. *quod dicitur*, or, λέγεται γὰρ, μαρτυρεῖται. The writer makes the appeal to Scripture, in this case, to confirm and enforce what he had just asserted.

The conclusion is now left for the reader to supply. In ver. 11, the writer had said, that the Levitical priesthood, and the system of law under which the people of Israel had been placed, were connected together. In ver. 12, he intimates that the connexion was so intimate, that whatever affected one would affect the other; and, consequently, that if the priesthood be changed, the law itself must be. " But the priesthood is changed," is the next proposition which he establishes, ver. 13—17. It follows, therefore, (and this is the conclusion which the reader is now to supply,) that the law is also changed.

The writer proceeds to give another reason why the ancient law must be repealed, or rather be superseded. One reason just given above is, that the priesthood is changed, which demands a corresponding change of the law. Another reason now to be given, is the inefficacy of the whole legal institution, in respect to spiritual pardon and sanctification.

Ver. 18. Ἀθέτησις μὲν γὰρ . . . . ἀνωφελὲς. *There is, moreover, a setting aside of the preceding law, because it was inefficient and unavailing.* Μὲν γὰρ, continuative, (as often,) *further, also, moreover, besides;* the transition being made to another argument, and μὲν γὰρ showing that the subject is continued, and something more added to it. Ἀθέτησις, *rejection, setting aside, abrogation;* a stronger word than ἀναλλαγή. Προαγούσης, literally, *preceding,* i. e. going before the Christian dispensation, i. q. the ancient law. Ἀσθενὲς καὶ ἀνωφελὲς are words of nearly the same import here. Ἀσθενὲς is said of that which has not *power* to accomplish any particular end proposed; and ἀνωφελὲς is said of that which proves to be neither useful nor availing, for the purpose to which it has been applied. The meaning here is, that the ancient law, with all its ritual, had proved to be altogether incompetent to effect the τελείωσιν mentioned in ver. 11, i. e. the purification of the sinner, and that peace of conscience which is inspired by the well-grounded hope of pardon for sin: compare ver. 19; and ch. ix. 9, 14; ch. x. 1—4. The two words ἀσθενὲς and ἀνωφελὲς increase the intensity of the affirmation. The epithet σαρκικῆς, in ver. 16, is of a similar nature.

Ver. 19. Οὐδὲν γὰρ ἐτελείωσεν ὁ νόμος, *for the law perfected nothing*. Οὐδὲν, neuter gender, is used here for οὐδένα, masculine, i. e. *no one*; just as τὸ ἔλαττον, in ver. 2, means the *superior person*, i. e. Melchisedek. Τὸ πᾶν and πάντα are repeatedly used, by John, for πᾶς and πάντες, and so of other adjectives. Ἐτελείωσε means, *did not effect a τελείωσις, did not purify and pacify the consciences and minds of sinners*. We have no one English word, which corresponds at all with the force of the Greek original; and we must therefore content ourselves, either with a kind of literal rendering of it, or with a periphrasis, leaving the explanation for notes.

Ἐπεισαγωγὴ δὲ .... τῷ Θεῷ, *but the introduction of a better hope* [does]. Ἐτελείωσε is implied after ἐλπίδος, by the laws of grammar. *The introduction of a better hope does perfect men*, i. e. it inspires them with well-grounded hope of pardon, and " purifies their consciences from dead works, so that they may serve the living God." ch. ix. 14. Ἐπεισαγωγὴ, *superinduction*, is said of one thing which is introduced in the place of another; e. g. in this case, of the gospel, which was superinduced upon the Mosaic law. Ἐλπὶς κρείττων means *a better source or ground of hope*, viz, the gospel was a better ground of hope to the sinner than the law, Δι' ἧς, *by which, by means of which, through which*, i. e. in the way disclosed by the gospel, ἐγγίζομεν τῷ Θεῷ, *we draw nigh to God, we have access to God*. Under the ancient law, the high priest only entered the holy of holies, to procure pardon for the people. Under the gospel, the way is opened by Jesus, for all penitent sinners to " come boldly to the throne of grace," ch. iv. 16, in order to obtain the blessings which they need. Ἐγγίζω is frequently construed with the dative, in Hellenistic Greek; see Winer's Gram. § 24. 4. Septuagint, Gen. xxvii. 21 ; Exod. xix. 22.

Ver. 20. Καὶ καθ' ὅσον οὐ χωρὶς ὁρκωμοσίας, *further, since not without an oath*, supply ἱερεὺς γέγονεν Ἰησοῦς from the latter part of the following phrase, which is the antithesis of this. Καθ' ὅσον, in this case refers to κατὰ τοσοῦτον in ver. 22; and the intervening phrases are added by the writer, only by way of explanation and comparison. It is difficult, if not impossible, to give the exact features of the original here, in any copy. The argument of the writer stands thus: " The gospel is a *better* source of hope; for, *as much* (καθ' ὅσον) as the appointment of a priest, by an oath, exceeds, in solemnity and importance, an arrangement to take the office merely by descent, *so much* (κατὰ τοσοῦτον, ver. 22) does the new covenant, of which Jesus is the sponsor, exceed the old." Ὁρκωμοσία does not differ in meaning from ὅρκος, unless it be, that the former applies rather to the *act* of taking an oath, being derived from ὅρκος and ὄμνυμι.

Ver. 21. Οἱ μὲν . . . γεγονότες. *for they*, i. e, the Levites *became priests without an oath*. Μὲν γὰρ often means, *indeed, in fact, verily;* but here μὲν is only the sign of *protasis*. The Levites were priests in consequence of being the descendants of Aaron; Jesus became a priest only by special appointment, sanctioned by an oath, as follows.

Ὁ δὲ μετὰ ὁρκωμοσίας . . . Μελχιζεδέκ, *but he* [Jesus, became a priest] *with an oath, by him who said to him*, " *The Lord hath sworn, and will not repent; Thou art a priest for ever, of the order of Melchisedek*," Ps. cx. 4. Μεταμεληθήσεται signifies, *to regret, to alter one's mind or purpose through regret;* and simply, *to change or alter one's purpose*.

Ver. 22. Κατὰ τοσοῦτον . . . Ἰησοῦς, *Jesus is the surety of a covenant so much the better.* On κατὰ τοσοῦτον, see above. Διαθήκη (בְּרִית) means, *covenant, promise, disposition, arrangement, testament;* consequently, when applied to the ancient Jewish law, or to Christianity, it means, *dispensation, economy*. Κρείττονος means, *better* than the ancient διαθήκη; i. e. the hope inspired by the new διαθήκη is as much better than the ancient διαθήκη could inspire, as the new διαθήκη is superior to the old. Ἔγγυος, *sponsor, pledge, surety*. Many critics have supposed, that this word is chosen here, on account of its likeness to ἐγγίζομεν in the nineteenth verse; so that it constitutes a kind of παρονομασία with it. However this may be, the word is altogether appropriate to the writer's purpose. He had spoken of a *better hope*, in ver. 19. It was natural to ask, What is the ground, or security, that this hope would be realized? This is answered by the assurance, that Jesus is ἔγγυος for the dispensation which supports it.

The writer now proceeds to add another reason why the Levitical priesthood must be considered as far inferior to that of Jesus. As men in a frail and dying state are constituted priests, under the Levitical law, the consequence is, that the priesthood is liable to continual change, and must necessarily pass from the hands of one to another, in a short time. Not so, in the case of Christ; who, being exalted above the heavens, and constituted high priest in the temple not made with hands, hath an immutable priesthood ; subject to no succession.

Ver. 23. Καὶ οἱ μὲν πλείονες .... παραμένειν, *again, those priests,* viz. descendants of Aaron, *are many, since by reason of death they cannot be permanent.* Πλείονες refers to numbers consituted by repeated succession ; not to the number of priests existing at any one time. Θανάτῳ is put in the dative, as signifying the means. The writer, doubtless, intends, that the comparison here shall be referred to the high priest's office in particular ; for he is all along considering Jesus as ἀρχιερεὺς. The number of priests, in general, is stated by Josephus to have been fifteen hundred. Contra Apion. I. 22.

Ver. 24. Ὁ δὲ, διὰ τὸ μένειν .... ἱερωσύνην, *but he, because he continues* [a priest] *for ever, has a priesthood without succession.* That μένειν here refers to priesthood, and not to simple duration of life, seems to me quite clear, from comparing ver. 3, (ad finem,) 17, and 21. The very object of the writer is, to show the difference between the order of Christ's priesthood and that of the Levites. To say that Christ lives for ever, in the world above, is to say no more than what is equally true of the sons of Aaron, who surely are immortal beings. But to say that he continues a perpetual priest, and that his office is therefore subject to no transfer and succession like theirs, is saying what is altogether adapted to the writer's purpose, and perfectly accords with the assertions in the verses to which a reference has just been made. The reasoning stands thus : Jehovah has, by an oath, constituted the Messiah ἱερέα εἰς τὸν αἰῶνα ; and because he is thus constituted perpetual priest, his priesthood has not, like that of Aaron, any succession in office.

'Απαράβατον is altogether an appropriate word here, and more significant than αἰώνιον or ἀτέλευτον would be. The writer had just said, " The Levitical priesthood admits or demands many (πλείονες) priests in succession, because death is continually removing them from office." On the contrary, Christ being appointed to a perpetual priesthood, his office is here declared to be ἀπαράβατος, i. e. it demands or admits no transition to another, no successor in his place. Παραβαίνω means, *to pass over, to pass on ;* and, when spoken of an office, it signifies, *to pass into the hands of another person.* 'Απαράβατος is, therefore, *incapable of transition ;* which is the very shade of meaning that the writer's argument demands. So Theophylact and Œcumenius : ἀπαράβατον, ἀδιάδοχον, *without succession.*

Ver. 25. "Ὅθεν καὶ σώζειν .... Θεῷ, *hence, also, he is able always to save those who draw nigh to God through him*, i. e. approach the throne of grace (ch. iv. 16) in his name, or on his account, trusting in him as their priest and intercessor. "Ὅθεν, *whence*, i. e. because he is a perpetual priest. Σώζειν, *to save*, means here, *to deliver from condemnation and punishment*. This the high priest did, in regard to God's external government over the Jews, when he went into the most holy place, and made expiation for the sins of the people. Christ, as a priest in the heavenly world, is able to do this; and to do it, εἰς τὸ παντελὲς, *unceasingly, always*, so long as there are any who need pardon, and who can obtain it.

Πάντοτε ζῶν, *ever living*, i. e. always abiding or continuing a priest; compare ver. 3. 8. 17. 21. 24. Ζάω, *to live, to endure, to be perennial;* as frequently before. The mere *continual existence* of Christ is not at all the question here, but the perpetuity of his priesthood; so that ζῶν plainly refers to his ever living or continuing as a priest, in which capacity ἐντυγχάνειν ὑπὲρ ἡμῶν, as follows.

Εἰς τὸ ἐντυγχάνειν ὑπὲρ αὐτῶν, *to intercede for them*, or rather *to interpose in their behalf.* The proper meaning of ἐντυγχάνω is, *to go to any one, to approach him, to meet him*, for the sake of accusing, defending, convicting, or delivering any person, or of transacting any business which has respect to him. Here, it is plainly in the sense of *aiding, defending*, or *delivering;* as the preceding σώζειν clearly indicates. It means here, also, to do something, or to interpose, in such a way as is appropriate to the priest's office. But *to intercede*, in the sense of *making supplication*, is not appropriate to any part of the priests' office under the Levitical law; at least, not to any which the Scriptures have presented to our view. The reader will search in vain for any direction to the priests, under the Jewish economy, to perform such a duty as priests; and all the testimony we have to show us that the priests did make intercession, is what Philo says of their duties, Legat. ad Caium. II. 77, p. 591, (edit. Mangey;) see on ver. 27. Even the passage in Luke i. 9, 10, seems to indicate nothing that solves the question. We must, therefore, understand ἐντυγχάνειν here, in a more *general* sense, and refer it to *any* aid which Christ as high priest extends to those who approach God, confiding in him, ch. iv. 16. He is able, σώζειν αὐτοὺς, because he is a perpetual priest, ἐντυγχάνειν ὑπὲρ αὐτῶν, i. e. *to interpose in their behalf, to procure for them such aid* as they may need. So the priests, under the Levitical dispensation, were the *internuntii* between God and the people, and procured blessings for them, not only by presenting the offerings which they brought, but by inquiring of the Lord for them, or consulting his holy oracle. I acquiesce, therefore, in the *general* idea of ἐντυγχάνειν here, viz. *interposing in our behalf, assisting;* and I believe, that all attempts to draw from the word any thing more than this, is substituting imagination for well-grounded reasoning.

The writer, having now commented on the priesthood of Christ as compared with that of Melchisedek, and having also made some deductions from the nature of Christ's priestly office as thus exhibited, which are much to his purpose, resumes the subject which he had dropped at ch. v. 10, and which he had first proposed in ch. v. 2, 3. In ch. v. 7—9, he had shown the similarity between Christ and the Jewish priests, in regard to the power of sympathizing with the suffering, inasmuch as both he and they were sufferers themselves. But he did not intend that the ἀσθένεια of the Jewish priests should be predicated of Jesus in *all* respects. To guard against this, our author again introduces the topic here, and shows how far superior the priest of the new covenant is, in a *moral* respect, to the priests of the old.

Ver. 26. Τοιοῦτος γὰρ ἡμῖν ἔπρεπεν ἀρχιερεύς, *moreover, such a high priest was needful for us.* Πρέπω signifies, ordinarily, *that which is becoming, proper, fit.* But here ἔπρεπε seems plainly to be equivalent to τὸ ἀναγκαῖον; as in Matt. iii. 15. So Luther, sollten wir haben, *we must have.* So Ernesti, Calovius.

Ὅσιος, *holy,* not merely קָדוֹשׁ here, but צַדִּיק חָסִיד, תָּמִים; for *moral,* internal holiness or purity of nature is intended. Ἄκακος, *harmless, qui malum non fecit,* whose external conduct towards others corresponds with internal, ὁσιότης.

Ἀμίαντος, *undefiled,* has reference to the ceremonial purity which was peculiarly required of the Jewish high priests. Ἀμίαντος has here, however, a *moral* sense, and expresses, summarily and with intensity, the ideas conveyed by ὅσιος and ἄκακος. Κεχωρισμένος ἀπὸ τῶν ἁμαρτωλῶν, *separated from sinners,* i. e. removed from all that could contaminate or render impure; diverse from sinners; unlike to them. It is nearly synonymous in its meaning with ἀμίαντος, and is added (as is usual in such cases with the sacred writers) for the sake of intensity.

Ὑψηλότερος τῶν οὐρανῶν γενόμενος, *exalted above the heavens,* i. e. seated at the right hand of the majesty on high, ch. i. 3. Compare Phil. ii. 9. Colos. i. 18. Heb. ii. 9; viii. 1. Rev. v. 12. Matt. xxv. 31.

By these assertions, the writer designs to show his Hebrew readers, that Christ was, in all personal respects, exalted above the Jewish high priests. They were " compassed with infirmities," but he was spotless; if they were ceremonially undefiled, he was morally so; if they were placed in an exalted station, he was infinitely above them, being like Melchisedek, king as well as priest, inasmuch as he was raised to the throne of God above the heavens, ch. i. 3. To finish the comparison, he goes on to say, that, in consequence of his perfect purity, he needed no expiatory offering for himself, as the Jewish high priest did.

Ver. 27. *Ὃς οὐκ ἔχει* .... *λαοῦ*, *who has not, like the high priests, any daily necessity of offering sacrifices, first for his own sins, and then for those of the people.* Many doubts have been raised by critics, about the meaning of καθ' ἡμέραν here, because they have supposed that the high priest officiated in person, only on the great day of atonement. But that these doubts are without any good ground, may be seen by consulting Lev. vi. 19—22. Numb. xxviii. 3, 4. Philo, who was contemporary with the apostles, says, ἀρχιερεὺς, κατὰ τοὺς νόμους, εὐχὰς δὲ καὶ θυσίας τελῶν καθ' ἑκάστην ἡμέραν, *the high priest, agreeably to the laws, makes daily supplications and sacrifices,* see on ver. 25. It happens in this case, as in all others of a like nature which occur in our epistle, that the deep and accurate knowledge of the writer, in respect to every thing which concerned the Jewish dispensation, becomes apparent, just in proportion to our knowledge of the usages which really existed under that dispensation.

Τοῦτο γὰρ .... *ἀνενέγκας, for this he did, once for all, when he offered up himself.* Ἀναφέρω is like the Heb. הֶעֱלָה. Προσφέρω is also used in a similar sense.

Ἐφάπαξ, literally *for once, einmal;* but, according to usage, it denies a repetition of the act or thing to which it relates, and so means *once for all.*

Ver. 28. Ὁ *νόμος γὰρ* .... *ἀσθένειαν, now the law constitutes men high priests, who have infirmity.* Γὰρ may here mean *truly, indeed;* but the connexion is better kept up by the version which I have given it.

Ἔχοντας ἀσθένειαν, here means, those who have infirmity of a moral nature, i. e. who commit sin, who are sinners; so also in ver. 2.

Ὁ *λόγος δὲ ὁρκωμοσίας . . . τετελειωμένον, but the word of the oath, which was subsequent to the law*, [constitutes as high priest] *the Son, who is for ever exalted to glory.* Ὁ λόγος τῆς ὁρκωμοσίας is the same as ὅρκος, or ὁρκωμοσία in ver. 20. The writer refers to Ps. cx. 4. *The word of the oath*, i. q. the oath that was uttered.

Υἱὸν εἰς τὸν αἰῶνα τετελειωμένον. On τελειόω, see ch. ii. 10, τελειῶσαι. I regard the expression as designed here to convey, for substance, the idea of a state of the highest perfection and exaltation, which forbids the supposition that he can have such ἀσθένειαν as the Jewish priests.

CHAPTER VIII.

Ver. 1. Κεφάλαιον δὲ ἐπὶ τοῖς λεγομένοις, *the most important thing, however, in regard to what we are now treating of, is.* That κεφάλαιον has such a meaning as is here assigned to it, is beyond any reasonable doubt. So Suidas, referring to this passage, says, Κεφάλαιον, ἐκεῖ, τὸ μέγιστον. So Theophylact, on this verse, ἵνα εἴπω τὸ μέγιστον καὶ συνεκτικώτερον, *that I may say the greatest thing and the most comprehensive.* So Theodoret understood κεφάλαιον; for he says, τὴν μεγίστην τιμὴν τελευταίαν κατέλιπε, *he reserved the greatest honour until the last.* So Philo, τὸ κεφάλαιον τῶν ἀνδρῶν τῶν πολεμιστῶν, *the head of the warriors.* So the classic authors also, as may be seen in Schneider, and in any good Greek Lexicon; to which may be added, many of the most distinguished among late critics on our epistle, such as Zachariæ, Michaëlis, Heinrichs, Storr, Dindorf, Schulz, Iaspis, and others. The context, also, renders it quite plain, that such must be the meaning, and that κεφάλαιον does not here mean, *sum*, or *summary*, in the sense of *recapitulation* or *contents*: for what follows is no *recapitulation* of what precedes, but a new topic, exhibiting a different attitude or view of Christ's priesthood. In the preceding chapter, the apostle has treated of the superiority of Christ's priesthood, in respect to duration and succession. He has shown, also, that Christ was made priest by the solemnity of an oath, while the Levites were not introduced to their office by such a solemnity. The priesthood of the latter was liable to continual interruption and vicissitude, from the frail and dying state of those who were invested with the office of priest; while the perpetuity of Christ's priestly office was never exposed to interruption from causes of this nature. Finally, the Jewish priests were themselves not only peccable, but peccant men, and needed to offer sacrifices on their own account, as well as for the sake of others; while Christ was holy, and perfectly free from all sin and exalted to a glorious state in which he was placed for ever beyond the reach of it, so that his sacrifice would endure solely to the benefit of sinful men.

Thus much the writer has already said, respecting the nature of the office conferred on Christ, and his qualifications to discharge the duties of it. He now comes, in ch. viii.—x., to the consideration of the duties themselves, viz. the nature of the sacrifice which Jesus offers; the place where it is offered; the efficacy which it has, to atone for sin; and the difference, in regard to all these points, between the sacrifice offered by Christ, and that which was presented by the Jewish priests. This topic, then, differs from those which were discussed in ch. vii. Κεφάλαιον, therefore, does not mean *recapitulation* here, although there can be no doubt that the word itself is capable of conveying such a sense, if the nature of the case demanded it.

Moreover, from the circumstances just presented, it is evident that what follows is the Κεφάλαιον, *principal thing*, which belongs to the topic of the writer. The dignity of an office, and the particular qualifications of the person who is to be invested with it, are things which in their own nature are subordinate to the great end which is to be accomplished by the office itself. They are only subordinate *means* of bringing about the end of the office; while this end or design itself, must, from its own nature, be regarded as the *principal thing*, κεφάλαιον.

'Επὶ τοῖς λεγομένοις, *in respect to*, &c. That ἐπὶ often has this sense, may be seen in the lexicons. Λεγομένοις, present participle passive, means, *the subjects now spoken upon or discussed*. Τοιοῦτον ἀρχιερεὰ. *such a priest*, viz. as had been described in the preceding chapter; see ch. vii. 26.

'Ὃς ἐκάθισεν ἐν δεξιᾷ, κ. τ. λ., see on ch. i. 3. ult. It is quite possible, that the writer, in using ἐκάθισε here, may intend tacitly to introduce a comparison between Christ as a priest, performing the duties of his office, *seated* on a throne of majesty, and the high priest of the Jews, who, in the discharge of all the duties of his function, *stood* before the Lord. But I do not think the point clear enough to be insisted on. Thus much is clear, viz. that the writer means to show the very great difference between Christ and the Jewish high priest, by adverting to the fact, that the one is seated on the throne of God in the heavens, while the other only ministers on earth, in a temple reared by the hands of men. This last idea he proceeds more fully to develop in—

Ver. 2. Τῶν ἁγίων λειτουργὸς, *a minister of the sanctuary*, i. e. of the adytum, sanctum sanctorum הַקֹּדֶשׁ ; in other words, the high priest of the temple above, having access to הַקֹּדֶשׁ, *the holy*, or *most holy place*. 'Αγίων may also mean, *of holy things*, i. e. ἁγίων ἀληθινῶν, of the truly sacred or holy things in heaven. But I prefer the former sense ; as the comparison thus becomes more direct with the Jewish high priest. Λειτουργὸς means, *a public minister, qui publicis officiis præest*, vel. *munera publica præstat*. Says Ulpian, the Scholiast upon Demosth. contra Septin., λεῖτον, ἐκάλουν οἱ παλαιοὶ τὸ δημόσιον, *what was public, the ancients called* λεῖτον. The ending -ουργὸς comes from the verb ἔργειν, *opero, officio fungor*.

Καὶ τῆς σκηνῆς τῆς ἀληθινῆς, *the true tabernacle*, means, that which is spiritual, immutable, and eternal in the heavens ; and which therefore is called *true* or *real*, in distinction from the earthly tabernacle that was made by the hands of men, and was of materials earthly and perishable. The tabernacle in heaven is the *substance* ; that on earth, the image or type. Hence the former is, by way of distinction, properly named ἀληθινῆς, i. e. *real*, or *that which truly and permanently exists*.

What is intimated by this appellation, is now more fully expressed. Ἣν ἔπηξεν ὁ Κύριος, καὶ οὐκ ἄνθρωπος, *which the Lord constructed or reared, and not man;* i. e. the true or heavenly tabernacle is not material, was not formed by human architects, but reared by the immediate power of God. Whether the writer means here to speak of an actual heavenly structure, having physical form and location, is a question which will be brought up by ver. 5, below.

Ver. 3. Πᾶς γὰρ ἀρχιερεὺς ...... καθίσταται, *now every high priest is appointed to present oblations and sacrifices;* i. e. it enters into the very nature of such an office, that duties of this kind must be performed by him who sustains it ; see the original proposition of this subject, in ch. v. 1. Δῶρα, *oblations* or *gifts* that were without blood ; such as the first-fruits of grain, vegetables, &c. Θυσίας, *animals slain for sacrifice*. Both were presented to God by the priest, who acted as the *internuntius* between Jehovah and the offerer.

Ὅθεν ἀναγκαῖον ...... προσενέγκῃ, *whence, it is necessary that this* [high priest] *also have some offering to present;* i. e. if Christ be high priest, and if such an office is necessarily connected with the duty of presenting some offering, then Christ, of course, must present one

What the oblation made by Christ is, he tells us more fully in ch. ix. 11—14. 25. 26.

Ver. 4. The apostle proceeds to show the reason, why Christ is a priest in the tabernacle above, and not in that on earth. Εἰ μὲν γὰρ ἦν...... δῶρα, *but if he were on earth, then he could not be a priest, because there are priests appointed by law, who present oblations according to the law.* The argument is thus : " The Scripture calls Christ, ἱερεὺς εἰς τὸν αἰῶνα ; but this he could not be on earth, inasmuch as there are already ἱερεῖς there, by divine appointment; consequently, he is ἱερεὺς in the temple above, and must present his offering there. Δῶρα means here *oblations of every kind,* comprehending the same things as δῶρὰ τε καὶ θυσίας in ver. 3.

Ver. 5. Οἵτινες ὑποδείγματι ...... ἐπουρανίων, *the same who perform service in* [that tabernacle which is] *a mere copy of the heavenly* [sanctuary.] Compare ver. 2, and ch. ix. 24. Ὑπόδειγμα means, *image, effigy, copy, resemblance, imitation ;* all designating the idea, that the earthly temple stands related to the heavenly one, only as a painting or picture of any thing does to the object itself. The heavenly σκηνὴ is ἀληθινὸς ; the earthly one, σκιαρὰ.

Σκιὰ, *shadow, slight and imperfect image, sketch ;* distinct from εἰκών, *a picture completed, an accurate resemblance.* It is also the correlate antithesis of σῶμα, *body ;* see Col. ii. 17. Σκιὰ I have construed as qualifying ὑποδείγματι, and rendered both words, *mere copy,* i. e. I have construed them as a Hendiadys. The meaning is, that it is *only a resemblance,* i. e. the earthly tabernacle is but a *shadow,* a *mere imperfect effigy,* of the heavenly one. Consequently, the office of priest in the latter, is far more elevated than the like office in the former.

Τῶν ἐπουρανίων, i. e. ἁγίων, *sanctuary.* So in ver. 2, ἁγίων λειτουργὸς, i. e. ἁγίων [τόπων] λειτουργὸς, *a minister of the holy of holies,* or, *of the most holy place.*

Καθὼς κεχρημάτισται ...... ὄρει, *for Moses, when about to build the tabernacle, was divinely admonished ;* " See now," said he, " that thou make all things according to the pattern showed thee in the mount."

Χρηματίζω means, *to give oracular responses,* or, *to make communications to men in any supernatural way.* It is spoken, *actively,* of God, and not of men. So Phavorinus, χρηματίζειν, λέγεται ἐπὶ Θεῶν· τὸ δὲ διαλέγεσθαι, ἐπὶ ἀνθρώπων. In the passive voice (as here) it means, *to receive divine responses* or *communications, of any kind.*

'Επιτελεῖν, to complete, finish, perform, do, make. Φησὶ, viz. God saith, in Exod. xxv. 40 : compare Exod. xxv. 9 ; xxvi. 30 ; xxvii. 8. Numb. viii. 4. 1 Chron. xxviii. 11. 19. Acts vii. 44. The Hebrew word, to which τύπον here corresponds, is תַּבְנִית, *model, sketch, delineation, form*. Τύπος means, *model* or *form* here ; as it often does. Ὄρει refers to Mount Sinai ; for it was during the theophany there, that communications were made to Moses on the subject of building the tabernacle ; see Exod. xxiv. 18 : compare ch. xxv. 9. 40 ; xxxi. 18 ; xxxii. 1. See EXCURSUS XV.

Ver. 6. Νυνὶ δὲ διαφορωτέρας τέτευχε λειτουργίας, *but now has he obtained a service of a more excellent nature ;* i. e. since he is not a priest in the earthly temple, but in the heavenly one, he has an office [πόσῳ] διαφορωτέρα, [so much] *more exalted*, viz. than that of the Levitical priests.

Ὅσῳ καὶ . . . μεσίτης, *as much more, as the covenant, of which he is the mediator, is superior* [to the ancient one,] *being sanctioned with better promises*. Πόσῳ must be understood in the clause preceding this, viz. πόσῳ διαφορωτέρας, in order to make out the comparison which its correlate ὅσῳ implies, in the latter. Νενομοθέτηται, *is sanctioned*, i. e. is promulgated and established with all the solemnity and stability of a law. The *better promises* follow, viz. in ver. 8—13. The imperfection of the first covenant, and the perfection of the second, is disclosed further, in ch. ix. 9—14 ; x. 1—22 ; xiii. 9—14. From these passages it appears, that the first covenant promised only external purification, and the civil or ecclesiastical pardon of an offender who complied with the rites which it enjoined ; but under the new covenant, real pardon of sin by God is to be obtained, with purification and peace of conscience, the hope of eternal life, and union at last with the assembly of the redeemed in a better world.

The sentiment of the apostle, then, in our verse, stands thus : " The office with which Christ is invested as a priest, or his priestly function, is as much superior to that of the Levitical priests, as the covenant under which he holds his office excels, in the blessings which it promises, the covenant introduced by Moses."

Ver. 7. Εἰ γὰρ ἡ πρώτη . . . τόπος, *moreover, if that first* [covenant] *had been faultless, then no place for the second would have been sought*. Ἡ πρώτη, sc. διαθήκη, means here, the Jewish dispensation or economy. Ἄμεμπτος, *without fault, free from defect*. The meaning is, not that the Mosaic economy had *positive* faults, viz. such things as were palpably wrong or erroneous; but that it did not contain in itself all the provision necessary for pardon of sin, and the rendering of the conscience peaceful and pure; which the gospel does effect. See on ch. vii. 19, and compare ch. ix. 9—14. 23. 24; x. 1—3. 10—14. The law, then, was not τέλειος, i. e. ἄμεμπτος; nor was it designed to be any thing more than a dispensation *preparatory* to the gospel.

Ἐζητεῖτο τόπος, *no room had been sought*, or, *no provision had been made, for a second*, i. e. for a new covenant, or, the gospel dispensation.

Ver. 8. Μεμφόμενος γὰρ αὐτοῖς λέγει, *but, finding fault* [with the first covenant,] *he says to them*, i. e. the Jews. The passage is capable of another construction, viz. *finding fault with them*, i. e. the Jews; in which way a majority of the commentators, with Chrysostom, have understood it, Μέμφομαι can undoubtedly govern αὐτοῖς in the dative; but still I prefer the other construction. The apostle says, "The former covenant was not ἄμεμπτος." He goes on to prove this: but how? by quoting a passage from Jer. xxxi. 31—34. But what does this passage contain? Μέμφεται, says the apostle, i. q. μεμφόμενος ἔστι, i. e. it affirms that the law is not ἄμεμπτος; for these two words are plainly connected as *antitheses*, by the writer. If so, then μεμφόμενος applies to διαθήκῃ, and not to αὐτοῖς; and so I understand it. If the ellipsis be supplied, it will read, μεμφόμενος αὐτῇ sc. διαθήκῃ. In such a case, αὐτοῖς is governed by λέγει.

In addition to the argument thus drawn from the writer's purpose, I would also suggest, that the whole of Jer. xxxi., which precedes the passage quoted, is made up of consolation and promise, instead of reproof or finding fault. The *imputation of defect*, then, must be such an imputation, in this case, as is implied in the passage quoted. But in this, the declaration that a new covenant should supersede the old one, implies, of course, that the old one had failed to accomplish all the objects to be desired, i. e. it was defective.

The apostle evidently understands the passage quoted, as originally having respect to the gospel dispensation; nor can I perceive any good reason why it should not be so understood. There is the same objection, that any prophecy whatever should be understood as having regard to this dispensation, as there would be to this being so understood; consequently, there is sufficient reason why this should be understood as the apostle has explained it, unless we reject altogether the idea, that any truly prophetic declarations of such a nature can and do exist.

'Ἰδοὺ ἡμέραι ...... καινήν, *behold the days are coming, saith the Lord, when I will make a new covenant with the house of Israel and with the house of Judah.* 'Ἰδοὺ corresponds to the Hebrew הִנֵּה, and is used to excite the particular attention of the persons who are addressed, to any thing or subject. It is Hebraism, and not of classic usage; at least not in any measure so frequently employed in the classics, as by the writers of the New Testament. 'Ἰδοὺ is accented on the ultimate, to mark it as an *adverb*, and to distinguish it from ἴδου 2. aor, imp. of the verb εἴδω.

'Ἡμέραι ἔρχονται is equivalent to the Hebrew יָמִים בָּאִים, which is used indefinitely for any future period, whether near or remote. The simple meaning of the expression is, "At some future period I will make," &c.

'Ἐπὶ τὸν οἶκον 'Ἰσραὴλ καὶ ἐπὶ τὸν οἶκον 'Ἰούδα, i. q. in Hebrew בֵּית יְהוּדָה וְיִשְׂרָאֵל, i. e. *house, family, tribe,* or *nation of Judah and Israel.* The meaning is, with all the twelve tribes, i. e. the whole of the Hebrew nation. 'Ἐπὶ τὸν οἶκον, i. q. ἐπὶ τῷ οἴκῳ, see Wahl's Lexicon on ἐπὶ, No. 8. a. In the Septuagint, the passage reads, καὶ διαθήσομαι τῷ οἴκῳ 'Ἰσραὴλ καὶ τῷ οἴκῳ 'Ἰούδα διαθήκην καινήν.

Διαθήκην is commonly employed by the LXX., in order to translate בְּרִית. The general idea of διαθήκη is, *disposition* or *arrangement* of any kind, or in regard to any matter; from the verb διατίθημι, *to dispose of, to arrange.* Hence, it is sometimes employed by classic writers, in the sense of *fœdus, compact,* or *covenant* between two parties; but not so in the New Testament. Like the Hebrew בְּרִית, (to which, according to the *usus loquendi* of the New Testament, it generally corresponds,) it often means *law, precept;* even particular precept, as in Acts vii. 8, the precept of circumcision; in Rom. ix. 4, αἱ διαθῆκαι, *the tables of the law,* i. e. the ten commandments; compare Deut. iv. 13, where בְּרִית is explained by עֲשֶׂרֶת הַדְּבָרִים, *the ten commandments;* compare also Deut. ix. 9. 11. So Heb. ix. 4, κιβωτὸν τῆς διαθήκης, *the ark* which contained the διαθήκην, i. e. the two tables of the ten commandments, (i. q. אֲרוֹן בְּרִית־יְהוָה, Numb. x, 33;) and afterward, in the same verse, αἱ πλάκες τῆς διαθήκης, *the* [stone] *tablets containing the ten commandments.* The general idea of *law, precept, statute,* is very commonly annexed to בְּרִית in Hebrew, where the Septuagint renders it by διαθήκη; e. g. Exod. xix. 5, et al. sæpe. Both in classic authors, and in the New Testament, it has also the meaning of *last will, testament;* e. g. Gal. iii. 15. Heb. ix. 16, 17.

Most frequently of all, is בְּרִית in the Old Testament, and διαθήκη in the New, employed to designate a *promise, compact,* or *agreement* on the part of God with his people, that, on condition of doing thus and so, blessings of such and such a nature shall be bestowed upon them. It comes, in this way, very commonly to designate *the whole Jewish economy,* (as we call it,) with its conditions and promises ; and by the writers of the New Testament it is employed, in a similar way, to designate *the new economy* or dispensation of Christ, with all its conditions and promised blessings. Thus, ἡ παλαιὰ or πρώτη διαθήκη means, *the Jewish dispensation* ; and ἡ καινὴ διαθήκη means, *the Christian dispensation.* The idea often annexed by readers to the word *covenant*, viz. *mutual compact,* and a *quid pro quo* in respect to each of the parties, is not the scriptural one. The meaning altogether predominant is *an arrangement* on the part of God in respect to men, in consequence of which certain blessings are secured to them by his promise, on condition that they comply with the demands which he makes, i. e. obey his precepts. Διαθήκη, then, embraces both *precept* and *promise ;* and may be used for either, or for both at the same time, *pro re natá ;* and it often is so used in the Old Testament, and also in the New.

In our text, διαθήκην καινὴν means, *a new arrangement* or *disposition* made by Christ, i. e. one which has, in some respects, new conditions and new promises.

Ver. 9. Οὐ κατὰ τὴν διαθήκην, κ. τ. λ. This clause is explanatory of the word καινὴν in the preceding verse. The meaning is, " The covenant which I will make, at a future period, with the Jewish nation, (i. e. the dispensation under which I will place them,) shall be different from that which I made, when I brought them out of Egypt."

Ἐν ἡμέρᾳ ἐπιλαβομένου μου τῆς χειρὸς αὐτῶν, Heb. בְּיוֹם הֶחֱזִיקִי בְיָדָם. Χειρὸς, in the genitive, is governed by the force of ἐπὶ in composition with λαβομένου ; so ἐπιλαμβάνειν τῆς χειρὸς, *to take by the hand, to lead, &c.* Ἐξαγαγεῖν, *to bring* or *lead out,* εἰς τὸ being understood before the infinitive here. Both words together mean, *assisted* or *helped to come out.* This clause is added by the writer, in order to show plainly, that he means the διαθήκην, which was made when Moses led the Israelites out of Egypt, through the wilderness, toward Canaan.

Ὅτι αὐτοὶ οὐκ ἐνέμειναν ἐν τῇ διαθήκῃ μου, *because they did not keep my covenant.* The Hebrew is, אֲשֶׁר הֵמָּה הֵפֵרוּ אֶת־בְּרִיתִי, *because they violated my covenant,* i. e. failed to perform the conditions on which I promised to bestow blessings upon them. The Greek οὐκ ἐνέμειναν is a version *ad sensum*, but not *ad literam*. Μένω or ἐμμένω means, among other things, *to persevere, to be constant, to continue firm,* or *stedfast* in any thing. The Greek expression, οὐκ ἐνέμειναν is softer than הֵפֵרוּ; and as οὐκ ἔμειναν conveys, for *substance*, the same idea as הֵפֵרוּ, we may well suppose it was preferred to a stronger expression by the writer of our epistle, while he was addressing himself to his Jewish brethren. Ὅτι οὐκ ἐνέμειναν assigns a reason why a new covenant was to be made, viz. because the old one is broken, and because it has not been kept on the part of the Jews, and will not be kept, therefore a new one, on different conditions and with better promises, shall be made.

Κἀγὼ ἠμέλησα αὐτῶν, Hebrew וְאָנֹכִי בָּעַלְתִּי בָם, (English Version) *although I was an husband to them*; Gesenius, *although I was their Lord;* both according to a sense of בַּעַל, which is a usual one. But that the Septuagint have given a correct version here, and the apostle properly adopted it in our text, is very probable. The Arabic بَلْ ب (בַּעַל בְּ) means, *to loath, to reject with loathing*; see Castell Lex. on بَلْ. In this sense, it is probable, בַּעַל בְּ is used in Jer. xxxi. 32, and, as some think, in Jer. iii. 14. So Abul Walid, Joseph Kimchi, and Rabbi Tanchum, understood the word in ch. xxxi. 32; and in like manner many modern critics. The Greek ἠμέλησα means, *to neglect, to disregard, to treat with neglect,* and is, (like οὐκ ἐνέμειναν) a softer expression than the corresponding Hebrew one, while it conveys for substance the same idea. The Septuagint, in their rendering of בָּעַלְתִּי בָ appear to have preserved an ancient meaning of the word בָּעַל, the correctness of which the Arabic is a pledge for, at the present time.

The *disregarding*, or *treating with neglect* (ἠμέλεσα,) here spoken of, has reference to the various punishments inflicted upon Israel for their wickedness, instead of the blessings which they would have received, had they been obedient.

Ver. 10. Ὅτι αὕτη ἡ διαθήκη . . . κύριος, *but this is the covenant which I will make with the house of Israel, after those days, saith the Lord.* Ὅτι *but*, so the Hebrew כִּי, Ps. xliv. 23; cxxx. 4. Job xiv. 16, al. The Lexicons are imperfect in regard to this word, Οἴκῳ Ἰσραήλ, *house of Israel* in this verse means, the Jews in general, the Israelitish nation, for so the whole nation is often named, in the Old Testament and in the New.

Διδοὺς νόμους μου εἰς τὴν διάνοιαν αὐτῶν, *I will put my laws upon their mind*, Hebrew בְּקִרְבָּם. For διδούς, the Septuagint has διδοὺς δώσω, meaning, I suppose, *deeply infix*. This sense of δίδωμι comes from the Hebrew נָתַן; see Wahl on δίδωμι, No. 8. Διδούς, like the present participle in Hebrew, is used for the future δώσω. To *place* or *put laws upon their minds*, of course means to inscribe or engrave them, as it were, i. e. deeply to infix them. Καὶ ἐπὶ καρδίας αὐτῶν ἐπιγράψω αὐτούς, *and I will engrave them upon their hearts*, or, *inscribe them upon their hearts*; an expression parallel to the preceding, and of the same import. The meaning of both is, I will give them a lasting spirit of obedience to my laws, so that they will no more violate them as they have done; i. e. the new covenant shall be distinguished from the old, by a higher and more permanent spirit of obedience in those who live under it.

Καὶ ἔσομαι αὐτοῖς . . . λαόν, *and I will be their God, and they shall be my people;* i. e. I will grant them peculiar protection and blessings, and they shall be peculiarly obedient and devoted to me. Compare Rev. xxi. 3, 4. 7. Zech. viii. 8. For the meaning of the Hebrew idiom, εἰς Θεὸν and εἰς λαόν, see on Heb. i. 5.

Ver. 11. Καὶ οὐ μὴ διδάξουσιν . . . . κύριον, *no one shall teach his own fellow-citizen, nor any one his brother, saying, Know the Lord.* For τὸν πολίτην, various manuscripts and editions have τὸν πλησίον. The original Hebrew is, אֶת־רֵעֵהוּ וְאִישׁ אֶת־אָחִיו וְלֹא יְלַמְּדוּ עוֹד אִישׁ which, interpreted agreeably to a well-known Hebrew idiom, means simply, *one shall not teach another;* for אִישׁ and רֵעַ as well as אִישׁ and אָחִיו simply denote *each other*, or *one another*, when thus coupled together. Τὸν πολίτην, in our text, corresponds to the Hebrew רֵעֵהוּ; and this word the Septuagint almost always render by πλησίον. This is the ground, probably, why the reading πλησίον has been preferred by Bengel, Carpzoff, and some other critics. But πολίτην is in the best manuscripts; and Wetstein, Griesbach, Matthiæ, Rosenmüller, Knapp, Heinrichs, Tittmann, and others, prefer it. The Septuagint, moreover, render רֵעַ by πολίτης, in Prov. xi. 9; xxiv. 28. Whether, however πλησίον or πολίτην be adopted, the sense is not changed. The meaning of the whole phrase, is simply what the Hebrew idiom allows it to signify, viz. "One shall have no need to teach another." The repetition of the sentiment, by τὸν πολίτην αὐτοῦ and τὸν ἀδελφὸν αὐτοῦ, belongs merely to the poetic parallelism of the original Hebrew, which expresses the same thought in two different ways, as is constantly done by the synonymous parallelisms of the Old Testament.

"Ότι πάντες . . . μεγάλου αὐτῶν, *for all shall know me, from the least to the greatest*, i. e. all of whatever rank or condition, high or low, rich or poor—all classes of people, shall have a knowledge of God. Μικροῦ and μεγάλου here refer to *condition*, rather than *age*.

The writer does not mean that religious instruction will be altogether *superseded*, when the happy period arrives of which he speaks; but that, inasmuch as the laws of God will be *infixed upon* the hearts of his people, and engraven upon their minds, none will be ignorant, as in former times, of his true character and the requirements of his law. The words are not to be urged to a literal explanation. The meaning of the whole plainly is, that the knowledge of true religion, or of God, should become universal, under the *new covenant*, so that no one might be found, who could properly be addressed as knowing nothing of the true God. The implication, moreover, contained in this, is, that under the *old covenant* many had been thus ignorant; a fact highly credible, considering the frequent lapses of the Jews into a state of idolatry.

Ver. 12. "Ότι ἵλεως ἔσομαι . . . ἔτι, *for I will be merciful in respect to their iniquities, and their sins and their transgressions will I remember no more.* Ἵλεως, *propitious, mild, clement,* governs the dative ταῖς ἀδικίαις, and (like אָסְלַח to which it corresponds) designates the idea of *readiness to pardon,* or, *to deal mildly* with offenders.

Τῶν ἀνομιῶν αὐτῶν is not in the Hebrew, nor in the common Septuagint, nor Vulgate, Syriac, Coptic, Ethiopic. The Hebrew has only לְחַטָּאתָם, to which τῶν ἁμαρτιῶν αὐτῶν answers, in our text. It is difficult, or rather impossible, now to determine whether τῶν ἀνομιῶν αὐτῶν was originally inserted by the writer of our epistle, or crept in afterwards from some edition of the Septuagint which contained it. But whether it be admitted or excluded, it makes no difference in the *sentiment* of the passage; the first clause of which is the first member of a poetic parallelism, to which the second clause corresponds, echoing the same sentiment. Ἵλεως εἶναι ταῖς ἀδικίαις means, *to be forgiving, ready to pardon;* and οὐ μνησθῆναι τῶν ἀνομιῶν means, *to pass sins by unpunished, to treat offenders as though their sins were forgotten.* The expression applied to God, is altogether *anthropopathic;* but so are most other expressions which speak of him as acting in relation to such subjects.

Thus far the quotation from Jeremiah, in order to prove that a *new covenant,* better than the Mosaic one, was to be made with the people of God. The writer now adds, as a comment on what he had quoted—

Ver. 13. Ἐν τῷ λέγειν . . . . πρώτην, *in saying a new* [covenant,] *he represents the first* [covenant] *as old.* Of course, if a new one is to take the place of the former one, the former is considered as obsolete. Πεπαλαίωκε, like the Hebrew Piel and Hiphil, means *to represent a thing as old*, or, as *superannuated;* for in no other sense did the words just quoted make the former covenant old.

Now follows the deduction of the apostle from this. Τὸ δὲ παλαιούμενον . . . . ἀφανισμοῦ, *now that which has become old, and is advancing in age, is near to dissolution.* Παλαιόω is more usually applied to *things*, and γηράσκω to *persons*. The use of two synonymous words here, serves merely to strengthen the representation, and is equivalent to saying, "That which is very old."

Ἀφανισμοῦ, literally, *disappearing, vanishing.* Applied to a law or dispensation, it means *abolition* or *abrogation.* The argument of the writer is thus: " What is very old is near dissolution ;" but the prophet Jeremiah has represented the former covenant as πεπαλαιουμένην ; therefore it is near dissolution, or, it is about to be dissolved or abrogated.

CHAPTER IX.

For an illustration of the course of thought and reasoning in this chapter, see above, p. 351, seq.

Ver. 1. Εἶχε μὲν οὖκ καὶ ἡ πρώτη . . . κοσμικὸν, *moreover, the first* [covenant] *also had ordinances of service and a sanctuary of a worldly nature.* Οὖν, a sign of *transition* here, for a new subject is introduced. The force of καὶ here, is not easily described. I join it with εἶχε thus, " Besides what I have said about the first covenant, let me add, that εἶχε καὶ, *it also had* ordinances," &c. All three particles, μὲν οὖν καὶ, might be rendered, *and besides, and further, and I may add,* &c. ; but I prefer the manner in which I have rendered them. As to μὲν, it is the mere sign of *protasis ;* see below, on ver. 11.

Ἡ πρώτη, i. e. διαθήκη, compare ch. viii. 6, 7, 13 ; not ἡ πρώτη σκηνὴ, as some critics have supposed.

Δικαιώματα λατρείας means, *a service arranged, conducted, by rules* or *ordinances.* Λατρεία designates the public service of the temple or tabernacle; and δικαιώματα, the *rules* or *precepts* which regulated it.

Ἅγιον usually means *sanctuary* or *holy place*, in a general sense, and so it may be taken here, viz. for the whole temple. But it may also be understood, as referring to that spacious apartment of the temple, in which the various articles of sacred furniture were placed that are immediately mentioned, which, however, is called by the writer, ἅγια, in ver. 2. If it be the same as ἅγια, it is distinguished from ἅγια ἁγίων, in the third verse ; which means the apartment behind the veil, where the ark, &c. were deposited. Κοσμικὸν (from κόσμος) means, *pertaining to this world, of a terrestial nature*, i. e. material, the opposite of οὐ χειροποίητον in ch. ix. 11, 24, and i. q. χειροποίητον ; the opposite also, of 'Ιερουσαλὴμ ἐπουράνιος, ch. xii. 22 ; compare Rev. xxi. 2. Some critics have explained κοσμικὸν by *formosum, illustre*, because κόσμος sometimes signifies *ornatus,elegantia*. But the adjective which designates the meaning correspondent with these significations, is κοσμιος, and not κοσμικὸς.

Ver. 2 . Σκηνὴ γὰρ . . . πρώτη, *for an outer tabernacle was constructed*. Σκηνὴ evidently means here, only one apartment of the ἱερον or sacred building ; compare ver. 3, where another σκηνὴ is described. Ἡ πρώτη means, *that which first presents itself*, viz. to the worshipper as he enters the outer court of the building ; therefore *outer* σκηνὴ or apartment, the most holy place being the *inner* one. We might expect, according to the rules laid down by grammarians concerning the Greek article, that either σκηνὴ would have the article, or πρώτη would omit it. Constructions, however, of the same kind as σκηνὴ ἡ πρώτη are frequent in the New Testament; e. g. Rom. ii. 9. ἀνθρώπου τοῦ ἐργαζομένου ; ch. ii. 14, ἔθνη τὰ .... μὴ ἔχοντα ; ch. v. 5, πνεύματος ἁγίου τοῦ δοθέντος. See Rom. viii. 33, 34. 1 Cor. ii. 7. Gal. iii. 21. 1 Thess. i. 10. 1 Tim. vi. 13. 2 Tim. i. 8, 9. 14. Heb. vi. 7, &c. See Gersdorf's Beiträge, p. 355, seq. It happens in this case, (as in regard to most of the *definite* rules laid down about the use of the Greek article,) that investigation shows the principle assumed to be by no means uniform, and that the Greek writers were less regular in regard to this matter, than the grammarians would fain have us believe. For the dimensions, &c. of the various σκηναὶ, or apartments of the temple, see 1 Kings vi.

Ἐν ᾗ ἥ τε λυχνία .... ἄρτων, *in which* [apartment] *was the candlestick, and the table, and the show-bread*. For a description of the candlestick, see Exod. xxv. 31—39 ; xxxvii. 17—24. The Hebrew word answering to λυχνία, is מְנוֹרָה. The τράπεζα is described in

Exod. xxv. 23—39. The design of the table was, that the bread which was consecrated to the Lord might be placed upon it. Πρόθεσις τῶν ἄρτων, *the exhibition of the bread*, viz. before Jehovah, is described in Exod. xxv. 30, and Lev. xxiv. 5—9. The earlier Hebrew name was לֶחֶם הַפָּנִים, *presence-bread*. It is also called עָרֻךְ לֶחֶם, and לֶחֶם הַמַּעֲרֶכֶת, *the arrangement of bread*, or, *the bread arranged*, in reference to the manner in which it was exhibited upon the table; see Lev. xxiv. 5, 6.

The altar of incense is omitted in this catalogue of sacred utensils: as it is omitted in the draft for building the tabernacle by Moses, in Exod. xxv. But it is mentioned in Exod. xxx. 1, and xxxvii. 25—28; xxxv. 15. So also the altar of burnt-offering is omitted, in Exod. xxv. although it is mentioned in Exod. xxxv. 16; xxxviii. 1; and many other utensils of the tabernacle also are omitted in Exod xxv. which are mentioned in Exod. xxxv. Our author expressly says (ch. ix. 5,) that he shall not attempt to mention all the particulars of the sacred apparatus for the temple service.

"Ητις λέγεται ἅγια, *which is called* ἅγια, i. e. מִקְדָּשׁ, קֹדֶשׁ, *the holy place, the sanctuary*; a different apartment in the ἱερόν or sacred enclosure, from the ἅγια ἁγίων mentioned in ver. 3. "Αγια in our text, is plural; for the singular feminine is written ἁγία, (with the accent on the penult.,) not ἅγια. The writer means to say that ἡ σκηνὴ πρώτη; *the outer apartment*, of the temple, was called ἅγια. The plural is used here in order to designate one apartment in the temple, just as it is in ἅγια ἁγίων (not ἁγία ἁγίων,) ver. 3; and both are conformed to a usage that is common in Hebrew, which not unfrequently employs the plural to designate the *sanctuary*. E. g. Ps. lxxiii. 17, מִקְדְּשֵׁי־אֵל, i. e. ἅγια Θεοῦ. Ps. lxviii. 36, מִקְדָּשֶׁיךָ, ἅγιά σου. Lev. xxi. 23, מִקְדָּשַׁי, ἅγιά μου, &c.

Ver. 3. Μετὰ δὲ τὸ δεύτερον καταπέτασμα, *and behind the second veil*. A description of this veil is given, in Exod. xxvi. 31—33; xxxvi. 35, 36. As the inner veil is here called δεύτερον, the necessary implication is, that there was a πρῶτον also, and accordingly we find it described in Exod. xxvi. 36, 37; and Exod. xxxvi. 37, 38. The Hebrew name of the *inner* veil (which separated the most holy place from the ἅγια or common sanctuary,) is פָּרֹכֶת, as given in Exod. xxvi. 31—33, and in the corresponding Exod. xxxvi. 35, 36; also Lev. xvi. 2. The Hebrew name of the *outer* veil, which served as a *door* for the tabernacle, i. e. which covered the entrance passage to the first ἅγιον, is מָסָךְ. The former is called καταπέτασμα by the Septuagint, (as the apostle calls it in our text.) in Exod. xxvi. 31. 33. Lev. xvi. 2. Exod. xxxvi. 35, and also by the evangelists, Matt. xxvii. 58. Mark xv. 38. The latter, both καταπέτασμα and ἐπίσπαστρον, in the passages connected with those just cited. There was a third *external* covering or curtain for the tabernacle, (called יְרִיעָה, יְרִיעוֹת, in Exod. xxvi. 1, 2. seq.,) which Dindorf says was a *third veil;* but which, manifestly, Paul does not reckon to be such ; nor Moses, in the passages above cited.

Σκηνὴ ἡ λεγομένη ἅγια ἁγίων, *the apartment which is called the holy of holies*, i. e. the most holy place, i. q. קֹדֶשׁ הַקֳּדָשִׁים, a common form of expression in Hebrew, in order to denote *intensity*. In regard to ἡ λεγομένη, after σκηνὴ without the article, see on ἡ πρώτη above. Κατεσκευάσθη is understood after σκηνή ; see in ver. 2, where it is expressed. The inner sanctuary was called *most holy*, because there was the ark of the covenant, the mercy seat, &c. ; and there the presence of Jehovah, (which the Jews in later times called שְׁכִינָה,) was peculiarly manifested, so that this was regarded as his particular dwelling place, מְעוֹנָה.

Ver. 4. Χρυσοῦν ἔχουσα θυμιατήριον, *containing the golden censer*. See Excursus XVI.

Καὶ τὴν κιβωτὸν .... χρυσίῳ, *and the ark of the covenant, covered on every part with gold*. Κιβωτὸς was a *coffer* or *chest*, made of wood, and covered with laminæ of gold ; a description of which is given in Exod. xxv. 10—16 ; xxxvii. 1—5. It is called *the ark of the covenant*, because in it were deposited the two *tables of the covenant*, (בְּרִית, see on διαθήκην in ch. viii. 8. and compare Deut. iv. 13 ; ix. 9. 11 ;) which tables are also called *the two tables of testimony*, i. e. of statutes, שְׁנֵי לְחֹת הָעֵדוּת, Exod. xxxi. 18. Both the terms בְּרִית and עֵדוּת plainly mean, *laws, statutes, or precepts*, in this case, and both refer principally to the ten commandments ; see 1 Kings viii. 9, and Deut. x. 1—5. 2 Chron. v. 10 ; vi. 11.

Ἐν ᾗ στάμνος χρυσῆ ἔχουσα τὸ μάννα, *in which* [ark] *was a golden pot containing the manna*. The fact to which this alludes, is described in Exod. xvi. 32—34 ; where the στάμνος is called simply צִנְצֶנֶת, that is, *pot, urn, vessel for safe keeping*. Nothing is said, indeed, of its being *golden* in the Hebrew ; but the Septuagint render צִנְצֶנֶת, by στάμνον χρυσοῦν. Of the fact that it was so, no one will be disposed to doubt, who reads a description of the furniture of the most holy place, and finds that almost every thing within it was either pure gold, or was overlaid with gold : e. g. the ark, Exod. xxv. 11 ; the mercy-seat, ch. xxv. 17 ; the cherubim, ch. xxv. 18; the pillars and hooks for the veil that separated the inner sanctuary from the other, ch. xxxvi. 31, 32. Who now can rationally suppose, that the urn containing manna, and the censer used on the great day of atonement, were not also *golden?* See Excursus XVII.

Μάννα ; see on this word, Rosenmüller, on Exod. xvi. 15; where the various derivations of the word are considered ; the various species of manna described ; and the fact shown, that the supply of this food for the Israelites in the wilderness, was understood, by the writer of the narration in Exodus, to be miraculous.

Καὶ ἡ ῥάβδος Ἀαρὼν ἡ βλαστήσασα, *and the rod of Aaron which budded.* See Numb. xvii. 1—10, and what is said respecting this rod and the pot of manna, in Excursus XVII.

Καὶ αἱ πλάκες τῆς διαθήκης, *the tables of the covenant,* means the stone tablets on which the ten commandments were inscribed, and which were deposited in the ark, Exod. xxxi. 88 ; xxxii. 16 ; xxxiv. 28, where *the words of the covenant* are expressly said to be *the ten commandments;* Deut. x. 1, 2. 1 Kings viii. 9. 2 Chron. v. 10. The writer asserts, therefore, that the pot of manna, the rod of Aaron, and the two stone tablets on which the ten commandments were inscribed, were all laid up originally in the κιβωτός.

Ver. 5. Ὑπεράνω δὲ αὐτῆς χερουβὶμ .... τὸ ἱλαστήριον, *and over it* [the ark] *were splendid cherubim, which overshadowed the covering of the ark.* See the description of the cherubim in Exod. xxv. 18—20. 1 Kings viii. 6, 7. 1 Chron. xxviii. 18. That cherubim were *symbolical* images or representations, is quite plain from comparing the various descriptions given of them in different passages of scripture ; e. g. Exod. xxv. 18—20; xxvi. 31. 1 Kings vi. 23—39. 32 ; and Ezek. i. and x. particularly ch. x. 20—22. I understand the word δόξης as referring to the *splendour* of these symbolical figures, which were covered with gold throughout, Exod. xxv. 18—20. 1 Kings vi. 28. Some understand δόξης of the glory which was displayed under and around them ; to which they suppose a reference to be made in Ps. lxxx. 1, [2.]

Κατασκιάζοντα refers to the outstretched wings of the cherubim over the ἱλαστήριον, as described in the passages above quoted. Ἱλαστήριον here means, the *lid* or *covering* of the κιβωτός, which was pure gold, Exod. xxv. 17, 21. In Hebrew it is called כַּפֹּרֶת, which the LXX.

have rendered ἱλαστήριον in Exod. xxv. 17, 21. As כָּפַר means, to *over sin*, i. e. to *make atonement* for it, so כַּפֹּרֶת may very naturally be rendered ἱλαστήριον, since it was by sprinkling blood upon this ἱλαστήριον, by the high priest, that atonement was made, Lev. xvi. 14. Ἱλαστήριον, understood in reference to this, might be translated, *the place* or *instrument of propitiation*, or (with our English translators) *mercy-seat*. It was over this that the divine glory was seen, i. e. a supernatural, excessive brightness ; and hence God was supposed to be seated on it, as his throne, and from it to dispense his mercy, when atonement was made for the sins of the people, by sprinkling it with blood. Hence our appellation, *mercy-seat*.

Περὶ ὧν .... μέρος, *respecting which things, it is not my present design to speak with particularity.* Ὧν here refers to the various articles of sacred furniture, which he had just been mentioning. He means to say, that a particular description of these, and of all the various utensils of the sanctuary, is not what he intends to give ; i. e. he shall content himself with merely having suggested those which were already named.

Ver. 6. Τούτων δὲ οὕτω κατασκευασμένων, *now these things being thus prepared*. Κατασκευάζω is also, *to build* or *construct*. But in our phrase it means more. It designates not only the *fabrication* of the various utensils above named, but the adaptation of them to their respective purposes, and the arrangement of them in the order which the rites of the sanctuary required.

Εἰς μὲν τὴν πρώτην . . . ἐπιτελοῦντες, *the priests, performing the services, entered continually into the outer tabernacle.* Πρώτην, that which is *first* approached, i. e. *outer*, as in ver. 2 above. Λατρείας, *public religious services ;* see on ver. 1, above. Διαπαντὸς, *every day, without intermission, constantly and often.* This the priest did, to make the morning and evening oblations and sacrifices ; and also to present the private offerings of individuals. Μὲν is the usual sign of the *protasis* of a sentence here ; to which δὲ, in the *apodosis*, ver. 7, corresponds. Μὲν, in such a case, is incapable of a translation that corresponds with its use in the original. It is easy to see, that there is not only a correspondence between the two parts of the sentence above mentioned, but also an antithesis between them.

Ver. 7. Εἰς δὲ τὴν δευτέραν .... ὁ ἀρχιερεὺς, *but into the second* [viz σκηνὴν, tabernacle, apartment,] *the high priest only* [entered,] *once in a year ;* compare Lev. xvi. 2. Δευτέραν implies σκηνὴν. Ἅπαξ means either simply *once*, as ἅπαξ καὶ δὶς, *once and again;* or it means *once only, once for all;* which is the meaning of it here, and in several other passages of this epistle. Τοῦ ἐνιαυτοῦ is the genitive of time: the genitive being commonly used in order to designate the time *when* or *how often*. On the great day of atonement, it appears that the high priest went thrice into the inner sanctuary, Lev. xvi. 12. 14, 15; to which may be added once more, in order to bring out the golden censer; which accords well with the Jewish tradition, viz. that the high priest entered the sanctuary *four* times, on the great day of expiation.

Οὐ χωρὶς αἵματος, *not without blood.* See Lev. xvi. 14, 15, by which it appears, that the blood of a young bullock, Lev. xvi. 3, and of a goat, was brought into the most holy place, by the high priest, on the great day of atonement, and there sprinkled seven times upon the mercy-seat and before it.

Ὃ προσφέρει .... ἀγνοημάτων, *which he presented for his own sins, and for those of the people.* See Lev. xvi. 6. 11. 14—16. Προσφέρει designates the act of presenting the blood before the Lord, as indicated in Lev. xvi. 14—16. That the priest was to make atonement for himself, as well as for the people, is expressly declared in the verses above referred to. Ἀγνοημάτων Wahl renders, *sins of ignorance.* But plainly it is not necessarily limited to this confined sense. It means, *fault, error, sin,* generally considered. So in Judith v. 20. Sirach xxiii. 2; li. 19. Tobit iii. 3. 1 Macc. xiii. 39. The LXX. have sometimes used it to express the Hebrew מִשְׁגָּה, from שָׁגָה, *to err.* In Lev. iv. 2. 13. 22. 27, sins בִּשְׁגָגָה, *through precipitancy,* are mentioned, and atonement is directed to be made for them, by sprinkling blood before the mercy-seat, Lev. iv. 6. 17. But this mode of making atonement, and this limitation of the kind of offences for which it was to be made in this peculiar way, seem to have been afterwards changed, and limited in a different way, on the occasion of the death of the sons of Aaron, Lev. x. 1, 2; xvi. 1, 2. It would seem, from Lev. iv., as if the sins בִּשְׁגָגָה had a special atonement made for them, in the inner sanctuary, *without limitation* as to the number of times that the high priest might go there. But Lev. xvi. 2, *restricted* this custom; so that atonement for sin of any kind was made, before the mercy-seat, only *once* in a year, agreeably to Exod. xxx. 10.

Ver. 8. Τοῦτο δηλοῦντος ... ὁδὸν, *the Holy Spirit signifying by this, that the way to the most holy place was not yet laid open.* The

Holy Spirit here mentioned, is that Spirit which guided the ancient prophets; which taught Moses what arrangements to make for the service of God; and which signified, by these arrangements, what the apostle here affirms. Τοῦτο I construe with διὰ understood, viz. *by this;* so Ernesti and Dindorf, *his rebus;* Storr, *wodurch, whereby.*

Τὴν τῶν ἁγίων ὁδὸν means, *the way to the heavenly or upper sanctuary.* Through Jesus only, Jews and Gentiles have free access, at all times, to the mercy-seat of heaven : compare Eph. ii. 18. Heb. iv. 16 This way was before obstructed by numerous ceremonial rites, and limited as to times and persons. Of necessity such was the case.

Ἔτι τῆς πρώτης σκηνῆς ἐχούσης στάσιν, *while the first tabernacle had a standing;* i. e. so long as the Jewish dispensation lasted. Πρώτης σκηνῆς is here used, in the general or unlimited sense, for the tabernacle or temple, with its services.

Ver. 9. "Ἥτις παραβολὴ .... τὸν ἐνεστηκότα, *which* [has been] *a type down to the present time.* Παραβολὴ means, *symbol, similitude, image,* i. e. symbolical representation of any thing; which is also the meaning of τύπος. But in the English language, *type* is used not for similitude merely, but for something, under the ancient covenant, which was specially designed, on the part of God, to be a symbol of some person or event that was to exist or take place under the new one. Here, the preceding verse shows that the ancient tabernacle or temple was designed by the Holy Spirit to be a symbol, expressive of some important truths that had relation to the New Testament dispensation. Of course, the rendering of παραβολὴ by *type*, is appropriate to express the idea intended to be conveyed by the writer. Εἰς τὸν ἐνεστηκότα *down to the present time;* εἰς, *ad, usque ad :* see Wahl on εἰς, 2. a.

Καθ' ὃν δῶρα .... λατρεύοντα, *in which both oblations and sacrifices are presented, that cannot fully accomplish what is needed for the worshipper, in respect to his conscience.* Καθ' ὅν, *in which, during which,* viz. time ; see Wahl on κατὰ, No. 2. Δῶρά τε καὶ θυσίαι means, *offerings of every kind,* which were presented to God. For τελειῶσαι, see on τελείωσις, ch. vii. 11. The meaning is, "To render the mind of the worshipper secure of pardon for sin, and to produce that quiet which was connected with a well-grounded persuasion of this, and that moral purification which must accompany it." We have no one word to express all this in English. I have come as near to it as I am able to do, in the version which I have given.

The whole verse shows very plainly, that our epistle was written while the temple rites were still practised; consequently, before A. D. 70. But by the phrase, τὸν καιρὸν τὸν ἐνεστηκότα, the writer particularly alludes to the age then present, in which the new or Christian dispensation had begun. The whole sentence is as much as to say, "The Jewish ritual, from the commencement of it down to the present moment, has never been, and still is not, any thing more than a *type* of the Christian dispensation, which has already commenced. All its oblations and sacrifices were ineffectual, as to removing the penalty due to sin in the sight of heaven, or procuring real peace of conscience.

Ver. 10. Μόνον ἐπὶ βρώμασι . . . ἐπικείμενα, *the ordinances of an external nature had respect only to meats, and drinks, and divers ablutions, enjoined until the time of reformation.* A passage very difficult in respect to its grammatical construction. Many writers have referred δικαιώματα to the δῶρα καὶ θυσίαι, mentioned in the preceding verse; and then have found difficulty enough, (as well they might,) in accounting for it, how *oblations* and *sacrifices* could consist in meats, and drinks, and *various ablutions*. To me it seems quite evident, that ver. 10 is designed to signify something additional to that which is mentioned in ver. 9; although the construction is asyndic, i. e. καὶ is omitted before μόνον. Ἐπὶ βρώμασι . . . . βαπτισμοῖς, I understand as a clause qualifying δικαιώματα, i. e, it stands in the place of an adjective designating wherein the δικαιώματα consisted; while σαρκὸς supplies the place of another adjective, denoting to what the δικαιώματα had relation, viz. to the *flesh* or *external part* of man. *Meats* and *drinks* have respect to that which was clean and unclean, under the Jewish dispensation; and not (as some critics interpret the words) to the meats and drinks offered to the Lord. Most evidently, βαπτισμοῖς refers to the ceremonial ablutions of the Jews, which had respect to external purification; and βρώμασι καὶ πόμασι seem plainly to respect the same kind of purity. Besides, all this agrees perfectly with the scope of the writer. He had denied that the penalty, due to sin in the sight of God, could be removed by any of the *temple offerings*, ver. 9; and in this verse he denies that the moral expiation required could be effected by any or all of the rites pertaining to *external purification*. Consequently, there was, according to him, nothing in the Jewish ritual, which could effect an atonement such as the sinner needed.

Μέχρι καιροῦ διορθώσεως ἐπικείμενα, sc. ἦσαν. This clause, many interpreters have placed first in order in the verse, in the translations which they have made; but this is unnecessary. It must be admitted, that the construction in this case is very difficult, and far from being clear. The *intention* of the writer seems to be the best guide; for, interpret as you please, the grammatical difficulties are about the same. I regard the whole in this simple light. Ver. 8 and 9 mention the tabernacle, (which of course includes the temple, for the latter was only a substitute of the former,) and declare that the same, with all its apparatus and rites connected with it, was only a παραβολὴ, i. e. *a symbol* of something real and ultimate, under the new dispensation. Two particulars, or rather, two classes of things, belonging to the ancient ritual, now seem to strike the writer's mind. First, the δῶρα καὶ θυσίαι offered to God, ver. 9; and secondly, the various meats and drinks, distinguished into clean and unclean, to which men under the Levitical law must have respect, and the divers ablutions which they must practise. "The ordinances pertaining to the flesh," says he, "which respect only meats and drinks, and divers ablutions, are imposed until the time of reformation," i. e. they are all of a temporary nature, and therefore are plainly to be abolished. I regard the last part of this affirmation, viz. that which asserts the *temporary* nature, (and therefore inadequate) nature of meats and drinks and ablutions, as corresponding with the μὴ δυνάμεναι κατὰ συνείδησιν τελειῶσαι τὸν λατρεύοντα of the ninth verse. Thus, both together declare the inadequacy and temporary nature of the ancient ritual, and lead the mind of the reader to expect a new one; which the writer goes on immediately to propose, in ver. 11.

Those who have referred δικαιώματα ἐπικείμενα to δῶρα καὶ θυσίαι, have been greatly perplexed in adjusting the reading of the word ἐπικείμενα; for in ver. 9, we have δυνάμεναι (feminine) referring to θυσίαι. They propose that we should either read δυνάμεναι—ἐπικείμεναι, or else δυνάμενα—ἐπικείμενα, so as to make them agree. But all this difficulty arises from connecting δικαιώματα with that to which it does not belong; as we have seen above.

Most Codices and Versions read δικαιώμασι, instead of δικαιώματα; but the latter is preferred by Knapp and others, and admitted to be of equal, or nearly equal, authority by Griesbach; and it seems to me to make better sense, and to afford a more easy construction, than δικαιώμασι.

Καιροῦ διορθώσεως plainly means, *the time of the gospel dispensation*, called χρόνων ἀποκαταστάσεως, in Acts iii. 21. Compare Mal. iii. 1; v. 5, 6. Isa. lxvi. 22; lxv. 17; li. 16.

Thus much for the description of the earthly tabernacle and its sacred utensils, together with an exhibition of the inefficacy of the whole in respect to meeting the wants of sinners, and also an avowal of their temporary nature. They were intended only as the introduction to a new and better dispensation. Μὲν, in ver.11, is the sign of *protasis*, and is the correlate of δὲ in ver. 10, where the *apodosis* begins. All that follows ver. 1, on to ver. 10, is only a particular description of what is mentioned in general terms in ver. 1, and is subjoined for the sake of illustration and impression. Ver. 10 is plainly the sequel to ver. 1, and nearly related to it.

The writer now proceeds to shew, that the tabernacle in which Christ officiates, is οὐ χειροποίητος not κοσμικὸς, like that of the Jews. The antithesis between the old and new tabernacles, their services, and the respective efficacy of them, is carried on, by the apostle, through the remainder of chap. ix. and down to chap. x. 19.

Ver. 11. Χριστὸς δὲ παραγενόμενος . . . ἀγαθῶν, *but Christ being come, the high priest of future blessings*. Χριστὸς . . . παραγενόμενος is nominative to the verb εἰσῆλθε in ver. 12.

Ἀρχιερεὺς τῶν μελλόντων ἀγαθῶν, literally, *a high priest of good things future*, i. e. *of future blessings*. The meaning is, plainly, " The high priest, who procures future blessings." The principle of interpretation is the same that is adopted in such phrases as the following : viz. *the God of peace*, i. e. who procures or bestows peace ; *the God of consolation*, i. e. who bestows consolation ; *the God of grace*, i. e. who bestows grace ; ἄρτος τῆς ζωῆς, i. q. ἄρτος τὴν ζωὴν διδοὺς, &c. Christ is here called, *the high priest who procures future blessings*, by way of comparison with the Jewish high priest, who was μεσίτης (ch. viii. 6,) or ἔγγυος (ch. vii. 22,) between God and the people, and was the medium through which blessings were procured from God.

Διὰ τῆς μείζονος . . . τῆς κτίσεως, *through a greater and more perfect temple, not made with hands, that is, not of this* [material] *creation*. Σκηνὴ here, as in ver. 2, most probably means, *the outer apartment* or *court* only of the heavenly temple. So we must understand it, if we render διὰ *through*, as the best commentators and lexicographers do, in this case. But to give it *material* form and shape, would be nothing less than to make it χειροποίητος; although the writer of our epistle expressly says, " it is οὐ χειροποίητος." It is unnecessary, then, to inquire precisely what there is, in the heavenly world, which constituted, *materialiter*, this *greater and more perfect outer sanctuary*, through which Jesus passed, when εἰσῆλθεν ἐφάπαξ εἰς τὰ ἅγια, ver. 12. The comparison is made with the high priest of the Jews, who passed through the outer sanctuary, when he entered into the inner one, upon the great day of atonement. The probability is, that the writer compared, in his own mind, the *visible heavens*, (through which Jesus passed in his ascension on high, (ch. iv. 14 ; vi. 20 ; viii. 1, 2,) with the veil which separated the *outer* sanctuary of the Jewish temple from the *inner* one ; the clouds or sky, (which conceal the temple above from our view,) being resembled to the veil of the inner temple. Be this as it may, he explicitly declares that he does not mean a *material* sanctuary, visible to the natural eye, and corresponding in this respect to that upon the earth ; for he says, it was οὐ χειροποίητος. And lest this should not be sufficient to prevent misapprehension, he adds, οὐ ταύτης τῆς κτίσεως, i. e. not of *the visible material creation*, or, *not* (like this creation) *visible* and *material ;* which is plainly implied by ταύτης.

The version of διὰ by Dr. Schulz, (vermöge, *by virtue of,*) I am not able to comprehend. In what sense can it be said, that Christ, εἰσῆλθεν ἐφάπαξ εἰς τὰ ἅγια, αἰωνίαν λύτρωσιν εὑράμενος, BY VIRTUE OF *a greater and more perfect tabernacle, that was not material?* which is the same as to say, " He entered into the adytum of the tabernacle above, *by virtue of* the same tabernacle." I do not aver that this has no meaning ; but I readily confess my inability to discover what the meaning is. It would be well for Dr. Schulz, who has appended so many interrogation and exclamation points, to extracts made by him from Storr's version of our epistle, and from his notes upon it, to defend, or at least explain, such a version as that which gives occasion to these remarks.

There is, indeed, another construction of διὰ, in this case, which, if it might be applied, would give a meaning that is tolerable. Διὰ is often put before the genitive of a noun which indicates the *manner*, or the *circumstances*, in which any thing exists, or takes place, or is effected ; as all the lexicons will show. In 2 Cor. v. 10, the apostle says, " We must all appear before the judgment-seat of Christ, in order that every one may receive, τὰ διὰ σώματος, [according to] *the things done* IN *the body.*" But, strictly considered, διὰ does not signify *place* here ; for διὰ σώματος means, *in a corporeal condition.* Now, if we render the phrase in Heb. ix. 11, thus, *in a greater and more perfect temple*, we make διὰ indicate the *place where* simply. To render it thus, I find no sufficient authority ; for διὰ is used only to denote the place *through which*, or *by which* one passes. See Wahl, διὰ I. 1. a. And besides, the *circumstances* which attended Christ's going into the most holy place, are noted in ver. 12 ; so that it is hardly to be expected that they are to be found here. There, διὰ is used in a way that is not at all uncommon; e. g. "Christ entered the eternal sanctuary, οὐ δί αἵματος τράγων καὶ μόσχων, but διὰ τοῦ ἰδίου αἵματος." I cannot see, therefore, how διὰ μείζονος καὶ τελειοτέρας σκηνῆς can be construed in the way of indicating *the circumstances in which*, or *the means by which*, Christ entered the eternal sanctuary. Of course, διὰ, in the case under consideration, must, after all, be construed *through*; and be understood as having reference to the passage *through* the πρώτη σκηνή, in order to enter the δευτέρα σκηνή.

Ver. 12. Οὐδὲ δι αἵματος .... τὰ ἄγια, *not with the blood of goats and of bullocks, but with his own blood, he entered once for all into the sanctuary.* The Jewish high priest, on the great day of atonement, carried with him into the inner sanctuary, first, the blood of a bullock, and sprinkled it upon the mercy-seat, Lev. xvi. 14; then the blood of a goat, which he also sprinkled upon the mercy-seat, Lev. xvi. 15. Christ did not carry with him the blood of bullocks and goats, into the heavenly sanctuary, in order to make atonement; but he presented his own blood there, in order to make expiation. But this is not to be understood *literally*; for as the sanctuary itself was οὐ ταύτης τῆς κτίσεως, or οὐ χειροποίητος, so the Saviour's blood, which was shed upon Calvary, was not *literally* taken and carried by him into the heavenly temple. All that is *material*, is only a figure or emblem of that which is *spiritual* or *heavenly*. That διὰ before αἵματος means *with*, *cum*, בְּ, is quite clear, from the nature of the case, and from comparison with Lev. xvi. 14, 15. 2 Cor. ii. 4. Rom. ii. 27; xiv. 20; viii. 25. Heb. xii. 1. Δέ is adversative, *but*, when it follows a negative particle, as οὐδέ is here. Ἐφάπαξ means here, *once for all, once only*.

Αἰωνίαν λύτρωσιν εὑράμενος, *obtaining eternal redemption*. Εὑράμενος is not an Attic form of the first aor. middle. It seems to be an Alexandrine form, made after the analogy of the 2 aor. εὗρα; see Winer's Gram. § 9. d. Εὑρίσκω often means, *to obtain* or *acquire* any thing. Here, the act of entering the eternal sanctuary and presenting his own blood, is considered as the means by which the eternal redemption of sinners is obtained or accomplished. Λύτρωσις, in the New Testament, means, *liberation* or *redemption*; i. e. *liberation* from the penalty due to sin, or *redemption* from the bondage and penalty of sin. It is called αἰωνίαν, because the redemption obtained is eternal in its consequences, or because it is liberation from a penalty which is eternal, and introduction to a state of endless happiness. The λύτρωσις effected by Christ, needs no repetition; when once made, the consequences are eternal ; as we may see in ch. ix 24 —28 ; x. 1, ? 11 —14.

Ver. 13. Εἰ γὰρ τὸ αἷμα .... κεκοινωμένους, *for if the blood of bulls and of goats, and the ashes of a heifer sprinkling the unclean.* The blood of bulls and of goats, as employed for the purpose of purification or expiation, is described in Lev. xvi. 14, 15. It was also shed, on other occasions, as a sin-offering, Lev. i. 2—5. 10. 11. Ταύρων in our verse, corresponds with μόσχων in ver. 12. Both words mean a bullock, or a beeve : and the Septuagint employ both Greek words to translate the Hebrew שׁוֹר and פַּר. E. g. ταύρος for שׁוֹר in Gen. xlix. 6, and for פַּר in Gen. xxxii. 16 [15] ; μόσχος for שׁוֹר in Prov. xv. 17, and for פַּר in Lev. iv. 3—5.

Σποδὸς δαμάλεως, κ. τ. λ. See an account of the manner in which these ashes were prepared, in Numb. xix. 2—9. In the last verse, the ashes are directed to be kept *for a water of uncleanness,* לְמֵי נִדָּה, i. e. to be mixed with water which was to be sprinkled on the unclean, that they might be purified. It is also called, in the same verse, חַטָּאת, *a sin offering,* or (as our English version has it) *a purification from sin,* meaning a *means of purification.* So in Numb. xix. 13, 20, the person who had defiled himself, and neglected to have the מֵי נִדָּה sprinkled upon him, is pronounced unclean. Storr applies ῥαντίζουσα to αἷμα, as well as to σποδὸς. But, setting aside the difficulty of the grammatical construction as to concord, it does not appear, that the sprinkling of blood upon the unclean was a usual part of the Levitical rites of purification. The blood was sprinkled upon the mercy-seat, and on the horns of the altar, and poured out before the altar. Nor is there any need of the construction which he adopts ; for the sense is unembarrassed, if we follow the usual grammatical construction. ʻΡαντίζουσα is indeed feminine, and σποδὸς masculine. But such anomalies in concord are very common in Hebrew, see Gram. § 189, 5, 7. Besides, as the latter noun here (δαμάλεως) is feminine, it happens, as in some other cases of the like nature, that the grammatical concord, as to gender, is regulated by the latter of two nouns in regimen.

Ἁγιάζει ...... καθαρότητα, *sanctifies in respect to external purification.* Ἁγιάζει, used in respect to external rites, denoted that the person rendered ἁγιαζόμενος was clean or purified from all ritual uncleanness, i. e. that he had performed all the necessary rites of external purification, so that he could draw near to God, as a worshipper, in a regular manner. Thus much, our author avers, was accomplished by the ceremonial rites of the law. If so, then greater efficacy is to be attributed to the sacrifice made by Christ, as he proceeds to declare.

Ver. 14. Πόσῳ μᾶλλον . . . ἔργων, *how much more shall the blood of Christ, who, in an eternal spiritual nature, offered himself without spot to God, purify our consciences from dead works.* In ver. 11, 12. Christ is represented as entering the heavenly sanctuary, *with his own blood*, in order to expiate the sins of his people, or to procure λύτρωσιν for them, i. e. deliverance from the penalty of the Divine law. It is, then, in the heavenly world, in the tabernacle *not made with hands*, that the offering of our great High Priest is made. There he has presented himself, in his heavenly or glorified state, in his eternal spiritual condition, or possessed of an eternal spiritual nature, as the victim that had been slain, ch. x. 10—12; i. 3; vii. 27. Rev. v. 9. Eph. v. 2; and there his blood, that had been shed, is virtually offered to make atonement; not *literally*, but *spiritually*, i. e. in a manner congruous with the spiritual temple in which he ministers.

Nearly to this purpose did Theophylact, long ago, explain this difficult passage. His words are, " Οὐκ ἀρχιερεὺς τις προσήνεγκε τὸν χριστὸν, ἀλλ' αὐτὸς ἑαυτόν· καὶ οὐ διὰ πυρὸς, ὡς αἱ δαμάλεις, ἀλλὰ διὰ πνεύματος αἰωνίου, ὥστε καὶ τὴν χάριν καὶ τὴν ἀπολύτρωσιν διαιωνίζειν," i. e. No high priest made an offering of Christ, but he of himself; and this, *not by fire*, as the heifers [were offered,] but *by an eternal Spirit*, so that he might render grace and redemption eternal. See EXCURSUS XVIII.

Ἑαυτὸν προσήνεγκε. The apostle seems to use σῶμα, ἑαυτὸν, and αἷμα, as equivalent in regard to the sacrifice which Christ offered; see and compare Heb. i. 3; x. 10; ix. 12. 14; x. 19; ix. 26. The reason of these different expressions may be found in the nature of the Jewish ritual. When the blood of an animal was presented before God, in order to make atonement, the body was also consumed by fire, so that the whole was offered in sacrifice. See Lev. iv. 6—12, 17—21. The use of either the three words σῶμα, ἑαυτὸν, αἷμα, as designating the sacrifice of Christ, implies all that would be designated by employing the whole of them; i. e. when his *blood* was shed, his *body* was slain, i. e. *he himself* was slain.

Ἄμωμον, *spotless*, an evident allusion to the Jewish victims, which were required to be without spot or blemish. No other could be accepted of God. So Christ, who was " holy, harmless, undefiled, and separate from sinners, ch. vii. 26, was ἄμωμον, i. e. a *perfect* victim, a *lawful* or *acceptable* one

Καθαριεῖ τὴν συνείδησιν ἡμῶν ἀπὸ νεκρῶν ἔργων, *shall purify our conscience from deadly works.* Καθαριεῖ is the Attic future for καθαρίσει. Συνείδησιν does not mean simply the conscience as a faculty of the soul, bnt *the mind* or *conscious power* of men, i. e. the internal or moral man. Νεκρῶν in such cases usually means *deadly*, i. e. having a deadly, destructive, condemning power. This may be the meaning here; and so it is more usually taken, and so I have translated it. But as in ver. 13, the writer has made mention of the *ashes of a heifer*, as one of the means of effecting external purification; and since, in Numb. xix. 11—19, these ashes are described as particularly intended to cleanse those who had been polluted by the touch of *dead bodies*; may it not be supposed, that there is an allusion in the term νεκρῶν here to that fact? *Dead works,* in this sense, would be such as pollute the soul, as dead bodies did the persons of the Jews. *Dead works,* then, may mean *sinful* works; for it is from the pollution of sin that the blood of Jesus cleanses.

Εἰς τὸ λατρεύειν Θεῷ ζῶντι, *so that we may serve the living God;* another allusion to the Jewish ritual. Before persons, under the ancient dispensation, could present themselves in the presence of the Lord acceptably, they must have been subjected to ceremonial purification. What this *prefigured,* the blood of Jesus *effects.* It takes away the sinner's moral pollution, i. e. Christ removes the penalty to which he was obnoxious, and sanctifies, by the Spirit, the soul of the penitent sinner; and thus he may draw near to God, and offer him an acceptable service. He is *clean,* in a sense as much higher than the Israelite was who had purified himself only externally, as the efficacy of Jesus' blood is greater than that of goats and bullocks.

Ver. 15. Καὶ διὰ τοῦτο διαθήκης καινῆς....κληρονομίας, *on this account also, he is the mediator of a new covenant, in order that, his death having taken place for the sins* [committed] *under the former covenant, they who have been called might receive the promised blessing of the eternal inheritance.* A passage about which much difficulty has arisen, and a variety of interpretations been proposed. Διὰ τοῦτο, I understand as referring to the sentiment in ver. 14. The sentiment stands thus: " As Jewish sacrifices rendered the offerer externally clean; so the blood of Christ purifies the moral or internal man, and removes the consequences of sin. On this account, (διὰ τοῦτο,) i. e. because the sacrifice of Christ produces an effect such as the Jewish sacrifices did not, he

2 F

may be justly called the *mediator of a new covenant*, differing greatly from the old." Compare Heb. viii. 6—8. 13; vii. 15—19.

Διαθήκης καινῆς μεσίτης, means, *the author of a new covenant*, or the *internuntius*, מַלְאָךְ, who (so to speak) negociated such a covenant between God and man. See Gal. iii. 19, where Moses is called the μεσίτης of the former covenant.

" But of what avail," the Hebrews would very naturally inquire here, " can this *new covenant* be, to all those who have lived in former ages, under the Mosaic dispensation? You affirm that the ritual of the Mosaic law had no power to remove the spiritual penalty of guilt; do, then, the patriarchs, and prophets, and just men of past ages, still lie under the imputation of the sins which they committed?" By no means, answers the apostle. A new and better covenant than the Mosaic one has been instituted, under which real spiritual pardon for offences is obtained, which avails to them as well as to us at the present time.

"Οπως, κ. τ. λ. *so that the death of Christ having taken place, for redemption from the punishment due to transgressions committed under the ancient covenant, those who have been called might be made partakers of promised eternal blessings.* Θανάτου means, *the death of Christ*. Τῶν παραβάσεων is governed in the genitive by the force of ἀπὸ in composition with λύτρωσιν; and it means here, the *effects of transgression*, i. e. punishment, penalty; just as the Hebrew חַטָּאת and עָוֹן mean, not only *sin*, but the *penalty* due to it. Οἱ κεκλημένοι (like ἐκλεκτοὶ) means, those who are *called, invited*, viz. to an actual participation of the heavenly inheritance. It is, of course, understood, that only those who are pious have such an inheritance *promised* to them. Compare κλήσεως ἐπουρανίου μέτοχοι, in Heb. iii. 1. Οἱ κεκλημένοι here refers to just men, of the times which preceded the gospel dispensation, or new covenant; as the antecedent member of the verse clearly shows. Τῆς αἰωνίου κληρονομίας, as a genitive, depends on ἐπαγγελίαν, not on κεκλημένοι, although such a separation is somewhat unusual; see on ver 16, θάνατον....διαθεμένον. Ἐπαγγελίαν is best translated here, as in ch. vi. 12. 15. 17; ch. x. 36; ch. xi. 13, &c. *promised blessings*, or *proffered good*. The inheritance is called eternal, (αἰωνίου,) because the blessings procured by a Saviour's blood, for those who lived under the ancient dispensation, are of a spiritual eternal nature, see ver. 12. Such blessings could not be obtained by any of the rites of the old covenant; it is only by virtue of what is done under the new, by Jesus, that the ancient worthies came to the possession of them.

The sentiment which this verse contains, respecting the efficacy of atoning blood in regard to the sins of preceding ages, has an exact parallel in Rom. iii. 25, where the blood of Christ is declared, by Paul, to have procured τὴν πάρεσιν τῶν προγεγονότων ἁμαρτημάτων, *the remission of sins committed in preceding times;* as is plain from the antithesis, τῷ νῦν καιρῷ, in the following verse. Both passages compared, form a striking coincidence of a peculiar sentiment, which is no where else so clearly and directly asserted.

Ver. 16. Ὅπου γὰρ διαθήκη . . . . διαθεμένου, *for where there is a testament,* (i. e. where a testament becomes fully so, ἰσχύει, *is valid,*) *the death of the testator must take place.* The occasion of here introducing διαθήκη, in the new sense of *testament,* is stated in the summary prefixed to ch. iv. 14, and need not be again repeated. The whole comparison of *testaments* (διαθῆκαι) among men, which confer a valid title to an *inheritance,* ver. 16, 17, most evidently springs from the mention of Christ's *death,* in the preceding verse, and of the confirmation thereby of the believer's title to a heavenly *inheritance.* It is as much as to say, " Brethren, regard it not as strange, that the death of Christ should have given assurance of promised blessings to believers—should have ratified the new διαθήκη, of which he is the author; other διαθῆκαι are ratified by the death of their respective testators, and only in this way." And then he goes on to show, that even the ancient covenant, though it could not be called a διαθήκη in all respects, so well as the new one, still was ratified in a manner not unlike the new one, viz. by blood, the emblem of death, ver. 18—22.

As the mode of illustration or comparison, in ver. 16, 17, depends entirely on the sense of the *Greek* word διαθήκη, and is not at all supported by any meaning of the Hebrew בְּרִית, it must be plain, that our epistle was originally written in Greek, and not in Hebrew, as some of the ancient, and a few of the modern, critics have supposed.

Φέρεσθαι, in the sense of *intervening, happening, taking place,* (which must necessarily be attached to it here,) has no exact parallel, that I can find, either in classic or sacred usage. It is, as to such a meaning, a true ἅπαξ λεγόμενον.

If the reader finds any difficulty in admitting, in ver. 15, the wide separation of ἐπαγγελίαν and κληρονομίας, he will now perceive a separation of the same nature, in respect to θάνατον and διαθεμένου, about the relation of which no possible doubt can be rationally entertained.

Ver. 17. Διαθήκη γὰρ ἐπὶ νεκροῖς βεβαία, *for a testament is valid, in respect to those who are dead*. 'Επὶ is not unfrequently employed to denote *after*, viz. in respect to *time*; e. g. Acts xi. 19, ἐπὶ Στεφάνῳ, *after the time of Stephen*, as Wahl renders it; and so Mark vi. 52, ἐπὶ τοῖς ἄρτοις, *after the loaves*, i. e. the miraculous feeding of several thousands with them. So in Phil. iii. 12, ἐφ' ᾧ, i. e. *ex quo tempore*, as Brettschneider renders it. But these cases are not altogether clear. In classic authors, however, ἐπὶ τουτοῖς, means, *postea*; so ἐπὶ τυφλῷ τῷ Δανδάμιδι, *after Dandamis became blind*, Lucian in Tox. See Vigerus, p. 620. Matthiæ, § 584. In accordance with this usage, many critics have translated the phrase under consideration thus: *a testament is valid after men are dead*, or, *after death*. This, no doubt, gives the general *sentiment* of the passage; but, after all, the explanation of ἐπὶ νεκροῖς in this way, is somewhat forced; and I prefer that given in the translation, which conveys the same sense, and is not exposed to any doubts with regard to *usage*.

'Επεὶ διαθέμενος, *since it is of no avail, while the testator is living*. Μήποτε is stronger than the simple negative μή; and one might well translate, *since it is of no avail at all*. 'Ισχύει, here first expressed, seems to be implied after διαθήκη, in ver. 16.

The amount of the comparison in ver. 16, 17, is as before stated, that as διαθῆκαι among men are ratified by death, so did the death of Christ, (which the writer had just mentioned, ver. 15,) ratify the new διαθήκη which he had made, and gave a valid title to the heirs who were to receive the inheritance.

Ver. 18. "Οθεν οὐδ'...... ἐγκεκαίνισται, *whence, neither the first* [διαθήκη] *was ratified without blood*.

"Οθεν, *whence*, i. e. seeing that a διαθήκη must be ratified by the death of the testator, and that the new διαθήκη has been ratified by the *death* of Christ, so as to make sure the *inheritance* to believers, verse 15; therefore ἡ πρώτη, &c. The meaning is, that since the *new testament* (καινὴ διαθήκη) was, like other testaments, to be rendered valid by the death of the testator, therefore the παλαιὰ διαθήκη, בְּרִית רִאשׁוֹן, which was the prototype and emblem of the new testament, was itself confirmed, and all the apparatus attached to it consecrated, by blood, the emblem of death. The writer does not mean to say, that διαθήκη, in the sense of *testament*, can be appropriately used to designate the ancient covenant ; but he means to aver, that as the καινὴ διαθήκη could be appropriately enough called so, and as the death of Christ was to sanction it, therefore the ancient διαθήκη prefigured this, by the use of consecrating blood. In other words, as almost every thing attached to the παλαιὰ διαθήκη was consecrated to God, and rendered acceptable to him by being sprinkled with blood, and the διαθήκη itself was ratified in the same way ; so under the καινὴ διαθήκη, the blood of Christ only consecrates all things and renders them acceptable to God, and his death has fully ratified the διαθήκη which he made.

The resemblance between the ancient διαθήκη and the new one, is plainly not *entire*. Moses, the μεσίτης of the ancient one, did not ratify it by his death ; for his death is never represented by the Scriptures in such a light. But as the new διαθήκη was, in respect to the death of its μεσίτης, to differ from the old one ; so, (our author means to say,) the old διαθήκη, which was in its nature typical or emblematical, did prefigure this very thing, by the use of blood ; i. e. the old *covenant* resembled the new *testament*, as much as the nature of the case permitted.

Πρώτη agrees with διαθήκη understood. Ἐγκεκαίνισται, *to initiate, to consecrate, to dedicate*, i. e. by appropriate rites, to declare a thing which is already completed to be now ready for its uses, and to devote or dedicate it to those uses. The sprinkling of blood upon the book of the law, and upon the people, was the rite performed by Moses, when he consecrated the book of the law as their statute book, and them as publicly and solemnly bound to observe its precepts.

Ver. 19. Λαληθείσης γὰρ πάσης ...... τῷ λαῷ, *for when all the commandment, according to the law, had been recited by Moses to all the people*. The πάσης ἐντολῆς, to which reference is here made, are the statutes contained in Exod. xx.—xxiii. These Moses first recited *memoriter* to the people, after they had been communicated to him by the Lord at Sinai, Exod. xxiv. 3. He then wrote them down, Exod. xxiv. 4, and afterwards, on occasion of solemnly renewing the covenant on the part of the people to obedience, he again recited them from the book of the law, (סֵפֶר הַבְּרִית,) Exod. xxiv. 7. Κατὰ νόμον most probably means here, *according to the written law*, i. e. just as they were in the book of the law. But νόμον may refer to a command which Moses received to communicate to the people the laws given to him, although this command is only *implied*, but not expressed in the Scripture ; in which case the meaning would be, that *agreeably to the divine command*, Moses read all the law to the assembled nation.

Λαβὼν τὸ αἷμα . . . ἐρράντισε, *taking the blood of bullocks and of goats, with water and scarlet wool and hyssop, he sprinkled both the book and all the people.* This passage has occasioned no small perplexity to commentators; inasmuch as Moses, in his history of renewing the covenant of the people, in Exod. xxiv., has said nothing of the blood of goats; nothing of the water and scarlet wool and hyssop; nothing of sprinkling the book of the law with blood. Whence then did the writer obtain these circumstances? That they were not matters of new revelation to him, seems pretty evident; for he plainly makes an appeal to circumstances, which he takes for granted are well known to the Hebrews whom he addresses, and about which, if he were to commit an error of statement, all his readers would be revolted.

1. *The blood of goats.* In Exod. xxiv. 5, it is said that Moses *sent young men, who offered burnt offerings* (עֹלֹת,) *and sacrificed sacrifices, peace offerings* (זְבָחִים שְׁלָמִים) *to Jehovah, even bullocks,* (פָּרִים). Now, although *goats* are not mentioned here, yet it is quite probable that the עֹלֹת on this occasion were goats; for עֹלָה is a *holocaust*, i. e. an offering *entirely* consumed by fire, while שְׁלָמִים were mostly eaten by the offerers. That goats were used for all kinds of sacrifices, as well as bullocks, is quite evident from mere inspection of the Levitical law. E. g. goats are named as an עֹלָה, Lev. i. 10; iv. 24. 28, et alibi. It is altogether probable, then, that the holocausts or עֹלֹת mentioned in Exod. xxiv. 5, as offered on the occasion of renewing the covenant, were *goats;* and were of course understood by a Jewish reader to be such, inasmuch as the שְׁלָמִים only are affirmed to have been *bullocks*.

2. *The water, scarlet wool, and hyssop.* That water was used as well as blood, in order to sprinkle various things, is clearly implied in Lev. xiv. 4—7, compared with Lev. xiv. 49—52. Numb. xix. 18. Ps. li. 7. Ezek. xxxvi. 25. The scarlet wool, (שְׁנִי תוֹלַעַת *scarlet*,) was connected with a branch of hyssop [אֵזוֹב,) in order to make a convenient instrument for receiving and sprinkling the blood and water. It is not, indeed, expressly mentioned in Exod. xxiv.; but it is doubtless implied; for this was the common instrument by which the rite of sprinkling was performed. So in Exod. xii. 7, direction is simply given to sprinkle the door-posts of the Israelites with blood; and afterwards, in ver. 22, it is mentioned, that this was to be done *with a bunch of hyssop*.

So in Lev. xiv. 4—7, the שְׁנִי תוֹלַעַת, i. e. ἔριον κόκκινον, and the hyssop, are mentioned as employed in the office of sprinkling ; and again, in Lev. xiv. 49—52. The hyssop is also mentioned in Numb. xix. 18. Ps. li. 7. It may well be presumed, that the reason why the writer of our epistle, and the Hebrews of his time, supposed that Moses made use of the water and hyssop and scarlet wool, in the lustration of the people, when the covenant was renewed, was because these were employed in the lustrations where sprinkling was performed, on other occasions. The convenience of the instrument in question, and the nature of the case, would very naturally lead to such an opinion ; and who can doubt that it is well grounded ?

3. *The book of the law.* Because nothing is said, in Exod. xxiv. 3—8, respecting the sprinkling of the book, many commentators, e. g. Grotius, Bengel, Kopp, Storr, and others, construe αὐτὸ τὲ τὸ βιβλίον with λαβὼν τὸ αἷμα, i. e. *taking the blood* .... *and also the book of the law.* So far as such a construction of the particle τὲ itself is concerned, this might perhaps be allowed ; for τὲ is sometimes employed, when it is not preceded by καὶ or δὲ, in the clause immediately antecedent; as in Acts ii. 33. To justify the method of interpretation now in question, Storr appeals to Heb. ix. 1, and xii. 2. But in the former case, τὲ is preceeded by καὶ ; and the latter is a case where two verbs are connected. But in our verse καὶ follows βιβλίον, and seems necessarily to connect it with πάντα τὸν λαόν. But to say of Moses, λαβὼν .... πάντα τὸν λαόν, will not be contended for. Michaëlis, Heinrichs, Dindorf,. Ernesti, and others, agree with the interpretation which I have given. Indeed, καὶ and τὲ seem to be as necessarily related here as *et* and *que* are in Latin ; and, in fact, they commonly sustain the same relation to each other. As to manuscripts, only one omits καὶ after βιβλίον ; and we are obliged, therefore, by the laws of criticism, to retain it, whatever difficulties it may occasion to the interpreter.

In regard to the fact itself, viz. that Moses did sprinkle the book with blood, no intimation of it is given in Exod. xxiv. 3—8. Yet nothing can be more probable, than that such was the fact. Aaron, and his sons, and their garments, were sprinkled with blood, when consecrated to the priest's office, Exod. xxix. 19—21. The blood of sacrifices was sprinkled upon the altar, Exod. xxix. 16. Lev. i. 5. 11 ; iii. 2. 13 ; also before the veil of the sanctuary, Lev. iv. 6. 17 ; compare Lev. vi. 27 ; vii. 14 ; viii. 15. 19. 24. 30 ; ix. 12. 18. et alibi. Philo, (de Vita Mosis B. p. 675,) has a passage which speaks of all the various apparatus of the tabernacle being anointed with holy oil, and the vestments of the priests being sprinkled with blood. So Josephus, also, speaks of sprinkling the garments of Aaron and his sons with αἵματος τῶν τεθυμένων, *the blood of the slain beasts*, and with spring water, and holy chrism. Lib. V. 6. 6. p. 334. edit. Havercamp. All this serves to show how common this rite of sprinkling with blood was in the Jewish ritual; so common, that the writer of our epistle seems, with those whom he addressed, to have considered it a matter of course, that when the people were sprinkled with blood, at the time of renewing their covenant to keep the precepts contained in the book of the law, Exod. xxiv. 8, the book itself, like all the sacred apparatus of the temple, was also sprinkled in like manner. Nothing could be more natural. The people were consecrated to observe the statutes of the book; and the book was consecrated, as containing that sacred code of laws which they were bound to obey.

If, however, after all, one is not satisfied that Paul drew his conclusions from the analogies and probabilities just stated, he may easily suppose that tradition among the Jews had preserved the remembrance of the particulars described in our verse, on account of the very solemn and important nature of the transaction with which they are connected. It would be easy to suppose, with some commentators, that these particulars were suggested in a miraculous way, by the Holy Spirit, to the mind of the writer. But this solution of the difficulty is not a probable one; because the writer evidently touches upon circumstances here, which he takes it for granted his readers will at once recognize and admit. If so, then these things must have already been matters of *common opinion* among the Hebrews; and consequently were not now first suggested to the writer of our epistle in a *miraculous* way. At all events, there can be no serious difficulty in the case. The fact that Exod. xxiv. 3—8 does not mention the particulars in question, can be no more proof that they did not take place, than the fact that the evangelists have not recorded the words of Christ, "It is more blessed to give than to receive," would prove that he did not utter them. Whether Paul and the Hebrews knew these things by tradition, or believed from analogical reasoning, cannot be important. Enough that they were facts, and were appealed to as such by the writer, with full confidence that they would be recognized by his readers.

To illustrate the principle, *de minimis non curat lex*, it may be remarked, that Paul says simply, λαβὼν τὸ αἷμα ; Moses, that "he took half of the blood," Exod. xxiv. 6. But, surely, if he did the latter, he did the former. Such expressions, no where either in sacred or profane writers, are to be tortured, in order to extract from them a metaphysical exactness : *verba—ne resecanda ad vivum.*

In the like manner, I interpret πάντα τὸν λαὸν. How, it has been asked, could he sprinkle three millions of people, with the blood of a few goats and bullocks? In such a way, I would answer, as "*all* Judea and Jerusalem went out to John, to be baptized of him in the river Jordan, *confessing their sins,*" Matt. iii. 5, seq. Must we now understand by this, that all the infants, the *non compotes mentis*, mutes, the sick, infirm, the aged, all females, or literally *all* males, repaired to John, to be baptized, and did *all* (infants and mutes with the rest) *confess* their sins to him? If not, then there is no difficulty in construing πάντα τὸν λαὸν, in the case now under consideration. *Moses sprinkled blood on the multitude of the people*, I take to be the simple meaning of the writer; not that all and every individual was actually and personally sprinkled. Some were actually sprinkled ; and these, being of the multitude, were representatives of the whole. Nothing is more common than to attribute to a body of men collectively, what belongs, strictly considered, only to certain individuals of that body. Thus, what the *government* of this country do, the *Americans* are said to do.

Ver. 20. Λέγων· τοῦτο τὸ αἷμα . . . . ὁ Θεὸς, *saying, This is the blood of the covenant, which God has enjoined upon you.* Another instance, in which the *letter* of the Old Testament is forsaken, and the *sense* merely retained. The original in Exodus xxiv. 8, is, הִנֵּה דַם־הַבְּרִית אֲשֶׁר כָּרַת יְהֹוָה עִמָּכֶם, *behold, the blood of the covenant which God has made with you.* But הִנֵּה means, *see here*, or *see this*, and is equivalent to τοῦτο used as a *demonstrative*. The verb כָּרַת is rendered by the LXX. διέθετο ; by our author, ἐνετείλατο. The reason of this probably is, that בְּרִית, in Exod. xxiv. 8, means *statutes, laws*, as it evidently refers to the preceding *statutes*, in Exod. xx.—xxiii. God *commanded* that the people should observe these; and with reference to this injunction, our author says, ἐνετείλατο.

Τὸ αἷμα τῆς διαθήκης means *the blood by which the covenant*, or, assent on the part of the people to the laws proposed, or rather, their promise to observe them, Exod. xxiv. 7, *was ratified.* So common was it, among the Hebrews, to ratify engagements by the blood of animals slain, **that** the usual idiom of the language is, בָּרַת בְּרִית, *to cut a covenant*, i. e. to sanction one by cutting an animal into two pieces, and passing between them. See Gen. xv. 10; xxxi. 54. Jer. xxiv. 18. Ephrem Syrus testifies, that the Chaldeans had the same usage, Opp. I. p. 161 ; as also Hacourt does, in respect to the Arabians, Histoire de Madagascar, p. 98. 360. The meaning of such a transaction seems evidently to be, that the persons who make the engagements, by passing between the dissevered parts of the slain animal, virtually say, " If we preserve not our engagement faithfully, and without violation, then let us be cut in pieces, like the animal between whose dissevered parts we now pass." The sprinkling of blood on the people, Exod. xxiv. 8, was a solemnity of a similar nature. By it they were also ceremonially purified, and consecrated to God.

Ver. 21. Καὶ τὴν σκηνὴν .... ἐῤῥάντισε, *the tabernacle, also, and all the vessels for service, he sprinkled in like manner with blood.* Καὶ, although a kind of copulative here, still indicates another transaction different from that related in ver. 19 ; for when the people were sprinkled with blood, the tabernacle was not built, neither were the σκεύη λειτουργίας yet made. The setting up and consecration of the tabernacle, with its vessels, is related in Exod. xl. ; yet nothing is there related of sprinkling them with blood, but only of anointing them with holy oil, Exod. xl. 9—11. In the like manner, the *anointing* only of Aaron and his sons is there spoken of as a rite preparatory to entering upon the duties of their office in the tabernacle, Exod. xl. 12—15 ; while nothing is said at all of their being sprinkled with blood. But if we compare Exod. xxix. 20, 21, and Lev. viii. 24. 30, we shall see that it is certain that Aaron and his sons were sprinkled with blood, as well as anointed with oil. In like manner, it is probable, that the tabernacle and its furniture were sprinkled with blood, although Moses has not mentioned it in Exod. ch. xl. Josephus says, " Both the tabernacle and the vessels pertaining to it, [Moses sprinkled and purified] with oil, prepared as I have described, and with the blood of bulls and rams that were slain, one of each kind alternately, every day," Antiq. III. 8. § 6. This seems to indicate, that Josephus had the same view as Paul, in regard to purifying the tabernacle. The verbs in brackets, in the above translation, are drawn from the preceding clause, where we find ἔῤῥανεν ἀφαγνίσας, *purifying he sprinkled.* They belong to the sentence here translated, by *implication.*

In regard to the fact itself, we may observe, that it is rendered quite probable from analogy. Then, as to a knowledge of it by our author, nothing more is necessary, than the supposition that tradition had conveyed the knowledge of this, as well as of many other facts, down to the time of Paul. The writer evidently appeals to facts, which were believed by the Hebrews in general whom he was addressing; and facts which, although not stated in the Old Testament, are by no means improbable, and which no one surely has it in his power to contradict.

Ver. 22. Καὶ σχεδὸν ἐν αἵματι . . . νόμον, *indeed, every thing is, according to the law, purified by blood.* Καὶ, imo, vero, yea, indeed. Σχεδὸν πάντα, and not πάντα absolutely and simply; for some things were purified by *water*, Lev. xvi. 26. 28. Numb. xxxi. 24. some by fire and water, Numb. xxxi. 22, 23. But the exceptions were few, in which shedding of blood, or sprinkling of blood, was not required, in order to effect ceremonial purity. See on ver. 19.

Καὶ χωρὶς αἱματεκχυσίας οὐ γίνεται ἄφεσις, *and without shedding of blood there is no remission* [of sins.] See Lev. iv. 2—6. 13—17. 22—25. 27—30, and 31. 35. Under the Mosaic law, not every transgression could be atoned for; consequently, remission of the penalty which the law inflicted could not, in some cases, be obtained. See Numb. xv. 30, 31. It was only he that sinned through a degree of ignorance or inadvertency, who could bring his sin and trespass offering, Numb. xv. 27. 29; for cases of a different nature, compare Lev. iv. 2. 13. 22. 27. The חַטָּאת and אָשָׁם *sin* and *trespass*, were atoned for, in a civil and ecclesiastical point of view, by appropriate sacrifices, which bore the like names. But in this case, the remission was only from a temporal penalty or calamity. It was not possible that such sacrifices could atone for sin, as viewed by the righteous Governor of the world. Such the nature of the case seems plainly to be; and so the writer of our epistle has expressly declared, in ch. x. 4. God, as the king and head of the Jewish nation, granted remission of the penalty which the Jewish law inflicted in many cases, on certain conditions. But this had respect merely to the present world, and not to the accountability of transgressors, before the tribunal of the universe, in the world above. Even *temporal* forgiveness, however, could not be obtained χωρὶς αἱματεκχυσίας. It was thus, that these ὑποδείγματα shadowed forth, to the ancient church, the necessity of atoning blood, which possessed a higher virtue than that of beasts, in order to remove the penalty against sin, that was threatened in respect to a future world. So the writer proceeds to tell us in the next verse.

Ver. 23. Ἀνάγκη οὖν . . . ταύτας, *since, then, the images of heavenly things must needs be purified by such* [rites,] *the heavenly things themselves* [must be purified] *by better sacrifices than these.* Μὲν is here the mere sign of *protasis.* Ὑποδείγματα, *copies, effigies, images, resemlances, likenesses;* meaning the tabernacle and temple, with all their sacred utensils, &c. See on ch. viii. 5. Τῶν ἐν τοῖς οὐρανοῖς means, the *spiritual objects of the heavenly world,* of which the tabernacle, with all its apparatus and services, was only a symbol. See on ch. viii. 5. Τούτοις designates such things, i. e. such rites and means of purification, as had been described in the preceding context. Καθαρίζεσθαι refers to the ceremonial purification of the temple and its sacred utensils; e. g. of the most holy place, Lev. xvi. 15, 16. of the altar, Lev. xvi. 18. Exod. xxix. 36, 37; of the tabernacle, Lev. xvi. 20. 33. This was to be done, because the Israelites, sinful and impure, profaned these sacred things by their approach, Lev. xvi. 19; xv. 31. Numb. xix. 19, 20. And this being done, God vouchsafed his presence in the tabernacle, and promised to dwell among the Israelites, Exod. xxix. 43—46. All this was symbolical of the heavenly sanctuary and sacrifice. God permits sinners to hope for pardon and approach to him, only when they are sprinkled with the atoning blood of Jesus; and what was done on earth as a *symbol,* has been done in the heavenly world in *reality,* i. e. so as actually to procure *spiritual* pardon, and restoration to the Divine favour.

Αὐτὰ δὲ τὰ ἐπουράνια .... ταύτας. Δὲ is the sign of *apodosis* merely. It may be translated, *therefore, then;* but there is no need of rendering it, as our language does not demand like signs of protasis and apodosis with the Greek. Ἐπουράνια means the σκηνὴ ἀληθίνη, ἢν ἔπηξεν ὁ κύριος, ch. viii. 2, i. q. ἡ σκηνὴ οὐ χειροποίητος, ch. ix. 11. But how could the heavenly tabernacle, καθαρίζεσθαι, *be purified?* The grammatical construction of ver. 23, certainly requires us to supply this verb in the latter clause, since it is expressed in the former. But the word, of course, can be here used only in a *figurative* manner; for the ἐπουράνια are not *impure.* But as God was accessible to offenders, in his sanctuary on earth, only when atoning blood had been offered; so God, in his heavenly sanctuary, is accessible to sinners, only through the blood of Jesus there offered, and there consecrating a new and living way of access to the throne of mercy. It is in this sense, that the writer means to apply καθαρίζεσθαι, viz. that of rendering the sanctuary approachable by offenders, and affording assurance of liberty to draw near to God (ch. iv. 16,) rather than that of direct purification from uncleanness; which could not be predicated of the heavenly sanctuary. It is the *effect* of the purifying blood of Jesus, in regard to giving access to the heavenly sanctuary, which the writer means to compare with the purification of the tabernacle and its utensils; for the most holy place of the earthly tabernacle could be properly approached by offenders, only when atonement was made.

Ver. 24. That better sacrifices than those offered on earth by the Jewish priests, were required under the priesthood of Christ, necessarily results from the nature of the sanctuary in which Christ ministers. Οὐ γὰρ εἰς χειροποίητα ἅγια .... οὐρανὸν; *for Christ entered not into a sanctuary made by hands, which is only a copy of the true one, but into heaven itself.* It is the entrance of Christ, as a *priest*, into the heavenly sanctuary, of which the writer is here speaking. That Christ performs the office of priest in the heavenly sanctuary, the writer has already intimated several times; see ch. ix. 9. 11; viii. 1—4. 'Αντίτυπα *copy, image, effigy, form or likeness*, corresponding to the original τύπος, shewn to Moses in the mount, ch. viii. 5. 'Αληθινῶν means, *that which is real;* i. e. the original or heavenly sanctuary, of which the earthly one is a *mere copy*. In other words, they stand related as substance and shadow, or image. The *reality* is in heaven; the *emblem* or *mere similitude* of it, on earth.

Νῦν ἐμφανισθῆναι ... ἡμῶν, *thenceforth to appear before God in our behalf.* Νῦν means, from the point of time when he entered heaven as our high priest, onward indefinitely; and it implies, that his office was continued while the writer was then addressing his readers. 'Εμφανισθῆναι means, among other things, *to present one's self before a tribunal,* for the sake of accusing or defending. In the former case, it is followed by κατὰ, e. g. Acts xxiv. 1; xxv. 2. 16: in the latter, it takes ὑπὲρ after it, as in our text. The usual and full grammatical construction would be ὥστε ἐμφανισθῆναι. I have been able to find no similar usage of ἐμφανίζω, among the Greeks.

Τῷ προσώπῳ τοῦ Θεοῦ, the same as the Hebrew לִפְנֵי אֱלֹהִים, being altogether Hebraistic. The whole comparison is taken from the custom of the Jewish high priest, who, when he entered the most holy place, was said to *appear before God*, or to *draw near to God*, because the presence of God was manifested over the mercy seat, in the holy of holies, and God was represented, and was conceived of by the Jews, as sitting enthroned upon the mercy-seat. Now, as the high priest appeared before God, in the Jewish temple, and offered the blood of beasts for expiation, on the great day of atonement, in behalf of the Jewish nation; so Christ, in the heavenly temple, enters the most holy place with his own blood (ver. 12,) to procure pardon (αἰωνίαν λύτρωσιν) for us. This is what the writer means, by ἐμφανισθῆναι τῷ προσώπῳ τοῦ Θεοῦ ὑπὲρ ἡμῶν.

Ver. 25. But although there is a similitude between the atoning office of Christ and that of the Jewish high priest, yet there is a great difference, in some respects, between his manner of offering expiatory sacrifice, and that of the Levitical priesthood. Οὐδ' ἵνα πολλάκις . . . ἀλλοτρίῳ, *yet not that he may frequently repeat the offering of himself, like the high priest, who, every year, enters into the sanctuary with blood not his own.* This refers to the entrance of the high priest into the sanctuary, on the great day of atonement. Ἐν αἵματι ἀλλοτρίῳ, *with the blood of others*, i. e. with blood not his own; in distinction from the manner in which Christ entered the heavenly sanctuary, which was *with his own blood*, ver. 12. Two points of difference, then, are here suggested, between the Jewish offerings and that of Christ; the one, that they were *often* repeated, his was made but *once;* the other, that the high priest presented the *blood of goats and bullocks,* but Jesus, his *own blood.*

Ver. 26. Ἐπεὶ ἔδει . . . κόσμου, *for then he must needs have often suffered since the world began.* That is, since the blood of Christ is necessary to make atonement for sin, and to procure pardon for it from the righteous and spiritual Judge of men; and since the blessings procured by the death of Jesus must avail, as well to the benefit of the ages which preceded his coming, as to those which follow it, (see ver. 15, and Rom. iii. 25, 26;) it follows, that if his sacrifice had not been of a different nature and value from that of the Jewish priests, it must have been continually repeated, from the very beginning of the world, down to the time in which the writer was addressing his readers. We may of course add, that it must have continued to be repeated down to the end of the world, for the same reason. This passage serves then to show, that when Heb. ix. 15, and Rom. iii. 25, 26, are construed as having relation to the retrospective influence of the death of Christ, no doctrine foreign to the conceptions of our author is introduced; for the verse under consideration is plainly built upon the ground of such a retrospective influence.

Νῦν δὲ ἅπαξ . . . πεφανέρωται, *but now, at the close of the* [Jewish] *dispensation, he has, once for all, made his appearance, in order to* remove the punishment due to sin by the sacrifice of himself. Νῦν does not relate particularly to time here, but is a particle of opposition, in contradistinction to ἐπεί. Συντελείᾳ τῶν αἰώνων, the close of the Mosaic economy or period. Αἰών singular, and αἰῶνες plural, appear to be sometimes used in the same sense, in the New Testament; like οὐρανός and οὐρανοί, σάββατον and σάββατα, and some other nouns. For the meaning given to αἰών, see Wahl's Lexicon on the word.

'Αθέτησις signifies *putting away, removal, abrogation, annulling*, &c. 'Αμαρτία I understand here, as meaning *the penalty due to sin*; just as the Hebrew חַטָּאת means *sin*, and *the punishment*, consequences, *of sin*; and עָוֹן means, *iniquity*, and the *punishment*, i. e. consequences, *of iniquity*. It is true, indeed, that Christ came to save men from the *power*, as well as the *penalty*, of sin; but most evidently his death is here considered, by our author, as an expiatory sacrifice, by virtue of which the consequences of sin, i. e. the punishment due to it, are removed, and the sinner treated as though he were innocent.

Διὰ τῆς θυσίας αὐτοῦ : compare ch. i. 3 ; ii. 14 ; vii. 27 ; ix. 12. 14, 15 ; x. 5—10.

The whole comparison stands thus: "As the expiatory sacrifices under the law, which were annually offered, and therefore often repeated, procured remission of the temporal punishment due to offences under the Mosaic dispensation; so the sacrifice of Christ, and the blood which he presents, once for all, in the eternal or heavenly sanctuary, is effectual to procure spiritual pardon for all times and ages, past and to come." Nothing could exhibit the great superiority of Christ's priesthood over that of the Jewish, in a more striking point of light than this. The latter, by its offerings and atonements, procured only a remission of *temporal* punishment in the *present world;* the former, a remission αἰωνίου κολάσεως, (Matt. xxv. 46,) in the *world to come*.

Ver. 27. Καὶ καθ' ὅσον ...... κρίσις, *for since it is appointed unto men to die once only, and after this* [cometh] *the judgment*. Καθ' ὅσον is sometimes equivalent to καθώς, *since, as,* in this epistle; e. g. ch. vii. 20, compare ver. 22 ; and here it is plainly the same as ὡς or καθώς. 'Απόκειται, *repositum est, it is laid up for*, i. e. by Divine appointment, *it is reserved for*, or *it awaits* men once to die. The translation gives the meaning, but not with *literal* exactness. "Απαξ is here, *once for all, only once ;* for the object of this comparison is to show that as men die *but once*, so Christ, who had a nature truly human, and was in all things made like unto his brethren, (ch. ii. 17,) could die *but once*, (and not oftentimes,) in order to atone for sin.

Μετὰ δὲ τοῦτο κρίσις, i. e. men, having *once* died, go after that to a state of reward or punishment, to a final state, in which no more such changes as death makes can be suffered. The clause in question is added to the former part of the verse, in order to show that dying more than once is impossible, inasmuch as judgment immediately follows, with which is connected the immutable state of men. The implication contained in this verse, viz. that a state of trial in a future world, like to that which is allowed to men in the present world, is not to be expected, seems to be plain.

Ver. 28. Οὕτω καὶ ὁ Χριστὸς ...... ἁμαρτίας, *so Christ, also, after having once for all offered up himself, in order to bear the sins of many*. The writer had been labouring, in the preceding context, to show that the offering of Christ needed not, like that of the high priest, to be often repeated. Ver. 27 and 28, are designed to show that a repetition of the death of Jesus (who suffered in our nature) would have been inconsistent with the nature which he sustained, and contrary to all analogy. So the author; " Since men die *but once*, so Christ died or was offered up, προσενεχθεὶς, *but once*.

Προσενεχθεὶς (from προσφέρω) is a participle of the first aor. passive, and may be rendered *offered up himself*, or, *made an offering of himself*, inasmuch as the first aor. passive, frequently has a middle or reflexive sense, particularly when any verb lacks the first aor. of the middle voice, Buttmann Gram. § 123. Προσφέρω is a very general word in respect to offerings, and designates the action of the person who brings the sacrifice, or of the priest who presents it. As the sacrifice offered to God was first *slain*, and then presented; so the idea of an offering here necessarily involves the idea of the death of the victim offered. It is this implied idea of the death of the victim, that stands in comparison with the ἅπαξ ἀποθανεῖν of all men; i. e. as they die but once, so Christ died but once.

Πολλῶν, *many*, i. e. *all nations* without distinction, Jews and Gentiles, for ages past, and ages to come, ver. 15. 26. and Rom. iii. 25, 26. See the like representation, respecting the universality of the benefits offered through the death of Christ, in Matt. xx. 28; ch. xxvi. 28. Rom. v. 15. 19, compare ch. v. 18. John vi. 51; ch. iii. 16. 1 John ii. 2, &c.

'Ανενεγκεῖν ἁμαρτίας, to bear the sins, means, to bear the punishment, i. e. to suffer the penalty, due to sin. See Excursus XIX.

'Εκ δευτέρου . . . . εἰς σωτηρίαν, shall make his appearance, a second time, without a sin-offering, for the salvation of those who wait for him. 'Εκ δευτέρου has reference to ἅπαξ in the preceding clause. Christ appeared, and died *once* for sin; but when he appears *again*, ἐκ δευτέρου, it will not be to repeat his sufferings, i. e. to make again an expiatory sacrifice, but for the purposes of bestowing rewards on those who trust in him, and wait for his coming.

Χωρὶς ἁμαρτίας has been variously explained. But it is evident, that the expression has a direct reference to the preceding clause, i. e. either to προσενεχθεὶς, or to ἀνενεγκεῖν ἁμαρτίας. In the former case, ἁμαρτίας, in our clause, would mean *sin-offering*, like חטאת, אשם, because προσενεχθεὶς means, *he made himself an offering*. The meaning would then be, "but when Christ again appears, he will not make himself a sin-offering," i. e. his appearance will be χωρὶς ἁμαρτίας. So I understand the phrase. But if we construe χωρὶς ἁμαρτίας, as referring to ἀνενεγκεῖν ἁμαρτίας, then the supplement to the phrase will be χωρὶς [τοῦ ἀνενεγκεῖν] ἁμαρτίας. The meaning of this is, "Without again suffering the penalty due to sin." In either way, the sense amounts to about the same; for either method of interpretation makes the writer say, that Christ would no more suffer on account of the sins of men, but that, by dying once, he has perfectly accomplished the redemption of those who trust in him.

Τοῖς αὐτὸν ἀπεκδεχομένοις means, those who, renouncing the world, and resisting all the motives to swerve from Christian hope and faith, which the times presented, patiently wait for the rewards which the Saviour will finally bestow upon his followers. There is a tacit admonition to the Hebrews in this; for it is as much as to say, "Those only who do thus persevere, will be rewarded." Εἰς σωτηρίαν has reference to the future salvation or blessedness, which Christ will bestow upon his followers at his second coming.

The insufficiency of the Levitical sacrifices to procure spiritual pardon for sin, and the sufficiency of the sacrifice which Christ had offered, was one of the most important and interesting of all the points which the writer of our epistle had to discuss. The Hebrews in general placed full confidence in the efficacy of the Levitical sacrifices to purify them from sin—at least, to remove the penalty of it. Every person, who is conscious of sin, and knows that it subjects him to the penalty of the Divine law, must naturally feel a deeper interest in the question, Whether, and how, sin can be pardoned? than in any other. It was very natural for Jews who had been educated in the full belief of the efficacy of the sacrifices instituted by Moses, to cling to them as the foundation of their dearest and highest hopes, viz. the means of pardon, and restoration to Divine favour. It was an attachment to the Jewish ritual, built upon hopes of such a nature, which rendered the Mosaic religion so attractive to the Hebrews, and endangered their adherence to a Christian profession. There was much, too, in the pomp and solemnity of their rites, which served to interest the feelings, and delight the fancy, of the worshippers. It is on account of the strong attachment which they cherished for their system of sacrifices and purifications, that our author is so urgent in showing that real pardon with God could not be procured by any or all of these means. The blood of Christ only cleanses from sin, and procures acceptance for sinners with God, as their spiritual judge.

Accordingly, in ch. ix. he declares that the tabernacle, with all its sacred utensils and services, was only an *image* or *symbol* (παραβολή) of what is real and spiritual in the heavenly world, a *copy* merely of the σκηνή οὐ χειροποίητος, ch. ix. 9—11, or a mere ὑπόδειγμα τῶν ἐν οὐρανοῖς, ch. ix. 23. The Jewish sacrifices availed for nothing more than *external* purification, ch. x. 10. 13; while the blood of Christ purified the soul or mind (συνείδησιν) from the uncleanness of sin, and rendered it capable of offering acceptable service to the living God, ch. ix. 14. After adducing various considerations, to show how extensively the rites of the law, which required the exhibition and application of blood, prefigured that atoning blood which Jesus offered, to make expiation for sin, and that his death, once for all, was sufficient for this purpose, he proceeds, in ch. x. more deeply to impress the great subject of atoning sacrifice by Christ upon the minds of his readers, knowing that very much depended on the conviction which might be attained in respect to this point. Could they be persuaded, that Jesus had himself offered the only sacrifice which made real expiation for sin; and that this, once offered, was an all-sufficient sacrifice; then there could be no rational inducement for them to abandon their spiritual hopes, and return to their confidence in the rites of the Levitical law.

The repetition of this subject is for the purpose of suggesting some new arguments in order to enforce it; as may be seen in ver. 5—18.

CHAPTER X.

Ver. 1. Σκιὰν γὰρ ἔχων . . . πραγμάτων; *moreover, the law, which presented only an imperfect sketch of future blessings, and not a full representation of those things.* Σκιά and εἰκών are related, as the Latin *umbra* and *effigies* are. The former is an *imperfect sketch*, a *mere outline* (as we say,) a *slight representation* or *resemblance:* the latter is a picture or image filled out or completed, and made, in all its minuter parts, to resemble the original. Not that these words are always employed with a sedulous attention to these nice shades of signification ; but in the case before us they are so, for they are evidently contrasted with each other. The meaning of the writer is, "The law did not even go so far, as to exhibit a *full image* of future blessings, but only a *slight adumbration*. Ἔχων *having, containing, possessing, affording*, or (ad sensum) *exhibiting, presenting*, so as to accord with the nature of the image which follows.

Νόμος means here, *the sacrificial ritual law*, of which he had before been speaking ; the old בְּרִית, διαθήκη, which was to be abolished. The whole law of Moses, that is, the moral code which it contains, is not the subject of consideration or assertion here. Μελλόντων ἀγαθῶν, the same as in ch. ix. 11. Τῶν πραγμάτων, i. e. τουτῶν, viz. the *future blessings* just before mentioned.

Κατ' ἐνιαυτὸν . . . τελειῶσαι, *by the yearly sacrifices themselves, which are continually offered, can never fully accomplish what is needed for those who approach* [the altar.] By the κατ' ἐνιαυτὸν θυσίαις, the writer means particularly to designate those which were offered on the great day of national atonement ; which were considered the most sacred and efficacious of all, inasmuch as the high priest then entered the inner sanctuary, and presented himself before the mercy seat.

Προσφέρουσι, with a nominative not expressed, is equivalent to the passive voice here, as often elsewhere, agreeably to the Hebrew idiom.

Εἰς τὸ διηνεκὲς, *without cessation, continually*, they were repeated each successive year. The word is peculiar to this epistle ; and Schneider has omitted it in his Lexicon ; but Elian, Appian, Diodorus Siculus, and Symmachus, employ it.

Τοὺς προσερχομένους means, the worshippers who approach the altar, or the temple, or the Divine presence in the temple. The sense is for substance the same, whichever of these be understood. For τελειῶσαι, see on Heb. ix. 9, and vii. 11. The sentiment of the verse corresponds very exactly with that in ch. ix. 9, 10.

Ver. 2. Ἐπεὶ οὐκ ἂν ἐπαύσαντο προσφερόμεναι, *for otherwise*, i. e. if the sacrifices could have perfected those who presented them, *would not the offerings have ceased?* To προσφερόμεναι most critics subjoin εἶναι understood, which would be equivalent to the infinitive προσφέρεσθαι, rendering the phrase thus, "*They* (i. e. the sacrifices) *had ceased to be offered.*" The sense of the phrase, thus explained, is the same that I have given to it. But προσφερόμεναι [θυσίαι] ἐπαύσαντο seems to me more facile than the other construction.

Διὰ τὸ μηδεμίαν .... κεκαθαρμένους, *because the worshippers, once for all made clean, would have no longer been conscious of sins.* Λατρεύοντας designates those who brought the offerings or sacrifices, and on whose account they were presented to God, i. e. the worshippers. Ἅπαξ denotes here, as in the preceding chapter, *once for all ;* the nature of the argument demanding this sense. For if a worshipper at one time obtained pardon, or was made clean only in respect to *past* offences, (and surely expiatory sacrifices were offered only with respect to the *past*,) this would not prevent the dread of punishment at a future period, when new offences would have been committed. To be purified *once for all*, then, was necessary, in order to quiet the apprehensions of such a worshipper.

Κεκαθαρμένους, *purified, atoned for.* As καθαρίζω means, in Hebrew Greek, *to make expiation for, to purify by expiatory offering, to pronounce* or *declare one to be pure ;* so κεκαθαρμένους of course means, *those atoned for, those for whom expiation is made, those declared to be pure,* or *rendered pure,* and consequently restored to favour.

Συνείδησιν means not merely, *conscience,* but *consciousness, opinion, judgment, sentiment, apprehension.* Συνείδησιν ἁμαρτιῶν is *an apprehension of the consequences of sin,* or, *a consciousness* that one has subjected himself to them, *a consciousness of guilt.* Ἁμαρτιῶν may mean here, (as often before,) *punishment of sin, consequences of sin*, like the corresponding Hebrew חַטָּאת,עָוֹן, פֶּשַׁע; or it may mean *sin, guilt, transgression.* The writer, however, does not mean to say, that the pardon of sin takes away from him, who obtains it, the consciousness that he has once been the subject of moral turpitude. This the blood of Christ itself does not effect; and in heaven, the consciousness of this will for ever raise high the notes of gratitude for redeeming mercy. But pardon may and does remove the apprehension of penalty for sin ; or if by ἁμαρτιῶν we understand *sin, guilt,* simply, then, *to be made clean* (κεκαθαρμένους) from this, so as to have no consciousness of it, is so to be purified, as not to contract the stain of it.

Ver. 3. Ἀλλ' ἐν αὐταῖς . . . ἐνιαυτὸν, *nay rather, by these* [sacrifices] *yearly remembrance of sins is made.* Ἀλλὰ, *but rather, nay rather, quin, quinimo ;* or, (as I have rendered it in the version,) *on the contrary, but.* Αὐταῖς agrees with θυσίαις implied ; see in ver. 1. On the day of annual atonement, the sacrifices that were offered being of an expiatory nature, and being designed as propitiatory offerings, they were of course adapted to remind the Hebrews of the desert of sin, i. e. of the punishment or penalty due to it. As they continued to be offered *yearly*, so those who brought them must be reminded, through their whole lives, of new desert of punishment. The writer means, however, that a yearly remembrance of sin in a *spiritual* respect, not merely in a civil or ecclesiastical one, was made; for in this sense, the yearly atonement procured pardon. In the other, it did not; as he now proceeds to assert,

Ver. 4. 'Αδύνατον γὰρ ...... ἁμαρτίας, *it is, indeed, impossible that the blood of bulls and goats should remove the penalty due to sin.* 'Αφαιρεῖν ἁμαρτίας means, *to take away sin*, in the sense of *removing the penalty* or *consequences of sin*; for this is the subject of which the writer is now treating. That the author has reference to the consequences of sin in a future world, or to the punishment of it which God inflicts as the spiritual judge of men, is evident from the whole tenor of his discussion. One so profoundly versed as he was in all the Jewish ritual law, surely was not ignorant of the fact, that civil and ecclesiastical pardon for offences of various kinds, was every day procured by the blood of bulls and goats, and this, too, agreeably to Divine appointment.

Ver. 5. Nothing could be more directly in opposition to Jewish prejudices, respecting the importance and value of the Levitical sacrifices, than the assertion just made. Hence the writer deems it prudent to make his appeal to the Scriptures, for confirmation of what he had advanced. This he does by quoting a passage from Ps. xl., which he applies to the Messiah, and to the efficacy of the sin-offering made by him.

Διὸ εἰσερχόμενος εἰς τὸν κόσμον, λέγει, *wherefore, entering into the world, he* [Christ] *says;* i e. because the blood of goats and bullocks is *not* efficacious in procuring pardon for sin, Christ, when entering into the world, is represented by the Psalmist as saying, viz. in Psalm xl. 7, seq.

Θυσίαν καὶ προσφορὰν οὐκ ἐθέλησας, *in sacrifice and oblation thou hast no pleasure.* Θυσία means, *a sacrifice of some slain beast*, from θύω, *to kill*. So the corresponding Hebrew זֶבַח, from זָבַח, *mactare.* Προσφορὰ is *any thing offered* or *presented;* and here it means, other oblations than those of sacrifices, such as thank-offerings, libations, &c. The corresponding Hebrew מִנְחָה, *gift, present*, comes from the obsolete root כָּנָה, *to present*, Arabic کنی the same. Οὐκ ἐθέλησας, Hebrew לֹא חָפַצְתָּ, is capable of being translated, *thou hast not* required, or, *thou hast not desired, thou hast no pleasure in,* or *desire for.* The latter is, doubtless, the shade of meaning here. The sentiment is not, that God had not at all required sacrifices and oblations, for this he had done: but that they were, in a *comparative* sense, of little value; they were insufficient in themselves to accomplish the higher purposes of his spiritual law, and therefore he had no pleasure in them.

Σῶμα δὲ κατηρτίσω μοι, *but a body hast thou prepared for me.* A very difficult and much agitated expression. If we recur, in the first place, to the original Hebrew, we find the corresponding words there to be, אָזְנַיִם כָּרִיתָ־לִּי, *mine ears hast thou opened.* The verb כָּרִיתָ (from כָּרָה) means, primarily, *to dig, to hollow out,* e. g. a well, Gen. xxvi. 25; a pit, Ps. vii. 16; or pit-fall, Ps. lvii. 7; a sepulchre or grave, Gen. l. 5; 2 Chron. xvi. 14. The verb כָּרָה has also the meaning of *purchasing,* or *procuring,* e. g. water, Deut. ii. 6; particularly of procuring a supply of food and drink, 2 Kings, vi. 23; also of other things, e. g. a wife, Hosea iii. 2, where אֶכְּרֶהָ has a Daghesh euphonic in the כ. These are all the meanings of this word, which the Hebrew Scriptures present. In translating אָזְנַיִם כָּרִיתָ לִּי, then, we may render it either *mine ears hast thou opened,* which is only a small deflexion from the literal sense, (for *to dig* out a pit or well, is *to open* one;) or we may render it, *ears hast thou provided for me,* in which sense the LXX. seem plainly to have understood כָּרִיתָ, when they rendered it by κατηρτίσω. The former sense seems to be more analogical with the nature of the subject, and with the Hebrew idiom. The Hebrews speak of *opening the ears,* and *uncovering them,* in order to designate the idea of *prompt obedience,* of attentive listening to the commands of any one. E. g. Isa. l. 4, we have יָעִיר לִי אֹזֶן לִשְׁמֹעַ, *he excited my ear to hear;* and in ver. 5 is an equivalent expression, פָּתַח לִי אֹזֶן, *he opened mine ear,* which is explained in the corresponding parallelism, by וְאָנֹכִי לֹא מָרִיתִי, *and I was not refractory,* i. e. I was obedient. So גָּלָה אֹזֶן *to uncover, to disclose the ear,* means, *to communicate any thing,* or *reveal it to another;* e. g. 1 Sam. xx. 2. 12, 13; ch. xxii. 17. From such forms of expression, in Hebrew, with such a meaning, we may very naturally conclude that אָזְנַיִם כָּרִיתָ לִּי (in Ps. xl. 7,) means, *thou hast opened mine ears,* i. e. thou hast made me obedient, or, I am entirely devoted to thy service. And Ps. xl. 8, 9, which exhibits the consequence of having the ears opened, leads us almost unavoidably to make such a conclusion, respecting the meaning of the phrase in question.

If this view of the meaning be correct, then another interpretation, put upon the phrase by many critics, is not well founded. They render it, *mine ears hast thou bored through*. They suppose the expression to be figurative, and to be borrowed from the Hebrew usage of boring through, with an awl, the ear of a person who became the voluntary servant of another, as described in Exod. xxi. 6. Deut. xv. 17. *Mine ears hast thou bored through* would then mean, "I am, through life, thy voluntary servant," or, "I will be perpetually obedient to thee." This sense, it will be seen, agrees in general with that put upon the phrase by the other mode of explanation. But the source of explanation, here adopted, does not seem to be admissible. In Exod. xxi. 6, the verb *bore through* is רָצַע, (not כָּרָה, as in Ps. xl. 7;) and the instrument by which it is done, is named מַרְצֵעַ, *an awl*, a derivative of the verb רָצַע. So in Deut. xv. 17, the instrument named is the same מַרְצֵעַ, and the action of *boring through* is expressed by נָתַתָּה בְאָזְנוֹ, *thou shalt put it through his ear*, (not כָּרִיתָ.) That רָצַע and כָּרָה indicate very distinct actions, is sufficiently plain; for *to bore through* any thing, and *to dig* or *hollow out* a pit, grave, or well, are surely very different actions, indicated in Hebrew by verbs as different as the English *dig* and *bore through*. Moreover, in Exod. xxi. 6, and Deut. xv. 17, the singular אֹזֶן is used, and not as here אָזְנַיִם, *both ears*.

The original, then, in Ps. xl. 7. אָזְנַיִם כָּרִיתָ לִּי, means, *mine ears hast thou opened*, i. e. me hast thou made readily or attentively obedient; at least, this seems to be the meaning, if we make Isa. l. 4, 5, our exegetical guide. See EXCURSUS XX.

Ver. 6. Ὁλοκαυτώματα καὶ......εὐδόκησας, *in whole burnt-offerings and* [sacrifices] *for sin, thou hast no delight*. Ὁλοκαυτώματα means, *such offerings as were entirely consumed upon the altar;* so the corresponding Hebrew עֹלָה signifies. Περὶ ἁμαρτίας is an elliptical expression, answering to the Hebrew original חֲטָאָה, and which, completed, would be θυσίαι περὶ ἁμαρτίας, *sin-offerings*. Οὐκ εὐδόκησας, Hebrew לֹא שָׁאָלְתָּ, *requirest not, desirest not, demandest not, hast no pleasure in*.

Ver. 7. Τότε εἶπον, *therefore I said*, or, *then I said*. The first of these versions is approved by eminent critics. They suggest, that if τότε (Hebrew אָז) be referred to *time* merely, it seems very difficult to ascertain what is the precise meaning; for at what particular *time* was it, that God did not delight in whole burnt-offerings and sacrifices for sin? It may, however, be said, that the speaker here refers to the time when he s disclosing these views respecting sacrifices. Supposing this to be the case, τότε would mean *then*, i. e. immediately after this sentiment was declared; which would be very congruous with the context. If τότε be rendered *therefore*, the meaning will be, " because thou hadst no pleasure in sacrifices, *therefore* I said," &c. Strictly speaking, nowever, τότε is not *illative*. I prefer the other rendering.

'Ιδοὺ ἥκω .... Θέλημὰ σου, *Lo! I come, O God, to do thy will. (In the volume of the book it is written respecting me.)* 'Ιδοὺ ἥκω expresses the *readiness* of him who speaks, to obey the will of God.

'Εν κεφαλίδι βιβλίου is a much agitated expression. The Hebrew is simply בִּמְגִלַּת־סֵפֶר, *in the roll*, or *volume of the book*. But how does κεφαλίδι βιβλίου correspond to this? Κεφαλὶς denotes *the end* or *extremity* of any thing, as being *the head* or *summit* of it. The Hebrew סֵפֶר, βιβλίον, was a manuscript rolled upon a cylinder of light wood, at the extremity of which were *heads* or *knobs*, for the sake of convenience to those who used the manuscript. The *knob* or *head*, κεφαλὶς, is here taken as a *part*, which is descriptive or emblematic of the *whole*. Κεφαλὶς βιβλίου means, therefore, a βιβλίον or סֵפֶר, with a κεφαλὶς, i. e. a manuscript roll; which was the form of the Jewish sacred books, and is still retained in all their synagogues. It coincides, then, with regard to signification, very exactly with the Hebrew מְגִלַּת סֵפֶר, of which it is a translation.

But what volume of manuscript-roll is here meant? Plainly, the one which was already extant when the Psalmist was writing. If the Psalmist was David himself, (as the title of the Psalm seems to affirm,) the only parts of the Hebrew Scriptures then extant, and, of course, the only part to which he could refer, must have been the Pentateuch, and perhaps the book of Joshua. Beyond any reasonable doubt, then, the κεφαλὶς βιβλίου (מְגִלַּת סֵפֶר) was the Pentateuch.

But *what* is there written, and *how*, respecting the personage who speaks in the fortieth Psalm? Rosenmüller (on Ps. xl. 7.) translates the Hebrew כָּתוּב עָלַי (γέγραπται περὶ ἐμοῦ) by *prescriptum est mihi*, and appeals to 2 Kings, xxii. 13, for confirmation of this version. He compares, also, Gen. ii. 16. Ezra i. 2; where עַל is used after צִוָּה and פָּקַד, verbs of *commanding* or *enjoining*. Gesenius approves this version, but produces no other instances to confirm it, which are of the same kind. He appeals, indeed, to Esth. ix. 23, where אֶל is used after כָּתַב; and to Hos. viii. 12. 2 Kings, xvii. 37, and Prov. xxii. 20, where לְ is used after the same verb, in order to confirm this interpretation. But the three last cases plainly denote nothing more, than that the matter referred to was *written for the use of another,* or *addressed to him.* Such, too, is the case with the other example in Esth. ix. 23, as may be clearly seen by comparing Esth. ix. 20. With deference to the opinion of these very distinguished critics, I must still doubt, therefore, whether כָּתַב עַל means *præscribere alicui.* At most, there is only 2 Kings xxii. 13, which is apposite to establish this signification ; and even here the meaning in question is not *necessary ;* for הַכָּתוּב עָלֵינוּ may be rendered, with about equal significancy, *which was written in respect to us,* or *concerning us,* i. e. for our sake, or to regulate our duties. The LXX. then, who translated כָּתוּב עָלָי by γέγραπται περὶ ἐμοῦ, translated it agreeably to the usual idiom of the Hebrew. The apostle, in our text, has evidently recognized the correctness of this version. The difference in meaning, between *prescribed to me,* and *written concerning me,* is a considerable one in this case. The first version would represent the speaker as saying, " I come, O God, to do thy will, [i. e. my duty,] as I am commanded in the Scriptures to do." The second, " I come to offer my body, or myself, in place of the legal sacrifices ; for, in the Scriptures, [i. e. in the law of Moses,] this is written concerning me." Now, as to a choice of versions here, it will not be doubted, that the latter version accords with the reasoning and design of the apostle, or rather, that it is important to his purpose. The first version would not, indeed, contradict the design of the apostle ; for he might say, it is prescribed in the Scriptures, that the Messiah should do the will of God, i. e. make himself an offering for sin. Compare Luke xxiv. 25—27. 46. Acts xvii. 2, 3. 1 Pet. i. 11, 12. But I apprehend the meaning of the writer to be, that the *book of the law,* which prescribes sacrifices that were merely σκιαὶ or παραβολαὶ of the great atoning sacrifice by Christ, did itself teach, by the use of these, that something of a higher and better nature was to be looked for than Levitical rites. In a word, it pointed to the Messiah ; or, some of the contents of the *written* law had respect to him. So Michaëlis, Storr, and others. Still, γέγραπται περὶ ἐμοῦ may have respect to declarations in the Pentateuch, of a different and more direct nature. That there are such, Jesus himself affirms, John v. 46. So Paul, Acts xxvi. 22, 23. Gal. iii. 16, seq. Construed in either way, the amount of the phrase under consideration is, " In the law of Moses I am described as coming to do thy will," i. e. to offer my body as a sacrifice : compare ver. 10.

That the Hebrews, to whom the apostle addressed himself, would recognize such an affirmation, and feel the force of it, seems to be nearly certain, from the fact, that the writer without any hesitation addresses it to them, in order to produce conviction in their minds with respect to the point which he is labouring to establish. Certain it is, then, that both he and the Christian Hebrews to whom he wrote believed that the Jewish ritual had respect to the sacrifice of the Messiah, and that he was virtually revealed, in the law of Moses, as a suffering Saviour, making atonement for the sins of his people. Were this not so, then the argument in Heb. x. 5—10, would be destitute of any real foundation, and consequently of any force, as a proof of what the writer is labouring to establish.

'Ο Θεὸς, Heb. אֱלֹהַי, *O my God*. If the Messiah be considered as uttering this before his incarnation, and as *Logos*, then would it be an embarrassing circumstance to explain it, how in his simple *Divine* nature he could speak of " *my* God." But if considered as a prophetic anticipation of what he would say, during his incarnation, (and so it clearly seems to me the writer intends it should be considered) then ὁ Θεὸς, or ὁ Θεὸς μου, accords with the usage of the Saviour in addressing the Father, as disclosed in the Gospel; Matt. xxvii. 46, al.

Τὸ θέλημὰ σου. What this will is, see in ver. 10.

Ver. 8. Ἀνώτερον λέγων .... εὐδόκησας, *first, he says, " Sacrifice, and oblation, and whole burnt-offering, and* [offering] *for sin, thou desirest not, nor hast pleasure in them."* Ἀνώτερον, literally *above*, which is equivalent here, to *first*, or *in the first place*.

Ἅτινες κατὰ τὸν νόμον προσφέρονται *which are presented according to the law.* This is a parenthetic explanation, added by the writer, in order to show that the same legal sacrifices, in which the Hebrews were in danger of placing their confidence, were those which must be superseded by the death of Christ.

Ver. 9. Τότε εἴρηκεν .... τὸ θέλημὰ σου, *and then says, " Lo, I come to do thy will."* We might expect εἴπων here, instead of εἴρηκεν, for the *regular* construction of the sentence would seem to require it. But here is a sentence constructed in the Hebrew manner, which not unfrequently begins with a participle in the first clause, and then uses a verb in the second, when both stand in the same relation to the sequel of the sentence, see Heb. Gram. § 212. 2. It is evident here, that ἀνώτερον λέγων and τότε εἴρηκε both bear the same relation to ἀναιρεῖ, κ. τ. λ. the sense of which, I may add, is rendered quite obscure by the period which most editors of the Greek Testament have put before it.

Ἀναιρεῖ ... στήσῃ, *he abolishes the first,* viz. the sacrifices, &c.

that he may establish the second, viz. the doing of the will of God, or the offering of himself as a sacrifice for sin, ver. 10. That is, "doing the will of God," or obedience to him even unto death, or the offering up of his body, is represented by the Psalmist as a substitute for legal sacrifices, and as an arrangement which would supersede them.

It is quite plain, that ἀναιρεῖ, κ. τ. λ. is an inference drawn from the two declarations recited in the context immediately preceding ; for πρῶτον certainly refers to the legal sacrifices, and δεύτερον to the obedience of the Messiah. But the construction of the sentence (for clearly it is in fact but one sentence) is Hebraistic, as noted above, and not according to the rules of classical Greek ; and it affords a notable example, how far the style of our author is from the easy, rhetorical, flowing method, of which so much has been said by late critics ; and from that ἑλληνικότης, which even Origen ascribes to him.

Ver. 10. The writer proceeds to explain what is meant, in this case, by *doing the will of God,* and what is the efficacy of that obedience. Ἐν ᾧ θελήματι . . . ἐφάπαξ, *by which will expiation is made for us, by the offering of the body of Jesus Christ once for all.* Ἐν ᾧ θελήματι means, *by doing which will,* i. e. by whose obedience. Ἡγιασμένοι ἐσμὲν, *expiata sumus, conciliati sumus, purificati sumus,* literally, *we are consecrated,* viz. to God, which necessarily implies, *purified, atoned for;* see on ἁγιάζω under ch. ii. 11.

The latter part of the verse leaves no doubt, that the writer meant to refer the *obedience* in question, or *the doing of the will of God,* to " obedience unto death," to the voluntary sacrifice for sinners, which the Saviour offered upon the cross ; compare Phil. ii. 8.

The whole amount of the reasoning, in ver. 5—10, is this. " Ritual sacrifices for sin are not accepted by God, as sufficient to remove the penalty due to the moral turpitude of sin. But the obedience of the Messiah unto death, the offering of his body on the cross, is sufficient, and fully supersedes the other sacrifices."

If all this be true, it follows, of course, that what the apostle had affirmed in ver. 3, is true, viz. that it is impossible for the blood of slain beasts to remove the penal consequences of sin, when considered in the light of a *spiritual* offence, and as having respect to the tribunal of God.

Ἐφάπαξ, *once for all.* The idea conveyed by this, is carefully repeated again here, because it concerns a point, in respect to which the

Hebrews would be very prone to raise objections. "You affirm," they would naturally say, "that there is a resemblance between the sacrifice of Christ and the annual expiatory sacrifices by the high priest. But there is evidently a great dissimilitude; for the expiation made by the high priest was repeated *every year;* while Christ suffered *only once.*" The apostle meets this difficulty, by showing, from various considerations, that being *once* slain as an expiatory offering, was altogether sufficient to satisfy the demands of the case. Compare Heb. ix. 9—14. 25—28; x. 1—3; 10—14. Indeed, Christ, from the nature of the case, could die but once, ch. ix. 27, 28.

Ver. 11. Καὶ πᾶς μὲν ἱερεὺς .... θυσίας, *now every high priest stands performing daily service, and oftentimes presenting the same sacrifices.* Πᾶς ἱερεὺς, every, or any Levitical priest. Ἔστηκε, *stands,* denoting the attitude of those who are in waiting or attendance upon another, and keep the position of *standing,* both as a token of respect, and as a state prepared for ready service. It is only the perfect, pluperfect, aor. second active, and aor. first passive, of the verb ἵστημι, that have the intransitive meaning *to stand.* The other tenses are transitive, and mean, *to set, place, station,* &c. See Buttmann § 95, and Wahl's Lexicon, on the word; and compare, for a sense of the word like that above) Rev. vii. 9, 11; viii. 2.

Τὰς αὐτὰς ... θυσίας. The same daily sacrifices were repeated without intermission; see Numb. xxviii. 2—6.

Αἵτινες οὐδέποτε .... ἁμαρτίας, *which can never remove the penalty due to sin;* compare ver. 1—3. That ἁμαρτίας here means *penalty due to sin,* is plain; and that it may be properly so construed, no one will deny, who understands the full meaning of חַטָּאת, עָוֹן, and פֶּשַׁע.

Ver. 12. Οὗτος δὲ μίαν .... Θεοῦ, *but this* [priest] *having offered a sacrifice for sin of perpetual efficacy, sat down at the right hand of God.* In ver. 11, we have πᾶς ἱερεὺς, i. e. every priest of the common order, every Levitical priest; the antithesis is οὗτος, which refers to Christ, and which (if the ellipsis be supplied according to the grammatical construction of sentences) must mean οὗτος ἱερεὺς.

Εἰς τὸ διηνεκὲς means the same thing here as ἅπαξ in ch. ix. 26, 28; and ἐφάπαξ in ch. x. 10. I connect it with θυσίαν, and not (as Carpzoff) with ἐκάθισε. *A sacrifice for perpetuity,* is a sacrifice *once for all,* ἐφάπαξ, or, it is a sacrifice of perpetual efficacy, one that needs not to be repeated.

Ἐκάθισεν ἐν δεξιᾷ τοῦ Θεοῦ, see on Heb. i. 3. Ἐκάθισε here is opposed to ἕστηκε in the preceding verse. The latter denotes the attitude of a *servant*; the former, that of a *master* or *lord*.

Ver. 13. Τὸ λοιπὸν ἐκδεχόμενος .... ποδῶν αὐτοῦ, *thenceforth waiting until his enemies be made his footstool.* Τὸ λοιπὸν means, *for the rest,* viz. of the time; therefore the idea conveyed by λοιπὸν here is, *afterwards, thenceforth.* Ἐκδεχόμενος designates the attitude of *waiting* or *expecting.* The idea is, that the Messiah is seated on his throne, quietly expecting that his enemies will, in due time, be all subdued.

Οἱ ἐχθροὶ designates all those who are opposed to the character, doctrines, or reign of Christ. *To make them his footstool,* means thoroughly to subjugate and humble them; compare ch. ii. 8. 1 Cor. xv. 27, 28. See the origin of this phrase in the custom described in Josh. x. 24.

Ver. 14. Μιᾷ γὰρ προσφορᾷ .... τοὺς ἁγιαζομένους, *by one offering, then, he has for ever perfected those for whom expiation is made.* Μιᾷ προσφορᾷ, viz. the offering of his own body, ch. v. 10. Τετελείωκε, see on ch. ix. 9, and ch. x. 1. The meaning is, "He has for ever removed the penalty due to sin, and procured for those, who were exposed to it, that peace of conscience which the law could never give; compare ver. 1—4. Ἁγιαζομένους, see on ch. ii. 11; ix. 13; x. 10.

Ver. 15. Μαρτυρεῖ δὲ ἡμῖν ...... ἅγιον, *moreover, the Holy Spirit also testifies* [this] *to us.* Δὲ, *moreover,* a continuative of the discourse, here marking the transition to a new paragraph, in which appeal is made, by way of confirming what the writer had said. *The Holy Spirit* means, the Holy Spirit who speaks by the Scriptures; as the sequel shows, which is a quotation from the Scriptures. Ἡμῖν, *to us,* means, that the sentiment which the writer had been inculcating, the truths which he had declared, are confirmed by what the Holy Spirit says *to us,* i. e. to us and to all, in the Scriptures of truth.

Μετὰ γὰρ τὸ προειρηκέναι, *for after having first said,* viz. first in order, or in respect to time.

Ver. 16. Αὕτη ἡ διαθήκη, κ. τ. λ. See on ch. viii. 10, where is the same quotation. It is worthy of note, however, that even here, where the same passage is appealed to, the *words* are not all the same. In ch. viii. 10, we have τῷ οἴκῳ Ἰσραήλ; in ch. x. 16, αὐτούς; in the former, διδοὺς νόμους μου εἰς τὴν διάνοιαν αὐτῶν; in the latter, διδοὺς νόμους μου ἐπὶ καρδίας αὐτῶν; in the former, ἐπὶ καρδίας αὐτῶν ἐπιγράψω αὐτούς; in the latter, ἐπὶ τῶν διανοιῶν αὐτῶν ἐπιγράψω αὐτούς. *Non refert verbum, sed res ipsa.* The meaning of both is the same. *De minimis non curat lex.*

Ver. 17. Καὶ τῶν ἁμαρτιῶν, κ. τ. λ. (see on ch. viii. 12,) *then* [he says] *" Their sins,"* &c. Καὶ, *then,* here evidently marks the *apodosis,* or corresponding and concluding part of the sentiment, and stands as a kind of counterpart to πρὸ in μετὰ γὰρ τὸ προειρηκέναι, ver. 15; otherwise the sentence is an example of the *anacoluthon.* Compare ch. viii. 10—12, where the distance, at which τῶν ἁμαρτιῶν, κ. τ. λ. follows the first clause, justifies the translation here given to καὶ; a translation which, indeed, is frequently necessary in the writings of the New Testament, in order to render the connexion of the sense plain.

Ver. 18. The writer next proceeds to show for what purpose this quotation is here made, i. e. to express the sentiment, that under the new covenant, or gospel dispensation, absolute and *final* pardon is to be obtained. ῎Οπου δὲ ἄφεσις .... ἁμαρτίας, *now where there is remission of these, there is no more offering for sin.*

῎Αφεσις here means *spiritual pardon,* or *remission,* on the part of God, as judge and ruler of the world. Τούτων, i. e. τούτων ἁμαρτιῶν καὶ ἀνομιῶν, mentioned in the preceding verse. Οὐκέτι, i. e. offering is no more needed, is no more presented.

This circumttance makes a great difference between the new covenant and the old one. Under the latter, sacrifices must be perpetually repeated; and, after all, only *civil* and *ecclesiastical* pardon was to be obtained by them. Under the former, one sacrifice is sufficient, and avails to procure, for all nations, and all ages, spiritual pardon or remission of the penalty threatened to be inflicted in a future world. Well might the apostle call this *a new covenant.*

The writer having gone through a comparison of the new dispensation with the old, and having shown, that whether Christ be compared with angels, who were the mediators of the Mosaic law, or with Moses himself, or with the high-priest of the Hebrews, he holds a rank far above them; having also shown, that whether the temple in which he ministers be compared with that at Jerusalem, or the sacrifice which he offers be compared with those sacrifices presented by the Jewish priests, either as to its exalted nature, its spiritual efficacy in respect to procuring pardon for sin, or the duration and extent of its effects, the Mosaic institutions are nothing more than the *shadow,* of which the Christian ones are the *substance;* he now proceeds to the hortatory and admonitory part of his epistle. In this, various subjects are presented, which the circumstances of those whom he was addressing rendered it expedient to consider. All that was peculiarly attractive to the Jew, in the Mosaic ritual; all that served to allure him away from his adherence to Christianity, and expose him particularly to the danger of apostacy, the apostle has brought into view, in the preceding part of our epistle, with a design to show, that however attractive or important these things might in themselves be, there was something still more so in the Christian religion, something of which the Jewish religion offered only a shadow or adumbration. Nothing could be more apposite, then, to the case in hand, than the argument of the apostle, in the preceding part of this epistle.

The practical application which follows, is designed to excite those whom the writer addresses, to constancy and perseverance in their Christian profession, to dehort them from apostacy, and to warn them against its tremendous consequences. With his warnings, however, the apostle intermingles a great deal of encouragement and promise, in order to excite in them an earnest desire to obtain the rewards which would be bestowed on all who remained faithful to the end of their course.

He begins the hortatory part, by an appeal to the great encouragement which the present privileges of the Hebrew Christians afforded them, to persevere in their Christian profession.

Ver. 19. Ἔχοντες οὖν, ἀδελφοὶ .... Ἰησοῦ, *since then, brethren, ye have free access to the sanctuary, by the blood of Jesus*. Οὖν, *then, therefore*, or *since then*. Παῤῥησία, in its first acceptation, means *boldness of speech*, or, *the liberty of speaking without restraint*. But the word is also used to designate *freedom from restraint* generally considered; which is plainly the case here. Παῤῥησίαν εἰς τὴν εἴσοδον, literally, *freedom in respect to entrance*, i. e. free access, unrestrained liberty of approach. Ἁγίων, i. e. ἀληθινῶν, the heavenly sanctuary, or, the presence of God, compare ch. ix. 24. Ἐν τὸ αἵματι Ἰησοῦ denotes, the means by which this access is procured, agreeably to what has been shown in ch. vii.—x.

Ver. 20. Ἣν ἐνεκαίνισεν....ζῶσαν, *in a new and living way, which he has consecrated*. Ὁδὸν I take to be the accusative of *manner*, construed with κατὰ understood; or it may be considered as a repetition of εἴσοδον, and in apposition with it. Πρόσφατον means *recent*, and has reference to the way *lately* opened by the new covenant or gospel dispensation. The *way* is called *new*, however, not merely because of this, but also, because those who draw nigh to God in it, have liberty of access in their own persons, to the mercy-seat, and there obtain pardon, by means of a sacrifice altogether different from that which was offered for worshippers by the Jewish priests.

Ζῶσαν, i. q. ζωοποιοῦσαν, i. e. εἰς ζωὴν ἄγουσαν, *leading to life*, con-

ferring life or *happiness*. So ζάω is often used in the New Testament. But it may mean here, *perennial, perpetual*, (a frequent sense of ζάω in the Hebrew Greek ;) and this would be altogether congruous with the preceding context, which insists on the *perpetuity* of the sacrifice of Christ. On the whole, I prefer the former sense. So Theophylact, who assigns the following reason for the epithet ζῶσαν, viz. ὅτι ἡ πρώτη ὁδὸς θανατηφόρος ἦν, i. e. because that any one who entered the inner veil of the temple was punished with *death*. But, here, viz. under the gospel, it is the way to *life*.

Ἐνεκαίνισε, *consecrated, dedicated*. To consecrate a way, is to open it for access, to dedicate it to use. So Jesus opened the way of access for sinners to the eternal sanctuary, in which, if they go, they may obtain free access to God, and pardon for all their offences.

Διὰ τοῦ καταπετάσματος . . . σαρκὸς αὐτοῦ, *through the veil, that is, his flesh*. I translate these words literally, because I am not well satisfied that I understand their meaning. The opinions of all the commentators, it would be tedious, if not useless, to recite. The principal interpretation, in which the most distinguished of them unite, is, that, as the veil of the temple must be *removed* in order to enter the inner sanctuary, so the body of Jesus must be removed (by death,) that we might have liberty of access to the sanctuary above. An exegesis which, while the facts to which it alludes are true, still presents a comparison incongruous at first view, and seemingly requires a distorted imagination, to recognise it with any degree of satisfaction.

I could more easily acquiesce in the idea, that there is a kind of *paronomasia* here, in respect to the word διὰ. The form of it may be thus expressed. " As the most holy place in the earthly temple could be approached only *through* (διὰ) the veil, i. e. through the aperture which the veil covered; so the heavenly sanctuary is approached only *through* (διὰ implied) *the flesh*, or *body of Jesus*." In this last case, διὰ (if employed as here supposed) would mean, *by means of, because of, on account of*, viz. by means of the body of Jesus sacrificed for sin, see ver. 10. The paronomasia would consist in using διὰ, in the first case, in the sense of *through* with respect to *place ;* and, in the last case, in the sense of *through* with the signification of *by means of*. Instances could easily be accumulated, where the same word is employed in different senses, in the same sentence. E. g. " Let the *dead* (νεκροὺς) bury their *dead*," (νεκροὺς,) Luke ix. 60 ; where νεκροὺς, in the first case, means *morally dead ;* in the second, *physically dead*. So

2 Cor. v. 21, " He hath made him to be a *sin-offering*, (ἁμαρτίαν,) who knew no *sin*," (ἁμαρτίαν.) In like manner the apostle might say, " As the Jews had access to the inner sanctuary of the temple, διὰ καταπετάσματος, *through the veil*, so Christians have access to the heavenly sanctuary," διὰ σαρκὸς, i. e. διὰ προσφορᾶς σαρκὸς Ἰησοῦ, compare ver. 10. And, although I would not admit paronomasia, except in cases where there are urgent reasons for it, it seems to be more tolerable here, than the other method of interpretation suggested above, and is certainly in harmony with the *principles* of the *usus loquendi* of the sacred writers.

But, after all, the mind still seems to feel a want of definite satisfaction, in regard to either of the methods of interpretation above proposed. May I be allowed, in a difficulty of such a nature, to propose at least for consideration, a third method of interpreting the expression τῆς σαρκὸς αὐτοῦ?

In John i. 14, it is said, " The Word became flesh, σὰρξ; to which the writer adds, καὶ ἐσκήνωσεν ἐν ἡμῖν. In 1 Tim. iii. 16, we have Θεὸς ἐφανερώθη ἐν σαρκὶ, supposing the reading to be correct, (and the evidence seems to me quite in its favour, and so Dr. Knapp has judged.) In Rom. i. 4, a broad distinction is made between the nature of Christ κατὰ σαρκὰ and his nature κατὰ πνεῦμα ἁγιωσύνης; and in Rom. ix. 5, Christ is said to have descended from the Jewish fathers κατὰ σαρκὰ, while he is at the same time ὁ ἐπὶ πάντων Θεὸς. In Phil. ii. 6, Christ, who was ἐν μορφῇ Θεοῦ,—ἐκένωσεν ἑαυτὸν, μορφὴν δούλου λαβὼν. In all these, and in many more passages which might easily be added, the human nature or body of Christ seems to be regarded as a kind of temporary tabernacle, or *veil* of the Divine nature which dwelt in him. May not our author, in the verse under consideration, have had such an idea in his mind, when he wrote τοῦ καταπετάσματος, τοῦτ' ἔστι, τῆς σαρκὸς αὐτοῦ? The idea would seem to be this; " As the veil of the temple concealed the glory of Jehovah, in the holy of holies, from the view of men, so Christ's flesh or body screened or concealed the higher nature from our view, (which dwelt within this veil, as God did of old within the veil of the temple.)" If, on this account, the apostle calls Christ's flesh *a veil*, then we may easily make out the sense of the verse before us. It would stand thus: " As God dwells behind the veil, in his earthly temple; so God dwells behind the veil of Jesus' body, in his spiritual temple, i. e. he can be approached only through the medium of this, or by means of this." So the context which precedes; " free access to the sanctuary is ἐν αἵματι Ἰησοῦ." That the writer had in his mind a design to compare the veil of the Jewish temple, as the medium between the worshipper, and the visible presence of Jehovah, to the body of Christ (σὰρξ αὐτοῦ) as the medium of access to God, or what must interpose between God and him, and this specially in reference to Christ's sufferings and death, seems to be, on the whole, quite clear. But which of the ways now proposed will best present this general idea, or whether any of them are sufficiently grounded, to be fully admitted, is a question on which the reader must be left to judge for himself. My own apprehension, on the whole, is, that the occasion of calling Christ's flesh a *veil*, or of comparing it to a *veil*, lies in the views stated under this last explanation; while, at the same time, the actual comparison of the veil of the temple and of Christ's body, is confined to the single point, that *each is a medium of access to God*. If you say, " The comparison is, in most respects, without grounds of analogy, and the two things widely dissimilar;" my answer is, that there is as much congruity in it, as there is in the comparison between the *physical* death of Christ, in Rom. vi., and the *moral* death of believers to sin, to which the former is there compared. Indeed, between all objects of comparison, when God or Christ is one of these objects, there must of course be a dissimilarity that is exceedingly great in some repects, although there may be an analogy in some others.

In whatever light our passage is viewed, it will be conceded, that its language is far from being in that *easy flowing* style, which has been so often asserted of our epistle.

Ver. 21. Καὶ ἱερέα ......Θεοῦ, i. e. καὶ ἔχοντες ἱερέα, κ. τ. λ. the participle being *implied*, which was expressed at the beginning of ver. 19. Compare ch. iv. 14; v. 10; vii. 17. 20. 26; viii. 1. Ἱερέα μέγαν is the same as כֹּהֵן גָּדוֹל, *high priest*, a Hebraism. Ἐπὶ τὸν οἶκον τοῦ Θεοῦ, compare iii. 1—6. It designates here the *spiritual house* of God, i. e. Christians.

Ver. 22. Προσερχώμεθα, *let us draw nigh*, i. e. τῷ Θεῷ, which is implied. The manner of the expression is borrowed from approach to the most holy place in the temple, where God peculiarly dwelt.

Μετὰ ἀληθινῆς......πίστεως *with a true heart, in full confidence*. Ἀληθινῆς means, *sincere, faithful, true*, and designates sincerity of Christian profession, faithful attachment to Christianity, in opposition to an insincere or an apostatizing state of mind. Πληροφορία means, a *full measure*. Πληροφορίᾳ πίστεως means, *unwavering, undoubting faith*, a *fulness of faith*, which leaves no room for *apostacy* or scepticism. How exactly this exhortation was adapted to the state of the Hebrews, it is easy to perceive.

'Ερραντισμένοι . . . . πονηρᾶς, *being purified as to our hearts from a consciousness of evil*, literally, *being sprinkled as to our hearts*, &c. The expression is borrowed from the rites of the law, agreeably to which very many ceremonial purifications, as we have seen, were made by the sprinkling of blood either upon persons or utensils, This was *external*. But when the writer says here, ἐῤῥαντισμένοι τὰς καρδίας, he designates *spiritual*, *internal* purification, and shows that he is not speaking of any *external* rites. This *internal purification* is effected by the blood of Jesus, with which Christians are figuratively said to be sprinkled. But the construction, ἐῤῥαντισμένοι . . . ἀπὸ . . . shows that the participle ἐῤῥαντισμένοι is to be taken in the secondary or metaphorical sense, i. e. *purified from, cleansed from*.

Συνειδήσεως πονηρᾶς, *a consciousness of evil*, or, *a conscience oppressed with evil* or *sin*. Perhaps both senses are included; for both are characteristic of Christian sincerity and full faith, which is incompatible with a consciousness of evil designs, and which frees men from an oppressive sense of past evil, by inspiring them with the hopes of pardon.

Ver. 23. Καὶ λελουμένοι . . . καθαρῷ, *having also our bodies washed with pure water;* another expression, borrowed from the frequent washings prescribed by the Levitical law, for the sake of external purification. See Exod. xxix. 4; xl. 31, 32. Lev. xvi. 4; also ch. vi. xiv. xv. et alibi. It seems to me, that here is a plain allusion to the use of water in the initiatory rite of Christian baptism. This is altogether consonant with the method of our author, who is every where comparing Christian institutions with Jewish ones. So, in the case before us, he says, "The Jews were sprinkled with blood, in order that they might be purified so as to have access to God; Christians are internally sprinkled, i. e. purified by the blood of Jesus. The Jews were washed with water, in order to be ceremonially purified so as to come before God; Christians have been washed by the purifying water of baptism." So Ananias exhorts Saul to be baptized, and *wash away his sins*, Acts xxii. 16. In this latter case, and in that before us, the phrase is borrowed from the legal rite of washing for purification. In Heb. x. 23, no particular stress is to be laid on the mere external rite of *washing the body;* for the connexion shows, that the whole is designed to point out the *spiritual* qualifications of sincere Christians for access to God. But the manner of expression turns wholly upon a comparison with the Jewish rites.

Κατέχωμεν τὴν ὁμολογίαν . . . . ἐπαγγειλάμενος, *let us hold fast the hope which we profess; for faithful is he who has promised.* Ὁμολογίαν means, *profession* or *confession of the Christian religion*, which is here called ἐλπίδος, in reference to the hopes which it occasions or inspires. The idea is, "Let us firmly retain our profession of that religion which fills us with hope respecting future rewards and happiness."

Πιστὸς γὰρ ὁ ἐπαγγειλάμενος, i. e. let us firmly adhere to our religion, because God, the author of those promises which it holds forth, will certainly perform them; he is *faithful*, i. e. true to his word, and altogether worthy of confidence in respect to his promises.

Ver. 24. Καὶ κατανοῶμεν . . . . ἔργων, *let us also bear in mind one another, so as to excite to love and good works.* Κατανοῶμεν, consider attentively, have a regard to, think upon, or bear in mind. The writer means, that it is the duty of the Hebrews to cherish a mutual spirit of interest or concern for each other; and this, in such a way as would be the means of mutually exciting each other to more distinguished benevolence and good works. The perils to which they were exposed, rendered such advice very timely.

Ver. 25. Μὴ ἐγκαταλείποντες . . . . παρακαλοῦντες, *not forsaking the assembling of ourselves together, (as the custom of some is,) but admonishing* [one another.] Ἐγκαταλείποντες is in the same construction with κατανοῶμεν in ver. 24, and consequently agrees with ἡμεῖς understood. Ἑαυτῶν relates to the first person plural here; as it does elsewhere, e. g. Rom. viii. 23. 1 Cor. xi. 31. 2 Cor. i. 9; x. 12. 14. In like manner, παρακαλοῦντες requires ἀλλήλους to be mentally supplied after it; which is expressed after κατανοῶμεν. That παρακαλέω means *to admonish*, any common lexicon will show. The whole sentence is in the usual manner of the writer, who very frequently employs κοίνωσις in warnings and admonitions.

Καὶ τοσούτῳ μᾶλλον . . . ἡμέραν, *and this* [do] *so much the more, as ye see the day approaching.* That is, be more earnest and constant, in mutual admonition and efforts to excite each other to Christian diligence and perseverance, in proportion as the time draws near, when the judgments denounced against the Jewish nation, by the Saviour, will be executed. Ἡμέραν, *day*, is doubtless an elliptical expression for ἡμέραν κυρίου, יוֹם יְהֹוָה; a very common expression of the Hebrew writers, for a time of distress, of chastisement; a time in which God executes the threats which have been uttered by his prophets. Compare Psalm xxxvii. 13. 1 Sam. xxvi. 10. Ezek. xxi. 25; xiii. 5. Job xviii. 20; xxiv. 1. Amos v. 18. Jer. xxx. 7. Joel i. 15. Isa. ñ. 12. Rev. xvi. 14, et alibi. Now, as Christ had foretold the destruction of the Jewish temple and nation, (which could not be unknown to the Hebrew Christians,) what could be more natural than for the apostle to say—" Brethren, do every thing in your power to guard against apostacy. And this the more, because a return to Judaism would now be very ill-timed; the season is near, when the Jewish temple and state are to be destroyed." All this is surely very apposite to the case in hand.

But if we should suppose (with not a few of the recent commentators) that the writer here alludes to the day when Christ should reappear, and commence a visible reign on earth, (which they suppose the apostles to have believed in common with many individual Christians of early times,) then I could not perceive so much force in the apostle's argument. It would run thus : " Be very strenuous in using all means to guard against defection from Christianity to Judaism ; and this so much the more, because, in a little time, Christ will commence his visible reign on earth." I will not deny, that the hope of reward for perseverance in Christian virtue, to be bestowed under this new order of things, might be used as an argument to dissuade from apostacy ; but plainly, the argument as above stated is more cogent, and more to the writer's purpose. How it can be proved to any one, after he has read and well considered Paul's second epistle to the Thessalonians, that this apostle believed in the *immediate* and *visible* advent of Christ, is more than I am able to see.

For these reasons, I hesitate not to apply the phrase, ἡμέραν ἐγγίζουσαν, to the time in which the Jewish state and temple were to be brought to an end.

Ver. 26. Ἐκουσίως γὰρ .... Θυσία, *moreover, should we voluntarily make defection from our religion, after receiving the knowledge of the truth, no more sacrifice for sin remaineth.* Ἐκουσίως, I apprehend, is not to be construed here with *metaphysical* exactness, but has reference to the common and acknowledged distinction in the Jewish law between the sins of oversight or inadvertence, (שְׁגָגָה,) and those of presumption. For the first class, see Lev. iv. 2. 13. 22. 27. Numb. xv. 27—29; for the second, Numb. xv. 30, 31, where the presumptuous offender is described by the expression, אֲשֶׁר יַעֲשֶׂה בְּיָד רָמָה, *who acts with a high hand.* That this is the kind of offence to which the apostle alludes, is evident ; for he distinguishes it expressly from the *sin of oversight* or inadvertence,

(שְׁנֶגְדָּה,) by saying, that it is committed after being enlightened by the gospel. Ἑκουσίως means then, *deliberately, with forethought, with settled intention,* and not by merely sudden and violent impulse, or by oversight.

That ἁμαρτανόντων, in this case, refers to the sin of *apostacy,* is quite plain from the context and the nature of the case, as well as from the object which the writer has in view. Ἀληθείας, *true doctrine,* i. e. the gospel, Christian instruction.

Οὐκ ἔτι .... θυσία, i. e. if you make defection from Christianity, and renounce your hope and trust in the atoning sacrifice of Christ, no other is provided, or can be provided, for you. No other makes real atonement for sin; this being renounced, therefore, your case is desperate. The sacrifice under the new covenant is never, like the Jewish offerings, to be repeated. Apostacy from your present religion, then, is final perdition.

Ver. 27. Φοβερὰ δέ τις . . . ὑπεναντίους, *but a kind of fearful expectation of punishment, yea, of burning indignation* [awaits us,] *which will consume the adversaries.* Κρίσεως often means, *condemnation,* and sometimes the consequences of it, i. e. *punishment,* as here. Ζῆλος πυρὸς is equivalent to the Hebrew אֵשׁ קִנְאָה, Zeph. i. 18, which means *vehement displeasure, severe punishment, fierce flames.* Both ἐκδοχὴ and ζῆλος are nominatives to ἀπολείπεται understood. Ἐσθίειν, *consume, devour, destroy,* like the Hebrew אָכַל, Deut. xxxii. 22. So Homer, Il. xxxiii. 182, πάντας πῦρ ἐσθίει. Ὑπεναντίους designates all *who oppose themselves* to the character, claims, and kingdom of Christ.

Ver. 28. Ἀθετήσας τις . . . ἀποθνήσκει, *whosoever violated the law of Moses, suffered death without mercy, in case there were two or three witnesses.* The meaning is not, that *every* transgression of the Mosaic law was punishable with death, but that in all the cases which were of a capital nature, death without reprieve or pardon was inflicted, where sufficient testimony could be had. See Numb. xv. 30, 31.

Ἐπὶ δυσὶν ἢ τρισὶ μάρτυσιν, see Deut. xvii. 6; xix. 15. The Hebrew עַל פִּי is rendered ἐπὶ by the LXX.; and well, for ἐπὶ denotes, *in case that, on the condition that,* any thing is done, or happens. The meaning plainly is, " provided two or three witnesses testify to a crime worthy of death."

Ver. 29. Πόσῳ, δοκεῖτε . . . καταπατήσας, *of how much sorer punishment, think ye, shall he be counted worthy, who hath trodden under foot the Son of God?* Δοκεῖτε implies an appeal, on the part of the writer, to the conscience and judgment of his readers, who, it is taken for granted, will decide according to his own views in respect to the point in question. 'Ἀξιωθήσεται is applied either to desert of reward, or of punishment; just as we say, in English, "The man is worthy of reward," or "worthy of death."

Καταπατήσας signifies, *to treat with contempt, to spurn at, to treat with contumely.* Apostasy from the Christian religion implies this; and the peculiar criminality of it is here argued, from the superior claims which Christ has, on every account, to regard and fidelity.

Καὶ τὸ αἷμα .... ἡγιάσθη, *and hath regarded the blood of the covenant, by which he hath been consecrated, as unclean.* The mode of expression is taken from the Jewish rites. When the people of Israel renewed their covenant with God, Moses sprinkled them with blood, Heb. ix. 19, 20; Exod. xxiv. 8. This is called *the blood of the covenant.* So, under the new covenant, when Christians are consecrated to the service of Christ, and make an open profession of his religion, (as the people of Israel did of theirs,) they are figuratively said to be sprinkled or cleansed with the blood of Jesus: compare Heb. ix. 14; x. 22; xiii. 20. 1 Cor. xi. 25. 1 John i. 7. 1 Pet. i. 19. Rev. i. 5. And as they enter into covenant with Christ at such a time, pledging themselves to obedience and fidelity, so the blood with which they are said to be sprinkled, is called the *blood of the covenant.* The *sense* of the expression is plainly *spiritual,* but the *form* of it is borrowed from the Jewish ritual.

Κοινὸν ἡγησάμενος, regarding it as *common* or *unclean,* i e. as blood not consecrated, but like any common blood; therefore, as having no consecrating or cleansing power, as not having set apart those, who were sprinkled with it, for the peculiar service of God in the gospel, nor laid them under peculiar obligations to be devoted to the cause of Christ.

'Ἐν ᾧ ἡγιάσθη, *by which he has been consecrated,* i. e. to Christ, set apart for his service; another expression, borrowed from the Jewish rite of consecrating things to the service of God in the temple, by sprinkling them with blood. See on ch. ix. 22.

Καὶ τὸ πνεῦμα τῆς χάριτος ἐνυβρίσας, *and hath done despite to the Spirit of grace.* 'Ενυβρίσας designates the idea of *treating with spite,* or *malignity,* or *contempt;* and is nearly equivalent to καταπατήσας above. Πνεῦμα τῆς χάριτος means, either the *gracious Spirit,* or *the Spirit who bestows grace,* i. e. religious spiritual favours and gifts.

Compare 1 Cor xii. 4—11. But many commentators interpret πνεῦμα τῆς χάριτος as meaning simply *grace, or gospel blessings.* But this does not accord with the idiom of our epistle; comp. ch. vi. 4, where apostates are described as having been μετόχους πνεύματος ἁγίου. The question, however, whether πνεῦμα here means *agent* or *influence,* is not so easily settled; for the sense is good and apposite, interpreted in either way. I incline to adopt the former meaning.

Ver. 30. This awful warning the apostle follows up with a quotation from Scripture, descriptive of the tremendous nature of the punishment threatened. Οἴδαμεν γὰρ .... Κύριος, *surely we know him who hath said, To me belongeth punishment, I will inflict it.* The passage is quoted from Deut. xxxii. 35, לִי נָקָם וְשִׁלֵּם, *to me belongeth punishment and retribution.* Ἐκδίκησις, like the Hebrew נָקָם, literally means *vengeance, revenge.* But as this is evidently spoken of God only ἀνθρωποπάθως, the meaning is, that God does that which is analogous to what men do when they avenge themselves, i. e. he inflicts *punishment.* The idea is rendered intense, by the subsequent intimation, that the almighty, eternal God will inflict such punishment.

Λέγει Κύριος are words of the apostle, not of the Hebrew Scriptures, and are probably added here, to show the end of the quotation made, and to enforce the threatening; for in the same way, the Hebrew prophets often expressed themselves when they uttered comminations, adding to them נְאֻם יְהוָֹה, *thus saith Jehovah.*

Καὶ πάλιν . . . λαὸν αὐτοῦ, *and again, " The Lord will judge his people."* This quotation may be either from Deut. xxxii. 36, or Psalm cxxxv. 14, both places containing the same expression. If it be from the former place, then it is on account of the clauses that intervene between the first quotation and this, that the writer says, καὶ πάλιν. If from the latter, then the reason for subjoining καὶ πάλιν, is still more evident.

Κρινεῖ means here, as often, *to pass sentence of condemnation, to subject to punishment, to punish.* The corresponding στίχος, in the Hebrew, clearly shews that such is the sense of the original יָדִין; for it runs thus, both in Deut. xxxii. 36, and Ps. cxxxv. 14, וְעַל עֲבָדָיו יִתְנֶחָם, *and on his servants will he take vengeance.* Probably the expression in Psalm cxxxv. 14, is a mere quotation of Deut. xxxii. 36.

Ver. 31. Well may the writer add, φοβερὸν .... ζῶντος, *it is a fearful thing to fall into the hands of the living God.* Ἐμπεσεῖν εἰς τὰς χεῖρας, נָפַל בְּיַד, means, *to be at the disposal of his vindictive power,* i. e. **of** his punitive justice. It is a Hebraistic mode of expression, for the classic writers say, πεσεῖν ὑπὸ τὰς χεῖρας Ζῶντος probably here means, *ever-living*, as it commonly does elsewhere, when applied to God. This idea, moreover, augments the dreadful nature of the punishment; which is altogether apposite to the writer's design.

Ver. 32. The writer now proceeds to enforce his admonition against apostacy, by holding up to the Hebrews encouragement to persevere from the experience of former days, when they remained steadfast amid many trials and sufferings.

'Αναμιμνήσκεσθε δὲ τὰς πρότερον . . . παθημάτων, *call to mind, now, former days, in which, after ye were enlightened, ye endured a great contest with sufferings.* That is, " Faint not, be not discouraged, at the prospect of trials. Look back to the time when ye patiently endured severer trials than ye now suffer, and still persevered. Continue to do as you have already done."

'Ημέρας, like the Hebrew יָמִים, is often used for *time, season*, indefinitely. Φωτισθέντες refers to the illumination which they received, when the knowledge of the Christian religion was first imparted to them. What the ἄθλησις παθημάτων was, is explained in the verses which follow.

Ver. 33 Τοῦτο μὲν . . . θεατριζόμενοι, *partly because ye were made a public spectacle, both by reproaches and afflictions.* Τοῦτο μὲν . . . . τοῦτο δὲ correspond, and when thus related, bear the sense which is here given to them. 'Ονειδισμοῖς refers to the reproachful appellations and language, addressed to Christians by their persecutors; θλίψεσι, to the various sufferings inflicted upon them by the same. In this way, they were exposed to public view, θεατριζόμενοι, i. e. held up to the world as persons worthy of reproach and ill-treatment, or made a spectacle to the world as sufferers of these things, and thus loaded with disgrace.

Τοῦτο δὲ . . . γεννηθέντας, *and partly because ye were associated with those who were thus treated.* That is, a part of their ἄθλησις consisted in the sympathy which they were called to exercise towards others who were reproached and persecuted. 'Αναστρέφομαι I have rendered as having a passive sense here, viz. *who were thus treated;* and so many critics render it. Still it would be difficult to find a classical example of giving to this verb a *passive* sense, inasmuch as it is commonly used in the *middle* voice, and employed as a verb neuter deponent. I have translated *ad sensum*.

Ver. 34. Καὶ γὰρ . . . συνεπαθήσατε, *for ye did truly sympathize with those who were prisoners.* Instead of δεσμίοις, prisoners, some manuscripts and editions, with several of the fathers, have δεσμοῖς μου; which is the reading of the received text, and is preferred by Matthiæ, Michaëlis, Carpzoff, Noesselt, and others. But δεσμίοις has the weight of authority in its favour; it is sufficiently consonant with the context; and it is, perhaps, on the whole, more natural to suppose the writer to have spoken of "sympathizing with prisoners," than "with bonds." There is no important objection, however, to the latter expression; and if Paul be the writer of our epistle, δεσμοῖς μου gives a very emphatic meaning.

Καὶ τὴν ἁρπαγὴν . . . προσεδέξασθε, *and cheerfully endured the plundering of your own property.* This was a part of the θλίψεις which they had suffered in former times.

Γινώσκοντες ἔχειν . . . μένουσαν, *knowing that ye have for yourselves, in heaven, a possession of a better and more lasting nature.* Ἑαυτοῖς, dativus commodi. Ὕπαρξιν, *any thing possessed, estate, property.* Κρείττονα, *better* than earthly possessions, i. e. spiritual, heavenly, not material and earthly. Μένουσαν, *enduring, permanent,* not perishable, fleeting, temporary, like all earthly possessions.

Ver. 35. Μὴ ἀποβάλητε . . . μεγάλην, *cast not away then your confidence, which will obtain a great reward.* That is, act as you formerly did, and thus gain possession of the κρείττονα καὶ μένουσαν ὕπαρξιν.

Ver. 36. Ὑπομονῆς γὰρ . . . ἐπαγγελίαν, *ye have need, no doubt, of patience, in order that when ye have done the will of God, ye may receive the promised blessing.* Patience they needed, because of the many trials and temptations to which they were still exposed. Γὰρ, *surely, truly,* and, (which is equivalent,) *it is true, no doubt.* The writer means as much as to say, "I readily concede, that patience is requisite, in your present circumstances, in order that you should persevere." *To do the will of God,* here, is to obey the requirement, to believe and trust in Christ. Ἐπαγγελίαν *thing promised, reward proffered;* for the *promise itself* they had already received. Ἐπαγγελίαν here, and μισθαποδοσίαν in ver. 35, both refer to the ὕπαρξιν κρείττονα καὶ μένουσαν mentioned in ver. 34, and which is there represented as promised to them in case of obedience.

Ver. 37. Ἔτι γὰρ μικρὸν .... χρονιεῖ, *however, yet a very little while, and he who is coming will come, and will not delay.* That is, the Messiah (ὁ ἐρχόμενος) will speedily come, and, by destroying the Jewish power, put an end to the sufferings which your persecutors inflict upon you. Compare Matt. xxiv. Ὅσον ὅσον is an intensive form of expression, which is applied either to things great or small, like מְאֹד מְאֹד. It is employed in the like way, however, by the classic Greek authors. The whole phrase resembles that in Hab. ii. 3, כִּי בֹא יָבֹא לֹא יְאַחֵר, *for it*, (viz. the vision) *will surely come to pass, it will not delay*. If, however, it be an actual quotation, the application of the words is different from that of the original, and the writer designed merely to use the language to express his own ideas. In fact, the Septuagint version of the passage in Habakkuk, differs slightly from the words used by the apostle. It runs thus, ὅτι ἐρχόμενος ἥξει, καὶ οὐ μὴ χρονίσῃ. It seems quite probable, (considering the quotation from Hab. ii. 4, which follows,) that the apostle had the Hebrew expression above quoted in his mind. But it seems equally plain also, that he has made use of it only as the medium of expressing his own particular idea, and not as a designed quotation used according to the exact idea of the original. I have marked it as a quotation, however, in my version, because the *words* appear to be quoted.

Ver. 38. Ὁ δὲ δίκαιος ἐκ πίστεως ζήσεται, *the just, too, shall live by faith*. In Hab. ii. 4, it is : וְצַדִּיק בֶּאֱמוּנָתוֹ יִחְיֶה, which (if rendered according to the accents) will be, *The just by faith shall live*, i. e. the just man who has faith shall be preserved. The expression in our verse is capable of the same translation, and Dr. Knapp has pointed it so as to be construed this way. But I apprehend, after all, that this is not the meaning of either the Hebrew or Greek phrase. *Faith* is put here as the means of preservation, in opposition to *apostacy* or defection, in the other part of the verse, which is the means of destruction or disapprobation. "A persevering confidence or belief in Christ," (the writer means to say,) "will be the means of preservation, when the Lord shall come to execute his judgments upon the Jewish nation." So the LXX. understood the phrase, which they have rendered ὁ δὲ δίκαιος ἐκ πίστεώς μου ζήσεται; as if they read בֶּאֱמוּנָתִי instead of בֶּאֱמוּנָתוֹ. The meaning of ἐκ πίστεώς μου, must of course be, *by faith*, or *confidence in me*, which expresses the condition of being saved, rather than the peculiar character of the person who is saved. I understand the expression, in Hebrew and in our epistle, in a similar way. If the apostle meant to quote here, it is evident that he has not adhered to the text of the Septuagint.

Καὶ ἐὰν ὑποστείληται . . . ἐν αὐτῷ, *but if any one draw back, my soul hath no pleasure in him*. I hesitate whether to translate καὶ here as the disjunctive *but*, or to consider it as an elliptical expression for καὶ λέγει, i. e. καὶ λέγει ὁ Θεὸς vel ἡ γραφή. The latter resembles the usage of this epistle; see ch. i. 10 : ch. x. 17. The former sense, (καὶ, *but*,) is quite common in the New Testament writers. Either method of interpretation is consistent with idiom, and with the scope of the writer. I have, on the whole, preferred the *antithetic* form of the sentence, and rendered καὶ, *but*.

'Εὰν ὑποστείληται, κ. τ. λ. seems plainly to be a quotation from Hab. ii. 4. The apostle, however, has changed the order of the verse, quoting the latter part of it first, and the former part last. The original Hebrew runs thus, הִנֵּה עֻפְּלָה לֹא יָשְׁרָה נַפְשׁוֹ בּוֹ, *behold, the scornful, his mind shall not be happy*; or (as Gesenius translates) *See! he whose soul is unbelieving shall, on account of this, be unhappy*. The LXX. who have rendered the Hebrew in exact accordance with the words of our epistle, must have read נַפְשִׁי here, as they did בֶּאֱמוּנָתִי in the clause preceding. This is the more probable reading, but it cannot now be critically defended. We can only say, therefore, that the quotation of the apostle is, on general grounds, *ad sensum*, but not *ad literam*. The sentiment of the Hebrew is, that the scorner or unbeliever of that day should be unhappy; the sentiment of the apostle, that the unbeliever, i. e. the apostate Christian who renounces his religion, shall incur Divine disapprobation. The same *sentiment* lies at the foundation, in both cases. Such disapprobation the last clause expresses, οὐκ εὐδοκεῖ ἡ ψυχή μου ἐν αὐτῷ, where the negative form of expression is employed (as often in sacred and also classical writings) instead of the affirmative, i. e. " he shall be an object of my displeasure."

Ver. 39. 'Ημεῖς δὲ οὐκ . . . ἀπώλειαν, *but we are not of those who draw back to destruction*. 'Υποστολῆς is the abstract noun, *shrinking back, timidity, withdrawing*; and (as is common) the *abstract* is here put for the *concrete*, i. e. for persons who withdraw or shrink back, viz. from their Christian profession. The consequence of such withdrawing is ἀπώλεια ; see ver. 26, 27.

'Αλλὰ πίστεως, εἰς περιποίησιν ψυχῆς, *but of those who believe to the salvation of the soul*. Περιποίησιν means literally, *obtaining, acquiring, possessing*. But as it is here placed in antithesis to ἀπώλειαν, it plainly means, *saving* or *salvation*. Πίστεως, *faith, belief*, is an abstract noun used instead of a *concrete*, in the same manner as ὑποστολῆς above.

COMMENTARY ON HEB. XI. 1.   477

Having mentioned *faith,* or *belief, confidence,* as a peculiar and most important characteristic of those who persevere in the Christian religion, so as to secure their salvation; the writer now proceeds, with great force and propriety, to make his appeal to the Old Testament Scriptures, in order to show that *faith* or *confidence* in the Divine promises has, in all ages, been the means of perseverance in true religion, and consequently of salvation. In ch. x. 34—39, the apostle had exhorted his readers to persevere in waiting for the rewards of a future world, ὕπαρξιν ἐν οὐρανοῖς κρείττονα καὶ μένουσαν . . . μισθαποδοσίαν μεγάλην . . . τὴν ἐπαγγελίαν. He now goes on to show more fully, that the very nature of *faith,* and the character of *believers,* demand this. All *believers,* in every age, have done so: and the Hebrews ought to follow their example. See, on the nature of the faith brought to view in this chapter, p. 129. et seq.

CHAPTER XI.

Ver. 1. The general nature of *faith* is first explained. Ἔστι δὲ πίστις . . . βλεπομένων, *now faith is confidence in respect to things hoped for* [and] *convincing evidence of things not seen.* Ὑπόστασις, *confidence, confident expectation.* Others, with Chrysostom, " Faith gives reality or substance to things hoped for." The sense is good; but the shade of meaning is not exactly hit. If this were the idea of ὑπόστασις, we might expect the antithetic word to be ἀσωμάτων or ἀνύλων *incorporeal* or *immaterial things,* instead of ἐλπιζομένων. The use of ὑπόστασις, in the sense of *confidence, &c.* belongs to the later Greek, and is frequent in the New Testament. This sense is evidently appropriate here. The writer had just been exhorting his readers not to cast away their *confidence* or *boldness,* which would ensure a great reward, ch. x. 35. If any one should object to this exhortation, that the objects of reward were all *future* and *unseen;* the reply is, that " the very nature of belief or faith implies confidence in respect to objects of this nature. All the patriarchs and prophets possessed *such* faith." Ἐλπιζομένων means, *things future which are the objects of hope,* and not of present fruition. The things future are the rewards which have just been mentioned above.

Ἔλεγχος, *demonstration, proof, convincing evidence.* This last idea I have expressed in the translation. The meaning is, that faith in the Divine word and promises is equivalent to, or supplies the place of, proof or demonstration, in regard to the objects of the unseen world, i. e. it satisfies the mind respecting their reality and importance, as proof or demonstration is wont to do.

That the faith here brought to view, and adverted to through ch. xi. is not *specifically* what some theologians call *saving faith*, viz. faith in Christ in an appropriate and *limited* sense, is evident from the nature of the examples which are subjoined by the writer; e. g. ver. 3—5. 7, 8. 11, &c. In this chapter, faith is *belief* or *confidence* generally in Divine declarations, of whatever nature they may be; for it does not always have respect even to *promises*, or to the *future ;* e. g. ver. 3. Now, the same confidence in what God declares, respecting subjects of such a nature as are brought to view in this chapter, would lead the person who exercises it, to confidence in all which God might declare respecting the Messiah, and consequently to belief in Christ. It is then called by theologians, *saving faith.* But it should be remembered, that this is only a convenient *technical* phrase of modern theology; not one employed by the sacred writers. The true and essential nature of faith is, *confidence in God, belief in his declarations ;* and whether this be exercised by believing in the Scripture account of the creation of the world ; or, as Abel, Enoch, Noah, Abraham, Sarah, and others, exercised it, in respect to specific objects; or, by believing on the Messiah ; it is evidently *the same disposition of mind* in all cases. It is *confidence in God*. It is, therefore, with perfect propriety, that our author here excites the Hebrews to persevere in their Christian faith, by various examples which exhibit the power of faith in the ancient worthies, as a principle of pious and virtuous belief and action.

Ver. 2. Ἐν ταύτῃ γὰρ ...... πρεσβύτεροι, *on account of this, moreover, the ancients were commended.* Μαρτυρέω not unfrequently means, *to applaud, praise, commend, openly signify approbation.* See Wahl's Lexicon, No. 2. This is evidently the sense of the word here.

Ver. 3. Πίστει νοοῦμεν . . . γεγονέναι, *by faith we perceive that the worlds were formed by the word of God, so that the things which are seen were not made from those which appear.* Πίστει, *confidence*, in the account which the Scriptures (viz. Gen. i.) give of the creation. It is confidence in *God*, too ; for there could be no other witness of what was then done; at least, there could be none of the human race. Νοοῦμεν, *we perceive, apprehend, attain to an apprehension of.* Κατηρτίσθαι, *ordinare, disponere,* not simply to create or bring into being, but also *to fit, prepare, form,* i. e. reduce to form and order. Ἀιῶνας, *worlds,* i. e. the universe, עוֹלָמִים; see on Heb. i. 2. That αἰῶνας, in this case, cannot mean *seculum* or *ævum,* is sufficiently plain ; for in what tolerable sense could the writer say, that seculum or ævum *was not made* ἐκ φαινομένων, i. q. was made ἐκ μὴ φαινομένων, or, *out of nothing?* That the assertion in the negative form, is of the same import as if it were of the positive form, might be easily shown by appeal to a multitude of the like cases of λιτότης, in the Scriptures. "John confessed, and *denied not,* but confessed," John i. 20; where οὐκ ἠρνήσατο plainly conveys the same idea as ὡμολόγησε. As to classical usage, the commentary on the next clause may be consulted. In what sense, too, could *seculum* or *ævum* be called βλεπόμενα? This word means, *objects visible to the sight,* or *palpable to the senses,* i. e. material objects. Φαινόμενα means the same thing; there being no more difference between the two words, in Greek, as characterising objects, than there is between *seen* and *apparent* in English. The assertion of the writer then is, that "visible objects, i. e. the visible creation, did not spring from objects that were apparent," i. e. that the visible creation was not made out of matter before existing; which is the same as to say, that the world was created, brought into existence by the word of God simply, and was not a mere reducing to order materials that before existed; see on the succeeding clause of the verse, in the sequel. At all events, the idea of a *seculum* or *ævum* "being *framed* (κατηρτίσθαι) by the word of God," presents an incongruity of which no example can be found in the sacred writers. Equally incongruous would ἐποίησε τοὺς αἰῶνας, in ch. i. 2, be, if αἰὼν were to be rendered *seculum*. Ῥήματι Θεοῦ, *the command of God;* compare Gen. i. 3. 6. 9. 11. 14. 20. 24. 26. Ps. xxxiii. 6. 2 Pet. iii. 5.

Εἰς τὸ μὴ ἐκ φαινομένων τὰ βλεπόμενα γεγονέναι, a controverted, and somewhat difficult expression. If we construe it as the text now stands, the μὴ must naturally be joined with γεγονέναι, and it must be rendered, *so that things visible were not made of things which do appear.* Accordingly, Pierce insists on this construction, and maintains that the sense is, "So that things visible might appear not to have been made of things apparent, i. e. out of pre-existing matter."

Those who adopt a different construction of the passage maintain, that εἰς τὸ μὴ ἐκ φαινομένων may be translated, as if it were written εἰς τὸ ἐκ μὴ φαινομένων. That such a metathesis of the negative μὴ, or its equivalent οὐ οὐκ, is allowable, or at least that it is not uncommon, they endeavour to show by appealing to examples; e. g. 2 Macc. vii. 28, ὅτι οὐκ ἐξ ὄντων ἐποίησεν αὐτὰ ὁ Θεός, which plainly means, "God made them [heaven and earth] from things that do not exist, i. e. out of nothing. So Arrian, exp. de Alex. VII. 23, "These things I do not blame, unless that οὐκ ἐπὶ μεγάλοις μεγάλως διεσπουδάζετο, *he was too much occupied with small matters;* where οὐκ seems to qualify μεγάλοις. Plutarch, Pædagog, IX. 15, " I should say that promptitude of speaking on any matter is not to be altogether disapproved; nor, on the other hand, ταύτην οὐκ ἐπὶ ἀξίοις ἀσκεῖν, *is it to be practised in respect to trifling subjects.*" So the Greek οὐκ ἔφη εἶναι, *he said he would not come.* Arrian, Anab. I. 5, 6, οὐκ ἔφη χρῆναι ἐν λόγῳ τίθεσθαι Αὐταριάτας *he said that the Autariatae were not to be put into the account.* Polyb. p. 1331, τοὺς μὴ φάσκοντας ἀπολύειν, *saying that they were not to be absolved.* If the examples where φημὶ is used be abstracted from the others, there are still a sufficient number, they aver, to show that a metathesis of the negative particle μὴ is not without parallels.

Chrysostom also transposed μὴ here, and found no difficulty in it. He paraphrases it thus, ἐξ οὐκ ὄντων τὰ ὄντα ἐποίησεν ὁ Θεός· ἐκ τῶν μὴ φαινομένων, τὰ φαινόμενα· ἐκ τῶν μὴ ὑφεστώτων τὰ ὑφεστῶτα. So the Vulgate, Erasmus, Luther, Wolfius, and most of the later interpreters.

That the metathesis of μὴ, in this case, so as to construe it in connexion with φαινομένων, may be admissible, there can, indeed, be but little doubt. Yet it is, after all, unnecessary; for the phrase plainly has the same meaning, when translated agreeably to its present arrangement, if the nature of such a λιτότης be well understood. There is no need of understanding the examples cited from the classics in a different way. And, indeed, take them which way we will, (either by way of metathesis in respect to the οὐκ or μὴ, or of joining the negative with the verb or participle that follows,) the sense, all must admit, is plain, and is substantially one and the same. These examples, it must also be admitted, cast sufficient light upon the sense of the passage, Heb. xi. 3, so as to require no hesitation about admitting a meaning so well supported by parallel examples, and which, indeed, the context seems to demand.

We may also compare phraseology of a like nature, to be found in other parts of Paul's writings. In Rom. iv. 17, he says, " God restores the dead to life, and calls τὰ μὴ ὄντα ὡς ὄντα," i. e. summons [to fulfil his own purposes] things that do not exist, as though they did exist. In like manner, Philo, in Lib. de creat. mundi, p. 728, says, τὰ γὰρ μὴ ὄντα ἐκάλησεν ὁ Θεὸς εἰς τὸ εἶναι, *things which existed not, God called into existence.* That μὴ φαινομένων is equivalent to μὴ ὄντων, needs not to be formally proved. So in Hebrew, נִמְצָא *quod invenitur,* is a customary expression for *ens,* or *existens;* and לֹא נִמְצָא, for *res non existens, nihilum.*

On the whole, then, we must regard the phrase in question as equivalent to the expression in our language, "The visible creation was formed from nothing," i. e. it came into existence by the command of God, and was not formed out of any pre-existing materials. *Deus ex nihilo mundum fecit*, conveys the same idea. Such a phrase does not mean, that *nothing* was the *material* out of which the world was constructed, for there would be no sense in this; but it merely denies that any such *material* existed. This entirely agrees with the preceding clause of the text, which asserts that the command of God brought the universe into existence; and this is altogether confirmed by Gen. i. Here Moses represents, in ver. 1, the heavens and earth as first brought into existence by Divine power, and afterwards as *formed* and *arranged* into their present order; compare Gen. i. 1, with Gen. i. 2, and the sequel of the chapter. In fact, if the *manner* of assertion in our text be strictly scanned, it will be found to be more exact and philosophical than the Latin, *ex nihilo Deus mundum fecit*, or the English, *God made the world out of nothing*. Each of these phrases presents the *seeming* incongruity of asserting, that nothing was the *material* out of which the world was made. But our author is more strictly conformed to philosophical propriety, when he says, "Things visible were not made out of things that are visible," i. e. the visible creation was brought into existence by the word or command of God simply, and was not formed or fitted up out of any pre-existing materials. Exactly so do we find the assertion in 2 Macc. vii. 28, οὐκ ἐξ ὄντων ἐποίησεν αὐτὰ ὁ Θεὸς, *God did not make them* [heaven and earth] *out of things existing*, i. e. he strictly created them.

Well may it be suggested, that faith in the *divine* word was requisite to believe this; inasmuch as Thales, Plato, Aristotle, and other eminent philosophers, who followed not the *divine* word, indulged in speculations about the creation of the world, which were either very visionary, or quite different from the view which Moses has given.

Ver. 4. Πίστει πλείονα .... τῷ Θεῷ, *by faith Abel offered to God a better sacrifice than Cain*. Πλείονα, better, more excellent; so frequently, e. g. Matt. vi. 25. Luke xii. 23. Matt. xii. 41, 45. Mark xii. 33. Luke xi. 31. Heb. iii. 3. Rev. ii. 19.

On what account the sacrifice of Abel was more acceptable, commentators have speculated much, and assigned a great variety of causes. But it may be asked, Does not our text contain a solution of this

482   COMMENTARY ON HEB. XI. 5.

question? Abel made his offering *in faith;* the implication is, that Cain did not.

Δί ἧς ἐμαρτυρήθη . . . Θεοῦ, *on account of which* [faith,] *he was declared to be righteous, God himself commending his oblations.* How this was done, is not said in Gen. iv. 4. But most probably it was by fire sent from heaven, which consumed the sacrifice; compare Gen. xv. 17. Lev. ix. 24. Judg. vi. 21. 1 Chron. xxi. 26; ch. xxvii. 1. 1 Kings xviii. 38. The appellation δίκαιος is given to Abel, in Matt. xxiii. 35. 1 John, iii. 12,

Καὶ δι αὐτῆς ἀποθανὼν ἔτι λαλεῖ, *and by it, though dead, he continues to speak.* Δι αὐτῆς, viz. by his faith. Λαλεῖ and λαλεῖται are both supported by good authorities. The latter is preferred by Grotius, Hammond, Schmidt, Valkenaer, Michaëlis, Storr, Rosenmüller, Bengel, Griesbach, Schulz, &c.; the former by Wetstein, Matthiæ, Heinrichs, Knapp, &c. and has the majority of manuscripts, versions, and editions, in its favour. Where the balance of authority is, on the whole, nearly equal, I cannot well hesitate to prefer λαλεῖ to λαλεῖται. The sense of the latter would be equivalent to μαρτυρεῖται, sc. *laudatur, is commended.* But this idea has been twice suggested before in the same verse, by μαρτυρεῖται and μαρτυροῦντος . . . Θεοῦ. It is hardly probable that it would be a third time repeated. But λαλεῖ, I apprehend, has reference to Gen. iv. 10, where the " voice of Abel's blood is said to cry to God from the ground." In Heb. xii. 14, also, our author represents the blood of Christ and of Abel as *speaking,* λαλοῦντι. The *form* of expression only, in our verse, seems to be borrowed from the thought in Gen. iv. 10; for here it is the *faith* of Abel which makes him speak after his death; viz. he speaks by his faith, to those who should come after him, exhorting and encouraging them to follow his example. In other words, his example of faith affords admonition and instruction to succeeding ages.

Ver. 5. Πίστει Ἐνὼχ . . . . ὁ Θεὸς, *by faith Enoch was translated, that he might not see death; and he was no more found, because God had translated him.* Τοῦ μὴ ἰδεῖν is equivalent here to εἰς τὸ μὴ ἰδεῖν, or διὰ τὸ μὴ ἰδεῖν. The Hebrew has לָקַח אֹתוֹ אֱלֹהִים, *God took him,* where our author uses μετέθηκε. The original, in Gen. v. 24, says nothing respecting the point, whether Enoch was translated alive, or after death. Καὶ οὐχ εὑρίσκετο is the Septuagint version of the Hebrew אֵינֶנּוּ, *he was not,* sc. he was no more among men. The idea, in the

Hebrew and Greek, is for substance the same; for οὐχ εὑρίσκετο means, *he was no more to be met with, he was no longer extant* (לֹא נִמְצָא) *among men.* But all the Targumists, viz. Onkelos, Jonathan, and the author of the Jerusalem Targum, understand Enoch to have been translated without dying. So the Comment. Bereschith Rabba, parasch. 25. f. 28. So, probably, the son of Sirach, ch. xlix. 14. I may add, that this is a very natural deduction from the brief notice of Enoch's translation in Gen. v. 24. *Early* death is commonly represented in the Old Testament as the punishment of sin; and that the wicked should not "live out half their days," was the persuasion of most good men in ancient times. If, then, Enoch died before translation, how could his removal to another world have been regarded as an evidence of his extraordinary piety? The texts to which Dindorf has appealed, in his notes added to the commentary of Ernesti, are very far from supporting the position, that the ancient Jews regarded premature death as a testimony of Heaven in favour of him who was the subject of it. Nor is there any need of Rosenmüller's concession here, viz. that the apostle, in his account of Enoch's removal, has accommodated himself to the Jewish traditionary opinions. It may indeed be, that a tradition existed among the Jews, that Enoch "did not see death." But that this was founded in *fact*, seems to be plainly deducible from the manner of the narration in Hebrew, and the state of opinion in ancient times respecting *early* death.

Πρὸ γὰρ τῆς .... τῷ Θεῷ, *he is commended, also, as having pleased God before his translation.* The Hebrew says, וַיִּתְהַלֵּךְ חֲנוֹךְ אֶת־הָאֱלֹהִים, *and Enoch walked with God,* which denotes a state of communion and friendship with God, and implies, of course, a complacency in the Divine mind with respect to him. The apostle, therefore, appeals to the *sense* of the Scriptures in this case, and not to the *words*. Nor does he mean to say, that the testimony respecting Enoch's pleasing God was given before his translation; but that testimony given, viz. in the Divine word, respects his having pleased God before his translation. Εὐαρεστέω governs the dative.

Ver. 6. The writer now suggests the grounds on which he builds the conclusion, that Enoch was translated on account of his *faith;* viz. χωρὶς δὲ πίστεως ...... εὐαρεστῆσαι, *but without faith it is impossible to please* [him.] The truth of this he rests upon his own declaration, and the common opinion on this subject, which he trusted that all his readers entertained.

Πιστεῦσαι γὰρ δεῖ ...... γίνεται, *for he who cometh to God must believe that he exists, and that he will reward those who seek him.* Προσερχόμενον τῷ Θεῷ designates *him who worships God, Dei cultorem ;* see ch. vii. 15. The phraseology is probably derived from going up to the temple to worship, in the sanctuary of which God dwelt by his peculiar presence. Some have understood the phrase as referring to an approach to God in the invisible world, in heaven ; but the idea here is like that expressed by the Hebrew phrase, *going to God, returning to him, &c.* which usually denote, " approach, in the present world, to his spiritual presence."

Τοῖς ἐκζητοῦσιν αὐτὸν, compare the Hebrew, דָּרַשׁ בִּקֵּשׁ אֱלֹהִים, which are employed to designate the worship and prayers of those who are piously devoted to the service of God.

The two fundamental truths of all that can properly be called religion, are here adverted to. The first is, a belief that God exists ; the second, that he is the moral governor of the universe, i. e. that he rewards those who are pious, and, consequently, punishes those who are not so. He who denies this, denies all that sanctions religion, and makes it binding upon the consciences of men.

Ver. 7. Πίστει ...... οἴκου αὐτοῦ, *by faith Noah, being divinely admonished respecting the future, with reverence prepared an ark for the safety of his household.* Χρηματισθεὶς, compare ch. viii. 5, and Gen. vi. 13, 14 ; ch. vii. 1—5. Μηδέπω βλεπομένων, i. e. the future flood, no signs of which were as yet visible. Εὐλαβηθεὶς may be taken either in the sense of *fearing,* viz. the destruction which was coming ; or it may be understood of the *reverence* which he paid to the Divine admonition. I have translated it as bearing the latter sense, since this makes most directly for the apostle's object, which is to exhibit the faith which Noah exercised with regard to the Divine warning.

Εἰς σωτηρίαν, *for the saving,* or *safety.* It is often applied to temporal security or deliverance, like the Hebrew יְשׁוּעָה.

Δἰ ἧς κατέκρινε .... κληρονόμος, *by which* [faith] *he condemned the world, and obtained the justification which is by faith.* Ἧς I refer to πίστεως, as do Sykes, Heinrichs, Dindorf, and others. Κόσμον means *wicked men, men of a mere worldly spirit;* as often, in the New Testament. Noah *condemned* these, by an example of faith in the Divine warnings, while the world around him remained impenitent and unbelieving. In other words, his conduct condemned theirs.

Ἐγένετο κληρονόμος, i. q. ἐκληρονόμησε, i. e. *obtained, acquired, became possessor of.* So Abraham is, in like manner, said to be justified by *faith* or *belief,* in Rom. ch. iv., viz. belief in the promise of God respecting a future seed. On account of Noah's *faith,* he was counted צדיק, δίκαιος, (compare ver. 4, above,) or, he was regarded, treated, as δίκαιος.

From this verse, then, we may conclude, that faith may be of a justifying nature, i. e. such as is connected with the justification or pardon of the individual who exercises it, without being specifically directed to Christ as its object; for here, the object of Noah's faith was, the Divine admonitions and comminations in regard to the flood. This only serves to show, that faith, in its *generic* nature, has been the same in every age; and that it is, essentially, *a practical belief in Divine declarations.*

Ver. 8. Πίστει καλούμενος.... κληρονομίαν, *by faith, Abraham obeyed, when called to go forth unto the place which he was to receive for a possession.* See Gen. xii. 1—4. Καλούμενος, *summoned, invited, bid.* Ἐξελθεῖν, viz. from his own country and kindred, Gen. xii. 1. Τόπον means *the land of Canaan, Palestine,* the future possession of which was promised to him. His *faith,* in this case, was manifested by believing in this promise.

Καὶ ἐξῆλθε .... ἔρχεται, *yea, he went forth, not knowing whither he was going.* Καὶ ἐξῆλθε adds intensity to the preceding ὑπήκουσε; and I have translated it accordingly. The meaning is, "he even went out, ignorant of the place to which he was going;" which serves to give a higher idea of the strength of Abraham's faith, than if we should suppose him to be well informed respecting the land of Canaan, before he went to it.

Ver. 9. Πίστει παρῴκησεν .... ἀλλοτρίαν, *by faith he sojourned in the land of promise, while it belonged to strangers.* Πίστει, *by faith* he did this, i. e. by confidence in the promises which God had made respecting the future possession of this land, and respecting his offspring, he was moved to sojourn in Canaan, while it belonged to foreigners. Ὡς, *while, when,* as often; see Wahl. Ἀλλοτρίαν means, *that which belongs to another, quod alieni est, non sui.*

Ἐν σκηναῖς κατοικήσας, ... αὐτῆς, *dwelling in tents, with Isaac and Jacob, who were likewise heirs of the same promise.* That is, the promise was made to Abraham and his seed. What was not fulfilled in him, was to have its accomplishment in them. Hence, συγκληρονόμων, *fellow-heirs, joint-possessors,* viz. with Abraham; the same promise being made to them as to him, respecting the land of Canaan, and their future posterity.

Ver. 10. Ἐξεδέχετο γὰρ....Θεὸς, *for he expected a city which hath foundations, whose builder and maker is God.* Θεμελίους ἔχουσαν, *firmly built, well founded.* The plural, Θεμελίους, augments the idea of firmness of construction. Δημιουργὸς means, originally, *one who labours for the public good*, from δῆμος *publicus, ad populum pertinens*, and ἔργον *opus.* Hence, secondarily, it is transferred to designate a *labourer* or *artificer* of any kind. It is often applied by the heathen writers to designate the Divinity; and by Philo, Josephus, and the Christian fathers, it is employed as an epithet of the true God. Here, however, it is used as nearly a synonyme of τεχνίτης; the latter conveying the idea of a *builder skilled in the rules of his art*, but δημιουργὸς meaning, more simply, *maker, builder, fabricator.*

The meaning of the whole verse most evidently is, that Abraham looked for a permanent abode in the heavenly country, i. e. his hopes and expectations were placed upon the world to come. It was faith in this, which was ἔλεγχος οὐ βλεπομένων, and which moved him to obey the commands of God, and to do and suffer whatever he required. The fact, then, that saints under the Old Testament were moved, in their conduct, by considerations that had respect to the invisible world, or an immortal state of existence, is plainly implied here, by the reasoning of the apostle. See ver. 14. 16.

Ver. 11. Πίστει καὶ αὐτή . . . ἔλαβε, *by faith, also, Sarah herself received the power of conception.* Πίστει, *by faith;* how, or when? For when God announced to Abraham, that he should have a son by Sarah (Gen. xviii. 10,) she seems to have been in a state of unbelief, Gen. xviii. 12. But although it is true that Sarah laughed on that occasion, and it must be admitted that this was occasioned partly by her incredulity, as Gen. xviii. 13—15 shows; yet the same thing is affirmed of Abraham, Gen. xvii. 17. The truth is, the first annunciation that a child would spring from them, occasioned, both in his and Sarah's mind, a feeling of incongruity, of impossibility that the course of nature should be so reversed. Subsequent consideration brought both to a full belief in the reality of the promised future blessing. The history of this is not expressly given in Genesis, with respect to Sarah, but it is implied.

Καὶ αὐτὴ Σάῤῥα, *Sarah herself also.* Καὶ αὐτὴ, in this case, refers particularly to the fact that Sarah was barren, Gen. xvi. 1, and that she was far advanced in old age, Gen. xviii. 11. The meaning is, that faith gave even to Sarah, unpromising as her condition was in respect to offspring, the power of conception, i. e. by faith she obtained this blessing. Εἰς καταβολὴν σπέρματος, words tortured to the disgust of every delicate reader, by some of the critics. Even Wahl says, " she received strength εἰς τὸ δέχεσθαι σπέρμα καταβεβλημένον (i. e. by Abraham,) εἰς τὴν μήτραν." Did this need any *supernatural* strength? I construe the phrase very differently. Καταβολὴ means, *foundation, commencement, beginning.* Now, what is the foundation, or commencement, σπέρματος, of offspring or progeny? Conception. The true idea of the phrase, then, appears to be fully given by the version above. In this view of the phrase, I observe, Dr. Schulz concurs, rendering δύναμιν εἰς καταβολὴν σπέρματος, by das Vermögen zur Empfängniss, *the power of conception.*

Καὶ παρὰ καιρὸν . . . ἐπαγγειλάμενον, *and this beyond the usual time of life; inasmuch as she regarded Him as faithful, who had thus promised.* Καὶ παρὰ καιρὸν, see Gen. xviii. 11. Ἐπεὶ πιστὸν, κ. τ. λ. which shews that the apostle considered it as quite certain that Sarah, like her husband, did come to full confidence in the Divine promise.

Ver. 12. Διὸ καὶ ἀφ' ἑνὸς, . . . πλήθει, *wherefore, even from one who was dead too, as to these things, there sprung* [a seed] *like the stars of heaven for multitude.* Διὸ, on account of which faith, viz. of Sarah, or, perhaps, of Abraham and Sarah. Καὶ ἀφ' ἑνὸς, *even from a single individual,* is a designed antithesis to the *multitude* who are afterwards mentioned. Consequently it heightens the description. Καὶ ταῦτα νενεκρωμένου means *incapable* (according to the ordinary laws of nature) *of procreation ;* καὶ . . . . . . νενεκρωμένου, i. e. not only *one individual,* but *one dead also.* See the same description, in Rom. iv. 19. Ταῦτα is governed by κατὰ understood. Καθὼς τὰ ἄστρα, κ. τ. λ. that is, a very great number; compare Gen. xv. 5; xxii. 17.

Καὶ ὡς ἡ ἄμμος . . . . . . ἀναρίθμητος, *and like the sand upon the shore of the sea, which cannot be numbered,* i. e. an exceedingly great multitude. Χεῖλος θαλάσσης, literally, *lip of the sea,* which means the *shore.* So the word is used by profane Greek writers also ; as *labium* is by the Latin ones. So the Hebrew שָׂפָה, Gen. xxii. 17, which compare.

Ver. 13. Κατὰ πίστιν . . . . . . ἐπαγγελίας, *these all died in faith, not having received the blessings promised.* Οὗτοι πάντες—who? Abraham, Isaac, Jacob, and Sarah, mentioned in ver. 8—12 ; for οὗτοι cannot well be here extended to all who are mentioned in the preceding part of the chapter, because the "promised blessings" were those which were assured to the Hebrew patriarchs. Ἐπαγγελίας, not *promises*, (for these they had received,) but *blessings promised*, according to the idiom of this epistle. What were these blessings, *heavenly* or *earthly* ? The sequel will answer this question.

Ἀλλὰ πόρρωθεν ...... γῆς, *but seeing them afar off, and joyfully anticipating them, they openly professed themselves to be strangers and sojourners on the earth.* The application of this whole verse to the expectation of the future possession of Canaan, and of a numerous progeny, would be admissible, were it not for the sequel, (ver. 14—16,) which plainly forbids such an application. In addition to the faith of Abraham, and other patriarchs, in the promises of God, which had respect to temporal blessings, I understand the apostle as here asserting that those ancient worthies also exercised confidence in God's word, respecting the blessings of the invisible world ; i. e. theirs was ὑπόστασις ἐλπιζομένων ...... οὐ βλεπομένων. Those things which are invisible to the corporeal eye, they saw with the eye of faith, and seeing, *hailed them with joy*, (ἀσπασάμενοι,) *welcomed them, greeted them,* or *anticipated them with gladness,* as we *joyfully greet* or *anticipate* the approach of a beloved friend, or of some distinguished favour. And, looking forward to them as their chief source of happiness, *they openly declared themselves to be only strangers and sojourners in the present world.* That γῆς, by itself, might refer to the *land of Canaan*, is plain enough ; but that it does so refer here, is rendered quite improbable by the sequel. The idea is plainly more general. Παρεπίδημος means, *a temporary resident among any people,* i. e. a sojourner.

Ver. 14. Οἱ γὰρ τοιαῦτα ...... ἐπιζητοῦσι, *now they, who thus profess, show that they are yet seeking for a country*. Ταῦτα λέγοντες, viz. *saying* or *professing* that they were strangers and sojourners in the earth. Πατρίδα, *a fixed or permanent place of residence,* i. q. πόλιν μένουσαν, ch. xiii. 14, or πόλιν θεμελίους ἔχουσαν in ver. 10, above. That this πατρὶς was not of an *earthly* nature, the writer proceeds to show.

Ver. 15. Καὶ εἰ μὲν ἐκείνης ...... ἀνακάμψαι, *for had they cherished the memory of that* [country] *from which they came, they had opportunity of returning* [thither.] That is, if their native country on earth (πατρὶς) had been an object of affectionate desire, they might have easily returned thither, and dwelt there. But this they did not; for,

Ver. 16. Νῦν δὲ ὀρέγονται ...... ἐπουρανίου, *but now, they were desirous of a better,* [country,] *that is, of a heavenly one.* Νῦν, i. e. while they were strangers and sojourners, during the time *then present*

The explanation of the writer, in respect to the country which the patriarchs sought, is so plain, that nothing can add to its perspicuity.

Διὸ οὐκ ἐπαισχύνεται ...... πόλιν, *wherefore God is not ashamed of them*, [nor] *to be called their God; for he hath prepared a city for them.* Διὸ, *because*, viz. because of the faith which they reposed in the promises of God respecting future happiness, or in regard to a πόλιν ἐπουράνιον or μένουσαν. *To be their God* means, to be their protector, rewarder, benefactor; compare Rom. iii. 29. Rev. xxi. 3. 7. Exod. iii. 6. Zech. viii. 8. Gen. xv. 1. Ἡτοίμασε γὰρ αὐτοῖς πόλιν, i. e. he will reward them, for he has in fact prepared a πόλιν, sc. ἐπουράνιον, for them. By ellipsis οὐκ ἐπαισχύνεται is omitted before Θεὸς ἐπικαλεῖσθαι αὐτῶν.

Ver. 17. Πίστει προσενήνοχεν . . . πειραζόμενος, *by faith, Abraham when tried, made an offering of Isaac.* Προσενήνοχε, *made an offering of;* for the act, on the part of Abraham, was *essentially* done when he had fully resolved to do it, and was proceeding to the complete execution of it, Gen. xxii. 1—10. Πειραζόμενος (like the Hebrew נִסָּה) means, either *to put to trial*, or *to tempt*, i. e. solicit to sin. Which of these senses the word must bear, in any particular passage, must depend on the character of the agent who occasions the trial or temptation, and the objects which he has in view. Beyond all question, נִסָּה in Gen. xxii. 1, and πειραζόμενος in our verse, are to be understood in the sense of *trial;* for God is the agent, and " he tempts no man," i. e. solicits none to sin, James i. 13.

Καὶ τὸν μονογενῆ .... ἀναδεξάμενος, *yea, he who had received the promises made an offering of his only Son.* Gen. xxii. 2. This clause is designed to augment the force of the description of Abraham's case. It was not simply that Abraham, in circumstances common to others, i. e. surrounded by several children, and without any special promises, made the offering in question; but it was Abraham, to whom God had repeatedly made promises of a numerous progeny; and it was Abraham's *only son*, i. e. only son of promise, who was the offering which he stood ready to make.

Ver. 18. Πρὸς ὃν . . . σπέρμα, *unto whom it had been said, After Isaac shall thy seed be named.* The Hebrew, in Gen. xxi. 12, is בְּיִצְחָק יִקָּרֵא לְךָ זָרַע׃, which means, *thy seed shall be named after Isaac*, i. e. thy seed, viz. the seed which is *promised* to thee, must descend only from Isaac. Neither Ishmael, nor the sons of Abraham by Keturah, could be progenitors of the *promised* offspring, and give name to them. The Septuagint and apostle have rendered the Hebrew preposition בְ, in בְּיִצְחָק, by ἐν, which there means, *according to, with reference to, after.* This is a third circumstance added, in order to augment the impression of the reader respecting the faith of Abraham. This patriarch, to whom promises had been made, not only offered up his only son, born of Sarah his beloved wife, but his only son, on whom all the promises of God respecting his future progeny were suspended.

Ver. 19. Λογισάμενος, ὅτι καὶ . . . Θεὸς, *counting that God was able to raise him even from the dead;* i. e. he believed, that, in case Isaac should be actually slain and consumed as a burnt-offering, God could and would raise him up from the dead, so that the promise made to him would be fulfilled. This was, indeed, a signal example of the strength of faith, and it deserves the commendation which the apostle bestows upon it.

There are not wanting, however, critics of the present time, who attribute this whole transaction of Abraham to his superstition, or his heathenish views of sacrifice, or to a dream which he erroneously considered as a divine admonition. And in regard to the interposition from heaven, which prevented his resolution from being executed, they aver, that the accidental discovery of a ram caught by the horns in a thicket, was interpreted, by the superstitious patriarch, as a Divine admonition to refrain from proceeding with his design. How different all this is, from the views of the author who wrote Gen. xxii., of Paul in Rom. iv., and of the writer of our epistle, need not be insisted on to any one, who does not make his own conceptions about the subject of religion and miracles the standard by which the sacred writers are to be tried.

Ὅθεν αὐτὸν .... ἐκομίσατο, *whence, comparatively, he obtained him,* or *whence, as it were, he obtained him.* It would occupy much room even to glance at the variety of interpretations which have been put on this somewhat difficult phrase. Instead of this, I will simply state the one which appears to me altogether the most probable and satisfactory. Paul, speaking of the procreation of Isaac, in Rom. iv., mentions Abraham as then νενεκρωμένον, and the νέκρωσιν τῆς μήτρας of Sarah. In ver. 12 above, the same apostle speaks of Abraham as νενεκρωμένον; and his description of Sarah, in ver. 11, implies the same thing. Now, as Isaac sprang from Abraham and Sarah, both κατὰ ταῦτα νενεκρωμένοι, what is more natural than to suppose, that in our verse this fact is adverted to? The sentiment seems to be this: "Abraham believed that God could raise Isaac from the dead, because he had, as it were, obtained him from the dead, i. e. he was born of those who (κατὰ ταῦτα νεκροὶ ἦσαν.) Then the whole presents one consistent and apposite sentiment. Abraham believed God could raise his son from the dead. Why? He had good reason to conclude so, for God had already done *what was equivalent to this*, or *like this*; he had done this, ἐν παραβολῇ, *in a comparative manner*, i. e. in a manner that would compare with rising from the dead, when he brought about his birth from those who were dead as to the power of procreation. Παραβολὴ means, *comparison, similitude*; ἐν παραβολῇ, *comparatively, in like manner, with similitude, as it were*. Thus all is easy, natural, and consistent. How forced the other methods of construction are, which have been employed here, the reader may determine for himself by consulting them.

It may be made a question, whether ἐκομίσατο refers here to Abraham's having *obtained* Isaac from the altar of burnt-offering, where he was as it were dead; or whether the word refers to Abraham's having *originally obtained* him, viz. at his birth. It may be applied to either; but the latter application is far more significant, and accords altogether with the context. The hints for this explanation I owe to Dr. Schulz, in his Commentary on the Epistle to the Hebrews.

Ver. 20. Πίστει περὶ μελλόντων .... Ἡσαῦ, *by faith Isaac blessed Jacob and Esau, in respect to the future*. Περὶ μελλόντων εὐλόγησε, literally, *blessed Jacob and Esau in regard to future things*. The sentiment is, "pronounced a blessing upon Jacob and Esau, in regard to their future condition;" which accords with the facts as related in Gen. xxvii. 26—40. It was faith in the promises of God, which enabled the dying patriarch to do this.

Ver. 21. Πίστει Ἰακὼβ .... εὐλόγησε, *by faith Jacob, when about to die, blessed each of Joseph's sons*. See Gen. xlviii. 15, 16. Ἀποθνήσκων here, like the present participle in Hebrew, has the meaning of the Latin future in *rus*. It was not in the act of dying, that Jacob blessed the sons of Joseph, as Gen. xlviii. 8—22 shows; but it was when on his death-bed, that both they and the twelve sons of Jacob were blessed by him: see Gen. xlvii. 31; xlviii. 2; xlix. 33.

Καὶ προσεκύνησεν .... αὐτοῦ, *and bowed himself upon the top of his staff*. This last action did not accompany the blessing of the sons of Joseph; at least it is not related in connexion with it, but as preceding it. See Gen. xlvii. 31; compare xlviii. 1. 15, 16. I regard it, therefore, as a *separate* transaction. Προσεκύνησε (Hebrew וישתחו) designates, as it would seem, *the act of worship* or *reverence*, paid to God, and occasioned by the grateful emotions of the dying patriarch, on account of the promise which his son Joseph had just made, to bury him with his fathers. That the Hebrew, יִשְׁתַּחוּ, and the corresponding Greek, προσεκύνησε, are sometimes employed simply and merely to designate an act of religious worship, is plain from 2 Kings v. 18. Gen. xxii. 5. 1 Sam. i. 3. That הִשְׁתַּחֲוָה generally means *worship or reverence, by bowing down toward the earth,* or even *to the earth,* is sufficiently plain; but that, in some cases, it also designates *worship* simply as a religious act, without necessarily implying a particular position of body, is sufficiently plain from 1 Kings i. 47, where it is said of David, in extreme old age, and confined to his bed, וַיִּשְׁתַּחוּ הַמֶּלֶךְ עַל־הַמִּשְׁכָּב, *he worshipped upon his bed*; a phrase constructed exactly like that in Gen. xlvii. 31; in both of which cases, Gesenius says, the act of worship is signified without bowing down. This is indeed clear from the nature of the position, and the infirmities of Jacob and David. If the reader wants evidence of a similar meaning of προσκυνέω, he may consult John iv. 20—24; ch. xii. 20. Acts viii. 27; ch. xxiv. 11, &c.

The only question of difficulty that remains is, whether the present vowel-pointing of the Hebrew, עַל רֹאשׁ הַמִּטָּה, *upon the head of the bed,* is probably more correct than the Septuagint mode of reading the Hebrew, viz. עַל רֹאשׁ הַמַּטֶּה, *upon the top of his staff.* I have no hesitation in preferring the latter punctuation; for what is רֹאשׁ הַמִּטָּה, *the head of a bed,* in the Oriental country, when the bed itself is nothing more than a piece of soft carpeting thrown down upon the floor? And what can be the meaning of Jacob's *bowing himself upon the head of the bed?* For, (1.) there is no evidence that Jacob was upon the bed, when Joseph paid him the visit recorded in Gen. xlvii. 28—31. It was *after* this, that Jacob was taken sick, ch. xlviii. 1, and sat up on his bed, when Joseph came to visit him, ver. 2. (2.) An infirm person, lying upon a bed, if he assumed a position such as to *bow himself,* would sit on the *middle* of the bed, and *not* upon the *head* of it. (3.) In all the Scriptures, the *head of a bed* is not once mentioned; and for a good reason, as the Oriental bed had, strictly speaking, no head. For these reasons, I must regard Jacob as leaning upon *the top of his staff* for support, when he conversed with his son Joseph; than which nothing can be more natural, for a person of his very advanced years. In this position he was when Joseph sware to him, that he would comply with the request which he had made in respect to his burial. This was so grateful to his feelings, that he spontaneously offered up his thanks to God for such a favour; q. d. *he worshipped upon the top of his staff*, i. e. leaning upon the top of his staff, he offered homage or thanks to God; just as David " worshipped upon his bed," i. e. did homage, or paid reverence to God, while on his bed, 1 Kings, i. 47.

That the *present* vowel-points of the Hebrew do not, in *every* case, give the most probable sense of the original, will not appear strange to any one who reflects, that they were introduced *after* the fifth century of our present era. All enlightened critics, of the present day, disclaim the idea that they are *authoritative*.

The apostle says, that *by faith* Jacob worshipped. I understand this of that confidence in God which he entertained, and which led him to trust, that all which Joseph had promised him, would be accomplished.

Ver. 22. Πίστει Ἰωσὴφ .... ἐνετείλατο, *by faith, Joseph, at the close of life, made mention of the departure of the children of Israel,* [from Egypt,] *and gave commandment respecting his own bones.* See Gen. 1. 24—26; Josh. xxiv. 32. Τελευτῶν, see on ἀποθνήσκων, in ver. 21. Ἐνετείλατο, i. e. he commanded that his bones should be carried up, out of Egypt, to the land of Canaan, when the Israelites removed thither. It was by faith in the promises of God, that Joseph spoke thus confidently respecting the future exodus of the Israelites, and gave directions respecting his bones, which could be executed only in case this exodus took place.

Ver. 23. Πίστει Μωϋσῆς .... αὐτοῦ, *by faith Moses, after his birth, was concealed for three months by his parents.* See Exod. ii. 2. What is attributed by our author to the *parents* of Moses, is there said to have been done by his mother. But doubtless it was with her husband's knowledge and concurrence; and even if it were not, there are many cases in Scripture, where what is done by one of any class or company of men, is attributed generally to the class or company; e. g. one evangelist says, that the *thieves* on the cross reviled Jesus; but another informs us that *one of them* did this. That πατέρας applies to both father and mother is well known, it being equivalent to our word *parents*.

Διότι εἶδον . . . βασιλέως, *because they saw that he was a goodly child, and did not fear the king's commandment.* Ἀστεῖον, Hebrew, טוֹב, *goodly, fair, beautiful.* Διάταγμα τοῦ βασιλέως, viz. the command of Pharaoh to destroy all the male children, Exod. i. 16 22.

It was faith, or confidence in Divine protection, which led them to perform such a hazardous duty.

Ver. 24. Πίστει Μωϋσῆς ... Φαραὼ, *by faith Moses, when arrived at mature age, refused to be called the son of Pharaoh's daughter.* Μέγας γενόμενος means, *become full grown, become adult, having attained the stature of a man.* Ἠρνήσατο, *refused, &c.*: no express act of this kind is related in the sacred history; but the whole account of Moses' conduct shows that he had, at this period, fully resolved upon leaving the court of Pharaoh, and embarking in the cause of the oppressed Israelites.

Ver. 25. Μᾶλλον ἑλόμενος ... ἀπόλαυσιν, *choosing rather to suffer affliction with the people of God, than to enjoy the pleasures of sin for a season.* Λαῷ τοῦ Θεοῦ, i. e. the Israelites, to whom this name is often given. Πρόσκαιρον ἁμαρτίας ἀπόλαυσιν, viz. the pleasures of living at the court of Pharaoh in princely magnificence.

Ver. 26. Μείζονα πλοῦτον ... Χριστοῦ, *counting reproach, like that which Christ suffered, as greater riches than all the treasures of Egypt.* That ὀνειδισμὸν τοῦ Χριστοῦ has the meaning here assigned to it, seems quite evident, if we consider, that the comparison between the reproach which Christ himself suffered, and the treasures of Egypt, would be inapposite here. The simple sentiment is, " Moses renounced pleasure and wealth, and endured suffering and reproach, because he believed in the promises which God had made of future good, and that he would deliver his people from the bondage of Egypt. So Christ, "though rich, for our sakes became poor," in order to redeem us from a bondage worse than that of Egypt. That Moses, then, counted *reproach like that which Christ suffered,* as preferable to the pleasure and wealth which he might have enjoyed at the Egyptian court, is plainly the meaning of the writer. Compare παθήματα Χριστοῦ, *sufferings like those of Christ,* in 2 Cor. i. 5. Such a use of the genitive case is by no means unfrequent.

Ἀπέβλεπε γὰρ εἰς τὴν μισθαποδοσίαν, *because he had respect to the retribution.* Ἀπέβλεπε means, *to look away from* present things, and *to have respect to,* or *look forward to,* future ones. The *retribution* of the invisible world is doubtless meant, here, by μισθαποδοσίαν. Compare ver. 13—16, and ver. 27. By faith in the proffered happiness of a future state, Moses was led to the acts of self-denial here adverted to.

Ver. 27. Πίστει κατέλιπεν ...... βασιλέως, *by faith he left Egypt,*

not fearing the indignation of the king. It has been disputed, whether it was the *first* or *second* time that Moses left Egypt, to which the writer here adverts. The *first* is related in Exod. ii., and was when he fled to Jethro in Midian. But as he fled, in this case, to save his life, which Pharaoh sought to destroy, Exod. ii. 14, 15, this cannot be the leaving Egypt to which the apostle refers; although Chrysostom, Theodoret, Theophylact, Œcumenius, and some of the modern critics, have understood it to be so. It must be the occurrences related in Exod. x.—xiv., to which our author refers. Τὸν θυμὸν τοῦ βασιλέως, see Exod. x. 28, 29.

Τὸν γὰρ ἀόρατον ὡς ὁρῶν ἐκαρτέρησε, *for he persevered, as one who sees Him that is invisible.* Ἐκαρτέρησε, *perduravit, fortiter* vel *patienter duravit,* if it relate to perseverance in a time of trial and suffering, as here. It does not of itself indicate endurance of suffering, but *holding out, persevering,* in any state or condition, *keeping up good courage and fortitude perseveringly* or *constantly.* Ἀόρατον, i. e. Him whom " no eye hath seen," viz. the invisible God ; an appellation frequently given to the Deity ; e. g. 1 Tim. i. 17 : compare Rom. i. 20. Col. i. 15, 16. In other words, a regard to that world which is seen only by the eye of faith, led Moses to quit Egypt in defiance of Pharaoh's injunctions.

Ver. 28. Πίστει πεποίηκε ...... αὐτῶν, *by faith he observed the passover, and the sprinkling of the blood, so that He who destroyed the firstborn might not touch them.* Πεποίηκε τὸ πάσχα, Hebrew עָשׂוּת פֶּסַח, which the LXX. translate ποιεῖν τὸ πάσχα. This means, (as we say,) *to keep* or *celebrate the passover.* The Hebrew פֶּסַח comes from פָּסַח, *to pass over, to pass by.* The Greek form πάσχα comes from the Aramæan Hebrew word, פַּסְחָא, which was the Jewish method of pronouncing פֶּסַח in later times, and to which the Greek word exactly corresponds. The account of the event to which the word πάσχα relates, may be seen in Exod. ch. xii. ; for the etymology, see ver. 11. 13. Ὁ ὀλοθρεύων τὰ πρωτότοκα, see Exod. xii. 12. Μὴ θίγῃ αὐτῶν, Exod. xii. 13 ; αὐτῶν, in the genitive, is governed by θίγῃ, as verbs of sense (touch) govern the genitive.

All this was done *by faith,* i. e. because Moses fully believed that what God had foretold would come to pass ; in other words, it was through confidence in the Divine declarations.

Ver. 29. Πίστει διέβησαν ...... ξηρᾶς, *by faith they passed through the Red Sea, as on dry land* The nominative to διέβησαν is οἱ Ἰσραηλῖται, which the writer leaves his readers to supply from the tenor of the narration. Instances of the like kind are not unfrequent, both in the writings of the Old Testament and of the New. See the history of the event, in Exod. ch. xiv.

Ἧς πεῖραν ...... κατεπόθησαν, which the Egyptians assaying to do, were drowned. Ἧς πεῖραν λαβόντες is an expression of peculiar construction. Ἧς πεῖραν means the attempt of which, viz. of passing through the Red Sea; so that ἧς πεῖραν λαβόντες is equivalent to ἧς διάβασιν πειράζοντες, attempting the passage of which. Κατεπόθησαν from καταπίνω, to swallow up, to engulf, to overwhelm, and hence, to drown. See Exod. xiv. 27, 28.

It was on account of confidence in the promise of God to bring the Israelites safely through the Red Sea, that they ventured to cross an arm of it, looking to him for protection from its waters. It is not to be supposed that every individual of the Israelites possessed such a confidence as is here described; but their leaders had it, and (as in other cases of a similar nature) it is predicated of the nation.

Ver. 30. Πίστει τὰ τείχη ...... ἡμέρας, by faith, the walls of Jericho fell down, after they had been compassed about for seven days. See Josh. vi. 12—20. It was in consequence of the promise made by God to Joshua, that Jericho should be taken after the Israelites had marched around it for seven days in succession, that these circuits were performed. It was *confidence*, then, in the Divine word, which led to the event in question. Κυκλωθέντα, Rosenmüller, Schleusner, Dindorf, and others, understand to have respect to *circumvallation*, or a siege of the city by surrounding it; altogether contrary to the meaning of the narration in Josh. ch. vi. For what can be the meaning of Josh. vi. 15, on the supposition that their interpretation is correct? Did the Israelites lay *seven sieges* to it in one day? Most evident is it, that the sacred writer considers the whole event of the taking of Jericho as *miraculous*; and all attempts to explain it away by supposing a regular *circumvallation*, and that the city was stormed by the troops of Joshua on the seventh day, are glosses forced upon the scripture by the sceptical philosophy of interpreters, not a simple explanation of the meaning of the sacred writers.

Ver. 31. Πίστει 'Ραὰβ....εἰρήνης, by faith, Rahab the harlot, having entertained the spies in a friendly manner, perished not with the unbelieving. Οὐ συναπώλετο, i. e. was preserved, the affirmative idea being conveyed (as often elsewhere) by the use of a negative form of expression. Ἀπειθήσασι refers to the inhabitants of Canaan, who treated the claims of the Israelites to that country with *contumacy*, and disbelieved what Jehovah had said respecting them. Ἀπειθὴς is *one who refuses to be persuaded, who is contumacious*. The event to which this clause relates is narrated in Josh. vi. 22—25.

Δεξαμένη, *having entertained, received,* viz. into her house. Μετ' εἰρήνης, *with amity, in a peaceable manner;* like the Hebrew, שָׁלוֹם, *friendship*, e. g. Ps. xli. 10. Jer. xx. 10; ch. xxxviii. 22. Obad. 7. Ps. xxviii. 3; compare Esth. ix. 30.

It has been doubted whether πόρνη, the appellation given to Rahab, here and in James ii. 25, means *harlot* or *hostess*. For the latter, Schleusner contends, in his Lexicon; as do also many commentators. The corresponding Hebrew word is, זוֹנָה, which they say comes from זוּן *pascere, alere,* so that זוֹנָה may well be explained merely as *one who furnishes others with nutriment,* i. e. a hostess. But this derivation is contrary to the laws of etymology; for זוֹנָה must come from זָנָה, *to commit whoredom*, and not from זוּן, *to feed*; so that the whole argument, on which this interpretation is built, falls to the ground. Besides, the *usus loquendi* both of זוֹנָה and πόρνη, is against such an interpretation.

Ver. 32. Καὶ τί ἔτι λέγω; *and what shall I say more?* or, *why should I recount examples any longer?*

Ἐκλείψει γάρ με .... προφητῶν, *for time would fail me, should I tell of Gideon, and Barak, and Sampson, and Jephtha, of David, and Samuel, and the prophets.* The history of these, see in the books of Judges and Samuel.

Ver. 33. Οἱ διὰ πίστεως .... βασιλείας, *who through faith subdued kingdoms*. That is, confidence in Divine promises respecting the deliverance of Israel, led them to war with and subdue the kingdoms of those who oppressed the Hebrew nation.

Εἰργάσαντο δικαιοσύνην, Hebrew עָשׂוּ צֶדֶק, or פָּעֲלוּ צֶדֶק, *practised justice, did that which was equitable and proper, carried the laws of justice into execution*, which latter seems to be the idea here.

Ἐπέτυχον ἐπαγγελιῶν, *obtained promised blessings,* i. e. as the reward of their confidence in God. Ἐπαγγελία means here, as generally in this epistle, *quod promissum est;* and refers to the various successes which, at different times, attended the obedient efforts and deeds of kings and prophets.

"Ἔφραξαν στόματα λεόντων, which probably refers to the history of Samson, Judg. xiv. 5—9; of David, 1 Sam. xvii. 34—36; and of Daniel, Dan. vi. 16—24.

Ver. 34. Ἔσβεσαν δύναμιν πυρὸς, *they quenched the violence of fire.* See in Dan. iii. 19—26.

Ἔφυγον στόματα μαχαίρας, *they escaped the edge of the sword.* Στόματα μαχαίρας, Hebrew פִּי־חָרֶב. The expression is frequent in Hebrew, and the equivalent one, στόμα μαχαίρας, is several times used in the New Testament. The phrase is of a *general* nature, and is therefore applicable to many cases in the Old Testament, where escape from imminent danger is related.

Ἐνεδυναμώθησαν ἀπὸ ἀσθενείας, *were restored to vigour from a state of infirmity.* Ἀσθένεια refers to the infirmity occasioned by sickness, or disease; not to the weakness of one army compared with another, or of one man compared with another. The case of Samson, then, in Judg. xv. 15, 19; ch. xvi. 19, seq. to which Dr. Schulz refers us, seems not to be such as the writer had in view; but rather such cases as that of Hezekiah, 2 Kings xx.

Ἐγενήθησαν ἰσχυροὶ ἐν πολέμῳ, *became mighty in war.* Cases of this nature, the books of Joshua, Judges, Samuel, Kings, and Chronicles supply in abundance.

Παρεμβολὰς ἔκλιναν ἀλλοτρίων, *overthrew the armies of foreigners.* Many cases of this nature are presented in the same books. Παρεμβολὰς means, *camps, encampments;* hence, *the persons who live in them,* i. e. armies. Ἀλλοτρίων, גֵּרִים, זָרִים, i. e. strangers to the Hebrews, and to the worship of the true God; hence, *foreigners, heathen.*

Ver. 35. Ἔλαβον .... νεκροὺς αὐτῶν, *women recovered their dead, by a resurrection.* Ἐξ ἀναστάσεως designates *restoration to life from a state of death, a renewed subsistence or existence, a resurrection;* which corresponds with facts, as related in Scripture; e. g. 2 Kings iv. 18—37. 1 Kings xvii. 17—24. Τοὺς νεκροὺς αὐτῶν, viz. *their dead children;* which is implied by αὐτῶν.

Ἄλλοι δὲ ἐτυμπανίσθησαν, *some were tortured and beaten.* Τυμπανίζω, *to tympanize,* means to stretch upon an instrument called τύμπανον, (the shape of which is not certainly known at present,) for the sake of giving the body an attitude of peculiar exposure to the power of cudgels or rods. It involves the idea of scourging or beating in this peculiar way; i. e. torture by stretching upon the τύμπανον and beating, were conjoined at the same time.

Οὐ προσδεξάμενοι . . . τύχωσιν, *not accepting liberation, in order that they might obtain a better resurrection.* That is, they declined accepting liberation from their torments on condition of renouncing their religion. They looked to a resurrection of the body, which was of a higher nature than merely the redeeming it for a while from temporal death; and in view of this, they refused to accept of liberation from their torments on the condition prescribed. They persevered, because their faith enabled them to regard as a certainty the future and glorious resurrection of the just.

Κρείττονος ἀναστάσεως, *better resurrection.* Better than what? Plainly, better than that which had just been mentioned, viz. resurrection to life in the present world merely; as in the examples of the children mentioned in 1 Kings xvii. and 2 Kings iv. It was not the hope of such a resurrection—the hope of merely regaining the present life, and being again subject to death as before—which led the martyrs suffering upon the τύμπανον, to refuse liberation. It was the hope of resurrection to a life of immortal happiness and glory, that led them to refuse liberation.

Ver. 36. Ἕτεροι δὲ . . . ἔλαβον, *others were tried by mockings and scourges;* literally, others were put to the trial of mockings and scourges. Ἐμπαιγμῶν refers to scorn, derision, and buffeting, which the victims of persecution experienced. Μαστίγων designates a method of scourging differing from that practised by the use of the τύμπανον. See 2 Macc. vii. 1. 2 Kings, ii. 23. 1 Kings, xxii. 24.

Ἔτι δὲ δεσμῶν καὶ φυλακῆς, *and also by bonds and imprisonment.* See 1 Kings, xxii. 27. Jer. xx.

Ver. 37. Ἐλιθάσθησαν.. ἀπέθανον, *they were stoned, they were sawn asunder, they were tempted, they perished by the murderous sword.* The instances mentioned in this verse, of suffering and death, are not distinctly recorded in the Old Testament; but were doubtless all of them realities, and often repeated under the terrible persecution of Antiochus Ephiphanes, and perhaps of Manasseh and others. The Jews have had a tradition, from time immemorial, that Isaiah was sawn asunder by the command of Manasseh.

The word ἐπειράσθησαν has been a stumbling-block to the great body of critics, both in ancient and modern times. The difficulty lies in the fact, that a word of a mere *generic* signification, and of a milder aspect, should be inserted in the midst of those which designate *specific* sufferings, and those of a high degree. Accordingly, it has been proposed to read, ἐπυράσθησαν, ἐπηρώθησαν, ἐπρήσθησαν, ἐπάρθησαν, ἐπυρώθησαν, ἐπράθησαν, ἐσπειράσθησαν, ἐσφαιρίσθησαν, ἐπηρεάσθησαν, ἐταριχεύθησαν, or ἐπειράθησαν; all of which are without any authority, while ἐπειράσθησαν is well supported. In such a case, conjecture, moreover, is out of the question, so long as the established reading will make any tolerable sense. In respect to the contested word, ἐπειράσθησαν, it seems to me that the great body of critics have overlooked a very obvious and intensive meaning of it, viz. that of *temptation to do evil ;* which, in the case presented by ver. 37, here, must mean " temptations presented by persecutors to the victims of their torture, in order to induce them to forsake their religion, and worship the gods of idolaters." Such was a common practice among the heathen persecutors of Christians. Not only life, but wealth and honour were frequently proffered, in the midst of torture most agonizing to the human frame, in order to tempt the martyrs to forsake their religion. Such a temptation as this, is by no means to be reckoned, under such circumstances, among the *lighter* trials of good men ; and to such an one, it is plain, our text may refer. Is it not probable that it has such a reference ? Compare the latter part of ver. 35. If so, this *locus vexatissimus* may be permitted to rest in quiet, not only as being supported by good authority, but as altogether significant, and entirely consonant with the writer's purpose.

Περιῆλθον ἐν ...... κακουχούμενοι, *they went about in sheep-skins and goat-skins, suffering want, afflicted, injuriously treated.* That is, driven out from the society of men, they were obliged to clothe themselves with the skins of animals ; to undergo all the wants and distresses to which such a condition reduced them ; and to submit to the injuries which were heaped upon them by their persecutors.

Ver. 38. Ὧν οὐκ ἦν ἄξιος ὁ κόσμος, *of whom the world was not worthy*, i. e. with whom the world could not bear a comparison in respect to worth; in other words, " who were of a character elevated far above that of the rest of the world." This is a *proverbial* expression, and plainly is to be included here in a parenthesis, as it is an ejaculation of the writer, interrupting the regular series of the discourse.

Ἐν ερημίαις ...... γῆς, *wandering around in deserts and mountains, in caves also, and dens of the earth.* A further description of persons banished from society, and wandering hither and thither, in order to find the means of subsistence, or to avoid the rage of persecution. Σπηλαίοις and ὀπαῖς include fissures of the rocks, and holes in the earth ; both of which were resorted to by these outcasts, for a shelter, when one was needed.

Ver. 39. Καὶ οὗτοι πάντες . . . . ἐπαγγελίαν, *all these, moreover, who are commended on account of faith, obtained not the promised blessing.* That is, they lived in expectation of some *future* good, of some promised blessing. They habitually, by faith, looked forward to something which they did not attain in the present life. Μαρτυρηθέντες, *commended;* as often before, in this epistle.

Ver. 40. Τοῦ Θεοῦ περὶ . . . . . . τελειωθῶσι, *God having provided some better thing for us, so that without us they could not fully obtain what was needed.* An exceedingly difficult verse, about the meaning of which there have been a multitude of conjectures. The only ones that deserve particular regard are, that the κρεῖττόν τι refers to the Messiah; or, that it refers to the happiness of the heavenly world. In the latter sense, some very respectable interpreters take it. But how is *heavenly blessedness* vouchsafed to later, more than to ancient saints? And in what sense can it be affirmed that the ancients could not, or did not, attain it without us? The object of the writer, through the chapter, has been to show, that the hopes of heaven, cherished by the ancient worthies, were firm and bright, through faith in the word of God. That they did, at last, actually attain the object of their hopes, surely will not be doubted. The "better thing reserved for Christians," then, is not a reward in heaven; for such a reward was proffered also to the ancient saints.

I must, therefore, adopt another exegesis of the whole passage; which refers ἐπαγγελίαν to the promised blessing of the Messiah. See Gen. xii. 1—3; ch. xvii. 1—8. I construe the whole passage, then, in this manner. "The ancient worthies persevered in their faith, although the Messiah was known to them only by *promise.* We are under greater obligations than they to persevere; for God has fulfilled his promise respecting the Messiah, and thus placed us in a condition better adapted to perseverance than theirs. So much is our condition preferable to theirs, that we may even say, Without the blessing which we enjoy, their happiness could not be completed." In other words, The coming of the Messiah was essential to the consummation of their happiness in glory, i. e. was necessary to their τελείωσις.

In ch. ix. 15, (compare ch. ix. 26, and Rom. iii. 25, 26,) the death of Christ is represented as having a *retrospective* influence upon past ages. The happiness, then, of the ancient worthies, is connected with Christ's coming and atonement. And to these, the writer seems to me to advert, when he says, μὴ χωρὶς ἡμῶν τελειωθῶσι, i. e. without wha has taken place in our days, their happiness could not be perfected, great and good as they were. If this be not his meaning, I am unable to discover it. And this meaning is altogether apposite to his purpose; for, as he had shown that *faith* was the means, to the ancient worthies, of perseverance, and of obtaining future happiness, even *before* the coming of the Messiah, he might well argue, that *since* his coming, there were more powerful motives to persevere in the faith which he had been commending. If the ancients did so, whose happiness was connected with something then future, and which was to happen only in later days, then surely Christians ought now to persevere, who have actually witnessed the performance of promised good, for which the ancients only hoped. The κρεῖττόν τι, then, seems to be, "the actual fulfilment of the promise respecting the Messiah;" in respect to which, later times certainly have a pre-eminence over the early ones; and on which, the expected happiness of early times was really dependent.

CHAPTER XII.

Ver. 1. Τοιγαροῦν καὶ .... μαρτύρων, *since now we are encompassed by so great a multitude of witnesses;* i. e. by so great a multitude of spectators. An allusion, as the sequel shows, is here made to the stadium of the Greeks and Romans, where the persons stood who were to engage in the exercises of their public games, surrounded by great multitudes of spectators. In a condition resembling this, the writer now places the Hebrew Christians whom he is addressing, and surrounds them with the multitude of worthies and martyrs, to whom he had been alluding in the preceding chapters. Νέφος is figuratively used for *multitude.* So the heathen writers also; e. g. Herod. VIII. 109, νέφος τοσοῦτο ἀνθρώπων. Eurip. Phœniss. 1321, νέφος πολεμίων. Hec. 907, τοιόνδε 'Ελλήνων νέφος, where the Scholiast explains νέφος by πλῆθος. Aristoph. Avib. στρουθιῶν νέφος. Hom. Il. ψ. 133, νέφος πεζῶν. Diod. Sic. III. 28, νεφέλη [i. q. νέφος] ἀκρίδων.

The writer proceeds to exhort the combatants to prepare for the contest before them. Ὄγκον ἀποθέμενοι πάντα, *laying aside every incumbrance.* Ὄγκος means *swelling, tumour, pride;* also, *weight, weightiness.* The reference here is to those who ran in stadium, and who laid aside all superfluous clothing, and disencumbered themselves of every thing which could impede their progress. The simple word, *weight*, would not be of sufficient latitude to convey all which ὄγκος means, in the passage before us. Every *impediment* or hinderance is to be laid aside, or, every *incumbrance* is to be avoided.

Καὶ τὴν εὐπερίστατον ἁμαρτίαν, *especially the sin which easily besets us*. Καὶ I understand, here, as a particle of connexion before the τὴν εὐπερίστατον ἁμαρτίαν, and that it signifies *even, truly*, and is adequate, in such a connexion, to the English word *specially*, or *in particular*. Εὐπερίστατον is a ἅπαξ λεγόμενον, the meaning of which has been variously explained. It is, in its composition, analogical with εὐπερίγραφος, εὐπερίπατος, εὐπερίχυτος, &c. Περίστημι means, *to stand round, surround*. Hence Chrysostom explains εὐπερίστατον by ἡ εὐκόλως περιϊσταμένη ἡμᾶς, *which easily comes*, or *stands around us*. So many modern interpreters understand the word; which, on the whole, seems to me most apposite. The ἁμαρτία which most easily beset the Hebrews, was undoubtedly *apostasy*, or defection from their Christian profession; against which the whole epistle is directed. They were under peculiar temptations to this sin, in consequence of the persecutions which they endured, and their former prejudices in favour of Judaism.

But other critics, ancient and modern, explain εὐπερίστατον in a somewhat different manner. Περίστασις, among other things, denotes, as Hesychius affirms, θλίψις, ἀνάγκη, μέριμνα. Hence Theodoret explains εὐπερίστατον, by δι' ἣν εὐκόλως τις εἰς περιστάσεις ἐμπίπτει, *by which any one easily falls into troubles* or *afflictions*. That is, " Lay aside the sin which will easily bring you into a state of punishment or distress." So some of the modern critics, also, explain the word; especially as the Greek ἀπερίστατον means, *not dangerous, free from vexation*. Hence, they conclude, εὐπερίστατον must mean the opposite of this, viz. *full of danger* or *trouble;* εὐ being intensive, as in εὐμεγέθης, εὐμήκης, &c. This is a very good sense, and well supported by analogy. It may therefore be safely admitted.

Others, Ernesti, Doederlin, et. al. prefer to render εὐπερίστατος by *quod patronos habet quod homines favent;* i. e. εὐπερίστατον is, with them, *well surrounded*, viz, by applauding multitudes. But the preceding sense is better supported than this, by analogy.

Δι' ὑπομενῆς .... ἀγῶνα, *let us run with perseverance the race set before us*. Ὑπομενῆς refers here, not so much to enduring patiently evils which might befall them, as to *holding out* in the race, *persevering in their efforts* until it was completed, and the reward secured. Ἀγὼν means, *any kind of contest*, any gymnastic exercise which was a trial of skill, or in which there was a competition. Here, plainly, it is limited to designate *a race*, by the accompanying τρέχωμεν. Πρόκειμαι is employed, by the classical writers, in the same way as here, viz. to designate the proposal of this or that ἀγὼν to the ἀγωνίσται.

The simple meaning of the whole verse, divested of metaphor, is, "Since so many illustrious patriarchs, prophets, and martyrs, who preceded us, have exercised faith, persevered in it, and obtained the rewards consequent upon it, let us, in like manner, rejecting every solicitation to renounce our hopes and our holy religion, persevere in the belief, and in the duties, which the gospel requires."

Ver. 2. That they may be excited to do this, he now refers them to the example of Christ himself. Ἀφορῶντες εἰς τὸν ......Ἰησοῦν, *looking to Jesus, the author and perfecter of our faith.* Ἀρχηγὸν, *author, leader;* here it means, " Jesus, who introduced the new religion, or the Christian faith, who first taught it, who led the way in it. See on ch. ii. 10. Τελειωτὴν, *he who completed* the system of faith or religion, which he had introduced. So it is commonly explained. It may be asked, however, whether the meaning of τελειωτὴν be not substantially the same with τελειωθεὶς, ch. v. 9 ; τελειῶσαι, ch. ii. 10 ; τετελειωμένον, ch. vii. 28 ; compare ver. 26 of the same. If construed according to this analogy, the meaning of the phrase would be, " Let us look, for an example, to Jesus, the author of our religion, now advanced to a state of glory." There is an objection, however, to this, arising from the clause in the last part of the verse, which seems to present the same idea. It is hardly probable that the writer has fallen into tautology.

That πίστις often signifies *the Christian faith* or *religion*, hardly needs to be mentioned.

Ὅς ἀντὶ τῆς .... χαρᾶς, *who, on account of the joy that was set before him.* This χαρὰ προκειμένη, was exaltation to the right hand of God in the world above, and the glorious reign which was to follow, as the last part of the verse shows. *The joy that was set before him*, was given to him when he had finished his course.

Ὑπέμεινε σταυρὸν ...... κεκάθηκε, *endured the cross, disregarding ignominy, and has sat down at the right hand of the throne of God.*

'Εν δεξιᾷ τε, κ. τ. λ., see on ch. i. 3. Αἰσχύνη means, *the shame* which others might heap upon him, i. e. *ignominy, disgrace,* or the ignominious punishment of the cross.

Sentiment : " Do as Christ, the author of our holy religion, did. For the heavenly reward proposed, he, with patience and perseverance, endured every kind of indignity and suffering, and has, in consequence of it, received a glorious reward. Follow in his steps, and participate in his glory."

Ver. 3. 'Αναλογίσασθε ..... ἀντιλογίαν, *consider, now, him who endured such opposition against himself from sinners.* 'Αναλογίσασθε means, *reflect on his example, take his case into consideration.* 'Αμαρτωλῶν refers here to the persecuting Jews of the Saviour's time, who thus evil entreated Jesus. 'Αντιλογίαν, רִיב, מְרִיבָה, *opposition, rebellion, contest against, contumely.* Contradiction is a term too soft to reach the full meaning.

"Ἵνα μὴ κάμητε .... ἐκλυόμενοι, *lest, becoming discouraged in your minds, ye grow weary.* 'Εκλύομαι means, *to become discouraged* or *despondent.* I join the participle ἐκλυόμενοι with ταῖς ψυχαῖς. So Wahl, on ἐκλύομαι. The verb ἐκλύω has the same signification, if the noun be omitted ; e. g. ver. 5.

Κάμνω means, *to become wearied, to be tired out.* The first step toward forsaking the Christian course, is to become *disheartened* in the pursuit of it. Next follows *weariness* in pursuing that, from which we do not hope or expect any certain good. This leads, of course, to an abandonment of the pursuit.

Ver. 4. Οὔπω μέχρις . . . ἀνταγωνιζόμενοι, *ye have not yet resisted unto blood, in your contest against sin.* The phrase, *ye have not resisted unto blood,* is not to be understood as representing the Hebrew Christians as making, or preparing to make, active and hostile resistance to their aggressors or persecutors. This is not the meaning of the writer. It was *figuratively* a contest, in which the Hebrews were engaged ; just as in ver. 1—3, he had represented it as a race, ἀγών. It was a contest with trial, temptation, affliction ; the result of being persecuted by the enemies of the Christian religion. But the struggle had not yet proceeded so far, that they were called to martyrdom, as others in ancient times had been. Many vexations had been suffered by them ; but the shedding of their blood had not yet commenced.

This could hardly be said in respect to the churches at Jerusalem, without limitation, where James and Stephen had actually suffered martyrdom, and others had been severely treated. Still, it might be said of the generation of Christians then living there.

Πρὸς τὴν ἁμαρτίαν, a controverted phrase. I understand it (simply in accordance with the nature of the context) as an *abstract* noun put for a *concrete*, i. e. ἁμαρτία for ἁμαρτωλοὺς ; an *usus loquendi* very common in both the Old and New Testaments. 'Αμαρτίαν, if explained thus, means, *persecutors*, v:z. those who inflicted injuries upon the Hebrew Christians ; and probably these were their own countrymen or nation, i. e. the Jews.

Ver. 5. Καὶ ἐκλέλησθε . . . διαλέγεται, *and have ye forgotten the exhortation which is addressed to you as to children?* Most interpreters render καὶ ἐκλέλησθε, without interrogation, *and ye have forgotten, ye must needs have forgotten*, &c. It seems to me more congruous with the apostle's manner of address, in this hortatory part of his epistle, to render it, (as Ernesti has done,) *interrogatively*. It loses nothing of its force, and gains in respect to the manner of address.

Υἱὲ μου . . . ἐλεγχόμενος, *my son, do not slight the chastening of the Lord, nor be disheartened when reproved by him.* 'Ολιγώρει, Hebrew תִּמְאָס, *contemn, slight, despise, disregard.* Παιδείας, in the sense of the Hebrew, מוּסָר, *chastening, rebuke.* Classic usage employs παιδεία in the sense of *instruction, discipline.* 'Εκλύου, Hebrew תָּקֻץ, from קוּץ, *fastidire*, also *metuere*, i. e. μὴ ἐκλύου, *be not timid, be not disheartened*, viz. as to going forward in your Christian course; forsake it not because you experienced trouble in pursuing it. The quotation is from Prov. iii. 11, 12, and in the words of the Septuagint.

Ver. 6. Ὃν γὰρ ἀγαπᾷ . . . προσδέχεται, *for whom the Lord loveth, he chasteneth, and scourgeth every son whom he receiveth.* Μαστιγοῖ δέ, κ. τ. λ. is after the words of the Septuagint, Prov. iii. 12. The Hebrew, as now read, gives a somewhat different meaning. It is thus: וּכְאָב אֶת־בֵּן יִרְצֶה, *and as a father* [chastens] *the son whom he loves.* The LXX. appear to have read וְכָאֵב, participle of כָּאֵב, or else כִּאֵב, in Piel. But no example of a *transitive* sense of כָּאֵב, in Kal, is to be found ; it means only, *to be afflicted, to feel pain.* Of the Piel form of this verb, no instance is found in the Hebrew Scriptures. Still the LXX. may have read וּכְאָב, *and pain*, viz. יִקְרֶה, *shall overtake* the son, &c. which gives the same sense (for substance) as μαστιγοῖ υἱὸν. In whatever way they read the Hebrew, in order to make their version as the version now is, and as the apostle has quoted, it preserves the *spirit*, though not the *letter*, of the original Hebrew.

That quotations are often made by the New Testament writers from the Old Testament, in a *general* way, *ad sensum*, and not *ad literam*, I have had frequent occasion to remark before, in commenting on our epistle. No one who attentively studies the New Testament can doubt this.

Ver. 7. Εἰ παιδείαν .... ὁ Θεὸς, *if ye endure chastisement, God dealeth with you as children.* Ὑπομένετε has the sense here of *enduring, undergoing, suffering;* and not that of *supporting, bearing up under, persevering.* Προσφέρεται (mid. voice) means *tractare aliquem.* So the classical writers also employ it. See Schneider and Schleusner on the word.

Τὶς γὰρ ἔστιν .... πατὴρ; *for what son is there, whom his father does not chasten?* That is, how can ye expect, although ye are *children,* not to receive any chastisement?

Ver. 8. Εἰ δὲ χωρὶς ἐστε .... υἱοὶ, *but if ye are without chastisement, (of which all children are made partakers,) then are ye spurious and not* [legitimate] *children.* Νόθοι means, *illegitimate* children. Υἱοὶ which is here the antithesis, of course means *legitimate offspring.* The meaning is, " If ye are not dealt with as all legitimate children are, it would follow, that ye are considered as not belonging to them." That is, if ye receive no chastening, then God does not acknowledge you as his spiritual children.

The design of the writer, in thus applying this text of scripture, is plain. He means to tell the Hebrews, that so far from being disheartened by their trials and afflictions, on account of their Christian profession, they ought to regard it as matter of encouragement, and as an evidence that God is acknowledging, by these, their filial relation to him.

Ver. 9. Εἶτα τοὺς μὲν ... ἐνετρεπόμεθα, *furthermore, we have had fathers of our flesh, who have chastised us, and we have yielded them reverence.* Τῆς σαρκὸς ἡμῶν πατέρας *fathers of our flesh,* i. e. of our natural bodies. The idea is, " the fathers of our *physical* nature, in distinction from our *spiritual* one."

Οὐ πολλῷ μᾶλλον ... ζήσομεν; *shall we not much rather yield subjection to the Father of* [our] *spirits, that we may live?* That is, when God chastens us for our good, in order that he may promote our final happiness, when he has so important an end in view; shall we not bow to his will, with cheerful subjection? Πατρὶ τῶν πνευμάτων, an antithesis of τῆς σαρκὸς ἡμῶν πατέρας, and therefore, plainly, ἡμῶν is implied after πνευμάτων. Numb. xvi. 22, אֱלֹהֵי הָרוּחוֹת לְכָל בָּשָׂר, *the God of the spirits of all flesh*, is a parallel expression. Ζήσομεν has the sense here, as often elsewhere, of *being happy;* like the Latin *vivere*, in *dum vivimus vivamus*.

Ver. 10. Οἱ μὲν γὰρ ... ἐπαίδευον, *they, indeed, chastened us for a little while, according to their own pleasure*. Πρὸς ὀλίγας ἡμέρας, i. e. during our childhood, our minority; which seems to me a much more natural sense than to say, with Heinrichs and Dindorf, "the fruit of their chastisement was only temporary." Κατὰ τὸ δοκοῦν αὐτοῖς, *according to their own pleasure*, intimates that they sometimes erred in their chastisement, or that it was sometimes *arbitrary;* but it is not so with that which God inflicts.

Ὁ δὲ ἐπὶ τὸ συμφέρον ... αὐτοῦ, *but he for our good, in order that we might be made partakers of his holiness*. That is, God never chastises *arbitrarily*, but always to promote the real good of his children, to make them more holy, and so more like himself. Compare 2 Pet. i. 4. Lev. xi. 44; xix. 2; xx. 2, 76.

Ver. 11. Πᾶσα δὲ παιδεία .... λύπης, *now all chastisement, for the present, seemeth not to be matter of joy, but of grief*. Πρὸς μὲν τὸ παρὸν, *during the present*, i. e. while it continues. Μὲν here corresponds to δὲ after ὕστερον in the next clause, i. e. there is protasis and apodosis.

Ὕστερον δὲ .... δικαιοσύνης, *but afterwards it yields the happy fruit of righteousness, to those who are exercised thereby*. Καρπὸν εἰρηνικὸν is a peculiar expression. Some resemblance to it may be found in James iii. 18. Isa. xxxii. 17. Gen. xxxvii. 4. The meaning of εἰρηνικὸν is to be gathered, by a comparison of it with the Hebrew שָׁלוֹם, which means, *good, happiness, welfare*. Εἰρηνικὸς, then, is *th_t which bestows happiness, or produces it*. This corresponds with the writer's design; who means to say, that afflictions, rightly improved, will be productive *of fruit that will confer happiness*, such fruit as *righteousness* always produces. So remote a position of δικαιοσύνης from καρπον, seems almost to indicate the necessity of repeating this word before it.

Ver. 12. Διὸ τὰς παρειμένας .... ἀνορθώσατε, *wherefore strengthen the weak hands, and the feeble knees*. Ἀνορθώσατε is often employed by the LXX. in order to translate the Hebrew כון, which means to *establish, to make firm, to strengthen*. Παρειμένας (from παρίημι) means *relaxed, let down*, consequently, *weak, enfeebled*. One might (as many interpreters have done) translate ἀνορθώσατε παρειμένας χεῖρας, by *lift up the hands that hang down.* But since the same verb applies to παραλελυμένα γόνατα, it is better so to render it, as to make the application to both congruous; which may be done without transgressing Hellenistic usage. The quotation is from Isa. xxxv. 3, where the Septuagint has ἰσχύσατε instead of ἀνορθώσατε.

The meaning of the verse is, "Since all your afflictions are dispensed by fatherly kindness, be of good courage, do not indulge any despondency, but persevere in the course which you have begun."

Ver. 13. Καὶ τροχιὰς ὀρθὰς .... ὑμῶν, *and make plain the paths for your feet.* In Hebrew, פַּלֵּס מַעְגַּל רַגְלֶךָ, *make even or level the path of thy feet*; Septuagint, ὀρθὰς τροχιὰς ποίει σοῖς ποσί, Prov. iii. 26. If the apostle has quoted here, it is *ad sensum*, not *ad verbum*. The meaning is, "Remove all obtacles, or disregard all obstacles, to your progress in the Christian course."

"Ἵνα μὴ τὸ χωλὸν .... μᾶλλον, *that what is lame may not be sprained, but rather be healed.* Τὸ χωλὸν is a neuter adjective, used for the abstract noun, *lameness*, and therefore of a generic signification, designating *that which is lame*, or *the members which are lamed.* Ἐκτραπῇ means, *to turn aside*: which, applied to the lame, is *to dislocate, distort, sprain, wrench,* the limbs which are *lamed.*

Ἰαθῇ δὲ μᾶλλον, i. e. it is better to make the paths smooth and plain, so that those who are lamed may walk with ease and safety, than to let them be rough and uneven, so as to endanger an increase of their malady.

The whole is a figurative expression, used by our author to convey the idea, that to go straight forward in their Christian course, regardless of any afflictions to which this may subject them, is the only way of safety for those who are in danger of halting.

The writer now leaves the subject, on which he had insisted so long and with such earnestness, and proceeds to remind the Hebrews of various duties to which their Christian profession, and the times in which they lived, rendered it necessary that they should pay a particular regard.

Ver. 14. Εἰρήνην διώκετε .... ἁγιασμὸν, *studiously cultivate peace with all men, and holiness.* Εἰρήνην means here, *a state of concord and amity,* the opposite of contention and broils. To contentions the Hebrew Christians must have been much exposed at this time, in consequence of the frequent injuries inflicted upon them by their persecutors. Διώκετε, *pursue with zeal* or *engagedness.* 'Αγιασμὸν, *holiness,* i. e. a pious upright life, or a life of consecration to God.

Οὗ χωρὶς .... Κύριον, *without which no one shall see the Lord.* Ὄπτεσθαι τὸν Κυριὸν, *to see the Lord,* denotes, *to come before him, to enjoy his presence, to be admitted to his favour.* Compare Matt. v. 8, and Wahl on ὄπτομαι, 2 b. See also 1 Thess. iv. 17. 2 Cor. v. 8. Phil. i. 23. John xiv. 3, 4; xviii. 24.

Ver. 15. 'Επισκοποῦντες μή τις .... Θεοῦ, *see to it, that no one fail of the favour of God.* 'Επισκοποῦντες, literally, *seeing;* but the sense is the same, and the translation more perspicuous, if a new sentence be made here, by adopting, as I have done, the imperative form of the verb *to see.* Μή τις, i. e. μή τις ᾖ, the verb of existence being implied. Ὑστερῶν is differently rendered by different interpreters. Ὑστερέω means *to come late, to arrive after the proper* or *favourable time,* and is so rendered here by some. But ὑστερῶν ἀπὸ ... is hardly capable of such a meaning, and plainly should be rendered, *be wanting in respect to, fail of, come short of, lack.* But what is χάριτος? Some answer, *the Christian religion;* and construe the whole phrase thus, " Guard well against the apostacy of any one from Christianity." But this warning has been so often repeated, and in terms so awful; and specially, as the writer appears, in ver. 14, to make a transition from his great subject, to the consideration of other things of particular importance to the Hebrew Christians; it may well be doubted, whether χάριτος has the sense thus put upon it. The writer had just said, that " holiness was indispensable to that happiness which God bestows." I understand him as now saying, " See well to it, that no one fail of obtaining that Divine favour which is the result of holiness;" and so connect it, as a hortatory adjunct, with the preceding sentiment.

Μή τις ῥίζα .... ἐνοχλῇ, *lest any root of bitterness springing up trouble you;* i. e. see to it, lest any person of vicious life and example should rise up among you. Many commentators refer this to *apostates.* They are the more inclined to this, because a similar expression is found in Deut. xxix. 17, which there characterises those who turn from the worship of the true God to that of idols. But, as it is far from being certain that our author designs to make a direct quotation in the present case, I should not consider this reason, as in itself of any considerable weight. Even if the *form* of expression be quoted, the application of it must depend, of course, upon the context. This respects not apostacy in particular, (as we have already seen,) but other sins to which the Hebrews might be particularly exposed. No doubt, the expression ῥίζα πικρίας comes from the Hebrew, פֶּן יֵשׁ בָּכֶם פֹּרֶה רֹאשׁ וְלַעֲנָה, *lest there be among you any root springing up*, [which is] *poison and wormwood*, Deut. xxix. 18. The expression there used to describe an idolater, viz. *root of poison and wormwood*, is here applied to any person of an unholy life and deleterious example, who is called ῥίζα πικρίας.

The consequence is next described. Καὶ διὰ ταύτης μιανθῶσι πολλοὶ, *and by this many be polluted.* That is, the bad example of some will have a pernicious, polluting influence on many. Guard well against it; for ἐπισκοποῦντες is implied before μή τις ῥίζα, κ. τ. λ.

Ver. 16. Μή τις πόρνος .... αὐτοῦ, *let there be no fornicator nor profane person, like Esau, who for one morsel of meat sold his birthright.* Πόρνος is explained as meaning *apostate, one making defection from the true religion to a false one*, by those who construe the whole of our context as relating only to apostacy. God often taxes his ancient people with adultery and fornication, in consequence of their having turned to the worship of idols. The meaning thus given to πόρνος may, no doubt, be philologically supported ; i. e. the word is capable of such an explanation. But, as I interpret the context in a different way, it appears to be more consonant with it, to take πόρνος as designating *any person who indulges in gross and sensual pleasures*, or, *who is of an abandoned character.* So our Saviour often speaks of the Jews as a *wicked* and *adulterous generation;* not *literally* adulterous, (although doubtless this was true of some,) but adulterous in the *figurative* sense of the word, viz. *sensual, vicious, abandoned, profligate*.

Βέβηλος is one *who scoffs at religion* or *sacred things, who disregards what is sacred* in the view of Heaven. The appellations πόρνος and βέβηλος may both be applied to Esau here, and probably are so. As to the application of πόρνος, see Gen. xxvi. 34, 35; and Gen. xxxvi. 2. In regard to βέβηλος, see Gen. xxv. 29—34. His birthright was not, indeed, a thing of religion ; but it was, in those days, a matter of great personal importance and advantage. The argument is from analogy : " Let no one give up himself to the gratifications of his lusts, as did Esau, to the great grief of his father, Gen. xxvi. 35; let no one despise the distinguished privileges which Christianity confers upon him, like Esau, who despised the privileges of his birthright, and parted with them for a mere morsel of food." In the case of **Esau, folly and** unbelief were very conspicuous; for the land of Canaan, as he well knew, had been promised to his ancestors for a possession; and, as the first-born son, he must, according to the custom of those days, have a peculiar title to it. So, those who reject the proffer of the heavenly inheritance, and renounce their duty as Christians, may, with more propriety still, be called βέβηλοι.

Ver. 17. Those, who conduct themselves in such a manner, will hereafter weep with bitter lamentations, when it is beyond their power to recover what has been lost. Thus was it with Esau. "Ιστε γὰρ ...... ἀπεδοκιμάσθη, *for ye know, that when he was afterwards desirous to obtain the blessing, it was refused.* See Gen. xxvii. 34—40. Εὐλογίαν, viz. the blessing of his father Isaac.

Μετανοίας γὰρ .... αὐτὴν, *yea, he found no place for a change of mind* [in his father], *although he sought for it with tears.* See Gen. xxvii. 35, 38, 40. Μετανοίας here refers to a *change of mind* in Isaac, who had given the blessing (appropriate to primogeniture) to Jacob. The writer evidently does not mean to say, that Esau found no place for repentance in himself. Αὐτὴν, sc. μετάνοιαν.

The sentiment of the whole is, " Guard well against indulging any fleshly appetites; above all, against slighting the blessings and privileges which Christianity proffers; lest, having done this, you come at last, when it is for ever too late, bitterly to mourn over your folly and wickedness."

Such watchfulness the Hebrews had the more reason to observe, since under the new dispensation every thing was of a milder aspect, and of a more inviting, encouraging nature, than under the old. The comparison between the two dispensations is continued through ver. 18—24. The writer begins with describing the nature of the ancient one. The whole passage has respect to Exod. ch. xx. and xxi. &c.; and Deut. ch. iv. and v.

Ver. 18. Οὐ γὰρ προσεληλύθατε .... ὄρει, *moreover, ye are not come to the mount which could be touched.* He means mount Sinai, which was an object palpable to the senses. Ψηλαφωμένῳ, *contrectabile, quod tangendum sit,* i. q. αἰσθητὸν, *quicquid sensu percipitur.* So Tacitus, Ann. III. 12, *oculis contrectare;* and Cicero, Tusc. III. 15, *mente contrectare.* The idea of *de cœlo tactus, thunder-struck,* is here assigned by some respectable expositors to ψηλαφωμένῳ; but without any good philological support. The Greeks use θίγειν and θιγγάνειν, to denote *the striking of thunder.* The Hebrews employ עֵנֶג, which the LXX. transl ιe by ἅπτεσθαι. But ψηλαφάω answers to the Hebrew בָּשַׁשׁ and מוּשׁ. Particularly in Talmudic and Rabbinic Hebrew, is מְשַׁשָׁא and מַמָּשׁ used to designate, *quod contrectabile est, quidquid sensu cognoscitur*. But, philology apart, the object of the writer in the antithesis between Sinai and Sion, plainly shews, that he means to designate the former as *corporeal, material;* the latter as *spiritual, invisible,* the object of faith, but not of the senses. Chrysostom has well drawn the comparison, when he says of Sinai, πάντα τοτὲ αἰσθητὰ, καὶ ὄψεις, καὶ φωναὶ; of Sion, πάντα νοητὰ καὶ ἀόρατα νῦν. If the reader has any difficulty about the above explanation of ψηλαφωμένῳ, a comparison of Exod. xix. 12, 13, with it, will hardly leave any doubt as to the meaning of our author, who seems plainly to have had in his mind the strict injunction then made, *not to touch* the mountain.

Καὶ κεκαυμένῳ πυρὶ .... θυέλλῃ, *and to flaming fire, and thick clouds, and darkness, and tempest.* As to the particulars of the appearance at Sinai here mentioned, see Exod. xix. 16—18; ch. xx. 18. Deut. v. 21—26.

Κεκαυμένω πυρὶ means not, simply, *fire,* but the burning of it, i. e. *flame;* see Deut. v. 23. 25. It may also be translated in connexion with ὄρει, sc. *the mount that burned with fire.* But probably it was not the design of the writer that it should be so taken; for, as he has arranged ψηλαφωμένῳ before ὄρει, while it qualifies it, in like manner he has arranged κεκαυμένῳ before πυρὶ, which it also qualifies.

Γνόφῳ, is probably the Æolic form of νέφος, i. q. νεφέλη, for which the Æolians use νόφος, or γνόφος. The LXX. use it to translate עָנָן, in Deut. iv. 11, et alibi. It is doubtless used by the LXX., and by the writer of our epistle, to designate *the thick dark cloud* that surrounded Mount Sinai when God appeared there. The word often means, *tenebræ*. Here it means, *the cause of darkness,* i. e. thick black clouds.

Σκότῳ, Hebrew חֹשֶׁךְ, or עֲרָפֶל, the darkness or gloom itself, occasioned by the cloud upon Sinai, and around it. Θυέλλη is designed, perhaps, to correspond to the Hebrew, עֲרָפֶל. If not, it is descriptive of the tempest that accompanied the dark cloud, the thunder and lightning of Sinai, Exod. xix. 16. 18; ch. xx. 18.

Ver. 19. Καὶ σάλπιγγος ἤχῳ, *and to the sound of the trumpet.* See Exod. xix. 16. 19. Probably the meaning is, *a voice like that of a trumpet,* i. e. very loud. In Deut. v. 22, it is called *a great voice;* in ch. iv. 12, it is called, *the voice of words,* i. e. articulate sounds; and in

2 L

ver. 33, *the voice of God.* From comparing all these passages together, it seems evident that the meaning is, " an articulate voice, loud like that of a trumpet."

Καὶ φωνῇ ῥημάτων .... λόγον, *and the voice of commands, the hearers of which refused that another word should be added to them.* Compare Exod. xix. 16. 19; and ch. xx. 18, 19.

'Ρημάτων, *things uttered* or *said.* But it applies to any sort of speech; and, among other specific significations, it has that of *command;* see Luke iii. 2. Acts x. 2; ch. xi. 14. Heb. i. 3; ch. xi. 3. So דָּבָר in Hebrew, e. g. Esth. i. 19. Josh. i. 13. 1 Sam. xvii. 29. Isa. viii. 10. Exod. xxxiv. 28. So also, אָמַר, *to command,* Esth. i. 17; ch. iv. 13; ch. ix. 14. 1 Chron. xxi. 7. See Wahl, on ῥῆμα.

'Ης οἱ ἀκούσαντες, κ. τ. λ. The exact shade of the writer's meaning is, " The hearers of which [voice] refused that a word should be added to *them,* viz. αὐτοῖς ῥήμασι, to those commands." In other words, the exceedingly loud sound of the voice inspired them with such terror, that they declined having any more commands addressed to them in this manner.

Ver. 20. Οὐκ ἔφερον γὰρ . . . λιθοβοληθήσεται, *for they could not endure the admonition, " Even if a beast touch the mountain, it shall be stoned."* See Exod. xix. 13. The Vulgate edition of the New Testament adds to this clause, ἢ βολίδι κατατοξευθήσεται. But no manuscript of any authority exhibits this phrase; nor any ancient version; nor any of the ecclesiastical Greek writers, Œcumenius excepted. It is, beyond all doubt, an addition of later times, taken from the Septuagint of Exod. xix. 13. Οὐκ ἔφερον, *they could not endure,* means, " they were greatly affected with the severity of this command, viz. so that they could not bear it without awe and terror."

Ver. 21. Καὶ—οὕτω φοβερὸν ...... ἔντρομος, *and—so terrible was the sight—even Moses said, " I fear and tremble."* Οὕτω φοβερὸν ἦν τὸ φανταζόμενον seems to me, plainly, an expression thrown in by the writer, in order to augment the description of the scene, which interrupts the regular narration, and is therefore to be construed as if included in a parenthesis. But, as the whole of ver. 20 and 21 is evidently a parenthesis, I have avoided the insertion of the parenthetic marks a second time, and noted the words included within the inner parenthesis by a dash at each extremity. Καὶ, which introduces the last clause here, καὶ . . . Μωϋσῆς, has the force of, *and even.*

But where is the history of Moses' trembling? Nowhere, in the Old

Testament is it expressly mentioned. It is implied, however, in Exod. xix. 16, where it is said, that " all the people in the camp trembled;" and Moses was with them, compare ch. v. 14. The fear mentioned Deut. ix. 19, was on a different occasion, though this passage has often been adduced as supporting the affirmation now in question. The particular history, to which our author here alludes, was doubtless a matter of tradition among the Jews of his day; marks of which are still extant, in the Rabbinical writings. See Wetstein, on Gal. iii. 19. L. Cappell, on Heb. xii. 21. Ἐκφοβὸς εἰμι καὶ ἔντρομος, means, *I am greatly afraid*.

Τὸ φανταζόμενον, (the neuter participle being used like a neuter adjective,) is to be construed as an abstract noun, sc. *species, appearance, sight*. This idiom is very common in the writings of Paul.

Ver. 22. Next follows the antithesis to all this scene of terror which accompanied the introduction of the ancient law. Worshippers, under the new dispensation, approach a scene of a very different nature. Ἀλλὰ προσεληλύθατε Σιὼν, *but ye are come to Mount Zion*. Not the literal Mount Zion, but the figurative, i. e. heavenly one. This is made plain, by the additional description which follows. Καὶ πόλει Θεοῦ ζῶντος, Ἱερουσαλὴμ ἐπουρανίῳ, *and to the city of the living God, the heavenly Jerusalem*. The epithet ἐπουρανίῳ here determines, of course, that a *spiritual Jerusalem*, a *heavenly city*, is meant. Compare Heb. xi. 14—16; ch. xii. 28; xiii. 14. Gal. iv. 26. Rev. iii. 12; ch. xxi. 2. 10.

Καὶ μυριάσιν, ἀγγέλων πανηγύρει, *and to myriads, the joyful company of angels*. So, beyond all reasonable doubt, this clause is to be pointed, and translated; for πανήγυρις is not to be joined (as some later critics have joined it) with ἐκκλησίᾳ, κ. τ. λ. The structure of the whole paragraph demonstrates this; for each separate clause of it, (in ver. 18, 19, 22—24) is commenced by καὶ, and continued (where any addition is made to it) by nouns in apposition, without any conjunctive particle before them. E. g. καὶ πόλει . . . Ἱερουσαλημ ἐπουρανίῳ·—καὶ κριτῇ, Θεῷ πάντων, &c. The same construction, beyond all reasonable doubt, is to be adopted in the clause under examination. Dr. Knapp has arranged it in this manner, in his able dissertation on Heb. xii. 18—24, in his *Scripta varii Argumenti*.

Μυριάσι, literally, *myriads*, i. e. ten thousands, used by the Greeks to signify *a great and indefinite number*. In respect to the number of angels, compare Rev. v. 11. Matt. xxvi. 53. Luke ii. 13. Dan. vii. 10. Πανήγυρις, among the Greeks, meant an assembly of men convened on a joyous and solemn occasion; e. g. on the occasions of their public feasts, &c. The mention of such an assembly of angels, shows that the writer intends to describe the objects of the *invisible* world, as seen with the eye of faith; not things palpable, not the objects of sense. He has, moreover, a design to contrast this joyful, solemn assembly of the angels, with that awful one which was present at the giving of the law upon Sinai. In respect to the presence of angels on that occasion, compare Ps. lxviii. 17. [18.] Deut. xxiii. 2. (Septuagint,) Joseph. Antiq. XV. 3. 5. Gal. iii. 19. Acts vii. 53. Heb. ii. 2. with the Note upon it.

Our English version joins μυριάσι with ἀγγέλων, and renders, " to an innumerable company of angels." It also joins πανηγύρει with ἐκκλησίᾳ, and renders, " to the general assembly and church," &c. But the latter is not permitted, on account of the manner in which the author has constructed the whole of his enumeration of particulars, in ver. 18, 19. 22, 23, which, as I have already observed, are each separated from the preceding one, by καὶ. If it be said, that " πανηγύρει, in order to be constructed with ἀγγέλων, ought to *precede* it," the answer is, that in ver. 19, σάλπιγγος ἤχῳ is constructed in the same manner as ἀγγέλων πανηγύρει here; as is also διαθήκης μεσίτῃ in ver. 24. The Greek admits no other correct grammatical mode of construction but that which is given in the translation.

Ver. 23. Καὶ ἐκκλησίᾳ . . . ἐν οὐρανοῖς, *and to the assembly of the first-born enrolled in heaven.* Ἐκκλησία, conventus, *a concourse or assembly of people.* It is not a mere ecclesiastical word, but designates, by usage, any kind of assembly *sacred* or *civil.* Here it designates the sacred assembly of the upper world. Πρωτοτόκων must not be literally understood here, but figuratively. Among the Hebrews, primogeniture conferred distinguished rights and privileges. Hence, figuratively taken, πρωτότοκος means, *any one who enjoys distinguished rights and privileges,* whether he is first-born in a literal respect, or not. Thus Israel, as beloved of God and highly valued, is called his *first-born,* Exod. iv. 22. In like manner, Ephraim is named, Jer. xxxi. 9. So the son of Sirach (ch. xxxvi. 12,) calls Israel. The same appellation of endearment is given to the predicted Messiah, in Ps. lxxxix. 27. In a similar sense, ἀπαρχὴ is used in James i. 18. I understand it here of those who had been most distinguished for piety and usefulness; such as patriarchs, prophets, apostles, martyrs, &c. Storr understands it as referring to the angels, and as descriptive of them; but without any good support from the *usus loquendi* of Scripture.

Ἀπογεγραμμένων, *enrolled*, a word employed by the Greeks to signify the inscribing of a person's name in a record, as a citizen, as a free man entitled to all the rights of citizenship. It marks, here, citizenship in the New Jerusalem, or the heavenly Zion. The ἐκκλησία of such, is that ἐκκλησία with which Christians are to mingle, in the full and final enjoyment of their privileges. In a sense somewhat different to this, saints, while on earth, are spoken of as having their names *written* (γεγραμμένα ἐγράφη, not ἀπογεγραμμένα) in the book of life: e. g. Luke x. 20. Phil. iv. 3. Rev. iii. 5; ch. xiii. 8; xvii. 8; xx. 15; xxi. 27; xxii. 19. Dr. Knapp interprets our text, as speaking of the saints on earth. But he appears not to have noticed the difference of the phraseology employed in reference to such; and certain it is, that the whole tenor of our passage has respect only to the *heavenly* city and assembly. *To be enrolled in heaven*, is to be entitled to all the privileges of a member of *the heavenly city*.

Καὶ κριτῇ Θεῷ πάντων, *and to the judge, the God of all*. Κριτῇ designates Him before whose tribunal all must appear, that enter a future world. But to Christians he is a merciful, not a condemning judge. So means the phrase *God of all*, viz. of *all angels*, and of *all* πρωτοτόκων just mentioned, and (by implication) of all saints. To say, "he is *their God*," means to affirm, that he acknowledges them with favour and approbation. Compare Eph. iv. 6. Rom. iii. 29. Heb. viii. 10; ch. xi. 16. Acts vii. 32. Exod. iii. 6. Zech. viii. 8. Rev. xxi. 37. In the same sense, I apprehend, is Θεῷ πάντων to be understood in our verse; and then all difficulty ceases. In entering a future world, Christians must, indeed, present themselves before the tribunal of the eternal Judge; but he *is* not a Judge severe and rigid; he is in an appropriate sense, *their God;* he will regard them with favour, he will treat them with kindness. Thus all is *inviting*, with respect to the heavenly Zion. The transposition made by our English version, *to God the judge of all*, is against the arrangement of the text, and fails to give the appropriate sense of the words. The meaning of ὁ ἐπὶ πάντων Θεός, Rom. ix. 5, is different from Θεὸς πάντων here, the former being " supreme God."

Καὶ πνεύμασι δικαίων τετελειωμένων, *and to the spirits of the just made perfect*, i. e. exalted to a state of final reward. This differs from ἐκκλησίᾳ πρωτοτόκων ἀπογεγραμμένων ἐν οὐρανοῖς, in that this latter phrase designates *the more conspicuous and exalted part* of the church invisible, (προτοτόκων,) such as patriarchs, prophets, apostles, martyrs, &c.; while πνεύμασι δικαίων embraces all saints, "of every kindred, and tongue, and people, and nation." See a like distinction in the heavenly world adverted to in Rev. iv. 4. That the *elders*, mentioned in Rev. iv. 4, were of those redeemed from among men, is proved by Rev. v. 8, 9. Then follows the πνεύματα δικαίων τετελειωμένα, in Rev. v. 13. The passage in our verse, understood in view of this, is intelligible, and needs none of the varying and endless conjectures which have been made respecting it; nor emendations of the text that have been proposed.

Τετελειωμένων, i. e having completed their probation, and arrived at their mature state, viz. a final state of glory. See on Heb. ii. 10.

Ver. 24. Καὶ διαθήκης . . . . Ἰησοῦ, *and to the mediator of the new covenant, Jesus.* See on ch. viii. 6; vii. 22, where the same idea is exhibited.

Καὶ αἵματι . . . . Ἄβελ, *and to the blood of sprinkling which speaketh better* [things] *than* [the blood of] *Abel.* Respecting the blood of Christ offered in the eternal sanctuary, see Heb. ix. 11—14, 23. In respect to sprinkling, see ch. ix. 13. 19. *Figuratively* or *spiritually*, no doubt, this is to be understood. Sprinkled with Jesus' blood, the worshippers in the sanctuary above may approach the presence of God, i. e. the inner sanctuary, confident of a gracious reception.

Κρεῖττον λαλοῦντι, instead of κρείττονα λαλοῦντι, for the weight of authority is, beyond all doubt, on the side of κρεῖττον. Literally rendered, κρεῖττον would be, *something better.* But this is less grateful to the English ear than the form of expression in the version. The meaning of the phrase seems to me quite simple and easy. The blood of Christ proclaims pardon and peace; the blood of Abel cried to God from the ground (Gen. iv. 10.) for the infliction of punishment upon his murderer. Παρὰ τὸν (not τὸ) Ἄβηλ, is an elliptical expression, for παρὰ τὸ αἷμα τοῦ Ἄβηλ. That the verb λαλεῖ is *understood,* in order to complete the grammatical sense of the phrase, is quite plain. The form of the sentence, however, must be varied in order to *express* this verb. It would be thus, ἢ τὸ αἷμα τοῦ Ἄβηλ λαλεῖ.

Such is the contrast between the former and latter dispensation. *There,* all is awful, terrible, and threatening; *here,* all is alluring, gracious, and animating. Who, now, can adhere to the former, and renounce the latter? Such is the nature of the argument presented by the writer. He next proceeds to warn the Hebrews, in the most solemn and affectionate manner, against a renunciation of their Christian faith

Ver. 25. Βλέπετε, μὴ....λαλοῦντα, *take heed that ye turn not away from him who addresses you.* Παραιτέομαι means, to deprecate, to decline, to endeavour to avoid, aversari, respuere, repudiare. But who is τὸν λαλοῦντα? The sequel of the verse clearly shows that Christ is meant, who came from heaven to instruct men, and warn them of their danger, or rather (with reference to the preceding verse) " who speaks to men by his blood."

To give efficacy to this warning, he adds an example. Εἰ γὰρ ἐκεῖνοι... χρηματίζοντα, *for if they did not escape* [punishment,] *who rejected him that warned them upon earth.* That after ἔφυγον, either δικὴν, ἀπώλειαν, or some such word, is to be supplied by the mind of the reader, is plain from the nature of the subject, and of the context. But who is τὸν χρηματίζοντα? Moses, I answer. The two dispensations are here compared, in respect to the penalty to be inflicted on the contemptuous and refractory. The legislator, or head of each dispensation, is introduced, as the person who addresses the laws or warnings of God to men. See the same sentiment in Heb. x. 28, 29.

Πολλῷ μᾶλλον .... ἀποστρεφόμενοι, *much more shall we* [not escape,] *if we turn away from him* [who warns us] *from heaven.* See a similar commination in ch. ii. 1—3; x. 28, 29. That χρηματίζοντα is implied after τὸν, results from common grammatical usage. Ἀπ' οὐρανῶν is meant to represent, either that Christ came from heaven and warned them, or that being in heaven he now warns them, viz. by his messengers. It is possible, however, that God is here meant by the writer, as he who warns them. But the antithesis between the head of the old dispensation and the new, in the passage, hardly admits of this construction.

The ellipses of οὐ φευξόμεθα after ἡμεῖς, is sufficiently plain from the nature of the sentence.

Ver. 26. Οὗ ἡ φωνὴ .... τότε, *whose voice then shook the earth;* viz. when, as with the sound of a mighty trumpet, waxing louder and louder, he spake on mount Sinai, so that the earth trembled: see on ver. 19, seq.

Νῦν δὲ .... οὐρανὸν, *but now he has promised, saying,* " *Yet once more, will I shake not only the earth, but heaven also.*" Ἔτι ἅπαξ corresponds to the Hebrew עוֹד אַחַת מְעַט, *yet once, after a little time,* Hag. ii. 6. The citation is from the Septuagint, but οὐ μόνον is an addition by the writer of our epistle, and is designed to give emphasis to the declaration. That the passage has respect to the changes which would be introduced by the coming of the Messiah, and the new dispensation which he would commence, is evident from Hag. ii. 7—9. Such figurative language is frequent in the Scriptures, and denotes great changes which are to take place. So the apostle explains it here, in the very next verse. Compare Isa. xiii. 13. Hag. ii. 21, 22. Joel iii. 16; ch. ii. 10. 31. Matt. xxiv. 29—31 : compare ver. 34.

Ver. 27. Τὸ δὲ, ἔτι ἅπαξ . . . σαλευόμενα, *now this " Yet once more," signifies a removing of the things which are shaken, as of created things, in order that the things which are not shaken may continue.* The manner in which the writer understood the figurative expression in question, viz. the shaking of the heavens and the earth, is here plainly declared. It denotes a great change, a μετάθεσις, *removal,* or *abolition,* of the things changed, i. e. of the Jewish dispensation. The language which had been literally applied to the quaking of Sinai when the law was given, is now figuratively applied, in the usual scriptural way, in order to denote a great change of a moral nature.

Ὡς πεποιημένων is a *locus vexatissimus.* It would be of little use to detail the various opinions upon it; most of which seem to have sprung from a misapprehension of the meaning of the paragraph in which it stands. Even Michaëlis and Storr interpret the passage as referring to changes in the *natural* world, at the end of time; most evidently, against the meaning of the writer. I understand πεποιημένων to designate simply *things made* or *created,* χειροποίητα, caduca, mutabilia; ideas necessarily implied by a term which designates *things of a corporeal and created nature,* as here. The writer means to say, that the ancient order of things, viz. the Jewish dispensation, will be *changed, removed, abolished,* in like manner as the objects of the natural creation. In other words, like them, it is *caduca, mutabilis, evanida ;* and, like them, it will undergo a change. It really seems that more difficulty has been made about the phrase in question, than was necessary.

All this change or abolition of the *old* dispensation was to take place, in order that a *new* one might be introduced, which shall undergo no change; ἵνα μείνῃ τὰ μὴ σαλευόμενα.

Ver. 28. Διὸ βασιλείαν . . . . παραλαμβάνοντες, *wherefore, having obtained a kingdom which cannot be shaken,* i. e. the gospel dispensation, the βασιλείαν τοῦ Θεοῦ, or τοῦ χριστοῦ, or τοῦ οὐρανοῦ, *a regnum immutabile.* Plainly the βασιλείαν ἀσάλευτον here, is the opposite or antithesis of σαλευομένων in the clause above, which must therefore mean, (in such a connexion) *the Jewish dispensation*. The new dispensation is not, ὡς πεποιημένων, *like the objects of creation*, i. e. is not mutable, caducous, but ἀσάλευτον, *immutable, not to be shaken, not to be changed*.

῎Εχωμεν χάριν . . . εὐλαβείας, *let us manifest our gratitude, (by which we may serve God acceptably,) with reverence and devotion*. ῎Εχωμεν χάριν, *gratiam habeamus*, i. e. *let us express, manifest, exhibit gratitude*, viz. for the *unshaken kingdom*, which we have received, with all its privileges, preferences, and blessings. Εὐαρέστως, *acceptably*, i. e. gratitude for such blessings is due to God, and to render it will be well-pleasing in his sight.

Μετὰ αἰδοῦς καὶ εὐλαβείας, *with pious reverence*, i. e. let us not only exhibit gratitude to God for the mercies of the gospel, but let us add to this *pious reverence* for his spotless and awful perfections. ᾿Ευλάβεια means, *piety, pious devotedness, the spirit of religious devotion;* and αἰδὼς means *reverence*. I take the two words as designed to convey an idea of the *intense* pious reverence which ought to be paid to the great God whom the gospel exhibits. The principle, that one of two synonymous nouns, in such cases, may be employed for the sake of *intensity*, hardly needs to be again stated; and that one of them may be employed in the room of an adjective is equally plain; so that, if we choose, we may translate, " with profound reverence."

Ver. 29. Καὶ γὰρ ...... καταναλίσκον, *for our God is a consuming fire*. If this be not a quotation, the image is drawn from the description of Sinai (ver. 18), which was still in the writer's mind. The idea is, that God, if called to punish unbelief, is not only surrounded by flaming fire, as he was on mount Sinai, but this is also πῦρ καταναλίσκον, *devouring, destructive, tormenting fire*. The awful punishment of unbelievers and apostates is set forth, by the expression in question, in a very striking manner. But probably the expression is a quotation of Deut. iv. 24, where it is employed by way of commination.

CHAPTER XIII.

Ver. 1. ῾Η φιλαδελφία μενέτω, *let brotherly love continue*, i. e. let it be constant, let it remain in exercise. I am, on the whole, disposed to believe that the writer means to say, " Let it continue to be as it has hitherto been;" for he has repeatedly commended them, in our epistle, for their social sympathies and brotherly feeling. Φιλαδελφία is the mutual love of Christians as such.

Ver. 2. *Τῆς φιλοξενίας μὴ ἐπιλανθάνεσθε, cease not to practise hospitality*, or, *forget not hospitality*. This was peculiarly a duty, in those times of persecution and distress, when many were suffering the loss of their means of subsistence, and were obliged to cast themselves on the charity of their brethren.

Διὰ ταύτης γὰρ .... ἀγγέλους, *for by this some have entertained angels unawares*. "Ἔλαθον ξενίσαντες, a truly Attic mode of expression; for the Greeks were wont to join the verb λανθάνω with the participle of another verb, when they wished to express the idea, that the action indicated by that other verb was done *unconsciously, undesignedly, without foresight*. Literally, the phrase may be translated, *some entertaining angels were ignorant*, viz. that they were doing so. See examples of the kind referred to in Gen. xviii. 2, seq. and Gen. xix. 1, seq. The meaning of the whole is, "Continue to practise hospitality, since greater honour and reward is consequent upon it, than you might be ready to suppose."

Ver. 3. Μιμνήσκεσθε .... συνδεδεμένοι, *remember those who are in bonds, as if ye yourselves were fellow-prisoners*. The writer had before adverted to their past sufferings under persecution, ch. x. 32—34; and also to their present trials, ch. x. 36; xii. 3—5. Here he exhorts them *to sympathize with those who are in bonds*, as if they themselves were in the like condition, because they were continually exposed to be thrown into prison. A high degree of sympathy is designated by the expression ὡς συνδεδεμένοι.

Τῶν κακουχουμένων .... σώματι, [remember] *those who are injuriously treated, as* [it becomes] *those who are themselves still in the body*. Ὄντες ἐν τῷ σώματι, i. e. daily exposed themselves to persecution and suffering; and therefore liable to need commiseration from others.

Ver. 4. Τίμιος ὁ γάμος...... ἀμίαντος, *let marriage be honourable among all, and the bed undefiled*. So it should be rendered, because the whole strain is hortatory. So Schulz, "Ehrenwerth sei allen die Ehe." It is capable of another version, viz. *marriage is honourable for all, &c.* Ἐν πᾶσι τίμιος may also be translated, *is altogether honourable*. The first method, however, of rendering the phrase, seems to me preferable; as it is then made to be congruous with the context.

The fact, that such an exhortation is here addressed to the Hebrews, shows, either that some of them were chargeable with a breach of the precept respecting chastity, or that they were in danger of becoming so. Polygamy and concubinage were practised all around them, and had been for time immemorial. The demands of Christianity, then, in respect to these practices, might seem a grievance to some of the Hebrew Christians, and probably they were tempted not to regard them, and needed caution.

Πόρνους δὲ...... Θεὸς, *but whoremongers and adulterers, God will punish or judge;* i. e. those who live in fornication, while unmarried, or commit adultery after marriage, will not escape Divine indignation.

Ver. 5. Ἀφιλάργυρος .... παροῦσι, *let your conduct be free from covetousness; and be content with what ye have.* Ἔστω is understood after ὁ τρόπος, for the sentence is hortatory. Τρόπος means *behaviour*, the same as ἦθος, *manner of life.* Ἀρκούμενοι τοῖς παροῦσι, i. e. indulge no greedy desires for earthly possessions, but cheerfully submit to the allotment of Providence in respect to these things.

Αὐτὸς γὰρ .... ἐγκαταλίπω, *for he hath said, I will never leave thee, nor forsake thee;* i. e. God hath promised to provide for you in the best manner, and you should put your trust in him. The phrase here quoted, may come either from Deut. xxxi. 6; Josh. i. 5; or 1 Chron. xxviii. 20.

Ver. 6. Ὥστε θαῤῥοῦντας .... ἄνθρωπος, *so that we may boldly say, " The Lord is my helper, and I will not fear. What can man do to me?"* The quotation is from Ps. cxviii. 6; where the Hebrew, which corresponds to Κύριος ἐμοὶ βοηθὸς, is יְהֹוָה לִי, *Jehovah is for me.* The verse is divided by the accents in Hebrew, as the translation above divides it. The apostle has given the sense exactly; ὥστε θαῤῥοῦντας ἡμᾶς, sc. εἶναι, which is implied after ὥστε. The meaning of the verse is, "Under whatever trials and difficulties we may be placed, we need not be filled with terror or painful apprehension ; for God will help us."

Ver. 7. Μνημονεύετε .... Θεοῦ, *remember your leaders, who have spoken unto you the word of God.* Ἡγούμενοι, *duces, præsides, leaders, guides, directors,* which here means *teachers,* as the explanatory clause that follows clearly shows. Λόγον τοῦ Θεοῦ, *the gospel.*

Ὧν ἀναθεωροῦντες .... πίστιν, *and attentively considering the end of their manner of life, imitate their faith.* That is, calling to mind the peaceful and happy death of those religious teachers among you, who gave you instruction respecting the word of life, imitate their faith, i. e. persevere in your Christian profession, as they did, to the very end of life.

Storr and others refer ἔκβασιν τῆς ἀναστροφῆς to *the sequel* or *reward* that ensued, in consequence of the manner of life which these teachers had led. But I cannot find reason enough to believe, that ἔκβασιν may be properly understood in such a sense. It is not improbable, that the writer refers here to the triumphant death of Stephen, Acts vii., and of James, Acts xii. He exhorts his readers to follow the example of those faithful Christian teachers, who had died a peaceful and happy death, although, perhaps, a premature one.

Ver. 8. Ἰησοῦς Χριστὸς . . . αἰῶνας, *Jesus Christ is the same yesterday, to-day, and for ever.* That is, Christ is always the same, always ready and willing to aid you in all your trials : compare ch. vii. 3. 15—17. 21. 25. 28; also ch. v. 6. 9; ii. 18; ix. 24; x. 12—14, 23. Ὁ αὐτὸς corresponds with סוּ ὁ αὐτὸς εἶ. Ps. cii. 28, [Septuagint, ci. 27,] in Hebrew, אַתָּה הוּא, which there designates *immutability* or *eternity*; for the parallel distich is, *Thy years shall not come to an end*. The absolute eternity of Christ, (a parte ante, et a parte post) is not here directly asserted ; but the simple object of the writer is, to show that " he ever liveth to aid his disciples." To refer the expression to Christian doctrine, and unite this verse with the one which follows, seems to me plainly a deserting of the obvious intention of the writer. Dr. Schulz construes the passage as I have done. Χθὲς, καὶ σήμερον, καὶ εἰς τοὺς αἰῶνας, is a Hebraism, used to express the *past*, the *present*, and the *future ;* and ὁ αὐτὸς, joined with these, denotes *immutability*.

Ver. 9. Διδαχαῖς ποικίλαις . . . παραφέρεσθε, *be not carried hither and thither by diverse and strange doctrines.* Ποικίλαις καὶ ξέναις designates doctrines *different, diverse,* from true Christian doctrine, and *foreign* (strangers) to it. Such were the doctrines of the Judaizing teachers, respecting many of their ceremonial observances and traditionary rites ; and to these the writer here adverts, as appears by the sequel. For παραφέρεσθε, some manuscripts and editions have περιφέρεσθε, which Ernesti, and some other critics, prefer ; but it is not supported by equal authority.

Καλὸν γὰρ χάριτι . . . περιπατήσαντες, *for it is good that the heart should be confirmed by grace, not by meats, by which those have not been profited who have been occupied therewith.* A difficult expression, about which there has been a great variety of opinion and conjecture. Χάριτι seems to me plainly to refer here to the *gracious truth* or *doctrine*, of the Christian religion. The writer had just said,

"Be not tossed to and fro by doctrines diverse and alien from Christianity." Next follows the assertion, "It is good to be established, [settled, confirmed] in the *gracious doctrines* of the gospel, rather than to put confidence in *meats*, &c. Construed in this way, all is plain and congruous. βρώμασι indicates the various kinds of meats, which were distinguished by the Judaizing Christians into clean and unclean; the first of which might be safely and properly eaten; but the second must be avoided, on peril of losing one's character for piety, and incurring the displeasure of God. All attention to this subject the writer regards as useless; and avers, that those who have been sedulously attentive to it, have reaped no spiritual profit from it. Περιπατήσαντες like the Hebrew הִתְהַלֵּךְ, means, *to be concerned with, to be occupied with, to bestow one's attention upon.* In regard to the *unprofitableness* of such an attention to meats, compare Heb. vii. 18.

Ver. 10. Ἔχομεν .... λατρεύοντες, *we have an altar, of which those have no right to eat, who render their service to the tabernacle.* A figurative expression, borrowed from the Jewish ritual, and accommodated to express the privileges of Christians. According to the usages of sacrifice, in most cases, some part or parts of the victims offered, were reserved for the use of the priests, and, in some cases, were to be eaten also by the offerer: see Lev. vi. 26. Numb. xviii. 9, 10. Lev. vii. 33, 34. Numb. vi. 19. Lev. vii. 15; ch. xix. 6. But the עֹלָה was a *holocaust,* i. e. an offering which was to be *entirely* consumed by fire; particularly, the עֹלוֹת offered on the great day of atonement, Lev. xvi. 14—16. 27; ch. iv. 3—12. The reference in our text is to those sacrifices, a part of which were eaten by the priests and the offerers, in so far as the writer alludes to *partaking* of them. But when he says, that "Christians have a sacrifice, of which those who pay their service to the altar have no right to partake," he means, that the benefits procured by the atoning sacrifice of Christ, do not belong, or will not be granted, to such as rest their hopes of salvation on the ritual sacrifices of the Jewish law, i. e. to such as continue to be disciples of Judaism, or turn back from Christianity to Judaism, and thus renounce the blessings procured for believers by the death of Christ.

Ver. 11. Ὧν γὰρ εἰσφέρεται ...... παρεμβολῆς, *moreover, the bodies of those animals, whose blood was carried into the sanctuary as a sin-offering, by the high priest, were burned without the camp.* See Lev. xvi. 11. 14—16. 27. The construction of the verse is peculiar; and, literally translated, would run thus, " The blood of which animals was brought into the sanctuary... the bodies of the same were burned," &c. To make the verse plain, the *arrangement* has been altered in the translation. Ἁμαρτίας, *sin-offering*, or περὶ ἁμαρτίας, [offering] *on account of sin*, which conveys the same idea. The object, in offering the blood of goats and bullocks in the most holy place, was to make atonement for sin. Παρεμβολῆς, *camp*, refers to the time when the Israelites were in the wilderness and all lived in encampments.

Ver. 12. Διὸ καὶ Ἰησοῦς .... ἔπαθε, *wherefore, Jesus also, in order that he might make expiation for the people by his own blood, suffered without the gate.* Ἁγιάσῃ, *might make expiation;* see on ch. ii. 11. Διὰ τοῦ ἰδίου αἵματος: compare ch. ix. 12. 14. 25, 26; ch. x. 19. Acts xx. 28. Eph. i. 7. 1 Pet. i. 19. Rev. i. 5; ch. v. 9. Ἔξω τῆς πύλης, viz. the gate of Jerusalem; for he was crucified on Calvary, which was *then* without the walls of the city, although it is *now* within them.

Ver. 11, 12, are designed as a comparison between the sacrifice on the great day of atonement, and the expiatory sacrifice of Christ. The blood of the former was presented before God, in the most holy place: the blood of the latter, in the eternal sanctuary above, ch. ix. 12. 23, 24 The bodies of the beasts, used for the former, were consumed or destroyed without the camp; the body of Jesus was sacrificed or destroyed, with out the gate of Jerusalem. The atoning sacrifice of Christians is analogous, then, to that of the Jews; but of infinitely higher efficacy; compare ch. ix. 13, 14; x. 4. 12.

The particular object, however, of ver. 11, 12, is to introduce Christ as an example of suffering, in order to impress upon the Hebrews the necessity of perseverance in their Christian profession, amidst all their trials and difficulties. But the manner of introducing this example, is altogether in unison with the analogies which are so often repeated in other parts of our epistle.

Ver. 13. Τοίνυν ἐξερχώμεθα....φέροντες, *let us, then, go forth to him without the camp, bearing reproach like his.* That is, "since Jesus suffered persecution, ignominy, and distress, let us follow him, even if we endure reproaches like those which he endured. Let us leave the camp, i. e. the dwellings of the Jews, or the profession of Judaism, and go over to the place where Christians dwell, although it be without the city." In other words, Let us adhere to the profession of Christianity, although it be counted as ignominious, and worthy of reproach. In respect to suffering *with* Christ, compare Rom. viii. 17. 2 Tim. ii. 10, 11. 1 Pet. iv. 13. 2 Cor. iv. 10. Rev. i. 9. That ὀνειδισμὸν αὐτοῦ means *reproach such as Christ suffered*, is plain from the object of the writer. Compare Col. i. 24, which is exactly in point; and see on Heb. xi. 26.

Ver. 14. Οὐ γὰρ ἔχομεν .... ἐπιζητοῦμεν, *for here we have no permanent city, but we seek for one yet future*. In ch. xi. 14, the writer calls the heavenly inheritance which the patriarchs sought, πατρίδα ; and afterwards, (ver. 16,) πόλιν. Here the appellation πόλιν is used, because the writer had just been alluding to Christians being thrust out, or going out of the city, viz. of Jerusalem, as Christ did, to suffer ignominy. The design of our verse is, to show the Hebrews, that it cannot be of any great importance, should they be exiled from their dwelling-places, and the habitations of their Jewish kindred; for, in this world, no habitation, no place of abode, can be μένουσα, *permanent, lasting*. By profession, Christians, like the patriarchs, were seeking πατρίδα ἐπουράνιον, and consequently, πόλιν μέλλουσαν, *an abode yet future*, a residence in the world to come.

Ver. 15. Δἰ αὐτοῦ οὖν . . . Θεῷ, *by him, therefore, let us continually present to God the sacrifice of praise*. Δἰ αὐτοῦ, viz. by Christ, i. e. let us present such an offering, by him who is our great High-priest; not a sacrifice of goats or bullocks, but a *sacrifice of praise*. In other words, "Let us, as Christians, offer praises to God for the blessings of the gospel vouchsafed to us."

Τοῦτ' ἔστι, καρπὸν . . . . ὀνόματι αὐτοῦ, *that is, the fruit of our lips ascribing praise to him*. The expression, *sacrifice of praise*, זֶבַח הַתּוֹדָה, is found in Lev. vii. 12. A phrase similar to *fruit of the lips*, is used by Hosea, ch. xiv. 3, Hebrew, נְשַׁלְּמָה פָרִים שְׂפָתֵינוּ, where Septuagint καρπὸν χειλέων. The meaning of our phrase is, *what the lips utter*, viz. when they ascribe praise (ὁμολογούντων) to God. So, Prov. xviii. 20, פְּרִי פִי, *the fruit of the lips*, i. e. what a man says, his words.

Ὁμολογούντων, like the Hebrew, הוֹדָה, means, *to praise, celebrate, publicly acknowledge*. Ὀνόματι is here, as commonly, a periphrasis for the agent to whom the name belongs, viz. God; so that the sense is the same as τῷ Θεῷ.

What follows τοῦτ' ἔστι, is added by the writer, in order to guard against the apprehension of any one, that he was exhorting them to offer the *ritual* sacrifices prescribed by the law.

Ver. 16. Τῆς δὲ εὐποιίας . . . Θεός, *moreover, forget not kindness, and liberality ; for with such sacrifices God is well pleased*. Ἐπιλανθάνω governs the genitive εὐποιίας and κοινωνίας. The same strain of language as before, is continued in this verse. *Beneficence*, or *kindness* toward the suffering, and *liberality* toward the needy, are called *acceptable sacrifices*, or, *such as God is pleased with*. The sentiment is, " duties like these, Christianity requires ; not the blood of bullocks and goats."

Ver. 17. Πείθεσθε . . . ὑπείκετε, *obey your leaders, and be subject to them*. Ἡγουμένοις, in ver. 7, above, is clearly used in the sense of *teachers*, who were, in fact, the *guides* or *leaders* of the Christian community. If there be any difference between πείθεσθε in this case, and ὑπείκετε, the first has reference to positive obedience, in regard to any directions given them; the second prohibits any opposition to the teachers, in the measures which they might adopt to promote the improvement and the order of their religious community.

Αὐτοὶ γὰρ ἀγρυπνοῦσιν . . . . ἀποδώσοντες, *for they watch over your souls, as those who must render an account*. Ἀγρυπνοῦσι, *watch ;* the image seems to be taken from the practice of shepherds, who watch with solicitude over their flocks, in order that they may preserve them from the ravages of wild beasts. See the like imagery employed, respecting the prophet Ezekiel, ch. iii. 17.

Ὑπὲρ τῶν ψυχῶν ὑμῶν, i. e. for you, לְנַפְשֵׁיכֶם. Ὡς λόγον ἀποδώσοντες, viz. to God, to whom " every one must give an account of himself;" particularly, every one put in a place of trust with regard to spiritual duties.

Ἵνα μετὰ χαρᾶς . . . . τοῦτο, [so obey] *that they may do this with joy, and not with grief; for this would be unprofitable to you*.

Ἵνα, κ. τ. λ. I cannot but connect with λόγον ἀποδώσοντες. The sentiment is, " That they may render their account with joy, because of the obedience which has been paid to their admonitions, and of the safety in which their flock are placed thereby." An account of successful labours will indeed be a joyful account, to the ministers of the divine word. In respect to grammatical construction, ἵνα seems to be connected with the verbs in the first part of the verse, viz. πείθεσθε . . . ὑπείκετε ...... ἵνα μετὰ χαρᾶς, κ. τ. λ.; but τοῦτο ποιῶσι necessarily refers to something already mentioned, which the *teachers* must do; and what is this but λόγον ἀποδώσειν? I have been constrained, therefore to supply the ellipse in the Greek here from the preceding context, and to translate, *So obey, &c.*

Μὴ στενάζοντες, literally, *not groaning*, i. e. not grieving; the effect being put for the cause. It is only a *negative* form of expression here, designed to repeat the same idea as is conveyed by μετὰ χαρᾶς, and to render it more intense. 'Αλυσιτελὲς γὰρ, another negative expression, which means as much as to say, " This would be very hurtful or noxious to you ;" i. e. should their Christian teachers be compelled to give an account of unbelief and want of subjection in them, the consequences would be distressing.

Ver. 18. Προσεύχεσθε περὶ ἡμῶν . . . ἀναστρέφεσθαι, *pray for us; for we trust that we have a good conscience, being desirous in all things to conduct ourselves uprightly.* The request of the writer, that he may have an interest in their prayers, shows the friendly feelings and confidence which he entertained respecting them. He appeals to the sincerity and uprightness of his Christian deportment, as an evidence that he might claim a Christian sympathy for himself. Ἐν πᾶσι, κ. τ. λ. augments, or renders intensive, the idea contained in the preceding clause.

Ver. 19. Περισσοτέρως δὲ . . . ὑμῖν, *and I request this the more earnestly, in order that I may speedily be restored to you.* This seems plainly to imply, that the writer was detained from paying those a visit whom he addressed, by some adverse circumstances, viz. either by imprisonment, sickness, or some like cause. It also implies, that he is known to them, and they to him; for it indicates that he had formerly been among them.

Ver. 20. Ὁ δὲ Θεὸς . . . Ἰησοῦν, *now, may the God of peace, that raised from the dead our Lord Jesus, who by the blood of an everlasting covenant, has become the great Shepherd of the sheep.* Ὁ Θεὸς τῆς εἰρήνης, *God who bestows happiness, auctor salutis.* The Greek εἰρήνη, in the New Testament, like the Hebrew שָׁלוֹם, means, every kind of blessing or happiness. Ὁ ἀναγαγὼν, *who brought up, raised up, restored.* Τὸν ποιμένα . . . τὸν μέγαν, compare John x. 11, 14—18.

Ἐν αἵματι διαθήκης αἰωνίου, some join with ἀναγαγὼν. But what can be the sense of *raising Christ from the dead by the blood of the everlasting covenant?* Almighty *power* raised him from the dead; not *the blood of the covenant*. Beyond all reasonable doubt, then, ἐν αἵματι, κ. τ. λ. characterises the great Shepherd, who " laid down his life for the sheep," John x .15 ; and who sanctioned a new testament or covenant by his blood, Heb. ix. 15—23. Matt. xxvi. 28. The meaning is, that " the great Shepherd is provided with, or (so to speak) carries along with him, *blood* sanctioning a covenant which is of perpetual force. So, in Heb. ix. 25, the high priest is said to have entered yearly into the most noly place, ἐν ἀλλοτρίῳ αἵματι, i. e. carrying with him the blood of bullocks and goats. See also Wahl's Lexicon, ἐν, No. 2. The phrase is plainly an allusion to the preceding discussion, in ch. ix. I have rendered it so as to prevent a mistake in regard to its true meaning.

Ver. 21. Καταρτίσαι ὑμᾶς ἐν παντὶ ἔργῳ ἀγαθῷ, *fit you for every good work*, i. e. prepare you in all respects to act worthily of the Christian name, enable you in all respects as Christians to discharge your duties. Εἰς τὸ ποιῆσαι τὸ θέλημα αὐτοῦ, *so that you may do his will*, i. e. perform all which he requires. This is of the same import as the dative with ἐν, in the preceding clause.

Ποιῶν ἐν ὑμῖν .... Χριστοῦ, *working in you that which is pleasing to him, through Jesus Christ*. That is, enabling you to perform all your Christian duties, which will be *acceptable*, εὐάρεστον ἐνώπιον αὐτοῦ, *pleasing in his sight*, טוֹב לִפְנֵי, *pleasing to him*. Διὰ Ἰησοῦ Χριστοῦ, i. e. may he do this, *for Christ's sake, through Christ*, or, perhaps, *by the influence of the Christian religion.*

Ὧι ἡ δόξα .... Ἀμήν, *to whom be glory for ever and ever, Amen*. The nearest antecedent to ᾧ, is I. Χριστοῦ; and to him, it seems to me, the doxology plainly belongs. Other examples, of a similar nature, may be easily shown; e. g. Rev. i. 6. 1 Pet. iv. 11. 2 Pet. iii. 18. Doxologies introduced into the midst of a letter, in this way, are characteristic of the writings of Paul.

Ver. 22. Παρακαλῶ δὲ ὑμᾶς .... παρακλήσε·ις, *moreover, I beseech you, brethren, to bear with this word of exhortation; for I have written briefly to you.* Ἀνέχω means, *to bear patiently with, to receive* or *permit with kind feelings, to put up with.* Λόγον παρακλήσεως is simply *exhortation.* Some refer this only to the last part of the epistle; but the whole is intermixed with hortatory admonitions. The writer, after speaking so plainly, and giving warnings so awful, endeavours to win those whom he addresses, to a patient toleration of his plain dealing.

Διὰ βραχέων, an usual Greek expression for *briefly, within a short compass.* "But how," it is asked, "could Paul say this, when this epistle is longer than any one of his—that to the Romans, and the first to the Corinthians, excepted?" But is it to be supposed, that those whom the apostle now addressed were acquainted with all of his other epistles; and that they would estimate the force of διὰ βραχέων, by a comparison of our epistle with them? It is much more reasonable to suppose, that the writer means to say, that he had written *briefly*, considering the importance and difficulty of the subjects of which he had treated. And who will deny this?

Ver. 23. Γινώσκετε .... ἀπολελυμένον, *know ye that* [our] *brother Timothy is sent away.* See, on the meaning of this, Introduction, pp. 92, seq.

Μεθ' οὗ .... ὑμᾶς, *with whom, if he speedily return, I shall visit you.* Μεθ' οὗ, *in company with whom.* Ἐὰν τάχιον ἔρχηται implies, that Timothy was then *absent.* Of course, ἀπολελυμένον cannot well mean *set at liberty.* But if the meaning be as I have rendered it, then is the reason plain why Paul should say, ἐὰν ἔρχηται. If Timothy was imprisoned at Rome, and *set at liberty* there, why should the writer (at Rome) speak of his *coming to him*? If in some other place, how should he know of his liberation, sooner than those whom he addressed?

Ver. 24. Ἀσπάσασθε πάντας .... ἁγίους, *salute all your leaders, and all the saints.* Ἀσπάσασθε means, Present them with my kind wishes, and my regard for their welfare. Ἁγίους, *those who are consecrated to Christ, professing Christians, saints.*

Ἀσπάζονται .... Ἰταλίας, *they of Italy salute you;* viz. the *Italians,* see Introduction, pp. 98, seq. This shows that the writer was in Italy; from which country he sends the kind greeting of Christians there.

Ver. 25. Ἡ χάρις μετὰ πάντων ὑμῶν, Ἀμήν, *grace be with you all, Amen;* a frequent form of benediction in the apostolic epistles. Χάρις means, *Divine favour* or *blessing.*

The subscription to this epistle runs thus: Πρὸς Ἑβραίους ἐγράφη ἀπὸ τῆς Ἰταλίας διὰ Τιμοθέου. Like most of the other subscriptions to the epistles, it is of no authority. It is demonstrably erroneous here; for how could Timothy write this epistle, when the author says, at its very close, that Timothy was *then absent*? The author of this subscription, one is tempted to think, had either read the epistle with very little care, or with very little understanding of its contents.

END OF COMMENTARY

EXCURSUS.

EXCURSUS I.

Heb. i. 2.—Δι' οὗ καὶ τοὺς αἰῶνας ἐποίησε.

THERE still remains a difficulty in this passage, (in common with Eph. iii. 9,) as to *the form of expression*, or, rather, as to *the object of the assertion*.

In John i. 3, it is said, πάντα δι' αὐτοῦ [λόγου] ἐγένετο; in 1 Cor. viii. 6, δι' οὗ ['Ιησοῦ Χριστοῦ] τὰ πάντα; in Col. i. 15, ἐν αὐτῷ [Χριστῷ] ἐκτίσθη τὰ πάντα; in Col. i. 16, τὰ πάντα δι' αὐτοῦ [Χριστοῦ] . . . . ἔκτισται; and in Heb. i. 10—12, σὺ κατ' ἀρχὰς . . . . τὴν γῆν ἐθεμελίωσας, καὶ ἔργα τῶν χειρῶν σου εἰσὶν οἱ οὐρανοί. In all these passages, the creation of all things is simply ascribed to Christ; just in the same manner, as in Gen. i. 1., God is said to have created the heavens and the earth.

The reader is desired to mark the *mode* of expression, in the passages above quoted; as it is important for him to have a distinct cognizance of it, in order that he may perceive the difficulty which I am about to state. If the Scriptures had no where ascribed the creation to any other than the Logos or Christ, and had employed, in ascribing it to him, only such language as that just quoted above, I cannot perceive that any interpreter of the sacred writings would have ever thought of ascribing creation to any other than to the Logos simply; I mean, that so far as the *Scriptures* are concerned, he never would have thought of ascribing any sentiment to them, in respect to this subject, but that which assigns creatorship simply and solely to Christ or the Logos. There is, plainly, no difference in the *mode of expression*, in the Bible, which asserts creatorship of God, or which asserts it of Christ. I must be understood, of course, to affirm this here, only of that class of texts which has just been quoted above.

But there is another view of this subject, which presents difficulties that cannot be surmounted without some effort. The Scriptures do indeed ascribe creatorship to the Logos; as we have seen. But do the sacred writers mean to ascribe it to him *absolutely*, in the *highest sense*, as his *sole* and *independent act*? Or, do they represent him as creating by direction of the supreme God, and under his superintendence? In other words, was the Logos the *original author* of the universe; or, was he only the *instrument* by which the *original author* brought it into being? —Questions easily asked; but answered with somewhat more difficulty, than unreflecting minds may at first imagine. All is to be resolved by what the Scriptures have taught us. So one and all, who profess any sacred regard for the Scriptures, must concede. What then say the Scriptures on this point of all points, in respect to the great question of the real nature of Christ? Is he Creator by virtue of his *own*, or by virtue of a *delegated* power?

One thing it appears somewhat important to consider, before we advance any farther in the investigation of this subject. If Christ were only the *instrument* employed by the supreme God to bring the creation into existence, and to arrange it in its present order, the sacred writers might assert, and might truly assert, that πάντα δι' αὐτοῦ ἐγένετο, or, ἐν αὐτῷ ἐκτίσθη τὰ πάντα. It may be said, with equal truth, that the church of St. Paul's in London was built by Christopher Wren, and that it was built by the monarch who was the procuring cause or author of the structure, and by whose direction, and at whose expense, it was reared. Every day, men familiarly employ language in this manner, ascribing the building of a structure, either to the owner, or to the architect, just as the nature of the case may require.

Do the Scriptures ascribe creation then to Christ, as *architect merely*; or, as *original author* and *deviser* of the whole? In other words, Is that class of texts, which ascribe creation to Christ, to be *modified* by admitting the idea, that creating by *delegated* power, i. e. (so to speak) as *architect only*, is meant; or, are these texts to be understood in their *highest* sense, viz. in the sense of ascribing to Christ or the Logos *original authorship, creating* in the *highest* sense?

To prepare the way for an answer to this question, we must make inquiry respecting a second class of texts, such as those which I shall now subjoin.

In Heb. i. 2, the writer asserts, that GOD *made all things* BY HIS SON; and in Eph. iii. 9, τῷ [Θεῷ] τὰ πάντα κτίσαντι διὰ Ιησοῦ Χριστοῦ,

GOD *created all things* BY JESUS CHRIST. The latter clause, διὰ I. Χριστοῦ, is indeed wanting in some Codices of good estimation, and is rejected by Griesbach from the text. But Knapp and Tittmann have inserted it, and the weight of authority seems to favour the admission of it. That the sentiment is not without a parallel, is clear from Heb. i. 2.

In these two cases, then, the assertion of the apostle is, that GOD made *all things* BY *his Son,* or, BY *Jesus Christ.*

Are these expressions, now, to be interpreted in such a way, as to qualify all the first class of expressions ascribing creatorship to Christ, so that they must be understood as asserting nothing more, than that he performed an *instrumental* or *ministerial* work only, and did not act as *original author* in bringing the universe into being? This is the simple question before us, divested of all extraneous constructions put upon either class of texts by opinions previously formed, or views adopted in consequence of reasoning *a priori.*

Whatever may be the answer to this question, it is evident that nothing of importance can depend, either in respect to Heb. i. 2, or Eph. iii. 9, on the word διὰ. It has often been asserted, that this preposition is employed, before the genitive case, only to designate a *secondary* or *instrumental* cause. But this is altogether incorrect, both in respect to sacred and classical usage; as even the common Lexicons of the New Testament will shew. The cause, whether principal or instrumental, may be, and often is, designated by διὰ before the genitive.

Δι' οὗ, then, might designate (by itself considered) the *principal cause* or *original author* of the worlds. This expression, however, does not involve the *nodus* of the difficulty, in the case before us. The assertion is not here, that *all things were made* BY *the Son,* but that GOD *made all things* BY *him.* In what manner, now, ought we to interpret this?

How the most noted commentators of the Greek church understood this difficult passage, is worth a serious inquiry. Chrysostom, in explaining it, says, " As the Father judgeth no one, but is said to judge by his Son, because he hath begotten him who is judge; so also he is said δημιουργεῖν δι' αὐτοῦ ὅτι δημιουργὸν αὐτὸν ἐγέννησε, *to create by him, because he hath begotten him who is the Creator.*" He then proceeds, " Εἰ γὰρ αὐτοῦ αἴτιος ὁ πατὴρ, πολλῷ μᾶλλον τῶν δι' αὐτοῦ γεγεννημένων, *for if the Father is the cause of him, much more of the things made by him.*" Hom. I. in Epist. ad Heb. p. 15. Vol. XII. Ed. Montfaucon. To the same purpose, Theophylact: " ἐπειδὲ δὲ αἴτιος ὁ πατὴρ τοῦ υἱοῦ εἰκότως καὶ τῶν ὑπ' αὐτοῦ γενομένων, *seeing the Father is the cause of the Son, he must surely be of the things made by him.*" Comm. in Heb. Tom. II. p. 650. edit. Venet. 1755. Here, also, the generation of the *Divine substance* of the Son is asserted, and the appeal is made to this doctrine as solving the difficulty of our text. But as the idea of self-existence, existence uncaused, and independence, enters *essentially* into all our conceptions respecting a nature *truly Divine,* and is a *sine qua non* in all our apprehensions of a *Creator,* it is difficult for us to concede that the Father can be the *cause* (αἴτιος) of the Son in his *Divine* nature, without, of course, admitting, that the Son, as *Divine,* must be a *dependent* being, a δεύτερος Θεὸς only, as many have called him. The explanation of these fathers, (who accord with most of the ancient ecclesiastical writers,) seems, then, only to remove one difficulty, by bringing forward another still greater. This explanation also is forced upon the text. The writer of our epistle does not say, nor intimate, that " God created all things by his Son, inasmuch as he is *the cause* (αἴτιος ἀρχή; as Chrysostom calls him) of the Son." Can it be proper to force on the sacred writer a mode of metaphysical explanation, drawn from the philosophy of later ages, and foreign to the simplicity of the Scriptures?

In modern times, the mode of explaining our text is founded on what the systems of theology denominate " *subordination* in respect to the persons of the Godhead." Thus Owen, on Heb. i. 2, says, " The joint-working of the Father and Son doth not infer any other subordination but that of *subsistence* and *order ;*" he means the hypostatical subordination of persons, or order of their existence in the Godhead. The amount of the explanation adopted by him and many others is, if I rightly understand it, that God the Father, in the order of *subsistence* (not of time) preceding the Son, did by the Son create the worlds. But whether this explanation renders the text any more *intelligible,* may perhaps be well doubted. Especially so, as Owen, on the same passage says, " The *same individual creating act,* is the work of the *Father* and the *Son ;* whose power and wisdom being *one and the same undivided,* so also are the works which proceed outwardly from them." But if the power and wisdom of the Father and Son are not only *one,* but the SAME UNDIVIDED ; on what, it may be asked, is founded the evidence, that a SUBORDINATION *of subsistence and order* exists in the Godhead ? If the *attributes* of the Godhead are *one and the* SAME *undivided,* how can we come at the *evidence* of a physical or metaphy-

HEBREWS I. 2.   537

sical SUBORDINATION *of subsistence* or *hypothesis?* Can such a subordination of subsistence be in any way known to us, except through the medium of the Divine attributes? But these are affirmed to be *one and the same undivided.* Are we able then to show what the distinction in *divine essence* is; or to define the *mode* in which the metaphysical *essence* of the *uncreated Being* exists! Where is the passage of Scripture which does this? I am aware that an appeal is here made to those texts which mention Father, Son, and Holy Spirit in *connexion;* and particularly to the *order* in which they are mentioned. But of these texts there are only three. The first is in Matt. xxviii. 19, where the order just presented is observed. The second is in 2 Cor. xiii. 13, where the Lord Jesus Christ is placed *first.* The third is in John v. 7; a text, which if not proved to be spurious, is at least thrown into a state so doubtful, that no considerate inquirer would at present think of appealing to it as authority.

Is then, we may well ask, the *order of subsistence* or *hypostasis,* (which is so much insisted on, and so often appealed to by the schoolmen,) a doctrine taught by the sacred writers? Or, rather, is it not one of the inventions of metaphysical philosophy, in order to remove apparent difficulties in the sacred text? Can any one point out the text of Scripture, in which God is presented in a *physical* or *metaphysical* manner, so that his essence or mode of subsistence, in itself considered, is offered to our consideration? If not—and if God, only in his relations to us, and the creation around us, *God as developed by his attributes,* and *not as he is in himself,* or considered in respect to his *internal essence,* be revealed to us in the Bible—why not contented with what the Scriptures have taught, without forcing sentiments upon the sacred writers which have been excogitated only by metaphysicians of later days?

Owen himself, after going through a protracted consideration of our text, with that good sense and humility for which he was so conspicuous, adds, "It is not for us to inquire much into or after the reason of this economy and dispensation. We cannot by searching find out God, we cannot find out the Almighty unto perfection." He means, "We cannot find out the economy of God's creating the worlds by his Son, and the doctrine of subordination which is implicated in this." Happy would it have been for the interest of humble and candid inquirers, had this sentiment produced its proper influence over all the writings of Owen himself, and of many other eminent and excellent men!

Will not most sober and intelligent inquirers, of the present day, agree in saying, that the *nature* and *modus of the distinction* in the Godhead is not an object of revelation, and that it is BEYOND the boundaries of human knowledge? Let those, now, who write or teach respecting this momentous and awful subject, act consistently with such an avowal, and very much of the perplexity, which is still occasioned by incautious assertions in regard to it, will be saved.

The ground which Owen and so many others have taken, to explain the phrase in Heb. i. 2, is not satisfactory, because it is built on the assumption, that we know that which is beyond the boundaries of human knowledge, and which, after much examination, I am compelled to believe is not revealed in the Scriptures.

The difficulty of our text, then, still remains. It would be presumption in me to promise a solution of it that will be satisfactory. But as the subject is so deeply interesting to all sincere and humble inquirers after the simple meaning of the sacred writers, I will venture to suggest a few considerations for reflection.

Words are the signs of ideas. Words are human, i. e. they belong to men; they are employed by them; and employed to designate, of course, the ideas which men have in their own minds. All these ideas are derived from sensation, reflection, or consciousness. The perceptible objects without us, and the mental phenomena within us, are all the objects from which we can derive ideas through the medium of observation. Reflection, or reasoning upon the knowledge derived from these, may lead us to many new ideas; all of which, however, have their basis in the perceptions of objects external or internal.

As words are merely *arbitrary* signs of ideas, so, when employed in their original sense, they can never signify more than the things for which they stand. But words may be employed *figuratively*. When we come, by reasoning or reflection, to the knowledge and belief that there exists a Being who created the world; who is himself uncreated, eternal, and immutable; who is not the object of perception by any of our senses; and for the description of whom, none of the words of our language were originally formed; we are then obliged to apply to the description of this Being, words already in existence. But these words, it is plain, must in such a case be used nearly always in a sense more or less qualified, and differing from their original and *literal* sense. Even in expressing our ideas of the *moral* attributes of the Supreme Being, where there is a particular resemblance between him and man formed in his image, we do not apply to the Divinity the most common words, in exactly the same sense as we do to men. When we say, *he is wise*, we do not mean that he acquired his wisdom, or possesses it, or exercises it, just in the *manner* that men do. We mean that there is, in his wisdom, something analogous to wisdom in men; something which selects the best ends, and chooses the best means of accomplishing them. But we do not mean to imply that the acts of selecting and choosing in the Divinity are, in all respects, analogous to our own.

We say, *God is omnipresent*. But we do not mean that he is present every where, in the same manner as human beings are present at any particular place. We do not mean that actual *physical* presence of body, or of substance, is necessary to his being present; in other words, we do not mean, that he is *physically* diffused through the universe. We mean, that at the same instant, he can act, and does act, any where, or every where. Here is *some* analogy between him and us. We must be *physically* present in order to act; and we say, therefore, that where he acts, he is present. This is true in some sense; but as to *manner*, how exceedingly different is his being present from our own!

We say, *God is mighty*. But when we speak of *might* in him, we do not associate with it the idea of firm sinew, of vigorous muscle, of robust body, of mature age, of perfect health; all of which enter into our apprehensions of consummate strength in man. We content ourselves with one simple point of analogy. God has power to do whatever he desires to do; or, he is almighty. In this respect his might or strength is like that in men; it is power to accomplish the objects which strength or might is adapted to accomplish. But the might of the Deity infinitely excels that of men in degree. Here is one point of dissimilarity. It depends, too, on very different causes for its exercise. Here is another. But still, we speak of power in God, as frequently as we do of power in men. The imperfection of language obliges us to make use of words in this way. But who that has any reflection will say, that the words which we apply to God are used *entirely* in the *same sense*, which belongs to them when they are applied to men?

In the same manner we might proceed in the consideration of every one of the Divine attributes, whether natural or moral. In regard to them all, we should find that there is only some one point of analogy on which our assertion rests, when we apply human language to the description of God; and that the *manner* in which he possesses or exercises any of his attributes, *physically* considered, is utterly beyond the boundaries of human knowledge; and, indeed, that it was never meant to be an object of assertion, by any intelligent man who makes assertions in regard to the Supreme Being.

If all this is well understood, we are now prepared to advance a step farther, and see our way clear. Nothing can be more evident, (I might say, self-evident,) than that the eternal, uncreated, uncaused, independent, infinite, and self-existent God, must, as to his *mode of essence* and *existence*, be unlike to temporary, created, caused, dependent, finite beings, with a derived existence. The very fact that God is as he has been just described, and man as he has been represented, necessarily forces this conviction upon us. Nothing can be plainer, then, than that all human language, formed at first merely to express human conceptions of finite and created objects, must in itself be altogether incompetent *fully* to describe the Divinity. Nor could any language formed by created beings be adequate to this purpose; for the plain reason, that no finite being could ever have a *full* conception of the infinite and uncreated Being.

All our language, then, when used to describe God, must be considered rather as analogical only, than as capable of being simply applied to him in its *usual* sense. Any description made by it, is only an *approximation* towards a full description of what is divine. This has been shown above. And could this be remembered and rightly applied, in all our discussions respecting the nature of the Supreme Being, it would save much of the difficulty and darkness which now embarrass this great subject.

No assertion, indeed, can be made respecting God, which, if its language be understood and applied *altogether* in the *same* sense in which it is understood and applied when made of man, will not lead to contradiction or absurdity. This is evident from such plain cases as those already presented; viz. God is wise; God is omnipresent; God is mighty. If there is still any doubt here, take another case. *God has knowledge.* This is certainly true. But with us, knowledge can be possessed only through the medium of corporeal organs of sensation; it is acquired successively; in time; within a limited space; by the aid of memory, of comparison, of reasoning, of imagination; and when needed for use, it is summoned by recollection. When we say, " A man has knowledge," we imply all these things by the use of these words. But if we say, " God has knowledge," do we mean to assert that he has corporeal organs of sense; that he gradually acquires ideas; that, limited by time and space, he does this; that he makes the *effort* of charging the memory with it; the *effort* of comparing, of reasoning of imagination, of recollection, in any manner like ours? Whoever says this is an *anthropomorphite* indeed; such an one, too, as is not to be often met with (I would fondly hope) in these days of better illumination respecting the exalted and spiritual nature of the Divinity.

From these obvious considerations, we may now proceed to examine the language of the sacred writers, in regard to the difficult point which suggested the subject of this Excursus. Two things seem to be equally the object of assertion in the holy Scriptures. The first, that there is but one God; the second, that the Logos, or higher nature which dwelt in Christ, is truly divine, or is truly God. Of the first, it would be superfluous to produce proofs here. The Old Testament is full of them; and the New as distinctly recognizes the same doctrine; see John xvii. 3. 1 Cor. viii. 4. 6. 1 John v. 20. Luke xviii. 19. Matt. xix. 17. A formal proof of the second point would be out of place in an exegesis designed only for the explanation of a particular phrase. It must suffice merely to advert to John i. 1. Rom. ix. 5. Tit. ii. 13. 1 John v. 20 : the two former instances of which are so express, that no critical ingenuity can avoid the application of the term *God* to Christ; the third, when examined by the principles of grammar and of the *usus loquendi* of the New Testament, is scarcely less certain; and the fourth has never yet been satisfactorily explained away.

But how can the Logos be truly God, and yet *be with God*, and be *the agent* BY WHICH *God made the worlds?* Here lies, it must be confessed, the very essence of all the difficulty which embarrasses so many minds; and on this point we must now venture to dwell with some particularity.

In the first place, our minds are embarrassed with the difficulty which such a statement respecting the Logos makes, in regard to the Divine *unity*. Let us see if the source of this embarrassment cannot be distinctly pointed out.

Trinitarians have been accustomed, for many centuries, to characterize the distinction in the Godhead by the word *person*. Whether this word was well or ill chosen, it is not my present object to inquire. Thus much is certain: many, perhaps even the greater part of men in Christian lands, have incautiously attached to this word, when used in respect to the Godhead, a sense nearly (if not quite) the *same*, as they attach to it in *common usage*. Not a few theologians and critics have, indeed, protested against such an application of the word ; and some of those, who have been most eminent for their stedfast adherence to the belief that the Saviour possesses a nature truly Divine, have raised their voice high against such an application of it; but, unfortunately for the cause of truth, this voice has been listened to only by some of those who were friendly to a belief in the doctrine of the Trinity. Others, with different views, have commonly thought proper to pay no attention to such a protest, but to take advantage, in their efforts to oppose the doctrine of the Trinity, of the arguments which might be put into their possession, by taking the word *person* in its usual acceptation.

If now we speak of the Logos as a *person ;* and of God the Father as a *person ;* and attach to the word *person* the sense that is usual in common parlance; then it is certain, indeed, that the difficulty which lies in the way of supposing the Logos to be truly God, and yet consistently maintaining the Divine unity, is altogether insurmountable. " Person is an intelligent substance," (if I may use the language of philosophy for the sake of definition.) " *Substance*," as defined by Baumgarten, a divine of the old school, of high orthodoxy, and of great metaphysical acuteness, " is that which can exist by itself, or unassociated with another thing;" *Substantia est id, quod potest existere ita, ut ponatur extra alterum,* Metaphys. 191. 36. 231—233. As defined by another logician and philosopher, famous for nice distinctions of definition, " Substance is that which exists, or may be supposed to exist, although it is connected with nothing else;" *Substantia est id quod est, aut esse posse putatur, etiamsi nulli alii sit junctum,* Ulrich's Inst. Log. et Metaphys. § 316. To apply the word *person,* then, in the sense which such definitions necessarily afford, to the distinctions in the Godhead, inevitably leads to Tritheism, and, of course, to a *virtual* rejection of the Divine unity. We may say, in *words*, that we believe God is one, although we assert that there are three persons in the Godhead, as just defined ; but nothing is plainer, than that in such a case we believe merely in a *specific unity*, not in a *numerical one*. Specific unity, however, might admit three thousand or three million divine beings, and yet consistently maintain that there is but one God ; that is, it might do so, provided we allow the advocates of it that there is a γένος Θεῖον, *genus divinum,* or genus of divinities. Human nature, for example, is *one;* there is *but one* nature of man; yet the individuals of this genus are without number. That such is not the unity which the Scriptures assert of the Godhead, I need not stop to prove.

He who consistently holds the *numerical* unity of the Godhead, must, beyond all doubt, protest against the application of the word *person* to designate the distinctions of the Divine nature, if that word is to be taken in its *logical* or *metaphysical* sense. For, however one may hold to *words* and *forms* of expression, it is plain, that while he makes *such* an application of the word person to the Godhead, he in *fact* admits Tritheism, although he may be far from any design or any consciousness of doing so.

The views which have now been presented, may serve to explain the reason why many find it so difficult, or (as they think it) impossible, to admit the true divinity of the Logos. "How can he," say they, "be the second *person* in the Godhead, and yet be *one* with the first? How can he be *with* God, and yet be God *himself?*"

And truly, it must be confessed, that this cannot be, provided the words in question are to be construed altogether *more humano,* i. e. in their *logical, common, usual* acceptation. But is it analogous, is it proper, to construe them thus? Does it develop a spirit of candid and fair inquiry, to insist that these terms shall be construed *altogether according to their common acceptation,* when there is not, as we have seen above, a single term significant of a Divine attribute, which we ever construe in such a manner?

If this be correct, (and I may venture to say it cannot be reasonably disputed,) then I see no very urgent reason why the use of the word *person,* in order to designate a distinction in the Godhead, should be rejected. It is true, it is not a word which is applied by the Scriptures to the Godhead, (for ὑπόστασις, in Heb. i. 3, does not mean *person;)* it is also true, that many well-meaning individuals have been misled by it in regard to their conceptions respecting the Deity, and that those who reject the doctrine of the Trinity have made great use of this word in order to render the sentiments of Trinitarians obnoxious; so that one might almost wish the word had never been introduced into ecclesiastical usage. But when the matter is examined to the bottom, it will be found that objections of a similar nature might be urged against the application of any *anthropopathic* expressions to God. The simple and the untaught may be easily misled by them, and often are so. How many, for example, believe that God is really angry, repents, &c., *more humano,* because such expressions are found in the Scriptures? Shall all such expressions be laid aside, because they are misunderstood or perverted? And if so, where shall we stop? for we have seen, that all language which is used in order to describe God, must be taken, of course and by necessity, in a *qualified* sense. The *abuse* of a thing is no valid argument against the *use* of it. Those, then, who believe in the existence of a real distinction in the Godhead, in case they are careful to protest against the *literal* application of the word *person* to designate this, may still continue to employ the word, if they think best; for it is exceedingly difficult (as all will confess who have thoroughly studied this subject) to exchange it for a better one, or for one that will so well correspond with the representations of the Bible in regard to such a distinction. Certainly no term can be substituted for it, which will not, in like manner, be obnoxious to more or less objections.

If those who reject all distinction in the Godhead will persevere still in maintaining, that to say there are *three persons* in the Godhead necessarily involves the doctrine of *Tritheism;* and if they will thus continue, at all events, to explain the word *person* according to its *literal* and *common* meaning, and to charge upon those who believe in the doctrine of the Trinity the absurd consequences derivable from this; then they may, indeed, display their strength of attachment to their own views, and perhaps their skill in logomachy; but where is that candour and fairness toward those who differ from them, which becomes all who are seeking in earnest to know the simple doctrines of the Scriptures?

Suppose now, when one says, *God possesses knowledge,* he should be asked in the tone of reproof, " What! Do you mean to assert that God has *physical* organs of perception; that he studies; that he charges his memory with ideas; that he compares; that he deduces conclusions; that he summons them up by the effort of recollection when he needs them? *Men* do *all* this, who have *knowledge;* but can all this be predicated of *God?"* Would any considerate man think these questions very reasonable ones; or feel himself compelled by them to abandon his assertion, " that God has knowledge?"

Apply, now, the *principle* concerned in this case, to the idiom in question. The apostle John says, that *the Logos was with God; was with him in the beginning;* and repeats this asseveration, John i. 1, 2. Christ says of himself, that *he was with the Father,* and partook of his glory, before the world had an existence, John xvii. 5. In another place, John asserts, that the *Son was with the Father,* 1 John i, **2**; and the

Saviour speaks of the Father, as *loving him before the foundation of the world*, John xvii. 24. He declares, that *he came out from the Father*, when he came into the world, John xvi. 28. In accordance with this idiom, Paul says, that *God created all things by Jesus Christ*, Eph. iii. 9; and that *he made the worlds by his Son*, Heb. i. 2. Now, if such texts are to be considered as altogether *insulated*, and the principles of analogy in other cases are not to be applied to the language which they exhibit, then the conclusion, that Christ, or the Logos, is a being *wholly distinct* from God the Father, is clear and inevitable. But are these texts to be construed in an *absolute, isolated* sense, and without any reference at all to others, which relate to the same connexion between Father and Son? Certainly not, if we follow the analogy of exegesis in all other cases. When John says, that *the Logos was with God*, he tells us, at the very same time, as if to guard us against erroneously concluding that he is a distinct, and separate, and different *substance*, that *he was God*. When the Saviour spake of the glory which he had with the Father before the world was, he had just been addressing the Father as the only true God, John xvii. 5. 3 : so that no one could rationally suppose him to assert the existence of more than one true God. If Paul tells us that *God created all things by Jesus Christ*, and that *he made the worlds by his Son*, he also tells us, that Christ is *God over all, and blessed for ever*, Rom. ix. 5; and that he is the eternal and immutable Creator of the heavens and the earth, Heb. i. 10—12. Christ tells us, that he who hath seen him hath seen the Father, John xiv. 9; that he is in the Father, and the Father in him, ver. 10; and that all which the Father hath is his, ch. xvi. 15. Now, whatever diversity between the Father and Son the first class of texts above quoted may seem to imply, it is plain that it is not of such a nature as to destroy the unity of the Godhead. Whatever the *distinction* in the Godhead may be, it is *not* that which makes *plurality;* it is not that which makes *personality*, in a logical, or merely human sense. But can we say what it is? Plainly not. A positive description is nowhere given in Scripture; and surely it would ill become us to pretend that we understand, without revelation, the uncreated substance, and *modus existendi* of the Godhead. All that we can understand by such expressions as *the Logos being with God, becoming flesh and dwelling among us,* and *God's making the worlds by him,* is, that there is a distinction in the Godhead, of some kind, which amounts to more than merely the different modes or ways in which the Divinity discloses himself to us. It is something which is not merely *nominal* or *logical;* which is not to be predicated merely of the external relations of the Godhead. It is something which renders it possible to affirm, in some sense or other, analogous to the usual meaning of the words, that *the Son was with God,* that *God created the world by him,* that *he became incarnate, &c.;* all which cannot be predicated, in the *same* sense, of the Father. Yet all this must be true, in such a *modified* sense as does not infringe on the real unity of God.

Who, now, will undertake to decide what metaphysical distinctions or relations there may be, in the uncreated substance of the eternal God; and what are consistent, and what not consistent, with his unity? None, we may believe, but those who are either presumptuous, or destitute of cool and sober reflection. But although the *nature of the distinction* in the Godhead be truly beyond the boundaries of human knowledge, (as plainly it is,) yet the *fact, that there is a distinction of some kind or other,* may be revealed. Indeed, that it is revealed, seems to be a necessary consequence of allowing the two classes of texts above quoted to be true, and to modify each other. On the one hand, *distinction* is not to be so held or asserted, as to infringe upon *unity;* and on the other, *unity* is not to be so held or asserted as to preclude the possibility of any *distinction.* Who has found out the Almighty unto perfection? Are not all analogies from created, finite, temporal objects, utterly incompetent to convey adequate ideas of the infinite and uncreated God? Must they not from their very nature be so? Yet men will insist on applying all the analogy, which language imports, to God, in the same way as to themselves. We always conceive, for example, of *different* beings having a finite nature, as separated by space, as existing in time, and as having their own peculiar properties. When, therefore, we read of the Logos being *with God,* we very easily associate with this expression the analogy of one human being in company with another, or of some created thing associated with another that is a separate one. Then we are ready to ask, How can the Logos be God? One cannot, indeed, show that he is so, if we will insist that all language is to be applied to him, simply according to the common application of it to human objects. But is such an application to be made? Can it be? John says, he is God; and Paul says, he is *God over all.* Then human language, of course, can only *approximate* to a description of him; the literal and full application of it, in designating his relations to the Godhead, is out of all question. Only very inadequate views of this subject, or the spirit of party, or that of disputation, can maintain the propriety of such an application.

We may come then to the conclusion, that when the apostle Paul asserts that *God made the worlds by his Son,* there is nothing in reality more difficult in this expression, than there is in those expressions which are found in the Gospel and first Epistle of John. Whatever may be the economy of the Godhead to which Paul refers, it is not one which denies, or virtually takes away, either the unity of the same, or the supreme creatorship (so to speak) of the Son; for this he most fully asserts in Heb. i. 10—12.

We have seen, by the passages above cited, that the apostles, John and Paul, accord in their views both with respect to the *distinction* and the *unity* of the Godhead, and to the divinity of the Saviour. As they held these truths in such a manner that they harmonized with each other, so ought we to do; and consequently we should not give such an explanation to the one, as to destroy the other. In a particular manner, we ought to be guarded against making any assertions or definitions which are built on the assumption, that we know in what the distinctions of the Godhead consist. Some of the efforts of the school-divines, on this awful subject, are not only contradictory to each other, but their views are inconsistent with the true nature of a Divine and *self-existent* Creator, as well as repulsive to the feelings of a cautious, impartial inquirer, who seeks after ideas of *things,* and not after mere *words.*

The suggestions now made, respecting the necessity of feeling that all our language when applied to describe the Deity must be restricted to a *modified* sense, are strengthened, by an examination of the descriptions in general of God, as given in the Bible by the sacred writers. They represent him, for example, as angry; as repenting; as being grieved at the heart; as laughing at the efforts of the wicked; as mocking at their calamities; as rejoicing; as weeping; as avenging himself; as possessing eyes, hands, feet, and all the parts of the human body; as descending and conversing with men; as appearing to Abraham, Moses, and many others; as ascending; as riding in the whirlwind and the storm; as walking on the sea; as shooting with a bow and arrows; as whetting his glittering sword, and bathing it in blood; as clothed with the habiliments of a warrior, or in those of royal magnificence; in a word, as possessed of all the sympathies, and exhibiting all the phenomena, of a man. The most unpractised reader of the Bible knows this is true, and that, more or less of it, is to be found on nearly every page of it. Yet who, that has any rational views of the true spiritual nature of God, ever supposes that any part of all this language is to be applied merely in its *primary* and *literal* sense to God? Yet, in every case of this nature, there is some *real* meaning in the language employed by the sacred writers. There is some point of analogy, between the *literal* meaning of the language as applied to *men*, and the *qualified* meaning of it as applied to *God*. When God is said to repent, the meaning is, that he acts in a manner analogous to that in which men act when they repent, i. e. he changes the course which he was pursuing. When God is said to whet the glittering sword, to bend his bow, and to take hold on vengeance, then he does that which is like what men do to their enemies, i. e. he punishes, he inflicts distress, he makes retribution for crimes. In all these and such like cases, the *manner* in which the Divine Being acts is not intended to be described; but the *fact* that he does act, is what is asserted by the use of such language as has just been mentioned.

No one can justly say, then, that there is no *real* meaning in such language when applied to God, unless it is taken in its *primary* and *literal* sense. Such an affirmation would betray profound ignorance of the nature of language, as used in a qualified sense, and also of the true character of God. For if all such language respecting him is indeed to be *literally* construed, then have the Scriptures cast no additional light on the *spiritual* nature of God, and he is still to be regarded, as the heathen represented him, viz. as one *altogether like ourselves*.

If it should be thought, that the class of expressions which are mentioned in the two preceding paragraphs, are essentially different from those before considered, viz. such as *God knows, God is mighty*, &c.; an examination of the whole matter will convince any one of his mistake. It is true, that the former class of expressions are more *obviously* figurative. We at once perceive, that, as God is not *flesh and blood*, they cannot be *literally* applied to him; i. e. we abstract from these expressions whatever pertains to *modus,* whatever is borrowed from our earthly material structure. But is it not equally true, that whatever pertains to *modus* is, in the other case, to be in the same manner abstracted? For example, when God is said *to know*, does it any more imply the human *modus* of knowing, than it implies the human modus of acting, when he is said to lift up his arm in order to smite an offender? Most clearly not. The truth is, that, when sifted to the bottom, it will be found there is no essential difference as to the qualified nature of the language in both cases. In both, you abstract the *modus*, before you apply it to God. In the one case, indeed, the metaphor is taken from our *corporeal* parts; in the other, from our *mental* powers; but this makes no difference in respect to the thing itself, except that in the former case the language is more obviously and strikingly to be qualified, than in the latter.

If, then, such expressions as those which have been considered, and all others which designate the natural or moral attributes of God, are, and must be, understood in a *modified* sense; then why is not the assertion that the Logos was *with* God to be understood in a similar way? The manner in which one *created* substance, as contemplated by us, is *with* another can surely afford no perfect analogy to explain the manner, in which the *self-existent*, the *uncreated* Logos is *with* God. And yet the most specious of all the objections to the true divinity of the Logos, are grounded on the full and *literal* application to him of such language.

One word, with respect to the *unity* itself of the Godhead. Is not this term, as well as all the others applied to the Divinity, to be taken in a *modified* sense? If any one will, for a moment, put aside the veil of *words*, and come to the simple contemplation of *things*, he will probably find himself much less able to tell what unity in the Godhead is, than he suspected. In the substances around us, proximity of parts united by some common influence, or subserviency to some common purpose, is essential to our idea of unity. A tree is *one*, because its several parts are intimately connected, are under an influence common to all, and are subservient to a common purpose, i. e. of producing fruit, or foliage. Other trees, indeed, of the like kind, are under the like influence, and subserve the like purpose; but the want of an intimate proximity of parts to the tree in question, is the ground why they are not *one* with it. One man, in distinction from many, consists of a corporeal frame thus intimately connected, and animated by an intelligent spirit. Every thing that has material parts is *numerically* one, only by an *intimate* conjunction of those parts.

But when we apply the term *unity* to spirit, and ask, What is that in which the unity of spirit consists? it will be found more easy to ask, than to answer the question. A spirit we do not suppose to have parts; certainly not, in such a sense as matter has, i. e. it is not divisible. God has no parts; he is a spirit. Proximity of parts, then, does not constitute his unity. Nor have we, nor can we have, any proof that homogeneousness, or simplicity of essence or substance, constitutes his unity. For, in the first place, we have no distinct idea of what the essence or substance (if I may be allowed the expression) of the Godhead consists; and, of course, we cannot predicate *physical* homogeneousness or simplicity of that, respecting which we have no distinct idea. In the second place, as the most insignificant portion of matter has never yet, so far as we know, received an ultimate analysis from the highest efforts of chemical philosophy, so that any one can venture to affirm what its simple substance is, and confidently declare that it is homogeneous, and one only, in regard to its component elements; will any one venture to say, that he has analyzed the Divine substance, (I speak it with reverence,) so as to be able, with certainty, to predicate physical homogeneous simplicity and unity, of the elements which compose it? How is it possible for us to make affirmations about the nature of that substance, of which, by our own confession, we are altogether ignorant? A man who at the present day should do thus, in any other science than that of theology, would be regarded as a mere visionary, or as a bigoted enthusiast for the party to which he belonged.

The qualities, then, of the substance or essence of the Godhead, or (to speak in other terms) the physical or metaphysical nature of the Deity, is that of which we are profoundly ignorant. We know there is one Omnipotence, one Omniscience, one Creator and Governor of the universe; but do we know the internal relations and modifications of his substance? Confessedly not. How, then, can we with propriety reject the testimony of revelation, that the Logos is God, because of objections which our philosophy deduced from *a priori* reasoning may raise, in respect to the unity of the Divine substance; all of which objections, too, are deduced from analogies that are taken merely from *material* and *corporeal* things? Truly, if the nature of these objections be examined, and the whole matter sifted to the bottom, by putting mere *words* aside for a while, and looking at *things*, it will be found, that we have less reason to confide in such objections, than some are ready to imagine.

The Christian, who holds that the Logos is truly divine, (and of course that he is *self-existent*, eternal, and independent,) holds to what Paul and John seem very plainly to assert; and he, who admits that there is a distinction in the Godhead, (the nature of which is not developed, but which is implied in such expressions as those in Heb. i. 2. John i. 1, 2,) stands on *scriptural* ground, and on that too which is proof against all assault. For how can it be proved, that there is *not* a distinction in the Godhead, the nature of which we confessedly do not understand ? If it be asked, How can it be proved there is one ? The answer is, by a *revelation*. If such a revelation has been made, (and the texts cited above, not to mention others, seem plainly to imply it,) then we are either bound to receive it, or to reject the authority of the sacred writers. Consistency must oblige us directly and fully to do the one or the other.

As for all the illustrations attempted by divines, ancient and modern, of the physical nature of the distinctions in the Godhead, drawn from finite, material, created objects, the bare mention of them is enough to show, that they must be imminently exposed to error. Who can draw any perfect analogies between *created* and *uncreated* beings, in regard to their *physical* nature and properties ? And all the terms, and names, and dogmas, which have resulted merely from *such* comparisons, may be rejected in a mass—*salvâ fide, et salvâ ecclesiâ ;* and they ought to be rejected, if we would not expose the awful mystery of the doctrine in question to doubts, if not to rejection, by men who are not influenced in their opinions by tradition, nor by the authority of the schools. When the simple *biblical* view of this subject is embraced, and the simple position of the sacred writers maintained, without adding to it any explanations or definitions merely of our own invention, then may more unity of opinion on this subject be expected among professed Christians ; and then will truth be less exposed to assault, from those who reject it.

We come, then, at the close of this protracted discussion, to the conclusion—that language, like that in Heb. i. 2, is subject to such modifications as other parts of the Scriptures and the nature of the case demand. In other words, we can rationally apply it to God and to Christ, only in a *qualified* sense, just as all other language must be applied to them, most obviously, in a qualified sense. Whatever depends on *modus,* must be abstracted. *Facts* are aimed at by the sacred writers, not the *modus* of them.

The expression in our text, therefore, according to every just law of exegesis, must be so taken, as to accord with other assertions of the apostle and other inspired writers. But these do not permit us to attribute the act of *creating* to any but God himself, i. e. the supreme God. To this act the ultimate appeal is made by the sacred authors, in order to distinguish the supreme God from all that is called **God** in heaven or on earth: see Rom. i. 20. Ps. xix. 1. Acts xiv. 15. Isa. xl. 25, 26; ch. xlii. 5—8; xliii. 15; xliv. 23; xlv. 18; xlvi. 9; xlviii. 12, 13, &c. Now, is it possible for the human mind to appeal to any decisive evidence of supreme Divinity, unless the act of creation be such? The Deity can be known at all, only by the development of his attributes; and no development ever made, or (so far as we can see) none which can be made, is so highly and decisively characteristic of "eternal power and godhead," as the act of creation. So thought Paul, Rom. i. 20; and so, until the whole structure of my mind is changed, must I think.

The being then who *created* the world, is *God to me;* and from the nature of my moral and mental constitution, he must be so. This is a point that admits of no explaining away. If, therefore, Christ created the world, he must be, what John asserts him to be, GOD; and what Paul asserts him to be, GOD OVER ALL. But in what sense God can be said to have created the world by Christ, i. e. what is the *exact* meaning of a phrase, which refers to an internal distinction, (as it would seem,) in the Divine nature, is beyond the reach of our conception, as to *modus*. Enough, that it has matter of fact for its ground, viz. that the Logos was truly Creator. Enough that *creatorship* is so spoken of in the Bible, that we are not at liberty to predicate it of any dependent being. This point fixed, (and if it be not, we have no decisive evidence on which we can rely, that Jehovah is God,) the sense of Heb. i. 2, and of other like passages, is to be understood in a *qualified* way, so as not to gainsay what is plain and certain. This is as much as can be said with safety; for the subject, to which such passages refer, is plainly one that, in most respects, is beyond the boundaries of human knowledge.

That the subject is not without difficulties, even in its scriptural position, is what every candid and unprejudiced man will be very ready to confess. But it is a noble remark of Garve, (on Cicero de Offic. Lib. I. p. 70,) "The better part of men do not, because they may discover a few difficulties which they cannot solve, regard the whole system of acknowledged truth as uncertain. They can be aware that there is some darkness mingled with light in their knowledge, without being terrified by the one, or blinded by the other."

The effort to explain *every thing*, to define *every thing*, has led to the unhappy consequence of introducing scholastic phraseology and definitions, in respect to every thing about the doctrine of the Trinity.

This not only bewilders many, but makes others believe that they have a knowledge of *things* because they can use abundance of technical *words;* while the opposition of another class, who can detect the inconsistency and emptiness of these terms, is excited against the whole doctrine. The day, however, is coming, if not already arrived, when mere *names* will be regarded by the church as of little worth, provided they do not convey *intelligible ideas.* For the good of the church, also, it may be hoped, that the time is very near, when men will learn to stop, in making their inquiries, WITHIN *the boundaries of human knowledge,* and *neither to assert nor deny that, about which they know nothing, and can know nothing.* Well was it said by a very sensible writer, " He who will not undertake to explain what is incomprehensible, but will seek to know where the boundaries of this begin, and simply acknowledge them when and where he finds them;—he does most to promote the genuine knowledge of truth by man."*

EXCURSUS II.

HEB. i. 2.—Δι' οὗ καὶ τοὺς αἰῶνας ἐποίησε.

It has been argued, that the expression, *God made the worlds by his Son,* necessarily contains an implication of *eternal sonship,* or *eternal generation ;* in other words, that Christ is the Son of God in his *divine* nature, and not simply considered as mediator. " How," it is asked, " could God make the worlds by his *Son,* if he had no son until four thousand years after the world was created?" The answer, however, is easy. How could " God create all things by *Jesus Christ?"* And yet the apostle asserts that he did, in Eph. iii. 9. Is not *Jesus Christ* the appropriate name of the *incarnate* Logos? Of the Saviour as possessing *our* nature? How then could the world have been created by him? The answer is, that in both cases, and in all similar cases, the words which describe the person are used as *proper names,* and thus designate the whole person, in whatever relation he is considered. The Logos, who created the world, was united with the human nature of Jesus— with the human nature of the Son of God, i. e. the Messiah. And as the names *Jesus Christ* and *Son of God,* are evidently terms used to

* Jacobi, Gotting. Recens. St. 197, anno 1764.

describe the *complex* person of the Saviour; so it is altogether accordant with the usages of language to say, that " God created the world by Jesus Christ," or, " by his Son ;" meaning, in either case, the Logos or higher nature united to Christ, or the Son. So we say, *Abraham is dead*, meaning, that part of him which is mortal is dead; *Abraham is alive*, meaning, that part which is immortal lives. We say, too, *Abraham was born in Ur, of Chaldea;* yet he did not receive this name until ninety-nine years after his birth there, for before this last period he was called *Abram*, not Abraham, Gen. xvii. 1. 5. This is analogical with saying, *God made the worlds by his Son;* although the Logos did not receive the name *Son* (except by prophetic anticipation) until he appeared in the flesh. Nothing is more common than to employ proper names, when once acquired, in order to designate the *whole person*, in all its different stages or modes of existence, without any reference to the time or manner of acquiring the proper name. At all events, if to say, that *God made the worlds by his Son*, necessarily proves that the Logos was *then* a *Son* when he made the worlds; the same reasoning will of course prove, that he was then *Jesus* and *Christ* also, i. e. a complex person having a human nature, because it is said, *God created all things by Jesus Christ.*

In the same manner, the expression of our Saviour, *What if ye should see the Son of man ascend up where he was before?* John vi. 62, would prove, if the reasoning on which we are animadverting be correct, that the Son of Man existed in heaven *before* he dwelt among men, i. e. that the *Word made flesh* did not assume this incarnate condition at the birth of Jesus, but possessed such a nature before, viz. while in the heavenly world. Now, as neither fact justifies such a supposition, nor the usages of language demand it, so the doctrine of *eternal* Sonship can never be built upon a principle of reasoning which stands upon such a very insufficient basis.

EXCURSUS III.

Heb. i. 3.—Ὃς ὢν ἀπαύγασμα τῆς δόξης καὶ χαρακτὴρ τῆς ὑποστάσεως αὐτοῦ.

What can be plainer, than that the description, in Heb. i. 3, necessarily applies to the *incarnate* Logos, to the Son of God as disclosing in our nature the Father to the world of mankind? A multitude of analogous texts might easily be appealed to; but those quoted in the Commentary are sufficient. It is plainly the manifestation of God which the Son makes, that occasions the Son's being described as ἀπαύγασμα and χαρακτήρ; both of which imply, of course, what is *visible* and *perceptible*. But the Logos before the incarnation, while simply divine, was neither visible nor perceptible. Nor can we, with any propriety of language, speak of him in that state, in which he was simply the invisible God, as being only the *image* of God, or only the *radiance* of his splendour, or merely the *likeness* of his substance. Ὑπόστατις αὐτοῦ, *his substance*, I regard as equivalent to *him, himself as he really is*; for this would seem to be the meaning of *substance*, in the case before us, and not the designation of the physical or metaphysical nature of the Divine *substance*, which neither Christ nor any of the sacred writers have represented to us, and of which the Logos is not an *image*, since he is ONE with the Father.

Others understand ἀπαύγασμα in the sense of *image, exact resemblance*, and δόξα as meaning, *Divine majesty*; thus making ἀπαύγασμα δόξης and χαρακτὴρ τῆς ὑποστάσεως αὐτοῦ synonymous. They appeal, by way of supporting this, to an expression in Philo, who calls the sanctuary of the temple οἷον ἀπαύγασμα τῶν ἁγίων καὶ μίμημα τοῦ ἀρχετύπου, *an image* (as they translate it) *of the* [heavenly] *sanctuary, and a resemblance of the archetype*. But here ἀπαύγασμα may well be rendered *radiance* i. e. *light emanated* from the heavenly sanctuary, in reference to the heavenly splendour which appeared in the most holy place. Philo de Plantat. Noe, L. II. p. 221. edit. Francofurt. The book of Wisdom calls wisdom ἀπαύγασμα φωτὸς ἀϊδίου, καὶ εἰκόνα τῆς ἀγαθότητος αὐτοῦ, *the radiance of eternal light, and the image of* [God's] *goodness*; which, although cited by them, is still less to the purpose of defending their opinion.

Ancient and modern commentators, who have construed these phrases as having respect to the *divine* nature and condition of the Son, have understood them as asserting an exact likeness between the Father and the Son, first in regard to *attributes* (δόξα,) and then in regard to substance or *essence* (ὑπόστασις.) I must, however, regard the phrase in question, as of the same nature, in respect to meaning, with the texts to which they have been compared in the Commentary; and we may surely find, in the analogy of the scripture and in the nature of the imagery, reason to justify this view of them. But as the explanation referred to has been so long insisted on, and so often repeated, it deserves at least some particular attention.

Theodoret has best exhibited the mode of argument, which is used to defend the sentiment in question. " Splendour (ἀπαύγασμα,)" says he, " comes from fire. It has fire as its cause, but is inseparable from the fire ; for fire and splendour proceed from the same source. If now it is possible, in respect to objects of sense, that one thing should be derived from another, and yet co-exist with that from which it is derived, you cannot doubt that God, the Logos, the only begotten Son of God, is begotten as a Son, and yet that he co-exists with him who begat him as Logos, which [Logos] is ἀπαύγασμα δόξης. For the *glory* and the *splendour* have one common source. But the glory *always* existed; consequently the splendour. Fire and splendour are of the same nature; then the Son is of the same nature with the Father. Moreover, since the image of *splendour* abundantly shows the co-eternal and co-essential nature [of the Son with the Father,] it has afforded occasion for the blasphemies of those who labour under the disease of Sabellius and Photinus. By another image, therefore, he [the apostle] refutes this blasphemy, since splendour does not exist in and of itself; for he adds, χαρακτὴρ τῆς ὑποστάσεως αὐτοῦ, κ. τ. λ." Theod. Comm. on Heb. i. 3.

In a similar manner, Chrysostom and Theophylact argue, calling the Son φῶς ἐκ φωτὸς. So the Nicene Fathers say, " the Son is φῶς ἐκ φωτὸς, καὶ Θεὺς ἐκ Θεοῦ. All these plainly borrow their phraseology from the expression, ἀπαύγασμα τῆς δόξης αὐτοῦ, which is referred by them to the *Divine* nature of Christ.

But how incompetent any *material* objects are, to afford just analogies of the *modus existendi* of a *Divine* and *uncreated* nature, need not be again insisted on in this place. We might well ask, Is not the sun the *cause* of light? And does not the *cause* exist *before* the *effect?* Again ; Is light in all respects *homoousian* with the source of light, the luminary from which it springs? Is the *radiance* of the sun, the *same* thing as the sun itself?

Chrysostom, Theophylact, and Gregory Nyssen, moreover, assert, that the expression, χαρακτὴρ τῆς ὑποστάσεως αὐτοῦ, necessarily implies an entire resemblance, in *all respects*, of the Son to the Father, with the exception of *separate hypostasis;* and this they maintain must be so, because the impression made by a stamp or die is exactly like the stamp or die itself. But it may be asked first, Whether the writer himself of our epistle makes, as these commentators do, the exception of *hypostasis* from the completeness of the resemblance asserted? Next, whether an impression is indeed, in *all* respects, like the die which made it? For example; is the *impression* solid, or of the same material with the stamp; or does it possess the same physical attributes; or is it coeval with it? Such assertions, therefore, though they may be oratorical enough, and please the fancy of hearers or readers, vanish away before the tribunal of examination, and serve only to show the incompetence of any earthly analogies to give a true representation of the *modus existendi*, or of the physical substance, of the Godhead. They also show the imprudence, nay, the *danger*, of employing such figures, in regard to a subject of so awful a nature.

There can be no doubt in the mind of any man who carefully examines, that the Nicene fathers and the Greek commentators, one and all, held that Christ as to his *Divine* nature was *derived* from the Father. So the Nicene creed, Θεὸς ἐκ Θεοῦ, φῶς ἐκ φωτὸς. So Chrysostom, commenting on the phrase in Heb. i. 13, κάθου ἐκ δεξιῶν μου, affirms, that " the apostle says this for no other reason, than that you may not suppose the Son to be ἄναρχον καὶ ἀναίτιον," i. e. *sine principio et sine causâ;* most evidently in the very spirit of the Nicene creed. Yet we may ask the question—we cannot help asking it, Is then the Son, who is *God over all and blessed for ever*—is he, in his DIVINE nature, *derived* and *dependent*? Has he, as *very God*, an αἰτία and an ἀρχὴ? And is it possible for us, to make the idea of *true* and *proper divinity* harmonize with that of *derivation*, and consequent *dependence?* No; it is not. The *spiritual* views of the nature of God, which are now generally entertained by enlightened men, forbid this; in fact, they render it absolutely impossible. But not so in the days of the Nicene council, and of the Greek commentators. That they believed in the *Divine* nature of Christ, I consider as altogether certain; but that their views of what is necessary to constitute a rational and defensible idea of a nature truly Divine, were correct, is what no one, I think, who has read their writings and judged for himself, will now venture to maintain. Their views of the Divine nature were built on the metaphysical philosophy of their day; but we are not bound to admit this philosophy as correct; nor is it indeed possible, now, for our minds to admit it.

EXCURSUS IV.

HEB. i. 3.—'Εκάθισεν ἐν δεξιᾷ τῆς μεγαλοσύνης.

To sit at the right hand of one on a throne, appears to have two meanings, both in profane and sacred usage.

1. It denotes *honour, friendship, peculiar approbation, a reward bestowed* on any one. Thus Solomon, when on his throne, directed Bathsheba his mother to sit at his right hand, 1 Kings ii. 19. Thus, in Ps. xlv. 9, the queen is represented as taking her place at the right hand of the king her husband. The mother of James and John requests of Jesus, that her two sons may sit, one on his right hand and the other on his left, during his reign, (ἐν τῇ βασιλείᾳ σου, Matt. xx. 20—23; compare Mark x. 36—40,) i. e. that they may occupy the highest places of honour under him as king. In other passages, Christ promises his disciples that they shall have thrones, in the world of glory, Matt. xix. 28; nay, that they shall sit down with him on his throne, even as he sits down with his Father on his throne, Rev. iii. 21. So Christians are said to have kingdom given to them, Rev. i. 6; they are a *kingly priesthood*, 1 Pet. ii. 9; they reign with Christ, or in life, 2 Tim. ii. 12. Rom. v. 17. James ii. 5. Matt. xxv. 34. Rev. v. 10. In all these and the like cases, honour, reward, an exalted state of happiness or glory, is represented by such expressions; but not actual *participation* in the *supreme* government of the universe.

2. To sit at the right hand of one enthroned, or to sit on a throne with one, also denotes *participation of command, authority*, or *dignity*. So the heathen often employed the phrase: e. g. Pindar represents Minerva as δεξιὰν κατὰ χειρὰ τοῦ πατρὸς καθεζομένην, *sitting at the right hand of her father* [Jove]; which Horace explains by her occupying *proximos Jovi honores*. Pind. Fragm. p. 50. ed. Schneider. Hor. Od. I. 12, 19. So Callimachus says of Apollo, that "he will honour the quoir who shall sing what is pleasant to him; since he is able to do this, ἐπεὶ Διὶ δεξιὸς ἧσται, *because he sits at the right hand of Jove*." Hymn. in Apoll. v. 28, 29. The Greeks called him, who participated with another in his kingly authority, σύνεδρος, πάρεδρος, σύνθρονος; although they also applied these terms to any member of a council, or of a deliberative judicial assembly. In the New Testament, when Christ is represented as sitting at the right hand of Divine Majesty, Heb. i. 3; or at the right hand of God, Heb. x. 12; or at the right of the throne of God, Heb. xii. 2, participation in supreme dominion is most clearly meant. Compare Acts ii. 32—36. 1 Pet. iii. 22. Rom. viii. 34. Mark xvi. 19. Phil. ii. 6—11. Eph. i. 20—23. At the same time, the comparison of these passages will show most clearly, that Christ's exaltation to the right hand of God, means, *his being seated on the mediatorial throne,* as the result and reward of his suffer-

ings, (see particularly Phil. ii. 6—11, and compare Heb. xii. 2;) and that the phrase in question never means, the *original* dominion which Christ as Logos or God possesses. The sacred writers never speak respecting the Logos, considered simply in his *Divine* nature, as being seated at the right hand of God; but only of the *Logos incarnate*, or the Mediator, as being there. So in our text, it is *after* the expiation made by the Son of God, that he is represented as seating himself at the right hand of the Divine Majesty. And that this *mediatorial* dominion is not to be considered simply as the dominion of the *Divine* nature of Christ as such, is plain from the fact, that when the mediatorial office is fulfilled, the kingdom of the mediator as such is to cease, 1 Cor. xv. 23—28. Moreover, that the phrase, *to sit at the right hand of God*, or *of the throne of God*, does not of itself mean, *original divine* dominion, is clear, from the fact, that Christ assures his faithful disciples they shall sit down with him on his throne, even as he has sat down with his Father on his throne, Rev. iii. 21. It is exaltation, then, in consequence of obedience and sufferings, which is designated by the phrase in question. See an excellent dissertation *De Jesu Christi ad dextram Dei sedente*, by the venerable Dr. Knapp of Halle, (νῦν ἐν ἁγίοις,) in Knappii Scripta varii Argumenti. Hal. 1824.

EXCURSUS V.

HEB. I. 5.—'Εγὼ ἔσομαι αὐτῷ εἰς πατέρα, καὶ αὐτὸς ἔσται μοι εἰς υἱόν.

A DIFFICULTY still remains, in regard to the application of 2 Sam. vii. 14, to Christ. In the very same verse, which contains the quotation made by the apostle, is contained the following expression: "If he commit iniquity, I will chasten him with the rod of men, and with the stripes of the children of men;" i. e. I will inflict such punishment as men receive on account of transgression. Can it well be said respecting the Son of God, "If he commit iniquity?" &c. Where can any analogy in Scripture be found, of such language applied to him? The answer must be, Nowhere. But by a nearer inspection of the whole prophecy, and by comparing it with other predictions of a similar nature, perhaps the difficulty presented may be diminished, if not removed. What hinders, that God should promise both *temporal* and *spiritual* blessings to David, in consideration of his piety? See 2 Sam. vii. 1—13. Why could he not promise him, that he should have successors on the throne, who should, like other men, fall into sin, and be chastened for it? And yet, that among those kings who should descend from him, there should be one, who was the Son of God in a peculiar sense, who was destined to a dignity—to a throne—of a most exalted nature? Such at least seems to be the exposition by the author of the eighty-ninth Psalm, ver. 29—37.

Compare this now with the promises made to Abraham, Gen. xii. 1—3; ch. xv. 1—6; xvii. 1—8. These passages certainly contain assurances, that Abraham should have a literal, numerous offspring, and that they should inherit the land of Canaan; see Gen. xv. 7—18. Yet they also contain assurances of a seed, in whom all nations should be blessed, Gal. iii. 14—17; and of a seed who should be the heirs of Abraham's faith, i. e. resemble him in regard to faith or belief, Gal. iii. 6—8. It may be difficult for us to ascertain, in some cases, where the *temporal* promise ends, and the *spiritual* one begins; and so *vice versâ;* because both are couched, as usual, in similar language. But this does not show that there is any absurdity, or any improbability, in the supposition that God may have promised, and that he has promised, blessings both spiritual and temporal at the same time. Did he not engage that David should have successors on his *earthly* throne; and also that he should have a Son who would sit on a *spiritual* throne; and have a kingdom, of which David's own was but a mere type! Luke i. 32, 33. Rom. i. 3, 4 Admitting this, our difficulty is diminished, if not removed. The "iniquity committed" is predicated of that part of David's seed who might commit it, i. e. his successors on the *national* throne; while the more exalted condition, predicated of his successor, belongs to him to whom was given a *kingdom over all.*

If you say, "Thus interpreted, the prophecy seems to be in a great measure general, and difficult to be *definitely* interpreted;" the answer is, So it was designed to be. The *general* idea only was intended to be communicated, of some future most distinguished progeny of David. Very much of our difficulty in interpreting most of the prophecies of the Old Testament, arises from aiming to make them more *specific* and *definite*, than they were originally intended to be. When we shall have thoroughly learned, that "the law made nothing perfect," we shall find **less** difficulty in the interpretation both of the Old and New Testament.

EXCURSUS VI.

Heb. i. 6.—Καὶ προσκυνησάτωσαν αὐτῷ πάντες ἄγγελοι Θεοῦ.

As nearly all the commentators on our epistle have admitted, that the one or the other of these passages is actually quoted by the apostle, the difficulties to which such a supposition is exposed should be stated. In Deut. xxxii. 43 [Sept.], the very words are found, which appear in our text. But (1.) They are found *only* in the Septuagint version; the Hebrew, and all the ancient versions, omitting them. (2.) The copies of the Septuagint itself are not agreed respecting them. The Codex Alex. reads υἱοὶ Θεοῦ, instead of ἄγγελοι Θεοῦ, and one Codex at Oxford omits the whole clause. (3.) The subject connected with this command to the angels, (if we admit the clause in the Septuagint to be a part of the sacred text), has no relation to the Messiah. The context celebrates the victory over the enemies of Israel, which God will achieve. After saying, that " his arrows should be drunk with blood, and that his sword should devour flesh, with the blood of the slain and of captives, from the time when he begins to take vengeance on the enemy;" the Septuagint (not the Hebrew) immediately inserts, εὐφράνθητε οὐρανοὶ ἅμα αὐτῷ καὶ προσκυνησάτωσαν αὐτῷ πάντες ἄγγελοι Θεοῦ. This, in the place where it stands, must needs mean, " Let the inhabitants of the heavenly world rejoice in the victory of God over the enemies of his people, and let them pay their adoration to him." But the Messiah does not seem to be at all alluded to, any where in the context; much less described as being *introduced into the world.* I should therefore think it very improbable, if the apostle meant to quote Scripture, that he meant to quote *this* Scripture, on the present occasion; for we have no knowledge, (unless it be implied in our text), that the Jews of his time were wont to apply this passage to the Messiah. Still, it is a *possible* case that he quoted the words of Deut. xxxii. 43, merely as fitted to express the idea which he intended to convey; just as we now borrow scripture language, every day, to convey our own ideas, without feeling it to be at all necessary to prove, in every case, that the same meaning was originally conveyed by the words which we employ, as we attach to them in our discourse. Such a use, it is well known, is not unfrequently made of passages from the Old Testament by the writers of the

New; and such an one, Storr maintains, is here made by the apostle, of the words of the Septuagint, in Deut. xxxii. 43.

The probability, however, all things considered, is in favour of a quotation, (if it be necessary to suppose a quotation,) from Ps. xcvii. 7, (Sept. Ps. xcvi. 7;) where the Septuagint has προσκυνήσατε αὐτῷ πάντες ἄγγελοι αὐτοῦ, as a translation of the Hebrew, הִשְׁתַּחֲווּ־לוֹ כָּל־אֱלֹהִים, *worship him, all ye Elohim*. Here αὐτοῦ, in the Septuagint, stands after ἄγγελοι, but in Heb. i. 6, it is Θεοῦ; and καὶ in our quotation, is wanting in the Septuagint. But any one who has compared the quotations of the New Testament from the Old, either with the Hebrew or Septuagint, must have seen that very few of them are *verbatim*. The variation here of the quotation from the original, is so small, and so entirely unconcerned with the sense of the passage, that the discrepancy will not be any hinderance at all to the supposition that Ps. xcvii. 7, may have been quoted. Yet the subject of this psalm does not, at first view, seem to be the Messiah. The universal reign of Jehovah, his victory over his enemies, the manifestation of his glory to all nations, and the confusion of idolaters, are celebrated in the context. The verse from which our quotation is made runs thus: " Confounded be all they that serve graven images, that boast themselves of their idols, προσκυνήσατε αὐτῷ πάντες ἄγγελοι Θεοῦ, כָּל־אֱלֹהִים;" i. e. "let all created things, which are the objects of worship, instead of receiving adoration, pay it to Jehovah. Jehovah alone is the proper object of religious homage."

Yet it is certainly a *possible* case, that this very psalm celebrates the coming and empire of Christ, who was, as Simeon says, Luke ii. 32, φῶς εἰς ἀποκάλυψιν ἐθνῶν, καὶ δόξαν λαοῦ σου Ἰσραὴλ, (compare Ps. xcvii. 6;) and whose coming was to destroy idolatry, and fill the hearts of the righteous with gladness, ver. 11, 12. It must be admitted, however, that if the ninety-seventh psalm was designed to be applied to the Messiah, it is one of those which are much less definite and plain in regard to such an application, than several others. The Jews, as Kimchi asserts, were wont to apply all the psalms, from Ps. xciii. to Ps. ci., to the Messiah. If such an explanation was current in the time of Paul, it would give additional force to the appeal here made. And even if Paul himself did not regard Ps. xcvii. as originally designed to be applied to the Messiah, he might still use the words of it as descriptive of a fact which took place at the time of the Saviour's birth. The Jewish Christians, whom he addressed, could not have been ignorant of what happened in regard to the angels, at the time of this birth. Supposing, then, that the original Hebrew of the ninety-seventh psalm only means, " Worship him, all ye who are worshipped, [כָּל־אֱלֹהִים;"] and that the LXX. translated this as it now appears in their version ; why could not Paul make use of their words, to describe facts which happened in later times ? If you say, " This would be only to foster an erroneous translation of the Hebrew by the LXX., and an erroneous application of it by the Jews :" the answer is, The fact itself is not an error; viz. that the angels worshipped the Saviour. The words of Ps. xcvii. 7, thus applied, designate what is really true. If the Jews, to whom they were originally addressed, were accustomed to apply them to the Messiah, then the use which the apostle makes of them would be the more impressive; and impressive of an idea founded in reality, viz. that the Son of God was the object of angelic worship.

That the apostle, however, designed any thing more, than merely to use a phrase well known to the readers of the Septuagint version, borrowed from Ps. xcvii. 7, and accommodated to express his own ideas, need not be supposed; and cannot, indeed, well be proved. But if any are not content with this, (which I should myself prefer, provided we allow it to be an actual quotation ;) then it is, certainly, very possible to suppose, that the ninety-seventh psalm relates to the coming and kingdom of the Messiah, and that the appeal to it for a proof passage relative to him, is strictly proper, and not difficult to be understood. In either way, the difficulty which offers itself to the mind, on the first examination of the text, is greatly diminished, if not wholly removed, so far as appeal, by way of quotation, is concerned.

For my own part, I do not regard it as *necessary* to suppose that the phrase in question is quoted at all. Surely it is not improbable, that the writer means only to say, " The Father, who introduced the Son into the world, said, προσκυνησάτωσαν, κ. τ. λ." The Christian Jews, who cannot be supposed to be ignorant of what had happened at the time of the Saviour's birth, could hardly doubt of the writer's meaning. Thus the difficulty of the text would be removed. But if a *quotation* be insisted on, then, with Storr, I am inclined, as before suggested, to regard it as simply using a Septuagint phrase, in order to convey the apostle's own ideas. Yet the exposition, which is founded on the application of the ninety-seventh psalm to the Messiah, and which explains our text as the quotation of an actual prophecy, is not impossible; and, perhaps, not even improbable.

One question, however, still remains. How could the LXX., and Paul after them, translate אֱלֹהִים by *angels*? It is admitted, that the great body of lexicographers and critics, in modern times, reject the sense of the word here given. But usage, after all, pleads in favour of it. The Septuagint render אֵל *(God)* by ἄγγελος, in Job xx. 15; and אֱלֹהִים, by ἄγγελοι, in Ps. viii. 6; xcvii. (xcvi.) 7; cxxxvii. 1. Paul follows them, by quoting Ps. viii. 6, in Heb. ii. 7; and also by quoting Ps. xcvii. 7, in the verse before us; i. e. supposing that he does actually quote it. Is not this sufficient evidence that there was a *usus loquendi* among the Jews, which applied the word אֱלֹהִים occasionally, to designate *angels*? It is admitted, that kings and magistrates are called *Elohim*, because of their rank or dignity. Is there any thing improbable in the supposition, that angels may be also called אֱלֹהִים, who, at present, are elevated above men? Heb. ii. 7. *Facts*, and not *suppositions*, are evidences of the *usus loquendi* of the Jewish writers.

EXCURSUS VII.

HEB. I. 10, 12.—Σὺ κατ' ἀρχας, κύριε, τὴν γῆν ἐθεμελίωσας, καὶ ἔργα τῶν χειρῶν σου εἰσὶν οἱ οὐρανοί. Αὐτοὶ ἀπολοῦνται, σὺ δὲ διαμενεῖς· καὶ πάντες ὡς ἱμάτιον παλαιωθήσονται, καὶ ὡσεὶ περιβόλαιον ἑλίξεις αὐτοὺς, καὶ ἀλλαγήσονται· σὺ δὲ ὁ αὐτὸς εἶ, καὶ τὰ ἔτη σου οὐκ ἐκλείψουσι.

IN regard to the body of the psalm, (Ps. cii.,) from which this whole quotation is taken, the majority of late critics agree in the opinion, that it does not *primarily* relate to the Messiah, but to Jehovah, absolutely considered. It is, no doubt, one of those psalms, the internal evidence of which does not so clearly and definitely determine the application of the whole composition, as does that of many others. Thus much, also, seems to be clear; there is nothing in the psalm, which *forbids* the application of it to the Messiah. Nay, there are several passages in it, which apply to him in a more apposite way than to any other personage. If we suppose the complaint (ver. 1—11) to be that of the church, previously to the appearance of its Redeemer, then does the sequel well agree with the promised redemption. In particular, ver. 15. 18 20. 22, describe the propagation and prosperity of true religion among the heathen. But when was such a diffusion of the true knowledge and worship of God to take place? Under the Jewish dispensation, or under the Christian? Surely, under the latter only. Compare, too, ver. 20, with Isa. lxi. 1, which the Saviour applies to himself, Luke iv. 17—21. Ver. 23, 24, of Ps. cii. renew the complaint of the church; and ver. 25—28, contain the answer, viz. that the Redeemer is the Creator, and immutable, and that the church shall be continued, and a godly seed be permanent. So I am inclined to explain the whole psalm; and so, at any rate, the writer of our epistle seems to have understood it. Certainly there is nothing that forbids such an explanation, when it is once admitted that the Messiah was at all the subject of prediction in ancient times, and that some of the psalms do actually contain such predictions.

But if any one prefers construing Ps. cii. as applicable merely to Jehovah, absolutely considered, then there is no serious difficulty with respect to our quotation. The application of the same words to the Son of God, which were originally spoken respecting Jehovah, is equivalent to saying, " What was affirmed by the psalmist of Jehovah, may be as truly affirmed of the Son." As the writer applies the words in this manner, it shows that he considered those whom he addressed as being accustomed to make such an application of them, and that they were willing to admit it; otherwise he could not have expected the argument to be acknowledged by them as a forcible one.

Admitting, now, that the apostle has correctly applied this passage to the *Son*, it follows that the Son possesses a nature *truly divine*. The act of creation is the highest evidence of such a nature, that is offered, or can be offered, to our minds; and the sacred writers appeal to it as such. See Rom. i. 20. Ps. xix. 1. Acts xiv. 15. Isa. xl. 25, 26; ch. xlii. 5—8; xliii. 15; xliv. 24; xlv. 18; xlvi. 9; xlviii. 12, 13. The force of the proof in question is not altered, whether you suppose the hundred-and-second psalm *originally* to relate to the Messiah, or not. If it originally related to him, then the application is clear and unembarrassed. If it originally related to Jehovah, simply considered, then the apostle asserts here, that what was said of Jehovah may also be applied, in the same manner, to the Son. Of course, the weight of the argument is the same in either case, as it respects the divine nature of Christ. Either would show the opinion of the writer to be, that the Son is eternal, and the creator of the universe; of course, that he is exalted beyond all measure above the angels, and is truly divine. For, as the same writer says, *He who made all things is God*, Heb. iii. 4.

We may observe, too, that this last argument is the climax of the whole, and completes the proof which the apostle adduces, to show the exalted dignity of the Son. He had intimated the same sentiment at the commencement of his epistle, ver. 2; but here he brings out into full light, the nature of his views respecting this subject. Whatever, then, may be the economy, according to which *God made all things by his Son*, it is *not* of such a nature as to exclude supreme Creatorship, and eternal existence, as belonging to the Son; both of which are asserted to belong to him by the passage before us.

EXCURSUS VIII.

HEB. II. 2.—Εἰ γὰρ ὁ δι ἀγγέλων λαληθεὶς λόγος.

THERE are two methods of explaining this. (1.) the apostle here speaks merely in the way of *accommodation* to the Jewish mode of representing this subject. The Jews attributed the giving of the law to *angels*, as mediators or *internuncii* between Jehovah and them; and they were accustomed to make high claims, in respect to the dignity and superior excellency of their law, on this account. The apostle here adverts to their views of this subject; and what he says amounts to this, " If every transgression of the law, which you regard as given by the mediation of angels, was punished," &c. In like manner, the same apostle says to the Galatians, " Who hath bewitched you?" without intending to teach us that he believed in the power of witchcraft. And so our Saviour speaks to the Jews, of " the unclean spirit that goes out of a man, and walks through dry [desert] places, seeking rest and finding none, but afterwards it returns with seven other spirits, and repossesses the same man," Matt. xii. 43. Now, as this is not intended to teach us, that impure spirits actually wander about in deserts, &c., so we are not obliged to understand the apostle as meaning anything more by the expression in question, than a reference to the Jewish mode of speaking and thinking relative to the subject of angels. But,

(2.) Another mode of explanation is, that the phrase contains a concession, on the part of the writer, of what was viewed *by him* to be matter of *fact*. This view I feel constrained to adopt, by a comparison of similar passages. In Acts vii. 53, Stephen says to the Jews, "Ye have received the law, εἰς διαταγὰς ἀγγέλων, *by the disposition* [order, arrangement] *of angels;*" and Paul, speaking of the law, in Gal. iii. 19, says, that it was διαταγεὶς δι ἀγγέλων, *arranged,* [disposed proposed,] *by angels.*

But here a difficulty is urged. God *himself* proclaimed the law to the Israelites, Exod. xx. 1. 19. 22. Deut. v. 4. How then can the law be said to be λαληθεὶς δι ἀγγέλων; Different ways of avoiding and of answering this difficulty, have been adopted. Some have denied that ὁ λόγος here means the law ; and they interpret it as referring to the different messages, which in the Old Testament are said to have been delivered by angels. Others have made a distinction between what was said directly to Moses by God himself, and what was *promulgated* [διαταγεὶς εἰς διαταγὰς,] as they say to the people at large, by angels. That the law of Moses is meant, is plain from a comparison of Heb. x. 28, 29, and ch. xii. 26 ; as well as from the nature of the comparison here proposed, between the old dispensation and the new one. And that the tenuous distinction made, in the second case, is unnecessary, every one who reflects well on the *usus loquendi* of Scripture will concede. God is very often said to do that, which instruments under his direction, or under the general arrangements of his providence, accomplish. This idiom proceeds so far, that even evil is ascribed to him in this way by one phrase, which another passage shows to have been perpetrated by an inferior agent: e. g. 2 Sam. xxiv. 7, it is said of Jehovah, וַיָּ֫סֶת *he moved* [or excited] David to go and number Israel; which crime was followed by tremendous punishment. Yet in Chron. xxi. 1, it is said of *Satan*, וַיָּ֫סֶת, *he moved* David to go and number Israel. So it is repeatedly said of Pharaoh, that *he hardened his own heart*, and that *the Lord hardened his heart*, in Exod. iv—x. So, according to the prophet, Jehovah smites the confederate Syrians and Israelites, Isa. vii.—ix. ; so in other passages, Jehovah is represented as smiting the nations of Judah, of Assyria, of Babylonia, of Egypt, of Tyre, of Moab, &c. Yet, in all these cases, *instruments* were employed. Solomon *built* the temple ; but he did not hew and lay the stones with his own hands, nor carve the goodly architecture. Nothing can be more erroneous, then, in most cases, than to draw the conclusion, that because the Scripture asserts some particular thing to have been done by God, therefore he did it *immediately*, and no instruments were employed by him. How much difficulty and contradiction, as well in theology as in interpretation, has such a mode of reasoning produced! In interpreting the principles of human laws, we say, *Qui facit per alium, facit per se*. Does not common sense approve of this, as applied to the language of the Scriptures? Nothing can be more evident, than that the sacred writers have expressed themselves in a manner which recognizes this principle.

If then we are pressed with the *literal* explanation of ὁ δι ἀγγέλων λόγος, and any one insists, that this can mean no less than that angels uttered audible sounds, when the law was given; all this may be conceded, and still no contradiction be found in the representations of Scripture, when its *usus loquendi* is well understood. *God did what the angels performed by his direction.*

Yet such a *literal* interpretation of this passage is hardly to be insisted on. Stephen, in Acts vii. 53, and Paul in Gal. iii. 19, assert only that the law was διαταγεὶς δι ἀγγέλων; which well expresses the general sense to be attached to an expression of this nature, viz. " the angels were *ministering spirits* or *assisted* at the giving of the law." Such was the Jewish tradition, in the apostolic age. Josephus says, " Our best maxims and most excellent laws we have learned of God, δι ἀγγέλων, Archæol. XV. 9. Philo, (Lib. de Decalogo,) states, that " there were present, at the giving of the law, visible sounds, animated and splendid, flames of fire, πνεύματα, trumpets, and divine men running hither and thither, to publish the law. Yet in another place he states, that " God only spake the law to Moses;" which, however, as we have seen above, is not inconsistent with the former representation.

In addition to all this, there is a passage in Deut. xxxiii. 2, respecting the legislation at Sinai, which seems to refer to the fact designed to be stated in our text. " The Lord came from Sinai, and rose up from Seir unto them [the children of Israel;] he shined from mount Paran, *he came with holy myriads*, (מֵרִבְבֹת קֹדֶשׁ)." By *the holy* myriads here mentioned, must be meant *the angels;* so that the Old and New Testament agree, in representing the angels as present when the law was given, and as being ministering spirits on the occasion.

That the Jews, and a multitude of Christians after them, have carried speculation to a repulsive length, on the subject of *angelic ministration* at the giving of the law, does not disprove the fact itself; much less are their extravagances to be imputed to the writer of our epistle. While some have maintained, that the angels made circuits round the camp of the Hebrews; others, that they excited the thunders, and lightnings, and tempest; some, that they blew the trumpets; others, that they caused the quaking of the earth; some, that they delivered the tables of the law to Moses; others, that they uttered audibly the words of the law; and others still, that they were mere spectators of the awful scene ; we may stand aloof from being thus wise above what is written, and content ourselves simply with what our author teaches us, and what the Scriptures confirm, viz. that angels did assist at the giving of the law, or were in some way employed by Jehovah, on the occasion of its being promulgated. This is all the text can be well interpreted as meaning, and all that is requisite for the argument of the apostle.

EXCURSUS IX.

Heb. ii. 6—8.—Διεμαρτύρατο δὲ πού τὶς, λέγων, Τὶ ἐστιν ἄνθρωπος, ὅτι μιμνήσκῃ αὐτὸν· ἢ υἱὸς ἀνθρώπου, ὅτι ἐπισκέπτῃ αὐτὸν ; Ἠλάττωσας αὐτὸν βραχύ τι παρ' ἀγγέλους· δόξῃ καὶ τιμῇ ἐστεφάνωσας αὐτὸν, (καὶ κατέστησας αὐτὸν ἐπὶ τὰ ἔργα τῶν χειρῶν σου·) πάντα ὑπέταξας ὑποκάτω τῶν ποδῶν αὐτοῦ.

Thus far the quotation from Ps. viii. But how, it is asked, can this apply to Christ in particular, when the author of this psalm evidently speaks of human nature, or man in general ? Many of the later commentators reply to this question, by conceding that the apostle uses the words of the psalm only in an accommodated sense, in order to express his own views of the superiority of Christ's human nature. But this answer does not meet all the demands of the case. It is evident, that the writer appeals to Scripture authority here, in support of the proposition which he had advanced, viz. that the human nature of Christ is superior to that of the angels. If, now, the passage contains nothing more than an assertion of that dignity which is common to all men, how would this tend to convince those to whom he wrote, that the human nature of Christ is superior to that of the angels ?

It is difficult, then, to avoid the supposition, that the eighth psalm was referred to the Messiah, by those whom the apostle addressed. Was it rightly referred to him as being prophetic of him, or not? Many commentators answer in the negative. But is there not some reason here, to adhere to the more ancient method of interpretation? Let the reader, now, peruse 2 Sam. ch. vii. through, and then direct his attention to ver. 17—29, in particular to ver. 18, 19. 26. 29. compared with the prophetic declarations of Nathan in ver. 12—16. Does not the frame of mind, in which David appears to have been on this occasion, correspond well with that described in Ps. viii. 5? Suppose now, that David, in surveying the works of creation, is, in the first place, deeply impressed with his own insignificance, in a comparative point of view; and then, in the next place, revolves in his mind the promises made to him, as recorded in 2 Sam. ch. vii. His mind is naturally led to dwell on the distinguished goodness of God, in exalting a creature so insignificant as himself, to honour so great as the prophet had promised to him. Among his posterity was to be one, who should be the Son of God, and on whom universal empire should be conferred, 2 Sam. vii. 12—16, compared with ver. 8—11. In view of such honours, how natural would be the expressions in Ps. viii. 6—10. In the person of this illustrious descendant, whom Nathan had promised to him, he could see with a *prophetic* eye, that the human nature would be exalted to universal dominion. No created thing was to be excepted from this dominion. As to the particulars enumerated in Ps. viii. 8, 9, they are plainly borrowed from Gen. i. 26, seq. and indicate nothing more than *universality of dominion*. They amount to saying, " The dominion originally assigned to man over the creation around him, and abridged by his fall, is to be *actually* conferred on human nature; and this, too, in a still higher sense, inasmuch as all things are to be subjected to the Messiah." In other words, not only is man to have such dominion as by his original creation he was designed to have, viz. over beasts, and fowls, and fishes, but nothing, in this case, is to be excepted. With such views as these, might not the royal psalmist well add, " How excellent is thy name in all the earth!"

Who, now, that admits the spirit of prophecy to have at all existed, can deny that David might have had such a view of his future Son? Nay, considering the use which the apostle has made of the passage in question, is not this explanation of the psalm a *probable* one?

I am disposed, then, to believe that the course of thought, in David's mind, was something like the following: " Lord, how insignificant am I, compared with the glorious works which the heavens display! Yet thou hast magnified thy goodness toward me in a wonderful manner. Thou hast not only formed me in thine image, and bestowed many blessings upon me, but promised me a Son, on whom distinguished glory and *universal* empire shall be conferred. Can it be, that human nature will be thus exalted? Adored be thy name through all the earth!"

What is there, now, in all this, which is any more improbable than any other prophetic declaration respecting a future Saviour, and Lord of the world?

But if any one refuses to admit these views, there is still a sense, in which all the saints are, through Christ, to be exalted above angels, and to have a participation in the dominion of the world. They are, as being united with the Messiah, as being his brethren (Heb. ii. 11,) to judge, i. e. rule [שפט, *κρίνειν*] the world, 1 Cor. vi. 2; to rule over the angels, 1 Cor. vi. 3: to have power over the nations, and rule them, Rev. ii. 26, 27; to sit with the Redeemer on his throne, Rev. iii. 21; they are made kings and priests unto God, and reign over the earth, Rev. v. 10. All this, however, is plainly spoken in a qualified sense; and such privileges are bestowed upon them only by virtue of their union with Christ, to whom supreme dominion belongs. In like manner we say, "The Romans held the empire of the world;" attributing to the nation what properly belonged to their prince.

Human nature, then, in the persons of the saints—in a special manner, of course, in the person of their Head or leader—is exalted to a state of precedence above the angels, to a state of universal dominion. Consequently, that Christ possessed a nature which was human, did not make him inferior to the angels, but (since this nature was to be thus exalted) superior to them. And thus the psalmist declared it should be.

If the whole passage be understood as limited principally to Christ, or as extending to the saints also, the point which the apostle aims to prove is established. But it is only by understanding the passage according to the first method of interpreting it, that we can well apply, in its full force, the sequel of the apostle's remarks. Indeed, what can be more evident, than that since the fall of our first parents, universal dominion, even over all the animal creation, has never been actually possessed by man? Christ only has it, in its full sense; and in him only have the words of Ps. viii. had a *πλήρωσις* in all the extent of their meaning. When we once admit that prophetic anticipations of Christ were possible, and matters of fact, is there any thing which creates a serious difficulty, in supposing them to have been actually entertained by David in respec to Christ, and to have been uttered in the psalm just mentioned?

EXCURSUS X.

HEB. II. 13.—Καὶ πάλιν, 'Εγὼ ἔσομαι πεποιθὼς ἐπ' αὐτῷ· καὶ πάλιν, 'Ιδοὺ ἐγὼ, καὶ τὰ παιδία ἃ μοι ἔδωκεν ὁ Θεός.

BUT how does the passage quoted relate to the Messiah? In Is. viii. 17, 18, the subject spoken of is the prophet himself, who declares that he will keep himself in the attitude of constant waiting, i. e. in expectation that the prophecies which he had just been uttering would be fulfilled; and he appeals to the *children*, to which had been given symbolical names, and which God had given to him as pledges that these prophecies would be fulfilled. It would seem, then, at first view, that our author had accommodated this passage, merely for the purpose of expressing his views of the subject before him. There can be but little doubt, however, that when our epistle was written, the Jews in general construed a part of the chapter of Isaiah in question, as having respect to the Messiah. Thus Paul, in Rom. ix. 32, 33, seems plainly to refer to Is. viii. 14, as the source of a part of his quotation; and this passage he treats as applicable to Christ. In a similar way, also, the passage under consideration, with the clause that follows, appears to be treated. Indeed, unless the persons to whom Paul wrote would readily refer the passage quoted to the Messiah, it is difficult to perceive how the quotation, in the shape in which it is here introduced, would present any argument to them in favour of the position, that men are the brethren of the Messiah. But still, the mode of reasoning, it must be owned, seems to be *argumentum ad hominem*, or *argumentum ex concessis*, rather than from the real nature of things, considered independently of the opinions of those to whom our author wrote. Critics, in modern times, have felt a difficulty in considering this species of argument as admissible by a sacred writer. The Christian fathers, however, had no difficulties of this sort; most of them freely admitted it.

The majority of Protestant critics have considered the passage of Isaiah now in question, as actually spoken in the person of the Messiah. This they have done, in order to avoid the necessity of admitting an *argumentum ex concessis*; which has been regarded by them, as incongruous with the character of an inspired writer. But in avoiding one difficulty, they have fallen upon another equally great; for all the laws of exegesis, which bid us to connect text with context, and to interpret a writer so as to make him speak connectedly and directly to his purpose, are put at defiance, when we interpret the words of Isa. viii. 17, 18, as *originally* having been spoken with *direct* and *primary* reference to the Messiah, or in his person. To admit such a violation, would be a more serious evil than to concede, with nearly all antiquity, that the apostles did sometimes employ the *argumentum ex concessis*, as in the case above stated.

One may liken this case to that of a missionary in Hindoostan, who, designing to shew the possibility and probability that God might manifest himself in the flesh, should appeal, in the course of his argument, for the sake of silencing objectors, to the Shasters, which inculcate the doctrine that Vishnu became incarnate. Would such an appeal be *morally wrong*? And if not, might not the writer of the Epistle to the Hebrews make use of the views of those whom he addressed, respecting a particular passage of Scripture, (although those views might not have been exegetically well grounded), in order to confirm them in the belief of a truth that was well grounded, and which he knew to be certain, by revelation, or by other Scriptures which had a direct bearing upon it? However one might decide the case by reasoning *a priori*, most men practically admit such methods of persuasion, and, in other things, are very ready to justify them. Whether we are willing, however, or unwilling to admit the fact presented before us, can surely never alter the fact itself. Thus much we may truly say, viz. that those modes of explanation, which, in order to get rid of a difficulty, set afloat all the fixed principles and fundamental laws of interpretation, cannot be admitted without the greatest possible danger to the Scriptures; yet, without the admission of such principles, the words of the passages in question do not appear susceptible of being construed as *originally* and *primarily* having had a *direct* reference to the Messiah.

After all, this view of the subject applies merely to the simple interpretation of the original *words* of Isaiah, ch. viii.; but not to the typical design which may have been attached to the *things* or *facts* there related. We know that in the preceding chapter, the birth of a child, to be called Emmanuel, who was to spring from a virgin, is predicted, (ch. vii. 14;) which birth was to be a proof to Ahaz, that within some three years (compare ver. 14 with 15, 16) the land of Judah should be delivered from the confederated kings of Israel and Syria, who had invaded it.

Originally, and *literally*, this seems applicable only to the birth of a child within that period of three years; for how could the birth of Jesus, which happened seven hundred and forty-two years afterwards, be a sign (אוֹת) to Ahaz, that *within three years* his kingdom was to be freed from his enemies? Such a child, it would seem, was born at that period; for, in ch. viii. 8. 10, he is twice referred to as if then present, or at least then living. In ver. 10, our English version has translated the proper name עִמָּנוּאֵל, and thus obscured the form of the original Hebrew.

Yet, in Matt. i. 23, the passage in Isa. vii. 14, appears to be cited, as containing a prophecy relative to the Saviour's being conceived in the womb of the virgin Mary. In what way, then, must we explain this? How was it a πλήρωσις of Isa. vii. 14? To these questions, two answers may be given. (1.) It may have been a πλήρωσις, in the same sense as Christ's being called out of Egypt (Matt. ii. 15,) was a πλήρωσις of Hos. xi. 1; i. e. the event, which happened in later times, bore a strong resemblance to the one which happened in earlier times; the latter event, too, was of such a nature, that the words of Scripture, applied to characterize the early event, might be applied with a πλήρωσις, i. e. with more *completeness*, with more force, more propriety, more energy, to the latter event, than to the earlier one. Just so, the application of a passage in the Old Testament is made to the slaughter of the infants at Bethlehem, in Matt. ii. 17, 18; compare Jer. xxxi. 15. In the same manner, many other passages of the New Testament are to be construed, which refer in a similar way to the Old Testament.

But if this answer be unsatisfactory, it may be added, (2.) That some of the extraordinary events themselves, related in Isa. vii. and viii., may have been designed by God, and probably were designed by him, to be typical or symbolical of a future spiritual salvation and Saviour. Why is this any more impossible or improbable, than that there were other types and symbols, under the ancient dispensation, of things which were to exist under the new one? The Immanuel then born, in an extraordinary way, and then by his birth and name a pledge of temporal deliverance to Judah from their enemies, might well be a symbol of Him who was to save his people from all their spiritual enemies, to bring in everlasting redemption; whose name, also, was truly, in a much higher sense, עִמָּנוּאֵל, GOD WITH US. If so, then the prophet, with his symbolical children, (Isa. viii. 18,) giving assurance of *temporal* deliverance, may have acted a part that was symbolical of a future prophet, who would proclaim *spiritual* deliverance. In all this, there certainly is nothing impossible. The laws of exegesis are not infringed by such a supposition. The *words* of the prophet have but one simple original meaning. They apply directly to the transactions with Ahaz. But the whole of these *transactions* may have been (may I not add, seem actually to have been?) designed to prefigure a greater prophet, and a greater deliverance. Unless we deny the *possibility* of prophetic symbol, we must admit the *possibility* of this. Its *probability* is deducible from the use which the New Testament writers make of these facts. They seem to consider them as having a relation to Christ. I grant the possibility of the exegesis which explains the whole as *argumentum ad hominem*. It might be justified by numerous appeals to the New Testament; and he who wholly denies this principle, only shows that he decides upon the subject by reasoning *a priori;* for the examination of *facts* cannot fail to convince any one who will patiently and thoroughly make it. But still it does seem to me more probable, taking the appeal in Matt. i. 23, to Isa. vii. 14, and the appeal in our text and context to Isa. viii. 17, 18, that the prophet and Immanuel here act parts which may be regarded in the light of *symbols*. The extraordinary birth of the child Immanuel, at that time, is the symbol of the future birth of a spiritual Saviour; and the prophet with his children announcing deliverance from the confederated enemies of Israel, is a symbol of him who was to " preach liberty to the captives," and whose spiritual children were to be the pledge, that all his promises of good should be fulfilled. Is there any thing unnatural or strange in all this ?

If now this be admitted, then the words of our text may not unaptly be applied to Christ. For as the type put his confidence in God, so did the antitype. As the type had children who were pledges for the deliverance of Judah, so has the antitype " many sons and daughters," the pledges of his powerful grace, and sureties that his promises in regard to future blessings will be accomplished. As the type confided in God, because he possessed a nature that was dependent and human, so the antitype must have a like nature in order to use the same language; and as the type bore the relation of parent to children that were pledges of future blessings, and therefore possessed a like nature with them, so the antitype had a community of nature with those who were his spiritual children, and who were pledges that all his promises should be performed. Compare 2 Cor. i. 22; v. 5.

Thus understood, the whole quotation may be regarded not only as justified, but as apposite. Still, if any refuse to consider it in this light, because, as they aver, they are unable to see how the words of Isaiah can be considered in the light of prediction ; this reason cannot be regarded as in itself sufficiently valid. The words employed in Isa. ch. vii. and viii., have, in themselves, I freely concede, no direct reference to the Messiah, but to things and events connected with the affairs of Ahaz and his people. Neither have the words a *double* sense; which can never be conceded, without destroying the very basis of all stable interpretation. Yet the *events* themselves, *events* connected with the *temporal deliverance* of God's people then, may be symbols of a subsequent and *spiritual deliverance* and *deliverer*.

But it any one refuses to admit even thus much, it will be difficult for him to show, that the writer of this epistle might not use *argumentum ex concessis* here, (i. e. appeal to those views of scripture, which they whom he addressed entertained,) in order to confirm in them a belief of what he certainly knew to be true; as well as the Saviour could appeal to the Jewish belief, respecting the wandering of unclean spirits, in desert places, and many of them taking possession of a man at one and the same time, Matt. xii. 43, seq.; or as well as the Saviour could say to the Jews, "If I by Beelzebub cast out demons, by whom do your sons cast them out?" Luke xi. 19. The difficulty is, in fact, no greater with the quotation under examination, than with many others in the New Testament. Understood in any of the ways that have been proposed, it forms no important objection against the sacred writings, or their divine authority; although considered in the light of *accommodation* simply, it would interfere with some of the modern theories of inspiration. But, as has already been stated, the ancient churches, high as their views were on the subject of inspiration, had no hesitancy, in general, to admit the principle, that the New Testament writers have, not unfrequently, applied the Old Testament Scriptures merely by way of *accommodation*. While, then, for myself, I must believe there is something more than accommodation in the passage under consideration, yet I should not feel it to be a just cause for want of charity towards another, who should adopt a different mode of explanation, and regard the passages cited to be merely an *argumentum ex concessis*.

It is a strong ground of confirmation, with respect to the symbolical exegesis which has been above proposed, that the prophecy in Isaiah, (which begins with the eighth chapter and ends with chap. ix. 7,) contains, at the close of it, most indubitable proofs, that the birth of the Messiah, and the "coming of his kingdom" was, on this occasion, distinctly before the mind of the prophet ; see Isa. ix. 1—7. The whole together, taken in connexion with what appears evidently to be the views of the New Testament writers, seems to leave but little doubt, that such as at all acknowledge the existence of prophecy and symbol, in respect to a Messiah who was to come, may recognize them both in the case before us.

EXCURSUS XI.

Heb. v. 7—Ὃς ἐν ταῖς ἡμέραις τῆς σαρκὸς αὐτοῦ, δεήσεις τε καὶ ἱκετηρίας πρὸς τὸν δυνάμενον σώζειν αὐτὸν ἐκ θανάτου, μετὰ κραυγῆς ἰσχυρᾶς καὶ δακρύων προσενέγκας, καὶ εἰσακουσθεὶς ἀπὸ τῆς εὐλαβείας.

But what was that which Christ feared? And how can it be said, that he was delivered from it? Questions which commentators, for the most part, have passed by, even without any serious attempt to answer them.

If, now, we turn to Luke xii. 50, we shall see, that a view of sufferings, then future, produced in the mind of Jesus an oppressive anticipation, a sensation of distress and dread. As the scene of crucifixion approached nearer, these sensations were evidently increased, until they became almost overwhelming; as we may see by consulting Matt. xxvi. 36—39. Luke xxii. 40—44. Mark xiv. 34—36. What the agonies of the cross, which Jesus endured, actually were, we can never fully know; but we may draw the conclusion that they were very dreadful, if we read the account of the complaint which they forced from him, as it is recorded in Matt. xxvii. 36. Mark xv. 34. It is, indeed, unaccountable, that a character such as that of Jesus, pure, spotless, firm, unmoved by opposition, and contumely, and persecution, and un awed by threatenings and dangers, during the whole course of his public ministry, should exhibit such a despondency, such an oppressive, overwhelming sense of pain and distress: I mean, it is unaccountable by any of the ordinary principles which apply to virtuous sufferers, who possess fortitude of soul. That Jesus possessed this quality in a most distinguished manner, we know certainly, from the whole tenor of his life, as portrayed by the evangelists. How, then, could he exhibit such an oppressive, overwhelming sense of dread, at the prospect of crucifixion? Thousands of men, nay, thousands of the more delicate sex, in prospect of like sufferings, or, apparently, greater ones, (such as the rack, the wheel, or flames occasion,) have been perfectly calm, collected, and even triumphant. The very thieves on the cross, at the same time with Jesus, exhibit no such signs of despondency and oppression. Thousands and millions of common men, without God and without hope in the world, have undergone sufferings greater than those of simple crucifixion, without even uttering a groan. Yet Jesus was not only supported by a consciousness of spotless innocence, but had before him the certain prospect of a speedy resurrection from the dead, of exaltation to the right hand of God, and of being a King and High Priest for ever, unto all his people. Still, he was in such an agony at the prospect of the cross, as to sweat as it were drops of blood, Luke xxii. 44. And when actually enduring the suffering which he had anticipated, his exclamation, Matt. xxvii. 46, shows that he had not overestimated the dreadful hour.

If Jesus died as a common virtuous sufferer, and merely as a martyr to the truth, without any *vicarious* suffering laid upon him, then is his death a most unaccountable event, in respect to the manner of his behaviour while suffering it; and it must be admitted, that multitudes of humble, sinful, weak, and very imperfect disciples of Christianity, have surpassed their Master, in the fortitude, and collected firmness, and calm complacency, which are requisite to triumph over the pangs of a dying hour. But who can well believe this? Or who can regard Jesus as a simple sufferer in the ordinary way, upon the cross, and explain the mysteries of his dreadful horror, before, and during the hours of crucifixion?

Such, then, was the εὐλάβεια, מוֹרָא, *object of dread*, to which our text adverts. But how was Jesus εἰσακουσθείς, *delivered from it?* Pierce, in his commentary, says, that he was delivered by being raised from the dead, and advanced to glory. But this would make the object of fear or dread to be, that he should remain in the state of the dead. This fear we can hardly suppose Jesus to have entertained, inasmuch as he had often foretold, to his disciples, not only his death, but his resurrection, and exaltation to glory. Nor could it be the sufferings of the cross that he was delivered from, for he endured them to a dreadful degree. What then was it, in respect to which he was εἰσακουσθείς, *heard* or *delivered?* The context necessarily limits the *hearing*, or *deliverance* to something in his petitions which appertained to *suffering*, which was an object of *dread.* What could it be, but the dread of sinking under the agony of being deserted by his Father? Matt. xxvii. 46. Great as his agony was, he never refused to bear it; nor did he shrink from tasting the bitter cup, Luke xxii. 42. Matt. xxvi. 39. And does not Luke xxii. 43, explain our εἰσακουσθεις ἀπὸ εὐλαβείας? " There appeared unto him an angel from heaven *strengthening him*, ἐνισχύων αὐτὸν." This was the only kind of deliverance he sought for, or, on the whole, desired; Luke xxii. 42, πλὴν μὴ τὸ θέλημά μου ἀλλὰ τὸ σὸν γενέσθω. The dread in question was, like all his other sufferings, incident to his human nature; and fact shows, that he suffered under it to a high degree; but he did not shrink from it, and so he was *heard*, or *delivered*, in respect to the object of his petition in regard to it.

In the explanation of a passage so difficult, confidence would be unbecoming. I can only say, If this be not the right interpretation of it, I am ignorant of its true meaning, and will most thankfully receive from any one a more probable interpretation.

EXCURSUS XII.

HEB. VI. 4—6.—'Αδύνατον γὰρ τοὺς ἅπαξ φωτισθέντας, γευσαμένους τε τῆς δωρεᾶς ἐπουρανίου καὶ μετόχους γενηθέντας πνεύματος ἁγίου, καὶ καλὸν γευσαμένους Θεοῦ ῥῆμᾶ, δυνάμεις τε μέλλοντος αἰῶνος, καὶ παραπεσόντας, πάλιν ἀνακαινίζειν εἰς μετάνοιαν.

BUT does the whole paragraph pertain to real Christians, or to those who are such only by profession? To the former, beyond all reasonable doubt. For how could the apostle so solemnly warn those who were *mere professors* of Christianity, against defection and apostacy? Defection from what? From a graceless condition, and from a state of hypocrisy. Such must be the answer, if mere professors, and not possessors, of Christianity be addressed. But mere professors, instead of being cautioned against defection from the state in which they are every where denounced in language of the severest reprobation. See Rev. iii. 15, 16, and the denunciations of the Saviour against the Pharisees.

EXCURSUS XII.

Moreover, the language employed to describe the condition of the person in question, shows that the writer is addressing those whom he takes to be real Christians. E. g. μετόχους.... πνεύματος ἁγίου, καλὸν γευσαμένους Θεοῦ ῥῆμα. Above all, πάλιν ἀνακαινίζειν εἰς μετάνοιαν ; for how could he speak of being AGAIN renewed by repentance, if he did not address them as once having been renewed by it?

The nature of the crime, too, and the awful denunciation with which it is threatened, shows that something *peculiar* is attached to the case which the writer is describing. Sinners, who have been taught the doctrines of religion, and yet renounce their *external* respect for it, are manifestly not without the pale of God's mercy; at least, they are not so considered in the Scriptures generally, and fact shows that they are not. It is a peculiar and aggravated case, then, which is here stated; and what other case can it be, than that of apostacy from a state of *saving* knowledge of Christ and his gospel? Nor is such a case at all without a parallel in the Scriptures. Manifestly such an one is stated in Heb. x. 26—32; also in 2 Pet. ii. 20—22; in Ezek. xviii. 24; xxxiii. 12, 13; iii. 20, and in many other passages of the Bible. It is implied in every warning, and in every commination addressed to the righteous; and surely the Bible is filled with both of these, from the beginning to the end. What is implied, when our Saviour, in his sermon on the mount, urges upon his disciples, i. e. the apostles as well as other disciples, (see Luke vi. 12—20,) the duty of cutting off a right hand, and of plucking out a right eye, that offends; and this, on penalty of being cast into hell? Matt. xxv. 29, 30. Is this penalty *really* threatened; or is it only a *pretence* of threatening, something spoken merely *in terrorem*? Can we hesitate, as to the answer which must be given to this question?

But if we admit the penalty to be really threatened, then the implication is the same as in the passage before us, viz. that Christians are addressed as exposed to incur the penalty of the Divine law by sinning. In our text, they are surely addressed as exposed to fall into a state, in which there is no hope of a renewal by repentance. Whatever may be true, in the Divine purposes, as to the final salvation of all those who are once truly regenerated, (and this doctrine I feel constrained to admit,) yet nothing can be plainer, than that the sacred writers have every where addressed saints in the same manner as they would address those whom they considered as constantly exposed to fall away, and to perish for ever. It cannot be denied, that all the warnings and awful comminations, (directed against cases of defection,) are addressed to Christians, in the New Testament, which could be addressed to them, supposing them to be liable, every hour, to sin beyond the hope of being renewed by repentance. Whatever *theory* may be adopted, in explanation of this subject, as a matter of *fact*, there can be no doubt that Christians are to be solemnly and earnestly warned against the danger of apostacy and consequent final perdition. What else is the object of the whole epistle to the Hebrews, except a warning against apostacy? In this all agree. But this involves all the difficulties that can be raised by metaphysical reasonings, in regard to the perseverance of the saints. For why should the apostle warn true Christians (and such he surely believed there were among the Hebrews, ch. vi. 9,) against defection and perdition? My answer would be, Because God treats Christians as free agents, as rational beings; because he guards them against defection, not by mere *physical* power, but by *moral* means adapted to their natures, as free and rational agents. Let every man speculate as he pleases on this subject, when he addresses Christians by way of warning, he will inevitably fall into the same modes of address. And plainly he ought so to do; for thus have all the sacred writers done, and thus did the Saviour himself.

EXCURSUS XIII.

Heb. vii. 3.—'Απάτωρ, ἀμήτωρ, ἀγενεαλόγητος, μήτε ἀρχὴν ἡμέρων μήτε ζωῆς τέλος ἔχων, ἀφωμοιωμένος δὲ τῷ υἱῷ τοῦ Θεοῦ, μένει ἱερεὺς εἰς τὸ διηνεκές.

The description of Melchisedek, in ver. 3, has been interpreted in a variety of ways, so as to give rise to many diverse opinions respecting the person introduced here by this name. I shall very briefly exhibit some of them, without delaying to examine them.

(1.) The Hieracitæ, (so called from Hierax, Epiphan. Hæres, LXVII.,) held Melchisedek to be the Holy Spirit. Jerome undertakes to confute them, Epist. ad Evagrium.

(2.) The Melchisedeciani, (the author of which sect was Theodotus, or Thomas,) held Melchisedek to be one of the δυνάμεις of God, emanated from him, superior to Christ, and after the model of which Christ was formed.

(3.) It is an ancient opinion, (as Epiph. Hæres. LXVII. testifies,) that Melchisedek was the Son of God, i. e. the Logos; the same who appeared to Abraham, and to the patriarchs, &c. This opinion was held by Ambrose; and it has been defended, in recent times, by Molinæus, Cunæus, Gaillard, Outrein, Hottinger, Stark, Petersen, and others.

(4.) Origen, and after him Didymus, held Melchisedek to be an angel.

(5.) Others have held that Melchisedek was a man formed before the creation, out of spiritual and not of earthly matter.

(6.) Melchisedek was Enoch, sent again to live on earth, after the flood. So Hen. Hulsius.

(7.) Melchisedek was Shem, the son of Noah. So Targum Jon. and Jerus.; so also Lyranus, Tostatus, Eugubinus, Cajetan, Genebrard, Torniello, Villalpandus, of the Catholic Church; and among Protestants, Peucer, Pelargus, Brughton, Melancthon, Rungius, and others.

(8.) Melchisedek was Job. So G. Kohlreis.

(9.) It is unknown who he was. So Lyser, Gesner, Baldwin, Crenius, Buddæus, and others.

(10.) Melchisedek was a righteous and peaceful king, a worshipper and priest of the most high God, in the land of Canaan; a friend of Abraham, and of a rank elevated above him.

This last opinion lies upon the face of the sacred record, in Gen. xiv., and in Heb. vii.; and it is the only one which can be defended on any tolerable grounds of interpretation. What can be more improbable, than all the opinions above mentioned, with the exception of this! The most popular opinion among them all, viz. that Melchisedek was Christ, would of course force us to adopt this interpretation, viz. that " Christ is like unto himself;" or, that a comparison is formally instituted by our author, *between Christ and himself;*—" cujus mentio est refutatio."

EXCURSUS XIV.

HEB. VII. 9, 10.—Καὶ, ὡς ἔπος εἰπεῖν, διὰ 'Αβραὰμ καὶ Λευὶ, ὁ δεκάτας λαμβάνων, δεδεκάτωται· ἔτι γὰρ ἐν τῇ ὀσφύϊ τοῦ πατρὸς ἦν, ὅτε συνήντησεν αὐτῷ ὁ Μελχισεδέκ.

FOR a Hebrew, this assertion would less need an ὡς ἔπος εἰπεῖν, than for us, whose modes of thinking and reasoning, in regard to genealogies, descent, and rank, are so very different from those of the Oriental nations.

Since Abraham was deemed, by his posterity, to be the patriarch and head of all his descendants, in such a sense as to hold a pre-eminence in rank above them, a proof that he acknowledged his inferiority to Melchisedek, by paying tithes to him, was a proof that his descendants must of course be inferior to Melchisedek. The statement in ver. 9 and 10, is built upon the Oriental modes of estimating descent and rank. Since Levi, who was of the posterity of Abraham, might be reckoned as then virtually in the patriarch; and since he descended from him, and therefore could not be regarded as of a rank above him, it would follow, according to the Jewish mode of reasoning, that the priesthood of Melchisedek was of a rank superior to that of Levi.

If it be said, " We do not need such considerations as these, to establish the superior priesthood of Christ; neither do we, in this manner, count upon genealogy, and descent, and rank :" I freely assent. But then I am not able to see, why this should at all detract from the propriety or the weight of the epistle to the Hebrews, viz. that the writer has fully met the exigencies of the case, which called forth the epistle itself; and met them in just such a way as was adapted to the condition of his readers, and the modes of reasoning to which they were accustomed. If they attached high importance and dignity to the Levitical priesthood, because the Levites descended from Abraham, (as they surely did,) and this opinion served to fill their minds with difficulty in regard to admitting that the priesthood of Christ could supersede that of Aaron; then was it directly to the writer's purpose to remove this prejudice, and to show them, that, according to their own grounds of argument and computation, Melchisedek must be superior to the Levitical priests, and to Abraham himself. If now, in doing this, (which all must admit was necessary and proper to be done,) the writer has met their prejudices with arguments specially adapted to this purpose, and the force of which they must acknowledge, if true to their own principles; and, at the same time, he has averred nothing which is adapted to inculcate error, or to mislead others who were educated in a different manner from the Hebrews; then has he done what every wise and prudent man ought to do, under circumstances like his. And if several of his arguments are not now needed by us, and cannot well be employed by us, at the present time, with any particular efficacy, this makes nothing against his discretion, or against the validity of his reasoning. We all enjoy the light which has been shed around us by the whole of the New

Testament. Of this the Hebrews had little or nothing. We are educated with views and feelings entirely different, in many respects, from those in which they were brought up. We do not, therefore, need to be addressed and reasoned with, in *all* respects, just as they did. Many of their prejudices we have not; many of their doubts with respect to the superiority of Christianity over the Mosaic religion, we never entertained. Many things, then, which were said with great force and propriety to them, by our author, cannot be addressed to us with the *same* pertinency, nor felt with the same power.

Let the reasoning in the epistle to the Hebrews be judged of equitably, by taking into view such considerations as these, and all difficulties of any serious import, will, as I am inclined to believe, be removed from the mind of a serious, candid, and intelligent reader. Such considerations, too, might have saved the many *inuendos*, (with which we meet, in not a few of the recent commentaries on our epistle,) that the writer has built nearly all his arguments upon *allegory* and *accommodation;* an accommodation which allows the whole force of all the erroneous methods of Jewish reasoning, and conforms to it, merely in order to prevent the apostacy of professed Christians. I cannot acquiesce in the *latitude* of this opinion; nor can I well admit, that a sacred writer would make use of an argument, which in its nature he knows to be wholly erroneous and destitute of force, for the sake of persuading men to embrace Christianity, or to continue in the profession of it. Would not this be " doing evil, that good might come?" But I feel no objection to admitting, that *argumentum ad hominem* may be employed, for the sake of confuting errorists, and exposing their inconsistency. The Saviour himself plainly resorts to this, in some cases; see Matt. xii. 27. Luke xi. 19. So in our epistle, it cannot be deemed irrelevant or improper, if the writer shows the Jews, that, from their own modes of counting descent, and reckoning precedence in regard to rank, Melchisedek, (and consequently Jesus,) was as a priest of an order superior to the Levites. For substance, this is done, in the chapter under examination. Yet there is nothing conceded here, which can in any way endanger the principles of truth. At the same time, after the explanations that have been made, it is hazarding nothing to say, that we now have more convincing arguments than those here used, to establish the superiority of Christ's priesthood. But let it be remembered, we owe them to the New Testament, which we have in our hands, and which the Hebrews had not. Many things, therefore, needed by them in their condition, and with the greatest propriety urged upon them, are less applicable and less important to us, merely because our circumstances differ so much from theirs.

If the reader wants confirmation, in regard to the statement above made, of the Jewish views respecting the *precedency* of Abraham, let him peruse Matt. iii. 9. John viii. 52—58. Luke xvi. 22—25.

EXCURSUS XV.

HEB. VIII. 5.—Ὅρα γάρ, φησὶ, ποιήσῃς πάντα κατὰ τὸν τύπον τὸν δειχθέντα σοι ἐν τῷ ὄρει.

IT has been asked, in what was this τύπος exhibited to Moses? Was it by ocular vision; or by suggestion to the mind; or by words communicated to Moses, descriptive of the form in which the tabernacle should be constructed? The answer to all such questions is very easy; viz. that the subject is beyond the boundaries of human knowledge, so that we can know nothing more respecting it, than what Moses himself has told us. But this is merely an assertion of the *fact*, that the τύπος was exhibited to him. He says nothing at all of the *manner* in which it was exhibited. Consequently, the *fact* is all that we can know: and surely it is all that we need to know; for of what importance to us can the *manner* be, in which this revelation was made? The passage in Acts vii. 44, which speaks of the τύπον that Moses ἑωράκει, determines nothing, as it is not said whether he *saw* in a bodily or mental manner; and the word ἑωράκει is plainly applicable to either. In 1 Chron. xxviii. 19, David, after having drawn a plan for the temple, says, *All, which is in the writing from the hand of the Lord*, i. e. made by Divine assistance; הִשְׂכִּיל, *he taught me, even all the work*, הַתַּבְנִית, τύπου, i. e. of the plan. Yet there was no ocular disclosure. Consequently, the words used in our text will not determine the *manner* of the communication to Moses; and therefore we are not to consider it as capable of being definitely determined.

It follows, of course, that the exhibition of a visible temple in heaven, to the view of Moses, of a temple having *form* and *locality*, cannot be assumed; unless we build upon that which has no foundation to support it. The most that we can know of this subject is, that on Mount Sinai, the Lord revealed to Moses the τύπον of the tabernacle which he was to build; and that this is merely a ὑπόδειγμα and σκιὰ of the heavenly one. Is it a ὑπόδειγμα, then, in a *material* sense, or in a *spiritual, moral* one? In the latter, without any reasonable doubt; for so the whole nature of the argument leads us to conclude. The apostle is not comparing one *material* tabernacle on earth, with another more magnificent one, of the same kind, in heaven; but a material earthly one, with one which the Lord made, which is οὐ χειροποίητος, and οὐ ταύτης τῆς κτίσεως, ch. ix. 11, i. e. which is spiritual and heavenly in its nature. The whole representation, then, comes to this: " In heaven are truly and really all those things which the Jewish tabernacle and temple, with all their rites and offerings, only adumbrated. What is *there*, is *reality* in the highest and noblest sense; what is *here*, is comparatively only *shadow* and *effigy*. Christ does really there, what the high-priest has been accustomed to do figuratively and symbolically here. The temple *here* faintly represents (is ὑπόδειγμα and σκιὰ of), real *spiritual* existences and occurrences *there*."

The very nature of the heavenly world, and of the apostle's argument, is sufficient to show, that this is all that can be rationally deduced from the language which he employs. It would be just as rational to maintain, that God has a local habitation, and a corporeal form visible to the eye, because the Scriptures speak of his *fixed dwelling place* in heaven (מְעוֹנָה), and of his hands, and eyes, and face, and heart, as it would be to suppose that the temple above, in which Christ ministers, possesses *form*, and is composed of *material substance*, like that which was built by the Jews. *This* was merely σκιὰ; *that* is ἀλήθεια, ὑπόστασις, i. e. of heavenly, spiritual, divine ὑπόστασις, not earthly, visible, local matter.

How to build the *earthly* tabernacle, Moses was instructed on the Mount. But whether a form of the same was presented to his vision, bodily or mental; or whether he was taught by words, what the τύπος should be, does not, (as we have seen), appear from Scripture; nor is it important for us to know. Enough to know, that the earthly tabernacle is related to the heavenly one, only as *shadow* to *substance;* and consequently, that our great High Priest above, is exalted to a rank unspeakably higher than that of the Jewish high priest.

All which Moses and the people of Israel saw upon Mount Sinai, the darkness, and smoke, the fire, the cloud, and the lightnings; the voice of the trumpet which they heard, and the quaking of the earth which they felt, (Exod. xix. 17—20; ch. xx. 18—21; xxiv. 1, 2. 9, 10. 15—18; Heb. xii. 18—21); were manifestly symbols merely of the Divine presence, adapted to inspire the people with reverence and awe. In the same manner, the תַּבְנִית, or τύπος of the tabernacle to be built, was a symbol of what is heavenly or divine. It may just as well be argued from the clouds, and darkness, and fire, and lightning, and thunder, and earthquake of Sinai, that all these belong *materially* and *formally* to the heavenly world, as that the τύπος exhibited to Moses was an actually *visible, material* part of heaven.

If, now, the tabernacle built by Moses, the greatest of all the Jewish prophets, Heb. iii. 2, was nothing more than an ἀντίτυπος of that in heaven, ch. ix. 23, 24; a mere σκιά of it, ch. viii. 5; then the temple built by Solomon, which was only an imitation of this, 1 Kings, viii. 10—19; 1 Chron. xxviii. 19; and that in after times, built by Zerubbabel, Ezra v. 1, seq. and which was less magnificent, ch. iii. 12, 13; must also be merely ἀντίτυποι and σκιαὶ of that temple, of which Jesus is the priest. Consequently, the greater dignity of his priestly office may be obviously inferred, from this comparison.

EXCURSUS XVI.

HEB. IX. 4.—Χρυσοῦν ἔχουσα θυμιατήριον.

THERE is great difficulty and much perplexity, among commentators, in regard to the θυμιατήριον here mentioned. Moses makes no mention of such a sacred utensil, as appertaining to the most holy place; neither does the description of Solomon's temple, (modelled after the tabernacle,) contain any information respecting it. Θυμιατήριον, in its general sense, indicates any thing which contains θυμίαμα, or *incense ;* so that it may be applied either to an altar of incense, or to any pot or vessel, adapted for offering incense by burning it. Josephus applies θυμιατήριον to the *altar of incense,* Antiq. III. 6. 8; and so some have applied the word, in the phrase under consideration. But it is a strong, if not conclusive objection to this, that the altar of incense was *before* the veil of the most holy place, and not *within* it, Exod. xxx. 1—6; ch. xl. 5. 26. Moreover, this altar is called, in Hebrew, מִזְבַּח הַקְּטֹרֶת, Exod. xxxvii. 25. 2 Chron. xxvi. 19. 16; מִזְבֵּחַ לִקְטֹרֶת,

Exod. xl. 5 ; or, מִזְבַּח מִקְטַר קְטֹרֶת, ch. xxx. 1. In Greek, it is named θυσιαστήριον, and θυσιαστήριον θυμιάματος. On this altar, moreover, daily offerings of incense were to be made, both morning and evening, ch. xxx. 1—8. The *horns* of it, once in each year, were to be sprinkled with blood, viz. on the great day of atonement ver. 10. But I am unable to find any place which declares that this altar was carried within the veil, on the day just named, by the priest who offered incense before the Lord. On the contrary, the incense offered on that day was strewed on a vessel of burning coals, or a censer, *i. e.* pan, or fire-pan, which the priest held in his hand, and carried with him into the most holy place, Lev. xvi. 12—14. The name of the vessel was מַחְתָּה, ver. 12. Exod. xxvii. 3 ; ch. xxxviii. 3. 1 Kings, vii. 50. 2 Chron. iv. 22. In ch. xxvi. 19, this vessel is named מִקְטֶרֶת, and again in Ezek. vii. 11 ; in both which places the Septuagint have θυμιατήριον. Now, nothing can be plainer, than that the מַחְתָּה and מִקְטֶרֶת were different from the *altar of incense*, מִזְבַּח הַקְּטֹרֶת. Upon this, on the morning and evening of every day, offerings of incense were made : and this altar *stood* before the veil, Exod. xxx. 6—8. On the day of atonement, also, the *horns* of it were to be sprinkled with blood, ver. 10 ; ch. xl. 5, 26. But the incense before the Lord, which was to be offered in the inner sanctuary, was offered upon a מַחְתָּה, *pan* of burning coals, Lev. xvi. 12. Uzziah was about to burn incense in this manner, when the priests withstood him, 2 Chron. xxvi. 16—19. Compare also the case of Nadab and Abihu, Lev. x. 1.

That the incense altar was *stationary*, is plain from the dimensions assigned to it in Exod. xxx. 1, 2 ; viz. a cubit (i. e. 1 ⅞ foot) long, and broad ; and two cubits in height. The removal of this by the high priest, into the most holy place, is out of the question, when we consider that it was made of solid materials, probably metal of some kind. But the censers (fire-pans) were hand utensils, constructed for the very purpose of taking coals from the altar of burnt-offering, (where the fire was never suffered to become extinguished,) for the various uses of the temple, Lev. xvi. 12. The whole difficulty then, in our verse, amounts to this, viz, whether the χρυσοῦν θυμιατήριον, here mentioned, was laid up or deposited in the most holy place. That there were several θυμιατήρια, or מַחְתֹּת, is certain, from Exod. xxvii. 3 ; ch. xxxviii. 3. That the מַחְתָּה, or θυμιατήριον, which was employed by the high priest, was χρυσοῦν, i. e. *gilded*, or (if you will) *golden*, is highly probable ; indeed, one would suppose quite certain, seeing that the altar of incense, (which was designed only for the every-day's offering of incense,) was to be overlaid with pure gold, Exod. xxx. 3. Much more may we well suppose, that the censer, (carried by the high priest into the ἅγια ἁγίων, on the most solemn of all days, viz. the day of atonement for the whole nation, was covered with gold, i. e. was χρυσοῦν, as the apostle calls it. Moses, indeed, has not given us any particular description of such a censer ; nor is it mentioned particularly in the description of Solomon's temple ; nor is it any where said in the Old Testament, that such a censer was laid up in the most holy place. But, as nothing can be more probable than that the censer was χρυσοῦν ; so nothing can be more probable than that it was deposited in the inner sanctuary. That a censer used for the most sacred of all the temple rites, on a day the most solemn of all the Jewish festival days, should be used for the common and every-day occasions of temple service, is highly improbable ; especially when we consider, that every thing pertaining to the service of the *inner sanctuary* was regarded in a light that corresponded with the designation of that place, viz. ἅγια ἁγίων, or קֹדֶשׁ קָדָשִׁים.

Besides, the writer of our epistle, so intimately acquainted with every thing that pertained to the temple, to its rites, and, indeed, to the whole Jewish economy, cannot be reasonably supposed to have mistaken the fact, relative to the materials of which the censer used on the great day of expiation was made, or to the place where it was deposited. How easily would those whom he addressed have detected his error, and been led, of course, to think lightly of his accuracy, when matters so obvious escaped his notice ! In short, all the objection against the account of our author is, that the Old Testament is silent in regard to the two particulars about the censer which he mentions, viz. that it was χρυσοῦν, and that it was deposited in the ἅγια ἁγίων. But surely *silence*, in such a case, is no *contradiction;* and the nature of the whole case is such, there can be no rational doubt that our author has made a correct statement. The want of correctness here, would have argued an ignorance on his part, which would have destroyed all his credit with those whom he addressed.

If any apology be needed for dwelling so long on this subject, any one may find it by consulting the commentators, and learning the difficulties which have been made about it, and the charges of inaccuracy, or failure of memory, which have been made against the writer of our epistle, on account of the clause χρυσοῦν ἔχουσα θυμιατήριον.

EXCURSUS XVII.

HEB. IX. 4.—Ἐν ᾗ στάμνος χρυσῆ ἔχουσα τὸ μάννα, καὶ ἡ ῥάβδος Ἀαρὼν ἡ βλαστήσασα, καὶ αἱ πλάκες τῆς διαθήκης

BUT there is another difficulty, in regard to the phrase under consideration. It is said, 1 Kings viii. 9, and 2 Chron. v. 10, that " there was nothing in the ark, save the two tables which Moses put therein at Horeb." This, no doubt, is true; but our author is speaking, in Heb. ix. 4, of the *tabernacle* as constructed and furnished by Moses, and not of the temple built some five hundred years afterwards; still less, of the second temple, which, after the burning of the first by Nebuchadnezzar, must have lacked even *the tables of the testimony* or law. These were probably destroyed at the time when the first temple was consumed; since we have no authentic intelligence respecting them afterwards. It is probable, too, that the first temple lacked both the *pot of manna*, and the *rod of Aaron;* at least, we have no account of their being deposited in it. The probability is, that the ark, during its many removals by the Israelites after it was constructed, and in particular during its captivity by the Philistines, 1 Sam. iv. 11; v. 1; vi. 1. 21, was deprived of these sacred deposits; for we hear no more concerning them. Be this as it may, our author is fully justified, when, in describing the tabernacle, he attributes to it what the Pentateuch does; and that the *pot of manna* and *Aaron's rod* were laid up in the most holy place, and in the *ark of the covenant,* may be seen in Exod. xvi. 32—34. Num. xvii. 10; (xvii. 25.) In both these passages, the Hebrew runs thus: *Laid up* לִפְנֵי הָעֵדוּת, *before the testimony*, i. e. either before the ark containing the testimony; or (which is altogether more probable,) *before the testimony itself*, i. e. the two tables which were in the ark. Consequently, they were laid up with the testimony, i. e. the two tables; and the account given by our author is strictly correct.

It will be recollected, too, that it is the tabernacle made by Moses that he is describing throughout. As this was patterned after that which Moses " had seen upon the mount," and was built by workmen who had particular Divine assistance, Exod. xxxvi. 1, it was, of course, regarded by the Jews as the most perfect structure of all that had been erected for the worship of God. Perfect as it was, however, the apostle labours to show, that it was a mere shadow or image of the heavenly tabernacle, in which Jesus ministers.

EXCURSUS XVIII.

HEB. IX. 14. —Ὃς διὰ πνεύματος αἰωνίου ἑαυτὸν προσήνεγκεν ἄμωμον τῷ Θεῷ.

Διὰ πνεύματος αἰωνίου is a difficult phrase, about the meaning of which a great variety of opinions have been formed. Some understand it of the Holy Spirit; and some manuscripts and versions read ἁγίου instead of αἰωνίου. But in what respect the Holy Spirit rendered the offering of Christ perfect, (ἄμωμον,) it would be difficult to show from other parts of the Scriptures; which contain, so far as I have been able to discover, no assertions of a doctrine analogous to this. Others, as Ernesti, Capell, Outrein, Wolf, Cramer, Carpzoff, &c. understand it of the *Divine* nature of Christ. But although the offering of Christ might be rendered of the highest value, on account of the dignity of his person, in consequence of the higher nature which dwelt in him; yet the sacred writers represent him as having made atonement in his *human* nature, not in his Divine, Heb. ii. 14. 17, 18. Col. i. 21, 22. Phil. ii. 6—8. Heb. x. 5. 10. 1 Pet. ii. 24. But, independently of this consideration, instances are wanting satisfactorily to prove, that πνεῦμα ἅγιον, or αἰώνιον, when applied to Christ, designates *simply his Divine nature as such*.

Others consider πνεῦμα αἰώνιον as designating the idea of a *victim*, the sacrifice of which had *perpetual* efficacy to procure the pardon of sin; which is the ground of the epithet, αἰώνιον. Thus Noesselt, in his essay on this passage, contained in his *Opuscula*. But in this case, no *usus loquendi* can be alleged, to justify such an interpretation.

Others, as Heinrichs, Schleusner, Rosenmüller, Koppe, Jaspis, &c. consider πνεῦμα αἰώνιον as *endless* or *immortal* life, comparing it with ch. vii. 16. They place this in antithesis to the perishable nature of the beasts that were slain in sacrifice, and which are mentioned in the preceding verse. The antithesis would then be thus: "If mere *perishable brutes*, slain in sacrifice, effected external sanctification; how much more shall the offering of Christ, endowed with *eternal* life, or, with an *immortal* spirit, purify the conscience," &c. To this view of the subject I was myself inclined, before I made special investigation of the word πνεῦμα, as applied to Christ. In doing this, I found, beside the present instance, two other cases, in which it is pretty evidently applied to designate his *glorified state*, in the world of spirits, in distinction from his state of incarnation and humiliation. Thus, Rom. i. 3, 4, κατὰ πνεῦμα ἁγιωσύνης designates a state of distinction from κατὰ σαρκὰ, the *human nature* of Christ, that was descended from David; ἐκ σπέρματος Δαβὶδ, κατὰ σάρκα ...... υἱοῦ Θεοῦ ἐν δυνάμει, κατὰ πνεῦμα. Κατὰ πνεῦμα ἁγιωσύνης here designates the condition, in which Christ was the exalted and *powerful Son of God*, υἱοῦ Θεοῦ ἐν δυνάμει, compare Phil. ii. 8, 9. Heb. ii. 9, 10; i. e. it is descriptive of that *spiritual majesty*, ἁγιωσύνη, הוד, עֹז, or *exaltation*, which belongs to the Saviour in the heavenly world. So 1 Pet. iii. 18, θανατωθεὶς [Χριστὸς] μὲν σαρκὶ, ζωοποιηθεὶς δὲ πνεύματι, i. e. *in his incarnate nature, subjected to sufferings and death; in his spiritual* [heavenly] *nature* or *condition, enjoying happiness and glory.* So in 1 Cor. xv. 45, *the last Adam*, i. e. Christ, is called πνεῦμα ζωοποιοῦν, in distinction from the ψυχὴ ζῶσα attributed to the first Adam. This could not be because Christ had an *immortal soul*, and Adam had only a living *animal* soul; for Adam too was immortal. It would seem, here, that πνεῦμα and ψυχὴ both designate a *spiritual* or *immortal* nature; but πνεῦμα here designates such a nature of a *higher* order; and the antithesis is more fully made by ζωοποιοῦν and ζῶσαν, *life-giving* and *living.*

With these texts I am now inclined to believe the one in our verse is to be classed; and that the sense is to be given to it, which I have just expressed, viz. in his *eternal* state or condition, i. e. his heavenly one, Christ presented his offering, &c. As to διὰ, there is no difficulty in making such a translation of it. It is frequently used with the genitive in order to denote the *quality, condition, circumstances*, or *means*, that have relation to any thing or person; e. g. 2 Cor. iii. 11, διὰ δόξης, i. q. ἐν δόξῃ in the other clause of the verse, and in ver. 8, 9, and equivalent plainly to ἔνδοξος. So Rom. ii. 27, διὰ γράμματος, *with the Scripture*, i. e. *having the Scripture*, διὰ περιτομῆς, *with circumcision*, i. e. *circumcised;* Rom. iv. 11, δι' ἀκροβυστίας, *uncircumcised;* Phil. i. 20, εἴτε διὰ ζωῆς εἴτε διὰ θανάτου, *whether living or dying.* Compare also διὰ in Rom. xiv. 20; ch. viii. 25. Heb. xii. 1. See Wahl on διὰ, No. 3, a. b. Matthiæ, § 580. e.

In confirmation of this exegesis, it may be added, that in ver. 11, 12, the blood of Christ is expressly affirmed to be offered by him in the heavenly sanctuary. If ver. 14 contains substantially a recognition ot the same or the like sentiment, (which it seems to do,) then διὰ πνεύματος αἰωνίου may well refer to the *eternal spiritual nature* or *condition of the Saviour in glory*, who presented himself, in the heavenly temple, with such a nature, as a spotless offering to God, and procured that pardon and purification which the sinner needs. With this interpretation Storr substantially accords, who renders διὰ πνεύματος αἰωνίου by "*in dem Zustande der ewigen Herrlichkeit*," or "kraft seines herrlichen Zustandes," *in the state of eternal glory*, or *by virtue of his glorious state*. That Christ was himself both the offering and the priest who presented it, is plain from Heb. ix. 11—14, and Eph. v. 2. Heb. x. 10.

Respecting a phrase so difficult as the above, much confidence would not be becoming. I have laid before the reader different interpretations; and if he is dissatisfied with that which I have preferred, he can choose another that will give him more satisfaction.

EXCURSUS XIX.

HEB. IX. 28.—Οὕτω καὶ ὁ Χριστὸς ἅπαξ προσενεχθεὶς, εἰς τὸ πολλῶν ἀνενεγκεῖν ἁμαρτίας.

THE importance of the phrase, and the many constructions put upon it that are inconsistent with the *usus loquendi* of the sacred writers, render it desirable accurately to determine its meaning. *To bear sin*, then, is to suffer the punishment due to it, i. e. to take upon one's self the consequences of sin, or to subject one's self to its consequences. The phrase is sometimes used for exposure to the consequences of sin; e. g. Lev. v. 17. 1, compare ver. 3—5; ch. vii. 18. *To bear iniquity*, (נָשָׂא עָוֹן) means also, *to be cut off from the congregation of God's people*, Lev. xx. 17. Numb. ix. 13; it means, *to die* or *perish*, Numb. xviii. 22. 32. Exod. xxviii. 43. Lev. xxiv. 15, 16. So it is sometimes employed as a general expression, to designate any kind of sufferings borne or inflicted in consequence of sin; as in Numb. xiv. 33, 34, where, in the thirty-third verse, *Ye shall bear your whoredoms*, means, Ye shall bear the consequences of them; just as in ver. 34, *Ye shall bear your iniquities*, means, Ye shall bear or endure the consequences of them. Thus is the phrase employed where the subject in question is one's own sins. But,

2. *To bear the sins of others*, is to bear or endure the suffering or penalty due to them. So in Heb. ix. 26, ἁμαρτίας means the conse-

quences of sin, or *penalty due to it*. In Lam. v. 7, Jeremiah represents the afflicted people of Israel as saying, " Our fathers have sinned, and are no more, and we have *borne their iniquities*," עֲוֹנֹתֵיהֶם סָבָלְנוּ. So in Ezek. xviii. 19, 20, *to bear the iniquity of another*, means, to die or perish on his account, ver. 20, compare ver. 17. Isa. liii. 4, *he bore our distresses*, חֳלָיֵנוּ נָשָׂא, *he carried* [or bore] *our sorrows*, סָבַל מַכְאֹבֵינוּ is explained in ver. 5, by *he was wounded for our transgressions*, מְחֹלָל מִפְּשָׁעֵינוּ, *he was smitten on account of our transgressions*, מְדֻכָּא מֵעֲוֹנֹתֵינוּ. So נָשָׂא means, *to suffer*, Prov. xix. 19. Micah vii. 9; as does the corresponding Greek word βαστάζω, in Gal. v. 10, and φέρω, in Heb. xiii. 13. ʼΑναφέρω has the same sense as φέρω and βαστάζω, when used in such a connexion, and corresponds to the Hebrew נָשָׂא and סָבַל. So Peter says of Jesus, ἀνήνεγκε—τὰς ἁμαρτίας ἡμῶν, *in his own body, on the cross*, 1 Pet. ii. 24; to explain which he adds, *by whose stripes ye are healed;* i. e. Jesus suffered the penalty due to our sins, in his own body, on the cross; and, by his sufferings, our obligation to the penalty ceases. The passage is quoted from Isa. liii. 4, 5, which has the same meaning as ch. liii. 11, 12 ; and here we have, *He bore their sins*, עֲוֹנֹתָם יִסְבֹּל, *he bore* [or carried] *the sins of many*, חֵטְא־רַבִּים נָשָׂא. A comparison of all these instances, (more might be adduced,) will serve to show how plain and uniform the scripture idiom is, in respect to the sense attached to the phrase *bearing the sin* either of one's self or of others. It always means, either " actual suffering of the consequences due to sin," or, " exposure to suffer them, obligation to suffer them."

That ἁμαρτίας, Heb. ix. 28, may mean, and does mean, *the consequences of sin*, or *penalty of it*, is plain, (1.) From the impossibility, that the passage here can have any other sense. The *moral* turpitude of our sins, Jesus did not take upon himself; nor remove it, (as it is in itself considered;) but the *consequences* of them he prevented, by his own sufferings. (2.) The corresponding Hebrew words, הַטָּאת, עָוֺן, and פֶּשַׁע, all mean, *punishment* or *penalty of sin*, as well as *sin*, or *iniquity* itself.

The sentiment of the clause, then, clearly is, that Jesus, by his death, (which could take place but once,) endured the penalty that our sins deserved, or bore the sorrows due to us. But this general expression is not to be understood, as if the writer meant to say, with philosophical precision, that the sufferings of Jesus were in *all* respects, and considered in *every* point of view, an exact and specific *quid pro quo*, as it regards the penalty threatened against sin. A *guilty conscience*, the Saviour had not; *eternal punishment*, he did not suffer; *despair of deliverance*, he did not entertain. It is altogether unnecessary to suppose that the writer meant to be understood here with metaphysical exactness. But, that *vicarious* suffering is here designated, seems to be an unavoidable conclusion, as well from the *usus loquendi* of the Scriptures, as from the nature of the argument through the whole of ch. ix. and x.

EXCURSUS XX.

Heb. x. 5.—Σῶμα δὲ κατηρτίσω μοι. Ps. xl. 7. אָזְנַיִם כָּרִיתָ לִּי, i. e. mine ears hast thou opened.

But how could the LXX. render the Hebrew expression here, by σῶμα κατηρτίσω μοι? And how could the apostle follow them in this rendering; and even build an argument on such a translation, in order to establish the proposition, that the blood of goats and bullocks could not avail to take away sin? Questions, which have exceedingly perplexed commentators, and over which most of them have chosen to pass in silence. It is, indeed, much better to be silent, than to speak that which is erroneous, or will mislead the unwary. Still the ingenious inquirer, who wishes to see every difficulty fairly met, is offended with silence on a subject of such a nature, and cannot well resist a secret inclination to attribute it more to want of knowledge, or to want of candour, than to real prudence and discretion. At least, we ought freely to confess our ignorance where we feel it, and not affect to be profoundly wise about things of which we may not venture to speak, or are not able to speak, either to our own satisfaction, or to that of others.

Cappell, Ernesti, and some other critics, strive to maintain the probability, that the Septuagint reading in Ps. xl. 7, was formerly ὠτίον κατηρτίσω μοι, which by some accident has been changed, and the text of the apostle, in the New Testament, adapted to it. But of this there is no proof. Indeed, there is manifest proof that the apostle originally wrote σῶμα in ver. 5, by a comparison with it of his expression in ver. 10.

The difficulty cannot be met, then, by a change of the text; much less by such a change, when it is not authorised by any of the laws of sound criticism, and is against the context.

Were it not that the Septuagint contains the expression σῶμα κατηρτίσω μοι, I should be inclined to believe that it was merely a parenthetic circumstance, thrown in by our author, in order to explain the object of his quotation. *In sacrifice and offering thou hast no delight,* says the personage who is speaking. But what is to take their place? is the natural inquiry. What shall be substituted for them? Σῶμα κατηρτίσω μοι, is the answer, i. e. my body, which I am to offer as a sacrifice, is to come in their place; this will be a sacrifice acceptable, efficacious. In short, if the Septuagint did not contain the expression, we might conclude that the writer of the epistle added it in order to convey the sentiment of the whole passage in some such manner as the following : " In sacrifice and oblation I have no pleasure;" *my body hast thou adapted,* viz. for oblation, i. e. as if the writer had said, " The speaker means, *that his own body was to take the place of* sacrifice and oblation."

But as the Septuagint text now is, we are compelled to believe that the apostle has *quoted* it, and applied it to his purpose. Has he then made any *substantial* part of his argument to depend on the clause in question? An important inquiry, which may go some way towards removing the difficulties that the clause presents.

In ver. 8, 9, the writer presents the argument deduced from his quotation, in the following manner. " First, he says, sacrifice, and offering, and holocausts, and sin-offerings, thou hast no delight in, neither dost thou desire; (which are offered agreeably to the requirements of the law;) next, he says, Lo, I come to do thy will! He abolishes the first, then, in order to establish the second." That is, he sets aside the efficacy of ritual sacrifices and offerings, and establishes the efficacy of a Saviour's *obedience* unto death; compare Phil. ii. 8.

Now, in this conclusion, there is nothing dependent on the clause σῶμα κατηρτίσω μοι. The antithesis of *legal offerings,* is *doing the will of God,* ver. 9, viz. the obedience of the Saviour in offering up his body, ver. 20. This last verse describes, indeed, the *manner* in which the obedience in question was rendered. But the argument, as expressed in the eighth and ninth verses, is not made to depend on the *manner* **of** the obedience; for the object of the writer here, is to show the nullity of the Levitical sacrifices for spiritual purposes, and the fact that the Old Testament discloses this, and intimates their abolition.

I must regard, then, the use of σῶμα κατηρτίσω μοι by the apostle, as rather an *incidental* circumstance, than as an essential one. He found it in the text of the Septuagint which he used. It was well adapted for the particular purpose he had in view; as it turned the mind of the reader to Christ, as the true expiatory victim, rather than to the sacrifices prescribed by the law. It was altogether accordant with the general tenor of the passage which he was citing, and the conclusion which he was to adduce from it. But he does not make (as we have seen) the force of his argument to depend upon it. Were this the fact, and were we to suppose (and we have no *critical* evidence for believing the contrary) that the Hebrew text stood, in his day, as it now stands; it would be a case in point, to prove the extent to which the sacred writers have deemed it proper to employ the *argumentum ad hominem*, and adapt their reasonings to the modes of explaining the Scriptures practised by their readers. As it now is, I do not feel that much dependence can be placed on it, to establish a proposition of this nature; for, on the whole, I must view the employment of the phrase, as found in the Septuagint, rather *incidental*, than *essential* to the writer's purpose. Still, thus much is clearly decided by the case before us, viz. that the apostles did not feel under obligation in all respects to adhere to a *literal* use of the sacred text, but quoted *ad sensum* rather than *ad literam*. Even σῶμα κατηρτίσω μοι may be brought within the general limits of an *ad sensum* quotation, as Storr has remarked; for *preparing a body*, in this case, is preparing it for an offering—to be devoted to the service of God. Now, this is a species of obedience of the highest nature. If a body were given to the Saviour, which he voluntarily devoted to death, Phil. ii. 8, then *were his ears* indeed *opened*, or, *he was truly obedient*. The implication of the phrase σῶμα κατηρτίσω μοι, in the connexion where it stands, is, that this body was to be a victim, instead of the legal sacrifices; of course, *a devotedness of the highest nature* is implied. *Ad sensum*, then, in a general point of view, the text may be regarded as cited; and this, oftentimes, is all at which the New Testament writers aim.

One more difficulty, however, remains. It is alleged, that Ps. xl. cannot well be applied to the Messiah. It rather belongs to *David* himself. How then could the writer of our epistle appeal to it, for a proof that the obedience unto death, of the *Messiah*, was to accomplish what the Jewish sacrifices could not, viz. a removal of the penalty due to sin?

That there are difficulties in the way of interpreting this psalm, as *originally* having had direct respect to the Messiah, every intelligent and candid reader must allow. For it may be asked, (1.) What was the deliverance from impending destruction, which Ps. xl. 2—3, [1, 2,] describes? On what occasion was the song of gratitude for deliverance uttered? ver. 4—6, [3—5.] (2.) How could the *iniquities* of him, " who knew no sin," take hold of him? ver. 13. [12.] (3.) How could the Messiah anticipate such troubles, as are alluded to in ver. 12—14. [11—13;] and particularly, how can he, who, when suspended on the cross, prayed that his enemies might be forgiven, be supposed to have uttered such imprecations as are contained in ver. 15, 16. [14, 15]?

To avoid the difficulties to which these questions advert, some have supposed, that the first and last parts of the psalm in question relate to David, while ver. .7—9. [6—8,] contain a prediction respecting the Messiah; at least, that they are spoken concerning him. But it is not easy to conceive how more than one person can be spoken of throughout the psalm, it being all of the same tenor, and throughout appearing to be made up of words spoken by a suffering person, who had indeed been delivered from some evils, but was still exposed to many more.

Others have maintained, that the whole psalm relates only to David; and that consequently the writer of our epistle *accommodates* his argument to the Jewish allegorical explanation of it, probably current at the time when he wrote. Among these are some, whose general views of theology are far from coinciding with those of the neological class of critics. But there is a difficulty in regard to this, which must be felt by every reflecting and sober-minded man. How could the apostle employ as sound and scriptural argument, adapted to prove the insufficiency of the Jewish sacrifices, an interpretation of Scripture not only allegorical, but without any solid foundation? And how could he appeal to it, as exhibiting the words of the Saviour himself, when David was the only person whom it concerned? If the Old Testament has no other relation to the Messiah, than what is built upon interpretations that are the offspring of fancy and ingenious allegory; then how can we show, that the proof of a Messiah deduced from it is any thing more than fanciful or allegorical? And was it consistent with sound integrity, with sincere and upright regard to truth, to press the Hebrews with an argument, which the writer himself knew to have no solid basis? Or if he did not know this, then in what light are we to regard him, as an interpreter of Scripture, and a teacher of Christian principles?

Considerations such as these questions suggest, render it difficult to admit the opinion under examination, without abandoning some of the fundamental principles, on which our confidence in the real verity of the word of God rests.

Nor does that scheme of interpretation, which admits a *double sense* of Scripture, relieve our difficulties. This scheme explains so much of the psalm, as will most conveniently apply to David, as having a *literal* application to him; and so much of it as will conveniently apply to the Messiah, it refers to him. Truly a great saving of labour in investigation, and of perplexity and difficulty, might apparently be made, if we could adopt such an expedient! But the consequences of admitting such a principle should be well weighed. What book on earth has a *double* sense, unless it is a book of designed *enigmas*? And even this has but *one real* meaning. The heathen oracles indeed could say, *Aio te, Pyrrhe, Romanos posse vincere;* but can such an *equivoque* be admissible into the oracles of the living God? And if a *literal* sense, and an *occult* sense can, at one and the same time, and by the same words, be conveyed; who that is uninspired shall tell us what the *occult* sense is? By what laws of interpretation is it to be judged? By none that belong to human language; for other books than the Bible have not a double sense attached to them.

For these and such like reasons, the scheme of attaching a double sense to the Scriptures is inadmissible. It sets afloat all the fundamental principles of interpretation, by which we arrive at established conviction and certainty, and casts us upon the boundless ocean of imagination and conjecture, without rudder or compass.

If it be said, that the author of our epistle was inspired, and therefore he was able correctly to give the *occult* sense of Ps. xl. 7—9, [6—8;] the answer is obvious. The writer, in deducing his argument from these verses, plainly appeals to an interpretation of them which his readers would recognize, and to which, he took it for granted, they would probably consent. Otherwise, the argument could have contained nothing in it of a convincing nature to them; as the whole of it must have rested, in their minds, upon the bare assertion and imagination of the writer.

May not the whole quotation, then, be merely in the way of *accommodating* the language of the Old Testament, in order to express the writer's own views? Such cases are indeed frequent in the New Testament. God says by the prophet Hosea, "When Israel was a child, then I loved him, and called my Son out of Egypt," ch. xi. 1. Now, this is not *prediction*, but *narration*. But when Matthew describes the flight of Joseph and Mary, with the infant Jesus, to Egypt, he says, "This took place, so that this passage of Scripture [in Hosea] had an accomplishment, ἵνα πληρωθῇ, κ. τ. λ." Now, here is, evidently, nothing more than a *similarity* of events ; so that what is said of Israel, God's son in ancient times, might be affirmed of his Son Jesus, in later times, in a still higher sense, and in a similar manner. May not the writer of our epistle have accommodated the language of Ps. xl., in a similar way ? May he not have merely expressed his own views in language borrowed from the Old Testament, without intending to aver, that (as it stands in the original Scriptures) it has the same meaning which he now gives to it?

This would indeed relieve, in a great measure, the difficulties under which the passage labours, if it could be admitted. But the nature of the writer's argument seems to forbid the admission of it. He had asserted (which was entirely opposed to the feelings and belief of most Jewish readers) that "the blood of bulls and goats could not take away sin." What was the proof of this ? His own authority; or that of the Jewish Scriptures ? Clearly he makes an appeal to the latter; and argues, that, by plain implication, they teach the inefficacy of Jewish sacrifices, and the future rejection of them. Consequently, we cannot admit here a mere expression of the writer's own sentiments in language borrowed from the Old Testament.

Another supposition, however, remains to be examined, in regard to the subject under consideration; which is, that Ps. xl. relates *throughout* to the Messiah. This is certainly a *possible* case. I mean that there is no part of this psalm which may not be interpreted so as to render its relation to the Messiah possible, without doing violence to the laws of language and interpretation. To advert to the objections suggested on page 398 : it may be replied to the first, that the enemies of the Saviour very often plotted against his life and endeavoured to destroy it, and that he, as often, escaped out of their hands until he voluntarily gave up himself to death. The thanksgivings, in the first part of Ps. xl., may relate to some or all of these escapes. If it be replied, that the writer of our epistle represents the psalm as spoken when the Messiah was εἰσερχόμενος εἰς τὸν κόσμον, *coming*, [i. e. about to come,] *into the world*, and therefore before his birth; the answer is, that the phrase by no means implies, of necessity, that the Messiah uttered the sentiments here ascribed to him, before his incarnation, but during it. Εἰσερχόμενος, *entering, being entered,* or *when he had entered* into the world, he said, Θυσιὰ, κ. τ. λ. That the Saviour prayed to God, gave thanks, made supplications and deprecations, as men do, need not be proved to any reader of the evangelists. On what particular occasion in the Messiah's life, the words in Ps. xl. 7—9, were uttered, it is needless to inquire. Indeed, that they were ever *formally* and *ad literam* uttered, it is quite needless to show; inasmuch as all which the psalmist intends by the expression of them is, that they should be descriptive of his true character; which would be such, that we might well suppose him to utter them, or, that they would be appropriate to him. In a word, the psalmist represents the Messiah as uttering them, merely in order to exhibit the true nature of the Messiah's character.

The second objection appears, at first view, more formidable. 'How could the *sinless* Messiah be represented as suffering for his *own iniquities.* Plainly, I answer, he could not be. The iniquities of others might be laid upon him; as the Scriptures plainly testify that they were, (1 Pet. ii. 24. Heb. ix. 28. Isa. liii. 4, 5. 12;) i. e. he might suffer on account of the sins of *others,* or in their stead; but as to sins of his *own,* he had none to answer for. The whole strength of the objection, however, lies in the version of the word עֲוֹנֹתַי (Ps. xl. 13,) which the objector translates *my iniquities, sins, transgressions.* But who that is well acquainted with the Hebrew idiom, does not know, that עָוֹן means, *punishment, calamity, misfortune,* as well as *iniquity,* &c.? David, when he was chased away from Jerusalem by his rebel son, calls his calamity his עָוֹן. *Perhaps the Lord,* says he, *will look favourably* בַּעֲוֹנִי, *on my calamity,* 2 Sam. xvi. 12; for his SIN it was not, in this case. Compare Psalm xxxi. 11. Isa. v. 18. A Concordance will supply other cases, particularly cases where the meaning is *penalty, punishment.* Analogous to the case of עָוֹן, we have seen to be that of חַטָּאת and פֶּשַׁע; see on ch. ix. 28, EXCURSUS XIX. In Ps. xl. 13, then, עֲוֹנֹתַי may, agreeably to the *usus loquendi,* be translated, *calamities, distresses;* and that these came upon the Messiah (הִשִּׂיגוּנִי,) will not be doubted.

So, in 2 Cor. v. 21, ἁμαρτίαν ἐποίησε, i. e. God *made* Christ *a sin offering,* or, subjected him to calamity; and in Heb. ix. 26, ἀθέτησιν ἁμαρτίας means, *a removing of the calamitous consequences of sin.*

The third objection may be very briefly answered. Nothing can be easier than to suppose the Messiah might, at any period of his public life, have anticipated severe trials, and have deprecated them; as we know full well, how strongly he deprecated his final sufferings when he was in the garden of Gethsemane. That he should *formally* and *literally* use the identical words of the fortieth psalm, was not necessary; but that he should have been in a condition, such as the language there describes, is all that is necessary to justify the application of the psalm to him.

In regard to the last objection, which has respect to the *imprecations* contained in the latter part of Ps. xl., they may be, and probably are, viewed in a different light by different persons. Considered as simple *maledictions*, they would be unworthy of the psalmist, or of the Messiah. But as *denunciations* against the impenitent and persevering enemies of God and of David, or of Christ, they present themselves to the mind in a very different light. David did frequently utter denunciations against his enemies. So did Christ against his; e. g. against the Scribes and Pharisees, against Jerusalem, and against the Jewish nation. Yet who will say, that this was for want of tenderness in him, or of benevolent feelings towards those who were his enemies? No one can say this, who considers the whole of his character, as represented by the evangelists. If then he might, and did in fact, utter denunciations against his enemies and persecutors, he might be represented as doing this by the psalmist, without any error committed in so doing.

The objections, then, do not appear to be of a conclusive nature, which are made to the application of the fortieth psalm to the Messiah. Still, I freely acknowledge, that had not the New Testament referred to this psalm, as descriptive of the work of the Messiah, I should have been satisfied, in general, with the application of it to David himself, or even to the people of Israel collectively considered. Yet a minute consideration of ver. 7, 8, [6, 7,] certainly might serve to suggest some difficulty, in respect to such an application. *Obedience* is there represented as the *substitute* for sacrifices. So the writer of our epistle understood it. And it is said to be written in the sacred volume, that this would be the case respecting the individual whose obedience is there described. Is this anywhere written respecting the obedience of David? Is the obedience of the Jewish nation anywhere represented as a *substitute* for sacrifices? Rather, did not a part of their obedience consist in offering them?

After all, however, the whole passage might, perhaps, be construed as merely affirming, that obedience is more acceptable to God than sacrifice, and that this is so declared in other Scriptures. Compare 1 Sam. xv. 2

Ps. l. 9, seq.; Isa. i. 11. seq. At least, this mode of interpretation must be admitted to be a *possible* one.

Let us grant, then, what cannot fairly be denied, that the fortieth psalm, according to general laws of interpretation, *might* be applied to David. Is it not equally plain, that there is nothing in it which may not, without doing any violence to the laws of language, be applied to David's *Son*, in a still higher and nobler sense ? After what has been suggested, in respect to this application, I shall venture to consider the application itself as possible.

Here then is represented a case of the following kind. A psalm composed by an inspired writer, is (in itself considered, i. e. the words or diction being simply regarded,) capable of an application to David, or to the Son of David, the Messiah. To whom shall it be applied by us? If there be nothing but simply the psalm itself to direct our interpretation, the answer must be, "To David;" for the natural application of the words of Scripture, (which in themselves are not necessarily predictions,) is to the persons in being when they were written. But if we have a good reason for making the application of them in a *prophetic* sense, to some future personage, then ought we to make such an application. Consequently, the question in respect to the application of the fortieth psalm depends on the fact, whether we have sufficient reason to construe it as *prediction*, i. e. as descriptive of a personage who was to appear at a future period, viz. of David's Son. In itself it is capable of such an explanation. Paul has actually made such an application of it. The nature of the case shows, too, that the Hebrews of that time were accustomed so to explain it; for otherwise, the argument of the apostle would not have been admitted as of any force by his readers. Whence did the Hebrews derive such an interpretation? Or, (which is of higher moment,) how could the apostle appeal to Ps. xl. 7, 8, for proof of the efficacy of Christ's obedience unto death, as well as of the inefficacy of ritual sacrifices ? This appeal, then, under such circumstances as show that the stress of his argument lies upon the meaning he gives to the passage of Scripture which he quotes, settles the question how the fortieth psalm is to be interpreted, with all those who admit the authority of the writer of our epistle, either as a teacher of Christian doctrine, or an expositor of the word of God. At all events, it cannot be shown, that the fortieth psalm has no original relation to the Messiah. To show that it is *capable* of another interpretation, is effecting nothing. The second psalm, and all other psalms relating to Christ, borrow their imagery—their costume, from the times when they were written, and the persons, manners, and customs then existing; and of course, in a greater or less degree, appear at first view to relate only to them. In describing the future King of the Jews, the writers of ancient times would naturally borrow their imagery from the kings of that day. But to affirm, that because they did this, they had reference, and could have reference, only to the kings of their times, would be a position as little consistent with the principles of language and interpretation, as it is with the numerous declarations of the writers of the New Testament.

It will be easily perceived, that in admitting the possibility of applying the 40th Psalm to David, I have admitted that verses 7 and 8 may be interpreted, as expressing merely the general principle, that *obedience is better than sacrifices*. But if we suppose, with the writer of our epistle, that David, when he composed this psalm, meant to intimate, that this obedience was to be " obedience unto death, even the death of the cross," then must it follow, of course, that the psalm is altogether inapplicable to David; for neither his obedience nor death, nor that of any other person, (the Messiah excepted,) could supersede the ritual of the Mosaic law, and prepare the way for its abolition. Supposing, then, the apostle to have rightly interpreted the words of Ps. xl., (and who shall correct *his* exegesis?) the impropriety of applying the psalm to David is plain; and the propriety of referring it to the Messiah needs no farther vindication.

FINIS

www.ingramcontent.com/pod-product-compliance
Lightning Source LLC
Chambersburg PA
CBHW052109010526
44111CB00036B/1578